D1614995

A TEXTBOOK OF
JURISPRUDENCE

A TEXTBOOK OF
JURISPRUDENCE

BY

GEORGE WHITECROSS PATON

Kt., B.A., B.C.L. (Oxon.), Hon. LL.D. (Glas., Syd., Q'land,
London, Tasmania, Monash, and Melbourne),
Hon. D.C.L. (Western Ontario), M.A. (Melb.)
OF GRAY'S INN, BARRISTER-AT-LAW

FOURTH EDITION

EDITED BY

G. W. PATON
AND
DAVID P. DERHAM

M.B.E., B.A., LL.M. (Melb.)
BARRISTER-AT-LAW
VICE-CHANCELLOR OF THE
UNIVERSITY OF MELBOURNE

OXFORD
AT THE CLARENDON PRESS
1972

Oxford University Press, Ely House, London W. 1

GLASGOW NEW YORK TORONTO MELBOURNE WELLINGTON
CAPE TOWN IBADAN NAIROBI DAR ES SALAAM LUSAKA ADDIS ABABA
DELHI BOMBAY CALCUTTA MADRAS KARACHI LAHORE DACCA
KUALA LUMPUR SINGAPORE HONG KONG TOKYO

First published 1946
Second edition 1951
Third edition 1964
Fourth edition 1972

Printed in Great Britain
at the University Press, Oxford
by Vivian Ridler
Printer to the University

PREFACE TO FOURTH EDITION

THE fourth edition has been prepared by Professor Derham and myself. Without changing the character of the book, the attempt has been made to discuss the issues of the present decade.

The most complete revision is in Chapters V and XV. There has been much recent controversy on the relationship that should exist between law and morals, and this naturally is most relevant in dealing with the question of the interests which the law should protect. Greater emphasis has also been placed on the relationship of economics and law. The chapter on the criminal law has been thoroughly revised, taking into account recent statistics and modern developments in criminology.

Many new cases and much recent writing have been noted, but as an example the following sections are mentioned: S. 5 Decisions on Rhodesian Independence with regard to Kelsen's theory; S. 8 The scope of functional jurisprudence; S. 11 Comparative law; S. 45 Precedent; S. 49 Statutes; S. 54 Law Reform; S. 68 An Act as a basis of liability; S. 90 The Bracket Theory (recent company failures); S. 96 Collective contracts and trade unions; S. 100 *Non est factum*; S. 107 Functional analysis is of the law of tort; S. 111 Exemplary damages; S. 118 Analysis of Property in the modern world.

I wish to thank Miss Judith Wilkins for assisting with typing and the checking of the proofs, and also my son, Major Frank Paton, who assisted with the proofs. I am indebted to the Clarendon Press for their courteous co-operation with an author at the other end of the world.

G. W. P.

PREFACE TO THIRD EDITION

WITH great regret I decided that the preparation of a third edition required more than the part-time energies of a somewhat pre-occupied administrator. My disappointment was, however, allayed by the fact that Professor D. P. Derham was willing to undertake the task. It is fair to state that the new work is entirely his, though I have agreed with every amendment and addition.

G. W. PATON

THE main aim in the preparation of this edition has been to maintain the objectives stated in the Preface to the first edition. In particular, I have tried to preserve the usefulness of the book to undergraduates, to keep the language as simple and direct as possible, and to reveal the important questions rather than to provide dogmatic answers.

If any new major theme is introduced it is derived from the work of the linguistic analysts as exemplified, so far as lawyers are concerned, by the work of Professor Herbert Hart at Oxford. That theme is introduced in § 4 (John Austin and the Imperative School). The influence of the linguistic analysts' views is demonstrated in the revised treatment of the Definition of Law in § 18, of the Concept of Legal Personality in § 61 and Chapter XVI, of the Concept of Possession in Chapter XX, and to some extent by the revision of § 45 (Precedent).

As the above remarks indicate, some substantial changes have been made in this edition. Two new sections have been added— § 10 (The Scandinavian Realists) and § 61 (Legal Personality—An Introductory Note). The following sections have been substantially rewritten and expanded: § 4 (John Austin and the Imperative School); § 7 (The Functional School); § 18 (The Definition of Law— Introduction); § 45 (Precedent); § 85 (The Nature of Legal Personality); § 90 (Theories of the Nature of Corporate Personality); and the whole of Chapter XXII (The Concept of Possession). The text and footnote references have been revised throughout; more than two hundred new references to cases and authorities have been made by way of replacement of old references or by way of addition; and a considerable amount of incidental new writing has been attempted interstitially.

In the preparation of this edition I am particularly indebted to the University of Chicago. The grant to me of a Senior Fellowship in Law and the Behavioural Sciences in the Chicago University Law School in 1961 made it possible for me to do the necessary background work with adequate library facilities available. I wish also to express my gratitude to Miss Deirdre Farrell who undertook endless typing tasks and assisted with the checking of proofs, and to Mrs. Barbara Hocking for her assistance in checking references and proofs, and in the preparation of the tables and index.

DAVID P. DERHAM

February 1963

PREFACE TO SECOND EDITION

THE writer is grateful to reviewers for the constructive criticisms given of the first edition. Attempt has been made to meet them without destroying the purpose for which this work was designed— a student text. To follow every attractive path would have destroyed whatever usefulness the book may possess. I am particularly grateful for the comments made by Professor Hanbury in the *Law Quarterly Review* and for friendly criticism from Professor W. F. Bowker and Professor Zelman Cowen. Much is also owed to the discussions which I have inflicted on my colleague, Professor Friedmann.

There has been a wealth of writing since the first edition went to press. Professor Stone has published the *Province and Function of Law in Society* and (with Professor Simpson whose untimely death we deplore) the three volumes of *Law and Society*. Professor Friedmann has produced a second edition of *Legal Theory* and Professor Keeton of *Elementary Jurisprudence*. American writing has maintained its flow and the *Twentieth Century Legal Philosophy Series* is making accessible the writings of other lands. Dr. Huntington Cairns has written on *Legal Philosophy from Plato to Hegel*. It is not possible to acknowledge in detail the debt owed to these works.

The substantial changes in this edition are as follows. Firstly, the material has been reorganized. What was Book V, 'Analysis of Law on the Basis of Interests', has been entirely rewritten and transferred to Book II dealing with the purpose of law. This links the two approaches to the problem of teleology—the historic natural law and the modern jurisprudence of interests. New sections have been added as follows: Bentham (§ 3), Comparative Law (§ 10), Post-Classical Law (§ 16), Custom (§§ 39–40, now treated in its proper place under the sources of law), Statute Law (§ 52), Sale and Hire-purchase (§ 96), Bailment (§ 124). In some sections gaps have been filled, e.g. a short discussion of Hobbes and Locke appears in § 31. In other sections the material has been recast. Judge Frank has convinced me that I was not altogether fair to the realists or constructive sceptics as he prefers to call them (§ 7). The war trials necessitate a different treatment of international law (§ 20). A more sympathetic treatment is given of the Catholic doctrine of natural law (§§ 30, 33)— I must confess gratitude to my friend, Mr. Frank Maher, who has

helped me to fill the gaps of my learning. The treatment of void acts
(§ 67) has been modified in deference to the views of E. J. Cohn and
Cheshire and Fifoot. The passing of the Criminal Justice Act has led
to changes in § 79. The analysis of the criminal liability of corporations (§ 89) takes account of the article by R. S. Welsh. The treatment
of mistake (§ 98) is recast after reconsidering the views of Cheshire
and Fifoot. The decision in *Read* v. *J. Lyons & Co.* and the Law
Reform (Personal Injuries) Act, 1948, bring into relief the conflict
between the older theories of tort and the modern principles of
insurance (§ 102). *Hannah* v. *Peel* is more fully considered in connection with possession (§ 122). The writer has also attempted to be
more positive in the general part of the work and not merely to
confine the treatment to the formulation of the problems involved.
There has also been a thorough revision of the text.

My wife, Miss F. M. Scholes, and Mr. A. R. Brown have assisted
me with the proofs and the checking of references, and I express my
gratitude to them. The publishers have succeeded in adding much
new matter without increasing the size of the book and of their many
courtesies to me I am appreciative.

G. W. P.

February 1951

PREFACE TO FIRST EDITION

THE writer of a textbook on Jurisprudence is faced with more difficult problems of method and of matter than is the case in any other
legal subject. Whatever the result, criticism is inevitable, for it would
not be easy to discover two persons who would solve in the same
way the problem of what a textbook on Jurisprudence should
contain.

The writer confesses frankly to using a somewhat pragmatic test.
This work is the outcome of teaching in a Dominion law school and
is based on what are considered to be the needs of students. It is also
limited by considerations springing from the capacity of the under-
graduate mind. Severe restraint has been exercised to keep the discussion within reasonable limits, and every endeavour has been made
to avoid using the traditional and imposing quadrisyllables which
give a superficial impression of learning. The easiest way to achieve
fame in jurisprudence is to write a learned tome which is so bafflingly
obscure that it reposes on the shelves unread. It is the conviction of
the writer that, while solutions in jurisprudence are extraordinarily
few, the fundamental questions may be stated in reasonably simple
language. As the purpose of teaching is not to dictate dogmatic
answers but to stimulate thought, the important thing is to make clear
exactly what the problems are.

It must be admitted that to deal with the problem of content satisfactorily three volumes would be necessary. The pure science of law,
functional jurisprudence, teleological jurisprudence—each demands
separate treatment at length. There is, however, a wealth of literature
on particular aspects of jurisprudence. There is little which attempts
to discuss modern views in a compass within the reach of students.
For such a purpose it is absurd to attempt to cover the whole field of
literature, or to load the text with multitudinous references to works
which are either inaccessible or in a language which the reader has not
mastered. Some knowledge of the great names of the past is necessary
in order to set the problem in perspective, but otherwise the literature
of jurisprudence should be used merely as a peg on which to hang
a discussion of such problems as are thought important.

It is easy for a textbook of jurisprudence, as Dr. Allen has said,
to become a treatise 'in which the subjects are *dully* classified and

subordinated'. This is a question on which the reader will have strong feelings.

It is impossible to acknowledge adequately the debt which one owes to others. Frequently the greatest debts are not consciously realized by the writer. Readers will discover the clear influence of Justice Holmes and of Dean Roscoe Pound. Much is owed to Dr. C. K. Allen for encouragement and the force of example. I am grateful to Professor Goodhart for reading the manuscript and to Professor Brierly for scanning the proofs. I have gladly accepted the suggestions made. My wife and Miss F. M. Scholes have assisted me with the proofs and preparation of the indexes. The publishers have willingly assumed the extra burden caused by the presence of the author at the other end of the world. I appreciate the skill used to minimize these difficulties.

G. W. P.

February 1946

CONTENTS

§ 2. THE SCHOOLS OF JURISPRUDENCE

It is common to separate jurists into various schools.[1] Such a classification is useful in so far as it is confined to an attempt to label in
a broad way some of the most significant approaches to the problem.
But it is clear that many writers will escape the confines of even the
broadest distinctions adopted.[2] If we make our classification too
complex it defeats its own object for the aim of classification is
clarity, and too rigid and detailed an enumeration of species leads
only to confusion. Those who desire a fuller treatment should turn
to the learned pages of Dean Roscoe Pound.[3]

The great modern controversy has concerned the boundaries of
jurisprudence and the methods it should employ. Poincaré has said
that 'nearly every sociological thesis proposes a new method which,
however, its author is very careful not to apply, so that sociology is
the science with the greatest number of methods and the least
results'.[4] The same gibe may, perhaps, be flung at modern jurisprudence. Jerome Hall writes: 'Discussions of methods are also apt to
be vague and even futile unless they are directly related to specific
studies in which they were used.'[5] If we may generalize the conflict—
always remembering that brevity as well as wit has its dangers—the
dispute today is between analytical jurisprudence (which may be
taken here to include the various imperative or positivist theories,
the pure science of law, and the Scandinavian realists), functional (or
sociological) jurisprudence, and teleological jurisprudence.[6] Some
concentrate on the abstract theory of law, wishing to discover the
elements of a pure science which will place jurisprudence on the sure
foundation of objective factors which will be universally true, not on
the shifting sands of individual preference, of particular ethical or

---

[1] Much of the material in this chapter is taken from an article by the author in
4 *Politica* (1939), 16.

[2] For example Professor Sethna, Professor of Jurisprudence at the Government Law
College, Bombay, founded the 'Indian School of Synthetic Jurisprudence' in July 1955.
His textbook of *Jurisprudence* (2nd ed., 1959) shows that he draws upon many sources
and many different schools for his work, but the result is more of an aggregation than
a synthesis.

[3] *Interpretations of Legal History*, 24 *Harv. L. R.* (1910), 591; vol. 25 (1911), 140,
489; vol. 50 (1936), 557. *Encyclopaedia of the Social Sciences* (Seligman and Johnson),
viii. 477.

[4] *Science and Method*, 19–20.

[5] In a paper submitted to the VIII Congress of the International Academy of
Comparative Law (1970).

[6] The historical school is not specifically mentioned in this enumeration, as its
method is necessary in many types of jurisprudence: J. Stone, *Province and Function
of Law*, 26–7.

sociological views. The functional jurist argues that, useful as such a pure science may be, it has definite limitations and that, since the very *raison d'être* of law is to furnish an answer to social problems, some knowledge of these problems is necessary even if we desire only to understand the nature of law. We can understand what a thing *is* only if we examine what it does. The teleological school emphasizes that a mere collection of facts concerning social life is of no avail. Law is the product of human reason and is intimately related to the notion of purpose—hence this school asks: what are the supreme ends which law should follow? Frequently this type of jurisprudence is described as philosophical. It is true that this is the method normally used, but philosophy itself overlaps all schools. Kelsen builds his pure science and Savigny his historical theory on a philosophic basis. Hence it saves confusion if we adopt another title, for we do not find the work of the philosopher in one school alone.

These schools are complementary rather than opposed. The dogmatic insistence of certain writers that there is one, and only one, road to truth has tended to obscure this fact.[1]

In the sections which follow we will consider the approach of these schools. But in order to understand historical developments of theory it is necessary to modify the purely logical approach. The work of Bentham provides a convenient starting-point.

§ 3. BENTHAM (1748–1832)

Full credit has not always been paid to Jeremy Bentham as the founder of the English analytical school. Bentham devoted almost his whole life to writing: but he was not so interested in publishing and one of his most important manuscripts on jurisprudence only reached the public in 1945. This treatise, *The Limits of Jurisprudence Defined*, written in 1782, was found by Professor Everett at University College, London, deciphered and then published. This work reveals how much of Austin is due to Bentham and emphasizes that Bentham was not only a writer on the end of law but an analyst who was interested in the mechanics of the legal system.

The many sides of Bentham's activity may be seen by reading the symposium, *Jeremy Bentham and the Law*.[2] His desire for reform

---

[1] Ehrenzweig, 64 *Harv. L. R.* (1950), 355–9.
[2] Ed. by G. W. Keeton and G. Schwarzenberger.

based on the doctrine of utility, his ambition for codification based on a hatred of judge-made law, gave his work a sense of mission. His approach to sovereignty was similar to that of Austin: his definition of law was wide enough to cover subordinate legislation and administrative regulation: his analysis of rights and duties puts forward in embryo what was once thought to be a discovery of the twentieth century.[1]

Bentham was a realist in temper, and impatient of the rhetoric with which Blackstone and other eighteenth-century writers confused the problem of the nature of law. He was bitterly scornful of the pretensions of natural law. But he had his own gospel, that of utility, and he wished to test every law to see if it led to the greatest happiness of the greatest number. He was attempting to examine keenly the structure, conceptions, and functioning of the legal system in order that outworn abuses might be swept away—that every privilege should be justified by utility.[2] He analyses legal terms (such as power, right, prohibition, obligation, property, and liberty) and attempts to show what, in fact, they mean in the world of practice. His work was intended to provide the indispensable introduction to a civil code.

Austin took from Bentham the tool of analysis which both wielded so well; Austin also adopted the theory of utility, but he regarded it as falling outside the sphere of jurisprudence proper. Finally, the two sides of Bentham's work each created a separate school—the pure analyst interested in the law as such and the teleological writer interested in the ends which law should pursue.[3] It was a disaster for English jurisprudence that Bentham's work was not taken in its entirety. Analysis is barren without a keen view of social policy: a study of the objectives of law is useless unless founded on an analytical appreciation of the *law that is*. But in the nineteenth century, for all Bentham's influence in the world of practical affairs, there was a tendency to deny this in the theory of jurisprudence.

§ 4. JOHN AUSTIN AND THE IMPERATIVE SCHOOL

In 1832 John Austin, after a course of lectures at the University of London, published a work which he entitled *The Province of Jurisprudence Determined*—and determined it was with great rigour of analysis. After his death he achieved greater fame and became the

---

[1] W. G. Friedmann, 64 *L.Q.R.* (1948), 341.   [2] Everett, op. cit. 49.
[3] It must not be forgotten that although Bentham was an individualist, his doctrine of utility carried within it the seeds of collectivism: Dicey, *Law and Opinion*, Lecture IX.

founder of what was popularly called the analytical school. This title is rather misleading as it suggests that analysis is the exclusive property of this school instead of being (as it is) a method used throughout jurisprudence. Hence Allen prefers to speak of the imperative school, for this emphasizes Austin's particular conception of law.[1] Austin does not fit exactly into any of the broad divisions we have laid down. In some ways he was a precursor of the pure science of law, for he drew the boundaries of jurisprudence somewhat narrowly. Austin was not unmindful of the part played by ethics in the evolution of law; indeed, he devoted several lectures to the theory of utility. But, finding works on jurisprudence full of confusion, Austin decided to confine jurisprudence to a study of law as it is, leaving the study of the ideal forms of law to the 'science of legislation',[2] or teleological jurisprudence as we should term it today. Austin's followers were even more rigorous than their master in confining jurisprudence to an analysis of the rules in force. We will discuss Austin's views under three heads: (a) the basis of jurisprudence, (b) the method of jurisprudence, and (c) the relation of law and ethics.

(a) The Basis of Jurisprudence

Austin's broad approach to law was to regard it as the command of the sovereign. Positive law is a general rule of conduct laid down by a political superior to a political inferior. The notion of command requires that there must be a determinate person to issue the command, and that there is an implied threat of a sanction if the command is not obeyed.[3] Austin's aim was to separate positive law sharply from such social rules as those of custom and morality. The emphasis on command achieved this end, for the rules of etiquette are not laid down by a definite person. Jurisprudence was the general science of positive law in the rigid sense in which Austin defined it. But if the law of each country is based on the commands of the sovereign person (or body of persons) in that country, on what is jurisprudence to be based? As each sovereign may command what he wishes, will not there be the utmost diversity between the legal systems? Is there any element of identity on which a general science can be based? If we take the legal systems of the world from China

---

[1] *Legal Duties*, 13–14.
[2] *Jurisprudence* (5th ed.), 32. Actually Austin speaks of his science of the *law that is* as the *philosophy* of positive law, but this usage is rather misleading.
[3] *Infra*, § 20, and H. L. A. Hart's introduction to *The Province of Jurisprudence Determined, etc.* (1954).

to Peru, we find the utmost conflict as to the content of the rules, the classification of the law, and the technical language in which it is expressed. Must not jurisprudence, therefore, be confined to a study of a particular system so that we will have English jurisprudence, French jurisprudence, and so on?

Austin did not deal clearly with this problem. He assumed, without any real investigation, that certain principles, notions, and distinctions were common to all systems of law. Some notions were universal because it was impossible coherently to construct a legal system without using them, e.g. the terms 'duty', 'right', 'injury', 'punishment', and 'redress'.[1] Some principles were common to all refined or mature systems because they depended on general principles of utility which modern nations accepted. If it were suggested that primitive nations often accepted views the opposite of those accepted today, Austin would have had no hesitation in confining jurisprudence to the more advanced systems.

Analysis reveals Austin's foundation to be rather unstable. Firstly, it is clear that there are no universal rules of law—'hardly a rule of today but may be matched by its opposite of yesterday'.[2] 'The moment we have disengaged some principle of which we think to say, with a sigh of relief, "Well, *that* at least is an indispensable element of all law", some patient investigator into the legal systems of the Houyhnhnms in the mists of antiquity will discover a fragment of stone or pottery which disturbs all our conclusions.'[3] Secondly, there are few concepts which are common to all legal systems, and if we confine our analysis to such as we think are universal, we run two dangers: firstly, if further research shows that there are no concepts which are common to all systems, then there is no basis for general jurisprudence at all; secondly, even if a few notions are proved to be universal, they form a somewhat narrow basis for a science of law. Much of what the Romans considered universal is today considered a mere accident of the particular conditions in which Roman law was developed. In the nineteenth century writers frequently deduced certain universal legal principles, but twentieth-century insight shows that these principles are not universal but were based only on the necessities of a capitalist economy that still emphasized *laissez-faire.*

---

[1] *Jurisprudence*, ii. 1073.

[2] Cardozo, *The Nature of the Judicial Process*, 26.

[3] Allen, *Legal Duties*, 4. There may be principles of law *generally* accepted, although not universally. Thus the Court of International Justice was bidden to draw on general principles of law common to civilized nations: Verdross, *Rec. Gény*, iii. 383.

Rules of property that were considered axiomatic in 1850 do not apply in Russia nor in many other countries today. Hence, doubts have been expressed whether it is possible to construct any basis for jurisprudence that will not be upset by changes in economic and social conditions.

The solution of the problem is that, although there are few (if any) *rules of law* that are universal, yet there may be universal *principles of jurisprudence*. The assumptions of jurisprudence are simple. In all communities which reach a certain stage of development there springs up a social machinery which we call law.[1] Jurisprudence is not primarily interested in cataloguing uniformities, nor in discovering rules which all nations accept. Its task is to study the nature of law, the nature of legal institutions, the development of both law and legal institutions and their relationship to society. In each society there is an inter-action between the abstract rules, the institutional machinery existing for their application, and the life of the people. Even if there were no common elements discoverable in the legal systems of the world, jurisprudence would still have the function of tracing the relationship between law, legal institutions, and the life of the people. Legal systems seem to have developed for the settlement of disputes and to secure an ordered existence for the community. They still exist for those purposes but in addition they are part of the social machinery used to enable planned changes and improvements in the organization of society to take place in an ordered fashion. In order to achieve these ends each legal system develops a certain method, an apparatus of technical words and concepts, and an institutional system which follows those methods and uses that apparatus. The pressure of social needs which the law must satisfy will vary from one community to another, but jurisprudence studies the methods by which these problems are solved rather than the particular solutions. Jurisprudence is founded on the attempt, not to find universal principles of law, but to construct a science which will explain the relationship between law, its concepts, and the life of society.

Austin did not analyse this problem acutely, for both he and many of his followers fell into the error of thinking that what was common to certain nations in the nineteenth century was a universal element of all mature systems. The emergence of Soviet Russia (with its legal

---

[1] Diamond, *Primitive Law*; Llewellyn and Hoebel, *The Cheyenne Way*; Hoebel, *The Law of Primitive Man.*

system based on a social philosophy that rejects capitalism) saves us from the mistake of considering that what is suitable for one particular economy is a universal rule. Jurisprudence must widen its scope, for if it is concerned only with universal *rules of law*, it will perish for want of material.

(b) The Method of Jurisprudence

Austin believed that the chief tool of jurisprudence was *analysis*. The emphasis on law as the command of the sovereign led to concentration on mature (or what he sometimes called 'civilized') systems, since it is clear that a sovereign with effective machinery for enforcing law can exist only when the State has reached a fairly high degree of development.[1] Today, however, it is increasingly recognized that, useful as analysis may be, it will not suffice to answer all the problems of jurisprudence. An analysis of the judicial method[2] shows that law is not a static body of rules, but is rather an organic body of principles with an inherent power of growth. The law that is, of which some of Austin's followers so proudly boast, cannot be too sharply divided from the law that ought to be, because where there is no authority, the judge is perpetually clothing with the robe of positive law the rule that he thinks *ought* to exist. Whence is the judge to draw his material? Some of the imperative school seem to proceed on the tacit assumption that all legal problems can be answered by analysis of the rules that exist and by deductions from them. This is too narrow a view. The principles of the common law did not descend from the clouds complete and fully developed: nor can we say that the creative period is yet over. Exaggerated positivism ignores the fact that law develops not by logic alone, but by drawing new values from the life of the community and by gradually reshaping the rules so that they accord with the standards of today.[3] We cannot always convict a dissenting minority in the House of Lords of an error in logic—what is frequently decisive is the judge's view of the purpose that law should achieve.

It cannot be suggested that such elementary truths were beyond the understanding of the imperative school, and one of the besetting vices of jurisprudence is to exaggerate the views of an opponent in order to show how ridiculous they are and incidentally how much wiser the writer is. What is here stressed is only that the analytic system based

---

[1] *Infra*, Ch. II. [2] *Infra*, Ch. VIII.
[3] *Infra*, § 46; K. N. Llewellyn, *The Common Law Tradition: Deciding Appeals.*

on Austin's teaching did not make sufficient allowance for the creative element in law and tended to magnify the static character of legal rules. It was considered possible to solve all legal problems by deduction from the actual rules of English law, eked out perhaps by careful borrowing from the Roman jurists.

(c) Law and Ethics

Austin, as we have said, distinguished jurisprudence, the science of the law that is (without reference to its goodness or badness), from the science of legislation which he based on the principle of utility. Many of his followers ignored entirely the latter study and proudly boasted that they studied the facts, keeping their feet on the ground instead of soaring into the clouds of misty speculation. When Austin wrote it was very necessary to delimit the sphere of jurisprudence because of the prevailing confusion. But we can see today that even the most positive member of the analytical school did not succeed in separating the *law that is* from ideal elements. The analyst did not discover his principles and classifications ready made but evolved them after long and patient study, and they depended not on the law of any one particular country, but on an idealized picture of English and Roman law. Unconsciously, the analysts laid down as the supreme end of law an ideal of logical harmony. Law was treated as a coherent system based on certain fundamental principles from which the particular rules may be deduced. Naturally, no system of law is perfectly self-consistent, but any rule that could not be fitted into the analyst's framework was dubbed an historical accident or a logical anomaly which (it was predicted) would soon disappear. Internal consistency is a desirable attribute of a legal system, for if it is logically interrelated it can be better understood, applied, and extended than if it is a mere chaos of particular rules. But the analyst assumed that logical self-consistency was the sole end of law. This was not stated in so many words, or its fallacy would have been apparent, but it was the underlying assumption on which the analytical school based their work. Clearly, law does not exist for the sake of consistency, for many a rule that is theoretically anomalous is based on sound views of public policy. The English law of tort would be more consistent if liability never arose in the absence of fault, but strong reasons of justice have led the law to create some instances of strict liability. One of the great virtues of the

Roman jurist was that he was unwilling to push a principle to its logical extreme if injustice would result.

Thus, criticism of the analytical school emphasizes two very significant truths for jurisprudence. Firstly, the *law that is* does not exist as a perfectly proportioned body of rules deduced from a few leading principles. The social pressures of the past have led to many convenient anomalies being adopted. Hence any attempt to reconcile the rules on logical grounds easily develops into a study not of the *law that is* but of the *law that should be*, if logic were to prevail. It is not suggested that it is wrong to attempt to render the rules as logically harmonious as possible. All that is stressed is that the analytical school, while proudly boasting that it treated only of the facts, set up an ideal of logical self-consistency by means of which it developed the law. Thus, the second point is that it is extraordinarily difficult for any school to resist setting up an ideal which can be made the basis for constructive criticism of the law. The analytical school boasted that they were treating only of the law that actually existed, but, unconscious as their ideal was, it was the real driving force of their work.[1] The influence of their work was such, however, that their insistence that lawyers should be concerned with the *law that is*, combined with the dogma that judges do not make law, led to a wasteful argument about whether or not judges do make law, and to the exclusion from legal studies in England for many years of many matters which are relevant when judges in fact do make law.

Perhaps the most significant recent development in England, following the imperative school with its origins in Austin's work, is the application to legal thinking of the methods of the linguistic positivists among the philosophers. The influence of Ludwig Wittgenstein[2] at Cambridge is accepted as having been the most significant in the development of those methods; but it is at Oxford that those methods are now most directly influencing juristic thinking—particularly since the appointment of H. L. A. Hart to the Oxford Chair of Jurisprudence in 1952.[3]

The analytical positivists influenced by those methods still affirm the Austinian belief that law can and ought to be made the subject

---

[1] 'Positivism is a Utopia': O. Kahn-Freund; Renner, *Institutions of Private Law*, 8.
[2] *Tractatus Logico-Philosophicus* (1922); *Philosophical Investigations* (1953); D. Pole, *The Later Philosophy of Wittgenstein* (1958).
[3] Hart, *Definition and Theory in Jurisprudence* (1953); Hart and Honoré, *Causation in the Law*; Hart, *The Concept of Law* (1961).

of study separately from morals;[1] that it can be seen as a system of
rules with a logic of its own capable of more satisfactory elucidation
than heretofore; and that the methods of linguistic analysis pursued
by the philosophers can be employed in jurisprudence to clear up
many puzzles which have troubled legal theorists, and to produce
clearer thinking for lawyers generally.

To provide an adequate brief explanation of the work of the
analytical and linguistic positivists is almost impossible, as it rests
on a background comprised of the work of a whole school of philosophers.[2] The main lessons for lawyers, however, lie in new insights
into the uses and meanings of words, the classification of things, and
into the peculiarities of the use of words in the logic of the law. Some
attempt to illustrate the method is made in later parts of this book.[3]
Perhaps the primary lessons, however, are to see that the traditional
(Aristotelian) way of going about the task of definition, by the assignment of a *res* to a genus and then to a species by reference to essence
and differentiating characteristics, is not only bad as a method of
definition in most areas of thought,[4] but is positively misleading and
confusing when applied to many legal terms, notions, or concepts.
The first step appears to be to distinguish between the two tasks: the
definition of words, and the description of things—however often the
one task must be performed to perform the other. If we are to avoid
confusion, we should limit the purpose of definition to the elucidation
of the meaning of words and we should not speak of defining things.

The second is to appreciate that words have many meanings
depending upon context and use: that they cannot be taken separately on the points of pins and given meanings as though they were
merely symbols in a naming process. The variations in use which
they enjoy may prevent the assignment of any single characteristic,
or group of characteristics, as fixing their *proper* meanings. Their
meanings, therefore, may only be elucidated, and satisfactory definitions provided, by examining the work that they do. This in turn
will usually require the analysis of facts also; and so a method which
at first sight appears to be concerned with words only, turns out

[1] Hart, 'Positivism and the Separation of Law and Morals', 71 *Harv. L. R.* (1958),
593: for a criticism of this position, see L. L. Fuller, 71 *Harv. L. R.* 630.
[2] From Russell, Carnap, and Wittgenstein in his earlier period to the later Wittgenstein, Moore, Ryle; see, for example, G. Ryle, *The Concept of Mind*; Nowell-Smith,
Ethics; J. Wisdom, *Philosophy and Psychoanalysis* (1953); and J. A. Passmore, *Hundred
Years of Philosophy* (1957).
[3] *Infra*, §§ 18, 62, 85 and Ch. XXII.
[4] R. Robinson, *Definition*, ch. vi.

to be concerned with things and the realities of the external world as well.

The third major step is to see that many words (and many legal terms are peculiarly illustrative of this, even though they may be nouns) are not used as names for things which are entities examinable in the external world at all; but are words with meanings which can only be accurately discerned by reference to the rules of the system within which they are used and to the use made of them in that system. Robinson[1] calls such words 'systematic words' and shows, for example, that you cannot answer the question 'what is a Swiss citizen?' by reference to any external entity or by reference to essence and *differentia*; but only by reference to rules which establish what human beings become or are Swiss citizens. Those rules will be rules of a particular legal system. And Hart makes the point that many legal terms used as nouns are not names for things, but are words used to make arguments, press claims, or draw conclusions, of law. Those arguments, claims, conclusions, can only be seen as acceptable or as valid, by reference to the rules of the appropriate system. Thus the meaning, and hence the definition of such words, can only be elucidated satisfactorily by studying the use of them within the system of reasoning concerned. As an example of this method Hart would explain the meaning of the word 'right' in the law in the following manner:

(1) A statement of the form 'X has a right' is true if the following conditions are satisfied:

(*a*) there is in existence a legal system.

(*b*) under a rule or rules of the system some other person Y is, in the events which have happened, obliged to do or abstain from some action.

(*c*) this obligation is made by law dependent on the choice either of X or some person authorized to act on his behalf so that either Y is bound to do or abstain from some action only if X (or some authorized person) so chooses or alternatively only until X (or such person) chooses otherwise.

(2) A statement of the form 'X has a right' is used to draw a conclusion of law in a particular case which falls under such rules.[2]

---

[1] *Definition*, 128–9.
[2] *Definition and Theory in Jurisprudence*, 16–17. The problem of definition is discussed by W. A. Wilson, 32 *Mod. L. R.* (1969), 361.

This approach has been subjected to sharp criticism already[1] and its exponents have been charged with mere playing with words and with saying nothing of importance for the solution of the real problems which face lawyers. There are, however, many problems which have defied solution by legal theorists. The claim made for the modern analysts is not that their methods will provide right answers to all those problems but that they will help to remove some of the obstacles which have prevented satisfactory solution of those problems in the past. As put by Wittgenstein, the aim is 'to show the fly the way out of the fly bottle'.[2] Where the fly will fly after escaping from the fly bottle is a separate question altogether.

§ 5. THE PURE SCIENCE OF LAW

Nearly a century separates the work of Hans Kelsen from that of Austin.[3] If Austin was driven to make his jurisprudence rigid because of the confusion of previous writers, Kelsen represents a reaction against the modern schools which have so far widened the boundaries of jurisprudence that they seem almost conterminous with those of the social sciences. But while Austin did not consciously formulate a detailed philosophy, Kelsen admittedly builds on the doctrine of Kant.[4] Most philosophers emphasize that jurisprudence must study the relationship between law and justice, but Kelsen wishes to free 'the law from the metaphysical mist with which it has been covered at all times by the speculations on justice or by the doctrine of *ius naturae*'.[5] He is thus a philosopher in revolt from the tendencies to which philosophy has led so many writers. He desires to create a pure science of law, stripped of all irrelevant material, and to separate jurisprudence from the social sciences as rigorously as did the analysts. The mathematician is not interested in the way in

---

[1] C. A. Auerbach, 'On Professor H. A. L. Hart's Definition and Theory in Jurisprudence', 9 *J. Leg. Ed.* (1956), 39; E. Bodenheimer, 'Modern Analytical Jurisprudence and the Limits of its Usefulness', 104 *U. of Penn. L. R.* (1956), 1080; I. S. Shuman, 'Jurisprudence and the Analysis of Fundamental Legal Terms', 8 *J. Leg. Ed.* (1956), 437; E. Gelner, *Words and Things* (1959).

[2] *Philosophical Investigations* 47e—quoted by Lloyd, *Introduction to Jurisprudence* (1959), p. xiv.

[3] *Allgemeine Staatslehre*; *Reine Rechtslehre*; *General Theory of Law and State*; 55 *Harv. L. R.* (1941), 44; *Annales de l'Institut de droit comparé* (1936), ii. 17; J. W. Jones, *Historical Introduction to the Theory of Law*, ch. ix; *The Pure Theory of Law*, 50 and 51 *L.Q.R.* (1934–5), 474, 517; *General Theory of Law and the State* (trans. A. Wedburg) (1946); *What is Justice?* (1957).

[4] But he modifies Kant's theories and adopts diverse elements from other writers: Martyniak, *Archives de phil. du droit* (1937, 1–2), 166.

[5] Kelsen, *Law, a Century of Progress*, ii. 231; Jones, 47 *L.Q.R.* (1931), 62.

which men think nor is he directly concerned whether his work is to
be used to build a bridge or to work out a new system to break the
bank at Monte Carlo: so the jurist, if he is to be scientific, must study
the legal rules abstracted from all social conditions. Kelsen refuses to
define law as a command, for that introduces subjective and political
considerations and he wishes his science to be truly objective.

First, Kelsen wishes to separate the realm of jurisprudence from
that of natural science. The latter deals with cause and effect: for
example, Newton attempted to formulate a general principle which
would describe what actually does happen to the apple when its stalk
is loosened from the tree. Law, on the other hand, does not attempt
to describe what occurs but rather to prescribe certain rules, to lay
down standards of action which men ought to follow. If X breaks the
criminal law, then he ought to be punished. The sole object of study
for jurisprudence is the nature of the norms (or standards) which are
set up by law. A legal system exists in order to impose obligations on
certain individuals; to know whether in a particular case an obligation exists, we ask whether the individual, if he disobeys a rule, would
suffer a sanction. But Kelsen does not take Austin's step of defining
law as a command of the sovereign. Law and the State are really the
same thing envisaged from different aspects. A legal order becomes
a state when it has developed organs for the creation, declaration,
and enforcement of law. When we look at the abstract rules we think
of the legal order; when we examine the institutions by which law is
put into effect we think of the State. But this is merely looking at the
same thing from two angles.

If, however, we cannot adopt the easy method of defining law in
terms of the State, by what can we distinguish a rule of law? Rules of
law cannot be tested by their content, the actual subject-matter with
which they deal, since law may cover any topic. The modern tendency
to regulate so many of the affairs of the private citizen means that the
sphere of law is daily increasing. Nor can we define law in terms of
justice, for many rules may be unjust, but they do not therefore cease
to be law. 'Justice is an irrational ideal'—that is, it cannot be clearly
defined by reason, and hence it is not a satisfactory concept for a
science of pure law.[1]

Kelsen finds the criterion in the way in which the rule is created.
A judge in a mock trial may pass the same sentence as the judge of
a properly constituted court, but the latter sentence has legal validity

[1] Kelsen, 55 *Harv. L. R.* (1941), 44 at 48.

because the prescribed conditions of the legal order have been fulfilled. Hence we must trace every legal act back to a norm which imputes legal validity to certain human behaviour. The imprisonment of Jones is justified because of the sentence of a criminal court: the court has this power because of the criminal code: the criminal code has legal effect because it was enacted by the appropriate legislative body, which is granted the power to legislate by the constitution. But how can we explain the legal force of a constitution? What is the legal basis of the power of the King in Parliament to change the law? Constitutions ultimately have an extra-legal origin. Even if the whole community unanimously agrees to accept a particular constitution, that agreement has no legal force, for until a constitution is adopted the methods by which law is to be created are not laid down.[1] A revolution may destroy an old constitution and create a new one, but such matters are beyond the sphere of jurisprudence which must posit an initial hypothesis or *Grundnorm* beyond which it cannot go. Once it has been accepted as a basis that the will of the King in Parliament ought to be obeyed, we may trace the validity of any particular legal rule; but to determine what is to be the initial hypothesis for any country we must go beyond jurisprudence, examine the world of reality, and discover an hypothesis that has some measure of correspondence with the facts. It would be futile to state as the initial hypothesis for the U.S.S.R. that the will of the Tsar ought to be obeyed. But it should be noted that the hypothesis need not *absolutely* correspond with the facts. In England the will of the King in Parliament ought to be obeyed, but no one supposes that every member of the community actually does obey the law on every occasion. This emphasizes again that law does not state what actually does happen, but lays down what ought to happen; yet if the legal order is to be effective, it must secure a certain measure of acceptance.

An interesting example by which to test Kelsen's theory is the Unilateral Declaration of Independence by Rhodesia. The Privy Council, as part of the English legal order, naturally decided against the validity of the Rhodesian emergency powers which had not been laid down in accordance with the *Grundnorm* the court accepted.[2]

---

[1] Cf. *Att.-Gen. for N.S.W.* v. *Trethowan*, [1932] A.C. 526; *Harris* v. *Minister of the Interior*, [1952] 2 S.A. 428 A.D.; *Minister of the Interior* v. *Harris*, [1952] 4 S.A. 769 A.D.; Sir Owen Dixon, 'The Common Law as an Ultimate Constitutional Foundation', 31 *A.L.J.* (1957), 240.
[2] *Madzimbamuto* v. *Lardner-Burke*, [1969] 1 A.C. 645; see also *Adams* v. *Adams*, [1970] 3 All E.R. 572, where a divorce granted in Rhodesia was not afforded recogni-

The Rhodesian courts looked at the problem in the light of the new legal order created by the declaration of independence, and relied partly on the theory of necessity and of the actualities of politics.[1] In other words, these courts in effect accepted a new *Grundnorm* for Rhodesia.

The sphere of jurisprudence, then, is a study of the nature of this hierarchy of norms, the validity of each norm depending on its being laid down in accordance with a superior norm until we reach the initial hypothesis which jurisprudence can only accept and cannot hope to prove. The initial hypothesis is abstract, but as we descend the ladder the norms gradually become more concrete until we reach the final norm which imposes an obligation on a particular individual, e.g. either by the judgment of a court, the order of an administrative officer, or the making of a contract between two citizens. In essence these three operations merely carry out a superior norm and impose constraint on individuals.

It is difficult to appreciate the significance of Kelsen's work until the application of the theory is understood,[2] but for the present we are concerned only with the bearing of his theory on the problem of the boundaries of jurisprudence. The subject-matter for jurisprudence is the legal norm emptied of all practical content, all questions of ethics or social philosophy being beyond the jurist's ken. His claim that he has created an impartial and universal science is justified, but are we not left with the dry bones of the law deprived of the flesh and blood which give them life? The great value of his work is its critical force, since he ably shows that many writers have clothed with the glory of first principles of jurisprudence what are only their own prejudices. Kelsen is not alone in his disgust at 'politics masquerading as jurisprudence', at those who object to state regulation of labour conditions because it interferes with the onward march of the neo-Hegelian idea that law must give increasing freedom to the individual will. Kelsen is correct in showing that law is a weapon that may be used to effect many ends—indeed, it is curious to see that his impartiality in the conflicting social problems of today has led conservatives to call him a dangerous radical and the revolutionaries to dub him a reactionary. Kelsen's work is also valuable in its emphasis that in

tion in England, as the Rhodesian judge had not, according to the English *Grundnorm*, been validly appointed.

[1] J. M. Eekelaar, 32 *Mod. L. R.* (1969), 19; R. W. M. Dias, 26 *Camb. L. J.* (1968), 233. A most useful study is that of J. W. Harris, 29 *Camb. L. J.* (1971), 103.

[2] *Infra*, §§ 21, 75–6, 90, 99.

executing the norms of law the judge has much discretion—it is impossible for any general rule to provide for all contingencies, and the general rules must be made precise by those who have the duty of applying them. But, in order to maintain the air of impartiality, Kelsen regards as outside the scope of jurisprudence all discussion of natural law, and all examination of the sources whence the judge draws his rules when there is no authority in point.[1] This leaves the science of law very 'pure', but deprives it of all interesting contact with life itself. Indeed, what we obtain from this method is not a theory of legal development but simply the formal principles of juristic thought.[2] To exclude the whole of sociology and of ethics leaves jurisprudence but a mental exercise in abstract notions. The objection to Kelsen's pure science of law is that if the premises are rigidly followed, the result is too formal to be of service to jurisprudence; if the jurist goes beyond his premises, the method is destroyed. Kelsen would be very impatient of any argument that jurisprudence should serve the needs of life—its aim in his eyes should be to enable us to understand the nature of law and the State. But the point made here is that Kelsen's method does not even give us a true picture of law, for jurisprudence must go beyond the formal hierarchy of norms to study the social forces that create law. The doctrine of natural law has certainly been abused, but is jurisprudence, therefore, to ignore the whole question of ethics? Indeed, Kelsen himself goes beyond the limits of his method in discussing the nature of international law and really bases his view on the ideal of the legal unity of the world.[3] Nor can we understand the real nature of the State by regarding it in a purely formal light.[4] The philosophic difficulties involved in Kelsen's clear separation of the legal world of norms from the world of reality cannot be here discussed,[5] but it may be pointed out that, however pure his science is kept, the initial premiss for any legal order can be discovered only by a study of the facts in that particular community.

No one can doubt that Kelsen has made an original and striking contribution to jurisprudence. In 1832 Austin cleared away much

---

[1] H. Lauterpacht, in *Modern Theories of Law*, 105 at 133.

[2] F. Hallis, *Corporate Personality*, 56–7. On the other hand, Kelsen recognizes the validity of other methods, e.g. sociological jurisprudence. His concern is really to establish the validity of his pure science as the best, although not the only, approach: 55 *Harv. L. R.* (1941), 53.

[3] *Infra*, § 21. Formally Kelsen saves his method by verbally recognizing that this is not the only alternative: Lauterpacht, op. cit. 129.

[4] Carré de Malberg, *Confrontation de la théorie de la formation du droit par degrés*.

[5] Wilson in 1 *Politica* (1934–5), 54.

dead wood, and a century later Kelsen with critical acumen exposed   NB
many fallacies. But the aim of the pure science of law is a narrow
one, and it must be complemented by other and broader approaches.

§ 6. The Historical School

The historical school antedates the work of Kelsen, but the reason
for postponing discussion of the historical thesis is that, in opposition
to the doctrine of the pure science of law, the historical school considered law in direct relationship to the life of the community and
thus laid the foundation on which the modern sociological school has
built. The eighteenth century was an age of rationalism; it was believed possible by arm-chair deliberation to construct a universal and
unchangeable body of laws that would be applicable to all countries,
using as a premiss the reasonable nature of man.[1] The historical
school in part was a result of that surge of nationalism that arose at
the end of the eighteenth century. Instead of the individual, writers
began to emphasize the spirit of the people, the *Volksgeist*. In 1814
a programme for the school was enunciated by Savigny.[2] The central
question was 'how did law come to be?' Law evolved, as did language, by a slow process and, just as language is a peculiar product
of a nation's genius, so is the law. The source of law is not the
command of the sovereign, not even the habits of a community, but
the instinctive sense of right possessed by every race. Custom may be
evidence of law, but its real source lies deeper in the minds of men.
'The living of law' is the secret of its validity. In those matters with
which he is directly concerned every member of the community has an
instinctive sense as to what is right and proper, although naturally
he will have no views on matters which are beyond his experience.
Thus the mercantile community will have an intuitive appreciation
of the rules that should govern bills of exchange, a peasant of the
doctrines that should be applied to agriculture. Such is the approach
of the historical school, and it naturally led to a distrust of any
deliberate attempt to reform the law. Legislation can succeed only
if it is in harmony with the internal convictions of the race to which
it is addressed. If it goes farther, it is doomed to failure.[3]

---

[1] *Infra*, § 33.
[2] *On the Vocation of our Time for Legislation and Jurisprudence*: H. Kantorowicz,
53 *L.Q.R.* (1937), 326.
[3] Chinese philosophy approaches law in much the same spirit: cf. J. Escarra,
Archives de phil. du droit (1935, 1–2), 70. Marxist dialectical materialism argues that
the law is a product of social change—but for different reasons.

The contribution of the historical school to the problem of the boundaries of jurisprudence is that law cannot be understood without an appreciation of the social milieu in which it has developed. The slow evolution of law was stressed and its intimate connection with the particular characteristics of a people. Ever since Savigny wrote, the value which jurisprudence can gain from a proper use of the historical method has been well recognized, and in England Maine[1] and Vinogradoff[2] have kept the interest in these problems alive. Writers of legal history such as Pollock and Maitland[3] or Sir William Holdsworth[4] have provided surveys whose value for the jurist lies in the clear demonstration of the close connection between the common law and the social and political history of England.

In particular, the historical school destroyed for ever the shibboleth of immutable rules of law, discovered by abstract reason: they demonstrated that, just as in the case of the human body, transplants of legal systems or constitutions may be defeated by the immunological reaction of the receiving country.

But in Savigny's particular presentation there were exaggerations of which the historical method must be freed if it is to play its true part. Firstly, some customs are not based on an instinctive sense of right in the community as a whole but on the interests of a strong minority, for example, slavery.[5] Secondly, while some rules may develop almost unconsciously, others are the result of conscious effort—our modern trade-union law was not achieved without much struggle. The flood of legislation in the twentieth century connected with what has become known as the 'Welfare State' marks the denial of Savigny's views in practice if not in theory. Law has been used to plan the future deliberately and not merely to express and order the results of past growth. Thirdly, the creative work of the judge and jurist was treated rather too lightly. The life of a people may supply the rough material, but the judge must hew the block and make precise the form of law. It is possible to exaggerate the 'great lawyer' interpretation of history, for in a sense all men are children of the age in which they live, but to regard the judge as a mere passive representative of the *Volksgeist* is just as dangerous. Both in equity and in the common law we can still trace the influence of the masters of the past, and any layman would be surprised if told that

---

[1] *Ancient Law.*   [2] *Outlines of Historical Jurisprudence.*
[3] *History of English Law before the Time of Edward I.*
[4] *A History of English Law.*   [5] C. K. Allen, *Law in the Making,* chs. i and ii.

he had an instinctive sense of right concerning the rules of contingent remainders or the subtle refinements of the doctrine of equitable waste. Fourthly, imitation plays a greater part than the historical school would admit. Much Roman law was consciously borrowed, and when the success of the French Code was acknowledged, other nations laid it deeply under debt. When the East began its rapid assimilation of Western ideas, it borrowed freely from the codes of Germany and France.[1] Savigny himself could never quite exorcize the ghost of the reception of Roman law in Germany; the thesis that the jurists, in weaving Roman rules into the customary law, were mere representatives of the *Volksgeist* would have been ridiculed by the peasants who accused the *doctores iuris* of depriving the tenant of his customary rights in land by the introduction of foreign rules. Lastly, Savigny encouraged what Pound has termed 'juristic pessimism'—legislation must accord with the instinctive sense of right or it was doomed to failure. Hence conscious law reform was to be discouraged. There was sometimes a tendency to think that once the evolution of a rule had been traced, this description justified its existence. It is fatally easy to accept abuses in that to which one is accustomed, for 'nothing binds [*sic*] the vision so much as custom and habit. There was a time when the criminal law of this country was in a state which would have been a disgrace to a half-civilized community and . . . judges in high authority and writers . . . wrote about it that it was the perfection of human wisdom.'[2] The historical method in jurisprudence, therefore, should be supplemented by a critical approach based on a philosophy of law, in order that a true perspective may be maintained. Evolution is not necessarily progress, and one of the best aids to our own short-sightedness in dealing with the familiar common law is an acquaintance with many systems. This is well recognized by those who pursue the historical method today.

---

[1] An interesting account of the latent conflict between a borrowed code and a national tradition is that of Pound, 61 *Harv. L. R.* (1948), 749.

[2] Per Greer, L.J. *Leon* v. *Casey* (1932), 48 T.L.R. 452 at 455. It is easy, however, to exaggerate the 'juristic pessimism' of the historical school. Savigny's real point was that a code was impossible without the labour of many generations of jurists in order to distinguish the living law from what was dead: see J. W. Jones, *Historical Introduction to the Theory of Law*, 58.

§ 7. The Functional School

Dean Pound[1] is usually credited as being the American leader in the school of sociological jurisprudence, but it is unfortunate that the term 'sociological' was never used in this connection—to speak of the functional method would have been more accurate and less confusing. The fundamental tenet of this school is that we cannot understand what a thing is unless we study what it does. It is, perhaps, a penetrating study of the judicial method that has led these writers to urge the widening of the boundaries of jurisprudence. It is generally recognized today that the judicial process does not supply answers to concrete problems with the inevitable accuracy of an adding-machine. Where there is no authority in point, 'the inarticulate major premiss' or the 'social picture' of the judge may determine which of two competing analogies should be adopted. Too large a role has been assigned by some to the 'inarticulate major premiss', and too little attention given to the effect upon judges of their immersion in the common law system.[2] If the judge entirely ignored questions of social interests, of expediency and practical convenience, however, any system of law would become unendurable. But what attitude should jurisprudence take to this awkward question of the values that direct the development of law? Kelsen would expel them in order to retain the scientific method, but Pound considers that they must be analysed thoroughly in order to understand legal development—and an appreciation of legal development he considers a key to the nature of law. To Pound law is more than a set of abstract norms or a legal order—it is also a process of balancing conflicting interests and securing the satisfaction of the maximum of wants with the minimum of friction.[3] The analogy of social engineering is one which Pound uses more than once. Pound's work is well balanced, marked by tolerance and shrewd scepticism. To those who delight in controversy for its own sake he administers a just rebuke—'in the house of jurisprudence there are many mansions. There is more than enough room for all of us and more than enough work. If the time and energy expended on polemics were devoted to that work, jurisprudence would be more nearly abreast of its tasks.'[4] He expects no new heaven

---

[1] *The Philosophy of Law*; *Interpretations of Legal History*; *Outlines of Jurisprudence*; *Jurisprudence* (1959). The most understanding survey of Pound's writing is that of J. Stone, *Province and Function of Law*, 355 et seq.
[2] Sir Owen Dixon, 'Concerning Judicial Method', 29 *A.L.J.* (1956), 468.
[3] *Interpretations of Legal History*, 156.   [4] 44 *Harv. L. R.* (1930–1), 711.

by a stroke of the pen but urges that the jurist should study the actual social effects of legal institutions and endeavour to make legal rules really effective for the purpose for which they were designed. Law in action may be very different from law in books.[1]

What, however, is the criterion that should be applied in reaching a compromise between conflicting interests, for inevitably some must be sacrificed? Pound's view is essentially relativistic, for he emphasizes that the jurist as such has no divine charter to determine the ends which law should pursue but can only tentatively effect compromises valid for his time and generation because they are based not on absolute ideals but on the views held by that particular community at the moment.[2]

The left wing of the functional school is frequently termed the realist school. In the sense of a body of men agreeing on defined principles, no such group exists. But certain writers show a common approach to the problems of law, and the term 'realism' has been chosen to describe the method.[3] The realists trace their intellectual ancestry to the scepticism of Holmes J.[4] Pound is regarded as having seen the truth but as having failed to apply it effectively to jurisprudence.[5] The great merit of these two jurists was the balance and proportion of their work, for due weight was given both to the logical structure of the law and the influence of social forces. The realists, however, emphasize the element of uncertainty in law and the part played by the personal characteristics of the judge. Law is defined not as a set of logical propositions but in terms of official action. Law is what courts (or other officials) *do*, not what they *say*. Until a court has passed on certain facts, some realists argued, there is no law on the subject yet in existence, for the opinion of lawyers is only a guess as to what the courts will decide. Since law is defined in terms of official action (and not of the rules which should guide action), it follows that any force that will influence a judge in reaching a decision (whether corruption, indigestion, or partiality for the other sex) is a fit subject for jurisprudence. Much scorn is poured on the classical[6]

---

[1] Pound's six-point plan is laid down in 25 *Harv. L. R.* (1911–12), 513.

[2] *Infra*, § 36.

[3] Judge Jerome Frank, *Law and the Modern Mind*; for a bibliography of realist writings see G. N. Garlan, *Legal Realism and Justice* (1941), 135–43.

[4] 'I always say that the chief end of man is to form general propositions—adding that no general proposition is worth a damn', *Pollock–Holmes Letters*, ii. 13.

[5] 'If ever a man hid his light under a bushel it was Pound': Judge Frank, 80 *Univ. of Pa. L. R.* (1931–2), 19.

[6] Apparently Frank regarded any jurist as 'classical' who did not accept his thesis.

jurists for being deceived by what the courts said they were doing instead of examining what they actually did. The formal rules of law can have little weight in legal evolution—any rule is unsatisfactory because human relationships are too numerous and complex to be confined within a formula, because society is always changing, moral judgments are developing, and the law therefore is in a state of flux.[1] Words cannot accurately depict reality and rules have no meaning apart from their application in a particular case. Judge Frank accused the classical jurists of legal fundamentalism, of verbalism, of scholasticism, of childish thought ways, of worshipping rules, and of exaggerating the element of certainty in law.[2]

The early writing of the realists was frequently misinterpreted: now that sufficient time has passed it is easier to see it in a true perspective. Although they began earlier, the great arguments started by realist writing took place in the twenties and thirties of this century. Those were decades of philosophical, political, and economic upheaval throughout the world. The First World War had shattered the established order of European society and government, and the great depression of the 1930s presented the world, and particularly the United States of America, if not with new problems, with demands which had never been met adequately before. Most of the more widely read realist writers did not deny the importance played by rules of law in the effective operation of legal systems.[3] They did deny, however, that the study of the authoritative pronouncements of those placed within a legal system to make them, whether legislative, judicial, or otherwise, provided a sufficient explanation of the operation of a legal system. As has been seen, they took this denial so far as to define law as what officials do, rather than to define it by reference to the rules which are established (inter alia) to control and guide what officials do. They were almost universally agreed in rejecting, or at least in being suspicious of, any a priori logic and in accepting an instrumental logic.[4] They were pragmatists. However united they may have been in their rejection of then orthodox and absolutist explanations of law and legal systems, their particular interests took them off in widely divergent directions.

Some[5] attempted to establish a method by which the problems of law and legal development could be made objective, descriptive, and

[1] A. Kocourek, Rec. Gény, ii. 459.   [2] Law and the Modern Mind, 41, 57, 69.
[3] K. N. Llewellyn, The Bramble Bush (1951), foreword, 9–10; The Common Law Tradition: Deciding Appeals (1960).   [4] J. Dewey, Logic (1938).
[5] Like W. U. Moore, H. Oliphant, and perhaps W. O. Douglas.

factual. They approached law as a social science and, largely ignoring the rules which were said by many to be the law, they attempted to investigate the facts and decisions and consequences of legal activities, and so, by statistical methods, to produce new and objectively valid criteria for prediction on the one hand and evaluation on the other.[1] Others made the main burden of their attack the indeterminacy of language and the impossibility of providing certainty in particular official action by the framing of general rules. In this they were excited and encouraged by the growing study of semantics by thinkers outside the law.[2] Others concentrated upon the search for the real factors which control judicial decisions after assuming, or in some instances demonstrating, that the authoritative rules of law pronounced by judges as reasons for their decisions did not, in fact, control but were more in the nature of rationalizations made after a decision had been reached on other grounds. For these, various psychological theories were important and a new link with the behavioural sciences was established in the examination of the judicial process.

K. N. Llewellyn concentrated rather on the uncertainty in the actual operation of the rules in appellate courts—he wished to make a 'sustained and realistic examination of the best practice and art of the best judges and their judging'[3] and he has, in fact, in a major work attempted just such a study.[4] Similarly, W. W. Cook submitted the basic rules of private international law to an incisive analysis which showed that what appeared on a superficial glance to be certain was full of inherent ambiguity.[5]

Judge Frank divided the realists into two groups: 'rule-skeptics' and 'fact-skeptics'.[6] The 'rule-skeptics' were those who concentrated on appellate courts and on the nature and uses of legal rules.[7] The 'fact-skeptics' were those who concentrated on trial courts and who found the major cause of legal uncertainty in the uncertainties of fact

---

[1] For a criticism of this work see H. Kantorowicz, 'Some Rationalism about Realism', 43 *Yale L. J.* (1934), 1240, 1246.

[2] Ogden and Richards's book, *The Meaning of Meaning*, seems to have had a profound influence upon them.

[3] 40 *Col. L. R.* (1940), 581 at 614.

[4] *The Common Law Tradition: Deciding Appeals* (1960).

[5] *The Logical and Legal Bases of Conflict of Laws.*

[6] It may be that Judge Frank was the only prominent member of the second group.

[7] Frank said, 'Some (not all) of this group (Oliphant being the most conspicuous here) espoused the fatuous notions of 'behaviouristic psychology'. Some (not all) of these 'rules-skeptics' went somewhat further than Cardozo as to the extent of the existent and desirable power of judges to alter the legal rules.'—'Cardozo and the Upper Court Myth', 13 *Law and Contemporary Problems* (1948), 369, 384.

finding. Judge Frank claimed that the degree of legal uncertainty was far more extensive, in fact, than most legal scholars were prepared to admit.[1]

If, and in so far as, Judge Frank was emphasizing only the uncertainties introduced into the judicial process by the difficulty of finding the true facts, clearly few would disagree with him. It is the lower courts which deal with the great mass of litigation, and to a humble plaintiff it may not matter whether he loses because of a misunderstanding of the law or because of an error as to fact. If Frank's plea was that the courts should improve the techniques for finding facts, then he emphasizes a point that has not been sufficiently stressed in the past.[2] It is to be noted, however, that until he had had several years' experience as a judge both on trial and appellate courts, Judge Frank was just as vehement a 'rule-skeptic' as any of those he grouped under that name. To understand the judicial process we must, of course, use every aid. In any particular litigation it may be important to study the personality of the court before which the issue will come: but when we are considering the general development of the rules of law, individual peculiarities tend to cancel out.[3]

The realists had more in common than their rejection of much that they saw accepted around them. To a man they were reformers. As might have been expected in the 1920s, they found the law framed in terms of premises, concepts, and principles drawn from religious, philosophical, and metaphysical thinking of past centuries. In the main, they found methods characteristic of eighteenth-century rationalism and nineteenth-century utilitarianism, but still based in many parts upon medieval metaphysics. They attacked these bases. They insisted that to know what a thing is one must see what it does; that rules of law must be assessed by reference to their consequences. They saw law as but one method of social control and hence they argued that it could not be understood or developed rationally with-

[1] He said, 'So far as appellate courts and the legal rules are concerned, the views of the "fact-skeptics" as to existent and desirable legal certainty approximated the views of Cardozo, Pound, and many others not categorized as "realists".' 'Cardozo and the Upper Court Myth', *Law and Contemporary Problems* (1948), 369, 384.

[2] It is much easier to concentrate our attention on appellate courts. Judge Frank suggested that in an ideal law curriculum there would be a study based on first-hand observation of what courts, administrative agencies, and legislatures actually do. *Courts on Trial.*

[3] Some American writers regret that we have not sufficient evidence concerning the intelligence quotients of particular judges (167 *Annals of the American Academy of Political Science* (1933), 144) and of their psychological complexes. This would add a new terror to election to the bench.

out understanding its relationship with disciplines concerned with humanity and societies—politics, economics, psychology, sociology, and anthropology.[1]

The heyday of American realism was a time for free-swinging criticism of established ideas and established authority. It is not surprising that some of the realists' publications provoked such comments as: 'It was perhaps appropriate that the age of jazz should produce a jazz jurisprudence';[2] and 'the Bar has always studied the human personality of judges, but it has been too modest to dignify such research by the name of jurisprudence'.[3]

Perhaps the most immediate and most important influence of American legal realism was upon legal education. The aims and methods of law schools almost throughout the United States of America, both in the classroom and out of the classroom, underwent change. Classes were invited less and less to analyse the written opinions of judges to ascertain what the 'law on a point is', and more and more to examine the kinds of problems which are thrown up to be solved by the judicial system and to speculate about the kinds of thinking which would solve them best. This change affected profoundly the kind of materials used in legal education and in particular the content and format of American casebooks.[4] The concentration upon the problems to be solved rather than upon the formal and authoritative explanations of how they had been, or ought to be, solved, changed the whole nature of legal education. It forced upon law students a consideration of the interrelations between the study of law and the study of other social sciences. It brought into their field of vision the changes and developments in other social

---

[1] Perhaps the most succinct statement of the points the realists had in common is to be found in Llewellyn's 'Some Realism About Realism', 44 *Harv. L. R.* (1931), 1222. There Llewellyn concluded that the realists had the following in common: (*a*) A conception of law in flux; (*b*) a conception of law as a means to social ends; (*c*) a conception of society in flux; (*d*) for the purposes of the study in hand a separation of the *is* from the *ought*; (*e*) a distrust of traditional legal rules and concepts; (*f*) a distrust of giving too much importance to prescriptive rules in the decisional process; (*g*) a belief in the value of grouping cases in narrow categories; (*h*) an insistence on evaluation by reference to consequences; (*i*) a belief in the results which would be achieved by programmed and sustained research projects investigating the facts; and see Garlan, op. cit.

[2] C. K. Allen, *Law in the Making*, 3rd ed. 45. (This sentence does not appear in the 7th ed.)

[3] In the first edition of this book, 21.

[4] E. W. Patterson, 'The Case Method in American Legal Education: Its Origins and Objectives', 4 *Journal of Legal Education* (1951), 1; H. A. J. Ford, *The Evolution of the American Casebook*, 7 Res Judicatae 256; A. Ehrenzweig, 'The American Casebook: Cases and Materials', 32 *Georgetown L. J.* (1944), 244; B. Currie, 'The Materials of Law Study', 3 *J. Leg. Ed.* (1951), 331.

disciplines, such as sociology, psychology, politics, economics, and international relations, in a way that an earlier generation of law students had been able and sometimes encouraged to avoid.

Those changes brought with them their own disadvantages. A decline became evident among law students in their understanding and appreciation of the internal discipline and coherence of systems of law viewed as rules and principles. It may be that such a decline was inevitable in any case in a country where more than fifty ultimate courts of appeal may give differing final answers to a question of common law,[1] and that in a national law school it was already impossible to support the notion of a disciplined and authoritative body of law in the form of principles and rules which exist and operate apart from the men who apply them. If so it would be wrong to lay the decline mentioned wholly at the door of the realists. In any case during the 1920s and 1930s many changes in legal education were brought about as the result of efforts of law teachers who would not have called themselves realists.

It is not without significance to note that Thurman Arnold, one of the more colourful realist writers of the 1930s,[2] wrote recently: 'The ideal of a judiciary which discovers its principles through the enlightened application of established precedents dramatizes that most important conception that there is a rule of law above men. In that sense, law must be a "brooding omnipresence in the sky". This is an ideal which can never be attained, but if men do not strive for it the law loses its moral force';[3] and that he also wrote: 'Realistic jurisprudence is a good medicine for a sick and troubled society. The America of the early 1930s was such a society. But realism, despite its liberating virtues, is not a sustaining food for a stable civilization.'[4]

Now that the dust of earlier conflicts has settled, however, there seems to be less difference between the right and left wings of the functional school than was formerly supposed. The gospel of both is that the jurist must study the functioning of law in society: a realistic examination of the judicial process is obviously a part of such an approach. Inevitably, however, differences of emphasis will arise between various writers.

[1] *Erie R. Co.* v. *Tompkins*, 304 U.S. 64.
[2] *Apologia for Jurisprudence*, 44 *Yale L. J.* (1935), 729; *The Folklore of Capitalism* (1937); *The Symbols of Government* (1935), etc.
[3] 24 *U. of Chi. L. Rev.* (1957) at 634.
[4] Ibid. at 635.

§ 8. THE SOCIOLOGY OF LAW

Pound's sociological jurisprudence should be distinguished from what is now called the sociology of law. The natural confusion caused by the similarity of these terms is an added reason for preferring the name 'functional school' as the best description of the work of Pound.

Sociology of law is defined in many ways, but its main difference from functional jurisprudence is that it attempts to create a science of social life as a whole and to cover a great part of general sociology and political science. The emphasis of the study is on society and law as a mere manifestation, whereas Pound rather concentrates on law and considers society in relation to it.[1]

Thus Ehrlich[2] (1862–1920) builds on the foundations laid down by Savigny a broad theory that law depends on popular acceptance and that each group creates its own living law which alone has creative force. All that the judge does is to make precise and definite the raw material thus furnished by the community. He contrasts *living law* with the mere *norm for decision* laid down by the judge. To concentrate on the latter is to miss the real spirit of law. Codes may be technically in force in the sense that a court will apply their provisions if they are called in question, but frequently a community ignores the codes and lives according to rules created by consent. In parts of Austria the statute law has not greatly affected the real life of the community. The legislation of France and Rumania may be much the same, yet the law of the first differs very much from that of the second. Modern commerce has already gone far beyond the German Commercial Code. Hence to understand the legal life of a community the jurist must supplement his study of the code or the decisions of the courts by an analysis of the facts. 'To attempt to imprison the law of a time or of a people within the sections of a code is about as reasonable as to attempt to confine a stream within a pond. The water that is put in the pond is no longer a living stream but a stagnant pool, and but little water can be put in the pond.'[3] Any English writer would admit this but would consider that the courts gave a reasonably true picture of the living law. Ehrlich, however, draws the conclusion that jurisprudence is merely a branch of

---

[1] N. S. Timasheff, *Sociology of Law*; R. Pound, 'Sociology of Law and Sociological Jurisprudence', 5 *Univ. of Toronto L. J.* (1943), 1; G. Gurvitch, *Sociology of Law*.

[2] *Grundlegung der Soziologie des Rechts*, translated by Moll (1936) as *Fundamental Principles of the Sociology of Law*. [3] Ibid. 488.

sociology and extends the boundary of jurisprudence almost to absurd lengths. The first attempt must be to study living law just as the physiologist studies living tissue. It is not essential that law should be created by the State, or applied by the courts, or that there be a system of legal compulsion.[1] The real law consists not of propositions but of legal institutions created by the life of the groups within society—hence the importance of studying the factual institutions that create law. The custom of the past is the rule of the future. He considers that the jurist should study the factory, the bank, the railroad, the great landed estate, the labour union, the association of employers, and a thousand other forms of life. Every department in a factory should be studied so that no process of manufacture or sale should escape the jurist's eye. Rather breathlessly, one wonders if a lifetime would be enough to deal with one industry. Allen is tempted, without 'disrespect to the labours of a very learned, sincere, and original jurist', to term this kind of project 'Megalomaniac Jurisprudence'.[2] Some limit must be drawn, or jurisprudence, however great the zeal of its adherents, will dissipate its energies over too wide an area.

Huntington Cairns[3] also attempts to create a legal science with a dominant emphasis on sociology. He considers that modern jurisprudence is a 'meaningless and fruitless pursuit of a goal incapable of achievement'.[4] Jurisprudence is really an applied science, and no technology has ever succeeded unless it was based on the findings of a pure science. No universal propositions can be laid down concerning legal concepts or rules because they differ from race to race. If jurisprudence wishes to become scientific, it must create a science of society. The basis must be human behaviour as influenced by, and in relation to, disorder. It is impossible to discover how law operates unless we have greater knowledge of the factors that cause change in society and govern its evolution. When this is understood, jurisprudence as a technology can apply these rules to reach useful results. At present jurists are attempting to build a house before the foundations have been laid.

At this point it is convenient to make some general observations on the approaches of Pound, the realists, and Cairns.

Many have criticized these schools on the ground that they desire

---

[1] Op. cit. 24.   [2] *Law in the Making* (7th ed.), 32.
[3] *The Theory of Legal Science*; *Law and the Social Sciences.*
[4] *The Theory of Legal Science*, 11.

to teach a little of everything save the law. A textbook of sociology cannot be made a work on jurisprudence merely by changing the title. A knowledge of the properties of clay may be useful to a modeller, but twenty years spent in scientific analysis of this material would be a waste of artistic talent. Manning wittily caricatures the sociological jurist by comparing him with a professor of mathematics who, concerned about his country's bridges, urges his students to form the advance guard of creative engineering, and stresses that mathematics cannot be studied in isolation from town planning.[1] But might we not use another analogy? A medical professor says:

Anatomy is all you need to know. It is true that you will gain your knowledge from a dissection of the dead and in your practice you will be concerned with the bodies of those who, at least until they receive your merciful attentions, are still in the land of the living. It is true also that in the case of the patient psychological forces, business worries and married life may affect his health. But the study of these things is difficult and if we want an impartial science we must leave them alone. Austin our founder recognized that some of these things would affect your professional practice, but he wisely concentrated on anatomy alone. I advise you to do the same and to save your profession from having a little knowledge of everything save anatomy.[2]

Neither analogy is, of course, nor is it meant to be, exact, for each begs the question of what is meant by law.

It is submitted that the relationship between law and social interests may be usefully studied by jurisprudence for three reasons. Firstly, it enables us better to understand the evolution of law. What is needed is not a dogmatic assumption that economic self-interest (or some such force) has determined the evolution of law, but a penetrating analysis of the interaction between a tough and taught tradition, which has sanctified the logical structure of the law, and the immediate pressure of social demands. The absorbing task is to watch the struggle of modern social interests to secure expression in spite of the narrow confines of the decisions of the past. To attempt to explain the law on a purely logical basis is equivalent to interpreting a graph of the vibrations in a speeding motor-car without taking into account the surface of the road.[3]

---

[1] *Modern Theories of Law*, 219.   [2] Paton, 4 *Politica* (1939), 24–5.

[3] Vyshinsky, *Law of the Soviet State*, 81, supports the union of jurisprudence and the social sciences, though with the object of showing the merits of dialectical materialism; K. Renner, *Institutions of Private Law and their Social Functions*; A. V. Dicey, *Law and Opinion in England*.

Secondly, although man's views of ethics and of his social needs have changed as the centuries roll by, nevertheless the element of human interest provides a greater substratum of identity than does the logical structure of the law. Comparative law frequently illustrates that, while the legal theories of two systems may be as far apart as the poles, each may be forced for reasons of convenience so to modify the application of its theoretical basis that ultimately the practical results are not far removed. Many Roman decisions on the *Lex Aquilia* are surprisingly similar in effect to those of the English law of tort.[1] German law adopted a subjective theory of contract, English an objective, but each has been forced to adapt its theoretical basis to the needs of commerce.[2] In spite of differing theories, the English and Roman rules of possession were built up under the 'pressure of needs and circumstances which cannot have been wholly dissimilar'.[3]

Thirdly, although the view of Kelsen that the jurist should not discuss the question of social interests is attractive in that it encourages an impartial jurisprudence, yet such a study is essential to the lawyer to enable him to understand the legal system. As a mere question of terminology, it matters not how narrow is our pure science of law if it be supplemented by broader learning. But there is a danger that, if we regard jurisprudence proper as a pure science of law (in Kelsen's sense), the study of the broader questions will disappear from books that are perused by the lawyer.[4] We desire an impartial judge, but the law itself cannot be impartial (in one sense) for its very *raison d'être* is to prefer one social interest to another. Is the judge less likely to make a clear survey because the question of the social interests involved in a particular problem is freely canvassed instead of being the 'inarticulate major premiss'? Public policy is a less dangerous ground of judgment if the reasons for any particular application are clearly set forth,[5] since the very effort to justify a decision may limit the effect of prejudice.

The greatest achievement of the functional school is that it has

---

[1] Cf. *Dig.* 9. 2. 9. 4; H. C. Gutteridge, *Comparative Law* (2nd ed.), 49.

[2] E. J. Schuster, *Principles of German Civil Law*, 92.

[3] Holdsworth, *History of English Law*, vii. 460. It is not, of course, suggested that the element of human interest leads to identical solutions in the case of every system. Even over a period of one hundred years the common law shows surprising changes. The argument in the text is only that the pressure of social needs will frequently explain what, from the point of view of the logic of the law, may be a mere anomaly.

[4] Lord Simon, in conversation, once described the law as seen by practising lawyers and judges as 'knowledge in blinkers'.

[5] Cf. Lord Wright, *Radcliffe* v. *Ribble Motor Services Ltd.*, [1939] A.C. 215 at 239 et seq.

infused new life into both the study and the development of law. A promising beginning has been made which leads us to expect much in the future. The actual functioning of certain parts of the law has been intensively studied.[1] Perhaps the most valuable results are a new understanding of the judicial method and a broader outlook both in the universities and in the courts. A determined attempt is now made to teach law as a function of society instead of as a mere abstract set of rules, while the courts are canvassing freely the reasons of social policy which lie behind certain rules of law.[2] Probably no common law rule has ever received such sweeping condemnation as the doctrine of common employment received at the hands of the House of Lords.[3] The evil results of the rule were clearly laid down and, though unable to destroy it entirely, the learned Lords diminished its power as far as the fetter of precedent would allow. Administrative law, at first regarded as an intrusion, is now sympathetically studied in the light of the ends which modern government must achieve.[4] Psychology and psychiatry have revolutionized the approach to the problems of criminal law.[5] The real difficulties of constitutional law are now freely canvassed, and in America Brandeis, while at the bar, persuaded the Supreme Court that if an attack was made on the constitutionality of a statute (as being an unreasonable interference with life, liberty, or property), counsel should be permitted to introduce evidence from the social sciences

---

[1] As illustrations the following works may be mentioned: (a) in criminal law, see Jerome Hall, *Theft, Law and Society*, and the survey, *Criminal Justice in Cleveland*, directed and edited by Roscoe Pound and Felix Frankfurter; (b) study of the functioning of the law relating to injuries caused by motor vehicles—*Report of the Committee to study Compensation for Automobile Accidents to the Columbia University Council for Research in the Social Sciences*. It was discovered that if there was no insurance, the injured victim had only one chance in four of receiving anything; (c) studies of the effect of legal regulation on the habits of a population, e.g. Underhill Moore and C. C. Callahan, 53 *Yale L. J.* (1943), 1; (d) studies of corporation law, e.g. Berle and Means, *The Modern Corporation and Private Property*; (e) analysis of property in the modern world, K. Renner, *The Institutions of Private Law and Their Social Function*.

[2] Lord Atkin, *United Australia Ltd.* v. *Barclays Bank*, [1941] A.C. 1 at 29, referring to technical rules invented to meet requirements of the forms of action which have now disappeared, said: 'When these ghosts of the past stand in the path of justice, clanking their mediaeval chains, the proper course for the judge is to pass through them undeterred.'

[3] *Radcliffe* v. *Ribble*, [1939] A.C. 215. Parliament took the hint and abolished the rule.

[4] e.g. J. Dickinson, *Administrative Justice and the Supremacy of Law*; Jennings, *The Law and the Constitution*. Report of the *Committee on Administrative Tribunals and Enquiries* (The Franks Committee) (1957), Cmd. 218; K. C. Davis, *Administrative Law*; W. A. Robson, *Justice and Administrative Law*; M. D. Forkosch, *Administrative Law*.

[5] *Infra*, Ch. XV.

which would show the probable results of the legislation in question. The acceptance of the 'Brandeis brief' means that the courts frequently consider the real social problems instead of confining the argument to abstract logic.

All this must be placed to the credit of the functional and realist schools. But it must be confessed that the problem of method has not yet been solved. Huntington Cairns undoubtedly lays down a sphere that is too wide for jurisprudence in the lawyer's sense. But there is much in his contention that until social science itself progresses a functional jurisprudence is working in the dark.

The great success of the physical sciences contrasts strikingly with the meagre results secured by social studies. Hence arises the cry that, if only the rigorous method of the scientist were applied to the analysis of social life, then great progress would be made. But two points must be noted: firstly, no trick of method can secure for the social scientist the same accurate results secured by his colleague in physics or chemistry. The essence of the method of the physical sciences is controlled experiment by which the conditions are kept invariant save for one factor. For the sociologist it is rarely possible to achieve this test. Whether man has free will or not, he is a more complex study than an alpha particle, and we cannot hope to secure for the social sciences the rigid definitions and universal demonstrability of natural science.[1]

Secondly, the scientist merely observes facts: in society we are concerned not only with what is, but with the operation of standards dealing with what ought to be. It is impossible to draw a clear-cut line between the fact and the ideal, for each operates on the other. No controlled experiment could ever tell us what should be the end of law. Research may yield useful results which may guide our choice, but the ultimate reason for the choice of one form of social life rather than another is our philosophy of values. A wise community does not always accept that form of organization which will create most wealth—the cost in human suffering may be too high. But the choice between wealth and human suffering is not one that can be determined by research: it depends on the view of the community as to the purpose of life itself.

Thirdly, there is a great gap between research and its application.

[1] K. N. Llewellyn, 20 *N. Car. L. R.* (1941) ,1; M. R. Cohen, *Reason and Nature*; J. Michael and M. J. Adler, *Crime Law and Social Science*; J. Hall, *Annals of the American Academy of Political and Social Science*, clxvii (1933), 119; A. Nussbaum, 40 *Col. L. R.* (1940), 189; Lon. L. Fuller, *The Law in Quest of Itself*, 65.

In the physical sciences the advantages of the use of atomic energy are so great that nothing is allowed to stand in the way of its application: in the social sciences the application of research may conflict with ignorance or prejudice and thus action is retarded.

Hence advance in the social sciences cannot be rapid, and until they are more fully developed, it is hard to see that a comprehensive science of law can be created.[1] The jurist cannot cover the whole scope of social learning, and until there are clearer conclusions on which he can draw, he can only make tentative grasps at truth. This is stressed, not to belittle the work of Pound or Cairns, but to emphasize that progress must inevitably be slow and that the blame for this must not be laid on the lawyers alone. Psychiatry could be developed only after medicine had reached a certain stage, and if jurisprudence is a social science, it can make real advances only when better foundations are laid for sociology itself. So far we have ambitious programmes, some useful empirical results, the infusion of a new spirit into jurisprudence, and a more realistic analysis, but not the actual creation of a juristic science.

The difficulty of studying the sociological effects of the legal system is stressed by B. Abel-Smith and R. Stevens[2] in their survey of modern law. Too many aspects had not been studied in detail and there were enormous gaps in the statistical evidence available to them.

Let us take some examples of the problems which face modern society—poverty, the control of crime, the eradication of war and industrial strife. In each of these the law must play its part. In attempting to control poverty, we are not only in the hands of the economists, but also of our political masters. Can the ideal solution be imposed on the community, if it means further taxation? In the control of crime, further development and research in psychiatry and in the study of the effect of particular methods of punishment is a *sine qua non*. The problem of the eradication of war is discussed in 'Report from Iron Mountain on the Possibility and Desirability of Peace'.[3] The book is alleged to be a secret report to the President of the United States as to what would happen if peace—real peace—suddenly broke out. This, however, is merely the humorous vehicle for

---

[1] S. P. Simpson and R. Field, 32 *Virg. L. R.* (1946), 855; 22 *N. Y. Univ. L. Q. R.* (1947), 145.

[2] *Lawyers and the Courts* (1967); see also J. L. Montrose, *Precedent in English Law and Other Essays*, 357–64, who points out that all too often when the lawyer dealing with a specific problem turns to sociology, economics, or philosophy for guidance, he will receive little help.

[3] L. C. Lewin (1968).

a sober analysis of the actual effects on the American economy of the need to prepare for war. Fear of war creates an artificial demand and keeps the economy turning over. War creates unity (sometimes) and causes a psychological release. The point of the book (if I read it rightly) is not to justify war, but to emphasize that millions of dollars and the energies of thousands of men have gone into the 'war game', whereas little research has been done on the 'peace game'. What can take the place of war in stimulating research, medicine, and technology? The conclusion is that peace should be introduced slowly and after much thought, if we are to avoid chaos!

Functional jurisprudence, therefore, is a parasitic study which can develop only as fast as the social sciences. It needs money and men; and ironically enough society is willing to spend millions to put a man on the moon, but relatively little for the solution of social problems which are of far greater importance to the common man.

Above all we must remove from our study of society emotions and the easy acceptance of first principles which are not subjected to objective, critical examination. In 1638 the Jesuits in Peru discovered that quinine would alleviate the effects of malaria. The Faculty of Medicine at Paris forbad the use of quinine, as it was regarded as opposed to the first principles of medicine. It is needless to emphasize that the advance of medicine has been due to the substitution of cold scientific analysis for theoretical axioms. In social science, and in jurisprudence, we often try to clinch our arguments by the use of emotive words instead of by scientific analysis. A decision is 'progressive' or 'reactionary': a man is a 'liberal' or a 'communist'. Real advance will come when we reject the approach to virtue and vice which we see on the television screen. One author, surveying fifty years of American writing on Soviet criminal law, states: 'The American scholars, working in Soviet criminal law, have, by and large, tended to find what they wanted to find.'[1]

Lord Wilberforce satirizes some of the modern tendentious research: 'Pick out some examples of conduct which illustrate your thesis, omit all contradictory material and any statistical analysis, throw in a few newspaper snippets or attractive anecdotes and then re-state as a conclusion the thesis you started with. Is this good enough . . . ?'[2]

---

[1] Z. L. Zile, 70 *Col. L. R.* (1970), 194 at 216.
[2] 10 *J. Soc. Public Teachers of Law* (1969), at 259.

§ 9. THE TELEOLOGICAL SCHOOL

The teleological school regards the functionalists as laying down the pen when the task is only beginning. Pound believes that the end of law should be to satisfy a maximum of wants with a minimum of friction. The school we are now discussing would ask: 'What is meant by interests or the end of law? In the inevitable conflict of interests, what criteria should the law use in sacrificing one to another?' Pound himself was clearly interested in the end of law, but in his writing the two strands of relativism and absolute values are hard to reconcile.[1]

There are two fundamental points in the approach of this school. Firstly, it is argued that a proper answer must be given to the problem of the validity of law. Austin said that law was valid if it was the command of a sovereign, the realist if it was embodied in a particular decision of a court, but to the philosophers these seem rather superficial replies. Secondly, this school stresses that law is intimately related to justice, and that some attempt must be made to discover an absolute criterion by which law may be judged.[2] Consciously or unconsciously we all use ethical standards in criticizing the law. The analytical school set up an ideal of logical harmony, while even the pragmatic Pound assumes that law *should* satisfy as many social interests as possible. The iconoclastic realist is often moved by a burning passion for law reform, by a desire that law should be made a more effective weapon for social control. If we remain on the lowly level of fact, these are mere assumptions which cannot be proved—such views are based on ideals as to what law should be. In the same way, many criticize a distinction on historical grounds, thereby assuming that it is an ideal for law that historical continuity should never be broken—some historical jurists cling to the notion that all evolution is a progress to higher values. So far as the teleological school emphasizes that it is better to lay bare the unconscious ethical presuppositions of our thought, the argument is irrefutable. Ethics looked at comprehensively is merely a reasoned study of preferences, an endeavour to find a foundation for the judgments of value we are always making.

This school therefore asks: 'What should be the ideal end of law? What should guide us in developing the law?' The functional school shows somewhat the same interest, for Pound's doctrine of social

[1] *Introduction to the Philosophy of Law: Contemporary Juristic Theory.*
[2] Cf. Felix Cohen, *Ethical Systems and Legal Ideals.*

engineering assumes that law must be developed to meet changing social values.[1] But Pound expressly admits that philosophy has failed to provide an ideal scale of values and that the best the jurist can do is to proceed with the task of adapting law to the needs of his generation—the choice between conflicting ideologies is one for the community at large.

The teleological school is optimistic enough to consider that a reasoned scale of values can be discovered as a basis for legal development. The greater part of the work of this school lies in the realms of philosophy, and hence philosophical jurisprudence is a term that is frequently applied. But philosophy overlaps many schools of jurisprudence: we find traces of its doctrines in Savigny, Kelsen, and Pound, to name only three. The term teleological school is more appropriate, as it emphasizes the fundamental quest—the purpose[2] of law.

§ 10. THE SCANDINAVIAN REALISTS

In recent years interest has been attracted to a significant movement in legal theory in the Scandinavian countries by the publication in English of representative works by various Scandinavian authors. This movement has been labelled Scandinavian Realism. It is thought, however, that few Scandinavians, if any, would accept the label, nor would any of them accept as schoolfellows all those who have been lumped together by outsiders. Those best known to English readers are Olivecrona, Lundstedt, and Ross.[3] There are wide differences between them,[4] but they have it in common that they are all influenced by the philosophical works of Hägerström,[5] much as the English analytical positivists are influenced by the work of Wittgenstein. And the two influences have similarities, for both rejected traditional metaphysical thinking and both developed from philosophical bases of a positivistic kind.

Hägerström set out to destroy the notion that right–duty relations and legal obligations have any objective existence. He asserted that

---

[1] Pound emphasizes that even the concept of function implies a purpose: *Social Control through Law*, 132.
[2] *Infra*, Ch. IV.
[3] K. Olivecrona, *Law as Fact*; A. V. Lundstedt, *Legal Thinking Revised*; A. Ross, *On Law and Justice*.
[4] And between any one of them and other Scandinavian writers, e.g. F. Castberg, *Problems on Legal Philosophy*.
[5] See *Enquiries into the Nature of Law and Morals* (trans. C. D. Broad) (1953).

the idea of duty had no logical meaning. It was no more than the expression of a feeling which could be explained psychologically but which had no place in the logic of a legal system. In so far as such feelings are discovered in society, as they are, and are important to the working of a legal system, they cannot be said to be reasons for enforcing a law for they are the consequences of the operation of the law and have no existence independently of the law. By an examination of Roman Law, Hägerström sought to show how much 'word magic' was used in traditional legal forms to evoke feelings of duty or obligation. He insisted that arguments from justice and such general notions were merely emotional and were neither scientific nor of any objective or logical value.

His followers, in their various ways, carried that approach into an examination of law as they found it, seeking an objective and scientific explanation of the nature of law divorced from judgments of value and emotional attitudes. They said that they wanted to see what law was and how it worked as a social fact. This sounds rather like the language of American realism, and there are in truth some similarities between the two schools, particularly in their tendency to speak of rules of law as being properly tested by asking how well or ill they serve to predict the decisions of the authoritative agencies of the legal system. But there are wide differences between them none the less. The Americans, as has been seen, were mainly interested in the work of the courts, and they sought to understand all the factors relevant to decisions made by courts. The Scandinavians, on the other hand, seem to be more interested in developing a formal philosophy of law, seen as a body of rules, which will explain law logically and scientifically as a necessary part of the organization of society as a whole.

Lundstedt was the most extreme of the three writers mentioned and his work is likely to have less influence among English readers partly because of the extreme positions he took; but also because his work in English[1] is so difficult to read. Lundstedt made the mistake of dispensing with a competent translator. The value of his work is further affected by the extreme egotism of the author and the very personal reaction he had to his critics.

Lundstedt laughed at most of the traditional English theories of law. He rejected what he called 'the method of justice' and introduced his own 'method of social welfare'. Law is indispensable for the maintenance of human society. It needs no other basis, no higher

---

[1] His posthumous *Legal Thinking Revised* (1956).

explanation or justification. Its content should be determined by the requirements of 'social welfare'. Rights and duties are by-products of the maintenance of law and not things which are protected by the law, nor can they explain or justify the law itself. The science of law should treat law as having its own ends, its own logical demands. Only in this way can a true science be developed, and a realistic view of legal and social facts be obtained. Unfortunately, Lundstedt never seems to make quite clear how his 'method of social welfare' is to be used or what the details of the method are.

Olivecrona argues that the law to be understood must be studied as a social fact, but he does not go as far as Lundstedt does in rejecting as fantasy all talk about the normative nature of rules of law. He argues that rules of law have the character of 'independent imperatives' and that as such they do act as causal links in explaining the actual behaviour of officials and citizens working within a legal system. They do not, however, act as imperatives issuing from a formal or a human source carrying with them any binding force. The belief in the binding nature of law, except as a psychological and subjective feeling produced by habit and history in groups of people, is transcendentalism.

As an example of independent imperatives may be cited the Decalogue. It cannot be said that Moses is commanding us to do this or that. Nor is this supposed to be so. The words are said to be the commands of God. In reality the Decalogue is a bundle of imperative sentences, formulated several thousand years ago and carried through the centuries by oral tradition and in writing. They are nobody's commands, though they have the form of language that is the characteristic of a command.

The rules of law are of a similar character.[1]

The task then of the legal scientist is to study the actual working of a society and its legal system as a matter of objective fact and to understand the relations of cause and effect in the natural world. The real operation of law and of its so-called binding nature can then only be understood by reference to individual and group psychology.

Ross is as vigorous in his rejection of metaphysical thinking, and in particular of any kind of natural law thinking, as any of the other Scandinavians. He is, however, more easily understood and appreciated by English lawyers. He uses more illustrative examples which are familiar to English lawyers, and he shows a greater grasp

[1] *Law as Fact*, 43.

of traditional English legal theory. He examines in a not unfamiliar way a number of problems which have concerned English legal thinkers for a long time. While agreeing with the other followers of Hägerström that it is a fallacy to presuppose notions of justice and of pre-existing rights or duties which will justify particular legal rules, he does show how legal concepts such as 'rights', 'ownership', have a place in the logic of the law as organizing tools enabling simplification of a very large number of complicated conditioning facts and consequences. He sees rules of law, in so far as they have directive operation, as not aimed directly at controlling the behaviour of subjects but as directing the ways in which the official agencies of the legal system should decide issues. Thus, a rule of law is most commonly to be seen as telling a judge how to decide a case, not as telling a subject how to conduct himself.

At the same time he reduces the question of validity to one of predictability.

The test of the validity is that ... we can comprehend the actions of the judge (the decisions of the courts) as meaningful responses to given conditions and within certain limits to predict them—in the same way as the norms of chess enable us to understand the moves of the players as meaningful responses and predict them.[1]

He does not fail to see the apparent inapplicability of a predictive test for validity as applied to a judge. How can a judge decide what is valid law by reference to a prediction of what he will do?[2] Presumably, according to Ross, a judge will decide what is valid law by reference to his predictions of what other judges will do in the future. Ross does, however, seem to ignore the internal tests provided by most legal systems which enable judges to decide questions of validity by the application of constitutional rules not of a predictive kind.[3]

§ 11. COMPARATIVE LAW

Jurisprudence is usually distinguished from comparative law, though it is difficult to see how the former can exist without the latter.

[1] *On Law and Justice*, 35.
[2] Cf. H. L. A. Hart, 'Scandinavian Realism', 17 *Camb. L. J.* (1959), 233.
[3] For more extensive descriptions and criticisms of Scandinavian Realists, see H. L. A. Hart, op. cit.; F. Castberg, 'Philosophy of Law in the Scandinavian Countries', 4 *Am. J. of Comp. L.* (1955), 388; G. Marshall, 'Law in a Cold Climate', 1 *N.S. Juridical Review* (1956), 259; D. Lloyd, *Introduction to Jurisprudence*, ch. vii; W. Friedmann, *Legal Theory* (5th ed.), 304–11.

Legal history is also essential to jurisprudence, but no one maintains that the two are identical. There have been as many debates on the nature of comparative law as on that of jurisprudence—in some of the definitions comparative law is indistinguishable from comparative jurisprudence. Professor Gutteridge[1] emphasizes that comparative law denotes a method of study and research and not a distinct branch or department of the law. He distinguishes (*a*) descriptive comparative law, the main purpose of which is the provision of information, and (*b*) applied comparative law which has a definite object in view, e.g. the pursuit of uniformity of commercial law, or the desire to make the principles of private international law less diverse between the nations.[2] Comparative law is a relatively new discipline and its content is still a matter of dispute.

There is no *a priori* distinction between jurisprudence and comparative law. The two studies overlap the same field, although the point of emphasis is different. A collection of all the rules in the world relating to married women would be a useful piece of descriptive comparative law, but it would hardly be jurisprudence. Holland's view was that the scope of comparative law was practically limited to descriptive investigations—the material was then to be handed to the jurists who would 'set forth an orderly view of the ideas and methods which have been variously realised in actual systems'.[3] But advocates of comparative law have not been content with this lowly task, and the more they delve into the theory of the legal method, the more indistinguishable becomes the product from jurisprudence.

Comparative law is rapidly assuming greater prominence. The creation of the European Economic Community has focused attention on the need to understand the general principles of European law. The tortious liability of the E.E.C. is to be ruled by the general principles common to the laws of the member states. 'A jurist belonging to the Common Market must be a comparatist.'[4] European universities are now taking a much greater interest in this problem.[5] But attention cannot be confined to the European scene alone. The problems of the emerging states of Africa may compel attention to

---

[1] *Comparative Law*, ch. i.
[2] There is a third category of abstract or speculative comparative law, but Gutteridge thinks that its content, properly considered, would really fall into one or both of the heads set out in the text. See also R. David, *Traité élémentaire de droit civil comparé*.
[3] *Jurisprudence* (10th ed.), 8.
[4] See the survey by D. Tallon, 10 *J. Soc. Public Teachers of Law* (1969), 265 and at 270.
[5] R. H. Graveson, ibid. 273.

be directed to the merging of Eastern systems with the common law.[1] Islamic law governs five hundred million people, Hindu law more that four hundred million,[2] and Chinese law covers about one-fifth of the human race. Moreover, states such as Nigeria show the difficulty of moulding the application of the different strands of law into one system. The problem, therefore, has ceased to be an academic one and has become of the greatest practical importance.

Even considering law reform in England, the Law Commissions Act, 1965, expressly directed that the Commissioners were under a duty to obtain such information as to the law of other countries as would facilitate their task.

§ 12. The Scope of Jurisprudence

We have, therefore, many answers to the problem of the scope of jurisprudence. Kelsen, in his pure science, would divorce jurisprudence from ethics and sociology; Pound would study law in action, and the sociologist would turn to a science of society itself. The teleological school would plumb the depths of metaphysics to discover absolute values on which to build.

It is absurd to suggest that there is only one useful path for the jurist to tread. Each must work according to his own endowment, and individual preference will determine the issue. To the writer functional jurisprudence seems to offer the most useful results, though it is emphasized that these results still lie in the future, for until the social sciences are further developed, the jurist is greatly handicapped. Another major difficulty is the diversity of the actual legal systems and the lack of knowledge of many of the great codes of the past. Even if a complete copy of the Twelve Tables were discovered, we would know little of the life of the people that would explain the working of these rules. The results of the writing of this century are so far mainly destructive. Many false claims have been exposed. It is no longer hoped to discover universal rules of law, to create a rigid scheme of classification into which all legal systems can be fitted, or to discover a few general principles from which the answer to every legal question can be deduced. The real complexity of the problem is at last being recognized, and that at least is a gain. The ground has been cleared and lies ready for useful work in the future. Instead of seeking for immutable principles, jurisprudence attempts to discover

[1] J. N. D. Anderson, ibid. 245.
[2] Ibid. 246.

as much as possible concerning legal method, to study the concepts of the law, and trace the influence of the social forces upon their development. Jurisprudence is not primarily interested in discovering uniformities, for diversity may be even more important. If we put the emphasis not on the concepts of law but on the legal method used by varying societies to create order, to resolve disputes, and to further desired changes in society peacefully, the old bogy of the diversity of legal rules ceases to be a terror to jurisprudence, and becomes a most significant factor. All communities which reach a certain stage of development create a legal system to protect certain interests. As the community develops, the concepts of law will become more refined and the interests protected will change. No two countries will pursue precisely the same evolution, and no universal rules can yet be formulated to explain all legal changes. But although the problem is a difficult one, there is no reason why we should not attempt to answer it.

In short, jurisprudence is a functional study of the concepts which legal systems develop, and of the social interests which law protects. But the element of interest brings in the question of value. It is clear, therefore, that functional jurisprudence cannot be satisfactorily developed without a complementary study of the purposes for which society exists.[1]

[1] *Infra*, Chs. IV, V.

REFERENCES

ALLEN, C. K., *Law in the Making* (1964).
—— *Legal Duties*, 1.
FRANK, J., *Law and the Modern Mind.*
FRIEDMANN, W., *Legal Theory* (1967), Part II.
HARRIS, J. W., 29 *Camb. L. J.* (1971), 103.
JONES, J. W., *Historical Introduction to the Theory of Law*, ch. ix.
KELSEN, H., 55 *Harv. L. R.* (1941), 44.
LLEWELLYN, K. N., 40 *Col. L. R.* (1940), 581.
—— 44 *Harv. L. R.* (1931), 1233–56.
LLOYD, D., *Introduction to Jurisprudence.*
—— *Legal Philosophies of Lask, Radbruch, and Dabin* (trans. K. Wilk, 1950), (20th Century Legal Philosophy Series: vol. iv).
POUND, R., 50 *Harv. L. R.* (1937), 557, and vol. 51 (1938), 444, 777.
—— 25 *Harv. L. R.* (1911), 512–16.
RADBRUCH, G., 52 *L.Q.R.* (1936), 530.
REUSCHLEIN, H. G., *Jurisprudence: Its American Prophets.*
ROSS, A., *On Law and Justice.*
SCHLESINGER, R. B., *Comparative Law* (1960).
STONE, J., *Province and Function of Law*, chs. i, ii.

II

THE EVOLUTION OF LAW

§ 13. The Primitive Community

JURISPRUDENCE for long deserved the taunt that it boasted of universality while treating only of mature legal systems. Today, under the influence of the historical school, the researches of anthropologists are laid increasingly under debt.

Speculation has invented definite and simple lines of human evolution. Thus it was said that men lived first in the Stone Age, then the Bronze Age, and finally the Iron Age; that in marriage promiscuity came first, then one wife with many husbands, then one husband with many wives, and finally monogamy; in economic activity there is a simple advance from hunting to pastoralism, to agriculture, and then to the Machine Age. Anthropological research has shown that this is a fallacious simplification of the problem, which in reality is much more complex.[1] All races have not followed the same lines of evolution. Moreover, although there seems to be some correlation between the economic stage which a race has reached and the social institutions which it enjoys, this correlation is not perfect.[2] Few serious scholars today adopt the view that the whole of social life is determined by any one factor. Economic forces may be important, but they are not all-controlling and sometimes they fail to explain significant differences between two societies the economic basis of which is identical. Sociologists realize that the truth will be achieved, not by setting up one factor as a cause and regarding the rest of social life as a result, but in showing the interrelation between each of the forces which create society. Thus if economic means of obtaining a livelihood influence the social structure, social doctrines also influence economic forces.[3] The simple view which regards economic forces as all-powerful is now falling into that disfavour which has already

---

[1] The Aranda tribe in Australia is split into groups, some of which are matrilineal and others patrilineal; there seems no reason for this difference between societies with such economic and geographic similarity: T. G. H. Strehlow, *Aranda Traditions*, 71.

[2] L. T. Hobhouse, G. C. Wheeler, and M. Ginsberg, *The Material Culture and Social Institutions of the Simpler Peoples*.

[3] P. A. Sorokin, *Contemporary Sociological Theories* is an excellent survey.

become the fate of the religious interpretation of legal history. As yet, generalization is fraught with danger, for the lesson of modern social research is a critical attitude to all hypotheses.

Thus we must treat with suspicion any bold claim to plot a definite correlation between law and the culture of a society. That there is some relationship is obvious, for law is but a result of all the forces that go to make society. But there is a definite time-lag between the creation of new material culture (such as the machines of the industrial age) and the development of new social methods of control.[1] Law adapts itself slowly to new conditions—sometimes the development will be so retarded that a violent revolution is necessary. In other cases, one race may be able to draw on the experience of another and thus effect a comparatively rapid change. The variation in the 'cultural lag' of different systems can be explained only by an intensive study of each society in question—the answer cannot be found in economic forces alone.[2] Again, there are sometimes rapid jumps in legal evolution, because of direct borrowing—Japan has adopted modern commercial codes without passing through the intermediate stages which mark European law.[3] Some neo-Hegelians write as if there were immutable laws of legal evolution. Maine's generalization that the progressive societies have developed from status to contract ceases to be a convenient summary of certain features of legal history and is elevated to the rank of an historical truth.[4] Nineteenth-century individualism regarded all law as inevitably evolving towards greater freedom for the individual, but today the growth of collectivist theories shows that the legal pendulum is at present swinging back. Some have been so struck by the opposing tendencies in legal history that the theory of a cycle has been put forward. Legal institutions do not develop continuously along a single line, they grow and then decay. But the factors which create a cycle and the evidence that the decay of a society is inevitable are not yet clearly shown. Man develops and dies, as have many societies in the past, but there is no conclusive evidence that the social body must necessarily deteriorate.[5]

---

[1] K. Renner, *Institutions of Private Law*, is the classical exposition of the slowness of law in adapting itself to social change.

[2] Huntington Cairns, *Law and the Social Sciences*, 163–4, discussing the work of W. F. Ogburn, *Social Change*, and F. S. Chapin, *Culture Change*.

[3] As have so many other countries in recent years, e.g. India, Pakistan, and the other newly independent countries of Africa and Asia.

[4] *Infra*, § 87. Maine was careful to emphasize that he was speaking of what had happened 'hitherto'.   [5] P. A. Sorokin, op. cit. 728 et seq.

One warning may be given: there is always danger in interpreting primitive law by the use of categories or concepts suitable to a developed system. Native customary law may be unintentionally changed by the use of common law concepts in applying it.[1] However aware we are of the danger, the language which is the tool of the common lawyer deforms to some extent the explanation of the rules of primitive systems. We ask questions which would never have occurred to a primitive man.

A useful classification of types of societies adopts as a criterion the method employed in earning a living. What is called 'primitive law' covers communities in the following categories: Lower Hunters, Higher Hunters, Pastoralists, Advanced Pastoralists, First Agricultural Grade, Second Agricultural Grade, and Third Agricultural Grade. The most ambitious attempt to discover if there is any correlation between the economic stage which a tribe has reached and its culture and legal institutions is that of Hobhouse, Wheeler, and Ginsberg.[2] The main defect of sociology and historical jurisprudence is what has been termed the method of 'illustration'. A theory is invented and then the pages of human experience are searched for favourable examples. No theory can be proved by this method, since unfavourable examples are merely ignored. In order to obtain an objective result, these authors carefully classified all the data available on more than four hundred tribes. The results are very interesting, but certainly show the danger of rash speculation. In analysing the problem of the extent of self-help the tables show that although the use of a regular system of justice increases as the society develops, it is impossible to say that every tribe in the third agricultural grade has reached the same level of development.[3] There is no close correlation between the economic form and the legal institution—all that can be said is that most of the tribes that are advanced economically have also correspondingly developed their legal systems. But a much greater field of evidence must be available for scrutiny before any conclusive findings can be advanced.[4]

Bearing in mind all the difficulties that have been enumerated, we

[1] See J. L. Montrose, *Precedent in English Law and Other Essays*, 74 at 79.

[2] *The Material Culture and Social Institutions of the Simpler Peoples.*

[3] Thus in the case of the lower hunters, 40 per cent of the tribes have pure self-help and none of them have public justice as a regular system. In the third agricultural grade, 11 per cent have pure self-help and 41 per cent a regular system of public justice.

[4] The most valuable characteristics of the work of Hobhouse, Wheeler, and Ginsberg are the scientific detachment and the caution in drawing conclusions from data that are often shown to be exceedingly difficult to classify.

now proceed to discuss some of the most striking features in the evolution of law. The object is not to set down universal laws of legal evolution, but rather to study particular types of law: viz.

(*a*) Primitive law.
(*b*) Middle law.
(*c*) Classical law.
(*d*) Post-classical law.

§ 14. PRIMITIVE LAW

(*a*) Before the Era of Courts

It was once thought that the primitive native was automatically law-abiding and, therefore, had no need of a system of law. The *mores* of a tribe were regarded as a confused mass of usage, custom, and religion; it was said that there was no law, no individual property, no real means (save self-help) of enforcing any 'right' which an individual might think that he possessed. What keeps the community together is fear of the unknown, of the strange spirits that may punish man. What has been done once without evil result may be done again, but to innovate is to risk a supernatural sanction. Hence the native has no desire to break the customs of the community. Early law, therefore, springs from a religious sanction, the fear of the unknown, of the spirits that dwell everywhere.

But modern research has shown that this view needs correction. It is true that public opinion is always more powerful in a small community—it exercises much more influence in a tiny village than in a world capital. But Malinowski asks whether it is not contrary to human nature to accept any constraint as a matter of course.[1] All customs are not on the same level—some are followed because men choose to follow them either as a matter of convenience or because they have never dreamt of doing otherwise, but others cut across human desires and passions and hence require an effective machinery of enforcement. A member of a race that dwells in round huts would probably never think of constructing a square one. If he did build in a new style, his whim would not endanger the community life. But rules concerning adultery or rape may need a powerful sanction.

---

[1] *Crime and Custom in Savage Society* (1932), 10. An interesting survey is William Seagle, *The Quest for Law*; see also K. N. Llewellyn and E. A. Hoebel, *The Cheyenne Way—Conflict and Case Law in Primitive Jurisprudence.*

Malinowski considers that this is the germ of primitive law. There is no sanction in the Austinian sense—a penalty imposed by a determinate body—but the law does rest on a greater force than the vague pressure of public opinion. The very organization of the community protects the law. Apart from the community primitive man is helpless, and the ultimate sanction for the 'unclubbable' (not in the literal sense) man is expulsion or death—a sentence that will not be imposed by a predetermined tribunal but carried out by some members with the active approval of the rest. Even at a much later period when courts are fully developed, we still find a relic of the primitive expulsion in outlawry, which Brunner has described as the sentence of death pronounced by a community which has no police constables or professional hangmen.[1] The enforcement of economic obligations depends on a primitive anticipation of the 'stop list'—if one churlishly refuses to make a customary payment, no other member will help such a defaulter. If the Cheyenne Indians have a rule against individual hunting and it is broken, the offender is excluded from the tribe.[2]

There must be in all societies a class of rules too practical to be backed up by religious sanctions, too burdensome to be left to mere good-will, too personally vital to individuals to be enforced by any abstract agency. This is the domain of legal rules and I venture to foretell that reciprocity, systematic incidence, publicity and ambition will be found to be the main factors in the binding machinery of primitive law.[3]

At a very early stage the native distinguishes between a payment which is obligatory and one that is the result of generosity. There is undoubtedly here the germ of law, but whether such rules are strictly to be called law or not we leave for subsequent discussion.[4]

Before the advent of courts the sphere of pre-law (if we may invent the term) is fairly small. There are few rules concerning property but some concerning inheritance on death. There are rules of marriage (sometimes extraordinarily intricate as in the case of the Australian aborigines) which lay down the classes within which marriage may take place. Private wrongs are sometimes avenged by the victim,[5] in other cases compensation is payable. There are a few offences which are regarded as an outrage on the community as a whole, such as

[1] Outlawry was abolished in civil proceedings only in 1879, 42 & 43 Vict. c. 59, s. 3.
[2] K. N. Llewellyn and E. A. Hoebel, *The Cheyenne Way*, 9–10.
[3] B. Malinowski, *Crime and Custom*, 67–8.
[4] *Infra*, § 19. [5] H. I. P. Hogbin, *Law and Order in Polynesia*, ch. vi.

incest, witchcraft, and general 'incompatibility of temperament'. A simple economic structure requires few rules for its regulation.[1]

(b) Courts

About the end of the first agricultural grade institutions begin to appear which perform, often among others, functions which we would now recognize as those proper to courts. Before this it is rare to find definite institutions for the settlement of disputes, though a chief or patriarch may exercise a general control over the community. With the advent of the court the sphere of law becomes more definite, and the rules gradually more precise. The future history of law is largely bound up with the creation of definite institutions, which have power not only to apply the law to the settlement of disputes but also to create new law, and to secure the effective enforcement of such law as exists. Nevertheless, it is a long and slow evolution before there are institutions with the effective powers of the courts, legislatures, and the police mechanism of the modern State. If private violence is to be overcome, then the law must be enforced; but if law is to remain acceptable, then there must be machinery for its reform.

The orthodox theory is that the first task of the court is to moderate the blood feud and regulate self-help.[2] The *lex talionis* limits the aggressor to inflicting an injury similar to that which he received. Then appears the doctrine that the victim or his family may if they wish accept compensation, but that if it is not paid, physical violence may be inflicted. 'Buy off the spear or bear it.' As courts grow in power, the acceptance of compensation is made compulsory, save for certain offences which are regarded not as a mere private wrong but as an outrage against the community and deserving of punishment. Criminal law thus is definitely separated from civil law. For example, Roman law in 450 B.C. was in a state of transition from optional to compulsory composition.[3] Courts existed, but the methods of enforcement were still primitive, e.g. a claimant must himself secure the attendance of his opponent (apparently in the last resort by violence).[4]

---

[1] This is clearly brought out by K. N. Llewellyn and E. A. Hoebel, op. cit.

[2] For an account of a blood feud in 1914, see T. G. H. Strehlow, *Aranda Traditions*, 62; for self-help among the Cheyennes, see K. N. Llewellyn and E. A. Hoebel, op. cit. 194–5. Criminal procedure by way of appeal for murder was really a relic of the blood feud: Pollock and Maitland, *History of English Law*, i. 31.

[3] H. F. Jolowicz, *Historical Introduction to the Study of Roman Law*, 175.

[4] Similarly in Assyrian law. See G. R. Driver and J. C. Miles, *The Assyrian Laws*, 335.

Such institutions as *pignoris capio* and *manus iniectio* are obvious relics of an age of self-help. An analogy may be seen in the position of international law today—there are courts, but they do not have compulsory jurisdiction. Even if two nations submit their dispute to judicial decision, there is no machinery for the effective enforcement of decisions. In primitive communities the State finds difficulty in extending the control of the courts over the passions of men. Sometimes in order to persuade citizens of the value of the judicial process a bribe is offered, as in the fourfold damages awarded by Roman law against a thief caught in the act. In Assyria the State benefited itself by the forced labour imposed on criminals, gave as a *solatium* to the injured party a monetary compensation, and satisfied the desire for vengeance by the infliction of stripes.[1] But the ultimate reason for the triumph of royal justice is its efficiency, and the protection which it grants to those who would be too weak to stand alone.

In some respects this orthodox theory of legal evolution must be corrected. The distinction between civil and criminal law appears much earlier than is suggested.[2] But here once again we are faced with a difficulty of terminology. If the marks of criminal law are sentence by a court and the execution of the sentence by state officials, then it is a late development. But if we adopt as the test whether the wrong is regarded as a matter for a private individual only or for the community as a whole, then the distinction between criminal and civil injuries appears at the very birth of law. In some primitive communities definite rules of criminal law are enforced by superstitious practices—sorcery, or the supernatural consequences of taboo. To avoid confusing the issue by using our modern clear-cut terminology it would perhaps be preferable to speak of public and private delicts. Even in the most primitive tribes the community itself takes action against any one guilty of certain offences, e.g. incest, witchcraft, or bestiality. What is confusing is that modern man regards murder as *the* crime and therefore, if we find that murder is only a matter of private compensation, the conclusion is erroneously reached that there are no offences which the community itself punishes.[3]

Another criticism of the orthodox view is that of Diamond, who

---

[1] G. R. Driver and J. C. Miles, op. cit. 360. But, as is pointed out by the learned authors, the text says, 'they shall beat', etc., without specifying what 'they' means. The phrase apparently means that the stripes shall be inflicted by a person who has a right to do it—sometimes an officer of the king, sometimes the witness, sometimes an accuser (366). The Hebrews never seem to have had a public executioner (367).

[2] D. Daube, *Biblical Law*, 103.

[3] G. R. Driver and J. C. Miles, op. cit. 298.

denies that the *lex talionis* preceded the payment of compensation.[1] He considers that early law emphasized compensation for civil injuries and that corporal sanctions began to appear only in the codes of the middle period. Is not the truth somewhere between both views? The *lex talionis* in the sense of loosely regulated self-help belongs to primitive law and applies both to civil and criminal acts. But the direct infliction of corporal punishment by officials of the State belongs to a much later period.[2]

At first there is little notion of *legal duty*—the concept is rather that of *physical liability*.[3] At first it is the community rather than the individual who is responsible—it is only gradually that an individual's obligation is distinguished from that of the group to which he belongs. A debtor gives a hostage as security; if the debtor defaults, it is the hostage who is liable and not the debtor. Liability for debt does not mean execution against goods as in modern systems, but the physical liability of the hostage to be cut in pieces or sold into slavery —in a very real sense can a creditor 'take it out of the hide' of the debtor. When a debtor is allowed to give his own person as security, the creditor may take vengeance for any default directly upon him. The law of contract is not yet born—the debtor is regarded as one who wrongfully detains the creditor's property.[4] In early English law, debt (the action for money owed) was hardly distinguishable from detinue (the gist of which was that the defendant wrongfully refused to surrender a chattel to which the plaintiff had a right to immediate possession). The notion in early law is not so much one of legal obligation (that a person ought to do something) as that of liability (that he must pay or suffer punishment). In the law of delict we see the analogous notion of 'thing liability'. Deodand illustrates

---

[1] A. S. Diamond, *Primitive Law* (2nd ed., 1950), 304.

[2] For example see G. R. Driver and J. C. Miles, op cit. 346–7. Even when the State inflicts punishment, it may make the punishment fit the crime, e.g. a man loses his lips for kissing a married woman, the wife of a man who has seduced a virgin is delivered to the seduced girl's father for prostitution. Closely related are the 'mirroring' punishments: punishment of arson by burning, coining by boiling, removal of a boundary stone by ploughing off the offender's head. Cf. H. F. Jolowicz, *Cambridge Legal Essays*, 204. 'The Assyrian principle is talion, the child of the blood feud of which it restricts the ferocity, and the parent of the doctrine that the punishment must fit the crime': G. R. Driver and J. C. Miles, loc. cit.

[3] Cf. H. F. Jolowicz, *Historical Introduction to the Study of Roman Law*, 162–3.

[4] For sheer barbarity, see the dictum in *Dive* v. *Maningham* (1551), 1 Plowden 60 at 68: 'For if one be in execution, he ought to live of his own, and neither the plaintiff nor the sheriff is bound to give him meat or drink. . . . And if he has no goods, he shall live of the charity of others, and if others will give him nothing, let him die in the name of God, if he will, and impute the cause of it to his own fault, for his presumption and ill-behaviour brought him to that imprisonment.'

this tendency. If Paul took John's sword and slew Peter with it, the sword was forfeited. Later in English law, instead of losing the *res*, the owner could pay its value to the Crown. As late as 1842 in England a railway company was forced to pay deodand because of deaths resulting from a locomotive accident.[1] Deodand was independent of all notion of fault in the owner, for liability attached to the inanimate *res*. Where a slave or an animal was a 'wrongdoer', it was even more natural to attach liability. The noxal surrender of ancient Rome and the distress *damage feasant* of modern English law[2] illustrate this approach. The rules are far removed from any modern notion of fault. Wigmore cites the story of the killing of Baldur. All things had been sworn not to injure Baldur and the gods in sport threw missiles at him. But Loki was jealous, and learning that the insignificant mistletoe had not been sworn, he put a twig into the hands of Hodur the blind god and guided his aim; Baldur was killed and the innocent Hodur paid the penalty of death.[3]

There has been a gradual change from liability of the person to liability of the goods which a person possesses. This evolution of the law of execution against property is rather slow—thus in Roman law the right of *pignoris capio* is at first exercised only to put pressure on the debtor to pay his debt, for there is no right to sell or to use the *res*. When a court begins to grant execution against property, the tendency is for all the defendant's chattels to be seized, even if only a small sum is owing—to take only sufficient property to cover the debt seems an obvious procedure, but one that develops slowly.[4] Today, now that imprisonment for debt has been so largely restricted, liability is in effect limited to a man's property and future earning power. By the device of the limited company a man's loss may be confined to his investment in a particular venture, for the creditors can call on the funds of the company alone.

Primitive law is not rigid and inelastic, nor is it largely concerned with procedural details. It is in the middle period that excessive formality develops. Law begins with rather vague and elastic rules;[5]

---

[1] *Queen* v. *Eastern Counties Rly. Co.* (1842), 10 M. & W. 58. Deodand was abolished in England by the Deodands Act, 1846, 9 & 10 Vict. c. 62.
[2] Glanville Williams, *Liability for Animals*, 108.
[3] *Select Essays in Anglo-American Legal History*, iii. 483.
[4] H. F. Jolowicz, op. cit. 221.
[5] F. Pollock and F. W. Maitland, *History of English Law*, ii. 27, speaking of the *forma doni*, point out that it is a mistake to suppose that 'our common law starts with rigid, narrow rules about this matter . . . and rejects everything that deviates by a hair's breadth from the established models. On the contrary, in the thirteenth century it is elastic and liberal, loose and vague.' The common law of this period

technicality is really the result of a long period of development. Ehrlich points out that whether in art, religion, or law, whenever we find rigid forms and we are able to trace their history, we find that there has been a hardening of what was originally soft and flexible.[1] Although there was a natural tendency, in order to secure greater reverence for the law, to emphasize its antiquity, it is an exaggeration to say that primitive man regarded the law as unchangeable.[2] Indeed, a long period of discussion and indecision may precede action if a custom is broken: only slowly does the community evolve a practicable rule of enforcement. When technicalities appear in commercial transactions, in property, or in legal procedure, they 'mark the end of the period of primitive law'.[3] For example, the law of contract begins in a simple way and it is only in the middle period that it becomes technical and relatively fixed. Moreover, some legal systems remain relatively free from technicality even at a late stage of development.[4]

It may also be questioned whether primitive law was secreted in the interstices of procedure. Maine's dictum[5] has more reference to the middle era. A certain period of legal evolution is necessary before procedural rules can be developed, and indefiniteness rather than precision seems to be the mark of primitive proceedings.

(c) Codes

Codes begin to appear, usually, at some period after the third agricultural grade. If they are classified not according to their chronological date but according to the degree of internal development, early codes may be represented by the Salic law; the middle codes extend from the *Leges Barbarorum* of the reign of Charlemagne to the more developed laws of the Pentateuch and the Twelve Tables; finally, as an example of a late code we have that of Hammurabi (which incidentally is very early historically, the date being about 1914 B.C.).[6]

can hardly be regarded as primitive law, but it shows that fluidity may exist even in the early middle period.

[1] *Fundamental Principles of the Sociology of Law*, 259.
[2] A. S. Diamond, op. cit. 205.   [3] Ibid. 344.
[4] Chinese law, for example, is much less formal than Western systems. It is not sharply distinguished from ethics, but is regarded as the practical fulfilment of it. *Dura lex, sed lex* seems a strange maxim to the Eastern mind: J. Escarra, *Archives de phil. du droit* (1935, 1–2), 70. Lord Cooper emphasizes that Scots law is less formal than English: 28 *J. Comp. Leg.* (1946), Part III, 3–4.
[5] *Early Law and Custom*, 389.
[6] This is the arrangement adopted by A. S. Diamond, op. cit. 179.

Maine emphasized the influence of religion on early codes: 'there is no system of recorded law, literally from China to Peru, which, when it first emerges into notice, is not seen to be entangled with religious ritual and observance.'[1] A study of materials which have become accessible since Maine wrote shows that this view is too broad.[2] The codes of Hammurabi and of the Assyrians[3] are predominantly secular in character. It is true that in the Hebrew Pentateuch, in the Hindu Code of Manu, and in the Roman Twelve Tables religious sanctions are to be found.[4] Diamond, however, submits the Hebrew Code[5] to a precise analysis and shows that the early code was secular and that the sections showing religious influence are priestly additions of a later date.[6] The doctrine that the community punished certain offences only because of the religious notion that the community is thereby polluted may be supported by the Hebrew text that 'the land cannot be cleansed of the blood that is shed therein but by the blood of him that shed it',[7] but this text is probably also a late addition. Driver and Miles conclude that the Assyrian theory of punishment did not have a religious origin, nor is there any trace of the doctrine that crime is a pollution of the community.[8] The evidence is too meagre, however, to allow of dogmatic generalization.[9]

Proof, which Diamond attempts to give, that there is little or no direct religious influence in some early codes, does not determine the question for primitive law prior to the era of the codes. The question of the definition of religion in primitive times is nearly as difficult as that of law, but religion undoubtedly was one of the forces that went to create society and therefore the law. Maine's dictum is undoubtedly too wide, for he refers specifically to codes.

In all probability the codes did not create much that was new and were largely the result of a consolidation of scattered legislation. The view that all law is based on the work of one legislator is frequently accepted by primitive people, for example, Hebrew law was traced to Moses. But it is inconceivable that such a system was created by

---

[1] *Early Law and Custom*, 5.   [2] A. S. Diamond, op. cit., chs. vii and viii.
[3] G. R. Driver and J. C. Miles, op. cit. 346. Both the Roman pontiffs and the Indian Brahmins combined the characteristics of jurist, lawyer, and aristocrat.
[4] A. S. Diamond, op. cit. 85.   [5] Exod. 21: 1.
[6] His theory is that there was at first a clear-cut division between the jurisdiction of the priest and the ruler, but as the powers and wealth of the priesthood increased not only did they seize secular powers, but they also made priestly additions to what had been a secular code: *Primitive Law*, ch. xi.
[7] Num. 35: 33.
[8] *The Assyrian Laws*, 346–7. One possible trace of the doctrine that crime is a pollution is seen in relation to abortion.   [9] D. Daube, *Biblical Law*, 62.

one act. The codes are the result of gradual accretions to a short and primitive statement of the law—occasionally, to remove doubts, an authoritative version with some new matter is published by a law-giver.[1]

The use of writing has an important influence, for the sphere of law becomes more definite and there springs up a new professional class which is more numerous and more active than those who were the guardians of the oral tradition of the law.

§ 15. MIDDLE LAW

There are still relics of self-help in the middle period, but there is a tendency to prohibit it even more extensively than in mature law. 'Perhaps we may say that in its strife against violence [the law] keeps up its courage by bold words. It will prohibit utterly what it cannot regulate.'[2] 'In our own day our law allows an amount of quiet self-help that would have shocked Bracton. It can safely allow this, for it has mastered the sort of self-help that is lawless.'[3]

In this period we notice a gradual growth of rigidity and techni-cality. What are the causes of this curious love of formalism? It has been suggested that the formalism is a relic of traditional ceremonies of religious ritual,[4] that the parties desire a religious sanction, or that some ceremony is considered necessary to create a binding sense of obligation in the minds of the parties, or to impress the witnesses so that they are likely to remember the transaction. Vinogradoff suggests that we must go back even farther to the early agreements between the clans which were almost in the form of international treaties.[5] But no really adequate explanation of that curious love of formalism has ever been vouchsafed. The basic explanation may perhaps be found in the fact that most human beings find it much easier to learn a formal way of performing a complicated process, than to learn why the process must be complicated or to understand the complications.

'When primitive law has once been embodied in a code', Maine writes, 'there is an end to its spontaneous development', and there-

---

[1] 'Although English princes issued written dooms with the advice of their wise men during nearly five centuries, it seems all but certain that none of them did so with the intention of constructing a complete body of law': Pollock and Maitland, *History of English Law*, i. 26.

[2] F. Pollock and F. W. Maitland, op. cit. ii. 572.   [3] Ibid.

[4] H. J. S. Maine's theory was that the formalism of the Roman lawyer could be understood only if it is realized that the jurisconsult sprang from the pontiff or priest: *Early Law and Custom*, 26.   [5] *Historical Jurisprudence*, ii. 232–3.

after law is brought into harmony with society by three instrumentalities, legal fictions, equity, and legislation, which appear in the historical order in which they are enumerated.[1] This dictum needs some correction. It may be true that the *frequent* use of legislation to change, or to create new, law is a late phenomenon, but legislation appears very early. What are codes but legislation, and frequently they are mere consolidations of prior legislation.[2]

The use of fictions and equity is not confined to any one period. The fiction is useful at a time when legal stability is desired, but change in the application of the law is felt to be imperative. Maine defined the fiction in a very broad sense: 'any assumption which conceals or affects to conceal the fact that a rule of law has undergone alteration, its letter remaining unchanged, its operation being modified.' Thus in the *Actio Publiciana* of Roman law the formula ordered the *iudex* to assume that the period of prescription had already elapsed in order to give to the possessor in good faith a remedy which strictly was confined to him who was already *dominus*. The procedural fictions by which the English courts extended their jurisdiction are well known. But fictions are not confined to the past, for they still have their use today. What is quasi-contract but a legal fiction?[3]

Why do judges use this method? It is not, as Bentham suggests, a desire to deceive, for the fiction deceives no one. Nor is it an unbridled lust for power, although some of the fictions used to extend the jurisdiction of particular English courts are hard to defend. Partly it is 'economy of thought'—the desire to use old devices that have worked well instead of running the risk of innovation. Thus, under Scots law, dissolution of the marriage confers upon the wife a *ius relictae*, which is calculated as if the husband were already dead.[4] This device of the 'as if' can be used to extend new rules to old situations with a minimum of intellectual effort.[5] There is less apparent violence to accepted doctrines than direct reform would produce and, therefore, it is a useful weapon to a judiciary which wishes to maintain the view that its task is but to declare the law.[6]

---

[1] H. J. S. Maine, *Ancient Law* (ed. F. Pollock), 26, 29.
[2] A. S. Diamond, op. cit. 346.
[3] An interesting example of a recently developed 'fiction' in the form of an imputed licence—and of its demise in Australia—is to be seen in *Commissioner for Railways (N.S.W.)* v. *Cardy* (1960), 34 *A.L.J.R.* 134, particularly per Dixon C.J.
[4] *Selsdon* v. *Selsdon*, 50 *T.L.R.* 469. See also the discriminating speeches in *United Australia Ltd.* v. *Barclays Bank Ltd.*, [1941] A.C. 1.
[5] J. Dabin, *Technique de l'élaboration du droit positif.*
[6] Lon. L. Fuller, *Rec. Gény*, ii. 157.

Moreover, the legal fiction may prove a very useful agency of development. 'The fiction is the algebra of law and a picturesque form of algebra besides.'[1] Much law may be reduced to a heap of fictions piled one on top of another. Marriage may be regarded as a sale;[2] the first method of bequeathing an estate to one who is not a blood relation may be by adoption, then in the next stage a fictitious adoption may be posited as the legal basis of a will.[3]

The fiction serves its purpose, but it has serious defects. Firstly, sometimes sight is lost of the conditions under which the fiction was created and it is used to reach results that were neither contemplated nor desired.[4] On the whole the common lawyers used the device well, understanding the purpose for which the fiction was created and allowing it no further effect.[5] Can a wife, under the Scots fiction, after the death of the husband, claim a life interest belonging to her husband? If the fiction is applied logically she cannot, since, if the husband were already dead, the life interest would have ceased to exist. The House of Lords decided that the fiction should not be used beyond its real purpose—that is, to give the wife a right to share: the quantum of the share should be determined by the husband's actual wealth at the time of the divorce.[6] Secondly, it makes the law cumbrous and difficult to classify—thus an action for the seduction of a minor depends at common law on the fiction of the father's loss of service due to the resulting illness. Historically, the action gives compensation only for material loss, but today, if an action does lie, damages may also be given for the outrage to the family honour. The fiction of an implied contract was useful historically in creating a remedy for certain cases of unjust enrichment, but Lord Wright considers that the time has now arrived at which the fiction should be abolished and the law placed on the firm ground of a reasonable prin-

---

[1] Pierre de Tourtoulon, *Philosophy in the Development of Law* (trans. Read), 385.

[2] Historically the institution of marriage, however, probably preceded the development of the law of sale.

[3] 'At bottom all law is reduced to a series of fictions heaped one upon another in successive layers': Pierre de Tourtoulon, op. cit. 387.

[4] 'The danger attendant on all doctrines which are founded on presumptions, implications or fictions originally thought to be equitable is that they are apt to be extended by a process of logical development which loses sight of their origin and carries them far beyond the reach of any such justification as they may have originally possessed. This has been the case with the doctrine of common employment': per Lord Macmillan, *Radcliffe* v. *Ribble Motor Services Ltd.*, [1939] A.C. 215 at 235. See also note, 28 *Camb. L. J.* (1970), 213, discussing *Re Rodwell*, [1969] 3 W.L.R. 1115, which deals with the canonical fiction that an initially valid marriage, if avoided, is to be treated as void *ab initio*.

[5] Cf. Lord Wright, 6 *Camb. L. J.* (1938), 324.

[6] *Selsdon* v. *Selsdon* (*supra*).

ciple of unjust enrichment.[1] The difficulty is to determine the exact time when, and the method by which, fictions should be abolished—thus today there are three schools of thought concerning the utility of the fiction of the implied contract.[2] Sometimes the fiction is so firmly embedded that only a statute can destroy it—other fictions may slowly give birth to a new rule of law and then become only historical relics.

So far we have been dealing with the part played by the fiction in the evolution of law. But the term has uses other than its historical sense. Thus the brocard or legal maxim is sometimes called a fiction, e.g. the dead give seisin to the living. Although not legal principles in the true sense, these maxims play a real part in organizing legal knowledge. Especially before the days of writing, the use of 'catch phrases' minimizes the burden upon memory and a host of particular examples may be covered by the one generalization. Although these maxims are useful at a certain stage in legal evolution, they are very likely to be misused,[3] and a true basis for classification cannot be discovered until a theoretic study creates legal principles which can afford both cohesion and a capacity for development.

Somewhat akin to the maxim is the 'dogmatic fiction' which is used to classify law that already exists[4]—this clearly distinguishes it from the function of the 'historical fiction' which is to extend the law by bringing a new case within an old rule. Dogmatic fictions may range from the crude generalization of early times to such a developed concept as that of corporate personality. Some writers go to the extent of treating all legal concepts as fictions or tools of thought. A materialist approach suggests that everything which does not exist in the physical world is an invention of the mind—a fiction. The legal technique of creating concepts, rules, and principles is discussed below,[5] and this topic is mentioned here only for the sake of clarity. It saves confusion to confine the term fiction to its historical sense, to speak of maxims to convey the second sense, and to use 'legal constructions' as a general term to cover the tools of thought which the law creates in order to organize and classify its rules.

---

[1] 'Another generation of lawyers will have forgotten it, or if they ever remember it, will wonder why people troubled to discuss it except as matter of obsolete history': per Lord Wright, 6 *Camb. L. J.* (1938), 324.

[2] *Infra*, § 109.

[3] Per Lord Wright, *Lissenden* v. *Bosch Ltd.*, [1940] A.C. 412 at 435. The legal maxim that husband and wife are one person in law is very misleading, unless the necessary qualifications are made: Glanville Williams, 10 *Mod. L. R.* (1947), 16.

[4] J. W. Jones, *Historical Introduction to the Theory of Law*, 175.

[5] *Infra*, § 48.

Equity

In every system of law there is a conflict between two types of judicial mind—one glories in a strong decision which upholds the logical elegance of the law even at the cost of injustice or inconvenience,[1] another emphasizes that law exists for man and not man for law and that the rules must be so adapted that injustice is avoided.[2] If we like to use other language, we may emphasize the contrast between *strictum ius* and *aequitas*. In the early period the logical structure of the law has not yet sufficient rigidity to make this conflict prominent, but, once the era of formalism and technicality begins, we see the commencement of strife. Legal technique may become so absorbing that the game is played for its own sake, as in the heyday of the formalistic rules of English pleading.

In England lawyers are so accustomed to think of equity as the province of a separate court that the opposition between *aequitas* and *strictum ius* is perhaps exaggerated. Yet as late as the reign of Henry VII a Chancellor could, over the dinner table, suggest to the common law judges that, if they set their own house in order, the injunction which they feared would become unnecessary.[3] But the increasing technicality of the common law rendered the existence of the powers of the Chancellor a real necessity.[4]

In Rome the work of the praetor in modernizing the law, enforcing the requirement of good faith, emphasizing the intention of the parties rather than the form of the agreement, is somewhat similar in effect to that of the English Chancellor.[5] If we generalize from English and Roman law we may think with Maine of equity as any 'body of rules existing by the side of the original civil law, founded on distinct principles and claiming incidentally to supersede the civil law in virtue of a superior sanctity inherent in those principles'.[6] There is no doubt that the interference of equity with the law is more 'open and avowed' than in the case of the fiction which pretends to leave the letter of the

---

[1] In *R.* v. *Walcott* (1696), Shower 127, an attainder for treason was reversed because the words *ipso vivente* were omitted from the sentence. In 1908 in the U.S. a conviction for rape was annulled because the word *the* was omitted from the indictment: *State* v. *Campbell* (1908), 210 Mo. 202, noted 60 *Harv. L. R.* (1947), 406, and see *Internal Revenue Commissioners* v. *Hinchy*, [1960] A.C. 748.

[2] Cf. *In the Matter of Davy*, [1935] P. 1, where the court refused to apply a technicality when it would have defeated the plain intention of a statute, and *Rayboulds Pty. Ltd.* v. *Dodgshun*, [1953] *V.L.R.* 84.

[3] W. S. Holdsworth, *History of English Law*, v. 223.   [4] Ibid. ii. 345.

[5] But only somewhat: W. W. Buckland, *Equity in Roman Law*.

[6] *Ancient Law* (ed. F. Pollock), 12.

law as it is. But in other systems we do not find distinctions as clear cut as the English contrast of law and equity, and the Roman separation of *ius civile* and the praetorian law. In most continental countries the same word is used for law and justice.[1] Equity, so far as it operates at all, is a force working through and not in opposition to the law, and the continental lawyer finds it hard to grasp the exact relationship between equity and the common law. But let us not be too hasty in reaching conclusions, for even on the Continent we find a fundamental contrast made between positive law and natural law.[2]

§ 16. Classical Law

The classical stage is marked by a sudden flowering of legal genius. The community is economically well established, but rapid social developments have left the law far behind. The primitive rules, in spite of the use of the fiction, in spite of 'interpretation' which solemnly lays down that a sacred text means what it does not mean, are too undeveloped to serve the needs of the period. There is a danger that law may become a mere chaos of specific precedents, for, although rules are many, principles are few. There is need of classification, analysis, and synthesis. The dead law of the past must be cut away in order to allow future growth to be unhampered.

Hence the search for general principles which will explain the actual rules in force and provide a ground for future development, hence the analysis of the concepts which the law uses in order to achieve clarity. This was the work performed by the Roman jurists of the classical era and by the English judges and writers of the nineteenth century. The desire for a fully developed theory which can stand as a justification behind particular rules is not prompted only by an academic desire for completeness. A law that has a proper theoretical basis is more easily understood, applied, and extended than one which lacks such a foundation. Developed jurisprudence begins in the classical age.

The text-book shows the desire to organize, to classify, to search for the *ratio legis* which will explain and unify law instead of leaving it a mere collection of specific rules. The English law of tort, for example, was greatly developed through the influence of the writings of Pollock

---

[1] Cf. T. Leivestad, 54 *L.Q.R.* (1938), 95, 266, for the influence of this on the development of Norwegian law.   [2] *Infra*, Ch. IV.

and Salmond. But the search for principle may be carried out by a court as well as by an academic writer. Thus Blackburn J. explained several isolated rules of strict liability by a new principle which has shown great capacity for development—that he who uses his land in an unnatural or abnormal fashion which casts an excessive risk on his neighbour is strictly liable for any damage caused by the escape of dangerous things from his land.[1] But, where there is a legal concept which is used in many parts of the law, it frequently happens that there is no uniform development, for each court is interested mainly in the phase of the problem that directly concerns it. Thus the law of possession is very confused in English law, partly because it applies to real property, chattels, larceny, and prescription. The courts did not attempt a complete analysis and, unfortunately, before a leading text-book appeared,[2] a slipshod use of terminology was already too firmly entrenched to be dislodged. The law of bailment is in even a sorrier plight.[3]

The classical period cannot hope to stabilize the law entirely. But if the search for principle has been successful, the law can be adapted and modified to suit new conditions. The problem of reconciling stability and flexibility is discussed below[4]—here it suffices to remark that this is an ever-present problem for every age of legal evolution. But the classical period begins the creation of a developed *system* which is sufficiently mature to stand the strain of adaptation. This was the secret of the influence of Roman law upon European legal history. The Roman jurists were not gifted with speculative powers, but they did create a legal scheme of classification and a set of legal terms and concepts which were of great service to races whose native law was less mature. Moreover, the jurists had tested their legal principles, as they developed them, by applying them to hypothetical cases, so that there was a convenient intermixture of practical decision and logical theory. Paradoxically enough, had the *Digest* been a more perfect production, its influence would have been less. It represented, not a perfect set of rules, but the efforts of the classical jurists to show the reason behind the law. A study of it was an excellent training in legal technique, and the mind thus trained could apply the same method in the development of other systems.

---

[1] *Rylands* v. *Fletcher* (1866), L.R. 1 Ex. 265.
[2] F. Pollock and R. S. Wright, *Possession in the Common Law.*
[3] See G. W. Paton, *Bailment in the Common Law.*
[4] *Infra*, § 47.

§ 17. POST-CLASSICAL LAW

In the post-classical period society becomes more complex, and rapid development of the law is inevitable. We are too close to the evolution of the common law to make valid judgments, but in Roman post-classical law we find certain definite characteristics. Jolowicz[1] mentions: firstly, increasing reliance on equity at the expense of legal principle—there is lacking the desire to think out a new principle in place of the old and consequently a tendency to solve the issue merely by relying on phrases such as *benigne tamen dicendum est*. The desire to achieve justice is commendable, but there is too much of a tendency to take the intellectual short cut. Secondly, he finds a desire to protect the weak at the expense of the strong, even at the expense of general security and credit. This was obviously due in part to the influence of Christianity and a growing appreciation of the value of the human personality. Thirdly, there is the increasing emphasis on intent at the expense of form: an impatience of mere technicality which may defeat the ends of justice. Thus the bonds of precedent are loosened.[2] These tendencies are observable to some extent in our modern system of law.

It is easy to exaggerate the value of the analogy from the human organism which grows, reaches maturity, and then decays. Roman law after the post-classical period received a new lease of life through the reception and has left its mark deep on the modern world. But there is a tendency in mature systems, as economic and social conditions become more complex, to deal with new situations by statutes designed for a particular mischief only. A flood of such remedies leaves the law in a somewhat incoherent state. It is the task of the lawyer to point out how much the old order has changed and what reforms are necessary to make the body of the law again consistent with itself. It is easy to sneer at the desire for legal elegance, but if a system loses its underlying unity it becomes hard to teach and difficult to apply. Hence in the post-classical period there is a challenge to lawyers to study the basis of statutory law, as in the classical period attention was concentrated on the basis of case law. Otherwise law may cease to be a system and become a collection of *ad hoc* rules.

---

[1] H. F. Jolowicz, *Historical Introduction to the Study of Roman Law*, ch. xxix.

[2] e.g. the decision of the House of Lords in 1966 not to be bound by its own decisions; Lord Denning's view that the C.A. should not be bound by its own decisions; see in general R. Cross, *Precedent in English Law* (1968); *Bativala* v. *West*, [1970] 1 All E.R. 332, where Bridge J. distinguished a decision of the House of Lords.

At present the challenge is the stronger because of the influence of new social theories of collectivism and planning. How much of the classical conception of ownership remains, so far as real estate is concerned, in the light of statutes dealing with town and country planning? Has the nature of contract insensibly changed? Is the law of tort now more concerned with adjusting social risks than awarding damages on a basis of fault? These questions cannot be answered in a word, but they do demand examination if there is to be real understanding of the functioning of the law. Leaving aside debates of terminology, it is dogmatically stressed that no jurisprudence can be adequate unless it gives a better understanding of law, its evolution, and its social purpose. Legal purists may label the post-classical eras as degenerate: but that does not preclude us from studying the real nature of the world in which we live and attempting to make of law a more effective tool to achieve the ends which society demands.

The earlier Soviet jurists attempted to write the epilogue of the story of law. The thesis was based on the German individualist school which argued that the essential purpose of law was the protection of individual rights. Law existed to provide the basis for 'commodity exchange' between equals, and to protect property rights. Pashukanis deduced from this, firstly, that law, being merely the reflection of capitalism, would wither away when capitalism was destroyed, as its essential *raison d'être* had disappeared: secondly, that under socialism the whole national economy becomes the private business of the State—in other words, mere administration and not law.[1]

There was a lack of historical sense in this approach, which is curious because it claimed to be based on a study of history. Law as a weapon of society has served many ends and it was ridiculous to suggest that, because individualism disappeared, so would law. Moreover, there was a failure to appreciate that from a practical point of view the State cannot survive on a mere theory of administrative discretion—both the State and the citizen need some elements of predictability and certainty. The substance of law may change, but the need for a core of certainty still exists. Indeed, this was soon admitted by Soviet jurists and in 1934 Pashukanis fell into disgrace.[2] The only hypothesis on which we could conceivably imagine the

---

[1] R. Schlesinger, *Soviet Legal Theory*, ch. v. As Engels put it, with the abolition of classes rule over men would be replaced by administration over things: ibid. 161.

[2] Thus, recodifications of law began in the latter part of the 1950s—see W. Friedmann, *Legal Theory* (5th ed.), 375. Private property is increasingly allowed, so long as it does not relate to ownership of the means of production.

disappearance of the law would be the advent of the millennium. If every human being were perfect, there would be no need to use the crude compulsions of law to make social life possible. Until then, the more we have collectivism the greater the sphere of law. The instrumentalities set up by the State at least need the certainty of legal rules in their relations with each other. Moreover, important as the property element may be, it is not the sole sphere with which law deals. Even if no one covets his neighbour's possessions, he may still covet his neighbour's wife. Law may change its function in the socialist state, but no community can exist without it.

REFERENCES

BERMAN, H. J., *Justice in the U.S.S.R.* (1964).
CAIRNS, HUNTINGTON, *Law and the Social Sciences* (1935).
DIAMOND, A. S., *Primitive Law* (1950), 2nd ed.
—— *Evolution of Law and Order* (1951).
DRIVER, G. R., and MILES, J. C., *The Assyrian Laws* (1935).
—— —— *The Babylonian Laws* (1956).
HOBHOUSE, L. T., WHEELER, G. C., and GINSBERG, M., *The Material Culture and Social Institutions of the Simpler Peoples* (1915).
HOGBIN, H. I., *Law and Order in Polynesia* (1934).
JOLOWICZ, H. F., *Historical Introduction to the Study of Roman Law* (1932).
LLEWELLYN, K. N., and HOEBEL, E. A., *The Cheyenne Way* (1941).
MAINE, H. J. S., *Ancient Law* (ed. F. Pollock, 1924).
MALINOWSKI, B., *Crime and Custom in Savage Society* (1932).
REDFIELD, R., *The Primitive World and its Transformations* (1953).
SEAGLE, W., *The Quest for Law* (1941).

III

THE DEFINITION OF LAW

§ 18. INTRODUCTION

THE problems of definition are not as simple as they were once thought to be. According to a widely accepted method, the first task is to discover the genus to which a *res* belongs and then the particular characteristics which distinguish it from other species of the same genus. This method was combined with the notion that each *res* has an essence distinguishable from its other characteristics or mere incidents. The first step towards clarity, however, is to distinguish between the occasions when we are referring to words and those when we are referring to things or concepts.[1] This is frequently difficult because usually we are using words on both occasions. Robinson[2] asks '*Do we define things, or words, or concepts?*' In other words, are we to be *realists*, or *nominalists*, or *conceptualists*, about definition?

'When the notion of definition was invented by Socrates and Plato, only "real definition" was thought of. That is, it was always a *res* or things that required definition, never *nomina* or words or concepts.'

The first thing to notice about words and language is that their function is to aid communication between human beings. To describe and classify things is essential for the acquisition and communication of knowledge, but the definition of terms used or to be used is needed for the communication itself. It is convenient to distinguish between the two tasks in the interests of clarity. This is not to say that the traditional process of 'real definition' is not of value. But it has often caused puzzlement and fruitless argument by confusing the identification, description, and classification of things with arguments about the use of words. 'Real definition' (i.e. the assumption that when asked for a definition, what we are to define is a thing and not a word) has been valuable, although productive of confusion when applied to tasks to which it was not suited, because definition is perhaps most often seen as a matter of drawing lines or distinguishing between one kind of thing and another when language marks them off

---

[1] *Supra*, § 4.   [2] *Definition*, 7.

by using separate words to refer to them or so that language may do so in the future.[1] And the very word 'definition' suggests that the process is one of drawing lines or distinguishing.

It makes for clarity to distinguish between the definition of words on the one hand and the description or classification of things on the other, for a number of reasons. It is necessary to see that definition, even if confined to the definition of words, may be pursued in a number of different ways and for different purposes. For present purposes the mere equating of two words from different languages as having the same meaning may be ignored.[2] A clear distinction, however, should be drawn between what may be called lexical definition (reporting the meaning of words as actually used, or as they have actually been used), and stipulative definition (the 'explicit and self-conscious setting up of the meaning-relation between some word and some object, the act of assigning an object to a name (or a name to an object), not the act of recording an already existing assignment').[3] Both kinds of definition are constantly pursued in the ordinary work of the law, but confusion results if the differences between them are not kept in mind. Both kinds of definition, for present purposes, may be treated as nominal or word-thing definitions—that is, the assigning of a meaning to a word and in many cases the relating of a thing to a word which is said to refer to that thing. If that is the case then one method, and in many cases the most common method, will be to assign the meaning by describing or identifying the thing by one means or another.[4] Such description *may* be performed by assigning the thing to a well-recognized genus and specifying the distinguishing characteristics which it bears as contrasted with other things which fall within that genus.

Two things must be noted at this stage, however. First, that there are many words which are not in any real sense names for things which can be recognized as entities in the external world,[5] and whose meanings cannot be satisfactorily elucidated by this method; and second, that if this method goes to the traditional search for an essence on the assumption that all things have a simple essence which, once

---

[1] H. L. A. Hart, *Concept of Law*, 13.
[2] R. Robinson's 'word-word' definition, pp. 16 and 17.
[3] R. Robinson, p. 59.
[4] R. Robinson lists seven distinct methods for word-thing definition: (1) the method of synonyms, (2) the method of analysis, (3) the method of synthesis, (4) the implicative method, (5) the denotative method, (6) the ostensive method, (7) the rule-giving method, op. cit., ch. vi.
[5] See *supra*, § 4.

discovered, marks them off from all other things, then the method is bad.

It is bad because it is now realized that the nature of the external world is not Platonic. It cannot be explained by discovering a finite number of pure forms whose essence provides the classification for things; it is an infinite continuum. This is not to say that an essence may not be stipulated for clearly it can; but then it will be the product of a human decision. It will not be something discovered merely by observation and analysis. As the purpose of one observer differs from that of another so will his emphasis on different aspects of the thing observed. To a zoologist a horse suggests the genus mammalian quadruped, to a traveller a means of transportation, to the average man the sport of kings, to certain nations an article of food.[1] When a definition is produced which picks on one aspect as the essence of the thing in the light of the interests or purposes of the definer, then what has happened is a form of stipulation. The test of such a definition is whether it is useful for the particular purpose which the writer has in mind. The realization of this has led some to assert that to argue about definitions is merely to argue about words because you may define any word any way you please and you cannot be shown to be right or wrong in doing so.[2] But this goes much too far and may defeat the very purpose of the exercise, for the task is to enable communication to be improved and there are real limits to the practical acceptance of new language. And further, it goes too far because the mere reporting of the meaning of words as actually used is important in the work of the law. Many words used in the law are not names for things at all, but carry meanings which can only be understood, as has been pointed out,[3] by examining their use in the context in which they are used and by remembering that their meanings may vary strikingly in different contexts. 'The infinite diversity of human relationships with which the law has to deal transcends the limited resources of language, which is always trying to overtake the complexities of life and business and reduce them to categories.'[4]

---

[1] C. Morris, *How Lawyers Think*, 91–2.

[2] See Glanville Williams, 'International Law and the Controversy Concerning the Word Law', *British Year Book of International Law* (1945), 148; 'Language and the Law', 61 *L.Q.R.* (1945), 71, 179, 293, 384, and 62 *L.Q.R.* (1946), 387.

[3] *Supra*, § 14.

[4] Lord Macmillan, *Law and Other Things*, 149; see also W. A. Wilson, 32 *Mod. L. R.* (1969), 361. Thus a moving machine may be considered not in motion when it is moved by hand. Questions of degree always cause difficulty, as they sometimes raise mixed questions of fact and law.

Within a particular legal system, if we are asked: 'Is this particular rule law?', it may be possible to answer the question by reference to rules for identifying laws in that system. The question will be answered by reference to the rules of that system, and by putting the word 'law' in a sentence which can be tested as to its validity or invalidity as a conclusion of law. For example, it is the law that you must drive on the left-hand side of the roadway. This is a valid proposition of law in England because that rule is established under legislation made by Parliament and all rules established by Parliament are recognized as law. Thus the system may, and most systems do, include within itself rules which enable other rules to be recognized as legal or not. When someone asks 'What is law?' as a general question, however, he is asking something different. He may be familiar with the use of the word in ordinary language and he may be clear that there is in existence something called law; but he may be puzzled to know how to distinguish a system called a legal system from one not so called, or to distinguish a rule called law from a rule not so called, or to distinguish an institution called legal from one not so called. Or again he may really be asking a question about the nature of law so that he may understand it better, or about the purpose or purposes of law, or the history of law, or the source of law, or the content or form of law. A dispute over the answers to be given to such questions may spring from differing views of legal philosophy. Is law the whim of a despot or the protection of the liberty of the subject? This may be an argument over words, but it is a most important one. Many of the disputes in the past carried on as disputes over definition were really disputes over such questions of purpose or function or value.

If we pursue the task of defining law by the process of 'real definition' we find the method leads us into difficulties. 'There is no familiar well-understood general category of which law is a member.'[1] The attempts to find some common characteristics, or an essence, enjoyed by all the instances of what in ordinary uses of the word are accepted as laws, have all broken down at one point or another. Austin took the word 'law' and distinguished it, as applied to rules in systems which he recognized as legal, from its use in other contexts—as in Divine Law, laws of physics or chemistry. As has been seen, he fixed on the command of the sovereign as its distinguishing characteristic. But even to do this, of course, he had to recognize a legal system.

[1] H. L. A. Hart, op. cit. 15.

The problem of defining the term 'law' may be approached from the point of view of the theologian, the historian, the sociologist, the philosopher, the political scientist, or the lawyer. Most lawyers will approach the problem from inside a particular legal system. It is not surprising therefore that for the lawyers' purposes the investigation may stop at the point where that legal system provides authoritative tests for recognizing law from not-law. Those tests will be applied by some agencies of that legal system and hence we find lawyers defining law as 'the rules recognized and acted on by courts of justice'.[1] For lawyers working within a legal system such an answer may be sufficient for their purposes. But it does not assist those puzzled from a view outside a legal system as to the nature of law or the nature of legal systems. Hart says that for such people there have been three recurrent issues: 'How does law differ from and how is it related to orders backed by threats? How does legal obligation differ from, and how is it related to, moral obligation? What are rules and to what extent is law an affair of rules?'[2]

Much may be learnt about law by describing it in terms of its basis in nature, reason, religion, or ethics; by reference to its source in custom, precedent, or legislation; by its effects on the life of society; by the method of its formal expression or authoritative application; or by the ends that it seeks to achieve. But no definition in terms of any one of these provides an exhaustive means by which an inquirer could distinguish legal systems from other systems in all cases or legal rules from other rules in all cases. Pound has carried out an analysis which reveals the difficulties facing those who like their terms to be simple and clear cut.[3] Many attempts have been made to examine the problems relating to the definition of law.[4] It is futile to attempt to be exhaustive, but an analysis of a few typical definitions is a useful approach to the problem.

In preface, it should be pointed out that the word *droit* is even more ambiguous than the English term *law*. In its wide and objective sense *le droit* means the totality of the rules of law, and we sometimes find *droit objectif* (or natural law) opposed to a particular rule of positive law. Even when *droit* means positive law, the word carries an undertone of right or justice which is not present in the English term *law* to

---

[1] J. W. Salmond, 12th ed., 5.   [2] Op. cit. 13.
[3] 'Legal Essays in Tribute to MacMurray', 513.
[4] Most recently see H. Kantorowicz, The Definition of Law (1958), and H. L. A. Hart, Concept of Law (1961). Professor Hart's examination is probably the most penetrating presently available.

the same extent. In addition to these usages there is a purely subjective sense—thus *le droit d'auteur* means the right of an author. Hence particular caution must be used in translating any phrase in which *droit* occurs.

§ 19. LAW, ETHICS, AND POSITIVE MORALITY

A definition of law should establish clear distinctions between rules of law and rules of ethics, and between rules of law and such social rules as those of positive morality and of etiquette.[1]

To distinguish between law and ethics is fairly easy. Ethics is a study of the supreme good—an attempt to discover those rules which should be followed because they are good in themselves. Law tends to prescribe what is considered necessary for that time and place. Ethics concentrates on the individual rather than upon society; law is concerned with the social relationships of men rather than the individual excellence of their characters and conduct. Ethics must consider the motive for action as all-important, whereas law is concerned mainly with requiring conduct to comply with certain standards, and it is not usually concerned with the motives of men. It is too narrow, however, to say that ethics deals only with the individual, or that ethics treats only of the 'interior' and law only of the 'exterior', for ethics in judging acts must consider the consequences that flow from them and it is not possible to analyse the ethical duties of man without considering his obligations to his fellows or his place in society. It is equally misleading to concentrate upon those aspects of the law which are concerned directly with conduct and with 'exterior' factors in man's social relations,[2] to the exclusion of those which, explicitly or implicitly, are aimed at intention, motive, and the ends which men seek.

It is true, however, that law is more concerned with the social consequences of actions than with their effect on the character of the actor. Even when law bases liability on intention, there is a tendency to infer the intention from the conduct and to take a somewhat external view of the problem.[3] Law, in elaborating its standards, must not try to enforce the good life as such; it must always balance the benefits to be secured by obedience with the harm that the crude instrument of compulsion may do. There are many ethical rules the

---

[1] N. M. Korkunov, *General Theory of Law*, 41 et seq.
[2] See H. L. A. Hart, op. cit. 168–9.   [3] *Infra*, §§ 68, 82.

value of the observance of which lies in the voluntary choice of those who attempt to follow them. But there are other rules which it is essential for law to enforce for the well being of the community. Ethics thus perfects the law. In marriage, so long as love persists, there is little need of law to rule the relations of husband and wife— but the solicitor comes in through the door, as love flies out of the window. The *homo iuridicus*[1] who performs only his legal duties would be neither a pleasant neighbour nor a gracious friend— indeed, one would need to be exceedingly careful in doing business with him.[2]

Law thus lays down only those standards which are considered essential, whatever be the motive of compliance. In one sense law may be a 'minimum ethic', but frequently law has to solve disputes on which the rules of ethics throw very little light—where two persons, neither guilty of negligence, have suffered by the fraud of a third, who is to bear the loss? Ethics may suggest that the loss should be equally divided, but this is not a very practicable rule for the law which requires more definite rules for the passing of title and the performance of contracts.

The argument that the spheres of law and ethics are different, while it contains much truth, cannot be pushed too far, for while the sphere of ethics may remain the same, that of law will widen or narrow according to the particular social philosophy adopted by the community. What are today regarded as purely religious duties were once enforced by law; conversely, modern law will enforce many rules designed to save the individual from himself in a way that would have seemed absurd to a disciple of *laissez-faire*. There is no immutable boundary to the area of the operation of law.

Man is free to accept or reject the obligations of ethics, but legal duties are heteronomous, i.e. imposed on the individual without his consent. If a rule of ethics, which is in accord with positive morality, is broken, there may be the effective sanction of the pressure of public opinion, but ethical rules which are in advance of the views of a particular community are imposed by no earthly force.

It has been suggested that law creates both duties and rights,

---

[1] G. Del Vecchio writes interestingly on the concept of the legal man, the one who is guided only by his legal obligations, just as the economist treats the economic man who is guided only by self-interest: *Droit, Morale, Mœurs* (Inst. int. de phil. du droit), 1.

[2] This is illustrated by 'working to rule' in industrial disputes. Technical compliance with the letter and not the spirit may slow down any industry. The law operates effectively only if it is infused with a spirit of co-operation.

whereas ethics can create only duties.[1] This, however, may easily become a mere matter of terminology. If Jones is under an ethical duty to support his father, why cannot we say that the father has an ethical right to be supported? This right will not, or course, be enforced merely because it is decreed by ethics, and neither will breach of the duty be punished, but logically even in the case of ethics it is hard to conceive of a duty unless there is a corresponding right.

Positive Morality

Ethics deals with the absolute ideal, but positive morality is made up of the actual standards which are adopted in the life of any particular community. Positive morality, like law therefore, emphasizes conduct rather than states of mind; it is also similar to law in that it is imposed on the individual from without, for it has behind it the effective, if unorganized, sanction of public opinion. How many men would rather break the law than wear the wrong tie with a dinner jacket? Here we see the sanction behind a mere rule of etiquette, and the fear of ridicule or social ostracism protects strongly the more important rules of positive morality.

Various tests have been suggested to distinguish a rule of law from a mere dictate of positive morality. Firstly, a rule of law is imposed by the State; secondly, while there may be a sanction behind the rules of positive morality, it is not applied by an organized machinery, nor is it determined in advance. These two points are taken by Austin and we shall discuss them below.[2] Thirdly, some argue that the content of law is different from that of social morality: but, while it is true that law, having a different object, covers a different scope, there is no immutable boundary to its operation. Law, positive morality, and ethics are overlapping circles which can never entirely coincide, but the hand of man can move them and determine the content that is common to all or to two or confined to one. Ethics condemns murder, but it was once accepted both by positive morality and law. We do find a close relationship between the rules of law and those of positive morality, for the latter determine the upper and lower limits of the effective operation of law. If the law lags behind popular standards it falls into disrepute; if the legal standards are too high, there are great difficulties of enforcement. Thus the law has been ineffective in

[1] Thus the rules of law are said to be imperative-attributive, i.e. they impose duties and grant rights; cf. N. S. Timasheff, *Archives de phil. du droit* (1936, 1–2), 132; L. Le Fur, *Droit, Morale, Mœurs*, 56 et seq.   [2] *Infra*, § 20.

controlling monopolies and trusts, because it has not evolved a technique which can be effective against the strongly entrenched habits of business. The close relationship between law and the life of the community is shown by the historical school,[1] and if we admit that positive morality influences law, it must also be recognized that law in its turn plays a part in fixing the moral standards of the average man.[2] Fourthly, it has been suggested that the method of expression should be used as a test—rules of positive morality lack precision, whereas rules of law are expressed in technical and precise language. There is much truth in this, but the distinction is only relative; for early law is fluid and vague, and some social usages may be expressed very precisely, for example, the modes of address of those bearing titles. ·

Theoretically there may be some difficulty in determining the exact distinction between positive morality and law. In practice, however, the legal order provides machinery for the determination of difficult cases. If a sick relative, dependent on Jones for the needs of life, is so neglected by Jones that death results, is this a breach of a legal duty or merely an infringement of positive morality? In the modern State the court will supply the answer to this problem and draw exact lines of legal duty. For any legal system to be effective there must be provision for the clarification of these issues. Hence, in any given case, the practical distinction between morality and law is determined by the hypothesis laid down in the legal order itself. Logically it would be possible for a legal order to declare that all rules of positive morality should be regarded as law, and in that case the boundaries of each would be identical—but it would be absurd for the law to burden itself with multitudinous rules, many of which would be impossible to enforce.[3]

§ 20. THE IMPERATIVE DEFINITION

In his well-known analysis Austin first attempts to define the genus law and then to mark the *differentiae* which distinguish law as the subject-matter of jurisprudence.[4] In the broadest sense in which the term 'law' should be used, it signifies a command which obliges a person or persons to a course of conduct. Being a command, it must issue from a determinate person or group of persons, with the

---

[1] *Supra*, § 6.   [2] Cf. A. V. Lundstedt, *Legal Thinking Revised*, 217–68, 322–7.

[3] In China there seems to have been a less clear-cut distinction between morals and law than in most Western systems: for a discussion of the Chinese conception of law see J. Escarra, *Archives de philosophie du droit et de sociologie juridique* (1935, 1–2), 7.

[4] *Jurisprudence* (5th ed.), Lectures, I, V. (This work is hereafter cited as Austin.)

threat of displeasure if the rule be not obeyed. The person who receives the command must realize that there is a possibility of incurring some evil in the event of disobedience. This element of command clearly distinguishes a law from a mere rule of positive morality, since in the latter case the rule is not laid down by a determinate person, nor is there a *definite* threat of punishment.[1] But every command does not create a law, for we must distinguish between a particular order ('call me at dawn tomorrow') and an order laying down a general course of conduct ('call me at dawn every morning').[2] Austin, therefore, suggests that a statute issued by Parliament that corn then shipped and in port should not be exported would not be a law, since it relates merely to a specific case—but he agrees that in popular speech it would be called a law.[3] Generality is a normal mark of law because of the impossibility and undesirability of issuing particular commands for each specific act. Moreover, a law is normally general in another way, since we think of it as applying not merely to one person but to all members of the community or at least to all members of a particular class. Indeed, in the popular mind the notion of generality and uniformity in law is so accepted that the term law is metaphorically applied to the course of nature—thus we speak of the law of gravitation. Clearly this is quite a different use of the term, for the scientist attempts to describe what actually takes place, whereas a positive law prescribes what ought to be. Natural events were not affected by Newton's discoveries, whereas a positive law is designed to, and does, affect the wills of men. What is common to the two conceptions is the sense of order and uniformity. But it is difficult to prove *a priori* that order and uniformity are the marks of all positive law, for, if the leader of a small community decided each case not by rules but by his subjective sense of justice, few would go so far as to say that there was no law in the community.

Having thus discovered the genus law, Austin distinguishes the species which is of interest to the jurist—*positive law*, as he terms it. Positive law is laid down by the sovereign either mediately or immediately—it is a rule laid down by a political superior for a political inferior. Austin's theory of sovereignty is discussed below;[4] here it

---

[1] Although the unorganized pressure of public opinion may provide a fairly effective sanction.

[2] A law determines *acts of a class*, a particular command determines merely a specific act: Austin, i. 94.

[3] W. Markby, *Elements of Law* (6th ed.), 3, agrees with this approach.

[4] *Infra*, § 76.

is enough to say that he postulates, firstly, a political society, secondly, a superior in that society who is habitually obeyed by the bulk of the community and who is not in the habit of obedience to any other person or body.[1] The sovereign, of course, may consist either of one person or a number of persons.

Into a detailed criticism of the Austinian definition we do not propose to go, but there are three major points:

  (a) Should law be defined by reference to the State?
  (b) Is a definite sanction necessary before a rule can be regarded as law?
  (c) Should a definition of law contain a reference to the purpose of law?[2]

(a)

The definition of law in terms of the State possesses certain advantages. It gives a clear-cut and simple test. It solves in an easy manner conflict between various juridical orders, for example between Church and State. If only the State can create positive law, then the Church can have only such legal rights as the State grants to it. It gives an easy answer to the problem of the validity of law, since law is valid for the simple reason that it has been laid down by the sovereign. It is easy to mark the moment when primitive rules become law, for we have only to ask whether there is a determinate sovereign body that has issued a command. In the prevailing confusion of modern jurisprudence, clarity and simplicity are virtues to be prized.

There are, however, many critics of this solution. The historically minded have argued that the State is an incidental product of mature systems of law rather than the distinguishing characteristic of all law as such. It is said that historically law is older than the State and that, while mature systems normally develop a machinery for creating, applying, and enforcing the rules, law may exist even in the absence of such machinery.[3] In the Middle Ages an application of the Austinian definition gives a very small compass to law, for the innovating forces were the law of the Church, the law of the merchants, the law of the fief, and Roman law, and 'not one of these was Law in the Austinian sense'.[4] Del Vecchio suggests that those who define law in terms of the State should be forced to study history before writing

---

[1] Austin, i. 227.   [2] Infra, § 23, for a fuller discussion of this last point.
[3] Cf. F. Gény, Méthode, i. 202; G. Del Vecchio, Justice, Droit, État, 282.
[4] E. Jenks, Law and Politics in the Middle Ages, 62.

jurisprudence.[1] Austin, of course, can logically reply that he is entitled to define the term 'law' as he pleases. In the continuous evolution since primitive times some point must be chosen as that which marks the emergence of law. A monkey is not necessarily a man because he is descended from the same anthropoid ancestors, and we should not confuse the early beginnings of law with law itself. This is true, but the real issue is whether it is useful for jurisprudence thus to limit the use of the term 'law'. Anthropologists urge that primitive law serves the same function in early communities as does mature law today, and that the essence of law is its *function*, rather than the *form in* which it is created or the method by which it is enforced.[2] Law should be defined by the part it plays in the life of society, not by the historical accident that it is sometimes laid down by a sovereign. Must we deny that there is law where no sovereign exists? Malinowski argues that even in primitive societies there are rules behind which the community throws the whole weight of its organization.[3] The very structure of society is such that primitive man suffers if these rules are disobeyed. Although there is no intricate system of courts or police, nevertheless the community directly interests itself in securing the observance of those rules which it considers essential. If primitive man does not meet his customary obligations, then he knows that in future no one will help him. A primitive anticipation of the 'stop-list' can afford a very useful sanction. Apart from the community, primitive man is helpless, and the threat of expulsion or death is a salutary one for prospective offenders. Because in so many cases the community leaves primitive man to enforce his own rights by *self-help*, we must not leap to the conclusion that there are no rules breach of which is regarded as fatal to the community life.

Thus the thesis of the anthropologist is that law should be defined by function rather than form, by the part it plays in the life of society rather than by the method of its creation—in short, that law can be truly understood only if it is regarded as one of many means of social control.   *NB*

The argument whether primitive law is law properly so called may easily become one of mere logomachy. What is more important is that jurisprudence should study primitive beginnings for the light they throw on mature law. It may be primarily a question of

---

[1] *Justice, Droit, État*, 320.
[2] *Supra*, § 14. H. Kelsen also rejects the definition of law in terms of the State. A primitive tribe may have a legal order long before it has developed a state: 55 *Harv. L. R.* (1941), 66–7.   [3] *Crime and Custom*, 58.

convenience whether the term 'law' should be so widened as to include all societies traditionally described as primitive. The view taken in this work, however, is that it is more than a mere matter of convenience that the term 'law' should be used so as to include the enforceable normative rules of such primitive societies as have them. The view advanced is that law exists when rules can be articulated not merely as descriptions of what actually happens, but as accepted prescriptions for what ought to happen, and when they can be seen to be backed by some degree of enforcement by the community. The notion of enforcement by the community implies some mechanism for securing compliance with the rules in key cases—something more than individual redress even if such redress is approved by the community at large. Whether this mechanism must provide a specific sanction for each rule of law we now proceed to discuss.

(b)

Must the specific mechanism behind law be essentially a sanction? Austin emphasized that the sanction must consist in a fear of some evil. This is perhaps a natural conclusion if we define law in terms of command. Much law, however, is enabling rather than restrictive; although one law may abridge liberty, a second may give powers which otherwise a citizen would not possess. No man can surpervise the distribution of his estate after his death, but the law has granted power to a testator to determine, within limits, the destination of his wealth. Hence the observance of many rules is secured by the promise of reward (e.g. the fulfilment of expectations) rather than by a lurking sanction.[1] Bentham admitted the force of reward in securing the observance of law, but cynically observed that it was not as effective as pain, for the sources of pleasure are few and soon exhausted, whereas the sources of pain are innumerable and inexhaustible.[2] It is true that by the use of ingenuity the rules relating to wills may be expressed in terms of command—the order to the executor to carry out the provisions of the will, to the court to supervise the distribution, to strangers not to interfere with the property—but the most significant feature of testamentary law is the increased power given to the testator.

Psychologically, the sanction does not fully explain why law is

---

[1] B. Malinowski, introduction to H. I. Hogbin, *Law and Order in Polynesia*, p. lxv; A. L. Goodhart, *Transactions of the Grotius Society* (1936), xxii. 33.
[2] *Limits of Jurisprudence Defined*, 226, note.

obeyed. The sanction can be successful only if it is not necessary to employ it in all but marginal cases. Universal disobedience will rapidly destroy the whole basis of the legal order.[1] Law is obeyed because of its acceptance by the community, and while the sanction plays its part in dealing with a recalcitrant minority, the reasons for that acceptance lie deeper. Habit, respect for the law as such, and a desire to reap the rewards which legal protection of acts will bring— these are factors that are equally important. Hence, some define law in terms of rules that are mentally accepted by a population as binding. Academic preoccupation with the sanction leads to a false view of law. The idea of health does not at once suggest to our minds hospitals and diseases, operations and anaesthetics, however necessary these things may be to maintain the welfare of a community. The best service of medicine is the prevention of disease, just as the real benefit of law is that it secures an ordered balance which goes far to prevent disputes.[2] Austin's reply to this argument would be that he is attempting to define the formal mark of law and that, however interesting a discussion of the psychological reasons for the acceptance of law, that matter is germane to a sociological study of sovereignty rather than to jurisprudence.

There are some rules for which it is difficult to find a particular sanction. If one of the conventions of the constitution is not observed, it is not easy to find a precise penalty. Austin would not regard these conventions as law, since obedience cannot be enforced by court process. Some of these conventions,[3] however, are the foundation of the accepted legal order, and it is rather narrow to refuse to call them law merely because a specific sanction cannot be discovered. In fact these rules are effective because it is recognized that, if they are flouted, the legal order itself will break down. Indeed, if we take the sanction theory literally, there would need to be an infinity of sanctions. There should be a sanction against the judge if he does not apply a rule and a sanction against the official who should enforce the sanction against the judge, and so on.[4]

---

[1] Speaking of the law as applied to trade union members, O. Kahn-Freund, 33 *Mod. L. R.* (1970), 241, writes: '... sanctions cannot be applied to counteract the spontaneous conduct of amorphous masses. They can, however, be applied to regulate the conduct of organisations.'

[2] P. Vinogradoff, *Common Sense in Law*, 52.

[3] Conventions vary in strength. Roosevelt easily defied the convention that no President should serve more than two terms. But the conventions on which responsible government rests could be abandoned only by destroying the system itself: A. L. Goodhart, *Interpretations of Modern Legal Philosophies*, 296–7.

[4] J. P. Haesaert, *Théorie générale du droit*, 97.

Some of those who hold that the existence of the sanction is a necessary test of the existence of the law meet these objections by broadening the meaning of the term 'sanction' so as to include all forms of social pressure. This is wider than Austin would approve, since to him the sanction must be a definite threat by a determinate person. Moreover, such a wide use of the term means that the sanction does not provide a precise criterion, since even the rules of etiquette have public pressure behind them.

In the modern State the distinction between the sanctions of law and those of other social rules can, in the vast majority of cases, be clearly drawn. The sanctions behind positive morality are vague and indefinite, while those of law are usually pre-determined both in their nature and their conditions of application. Moreover, while a serious breach of a social rule may lead to exclusion from a particular set, the machinery of law possesses sanctions that are more effective— the defendant may be compelled specifically to carry out his duty, or he may be forced to carry out a subsidiary duty such as paying damages, or he may be branded as a criminal and sentenced to a fine, imprisonment, or death.[1]

In conclusion, it may be said that while it is difficult in theory to determine the precise nature of the sanction which must be attached to every rule of law, in practice there is no difficulty, for the legal order itself provides a method by which the boundary line is drawn between law and other social rules and in so doing determines what sanction is available. In the modern State the machinery of law is clear cut, but the farther back we go, the more confused the problem becomes. It is difficult to conceive of any legal system operating effectively without a sanction in the background—the weakness of international 'law' clearly illustrates this. But once a community is taught to observe the law, particular rules may be obeyed, even though there is no particular sanction attached to them. We cannot say *a priori* that a particular rule is law only if it has a specific sanction—the test is whether the rule is regarded as law by the particular legal order in question. Thus, it is universally admitted that the judge is bound by the law in deciding disputes, but there is no specific sanction in English law, save the rather drastic one of removal.[2]

The fundamental weakness in Austin's doctrine was his selection

---

[1] A. Desqueyrat, *L'Institution, le droit objectif et la technique positive*, 202; L. R. Siches in *Droit, Morale, Mœurs* (Inst. int. de phil. du droit), 160–1.

[2] A. L. Goodhart, *Interpretations of Modern Legal Philosophies*, 297.

of the notion of command as his basic test, instead of the wider notion of a 'rule'. If the difficult notion of a 'rule', with its dependent notion that things *ought* to be done or not done, is examined, 'the important similarities (hidden by Austin's concentration on the notion of a command instead of a rule) between primitive and developed systems and between municipal and international law could then emerge; and those who have been agonized by the question: "How can a fundamental constitutional law be law?" might be content when it is shown that a defining characteristic of a legal system just is that it includes a fundamental rule for the identification of the other rules of the system.'[1]

(c)

The third main criticism of Austin's definition is that it is superficial to regard the command of the sovereign as the real source of the validity of law. Many regard law as valid because it is the expression of natural justice,[2] or the embodiment of the spirit of a people.[3] A favourite conundrum asks whether law is valid because it is enforced or enforced because it is valid. The answer to both questions is 'Yes'; but to explain this paradox we must distinguish between a system of law as a whole and a particular rule.

If we are considering the legal validity of a system of law, it is clear that its positivity depends on acceptance, which may in turn depend directly or indirectly on enforcement. If I draw up an ideal code for Utopia, no degree of logical perfection or sweet reasonableness will give it the force of law—to deserve that description it must be applied in a particular community. Thus Kelsen recognized that his initial premiss must have a certain measure of correspondence with reality, and Austin's sovereign is not only *he who must be obeyed* (by the individual) but *he who in fact is obeyed* (by the bulk of the members of a given community). If a monarch, who by the constitution has the sole power to create law, flees, owing to revolt, and a new government is set up, the monarch loses the power to make new laws. A code drawn up in exile would not have the force of law, for the old legal order has been entirely destroyed. The validity of a legal system as a whole depends on the fact that it is accepted by, and therefore capable of enforcement over, a given community.

---

[1] H. L. A. Hart, in his introduction to Austin's *The Province of Jurisprudence Determined* (Library of Ideas, 1954), pp. xii and xiii; and see H. L. A. Hart, *Concept of Law.*   [2] *Infra*, Ch. IV.   [3] *Supra*, § 6.

On the other hand, if we are considering a particular *rule*, it is clear that it will be enforced only if it is valid, that is, in accordance with the structure of the legal system as a whole. The mere fact that a particular statute is ignored for a century does not (according to English notions) deprive it of the force of law: no court would listen to an argument that, since it had not been enforced, it was no longer binding. But, where a legal *system* is concerned, we can escape basing validity on effective operation only if we define law as the realization of natural justice or some other ideal. Law, however, is not only an ideal set of values, but also values which are applied in the life of a given community.[1] To say that a rule which is actually applied is not law because it conflicts with natural justice,[2] or to argue that an ideal which is nowhere applied is law, leads only to confusion. In emphasizing that positive law is such only if it is in effective operation in a particular community Austin makes an important point.

There are many incidental criticisms of Austin's definition which are discussed in the course of this work. Kelsen refuses to define law in terms of the State, for he regards law and the State as being essentially the same.[3] Public law and international law also raise difficulties. *Ex hypothesi*, in Austin's view, the sovereign cannot be legally bound by law—this problem, however, is best discussed in dealing with the relationship of law and the State.[3] At this stage the problem of international law will alone be discussed.

§ 21. The Problem of International Law

According to Austin's view international law is not positive law since there is lacking a determinate sovereign whom the nations of the world habitually obey. Perhaps on no point has Austin been so criticized as on his approach to this problem. But his conclusion follows irresistibly from his premises,[4] and many who criticize

---

[1] A. Ross, *Le Problème des sources*, 167. Austin, ii. 656, relates Murat's story that in some American states the judges and the bar met at the beginning of every term and decided what statutes of the preceding session they would enforce. Without accepting the story, we may use it as a test of the definition of law. Austin said that in this case a statute would not be law unless it was accepted by the court. If this power of the courts was tolerated by the community, the courts would be the sovereign in the Austinian sense.

[2] H. Krabbe, *The Modern Idea of the State*, denies the validity of a rule that conflicts with the instinctive sense of right of a community.

[3] *Infra*, § 76.

[4] C. A. W. Manning, *Modern Theories of Law*, 224, points out that in the end Austin agreed that international law was law properly so-called, although he still denied that it was positive law.

Austin show a disinclination to follow the only logical course and adopt a broader definition of law.

It is a question of degree whether any body of rules deserves the name of law. After the institution of the League of Nations and of the Permanent Court of International Justice, there was a tendency to over-estimate the effectiveness of international law, but the series of flagrant violations that began in the thirties of this century led to exaggerated pessimism. It is certainly inconvenient to follow Austin and deny the term law to the rules that apply to nations *inter se*, for there is a clear-cut distinction between international morality and international law. International courts use the language and technique that is employed by systems to which all admit that the adjective 'legal' is properly applied. There is the same reliance on authority, development of principle, discriminating use of analogy, and distinction—in short the same endeavour to build up a body of rules organically interrelated.[1]

The question whether the rules followed by primitive tribes are properly termed law may proceed in an atmosphere of academic calm, but the determination of the nature of international law has important practical results, for an admission that it is properly called law carries with it a greater sense of binding obligation. It is difficult to see how any community of nations can exist, save on the basis of rules of law —*ubi societas, ibi ius*. All these arguments of international lawyers contain some truth, but international law suffers from serious defects. It is very weak on the institutional side—there is no legislature, and, while a court exists, it can act only with the consent of the parties and has no real power to enforce its decisions. It may be possible to compare war to the self-help of primitive times, but as soon as law begins, the community regulates the cases in which self-help may be resorted to and the manner of its exercise. In international law the claimant of the right must still take the law into his own hands. Attempts have been made by the Covenant of the League of Nations, the Kellogg Pact, and the Charter of the United Nations to reduce the area of self-help, but humanity must travel far before there is an effective reign of law in international affairs.[2] It is true that the international law of peace is seldom broken, but once grave issues arise we see flagrant disregard of accepted rules. The public opinion of the world may be

---

[1] H. Lauterpacht, *Function of the Law in the International Community*.

[2] The theory of the just war is accepted by H. Kelsen, but even he recognizes the difficulties: *General Theory of Law and State*, 334. See also A. Nussbaum, 42 *Mich. L. R.* (1943), 453.

a factor not lightly to be ignored, but it is harder to deal with a nation that is a law-breaker than to expel a primitive man from his community—hence while primitive and international law both lack institutional machinery, the sanctions of the former are really more effective, since they are brought to bear on the individual and not on the nation. Law can be effective only if there is a community with an accepted scale of values. Nazi Germany denied that the State was bound by law in its dealings with states of another colour:[1] the same doctrine was originally put forward by Soviet thinkers, but the reality of international law is recognized by contemporary Soviet theory.[2]

One significant advance has been the setting up of courts to try war criminals.[3] This step has been hailed in most quarters as a vindication of the effectiveness of international law and the dawn of a new era when sanctions will be applied against law breakers.[4] It is certainly encouraging to see the attempt made to secure the observance of certain minimum rules, but optimism must be tempered by the following considerations.[5] Firstly, it is unlikely that the threat of a prosecution for a crime against peace (the waging of aggressive war) will ever deter a nation bent on conquest, for a crime against the peace is deliberately planned only where victory is expected. Secondly, so far as the rules of war are concerned, the principles are so uncertain that the individual is placed in a position of great difficulty. These rules are always obsolete as the machinery of international conferences is too cumbrous to develop them with sufficient speed. The submarine, the aeroplane, and the atom bomb were not envisaged when the earlier rules were laid down. Moreover, there is no international criminal court which can state the law authoritatively. For a submarine commander to kill survivors of a torpedoed vessel is a war crime:[6] the use of the atom bomb has been justified by the doctrine of military necessity. The defence of superior orders must inevitably be rejected: but the prosecution of a private for carrying out a specific order given by his superior reveals the dilemma in which the humble soldier is placed. If he disobeys the order, immediate punishment follows: if he obeys, he may be punished if his country is

---

[1] e.g. E. H. Bockhoff cited W. Friedmann, 2 *Mod. L. R.* (1938), 194 at 199.
[2] R. Schlesinger, *Soviet Legal Theory*, 285.
[3] The most authoritative account is the *History of the United Nations War Crimes Commission and the Development of the Laws of War* (H.M.S.O.). See also *Law Reports of Trials of War Criminals*, vols. i–xv.
[4] Lord Wright, 62 *L.Q.R.* (1946), 40; 19 *Temple L. Q.* (1946) contains a symposium.
[5] The writer discusses these problems more fully in 3 *Res Judicatae* (1947), 122.
[6] 'The Peleus Trial', *Law Reports of Trials of War Criminals*, i. 1.

defeated. Thirdly, the trials were conducted not by international courts in the full sense of the term, but by victors' tribunals. It is difficult to see what other policy could have been followed in the circumstances, but until there is a permanent international criminal court we cannot expect the defeated to have full confidence in the verdicts.[1] Fourthly, the real breach of order is the use of war itself. It is impossible to fight a modern war and observe the Christian principles of morality. We must be realistic and take account of the principle of military necessity, but that is a dangerous argument because it may be carried so far as to destroy all rules. All agree that the unnecessary infliction of death, suffering, and destruction of property should be forbidden, but that principle must be thoroughly worked out before it can create rigid rules.

Before international law can be effective, a reasonable alternative to war as a solution of international problems must be found. If international law is to be developed by the judicial method, we cannot criticize the courts for creating new rules. But the decisions in the war trials should be used as the foundation for further action and not left to stand as isolated instances. The rules of war must be codified and enforced by an impartial international tribunal. The United Nations realizes these problems. It is endeavouring to create an international community by such institutions as UNESCO, but progress is necessarily slow. Politically there is still a divorce between Russia and the western world and the iron curtain leads to misunderstandings which hinder or prevent creative effort.

The interest of these problems for jurisprudence is that they emphasize that law is ineffective without a real sense of community: that there must be machinery capable of developing the law speedily to meet new conditions: that there must be an authoritative tribunal which has the confidence of those subject to it and which has the command of force to back its decisions. It is too narrow to say that international law does not exist:[2] but in the present state of civilization it is tragically ineffective.

---

[1] F. B. Schick, 11 *Mod. L. R.* (1948), 290.

[2] The argument may easily become one of words, for whether international law is such depends on our definition of law: Glanville Williams, 22 *Brit. Y.B.I.L.* (1945), 146. While it may be futile to engage in terminological debates, it is essential to grasp the defects of the present system of international law. A brilliant treatment is that by the same writer, 61 *L.Q.R.* (1945), 71, 179, 293, 384; and 62 *L.Q.R.* (1946), 387.

The Relationship between International Law and the Law of the State

If we deny the existence of international law, then there is no real problem—the State possesses a body of law, while the rules binding nations are customary only. But, if international law is not a misnomer, what is the relationship between it and the law of the various states? Dualists solve the problem by saying that there is no conflict between them, since international law applies to states, and municipal law to individuals. But, as international law develops, this analysis is becoming increasingly difficult to apply.[1] The war trials showed that the sanctions of international law could be used against individuals. Monists argue that there cannot be two valid systems of law without some method of adjusting conflicts between them; thus Kelsen points out that a desire for a unified theory may lead either to the view that international law is supreme or else to the doctrine that the law of the State is the governing force and that international law is based merely on the consent of national sovereigns.[2] Enthusiasts for international law object that the doctrine of the supremacy of state law leaves little scope for international law. If the latter binds only because of consent, why may not that consent be withdrawn at any time? Moreover, the accepted theory is that international law binds a state even after a new government has been set up as the result of a revolution. There is no need for consent, any more than in the case where two new states are created by the partition of what was previously one state—the new states are bound by international law as a condition of their entrance into the family of nations.[3]

Theoretically, the view that international law is supreme is much more satisfying, since its tenets would then decide conflicts between states as to the extent of the operation of their particular legal systems. But, if we adopt the analogy of a federation,[4] we see that what is really supreme is the constitution itself which distributes certain powers to the central authority and others to the states or provinces. In the international sphere there is no constitution, but may there not be certain primary rules which mark out the sphere both of the laws

---

[1] H. Lauterpacht, 63 *L.Q.R.* (1947), 438; 64 *L.Q.R.* (1948), 97.

[2] *Annales de l'Institut de droit comparé* (1936), ii. 55. Finally H. Kelsen supports the theory of the primacy of international law, stating that the theoretic base for the primacy of international law was first discovered by the pure theory of law: 55 *Harv. L. R.* (1941), 68.

[3] J. G. Starke, 17 *Brit. Y.B.I.L.* (1936), 66; E. M. Borchard, *Rec. Gény*, iii. 328.

[4] For a scheme of federation for the democracies of the world see Clarence Streit, *Union Now.*

of the states and of international law itself?[1] Thus when the relationship between the legal systems of two states, or between the law of England and international law, becomes a matter of conflict, the primary rules (or the constitution of the world) could supply legal material according to which the conflict would be solved.

These abstract arguments have only a limited use. If the dogma is advanced that law can have no other source than the sovereign will of a state, then it may be justifiable to show that there is no *a priori* reason why other sources should not exist. But if we wish to discover the precise standing of international law today our analysis must be more concrete. Radbruch says that the primacy of international law is indispensable, since it is impossible to think of a 'space empty of law'. The answer is, not only that it is theoretically possible to conceive of this, but that the facts show that it may exist. Kelsen, finally, goes far beyond his premisses in supporting the primacy of international law and really gives to his formal theory an ethical core—the ideal of the legal unity of mankind at large.[2] We must not warp our analysis by wishful thinking. The notion of what ought to be undoubtedly affects what is, since if all men believed that international law should be given further scope, it would in fact soon develop. But to admit that the law carries into effect many of the purposes of ethics must not blind us to the distinction between the law that is and the law that ought to be, between the sordid realities of life as we know it and the vision that occasionally flies into the minds of even the most mundane of men. Whether at any given period there is international law, whether it is superior to state law, depends on an analysis of the facts—is it effectively in operation and does a specific mechanism exist for securing compliance? We cannot decide whether international law is supreme by weaving finely spun theories, for it may well be that there is no real international law in the fifteenth century and a very effective system in the twenty-first century.

§ 22. DEFINITION OF LAW IN TERMS OF THE JUDICIAL PROCESS

In America today the definition of law in terms of the judicial process is very popular. Holmes J. has said: 'the prophecies of what the courts will do in fact, and nothing more pretentious, are what I mean

---

[1] J. G. Starke, op. cit.
[2] J. W. Jones, 16 *Brit. Y.B.I.L.* (1935), 5 at 12.

by law.'[1] This definition has been seized upon by the realists and has coloured their whole approach to jurisprudence.[2] To Frank J. the law for any lay person with respect to a particular state of facts is a decision of a court, and 'until a court has passed on those facts, no law on that subject is yet in existence'. Prior to such a decision, the only law available is 'a guess as to what a court will decide'.[3] The realists push this approach to what they regard as its logical conclusion and law is treated as a collection of decisions and not as a body of rules.

Cardozo J. is on safer ground when he emphasizes that law is a basis for prediction rather than a mere guess: 'a principle or rule of conduct so established as to justify a prediction with reasonable certainty that it will be enforced by the courts if its authority is challenged is . . . a principle or rule of law.'[4]

The practical advantage of such an approach is that it emphasizes the fact that law is a process, that it is not a series of particular commands, but rather a body of principles slowly evolved by the decision of concrete cases. Cardozo's definition is slightly wider than the definition of law in terms of the State, since a court may exist even where there is no sovereign. Two points arise concerning this approach. Firstly, although useful as a description, it can hardly be accepted as a definition. Much law today never comes before the courts because recourse is prohibited, as can be seen in the rapidly growing body of administrative law. We are so accustomed to the development of law by the courts that we tend to forget that it may be developed and applied in other ways without ceasing to be law. It may be enforced according to the whim of a Minister who by statute is given the right to determine such questions with absolute finality. Secondly, the definition is but a modified form of Austin's, for it defines law in terms of the organ which creates it.

§ 23. DEFINITION OF LAW IN TERMS OF ITS PURPOSE

Salmond retains the emphasis on the judicial process, but considers that a reference to the purpose of law is essential. 'The law may be defined as the body of principles recognized and applied by the State in the administration of justice.'[5] Justice is the end of law, and it is

---

[1] *Collected Papers*, 173.   [2] *Supra*, § 7.
[3] *Law and the Modern Mind*, 46. On this theory the U.S. Supreme Court has been called 'the court of ultimate conjecture'.
[4] *Growth of Law*, 52; E. W. Patterson, 88 *Univ. of Pa. L. R.* (1939), 71,
[5] *Jurisprudence* (12th ed.), 5.

only fitting that an instrument should be defined by a delineation of
the purpose which is its *raison d'être*. This raises the question of the
relationship of law and justice. One theory defines law in terms of
justice, but from this it follows that an unjust law cannot exist, for if
it could, then on the premises there would be a fatal self-contradiction. Many writers have fallen into this simple trap. Thus earlier
theories of natural law put the emphasis on justice and denied the
validity of a law if it was opposed to natural justice. But slavery, condemned by natural law, yet existed in the legal systems of the time,
and, though the Romans recognized this difficulty, they never succeeded in solving it.[1] Law does not cease to be such merely because
it is unjust—if it did, who is to supply the criterion of injustice? Even
our modes of speech contain truths—the phrase *unjust law* has a
meaning, whereas the term *square circle* has not.[2] Is it accurate then
to define law by reference to a quality which actual laws in force may
lack? Is only that law which embodies what I like?

A second means of solving the problem of the relationship of law
and justice is to place all the emphasis on law and regard justice as
mere conformity to law.[3] But then we are depriving ourselves of
a criterion which may not be wholly subjective by which we may test
the operation of a legal system. In this sense law cannot be unjust,
since the term 'just' is defined only as that which is legal.

Each of these approaches is founded on false premises; we must
distinguish clearly between justice and law, for each is a different
conception. Law is that which is actually in force, whether it be evil
or good. Justice is an ideal founded in the moral nature of man.
The conception of justice may develop, as man's understanding
develops, but justice is not limited by what happens in the actual
world of fact. It is wrong, however, to regard law and justice as

---

[1] *Infra*, § 29. E. Bodenheimer, *Jurisprudence*, 19, regards law in its purest form as
that which reduces to a minimum the possibility of abuse of power by private individuals as well as by the government. The logical result of this is that law hardly
exists at all in a totalitarian state. Is not this a case of defining law as 'that which
achieves what I want'? Just because law is used for a purpose of which I do not
approve it does not cease to be law. Cf. G. M. Bergman, 57 *Yale L. J.* (1947), 55 at 71,
who defines law in terms of the will of the majority. The thesis is that justice is what
the community accepts and, as law is based on the majority will, law is founded on
justice.

[2] A. Desqueyrat, *L'Institution, le droit objectif et la technique positive*, 199. Is
an unjust law the negation of law? *Droit, Morale, Mœurs*, 48. N. S. Timasheff, *An
Introduction to the Sociology of Law*, 270, defines law as the overlapping part of
ethics and power.

[3] Jethro Brown, 32 *L.Q.R.* (1916), 180–1, suggests that justice as a concept of
jurisprudence is mere conformity to law.

entirely unrelated. Justice acts within the law as well as providing an external test by which the law may be judged, e.g. justice emphasizes good faith, and this conception has greatly influenced the development of legal systems.

Salmond's point really is not that law is justice, but that law is an instrument by which justice can be achieved.[1] It is not an adequate definition of medicine to describe it as a drug administered by a doctor because this ignores its real function (that of curing) and because medicine does not cease to be such just because it is prescribed by a layman.[2] But is the purpose of achieving justice as closely linked to law as is the desire of curing to the administering of medicine? Is defining law in terms of justice like defining a franc as a piece of money to be given to the poor? From the abstract point of view, it is possible to conceive of a legal system the dominant purpose of which was the infliction of injustice to satisfy the neuroses of an all-powerful tyrant. But such a ruler could make his rules effective only if he secured the co-operation of a sufficiently large part of the community to aid in enforcement. Some consideration must be paid to the desires of an army and the tolerance of a community. Moreover, if we leave the realm of the barely conceivable and study actual legal systems as we know them, we find that the most powerful rulers wisely left the *private* law of their subjects almost untouched. As the French adage has it, we can do everything with bayonets but sit on them. Law is one, and perhaps the most important, of the instruments for the achievement of such social purposes as win acceptance or tolerance from a sufficiently large section of the community to render enforcement possible.[3] We agree with Salmond that the purpose of law is essential to an understanding of its real nature; but the pursuit of justice is not the only purpose of law: the law of any period serves many ends and those ends will vary as the decades roll by.[4] To seek

---

[1] 'I am not afraid of being accused of sloppiness of thought when I say that the guiding principle of a judge in deciding cases is to do justice; that is, justice according to law, but still justice. I have not found any satisfactory definition of justice . . . what is just in any particular case is what appears to be just to the just man, in the same way as what is reasonable is what appears to be reasonable to the reasonable man': per Lord Wright, *The Future of the Common Law*, 114.

[2] Cf. P. Vinogradoff, *Historical Jurisprudence*, i. 117 n. 2.

[3] R. M. MacIver, *The Modern State*, 99, points out that every state has, as it were, a double framework—a code and a constitution, the thing administered and the agency of administration. Law grows quietly underneath, while the storms rage above. The most violent revolution may leave the bulk of the code untouched, although the power that administers it is changed.

[4] *Infra*, Chs. IV, V: cf. B. N. Cardozo, *Paradoxes of Legal Science*, 4: 'Nomos, one might fairly say, is the child of antinomies, and is born of them in travail.'

for one term which may be placed in a definition as the only purpose of law leads to dogmatism. The end that seems most nearly universal is that of securing order, but this alone is not an adequate description;[1] indeed, Kelsen regards it as a pleonasm, since law itself is the order of which we speak.[2] Dias makes the interesting point that when we are considering the concept of law at a definite period of time, the formal test is the most convenient, for it tells how a court on that day will decide. But if we are considering the historical sweep, natural law and ethics are just as useful in tracing the future evolution of law.[3]

§ 24. FORMAL DEFINITIONS OF LAW

Since the time of the ancient Greek philosophers, many writers have emphasized the relativity of law—there is scarcely a rule of today which may not be matched by its opposite of yesterday. A study of actual systems makes many despair of finding universal elements on which a definition of law can build. Kant attacked this problem by the application of his 'critical method'. It is not possible in a short section to expound one of the most difficult systems of philosophy ever conceived. All that can be achieved is to point out the bearing of Kant's method on the problem of defining law. To Kant the world of sensible experience is full of diversity and can of itself produce no principles which are universally valid. To define law we must distinguish between form and matter; the first being 'the complex of universally valid principles presupposed in any legal judgment, and the latter the changing world of social experience which those principles construe legally'.[4] To define law we should not study actual legal systems, but rather retire to the world of pure thought and discover those elements without which it is logically impossible to conceive of law at all.

---

[1] Many other ends have been suggested, e.g. security, order, the general good, the greatest happiness of the greatest number, the reconciliation of the will of one with the liberty of another. H. Lévy-Ullmann, *La Définition du droit*, 116–17, regards the definition of law in terms of its end as a surrender to subjectivism and to the individual arbitrariness of authors.

[2] 57 *Yale L. J.* (1948), 377. In his argument, however, there is a double use of the term *order*.

[3] R. W. M. Dias, 28 *Camb. L. J.* (1970), 75. There is not really such a gulf between L. Fuller and H. L. A. Hart as is sometimes supposed—see Hart, *Concept of Law*, 199. See also King, 24 *Camb. L. J.* (1966), 106, who distinguishes between the *law concept* used by the jurist to identify what is law, the *law idea* which explains law, and the *law theory*.

[4] F. Hallis, *Corporate Personality*, 31. For a concise account of Kantian legal philosophy see W. Friedmann, *Legal Theory* (4th ed.), 106–11.

The method may be illustrated by turning to the work of Rudolf Stammler.[1] He regards the philosophy of law 'as the theory of those propositions about law which have universal validity'.[2] The natural world shows us the working of cause and effect: law belongs to the realm which chooses ends and determines means. His first emphasis, therefore, is that law is a type of volition; or, to put it in other words, that inherent in law is the notion of purpose. Law exists to bind together the community; it is sovereign, and cannot be violated with impunity. Since by definition law exists to harmonize the purposes of individuals, law itself strives towards justice. The fundamental basis of law and of just law are, therefore, the same. The form of human society is external regulation, as social co-operation cannot be thought of in the absence of control—since law exists to co-ordinate, it can operate only by unifying all possible acts of men. This analysis does not depend on any particular theory of ethics or on postulates drawn from actual legal systems. When Stammler works out his theory he does not examine an actual society but postulates an ideal community in which everyone accepts as his own all those purposes of others which can be objectively justified. These principles of just law are based on the doctrines of respect (one must not treat another arbitrarily) and of participation (all must be allowed to share in the legal community). This picture of society is regarded as a determining form which will condition the rules in any particular group of men.

It is unfair to attempt to describe a great system of learning in a few lines. But despite all the skill and vigour of Stammler's work, it is hard to resist the conclusion of Gény[3] that his conclusions do not really depend on his premises—they are suggested by his particular prejudices and social views. Jurisprudence, in the hands of the formal theorist, is always faced with a dilemma: if it is true to the premises on which it is built, it remains in the pure heaven of logical concepts; if it attempts to descend to earth, then these concepts are explained according to the social picture of the writer. Thus Stammler has not really solved the relationship of just law and law. Does he

---

[1] *Rechtsphilosophie: Die Lehre von dem richtigen Rechte:* The Theory of Justice (trans. Husik).   [2] *Theory of Justice,* xx.

[3] *Science et technique en droit privé positif,* vol. ii, ch. vi. 'Stammler was apparently torn between his desire as a philosopher to establish a universal science of law and his desire as a teacher of civil law to help in the solution of actual cases. The result is an "Idea of Justice" which is a hybrid between a formal proposition and a definite social ideal, kept abstract and rather vague by the desire to remain formal'; W. Friedmann, *Legal Theory* (5th ed.), 185.

mean that just law effectively dominates law in every society? If so, the conclusion is demonstrably false. The abstract formulae produced are very subtle, but after all they are merely affirmed without being proved. The unity of the ideal community is merely a formal one in which there is logically no contradiction between the ends of each legal subject.

Whether we adopt the Kantian theory or not, there are points in Stammler's theory which any discussion of law must note. He rightly emphasizes that the notion of community is inherent in the nature of law: law could exist as a theory if Adam were the sole inhabitant of the globe, but law can exist only in fact if an actual society exists. Secondly, the realm of law and of the natural world are distinct. A natural law cannot be broken since it is merely a description of what invariably happens, whereas law is essentially normative in that it sets up a standard which men ought to follow. But while the dictates of law may be disobeyed, they cannot be disobeyed without risk. It is true that a wrongdoer may escape punishment, but the very notion of law is that it imposes itself on the will of the individual. In this sense law is autonomous and inviolable, for while man may be free to break the law, he is not free to evade its penalties. Thirdly, most systems do assume that law is a complete and exclusive system in itself. This raises the issue of *non liquet*—no judge is free to refuse to decide a case on the ground that legal authority provides no precise answer. The theory of the common law is that implicit in its legal principles is the answer to every conceivable legal problem.[1]

But we do not find that the legal systems of the world follow any *a priori* logic. The striving for justice may be the mark of ideal law, but it is not always the characteristic of actual systems. Stammler correctly emphasizes that inherent in law is the notion of purpose— but this purpose is determined, not by the logical principles of the academic jurist, but by the actual struggles of flesh and blood. The purpose of law is hardly a conditioning form which determines the rules of every community.

Del Vecchio follows the same Kantian method, but his writings are easier to follow.[2] He defines law as the objective co-ordination of possible acts among men, according to an ethical principle which determines them and prevents their interference.

---

[1] *Infra*, § 43.
[2] See the translation by J. Lisle, *The Formal Bases of Law.*

§ 25. DEFINITION OF LAW AS SOCIAL FACT

Duguit makes a determined assault on many of the traditional theories of jurisprudence.[1] He emphatically rejects any *a priori* method and prefers to draw his theories from an investigation of the facts of life itself. He wishes to separate jurisprudence entirely from ethics and metaphysics. Instead of beginning with a concept of the individual man and considering his rights against society, he thinks of man as living in society, bound by his own necessities to share the common life. Hence the foundation of law is not the right of the individual but the essential requirements of community life. Law arises because men live together and can only live together. Law does not depend on the will of the sovereign. Duguit rejects the notion of the personality of the State and says that a realist examination shows merely that certain persons govern and that others obey. But the governing class does not create law, for it arises directly out of the facts. Law does not lay down an absolute but only an hypothetical imperative: it does not say (as does ethics) that 'this end must be pursued because it is good in itself', but rather 'if such an end is not sought, this will cause a social reaction and lack of harmony'. The ruler is bound hand and foot by a law which he cannot change. You do not need to submit to the laws of rugby but, if you want to play, you must; if you break a rule, you may be sent off the field.[2] So it is with social life, with the important difference that, while a person may exist happily without playing rugby, no satisfying existence is possible for man save in the society of his fellows. Man must realize that, if he does not observe the canons of social life, he will suffer from the displeasure of his fellows. Society rests on the need for satisfying common interests (*solidarité par similitude*) and the need for division of work (*solidarité par division du travail*).

The actual rules which any society regards as fundamental will differ according to its state of development. There are, firstly, the economic norms which lay down the conditions under which a man may acquire wealth. Secondly, there are the moral norms. (In this sphere, however, we at once notice a difference from the orthodox approach which sharply separates the field of morality from that of law. To Duguit the only difference between morality and law is the

---

[1] *Archives de philosophie du droit* (1932, 1–2) is devoted to a study of L. Duguits' work; H. J. Laski, *Modern Theories of Law*, 52; C. K. Allen, *Law in the Making* (6th ed.), 574; J. W. Jones, 47 *L.Q.R.* (1931), 62.

[2] M. Réglade, *Archives de phil. du droit* (1932, 1–2), 21–67.

extent of public acceptance. Moral rules accepted by the whole community are rules of law; moral rules accepted only by the intellectual
élite are potential rules of law.) Thirdly, there is the legal norm which
has behind it an organized sanction. If, however, we limit rules of
law to those which are recognized by the government, we are basing
law on the will of the State, and this Duguit does not desire to do.
The State must be limited by law. Hence Duguit considers that a rule
becomes law, even before it is recognized by the State, if it has behind
it the effective support of the community. Legislation does not really
create law, but only defines that which already exists. The prohibition
of homicide was a rule of law before it was recognized by the State; it
was also a legal rule that the State must feed the starving even before
this humanitarian duty was embodied in legislation. Conversely,
a statute does not create law until it wins popular acceptance.

The foundation of law thus depends on the sentiment of solidarity.
But Duguit also recognizes a sentiment of justice which arises merely
out of the facts, and he describes it as a recognition by man, acquired
through a study of his own personality, of the necessity for fairness
and equality in the imposition of the rules on others. Solidarity, therefore, leads us to realize that a certain rule is essential to the life of the
community, justice that the rule should be enforced. Only a little
change of wording is necessary to transform this into the natural law
theory that the basis of law is in the reason and the moral nature of
man. Duguit refuses to admit this, for the sentiments of solidarity and
justice are not universal ideals but mere facts of which the jurist takes
note as he studies social life. Law, therefore, does not depend on the
will of the sovereign or the will of man, but on social realities. If we
postulate a general will as the foundation of law, Duguit thinks it is
too easy to make a transition to the will of the sovereign, and he
desires a law which will bind the ruler as well as the ruled.

But how is the sentiment of a community to be discovered? Duguit
grandiloquently declares that if law is only the will of the majority,
it is not worth the effort of study[1]—but as, save on simple issues,
unanimity is unlikely, what other method is possible if we are to avoid
despotism, benevolent or otherwise? Ultimately Duguit must fall
back on some system of majority rule—morals are translated into
law when they are effectively accepted by the bulk of a community.

The main criticism of Duguit is that, in founding law simply on
the facts, he fails to understand the true nature of ethical forces.

[1] L. Le Fur, *Archives de phil. du droit* (1932, 1–2), 197.

Sir Carleton Allen, after recognizing that Duguit has done good service to jurisprudence by emphasizing that law is essentially the product of social facts, adds: 'But he goes far beyond any sociological theory of law which has yet been advanced when he attempts to evaporate all ethical content out of law. . . . To banish the notion of *right* wholly from law, as M. Duguit seeks to do, is to make it meaningless, and to violate an instinct which is deep-seated in human nature.'[1] Solidarity may be filled with any content we desire, for it is not an end in itself but a mere means to the purposes which man wishes to achieve. Men may join together to collect the scalps of their neighbours or to preserve the peace of the world. A community of masters and slaves may have greater cohesion than a democracy. Again, while law is based on the facts, it is created only when men use their wills to choose between one set of facts and another. Rules are created because men say 'this is better than that', and because they agree to place their wills at the service of the chosen end. No theory is satisfactory which divorces law from the wills of men, the mainspring for the life of society.

In truth, as Duguit matured, he gave increasing emphasis to the sentiment of justice, and some of his own followers expressed regret that in the end he became entangled with that metaphysic which he had sworn to eschew. Although he denies that there are absolute ideals of justice, he really postulates as the basis of his theory the greatest possible co-operation of men for the highest possible ends. So interpreted, his doctrine is an unconscious natural law theory that law is based on the reasonable needs of the community life. But this phrasing uses terms which Duguit would have scorned.

§ 26. CONCLUSION

Lévy-Ullmann aptly says that a definition of law should have two aims: firstly, to make precise the meaning of law, and secondly, to call up in the mind of the reader a true picture of law and its operation.[2]

The existence of law presupposes a community. Implicit in the notion of community is the acceptance of a set of values dealing with the fundamental issues on which the existence of that society

---

[1] *Law in the Making* (6th ed.), 580, (this passage not in 7th ed.).

[2] *La Définition du droit*, 132 et seq. But this may be asking too much. Perhaps the most that can be asked is that the elucidation of the meaning will provide the tests which will enable a 'true picture' to be drawn.

depends.[1] In the absence of such agreement, men cannot act together effectively. When it reaches a certain stage of development the community sets up a legal order which determines the methods by which law is to be created, declared, and enforced. This machinery is naturally used by the most strongly organized section in order to effect their ends. Law is never ideal justice, but human justice defined by those who control the machine. What ends law has served is a question for legal history: what ends it should serve is a question for legal philosophy.

But in order to be really effective law demands, not only an active machinery for securing compliance with its rules, but also a method by which the changing conceptions of justice and the transfer of power from one class to another may be mirrored in the law itself. The sanction is a normal accompaniment of mature law, but it is impossible to lay down *a priori* that no rule of law can exist without a sanction. Certain constitutional conventions are normally regarded as an important part of the legal order although no precise sanction can be found. The sanction which exists is merely a realization that the convention lies at the foundation of the legal order itself.

Moreover, while the sanction may be important in order to explain why a particular rule is observed, it rarely explains the acceptance of the legal order itself. Terrorism, or the domination of a small community by a ruthless neighbour, may succeed for a time, but normally the sanction is effective only if it is necessary to use it in a limited number of cases.

There are thus two sides to law: from one side it is an abstract body of rules, from the other it is a social process for compromising the conflicting interests of men.

Law may shortly be described in terms of a legal order tacitly or formally accepted by a community. It consists of the body of rules which are seen to operate as binding rules in that community, backed by some mechanism accepted by the community by means of which sufficient compliance with the rules may be secured to enable the system or set[2] of rules to continue to be seen as binding in nature. A mature system of law normally sets up that type of legal order known as the State, but we cannot say *a priori* that without the State no law can exist.

---

[1] Compare A. L. Goodhart, *Trans. of Grotius Society* (1936), xxii. 40–1; F. W. Eggleston, *Search for a Social Philosophy*, 114.
[2] H. L. A. Hart, *Concept of Law*, 90–1, 228–31.

REFERENCES

AUSTIN, J., *Jurisprudence*, Lectures. 1, 5.
FULLER, L., *The Law in Quest of Itself.*
GOODHART, A. L., *Trans. of Grotius Society*, xxviii. 65.
HART, H. L. A., *Concept of Law.*
LÉVY-ULLMANN, H., *Éléments d'introduction générale à l'étude des sciences juridiques: la définition du droit.*
Modern Theories of Law (ed. Jennings).
POUND, R., in *Legal Essays in Tribute to McMurray* (ed. Radin and Kidd), 513.
ROBINSON, R., *Definition.*
STARKE, J. G., 17 *Brit. Y. B. of Int. Law,* 66.

BOOK II

THE PURPOSE OF LAW

IV

NATURAL LAW

§ 27. INTRODUCTION

AT first sight the problem of natural law may not seem very closely related to that of the purpose of law. But many theories of natural law attempt to define law in terms of purpose, and hence it is convenient to consider together many of the contributions of philosophy to these two problems.

§ 28. GREECE

The story of natural law begins with the philosophers of ancient Greece and its true meaning is still a matter of controversy today. The most diverse elements are gathered under the same label—Greek philosophy and medieval rationalism, Roman law and Christian theology, actual custom and moral intuition.[1] There is much confusion and crudity of thought, but the theory is concerned with two problems which are as vital now as when they were first formulated— what is the permanent underlying basis of law? what is its relationship to justice? Moreover, even if we think that many of the theories illustrate only 'another chapter in the history of human error', natural law has exercised great influence on legal development and some appreciation of it is necessary for an understanding of legal philosophy. To take only one example, 'no other philosophy moulded and shaped American thinking and American institutions to such an extent as

---

[1] G. D. Gurvitch, L'Expérience juridique (1935), 103, suggests that there are six uses of the term: (a) as a moral justification of all law; (b) as the a priori element of law; (c) as an ideal by which existing positive law can be judged; (d) as referring to immutable and not variable rules; (e) as 'autonomous' law valid because it is based on an ideal; (f) droit spontané as opposed to law fixed in advance by the State. These divisions seem to overlap a great deal.

did the philosophy of natural law in the form given to it in the seventeenth and eighteenth centuries'.[1]

To trace the history of natural law in detail would require a general history of jurisprudence and of political philosophy. For our purposes it is enough to discuss the light which typical theories throw on the problems of jurisprudence. Dominating all the doctrines of natural law is the thought that law is an essential foundation for the life of man in society and that it is based on the needs of man as a reasonable being and not on the arbitrary whim of a ruler.[2] 'The chief value of the older books on natural law for us of the present day does not lie so much in the systems they expound, as in the kind of legal thinking they exemplify.'[3]

The Greeks traditionally regarded law as being closely related both to justice and ethics.[4] Yet in the face of the diversity of the actual systems of the world, wherein was a permanent element to be found? The imaginative notions of Plato are still freely drawn on by modern thinkers,[5] and his *Republic* is a constructive attempt to discover the basis of justice. In the end, however, he rather underplayed the necessity for law in the sense of a body of binding propositions—the execution of justice was to be given to philosopher-kings whose education and wisdom was such that there was no need to shackle them by a higher law. Aristotle formulated more carefully the theory of justice.[6] He regarded justice as meaning either what is lawful, or what is fair and equal. Justice he divided into distributive and remedial justice. The first deals with the distribution of honour and wealth among the citizens and works according to the ratio of merit of the particular society in question.[7] A democracy will take different views from an oligarchy. In remedial justice the law looks to the nature of the injury, and attempts to restore the equality that existed before the wrong. Just action is a mean between acting unjustly and being unjustly treated. This definition, however, applies only to the position of the citizen—not that of the judge, for in making a decision, he is not in danger of being unjustly treated.

---

[1] E. Bodenheimer, *Jurisprudence*, 164.

[2] G. Del Vecchio, *Justice, Droit, État*, 134–5.

[3] Lon. L. Fuller, *The Law in Quest of Itself*, 103.

[4] P. Vinogradoff, *Historical Jurisprudence*, ii. 19.

[5] Indeed, H. Kelsen suggests that whatever has been taught about the essence of justice can be found in the works of Plato and Aristotle: *Interpretations of Modern Legal Philosophies*, 398–9.

[6] W. D. Ross, *Aristotle*, 209.

[7] H. Kelsen, *Interpretations of Modern Legal Philosophies*, 339, shows the weakness of this approach: it results only in the truism of 'to each his own'.

Aristotle also made a useful distinction between natural justice, which is universal, and conventional justice, which binds only because it was decreed by a particular authority. Thus it is a precept of natural justice that I must return what has been lent, but it is conventional justice that lays down whether the period of prescription is six or sixty years. To the Greeks the nature of a thing was discoverable not by studying its primitive form but rather its highest development. Hence to Aristotle the State was natural, since man was a political being who could realize his personality to the full only within such an organization.

The Stoics popularized the maxim, 'Live according to nature'. This did not necessarily mean 'in primitive simplicity'. A thing was in accord with nature when it was governed by its own leading principle, and in the case of man this was reason. The universe itself was governed by a reason similar to that which dwelt in man, and hence he who based his life on a rule of reason could face the world with confidence; for whether he understood or not the turn of fortune's wheel, a universe based on reason could not be hostile to him. The Stoic, perhaps in a superficial way, thus erected a popular theory of the unity of life out of the deeper elements of Greek thought.[1]

§ 29. ROME

The Roman classical writers used the Stoic theory as an ornament for their texts, without really weaving its implications into their theory of the law. As the Roman texts provided the basis for legal study for many centuries, it is not surprising that a theory of 'natural' law became established.

Gaius writes that every system of positive law can be divided into two parts: some rules are changeable because they depend on men's wills, others are universally accepted and immutable since they depend on reason.[2] Thus *ius naturale* was the fundamental basis of every legal system, for, however much conventional law may change, rules based on nature are beyond the power of man. But the Roman terminology became slightly confused. Great respect was paid to the work of the *praetor peregrinus* who had evolved rules to deal with transactions to which, because one of the parties was a foreigner, the rules of the *ius civile* did not apply. Sometimes this body of law was

---

[1] E. R. Bevan, *Stoics and Sceptics*, 47–9.
[2] *Dig.* 1. 1. 9; *Inst.* 1. 2; *Inst.* 1. 3.

given the name of *ius gentium*, which normally had the broader meaning of the actual common practice of mankind. But what was universally adopted by men was presumptively reasonable, and hence it was considered that the rules of *ius gentium* were in accord with natural law, or at least could be so treated until the contrary was proved. Thus, in Roman thought, there was a certain approximation between *ius naturale* (a philosophic theory of the fundamental element in all law) and *ius gentium* which had a twofold use: firstly, the actual common practice of mankind and, secondly, the particular rules which the *praetor peregrinus* had evolved for the use of foreigners.

But what did the Romans mean by nature or reason? Sometimes the jurists tried to draw rules from human nature itself.[1] Thus it was said that a usufructuary did not gain title to the young of a slave held in usufruct, for it was derogatory to human nature to deal with babies by the same rule of law that applied to animals.[2] But there is nothing immutable about this rule—indeed it was the institution of slavery itself that was opposed to the needs of man as a reasonable being. This contradiction always puzzled the jurists. If natural law prescribed that every man should be free, and if natural law was the fixed and immutable base of every system of positive law, how was it that all men recognized the practice of slavery?[3] The concept of man as a reasonable being may certainly provide us with ideal standards of value by which we may test the law in force, but, as civilization progresses, respect for human personality grows and the rules of law correspondingly develop. The search for *rules of law* that are unchangeable and universal is a futile one. As the Roman view got farther away from the deeper elements of Greek philosophy, it became superficial.

§ 30. The Christian Fathers

The Christian Fathers extended the authority of natural law by ascribing to it a divine origin, and even cited St. Paul as approving their doctrine.[4] This made it easier to pour practical doctrines into the mould of natural law, for the truths of revealed religion could

---

[1] N. M. Korkunov, *General Theory of Law*, 123.   [2] *Inst.* 2. 1. 37.

[3] See the confusion in *Inst.* 1. 2. The Romans also attempted to draw universal rules from the nature of the physical world, e.g. they said that by natural law the sea, running water, and the air are common property. But as man's control over nature grows, so do the rules of property. See N. M. Korkunov, op. cit. 123 et seq.

[4] Rom. 2: 14–15.

now be drawn upon. Hence it is not surprising that a theory of natural law should have great practical effect, since the element of reasonableness was interpreted in the light of Roman law (sometimes called *ratio scripta*) and the truths of Christianity. But, having forgotten Aristotle, the early writers treated the State as unnatural. Once, before the advent of sin, men had lived together in peace and happiness, needing not the constraint of government nor an exact division between *meum* and *tuum*. But with the fall of man, God created the State as a means of correcting the new tendencies to evil. Similarly, private property and slavery were instituted by God to correct the new sinful tendencies resulting from the fall of man. This illustrates the great gulf which separates the theory of the Christian Fathers from that of Aristotle who treated the State as a natural result of the social tendencies in man's nature.

§ 31. THE MIDDLE AGES

Why was the theory of natural law so popular in the Middle Ages?[1] There were reasons of conservatism and liberalism, of religion and of practical convenience. Firstly, we must realize that in the Middle Ages men defined law in a manner very different from that of Austin. Many today base law on will—whether it be the will of a sovereign or the general will of a community. Since the fall of Rome Europe was steering uneasily between the two dangers of tyranny and anarchy—Austinian theories might lead to the first, and, in the absence of a cohesive community, the doctrine of the general will may lead to the second. Men sought for a law that was based on something more enduring than the wills of men, that could provide an element of unity in the battle against chaos and an element of protection against the arbitrary will of a sovereign. In the Germanic community, the relationship between monarch and subject was expressed by the idea of mutual fidelity rather than unilateral obedience—the king was also subject to the law.[2]

Natural law satisfied the interests of conservatism, for it had a long and 'respectable' ancestry; it could be made to satisfy the demands of liberalism (or even 'the left') because no one knew exactly what it was and many radical propositions could be drawn from the needs of man

---

[1] A. J. and R. W. Carlyle, *Mediaeval Political Theory in the West*; O. F. von Gierke, *Political Theories of the Middle Ages* (ed. Maitland); W. Ullman, *The Mediaeval Idea of Law as represented by Lucas de Penna*.
[2] F. Kern, *Kingship and Law in the Middle Ages* (trans. S. B. Chrimes), 135.

as a reasonable being. Psychologically the theory was satisfying because the very chaos of the time made universalism precious, even in a theory. Generalizing minds in their search for some principle of unity seized on natural law as the easiest method of approach.[1] The theory satisfied the man of religion (for had not God revealed the truths on which natural law was based?),[2] and 'economy of thought' made it easier to tread the known paths of philosophy than to strike out afresh. Moreover, the infusion into the theory of many of the actual rules of Roman law was now bearing fruit.[3] Thus when the merchant pleaded that the rules of commerce should be based on natural law, he was not, contrary to the custom of his kind, engaging in philosophic mysticism, but arguing that the developed rules of Roman law should be adopted in place of the chaos of customary rules.

In the Middle Ages we find the germ of theories that later became of great practical importance. In searching for a principle by which the power of the State could be justified, writers evolved the theory of the social contract. There were many varieties of this doctrine, but the predominant medieval compromise was that the monarch was above positive law, but was bound by natural law.[4] This entails a complete break with the Roman view that natural law is the immutable and universal part of civil law. To the Middle Ages natural law may be the base on which positive law is built, but a tendency arises to regard natural law as a superior body of principles by the test of which the validity of positive law is to be judged. Thus even in this period we see the germ of the later theory of natural rights.

St. Thomas Aquinas (1225–74) is the most significant figure. He emphasizes that man's intellect and free will are the closest image of God in the material universe.[5] The eternal law governs the world through the will of God and according to His wisdom. For humanity this eternal law becomes the natural moral law, the basic rule being: act in conformity with your moral nature. The Decalogue provides

---

[1] 'The conception of absolute justice is one of the fundamental needs of the human mind': G. Del Vecchio, *Formal Bases of Law* (trans. J. Lisle), 14–15.

[2] Some argued that natural law depended on the will of God and hence that it was valid only because God had decreed it; the realists thought that it depended on God's nature, and therefore could not be changed, for if God changed his nature, would He still be God? O. F. von Gierke, op. cit. 75, 172, 173.

[3] Thus to Lucas de Penna in the fourteenth century, Roman law was the incarnation of reason and of culture; W. Ullman, op. cit. 75.

[4] Thus Azo believed that a rescript of the emperor contrary to natural law was void: A. J. and R. W. Carlyle, op. cit. ii. 32.

[5] M. J. Adler, *Essays in Thomism*, 205.

the contents of the natural law. This does not render the positive law superfluous—it is needed to work out the implications of the guiding natural law. Positive law should not conflict with natural law—if it conflicts, it is not law and does not bind the conscience of the subject. Thus law is reason and not the mere arbitrary whim of the ruler.

Adler points out that St. Thomas's theory has been misread, even by some of his followers, and that modern misunderstandings arise from the assumption that the term law is used in exactly the same sense in the phrases natural law and positive law. St. Thomas did not explicitly state that the word was used in two senses. The elements of truth in Thomism are more clearly seen if we adopt Adler's analysis:

(a) Natural law provides the *principles* which determine the ends of action—the first truths of the practical reason, which are universal;
(b) Secondly, there are the *precepts* which are derived from these principles, and are judgments about *means*;
(c) Thirdly, there are the rules of law which are the application of the precepts to changing circumstances—these rules are essentially variable as conditions change;
(d) Lastly, there are the decisions—the application of the rule to a particular case.

Natural law is not directive in the same sense as positive law: the former provides the ultimate end, the latter directs a certain course of action after considering all the circumstances here and now. Natural law binds the conscience: positive law binds because of a sanction, though if it is just it will also bind the conscience. Positive law is nothing else but an ordinance of reason for the common good, made by him who has the care of the community, and promulgated. Much confusion would have been avoided if the term law had been confined to positive law and another term used for the *ius naturale*, which essentially lays down general principles rather than detailed rules. The *principles of natural justice* is a phrase that expresses better the medieval notion.

§ 32. The Seventeenth Century

Grotius (1583–1645) is the most famous representative of the rationalist school. Natural law is based on the nature of man and his inward need of living in society.[1] To discover what are the rules of natural law we must see what is in accord with the rational and social nature of man and then test our conclusions by seeing whether the rule has been adopted by all nations or at least the most civilized.[2] In Grotius's whimsical language, human nature is the grandmother, natural law the parent, and positive law the child. Human nature makes us desire society and hence creates natural law, which in its turn recognizes contracts as valid and thus sanctifies the social contract which is the basis of the laws that Jack obeys. But he shared the naïve view that the principles of natural law could be deduced with ease—they are as evident as the physical objects we see with our eyes.

Grotius's most significant contribution was in the realm of international law. Appalled by the savagery of the wars of his time, he wished to discover a basis on which to build rules that would restrain the ferocity of states. What more inevitable than that he should turn to natural law? As even a society of robbers could hardly be preserved without the recognition of some mutual rights, surely that society which contains the greater part of the civilized world must recognize that there are inherent in each state rights which can give birth to a system of law. Stripped of some of its crudities, his doctrine is essentially sound—that a community between nations is possible only if certain rules be accepted as the binding basis of a common life. The passing of time has only underlined his argument.

Grotius had emphasized that man had an impelling desire for society and that natural law was an outgrowth of this characteristic. To Hobbes (1588–1679), however, man in a state of nature lived at war with his fellows and his life was solitary, poor, nasty, brutish, and short.[3] Hobbes was trying to build a theory on an anticipation of the findings of realism and empirical psychology. He emphasizes that he derives the rights of sovereign power from the principles of nature and according to the light of experience.[4] He claimed that he based his conclusions on the 'known natural inclinations of mankind'.[5] Distressed by the civil war, he wished to show that the true course lay in

---

[1] De Iure Belli ac Pacis, bk. I, ch. i. 10. 1. It is 'the dictate of right reason indicating that any act from its agreement with the rational and social nature (of man) has in it a moral necessity'.

[2] H. Grotius calls these methods the more subtle a priori and the more popular a posteriori: op. cit., bk. I, ch. i. 12. 1.

[3] A convenient summary of T. Hobbes's views is found in Huntington Cairns, Legal Philosophy from Plato to Hegel, ch. vii; M. Oakeshott, Hobbes's Leviathan.

[4] Leviathan, ch. xxxii.   [5] Op. cit. 466.

admitting the power of the State. Man must for self-preservation escape from the misery of anarchy. The passions that incline men to peace are fear of death: desire of such things as are necessary for commodious living and hope by their industry to obtain them. The 'articles of peace' are what others call the law of nature. 'A law of nature is a general rule, found out by reason, by which a man is forbidden to do that which is destructive of his life, or taketh away the means of preserving the same: and to omit that, by which he thinketh it may be best preserved.'[1] The fundamental law of nature is that every man ought to endeavour to obtain peace, as far as he has hope of obtaining it: and when he cannot obtain it, then he may seek, and use, all help and advantages of war. The second is that, if others are willing to follow the same rule, man should be content with so much liberty against other men as he would allow to others against himself. The third law of nature is that men perform their covenants made.[2] It is a striking commentary on the power of the tradition of natural law that such a realist as Hobbes, who broke with accepted tradition in so many ways, should still cast his theory in the language of natural law.

The only effective way to secure order was to reduce the warring wills of man by the imposition of a super-will which could command obedience. The sovereign was the sole source of law, was above it and alone had the power to change it. The laws of nature are contrary to our natural passions and there must be the 'terror of some power to cause them to be observed'.[3] But the foundation of the Commonwealth Hobbes finds in the agreement of men—this shows the influence of the theory of the social contract even on one who believed in absolutism.

Hobbes emphasized that law derived its authority from politically organized society. He did not ignore ethics for he admitted the ultimate force of ethical rules, but he sharply distinguished its sphere from that of law. Law existed, whether it be just or unjust, because it was laid down by the State. It is clear that Austin built on Hobbes. Hobbes's theory has two sides—as a formal theory of law it is still adopted by many realists. But it could easily be used to provide an ethical defence of absolutism, since Hobbes's analysis of man's nature left no hope for the creation of a general will save when it was

---

[1] Op. cit., ch. xiv.
[2] Hobbes altogether lays down nineteen rules of nature.
[3] Op. cit., ch. xvii.

imposed by force. His social contract is a *pactum subiectionis*, rather than a *pactum unionis*.

Hobbes's aim was to justify absolutism by contrasting it with the ills of the state of nature. Locke's[1] aim was to prove that government must necessarily be limited. Like Grotius, he believed that the moral rules could be easily discovered through reason. 'I doubt not, but from self-evident propositions, by necessary consequences, as un-contestable as those in mathematics, the measures of right and wrong might be made out, to anyone that will apply himself with the same indifferency and attention to the one as he does to the other of these sciences.'[2] Locke's inquiry is defined by him as follows: 'Political Power . . . I take to be a right of making laws with Penalties of Death and consequently all less Penalties, for the regulating and preserving of Property, and of employing the Force of the Community, in the Execution of such Laws and in the Defence of the Commonwealth from foreign Injury *and all this only for the publick Good.*' Pollock points out that the italicized clause gives the keynote to the whole Essay.[3] Locke emphasizes the imperfections of the state of nature: there is a want of established law, of an impartial judge, and of power to enforce rules—but he does not take such a gloomy view as Hobbes of the nature of man. He agrees with Hobbes that the organization of the State is essential, but the great difference lies in the fact that the surrender of liberty to the sovereign is not absolute but conditional— the power of the State 'can never be supposed to extend further than the common good'. His contribution, therefore, is that government is a trust for the benefit of men. The awkward question what was to happen if the ruler committed a breach of trust is skated over rather lightly.

§ 33. NATURAL RIGHTS

Even today, many theories of natural law have a religious base, but in the eighteenth century we notice an increasing secularization of the approach to legal and political questions. This ultimately makes more difficult the solution of the question whence comes the binding force of natural law, for the easy solution that it is based on the will of God does not prove acceptable to all men. But this period was too complacent for carping doubt—this was the 'golden century of human reason, when the miraculous was expected of it. In it was

[1] 1632–1704.   [2] Essay, IV. iii. 18; Huntington Cairns, op. cit. 349.
[3] *Essays in the Law*, 84.

found what the Middle Ages had found in religious faith, and what the nineteenth century was to find in science—a key to unlock all doors, a panacea for all the ills of the world.'[1] Great respect was paid to the achievements of Euclidean geometry. Why could not jurisprudence follow the same method and, after discovering the necessary axioms or self-evident principles, determine all its problems by rigorous deduction? But the actual contribution made was rather disappointing, and the attempt to distinguish between the rules that were fundamental and immutable and those that were merely convenient ended in failure.

In the eighteenth century the theory of natural rights became the spearhead of revolutionary activity. There had long been a tendency to set up natural law as a body of principles superior to positive law, and, if pursued too far, such a tendency may easily lead to anarchy. The doctrine arose that there were certain innate rights, arising from the very nature of man, which were beyond the assaults of positive law—in the famous words of the Virginian Declaration of Rights, 'all men are by nature equally free and independent and have certain inherent natural rights of which when they enter a society, they cannot by any compact deprive or divest their posterity'.[2] On the whole, theories of natural rights tended to be individualistic, to consider man as a unit rather than as a member of society. The Protestant revolt emphasized the liberty of the individual; and, economically, individualism was favoured by the rising middle class. Whatever started the spark that led to the French Revolution, the middle classes finally took control and impressed the vague theories of the philosopher with a bourgeois stamp. The liberty that was protected was that of the middle classes to run their businesses as they willed, that of the peasants to till their land free of the burdensome exactions of privilege.

There had long been a theory that natural law was immutable, and even today most theories of natural rights retain a trace of individualism. But times have changed, and hence the same gospel which was once the cry of the revolutionary is now the cliché of the conservative who wishes to check attempts on the part of governments to remedy inequalities.[3] Ritchie speaks of the grim delight with which

---

[1] J. Dickinson, *Administrative Justice and the Supremacy of Law*, 114.
[2] D. G. Ritchie, *Natural Rights*, 15; J. W. Jones in *Cambridge Legal Essays*, 228. Declarations of rights are not confined to the eighteenth century—the United Nations has produced a *Universal Declaration of Human Rights*.
[3] D. G. Ritchie, op. cit. 14–15.

Tom Paine would have listened to a Tory preaching the rights of man in 1891.[1] The middle classes, having won freedom, did not desire that freedom to be hampered by restraints imposed in the interests of the labouring classes. Thus the doctrine of natural rights has had great influence in America. The early American judges had a strong regard for the liberty of the individual. 'I cannot subscribe to the omnipotence of a state legislature. . . . An Act of the legislature (for I cannot call it a law) contrary to the great first principles of the social compact, cannot be considered a rightful exercise of legislative authority.'[2] The Fourteenth Amendment,[3] whatever may have been its object,[4] has been interpreted to give the courts power to safeguard natural rights and to declare unconstitutional any statute that unreasonably interferes with life, liberty, or property. Grant submits that the modern definition of due process is merely the natural law of Story and Field under a new name, that of reasonableness. Too often the courts tended to adopt fixed views of natural rights based on the doctrine of *laissez-faire* and boldly wrote these doctrines into the constitution itself.[5] Holmes J. has pointed out the dangers of this policy:

A constitution is not intended to embody a particular economic theory, whether of paternalism . . . or of *laissez-faire*. It is made for people of fundamentally differing views and the accident of our finding certain opinions natural and familiar, or novel and even shocking, ought not to conclude our judgment upon the question whether statutes embodying them conflict with the Constitution.[6]

Thus under the guise of the supremacy of law, America has achieved the supremacy of the judges,[7] and some of the political conflicts over Roosevelt's New Deal were transferred to the courts. Friedmann states that natural law thinking has dominated the Supreme Court more than any other law-court in the world.[8] It is true that the courts did not directly rely on a doctrine of natural right, but the inter-

---

[1] Loc. cit.
[2] Per Chase J., *Calder* v. *Bull* (1798), 3 Dallas 386, discussed by J. A. C. Grant, 31 *Col. L. R.* (1931), 56.
[3] Passed in 1868. No state shall 'deprive any person of life, liberty, or property without due process of law, nor deny to any person within its jurisdiction the equal protection of the laws'.
[4] 47 *Yale L. J.* (1938), 371.
[5] Thus in *Lochner* v. *New York* (1904), 198 U.S. 45, the majority decided that it was unconstitutional for the legislature to limit the hours of work in a bakehouse to ten hours a day.   [6] Ibid.
[7] J. A. C. Grant, 31 *Col. L. R.* 56; C. G. Haines, *Revival of Natural Law Concepts*, 176, 188.   [8] *Legal Theory* (5th ed.), 150.

pretation of what was an unreasonable interference with liberty or property was sometimes affected by the older doctrine that certain rights were fundamental or innate.[1]

Later the doctrine of natural law made the Supreme Court the active guardian of civil liberties such as freedom of the person, of thought, and of religious expression.[2] Moreover, the court has taken, since 1937, a more realistic approach towards new legislative experiments and the criticism that was justified earlier in the century is now out of place.[3]

On the other hand, the court has been so active in protecting personal rights that one school of thought attacks the Warren court for interventionism. Learned Hand, J. asks whether we could *a priori* determine that the court is more qualified to intervene on the question of personal rights than it was on the question of property rights.[4] An incisive attack was made on the activity of the court by Professor Bickel[5] as 'over interventionist in purpose, sloppy in reasoning and mistaken in result'. Judge Wright attempts to put the question in its historical perspective and defends the court.[6] All that is relevant for our purpose is to show that whereas in the early part of the century the court was being attacked by the liberals, it is now being attacked by the conservatives. This merely demonstrates the difficulties surrounding the interpretation of broad principles in a constitution.

It remains true that one disadvantage of any theory of higher law is that it is subject to abuse—thus the Nazis employed the higher law theory to undermine the position of certain classes of the community.[7] Is there a theory, however, which cannot be misused?

---

[1] R. H. Jackson, *The Struggle for Judicial Supremacy*, points out that only two acts of Congress were held unconstitutional by the court in the first seventy years of its existence. In the second seventy years, fifty-eight acts were set aside, and between 1890 and 1938 *State* legislation was set aside under the Fourteenth Amendment 228 times: see also C. G. Haines, in *Rec. Lambert*, ii. 286; W. Y. Elliot in the same volume at 324, and C. E. Clark at 311. The rising tide of collectivism led to greatly increased activity on the part of the court.

[2] W. Friedmann, *Legal Theory* (5th ed.), 143; and for accounts of the legal battles during the last decade in the United States of America over fundamental rights enshrined in the Bill of Rights and in the Fourteenth Amendment, see e.g. Learned Hand, *The Bill of Rights* (1958); W. O. Douglas, *The Right of the People* (1958); E. S. Corwin, *The Constitution and What it Means To-day*; J. Williams, *The Supreme Court Speaks* (1956), Part VI.

[3] A. S. Miller, 25 *Mod. L. R.* (1962), 641.

[4] *The Bill of Rights*, 50–1, cited Friedmann, op. cit. 149.

[5] *The Supreme Court and the Idea of Progress* (1970).

[6] 84 *Harv. L. R.* (1971), 769.

[7] Friedmann, *Legal Theory* (4th ed.), 352. This passage is omitted in the 5th ed.

§ 34. Modern Theories

The revolutionary character of natural law for a time led to the disappearance of the doctrine from official teaching. The Reformation had introduced diversities into the unity of European thought and the doctrine of the divine right of kings was unfavourable to any theory of a higher law. Moreover, the central thesis of the historical school was impressive—that it is impossible to determine the content of law *a priori*, for law is relative to time and place and is a peculiar product of each nation's culture. For all time the historical school disposed of the notion that immutable and universal *rules of law* could be discovered, and the recognition of the close relationship between man and the community has rendered less popular the attempt to discover rules drawn from the needs of man considered in isolation. But after the first flush of success had passed, men began to see that the historical school presented only a partial picture. To place the basis of law in an instinctive sense of right seems but to outline, instead of solving, the fundamental problem of the relationship of justice to law.

Hence to deal with the question of the rational and moral bases of law, new theories of *ius naturale* have arisen; but, thanks to the historical school, they are free from the worst vices of their predecessors. Instead of searching for immutable *rules*, the thinker attempts to find ideal standards or principles which will give direction to law, but also be capable of adaptation to different circumstances—hence the phrase, 'natural law with a variable content'. The same *principle* of justice may require one *rule* for London, another for Colombo. Although many theories of natural law were static, there is no inherent necessity why this should be so. Reason does not assume that the world remains the same, and a theory based on reason can easily be made progressive. The opposition between natural law and positive law is frequently solved by regarding the former as the ideal by which law should be tested, the latter as the actual law in force. Kant is the bridge between the earlier theories and those of today.

But there are still many different approaches, and it is perhaps unfortunate that the old terminology of natural law is used, for, at least in the Anglo-Saxon world,[1] there is a certain inbred hostility because of the crudities of the earlier theories—nor has all ambiguity disappeared today. But, whatever the terminology we use, the same

---

[1] Nevertheless, natural law had great influence in the formative period of American law: R. Pound, *The Formative Era of American Law*, ch. i.

problem must be faced. For all Bentham's scorn of natural law, his standard of utility is typical of much natural law writing and the actual term *utilitas* was used in the Middle Ages.[1] For those who wish to go beyond formal theories basing the validity of law on the will of the sovereign, or on an examination of the nature of legal systems investigated objectively whether as systems of rules or as systems of a more complex nature, there may be only three solutions —force, the will of the majority, or the needs of community life.[2] Thus Goodhart defines law as 'those rules of conduct on which the existence of the society is based and the violation of which, in consequence, tends to invalidate the existence of the society'.[3] This (in clearer language) is a solution similar to those of many natural law theorists, for the close relationship between law and the essential foundation of the community life is stressed. Le Fur describes natural law as law discovered by reason working by the light of ethics on the data provided by social facts.[4]

In the twentieth century we see the beginning of a functional and relativist approach. Theories of law become secularized: pragmatism emerges as a legal philosophy and the advance of science turns the minds of men into materialistic channels. New economic conditions and social philosophies made it impossible to apply literally the older doctrines, and until they could be restated in modern terms there was a tendency to reject them *in toto*. Moreover, Freud and the psychoanalysts introduced new theories of the human mind—the doctrine that we 'rationalize' our actions introduced cynicism towards absolute ideals. The first result of the widespread adoption of the functional approach was destructive—many lost their faith in reason and religion as the basis of natural law, but there was nothing constructive to put in its place. A functional theory is rightly interested in how the engine of a car works—but it does not help us in deciding the journey which the car is to take. Hence it was inevitable that there should be ultimately a renaissance of natural law.[5]

Natural law is rejected, for very different reasons, both by Kelsen and Kohler. Kelsen realizes that the fundamental thesis of natural law is that the validity of law is sought elsewhere than in a formal

---

[1] F. Pollock, *Essays in the Law*, 47 (although not precisely in Bentham's sense).
[2] L. Le Fur, in *Droit, Morale, Mœurs*, 55.
[3] *Transactions of the Grotius Society* (1936), xxii. 40.
[4] *Droit, Morale, Mœurs*, 55. The Austrian Code laid down that in default of authority problems should be resolved according to 'les principes juridiques naturels': M. F. Zoll, *Rec. Gény*, ii. 434.
[5] e.g. J. Charmont, *La Renaissance du droit naturel.*

postulate (e.g. the will of the sovereign). The jurist cannot accept two standards of validity, for in case of conflict his pure science would contradict itself. To Kelsen, justice is an irrational ideal, as it cannot be proved by rational cognition. If we are content with the formal approach, such a theory is unanswerable, but, since we can understand the development of law and its relationship to society only by digging deeper into the mind of man, we find the results of Kelsen's theory rather scanty. And when Kelsen treats of the problem of international law there seems to have crept in the 'ghost of natural law', for the primacy of international law is based on the needs of man rather than on any logical theory.[1]

Kohler[2] builds on the work of the historical school and adapts the premises of Hegel, but his modifications are so extensive that cynics say that there is little Hegelianism and less philosophy. Law is essentially a social fact and jurisprudence is a branch of that philosophy which deals with man and his culture—which term he defines as the greatest possible development both of human knowledge and of human control over nature. But culture is relative to time and place, and, as it varies, so must law. Evolution is thus the keynote of his work. 'There is no eternal law. The law that is suitable for one period is not so for another: we can only strive to provide every culture with its corresponding system of law. What is good for one would mean ruin to another.'[3] But Kohler does not regard law as being automatically created. Jurisprudence must be a creative science—the legal order must perpetually be creating new values which are in accord with the advancement of culture, and those who are far-sighted should struggle with the masses whose views are more mundane. He is therefore opposed to the *juristic pessimism* of the historical school.[4] History he treats as the evolution of an Idea which must triumph in the end, although there may be many periods of retrogression.[5] But there are two strands in his thought which are never quite reconciled —sometimes culture seems to mean the actual state of a given civilization, sometimes an ideal force fighting the powers of evil. On one page we read of men imbued with one ideal fighting men who stand

---

[1] H. Lauterpacht, in *Modern Theories of Law*, 130; C. H. Wilson, 1 *Politica* (1934), 54.

[2] *Lehrbuch der Rechtsphilosophie*, translated by A. Albrecht as *Philosophy of Law*.

[3] *Philosophy of Law*, 5.

[4] R. Pound, *Interpretations of Legal History*, 145; J. Kohler, *Philosophy of Law*, 26, 58-9.

[5] There is much that is 'illogical and unrhymed' in human history: after the triumph of reason, we see that of its opposite; there are 'pathological' periods.

for another; on a subsequent page we see culture almost as an entity in itself unfolding from the spirit of reason.[1] Kohler seems to make two points: firstly, reason (or the Idea of culture) lies at the basis of law; secondly, the actual rules must be adapted to the state of development of any particular society. Stripped of its Hegelian trappings, this is only to say that law is based on the needs of community life, on the reasonable demands of man as a civilized being. Thus, although Kohler expresses hostility to the doctrine of natural law, his basic ideas are somewhat akin to some modern forms of that theory: the jurist must draw from the civilization of his time those 'jural postulates' or necessary laws which are essential to achieve the purposes desired.[2]

The neo-Kantian approach is illustrated by Stammler, who seeks for the *a priori* form of law and of justice.[3] Stammler considers that the purpose of law is not to protect the will of one but to unify the purposes of all, to create a society in which each member will have adequate means of self-expression. But if this is the purpose of law, is it not also the purpose of just law, which attempts to effect a reasonable reconciliation of men's purposes? Hence a just law is that which agrees with the purpose of law as such. In seeking to elaborate the form of just law Stammler has no difficulty in showing the confusion and ambiguity of previous theories of natural law. But in order to secure certainty he takes the heroic step of rejecting the view that a basis for law can be discovered by analysing the nature of man—it can be found only by analysing the nature of law. There is no law of nature in the old sense of the word, but there may be formal principles implied in the notion of law which are universally true. Hence the cliché, 'natural law with a variable content', explains Stammler's view so long as we remember that his natural law is a mere logical form. What, however, of legal systems which are unjust? Stammler's reply is that 'individual misuse does not destroy the purpose which essentially lies in the thing itself'. A given body of law may fail to secure harmony, but the fact that Smith is an irrational idiot does not interfere with the accuracy of the statement that rationality is the characteristic of humanity. It is the striving towards just law that is the necessary mark of law—this is much the view of Salmond,[4]

---

[1] Castillejo y Duarte, *Filosofía del Derecho* (1910); appendix to J. Kohler's *Philosophy of Law*, 335. [2] *Infra*, § 36.
[3] *Die Lehre von dem richtigen Rechte: Theory of Justice* (trans. I. Husik); M. Ginsberg in *Modern Theories of Law*, 38; E. Bodenheimer, *Jurisprudence*, 168.
[4] *Supra*, § 23.

although the latter does not cumber his writing with the neo-Kantian technique. In fact Stammler produces only the formal principles of juristic thought. It is impossible to create principles of justice from the rules of logic alone, just as manipulation of the laws of architecture cannot produce a house without humble bricks and mortar.[1] Although it is claimed that the principles of just law are deduced from the premises, this plea would be rejected by many. Indeed, Stammler's method proves nothing concerning the nature of justice, and the only conclusion that we can draw is that even a philosophical technique does not make the writer immune from being influenced by his own prejudices.[2]

Gény seeks the foundation of natural law in the truths of religion.[3] He wishes to discover directive principles which will act as a guide to the judge where there is no authority in point.[4] Can the disturbing element of justice, ethics, social interest (call it what you will) be so reduced to order that it will prevent arbitrary caprice? As a philosophic basis Gény chooses so many elements from different streams of thought that it is difficult to weld his heterogeneous material into a consistent whole.[5] He denies that reason alone can solve the problems of the universe, for he emphasizes the part of intuition in enabling us to grasp reality. Firstly, he makes a confession of faith— the distinction between man and all other created things, the immortality of the soul, the existence of God and the communion between God and man. But he does not attempt to draw detailed rules from these principles. A very useful distinction is made between the *donné* —the substratum of objective truth which the jurist must accept since *ex hypothesi* it is unalterable—and the *construit*, where the activity of the jurist has free play within the limits set by the nature of things. Hence a modern doctrine of natural law can supply merely directive principles, which must be applied by the constructive work of the jurist, who must never forget that legal technique is not an end in

---

[1] F. Gény, *Science et technique*, vol. ii, ch. vi; M. Cohen, *Law and the Social Order*, 173.

[2] H. Goldschmidt, *Archives de phil. du droit* (1937, 1–2), 94.

[3] *Méthode d'interprétation et sources en droit privé positif*, and *Science et technique*; W. Friedmann, *Legal Theory* (1967), 184 et seq.

[4] *Infra*, § 46.

[5] He draws on scholasticism, Bergsoniani ntuition, and even positivism. Thus he has been labelled a neo-scholastic, an idealist, and even a realist because of his penetrating analysis of the judicial method (see Morris Cohen, *Law and the Social Order*, 300). He accepts part of Duguit's doctrine and some of the results of Stammler: he agrees with the neo-Hegelian that there must be a metaphysic at the base of law and with the sociological school that there should be a precise analysis of the milieu in which law operates.

itself but only a means of putting into effect the fundamental truths on which human life is based.

Since Gény expressly founds his doctrine on an intuitive religious faith, clearly it will prove unacceptable to those who reject such religious teaching. Moreover, in dealing with the application of law, Gény has too facile a belief in the possibility of discovering solutions that will be universally favoured. Even if all jurists adopted the New Testament as a basis, there would be many differences of opinions as to the proper application of that ethic to concrete cases. Gény recognizes this difficulty, but fails to solve the problem, and when he talks of socialist doctrines which contradict the tenets of natural law, he is letting dogmatism take the place of thought.[1]

The clearest modern Catholic exposition is that of Heinrich Rommen.[2] Law is not mere will—it is based on reason. But he rejects the excesses of the rationalists. The fundamental principles he finds to be 'What is just is to be done' and 'Give to everyone his due'. These directive principles he fills out with Christian teaching and a consideration of the rational and social nature of man. But he agrees with Gény that the farther we descend from these first principles to particular rules, the more difficult becomes the decision and the greater the controversy. He regards the legal institutions of private property and inheritance as part of the natural law, but decisions as to the exact forms of property and of inheritance are subject to economic conditions. Thus severe restrictions on private property may be necessary in certain conditions—property must be made to fulfil its real function of serving the individual. His doctrine does emphasize the moral supremacy of the natural law: but rejects the anarchial individualism of some earlier theories. Man exists only in society and he owes a duty not to disrupt the social structure. If a law is only unjust, it is the citizen's moral (as well as legal) duty to obey. Only those laws are devoid of obligation which are immoral.

Moreover, Rommen claims that there is no essential divergence between the historical and the natural law schools, if both are properly understood. All law must take account of the peculiarity of individual people and their legal genius, the course of historical development and

---

[1] The point made is not that socialist doctrines are right, but that to dismiss them as dogmatically as Gény does is not the impartial attitude which jurisprudence should adopt. What exactly does Gény mean when he speaks of social utility? See J. Stone, 47 *Harv. L. R.* (1934), 721 at 724; J. R. Commons, *Rec. Gény*, iii. 124. K. N. Llewellyn (in reviewing R. Pound, *Jurisprudence*) asserts that Gény has been misunderstood, that his 'method' is superb though his philosophy is weak.

[2] *The Natural Law* (trans. by T. R. Hanley).

economic evolution. Only the fundamental ends of society can be claimed as universal. On the other hand, politics cannot be divorced from the moral universe—natural law remains the criterion by which the justice of law is to be determined. 'Just as the real and the true are one, so too the true and the just are ultimately one. *Veritas facit legem*. . . . True freedom consists in being bound by justice.'[1]

The modern deification of the State leads naturally to a denial of the existence of natural law, since the State is placed above moral rules which bind the individual alone. Such an approach is not confined to modern Fascist theories, for its roots lie in the Hegelian conception of the State as an end in itself. Modern doctrines have carried to its logical end this older philosophy, and both Fascism and Communism condemned as outmoded and bourgeois any doctrine that natural law should bind or guide the law-maker.

Many democrats also deny the doctrine of a higher law on the ground that the wish of the populace should be supreme. With past examples in mind, natural law is sometimes regarded merely as a device to protect vested interests. But can democracy survive unless certain ultimate values are protected? One difficulty is that the word democracy is used in two senses: firstly, as meaning a system of government which gives full expression to the will of the people (in practice this means obedience to the majority); secondly, as meaning a system of spiritual values which recognizes that the will of the majority must be supreme but also stresses that the majority must respect the intrinsic dignity of human personality. Democracy cannot survive if it merely means the naked power of a chance majority—all action must be guided by the needs of the community as a whole. Whether we can prove the validity or not of ideals based on the unique value of human personality, it is unlikely that democracy will succeed unless they are respected. All attempts to establish absolute values on any other than a religious base have failed—but religion is essentially a matter of faith rather than intellectual proof. The nature of human communities seems to be such, however, that each to survive must recognize some fundamental values and must devise means to protect those values and, in the long run, not only to protect them but to permit them to grow and change.

[1] Op. cit. at 267.

§ 35. THE COMMON LAW APPROACH

Finally, let us consider the attitude of the common law towards these questions of value. We cannot adopt the easy solution of saying that the actual law in force lays down all the standards that are to be applied and hence that such problems need not trouble us. For, while of necessity there are many detailed rules which adopt certain ideals, there are two means by which modern views may influence the law laid down by the past: firstly, where there is no authority, the court's view of what is socially expedient will influence the law; and, secondly, many accepted rules lay down broad standards which are mere moulds that can be filled with changing contents. Thus public policy is 'a principle of judicial legislation or interpretation founded on the current needs of the community'.[1] The standard of reasonableness is elastic enough to be adapted to present views. Yet in applying these principles and standards, the English doctrine is that the judge should apply not his own view, nor even that of philosophy, but the opinion of the average right-thinking member of the community. If the House of Lords interpreted public policy by Marxian standards, there would not only be surprise but a feeling that the proper bounds of the court had been exceeded.[2]

Hence while there has been some repetition of natural law learning in the English books, the English judge prefers to use more humble tests. Bracton, Coke, and Blackstone use the doctrine of natural law as a rhetorical figment, but do not incorporate it into their theories of law.[3] Nevertheless, English law was open to the same ethical influence as were those systems that relied on natural law; but, where the continental lawyer would flourish a philosophy, the English jurist pins his faith to common sense,[4] natural justice,[5] reason,[6]

---

[1] P. H. Winfield, 42 *Harv. L. R.* (1928), 76 at 92.

[2] *Stuart* v. *Bell*, [1891] 2 Q.B. 341 at 350; *In the Estate of Bohrmann*, [1938] 1 All E.R. 271 at 279, per Langton J.; *Fender* v. *St. John-Mildmay*, [1938] A.C. 1 at 38 et seq.

[3] Bracton copies Azo, but his theories of natural law are not incorporated into his theory of law—see *Bracton and Azo*, Selden Society, vol. 8 (1894), 32–9. *Calvin's Case* (1610), 7 Coke 1a at 136 and *Day* v. *Savadge*, Hobart 85 at 87, state that natural law is immutable. See also *Bonham's Case*, 8 Rep. 107a at 114, for a trace of the view that even an act of Parliament cannot overturn natural law (but see T. F. T. Plucknett, *Statutes and their Interpretation in the Fourteenth Century*, 69–71). Blackstone, *Commentaries*, i. 38 et seq., after saying that natural law is supreme, admits that Parliament is omnipotent (i. 91). The most that can be said for any doctrine of fundamental law is that statutes which conflict with fundamental principles are strictly construed.

[4] Cf. du Parcq L.J. in *Smith* v. *Harris*, [1939] 3 All E.R. 960 at 967; *In re Piracy Iure Gentium*, [1934] A.C. 586 at 594. A. H. F. Lefroy has collected many instances of the use of such terms, 22 *L.Q.R.* (1906), 293; *Mogul Steamship Co.* v. *McGregor* (1889), 23 Q.B.D. 598 at 620; *Barker* v. *Herbert*, [1911] 2 K.B. 633 at 644–5.
[*Note 4 cont. and notes 5 and 6 overleaf.*]

convenience,[1] practical considerations,[2] public policy,[3] or humanity.[4] As Scrutton L.J. pithily observed: 'I am sure it is justice. It is probably the law for that reason.'[5] 'There may be no difference in logic, but I think there is a great difference in common sense. The law is the embodiment of common sense; or, at any rate, it should be.'[6] A decision that is hard to justify logically, but is based on pragmatic realism, is that of Stamp, J. in *Woollerton & Wilson Ltd.* v. *Richard Costain Ltd.*[7] The jib of a tower crane occasionally projected over plaintiff's land. It is no defence to trespass that no damage was caused, and hence plaintiff was granted an injunction, but its application was deferred until the expected date of completion of the building. There were no merits in plaintiff's claim, as they could not show damage, and the cost to the defendant in redesigning the method of erection of this building would have been substantial. But the lip-service paid to the doctrines of trespass was tempered by a desire to achieve substantial justice.

The whole conception of equity is, of course, akin to natural law, but the Chancellor postulated, not a philosophy, but rather an Englishman with a conscience slightly more sensitive than the average.[8] Bentham's hedonistic calculus fits in well with the practical

'Ratiocination is good, but common sense is necessary': per Evatt J., *R.* v. *Connare* (1939), 61 C.L.R. 596 at 620.
[5] A. V. Dicey, *Conflict of Laws*, 7th ed., Rule 186, cf. phrase 'natural justice' avoided; *R.* v. *Local Government Board*, [1914] 1 K.B. 160 at 199–200; *Moses* v. *Macferlan* (1760), 2 Burr. 1005 at 1012; *Mitford* v. *Mitford*, [1923] P. 130 at 137; *Valentini* v. *Canali* (1890), 24 Q.B.D. 166; *Dickason* v. *Edwards* (1901), 10 C.L.R. 243 at 255; *Igra* v. *Igra*, [1951] P. 404. For a discussion of the application of the principles of natural justice to a company limited by guarantee, see *Gaiman* v. *National Association for Mental Health*, [1970] 2 All E.R. 362.
[6] The reasonable man of the law of tort, the doctrine that statutes should not, if possible, be so interpreted as to lead to an unreasonable result: the frequent reliance on the 'reason of the thing'. *Rees* v. *Hughes*, [1946] 1 K.B. 517 at 526. St. Germain in *Doctor and Student* points out that the common law tends to rely on reason where the continental lawyer would speak of *ius naturale*. Contrast the pessimism of Neratius that the reasons underlying a legal system should not be inquired into too closely, otherwise much of what is certain would collapse: cited F. Schulz, *Principles of Roman Law*, 98.
[1] *Russell* v. *The Men of Devon* (1788), 2 T.R. 667; *Millar* v. *Taylor* (1769), 4 Burr. 2303 at 2312; *Townley Mill Co.* v. *Oldham Assessment Committee*, [1936] 1 K.B. 585 at 613. But where the rules are settled, the law cannot worry about 'collateral inconvenience': per Lord Sumner, *Rodriguez* v. *Speyer Bros.*, [1919] A.C. 59 at 132.
[2] e.g. fear of a flood of litigation—*Winterbottom* v. *Wright* (1842), 10 M. & W. 109 at 115.   [3] See the cases collected by P. H. Winfield, 42 *Harv. L. R.* (1928), 76.
[4] *Bird* v. *Holbrook* (1828), 4 Bing. 628 at 643.
[5] *Gardiner* v. *Heading*, [1928] 2 K.B. 284 at 290.
[6] Per Lord Denning, *SCM (U.K.) Ltd.* v. *W. J. Whittall & Son Ltd.*, [1970] 3 All E.R. 245 at 250.   [1970] 1 All E.R. 483.
[8] Equity is one of the most ambiguous terms of jurisprudence. See J. Austin, *Jurisprudence*, Lecture 33; C. K. Allen, *Law in the Making*, ch. v.

approach of the common lawyer. He is not interested in ultimate metaphysics but in framing a utilitarian test which could be used to encourage law reform.

The continental equivalent of public policy is the conception of *ordre public*, but it is interesting to contrast the English doctrine of public policy with the theory of natural law, for that throws light on the true nature of each. Compared with continental doctrines, the rule of public policy is practical and conservative, related to concrete cases rather than to abstract theory. It has been developed by dealing with actual abuses as they arose—hence public policy is disabling rather than constructive: it frequently prohibits, but rarely creates. The conception is peculiarly English and smacks of the particular genius of the common law. There are few bold leaps of doctrine, but step by step the territory has been mapped out. The doctrine is not individualistic, for (in theory at least) it considers the interests of the community rather than that of the parties before the court.[1] But in fact there is no investigation to discover wherein the interests of the community lie, the effect of a particular contract being assumed as self-evident,[2] and the application of the doctrine has sometimes been rather naïve.[3] The doctrine of public policy cannot be set in opposition to law (as was *ius naturale*), for it is part and parcel of the common law itself—it is respectable and respected. Nor could it be regarded as a universal or immutable body of rules, for the diversity of the heads of public policy is equalled only by the development of the rules under each head as circumstances changed.[4] Once cornering the market was regarded as 'a most heinous offence'[5]—now (if the operation be successful) it leads to universal admiration.

The common law determination of the ends that the courts should follow has thus been a work of practical adaptation to what are

---

[1] 'The law looks not to the probability of public mischief occurring in the particular instance, but to the general tendency of the disposition': per Lord Truro, *Egerton* v. *Brownlow* (1853), 4 H.L.C. 1 at 196.

[2] If a restraint of trade was reasonable as between parties, it was usually assumed that it was in the public interest. But Lord Hodson in *Esso Petroleum Co. Ltd.* v. *Harper's Garage*, [1967] 2 W.L.R. 871 at 900, regards 'public interest [as] being a surer foundation than the interest of private persons'.

[3] Did anyone ever suppose that the penalizing of illegitimate children would have any real effect on the prospective sinner?

[4] 'That unruly steed (public policy) now must be marked "aged" in the stud-book; but it gallops, nevertheless, with greater bounds than ever it did when the Common Law first ran it as a colt'—R. A. Eastwood and B. A. Wortley, *J. Soc. Public Teachers of Law* (1938), 23 at 30. For modern examples see *Beresford* v. *Royal Insurance Co. Ltd.*, [1938] A.C. 586; *Fender* v. *St. John-Mildmay*, [1938] A.C. 1; *Pigney* v. *Pointers Transport Services Ltd.*, [1957] 2 All E.R. 807.

[5] *R.* v. *Waddington* (1800), 1 East 143 at 155.

conceived to be the needs of the community rather than a philosophic study. It is akin to the spirit of Pound's analogy of social engineering —that the law should satisfy as many wants as possible with the least sacrifice.[1] But there can never be an exact correlation between the rules of law and the views of the average man. There are no precise methods of discovering what the community really thinks,[2] so we must trust the judge to be a typical representative of his day and generation.[3] Concerning many legal problems, we can hardly regard the average man as having any view at all. And occasionally the law has not hesitated to set a standard far higher than that actually observed. This method of the common law works well in times of quiet, but when there is rapid development the need for a deeper analysis is apparent. While jurisprudence may dispense with some of the jargon of the Continent, an appropriate dose of legal philosophy would stimulate the development of the subject. Even if we admit that philosophy has not yet evolved an acceptable scale of values, that its answers to the fundamental problems of jurisprudence are still confused, yet at least a study of philosophy shows us the futility of a dogmatic or unconscious assumption of a view that has already been shown to be false. Duguit is not the only writer who was most metaphysical when he attempted to divorce his writing from philosophy and ethics. Ignorance of the contribution of the philosopher causes us to stumble when we might walk with reflected light—even if the rays are not very powerful, they are preferable to the darkness which else would be our lot.

Whatever be the problems of philosophy, the law must actually translate a set of values into working rules of law. Pound points out, in reply to those who argue that a measure of values cannot be achieved, that the law has been forced to evolve a working test of values without waiting for all theoretical difficulties to be solved.[4] In this evolution the law cannot but be influenced greatly by the philosophy of life which a community holds.

---

[1] *Interpretations of Legal History*, 152. A realistic approach to the problem of trading with the enemy, so far as it related to Hong Kong under enemy domination, was taken by the Judicial Committee in *Hangkam Kwintong Woo* v. *Liu Lan Fong*, [1951] A.C. 707.

[2] J. Dickinson, 29 *Col. L.R.* (1929), 113 at 136: 'In truth it may well be doubted whether there is anything that may be called a customary or social opinion as to the right and wrong of perhaps most of the questions decided under modern conditions by a law court.' Cf. Hallett J. in *Chant* v. *Read*, [1939] 2 K.B. 346 at 357–8.

[3] Cf. P. H. Winfield, 54 *L.Q.R.* (1938), 155 and authorities there cited.

[4] *Contemporary Juristic Theory*, 81–2.

REFERENCES

BODENHEIMER, E., *Jurisprudence*, 103 et seq.
CAHN, E. N., *The Sense of Injustice*.
CARLYLE, R. W. and A. J., *History of Mediaeval Political Theory in the West*.
d'ENTRÈVES, A. P., *Natural Law—An Introduction to Legal Philosophy*.
FRIEDMANN, W., *Legal Theory* (1967), chs. vii–xiv.
GRANT, J. A. C., 31 *Col. L. R.* (1931), 56.
HAINES, C. G., *The Revival of Natural Law Concepts*.
KELSEN, H., *What is Justice?*
LEFROY, A. H. F., 22 *L.Q.R.* (1906), 293.
MAINE, H. S., *Ancient Law*, ch. iii.
MARSHALL, H. H., *Natural Justice* (1959).
POLLOCK, F., *Essays in the Law*, 31–79.
POUND, R., *Harvard Legal Essays* (1934), 357.
RITCHIE, D. G., *Natural Rights*.
ROMMEN, H. A., *The Natural Law* (trans. T. R. Hanley).
ROSS, A., *On Law and Justice*, chs. x, xi, xii.
WINFIELD, P. H., 42 *Harv. L. R.* (1928), 76.

V

LAW AS THE PROTECTION OF INTERESTS

§ 36. The Problems of a Jurisprudence of Interests

A GREAT part of this work concentrates on the analytical approach. For convenience, the law creates certain pigeon-holes (labelled: property, contract, tort, and so on) in which it may file the rather untidy facts of life. In discussing these concepts, the treatment emphasizes the logical theory of law, though an attempt is made to off-set this by considering the function of these concepts in the life of today.

It is possible to classify the law on an entirely different basis, using as a criterion the interests which law is intended to protect. There has been recently much writing on the 'jurisprudence of interests',[1] and this can hardly be ignored in any work which attempts to survey modern thought. Some of the writing is, however, confused because of a failure to state with precision the exact problem which is being discussed. Moreover, there has been too much rhetoric wasted in exaggerated claims of the originality of the 'jurisprudence of interests'. There is a broad gulf between the fanatics who worship legal conceptions for their own sake, and those who believe in a free law where the judge relies merely on his intuitive common sense and is free of all authority. But the great majority of writers and of lawyers fall between these two extremes. For stability there must be certain accepted conceptions and definite rules, and there must also be some flexibility. The real question is one of degree—how far should there be freedom to mould the rules to achieve the interests which society demands? Some modern writing proceeds on the hypothesis that the discovery that law exists to protect individual and social interests was vouchsafed to mankind only in the twentieth century. The barest knowledge of legal history, to say nothing of philosophy, suffices to show the fallacy of this assumption.[2] The real problem was well understood by the creative judges of the past.

[1] See in general J. Stone, *Province and Function of Law*, ch. xx; R. W. M. Dias, 28 *Mod. L. R.* (1965), 397.

[2] A balanced survey will be found in *The Jurisprudence of Interests*, trans. M. Schoch, which contains excerpts from the writings of M. Rümelin, P. Heck, P. Oertmann, H. Stoll, J. Binder, and H. Isay. An excellent review is E. J. Cohn, 13 *Mod. L. R.* (1950), 117, who shows that this school sought to keep legal science free of

Moreover, the modern jurisprudence of interests is merely another side of the theory of natural law—it is the attempt to examine the connection between the law and the needs of man as a reasonable being. Why did the change in terminology take place? Firstly, there were those who thought that natural law was a confused term, as so many theories were placed under its head: secondly, natural law was identified by many with Catholicism and immutable rules, whereas the new schools were often secular and relativist: finally, the jurisprudence of interests arose in opposition to the jurisprudence of conceptions. The latter was alleged to make law rigid and a plaything of logic: the much vaunted jurisprudence of interests was claimed as a functional study which placed law in its proper perspective as a means of protecting the interests of man and society. But it is important to realize that the jurisprudence of interests merely deals with the fundamental problems of natural law under a new set of terms.

In any discussion of interests, the following points should be distinguished:

1. There lie hidden in the phrase, 'the purpose of law', two problems that should be separated—firstly, what are the ends which law has achieved in the past and is achieving in the present—this is a question of fact, however difficult it may be to give a precise answer. Secondly, there is the question of the ends that law should pursue. In treating of legal history we must beware of thinking that law has developed as unconsciously as the flowers on the tree. Ihering has shown that will, conscious effort, and struggle precede the creation of many rules of law.[1] But it is an exaggeration to consider that man always has a logical reason for his action; we all frequently act first and think afterwards, not only when we jump to save our lives from a speeding car, but also when we create social customs. Even where a reasoned policy precedes the formation of a law or an institution, frequently the end achieved is different from that desired.[2] Again, it is superficial to simplify the problem and regard legal history as the evolution of one or even several ideas (such as freedom), for the graph of history does not show us a steady rise but a confused series of curves both up and down. No one social or economic force, no single

ethical valuations and asks how we can have a jurisprudence of interests without a scale of fundamental values.

[1] *Der Zweck im Recht.*
[2] P. de Tourtoulon, *Philosophy in the Development of Law*, 32–3, 39. This is sometimes referred to as the doctrine of the heterogeneity of ends.

logical idea, will explain to us the evolution of law; for law is a resultant of all the forces that go to make up the life of the community. Hence at the most we can expect to lay down mere generalizations, not immutable laws of history. Perhaps with further study it will be possible to show a greater measure of accuracy in the formulation of historical laws of legal development, but that day is as yet far distant. The happiest feature of modern thought is its tolerance and its scepticism; to realize the complexity of the problem is to be nearer a solution than to falsify reality by premature simplification.

Pound has attempted broad generalizations[1]—that in early times the object of law was mainly to keep the peace, and emphasis was laid on the rules whereby each was kept in his ordered place. With the arrival of an era of commercial expansion, the demand was for the greatest possible protection of liberty and self-assertion and for the removal of old restrictions. Finally, instead of emphasizing the freedom of the human will, the law began to interfere in economic matters in order to protect the interests of the weaker elements of society. This view is more accurate than that of some neo-Hegelians who treat legal history as showing the increasing freedom accorded to the human will. The laws of most modern countries today show an increasing tendency to interfere with the will of individuals in order to protect what are deemed to be higher interests—e.g. the right of the labourer to decent conditions of employment. There is, in all countries, an increasing socialization of law—town and country planning shows in a dramatic way the destruction of individual rights in order to achieve an ordered development.

2. What are the interests in a given country which are denied protection and yet are backed by a real demand? This is a more dynamic study, although its ambit is still confined by the political and social opinion of the country in question. It is the attempt to discover what Kohler and Pound have called the 'jural postulates' of our time—those values which civilization demands should be protected by the legal system. Logically, once we speak of civilization we are introducing a moral concept, which must be based, consciously or unconsciously, on a theory of values. Hence, although attempts are made to keep this study of the 'jural postulates' on a factual basis, the attempt is rarely successful, as the writer's picture of the ideal colours his actual reading of the facts. There is a good deal of 'cryptic evaluation' as Stone terms it.[2] Pound writes, and we may well agree with him, that the

---

[1] *Philosophy of Law*, ch. ii; *Harvard Legal Essays*, 357.   [2] Op. cit. 363.

interest in the individual life is the most important of all. This statement, however, really depends on a philosophy and not merely on
the 'facts'. A survey of the actual interests demanded by society
provides no basis for preferring one to another save that provided
by the strength of popular opinion. Only on a basis of absolutes can
we logically determine the priority and the relationship of the various
interests. Law that is in accord with the jural postulates of a particular
country will not necessarily be good law—each community will
obtain the kind of law it deserves.

The Universal Declaration of Human Rights[1] is really an attempt
to lay down the 'jural postulates' which the civilization of our day
demands. The Preamble treats the Declaration 'as a common standard
of achievement for all peoples and all nations' which states are under
a duty to implement. A survey of the rules actually enforced by the
various countries shows that the common denominator is very low:
the Declaration is not a statement of the interests actually protected
by particular nations but of the ideal values which the more sensitive
nations approve. As a programme of political objectives and of legal
reform, the document is valuable, but it cannot be regarded as throw-
ing light on what interests are actually protected.

3. What interests should the ideal legal system protect? This is a
question of values, in which legal philosophy plays its part. It is
essentially the problem of natural law, though other terminology
may be used. But, however much we desire the help of philosophy, it
is difficult to obtain. No agreed scale of values has ever been reached:
indeed, it is only in religion that we can find a basis, and the truths of
religion must be accepted by faith or intuition and not purely as the
result of logical argument.

The various doctrines as to what *should* be the end of law are nearly
as numerous as the writers who touch on the topic. Few writers can
avoid setting up an ideal end for the law. The analytical school unconsciously postulated an ideal of logical harmony; the historical
school assumed that evolution was progress; even such a positivist as
Duguit with his doctrine of social solidarity is really building on an
ideal of co-operation for the highest purposes. It might be thought
that the cynical realists were free of ethical drives, but through a great

---

[1] An accessible source is 27 *Can. B. R.* (1949), 203. J. E. S. Fawcett, *The Application
of the European Convention on Human Rights* (1969), points out that while the Universal Declaration has been a 'forlorn milestone', the European Convention has been
relatively successful, as the draftsmen were realistic rather than ambitious.

deal of their work runs a burning desire for legal reform.[1] The teleological school make an irrefutable point when they argue that it is better to lay bare the presuppositions of our thought, and subject them to analysis, than to be governed by unconscious prejudices. In any developing legal system it is really impossible to consider laws entirely without 'reference to their goodness or badness'. But the actual attempts to postulate an ideal end for law have not been very happy. Once men sought for self-evident principles or axioms from which the rules of law could be deduced, as are the theorems of geometry from Euclid's postulates. But the march of science has rendered us sceptical of self-evident propositions, and the story of natural law shows the danger of hastily drawing the ends of law from a superficial consideration of the demands of reason. The neo-Kantian uses the method of the *a priori*, but finds it difficult to relate his conclusions to the world of fact. Others base their view on religious faith. Neo-Hegelians often assume what they wish to prove. Morris Cohen concludes that, search where we will, we find either that the ideals set down are purely formal categories without any real content or that the writer merely assumes them as self-evident.[2]

Hence relativism has become popular. Jurisprudence should study the ends of law, but treat them frankly as hypotheses instead of accepted truths. Gustav Radbruch's work[3] has not received in England the attention it deserves.[4] He considers that legal philosophy should study legal values, but should not attempt to choose between them. The choice is not a matter of science but of conscience, hence tolerance is essential.[5] The antinomies cannot be resolved save by a practical compromise valid only for that time and place. Justice is one end of law and it has for its object the adjustment of relations between men: law cannot ignore ethics which concentrates on the individual rather than society, and it is not always possible to reconcile justice for society with proper consideration for the individual: law must achieve finality, security, and order. The law of prescription, by barring even just claims after the lapse of a certain

---

[1] M. J. Aronson, 4 *Univ. of Toronto L. J.* (1941), 90 at 105.

[2] *Reason and Nature*, 419. 'No ideal so far suggested is both formally necessary and materially adequate to determine definitely which of our actually conflicting interests should justly prevail.' See also *Le But du droit* (Inst. int. de phil. du droit); R. Pound, *Contemporary Juristic Theory*, ch. iii.

[3] *Lehrbuch der Rechtsphilosophie* (3rd ed., 1932); *Archives de phil. du droit* (1934, 1–2), 105. Cf. B. J. Cardozo, *Paradoxes of Legal Science*, 4: 'Nomos . . . is the child of antinomies and is born of them in travail.'

[4] W. Friedmann, *Legal Theory* (5th ed.), 191. See now *The Legal Philosophies of Lask, Radbruch, and Dabin* (trans. K. Wilk).   [5] Ibid.

time, sacrifices ethics in the interests of order; we frequently see a conflict between the logical structure of the law and the needs of an individual case. To Radbruch one of the gravest errors of philosophy is to ignore this triangular battle between the ends of law. A conservative will tend to emphasize security, while justice is the cry of the radical, and the individual, thinking only of his own case, may advocate an ethical approach.[1] This conflict can be solved only by the sovereign choice of each community, as it makes such practical adjustments as seem proper. Radbruch regards a purely theoretical attempt to solve the antinomy as leading only to false simplification. The law of a country is a tentative compromise between ideals that are logically irreconcilable. Relativism has been attacked as a 'give-it-up' philosophy,[2] but whatever its ultimate value, it is an interesting approach for jurisprudence; for even if the philosopher could prove the validity of a scale of values, that would not of itself influence actual legal systems, save in so far as that scale of values was accepted by the ruling classes in each community. Moreover, many writers miss the distinction between relativism as a method of jurisprudence and as an answer to the ultimate questions of existence.[3]

Some, after struggling through the labyrinth, suggest that jurisprudence has nothing to gain from a philosophic study of the end of law. But, though the problem cannot be regarded as solved, at least philosophy lays bare the issues and saves us from the dogmatism of ignorance.

In attempting to answer even the simplest of the problems relating to the protection of interests, the following difficulties emerge:

(a) Frequently the law (whether statute or precedent) does not specifically deal with the question of the interests which a particular rule is designed to protect and hence it may be a matter of dispute what interest a particular rule of law in fact protects. Hence the same rule may be classified by various writers under different heads. Instead of broad generalizations, we need microscopic analysis and research.

(b) Even where there is a deliberate policy behind the enactment of a statute, sometimes the actual result is the reverse of that intended. This illustrates the importance of studying the actual effects of law, as

---

[1] See W. Sauer, in *Rec. Lambert*, iii. 34; G. Burdeau, *Archives de phil. du droit* (1939, 1–2), 48, 49.

[2] R. Pound, *Contemporary Juristic Theory*, ch. ii. See also P. A. Sorokin, *The Crisis of our Age*, ch. iv.

[3] In his later writing, G. Radbruch emphasizes the need for a theory of minimum absolutes.

F

well as its formulation in the books: some statutes miss their intended effect because a convenient means of evasion is found. A converse to this doctrine is the deliberate manipulation of an old rule, designed to protect one interest, into the means of protecting another recognized at a later date. Partly this is done by the use of fictions—it represents economy of effort to adapt an old rule rather than to create a new one. Thus many personal interests were protected by creating a fictitious tinge of *property* in order that an established doctrine might be used. Moreover, a legal rule may remain unchanged in form, yet its social function may become entirely different.[1]

(c) The real problem is one of compromise. 'Unfortunately, the struggle for the rights of man consists of a struggle between the rights of man.'[2] Law does not create these interests—they exist already and the function of the law is to effect a delicate compromise between them. Hence particular rules frequently do not protect one interest, but rather determine the boundary between two clashing interests. It is easy to lay down a scale of absolutes—freedom of religion, freedom of speech, freedom of association: the real difficulty is that of *technique*, the working out of effective rules which will provide reasonable protection for each without endangering the others. If a particular religious sect attacks the State, or refuses to salute the flag, when does religious freedom cease and the interest of social security begin to operate? Freedom of property is a right to which many subscribe, but if laid down as an absolute right, it may stultify social progress. Hence an abstract bill of rights or table of interests cannot afford much direct help to the judiciary in their work from day to day. A broad objective may be provided but life is too complex to be adequately covered by abstract generalizations.[3]

There is a danger, moreover, in concentrating too much on abstract formulation—the real essential for society is to create a public opinion that will protect rights. It is well known that in England there is no higher law—no constitutional bill of rights—yet the temper of public opinion is such that minorities are well protected. On the other hand most nations would doubtless subscribe, as they did at San Francisco, to the generalities of human rights on paper. Indeed almost every dictatorship has done so. The most absolute of the South American governments

---

[1] K. Renner, *The Institutions of Private Law and their Social Functions.*
[2] F. R. Bienenfeld, *Rediscovery of Justice*, 68.
[3] This is recognized by the Universal Declaration of Human Rights, Art. 29, which emphasizes that everyone has duties to the community and that due recognition of the rights and freedom of others is essential.

have operated under constitutions with bills of right modeled after that of the United States. . . . If such examples appear to Americans to reflect only perverse foreign practices, it is sobering to recall that under our own Bill of Rights we protected slavery for three-quarters of a century and still protect racial segregation . . .[1]

Thus one of Pound's statements is that 'in civilised society men must be able to assume that they may control for beneficial purposes what they have discovered and appropriated to their own use, what they have created by their own labour and what they have acquired in the existing social and economic order'.[2] This is a statement of the interest in security of property, but the formulation shows the inherent difficulty of any generalization. Discovery can hardly give absolute rights, and even appropriation may need to be regulated. Again in modern society it is difficult, save in the simplest cases, to know what is created by a man's own labour, for economic arrangements are so complex.

(d) As Friedmann points out,[3] any such classification of interests is in the nature of a catalogue to which additions and changes have constantly to be made. The view of the function of the State has changed greatly, since Salmond originally described it as the administration of justice and the waging of war. The individualistic theories of natural law have been greatly modified. A survey of interests becomes quickly 'dated'. The postulates which Pound laid down in 1919 have ceased to represent the demands of today and in 1942 Pound modified his earlier formulation.[4] The discussion which follows shows how much development, and change of opinion, has taken place since the end of the war.

Clearly, as not all interests can be satisfied, we must make a choice. Pound suggests that in making this choice we must adopt a solution which will do least injury to the scheme of interests as a whole. This tacitly raises the whole question of values again.[5] It is inconceivable

---

[1] R. N. Baldwin, 243 *Annals of Amer. Academy of Political and Social Science* (1946), 134, but see now *Brown* v. *Board of Education of Topeka*, 347 U.S. 483 (1954), and the useful summary of the position at the end of the 1950s by E. S. Corwin, *The Constitution and What it Means Today*, pp. 268–71. Great changes are taking place, and rapidly. The protection of racial segregation is being diminished as the result of Supreme Court decisions interpreting the 'equal protection' clause of the Constitution of the United States (XIVth Amendment).
[2] *Outlines of Lectures on Jurisprudence* (4th ed.), 108.
[3] *Legal Theory* (5th ed.), 339.
[4] J. Stone, op. cit. 367–8; R. Pound, *Jurisprudence* (1959), vol. iii, pt. 4.
[5] Pound here presents a contradiction—his theory of social interests is relativistic. But he so fears the 'service state' that he attacks 'sceptical realism' or the 'give it up' philosophies. Friedmann, op. cit. 347–8.

that any machinery for sampling popular opinion could afford solutions of difficult cases—moreover, the law refuses to admit that it is a mere reflex of the actual behaviour of the community. The law admits that its standards cannot be too far removed from those of the community, but law attempts to lay down what men ought to do—not what the majority actually do.

To repeat, the jurisprudence of interests raises the same problem as does natural law. Are there any ideal values which can guide the law in its evolution and furnish assistance in the task of choosing the interests which are to be protected and the extent of that protection? This problem can be solved by the community only in the light of the particular philosophy which it adopts. Every jurist or judge has his natural law theory—the only difference is that some deliberately set it out and others hold it unconsciously. All individual life proceeds on a choice of values and so must the community. We cannot wait till philosophy solves its problems—urgent problems demand an immediate answer. The orthodox natural law theory based its absolutes on the revealed truths of religion. If we attempt to secularize jurisprudence, where can we find an agreed basis of values?

If the writer must make his own confession of values, of the interests which law should protect, he would start from the intrinsic worth of the human personality. The various ideologies provide little real assistance. Individualism places the liberty of man at the centre of the theory, but at the cost of ignoring economic realities—moreover, it encourages a ruthlessness towards the weak which may strengthen society by leading to their extinction but which can hardly be tolerated by anyone with a respect for human personality. Various theories of collectivism rightly place in the hands of the community itself the control of the most important economic forces, but this is frequently allied with the practice of treating the common man as a cipher who cannot be trusted to decide anything for himself. The question is one of tentative compromise rather than academic theory. The human mind is illogical. In Australia it has been almost an axiom that tramways, railways, telephones, and electricity supply companies should be under public control, but when nationalization of banking was suggested it assumed the importance of a major political issue.

It may be doubted whether any philosophy will ever solve the problem of the ethical relationship of the individual to the community. If we treat the individual personality as an end in itself, we must also admit that it is only in society that the true development of personality can be achieved. But how far may society go in sacrificing the individual in order to secure what are deemed social ends? How far can the interest of one be sacrificed to the interest of the many? The mysticism of Hegelianism provides too easy a justification of tyranny, for it regards the State as a moral end in itself in which the individual is submerged. As Friedmann writes: '. . . the values of human dignity and the development of the individual personality do not present us with ready-made solutions. . . . Legal philosophy can aid in the choice: it cannot and should not eliminate it.'[1]

Too much of the discussion of these issues has concentrated on the economic aspect of property. Clearly, one landowner cannot be allowed to prevent a plan for the development of a city. Any ultimate philosophy of values must place the property interest in its proper place. Some opportunity to enjoy the worldly things of this earth may be essential to the full development of human personality, but philosophy should adopt a functional theory which judges the institutions of a particular community by the part they play in assisting the common man to achieve fruition. But the spiritual values raise more delicate issues. How far may the community use force against one who conscientiously holds a religious view which that community finds inconvenient or even subversive?

Bentham would have tested every institution by asking whether it led to the greatest happiness of the greatest number. Philosophically it is easy to criticize this theory, with its emphasis on pleasure.[2] From the point of view of the individual, the greatest happiness is often achieved by ignoring 'pleasure' and losing self in the service of a great task. But as a working tool, Bentham's test has still great use if we reword it. Every law should be examined functionally to see if in the main it will assist in the development of the potentiality of the personality of the common man. Society must make its choice on an empirical basis: it cannot foresee the exact results of any reform but the ultimate justification for a particular society or state is in the quality—moral, intellectual, and personal—of the citizens it produces. Quality can be obtained only by some measure of diversity— education which produces 'factory-made minds' leads only to mediocrity.

[1] *Legal Theory* (5th ed.), 364.
[2] A. J. Ayer, *Jeremy Bentham and the Law* (ed. G. W. Keeton and G. Schwarzenberger), 245.

What interests of the common man need protection, if this end is to be achieved?[1]

Public, Social, and Private Interests

Pound[2] classifies interests under three main heads: individual, public, and social.

Individual interests are claims or demands or desires involved immediately in the individual life and asserted in title of that life. Public interests are claims or demands or desires involved in life in a politically organised society and asserted in title of that organisation. They are commonly treated as the claims of a politically organised society thought of as a legal entity. Social interests are claims or demands or desires involved in social life in civilised society and asserted in title of that life. It is not uncommon to treat them as the claims of the whole social group as such.

But Pound immediately points out that one cannot force every demand into one pigeon-hole—the same interest may be regarded from many angles. There is a public interest in preventing disorder, but the protection of the citizen is also an important individual interest. The learned writer emphasizes that when we wish to justify the triumph of one interest over another, there is a temptation to label one interest 'social' and the other 'individual' and then to claim that the interest of society is paramount. Dias considers that there is in the common law 'a detectable priority at least between considerations of public safety, sanctity of the person and property in that order'.[3] In time of war, public safety becomes inevitably a predominant interest.

Society has an interest in the welfare of each individual—if we push this view far enough then most individual interests become social interests. Conversely the individual has an interest in the proper functioning of the society in which he lives. A minimum subsistence level for citizens is an important individual interest, but both Pound and Stone classify it under social interests.

---

[1] See ch. vi of W. Friedmann, *Legal Theory* (1967), where there are discussed the principal antinomies of legal theory.

[2] 'A Survey of Social Interests', 57 *Harv. L. R.* (1943), 1. For a discussion of R. Pound's views see E. W. Patterson in *Interpretation of Modern Legal Philosophies* (ed. P. Sayre), 558.

[3] 28 *Mod. L. R.* (1965) at 406. Salmon L.J. considers that the rules relating to an occupier's liability to trespassers were based on the nineteenth-century view that rights of property, particularly in relation to land, were regarded as more sacrosanct than any other human right. He thought that the old doctrine should be buried: *Herrington* v. *British Railways Board*, [1971] 1 All E.R. 897 at 901.

An interesting discussion appears in the speeches of the House of Lords in *Home Office* v. *Dorset Yacht Co. Ltd.*[1] It is progressive penal policy to allow Borstal trainees as much freedom and responsibility as possible. If, owing to the negligence of the officers in charge, trainees escape from custody on an island and damage a yacht belonging to the plaintiff, can liability be imposed? There is the public interest in following a progressive policy and the private interest of property. The Lords decided the preliminary issue in favour of the private interest, but this did not require the Home Office to change its policy, for liability was to be imposed only if negligence were proved.

Stone rejects the division of public interests on the ground that they are really a particular form of social interests.[2] Indeed, this is partly recognized by Pound in so far as he classes the security of political institutions as a social interest.

The correct view is that logically no exact division can be drawn at all between social and private interests. This becomes clear when any attempt is made to distribute the various interests under these two heads. In fact in many catalogues we see that the same interest is classified twice, though this is partially concealed by the use of different terminology.

There is no point in prolonging a discussion of methods of classification. What is important is the realization that one rule of law may protect many interests and that a single interest may require many rules for its protection. Indeed, on the basis of an interest such as that of free association, it would be possible to give almost a whole course on English law. Association raises the problem of corporate personality and of clubs. Arising out of the latter, we may discuss the trust, co-ownership, agency, contract, tort—all are used in the attempt to protect the rights of the association. It would be possible to teach the law on a basis of interests—to look at it functionally instead of analytically.

The short survey of interests which follows is not meant to be complete but only to indicate the complexity of the rules which may be necessary to protect a particular interest and the antinomies which law must daily face in solving practical problems. A broad sweep provides the background for the analytical survey of the law, but

---

[1] [1970] 2 All E.R. 294. Liability extended only to property which the officer could reasonably foresee would be likely to be damaged—per Lord Diplock at 334.
[2] *Province and Function of Law*, 491.

abstract theories are good servants though bad masters. In *Russell* v. *Russell*,[1] a majority of the House of Lords held that a husband could not give evidence of non-access, as public policy protected the legitimacy of the child. If this rule were confined to cases in which legitimacy was directly in issue, there would be much to be said for it—but the rule was laid down in so wide a fashion that it upset the practice of the Divorce Court, created difficulties in criminal cases, and led to hair-splitting distinctions. The results of the rule have been criticized throughout the Empire[2] and it has been formally abolished in England,[3] New Zealand,[4] and in Australia.[5] So-called protection of social interests may be productive of great individual injustice.

Table of Interests

Social interests

1. The efficient working of the legal order.
2. National security.
3. The economic prosperity of society.
4. The protection of religious, moral, humanitarian, and intellectual values.
5. Health and racial integrity.
6. Environment.
7. Control of growth of population.

Private interests

1. Personal interests.
2. Family interests.
3. Right to economic benefits.
4. Political freedom.

Natural Law and Public Policy as Measures of Interests

The older theories of natural law were the traditional defenders of individualism, e.g. the doctrine of natural rights.[6] But there is no reason why the theory of natural law should be confined in this way. Indeed, the modern theories emphasize that natural law is a yard-stick of the validity of all possible interests. In the same way it is impossible

---

[1] [1924] A.C. 687.
[2] For a Canadian criticism see 23 *Can. B. R.* (1945), 536.
[3] Law Reform (Misc. Prov.) Act, 1949, 12 & 13 Geo. VI, c. 100.
[4] 22 *N.Z.L.J.* (1946), 1; Evidence Amendment Act, 1945, s. 1.
[5] Matrimonial Causes Act, 1959 (Commonwealth), § 98.　　　[6] *Supra*, § 33.

to regard public policy as protecting only one interest, or one type of interest. In some formulations of the doctrine it is emphasized that public policy does not consider the equities as between the individuals before the court, but the general tendency of the particular transaction in question. But it would not be correct to say that public policy ignored individual interests. The doctrine of public policy is rather naïve, however, and it has never been fully worked out so as to be an effective protection of social interests. Where the law comes into contact with economic theories, the result is not altogether happy. No evidence is given of what is in accord with public policy—this is left (in spite of some judicial doubts as to capacity)[1] to be decided by the judge on his knowledge of the world. The result of this is that the development of the doctrine has been rather haphazard as it has depended, firstly, on the accidents of litigation and, secondly, on the views of the judges before whom the problem arose. Especially in relation to economic problems, the law has failed to develop a consistent and realist theory.[2] Moreover, public policy has an essentially negative function—in the main it destroys certain types of agreements and transactions: only rarely can it be used to create a positive protection of interests.[3] Thus if a contract is held to be in restraint of trade, it is invalid; the court cannot cut down the provisions to allow reasonable protection to the purchaser of the goodwill of a business.[4] Natural law may claim to be the measure of all interests: public policy is only one of many doctrines used by the common law for the protection of particular interests.

The doctrine of public policy has suffered surprising changes in popularity and we cannot always connect these with changes in the attitude to individualism. In 1853, at a time when individualism was rampant, it is not surprising to see that the doctrine survived only by a narrow majority,[5] but today when collectivism is in the ascendant there is a tendency to hold that creative power is lost. The reference to the 'unruly horse'[6] is now classical and Winfield introduced a new metaphor by describing public policy as a football, which suffers the

---

[1] e.g. Best C.J., *Richardson* v. *Mellish* (1824), 2 Bing. 229 at 242; *Mogul Steamship Co.* v. *McGregor, Gow & Co.*, [1892] A.C. 25 at 45.

[2] F. Pollock, *Genius of the Common Law*, 94; A. L. Haslam, *Law Relating to Trade Combinations*, 198, 201.

[3] Cf. W. Friedmann, *Legal Theory* (5th ed.), 479.

[4] The Law Reform Committee of New South Wales advocates that a promise in restraint of trade should be unenforceable only to the extent that it is against public policy.

[5] *Egerton* v. *Brownlow* (1853), 4 H.L.C. 1.

[6] Per Burrough J., *Richardson* v. *Mellish* (1824), 2 Bing. 229 at 252.

ill fate of being kicked by everybody, although it is essential to the game.[1]

How far is the doctrine of public policy still creative, so that it can become a guardian of new interests? Maugham J.[2] (as he then was) expressed unwillingness to extend its ambit and Lords Halsbury[3] and Wright[4] doubted the power to create new heads of public policy. Lord Thankerton stated epigrammatically that the court should expound and not expand public policy.[5] Another form of the same problem is the question of the relation of the doctrine of precedent to decisions on public policy. This problem did not become of practical importance till the end of the nineteenth century, when the doctrine of precedent became finally fixed. Lord Wright said that 'public policy like any other branch of the common law is governed by the judicial use of precedents'.[6] On the other hand, Lord Watson considered that decisions on public policy cannot possess the same binding authority as decisions based on purely legal principles.[7] If we adopt this view too literally, public policy could protect only the interests recognized in the past. However, it is clear that the most strongly marked feature of the doctrine is the variability of its application. The attitude to restraint of trade, marriage, and illegitimate children has completely changed within a century, and is reflected in the decisions of the courts. A reconciliation can be sought only by using Lord Haldane's analysis[8] which points out that some doctrines based on public policy have crystallized into detailed rules while others have not, but have remained in the terms of a broad principle.

In truth it is artificial to speak of 'heads' of public policy, as if they were unalterably fixed by statute.[9] A glance at the views of public policy taken by learned writers illustrates that it is impossible to confine the luxuriant growth within the terms of any rigid classification. It is almost academic to ask whether the court can create a new head of public policy, for the statements in the cases are so broad that authority could be found for almost anything legitimately desired.

---

[1] 54 L.Q.R. (1938), 155.   [2] In re Hyde, [1932] 1 Ch. 95 at 99.
[3] Janson v. Driefontein Consolidated Mines Ltd., [1902] A.C. 484 at 491.
[4] Fender v. St. John-Mildmay, [1938] A.C. 1 at 40, and see per Lord Goddard C.J. in R. v. Newland, '. . . no additions are now to be made' [1954] 1 Q.B. 158 at 165.
[5] Fender's case (supra) at 23.   [6] Same case at 39.
[7] Nordenfelt v. Maxim-Nordenfelt, [1894] A.C. 535 at 553.
[8] Rodriguez v. Speyer Bros., [1919] A.C. 59 at 81.
[9] See per Windeyer J., Brooks v. Burns Philp Trustee Co. Ltd., [1969] A.L.R. 321; C. K. Allen, Law in the Making (7th ed.), 303 n. 2.

Between the creation of a new 'head' and the application of an old rule to new circumstances, it is impossible to draw any definite line. The case of *Neville* v. *Dominion of Canada News Co.*[1] at least shows flexibility. There was no previous authority which laid down that it was against public policy for a newspaper to accept money in return for a promise that it would not comment on the transactions of a particular person. As Stone points out, this question really raises that of the creative power of the judicial process in general,[2] and it is too dogmatic to assert that public policy can never be developed to protect new interests. One book asks whether the courts are too tied to the outlook of the eighteenth century: has the judiciary failed to adjust to the needs of the modern state and the modern economy?[3] Is it the task of the judges to achieve this, or of the legislature, or of both?

§ 37. SOCIAL INTERESTS

1. *The efficient working of the legal order*

This social interest lies at the basis of all others, in the sense that if order be lacking, then other interests cannot be realized. The repression of violence and self-help is an obvious necessity. The picture of international law shows the dangers of a party being a judge in his own cause and then taking action to secure rights by force. Whatever the philosophy of a particular community, this is an interest that must be achieved.

What is required under this head is a legal order which distributes power in such a way that the machinery can operate effectively and at the same time win the active support of public opinion. It is a waste of social effort to have a government the real foundation of which is brute force rather than consent. Here constitutional and administrative law play their part in distributing power and the rules of criminal law preserve order and respect for certain values.

The dilemma which every society must face is that between the creation of an omnipotent Parliament, which has effective powers of action in times of crisis but which may sweep away fundamental liberties overnight, and the establishment of a higher law beyond the reach of Parliament—a proceeding which may prevent real progress

---

[1] [1915] 3 K.B. 556.   [2] *The Province and Function of Law*, 500–1.
[3] B. Abel-Smith and R. Stevens, *Lawyers and the Courts* (1967).

or effective action in times of emergency. Those who live in a federation realize the difficulties created by a division of powers and by a constitution which, although capable of amendment in theory, is almost incapable of amendment in fact. The conflict between the two theories of law as power and as a means of curbing power is ever present. The solution of the problem cannot be found in abstract theory. Constitutions are created to suit the particular conditions of a country and cannot easily be transported to an alien environment. Indeed, the success of democracy depends on the intangible factors rather than on the theoretical rules. This is shown by the difficulties that have arisen in transplanting the English system of responsible government to other countries. The secret of the English success lies not in the method, but rather in the temper of public opinion. A working democracy cannot depend merely on the theory of majority rule, for a bare majority may be tyrannical and contemptuous of the rights of a minority. Democracy in the philosophic sense includes qualities of spiritual value, tolerance, and respect for human dignity.[1]

The existence of an efficient system for the administration of justice, impartial judges, and an effective system of enforcement—these are qualities the importance of which is clear. But it was too often forgotten that no legal order can function satisfactorily unless access to the courts is kept open for all citizens. The common law protected this access by a doctrine which, on grounds of public policy, invalidated agreements to oust the jurisdiction of the courts.[2]

'There must be no Alsatia in England where the King's writ does not run.'[3] Sometimes this doctrine may be used to defeat the policy which it was intended to protect. Public policy requires that a wife should not contract away her right to go to the courts for maintenance. In *Brooks* v. *Burns Philp Trustee Co. Ltd.*,[4] a wife, before the divorce was granted, accepted a sum in full settlement of all her claims. The divorce was granted and the husband paid the agreed amount until his death. The court held that the agreement was unenforceable against the executors. Thus the wife lost her right, by the application of a doctrine of public policy invented to protect her interest.

---

[1] See the discussion by K. N. Llewellyn, *Jurisprudence* (1962), ch. xii.

[2] *Scott* v. *Avery* (1856), 5 H.L. C. 811; *Lee* v. *Showmen's Guild of Great Britain*, [1952] 2 Q.B. 329. *Re Davstone Estates Ltd.*, [1969] 2 All E.R. 849. But it is not against public policy to agree to oust the jurisdiction of foreign courts, it seems: *Addison* v. *Brown*, [1954] 2 All E.R. 213.

[3] Per Scrutton L.J., *Czarnikow* v. *Roth, Schmidt & Co.*, [1922] 2 K.B. 478 at 488.

[4] [1969] A.L.R. 321.

Perhaps one of the most significant cases on 'ousting the courts' is *Anisminic Ltd.* v. *Foreign Compensation Commission*.[1] An Act of Parliament expressly declared that a determination of the Commission should not be called in question in any court of law. This seemed a clear provision, but the House of Lords held that the particular decision was a nullity, as it was made without jurisdiction.

The great difficulty in modern times is the cost of litigation. Schemes of legal aid exist in many countries, but in most cases the 'means test' provided is too harsh. The Poor Prisoners Defence Act, 1930, provided a good basis so far as the criminal law is concerned, and in civil cases the Report of the Rushcliffe Committee[2] led to the introduction of legislation in 1949[3] which greatly increased the scope of legal aid. But there are still many criticisms of its functioning, e.g. by the Law Society and the Citizens' Advice Bureaux; the extent of the real need is now being investigated at the London School of Economics.[4] There is today much more interest in these problems and also in the perennial problem of legal costs.[5] Even a perfect legal system cannot serve society if costs are beyond the reach of the average man.[6]

It is significant that two thousand administrative tribunals have been established in England which between them hear more cases than the High Court and the County Court combined. These tribunals provide a cheaper and more flexible procedure, but that, of course, was not the only reason for their establishment.[7] It would have been impracticable for the courts to deal with the mass of litigation engendered by modern developments.

Another suggested reform is nationalization of the legal profession. Many argue that if nationalization of medicine is essential for the provision of a proper health service to the community, nationalization of the legal profession is necessary for the provision of an adequate

---

[1] [1969] 2 W.L.R. 163. See the discussion by H. W. R. Wade, 85 *L.Q.R.* (1969), 198.
[2] Cmd. 6641, 1945; E. J. Cohn, 9 *Mod. L. R.* (1946), 58.
[3] Legal Aid and Advice Act, 1949, 12 & 13 Geo. VI, c. 51; Viscount Jowitt, 24 *N. Y. Univ. L.Q.R.* (1949), 757.
[4] M. Zander, *Lawyers and the Public Interest*, 244. See also Legal Aid Acts, 1960 and 1964.
[5] The sub-title to the book mentioned in the previous note is 'A Study in Restrictive Practices'.
[6] There has been much discussion whether in order to save costs the legal profession should be 'fused': see Zander, op. cit.; Lord Gardiner, in *Current Legal Problems, 1970*, 1. In Victoria (Australia) the profession was amalgamated by statute in 1890: but in fact there is a separate bar.
[7] B. Abel-Smith and R. Stevens, *Lawyers and the Courts*, 135–64, 315–48; Lord Wilberforce, 10 *J. Soc. Public Teachers of Law* (1969) at 256.

service of legal aid.[1] One obvious difficulty is that part of the work of the legal profession is to protect the citizen against the government, and security is diminished if the weapon of protection is entirely under state control. Another difficulty is that much of the expense in some lawsuits is the preliminary investigation and collection of evidence. Is a foreign corporation to be a *person* entitled to legal aid? In Russia the legal profession is organized through a *collegium*—a body which receives the fees of advocates and allocates to each a monthly salary. It is difficult to find expert evidence as to how the system works. The advocate is under a duty to defend any criminal case without fee when appointed by the court or by the executive of the college of advocates, and he must participate in the work of free legal aid.

The courts can function effectively only if they are protected by adequate rules. The judge should be immune from removal, save for misconduct. Judge, counsel, and witnesses must have absolute privilege so far as the law of defamation is concerned. Civil actions should not be available against witnesses, if the claim arises out of their evidence given in court, but an action may lie for abuse of the process of the court.[2]

The court must control effective process, e.g. power to summon a defendant, power to call witnesses, power to order execution when a judgment is not met. The power to commit for contempt (e.g. for disorder in court) is not meant to protect the dignity of the judge, but the inalienable right of the public that the courts should be left free to administer justice without obstruction or interference.[3]

It is these powers which distinguish common law courts from the International Court of Justice—the first have, and the second has not, effective power to enforce decisions, and to summon a recalcitrant party before the court. England has no constitutional bill of rights, but the temper of public opinion, and the creation of effective remedies against state departments if they act illegally, give a protection to the rights of the individual which is greater than that allowed by some countries which glory in their constitutional

---

[1] See e.g. B. Abel-Smith and R. Stevens, *Lawyers and the Courts*, 463. It is obvious that the effectiveness of a legal system must depend on the integrity and competence of the legal profession, and there must be adequate machinery for the investigation of complaints—see the *Justice Report on Complaints against Lawyers* (1970).

[2] *Roy* v. *Prior*, [1970] 2 All E.R. 729. 'Immunities conferred by the law in respect of legal proceedings need always to be checked against a broad view of the public interest': per Lord Wilberforce at 736.

[3] Per Salmon L.J., *Morris* v. *The Crown Office*, [1970] 1 All E.R. 1079 at 1086.

guarantees. A theory of individual rights is one thing, effective procedures for their protection are another. Thus the technical point whether discovery can be allowed against the Crown may in practice be decisive so far as the plaintiff's proof is concerned. The House of Lords in 1968 modified the rules to the advantage of the subject.[1]

2. National security

This interest concerns the relationship of a state with other states. All ideologies recognize the right of the State to protect itself, though theories may differ as to how that protection can best be achieved. Firstly, there is the predominant interest in maintaining peace, so far as is compatible with national honour and self-preservation. This is largely a political question, but there are rules of law directed to this end. The criminal law punishes certain acts which are likely to lead to ill-feeling between states, e.g. violation of the privileges of an ambassador; interferences in hostilities against a friendly power; a libel on a foreign power. Lord Mansfield once roundly said that 'no country ever takes notice of the revenue laws of another'[2] but in modern times an English agreement to smuggle whisky into the United States was held illegal as a matter of public policy based on international comity—otherwise a friendly government would have had just cause for complaint.[3] *A fortiori* any agreement which contemplates hostilities against a friendly power is unlawful.[4]

While it is not quite true to say that international law is part of the law of England, there is, nevertheless, a presumption that statutes should be interpreted, as far as possible, so as not to conflict with the rules of international law.[5]

Secondly, there is the interest in defence. The criminal law strikes at those who incite to public mutiny, disclose official secrets, or trade with the enemy. Modern 'total warfare' shows that there are practically no limits to the detailed regulation necessary to fit a community either for defence or offence. The availability of aeroplanes and missiles equipped with nuclear weapons means that hostilities cannot be confined to any 'front line' and almost every activity of the

---

[1] *Conway* v. *Rimmer*, [1968] A.C. 910.
[2] *Holman* v. *Johnson* (1775), 1 Cowp. 341 at 343.
[3] *Foster* v. *Driscoll*, [1929] 1 K.B. 470 at 510, followed by House of Lords in *Regazzoni* v. *K. C. Sethia (1944) Ltd.*, [1957] 3 All E.R. 286.
[4] *De Wütz* v. *Hendricks* (1824), 2 Bing. 314.
[5] *Zachariassen* v. *The Commonwealth* (1917), 24 C.L.R. 166.

population must be subordinated to the imperative need of self-preservation. National defence is, therefore, an interest which, of necessity, must in time of war be placed above many interests which are highly valued in time of peace. The conflict of ends is here obvious. In time of war the community must often forgo what in happier times would be regarded as its *raison d'être*.[1]

In time of peace the loyalty test for government service raises the same issues. It is one thing to dismiss those in the pay of a foreign power: it is another to act on rumour and unsifted evidence without any right of reply. The balancing of personal freedom and national security still remains an unsolved issue.[2] That the issue is not a minor one is illustrated by the fact that screening programmes apply to 13 million persons in the United States.[3] It is impossible to determine what dangers these programmes have averted, but it is beyond doubt that they have created 'an atmosphere of fear and insecurity, both in the public service and in other sectors of society, gravely disturbing men's confidence in the fairness of government and in the sense of justice of law'.[4] The question is not an easy one. In determining whether a man is a security risk, we are not asking whether he has committed a criminal act, but rather whether he is a *potential* criminal.

Conscription for military service, especially in time of peace, is an issue that has raised much controversy. In the U.S.A. and Australia the sending of conscripts to Vietnam has caused violent demonstrations.

3. *The economic prosperity of society*

The social interest (as does the individual) demands a society that is economically prosperous. This requires some security with regard to property, acquisitions, and transactions.[5] In other words the law of property and contract must function satisfactorily or else the real basis of economic life is absent. This does not necessarily mean that there must be capitalism and private property, but only that the legal order must provide a basis on which man can plan with relative security.

---

[1] *Liversidge* v. *Anderson,* [1942] A.C. 206; *Communist Party Case* (1951), 83 C.L.R. 1.

[2] E. V. Rostow, *The Sovereign Prerogative: The Supreme Court and the Quest for Law,* ch. viii.

[3] Rostow, op. cit. 273.   [4] Op. cit. 274.

[5] J. Stone, op. cit. 561. And note the realistic approach of the Privy Council in *Hangkam Kwingtong Woo* v. *Liu Lan Fong,* [1951] A.C. 707.

The theory of economic determinism suggests that legal theories are merely a reflection of the economic base on which the life of the community is built. This is an exaggerated view, but rejection of early crudities should not blind us to the great influence of these economic forces, and in a section concerned with the human interests protected by law, the economic philosophy held by a particular community is all-important. Russia protects interests very different from those of the capitalist world, and even if we take the history of England, there is a broad gulf between the *laissez-faire* of last century and the increasing national planning of today. The slave-owner, the landholder, the great industrialist, and now, finally, the working man, have each in turn sought to control the means by which law is created, and we can understand the reason for the laws of any particular epoch only by discovering what the controlling class thought all-important. The conflict today is between those who value the protection of property and individual freedom and those who would sacrifice both to the extent made necessary by the demand of the economically weaker classes for an assured protection in the present chaotic economic state of the world.

But it is not only in the creation of statute law that the philosophy of a community declares itself. In filling the gaps left by precedent, the judge will draw on those views which he considers are vital to the welfare of the community. English public policy shows a surprising swing from the individualism of last century. The courts in the past sometimes eviscerated statutes introducing new social experiments by arguing that it was a presumption of interpretation that the statute was not to be taken as interfering with vested rights of property save by clear words to that effect. But Parliament has so often interfered with vested rights that this presumption is losing much of its force. No one today could accuse the English courts of misunderstanding the great social experiments now being carried out. There is a real willingness to interpret the statute in the light of its social purpose.[1]

One task of the State is the development and conservation of natural resources. This is seen most clearly in an older civilization when the stress of war requires effective planning, determination of priorities, and economical uses of the resources that exist, and in new countries where either the task of development is beyond the

---

[1] D. Lloyd, *Current Legal Problems* (1948), 89, 101. It was not always so: cf. W. I. Jennings, 1 *Mod. L. R.* (1937), 111.

means of individuals or the State wishes to keep the necessary capital investments under public control. Typical problems in an agricultural country are the control of stock diseases, the eradication of pests and noxious weeds, the provision of irrigation, the reticulation of electrical power to the farms, and the prevention of erosion. To achieve these ends, great interference with the liberty of the individual landowner is necessary. Private property is no longer regarded as sacrosanct and the demands of town and country planning provide other illustrations of the disappearance of the right of the owner to do as he will with his own. 'It might even be said that it is almost a punishment to be a landowner. The pendulum has possibly swung too far in the interests of the community.'[1] Thus wrote one critic of the Town and Country Planning Act, 1947, although the writer admitted that some degree of planning is essential, in a country as congested as England,[2] for the proper development of economic resources.

The British people, almost without knowing it, are embarking upon one of the greatest experiments in the social control of their environment ever attempted by a free society. In the process they are putting old individual liberties in trust for the common good. The citizen surrenders his freedom to obstruct other people in the hope of gaining greater freedom from obstruction by other people, and he will judge the outcome by the degree to which his freedom in worthwhile matters is in fact enlarged.[3]

It is sometimes suggested that the function of a lawyer, in a settled and economically developed country, is the defence of the existing order. This has never been quite true. But in a developing country, with a newly achieved statehood and a developing economy, the lawyer must become 'an active and responsible participant in the shaping and formulation of development plans'.[4]

The economic prosperity of society is often deemed to demand the control of certain utilities by the State. There are various reasons for this: (a) some services can be more adequately carried on if there is a monopoly (e.g. the telephone), and such a monopoly should be sub-

---

[1] R. C. FitzGerald, 11 *Mod. L. R.* (1948), 411–12.

[2] There were at the time 766 persons to the square mile, whereas Germany and Italy had less than half that number, France a quarter, the United States had only 43, and Australia 2·43.

[3] *The Times*, 1 July 1948, leading article, cited with approval by R. C. FitzGerald, 11 *Mod. L. R.* (1948) at 428. But the great experiment was not easy to carry through successfully. The pendulum did swing back a little. All the aims of the Town and Country Planning Act, 1947, could not be achieved. See in general D. Heap, *An Outline of Planning Law* (1960).   [4] Friedmann, *Legal Theory* (5th ed.), 430.

ject to public control; (b) in some cases the development of the State
may demand the extension of a railway or the installation of hydro-
electric plants which, though essential for national development, will
not produce an economic return for a considerable time—hence it
is the State rather than the private investor which should be called on
to meet the cost; (c) in other cases national security may demand the
development of a particular industry which will be economically
wasteful in peace-time, but essential in time of war.

The public corporation has now become a common feature of
modern political life—it provides an interesting compromise between
the need for independence from political pressure in the conduct of
a utility and the need for ultimate control in the interest of the
community.[1]

The legal control of public companies is of growing importance.
The nature of the responsibility of directors and auditors has caused
dispute. The director is bound to act honestly and with reasonable
diligence, taking into account his own knowledge and experience.
There is a strict duty of loyalty and good faith, but rather lighter
obligations concerning skill.[2] Directors may properly leave certain
matters to another official or director.[3] There are strict duties concerning the prospectus, and a conviction may be recorded if the effect
of the prospectus is substantially misleading, even though each
sentence may be technically justifiable. What is left out may be as
important as what is placed in.[4]

The responsibility of the director is primarily to the company, not
to the employees or the public at large.[5] It has been argued that, at
least in the case of the large corporation, it should be recognized
that there is a duty to employees and the public in general.[6] The
general manager of B.H.P. Ltd. stated at a meeting of shareholders,
in answer to a question, that the company was responsible to four
sections of the community—shareholders, employees, customers,
and the public in general. This is a laudable approach, but is not yet
established in law.

In fact, the law has not yet caught up with the managerial

---

[1] Many features of the public corporation were first made clear by Australian
experience in the running of state railways and electricity commissions. In a young
country, such undertakings are frequently 'nationalized' from their inception: W.
Friedmann, 10 *Mod. L. R.* (1947), 233.

[2] Gower, *Modern Company Law*, 515; M. J. Trebilcock, 32 *Mod. L. R.* (1969), 499.

[3] *Huckerby* v. *Elliott*, [1970] 1 All E.R. 189.   [4] *R.* v. *Kylsant*, [1932] 1 K.B. 442.

[5] *Parke* v. *Daily News Ltd.*, [1962] 2 All E.R. 929.

[6] B. L. Murray, 7 *Univ. of Western Australia L. R.* (1966), 311.

revolution. The classical theory is that the board and the shareholders determine policy, and the executives administer within those guidelines. But the complexity of modern industry and the size of modern companies make it nearly impossible for the 'outside' director to understand all the issues involved.[1]

An illuminating series of reports was produced in Victoria into the affairs of Reid Murray Holdings Ltd. and its subsidiary companies, and this discusses the duties of directors and of auditors.[2] Directors are bound not only to be reasonably diligent, but also to consider the interests of the company on the board of which they are sitting at the moment, and not the interests of a group of companies as a whole. To lend money without security is not justifiable, merely because it will assist a subsidiary. Each company may have different shareholders and one must consider their interests.

With regard to auditors, B. J. Shaw reported that the 1961 accounts of Reid Murray Holdings Ltd. 'combined what was plain dishonesty with misleading exploitations of recognized accounting practices'. 'We have been greatly disturbed to find that thousands of people invested in the group in reliance, not upon their own judgment, but upon the advice of men who held themselves out in the community as skilled to give such advice.'[2] The accounting practices used were criticized as not giving a realistic picture of the situation.[3] A balance-sheet may be literally accurate, compiled according to accepted accounting practices, and yet be most misleading—because of what is not stated rather than what is.[4]

It is difficult to police all these matters. The appointment of company inspectors, after a company has been 'declared' under the Companies Act, comes after the event: and the declaration itself is not a step to be taken lightly, for inevitably it destroys the credit of the company. Moreover, the criminal sanctions of the Companies Acts, while producing valuable deterrents, often do not become really effective because a very expensive investigation may be necessary to satisfy the onus of proof.

The protection of investors and creditors is, therefore, a problem which has not yet been solved. Effective company legislation goes part—but only part—of the way.[5]

[1] F. J. Willett, 5 *Melb. Univ. L. R.* (1967), 481.

[2] Victoria: Parliamentary Papers 10856/68, 1468/65, 7859/66.

[3] B. L. Murray and B. J. Shaw, Victoria: Parliamentary Papers 10856/64, p. 107. Cf. R. Baxt, 33 *Mod. L. R.* (1970), 413.   [4] *R.* v. *Kylsant*, [1932] 1 K.B. 442.

[5] Companies Acts usually employ the 'philosophy of publicity' (requiring companies

The law relating to restrictive trade practices is an interesting example of the limits of effective legal regulation. The common law had reached the doctrine that no action lay for civil conspiracy, if (a) there was no specific unlawful act and (b) the combination was for the purpose of pursuing what the law regarded as a legitimate objective. The common law had, therefore, reached a dead end, for the 'stop-list', 'price fixing', and other means of industrial coercion were lawful, within the limits set by the previous sentence. Forcing an employer to dismiss a non-unionist was also legitimate, provided no breach of contract was induced.[1]

In the United States the Sherman Act in 1890 attempted to deal with combinations in restraint of trade, and this was followed by the Clayton Act of 1914. Opinions differ as to the effect of these statutes, but they certainly did not achieve all that their framers desired.

In England, the Restrictive Trade Practices Act, 1956,[2] started a new jurisdiction. The Act laid down the general principle that restrictive agreements are against the public interest, although they may be justified if it can be shown that the agreement serves the public interest or that its advantages outweigh the disadvantages. The court set up under the statute consisted of laymen as well as lawyers. It is not our purpose to canvass the detailed complexities of the legislation, but merely to examine the broad issues involved.

The court must not only study the present situation of the particular industry, but also forecast what the actual result of the restrictive agreement is likely to be in the future. It is absurd to say that because questions of policy are involved the issues are not justiciable—clearly the doctrine of public policy, as its name implies, has forced the common law courts to venture into these realms.[3] The real test is whether the legislature has been sufficiently precise in laying down the general principles which the court must apply.[4] Public interest is a wide concept which it is not easy to interpret. The English Act, unlike the American legislation, assumed that some restrictive agreements had redeeming virtues. Sir Kenneth Diplock writes: This does involve a value judgment on economic matters and it is at

to give certain information in prospectuses and balance-sheets) and the 'philosophy of regulation' (a mixture of administrative control and criminal sanction): G. Sawer, 44 *A.L.J.* (1970), 303.
[1] *Rookes* v. *Barnard*, [1964] A.C. 1129. See A. D. Hughes, 86 *L.Q.R.* (1970), 181.
[2] 4 & 5 Eliz. II. c. 68.
[3] R. B. Stevens and B. S. Yamey, *The Restrictive Practices Court* (1965).
[4] Op. cit. 43.

least debatable whether the judicial process does provide a suitable machinery for its determination.[1] Parliament obviously preferred that the issues should be determined by the court step by step. In the early cases, the cost of the proceedings was high, owing to the length of the trial—£30,000 would be an average cost for a thirty-day trial. It has been suggested that more systematic research by objective experts is necessary to throw light on the real issues involved, and that the adversary procedure of the court is rather a clumsy method.

The Restrictive Practices Court has certainly taken a broad view of the meaning of *agreement*. If this had been interpreted as a legally enforceable contract, the Act would have had little scope. There may be an 'agreement' for the purpose of the Act if it can be proved that eight companies made identical contracts with another.[2] The courts realistically refused to believe that this was a mere coincidence.

The early cases, at somewhat of a cost, laid down the general principles, but there was some restiveness in industry despite a general realization that the Act had worked well. Under the Restrictive Trade Practices Act, 1968, the Department of Employment and Productivity was given power to exempt from the necessity of registration any restrictive agreement which satisfied certain conditions, e.g. if it is calculated to promote the carrying out of an industrial project of importance to the national economy, to promote efficiency, or to improve capacity, provided that the restrictions are no wider than is reasonably necessary and that, on balance, they are in the public interest. Is this a transfer (at least partial) of decision-taking in this sphere from a court to the administrative processes of the Board of Employment and Productivity? Will a businessman prefer to talk in person to an administrator rather than through a lawyer to a court?[3] Is negotiation as to the terms of a particular agreement easier than trying to justify an existing agreement to a court? Only time will answer these questions.

Take-overs and mergers may be used as a means towards monopoly. Both may raise important questions for the national interest, if there is an attempt by foreign capital to gain control of a local industry.[4] Here there is a direct national interest in controlling this aspect of the economy. A developing country must balance the need for foreign capital against the fear of domination by foreign interests.

---

[1] *The Role of the Judicial Process in the Regulation of Competition* (1967).
[2] *Re British Basic Slag*, [1963] 2 All E.R. 807.
[3] See 32 *Mod. L. R.* (1969), 302.   [4] J. R. Peden, 44 *A.L.J.* (1970), 208.

The peaceful conduct of industrial relations is a most important social interest. At first the trade union was regarded with hostility by the law. The weapon of criminal conspiracy and the Combination Acts of 1800 made it difficult for a trade union to function. In 1824 the worst abuses of the Combination Acts were removed, but in 1825 the law was tightened and in effect left open the question of criminal conspiracy.[1] It was 1871 before this was removed.[2] In 1906 the Trade Disputes Act[3] freed unions from liability in tort, but individual members might be made liable for damages in tort for civil conspiracy. Finally the courts decided that an agreement for a legitimate economic objective, provided that it did not contemplate any specific illegal act, was not actionable in tort.[4] Now the trade union is regarded as a most valuable adjunct to ordered industrial relations, and in the Australian federal system may be registered under the Commonwealth Conciliation and Arbitration Act.

The exact statement of the law with regard to the liability of individual members of a union is still a cause of difficulty.[5] Inducing or procuring breach of contract, preventing performance of contract, or intimidation[6] may still create liability in certain circumstances. Many trade unions regard *Rookes* v. *Barnard*[7] as going behind section 1 (1) of the Trade Disputes Act of 1906 which gave immunity in tort to a person who commits an act in furtherance of a trade dispute if the act related only to a threat that a contract of employment will be broken or that he will induce another to break a contract of employment. These cases illustrate the conflict of interests in this part of the law, and again the legislature intervened with the Trade Disputes Act, 1965.

Australia, as early as 1904, established a court for Conciliation and Arbitration, but its jurisdiction was limited to industrial disputes extending beyond the limits of any one state.[8] It was confidently hoped that the conciliation procedures set down and the power to arbitrate would create 'a new province for law and order . . .'.[9] The

---

[1] Holdsworth, *History of English Law*, xiii. 346.   [2] 34 & 35 Vict. c. 31.
[3] 6 Edw. VII, c. 47.
[4] *Crofter Hand Woven Harris Tweed Co.* v. *Veitch*, [1942] A.C. 435.
[5] A. D. Hughes, 'Liability for Loss caused by Industrial Action', 86 *L.Q.R.* (1970), 181.
[6] *Rookes* v. *Barnard*, [1964] A.C. 1129; *Torquay Hotel Co. Ltd.* v. *Cousins*, [1969] 2 Ch. 106.   [7] *Supra*.
[8] There are also Wages Boards in the states with power to declare a minimum wage. Victoria was the first state to establish a Wages Board—1896.
[9] H. B. Higgins, appointed President of the Court in 1907, published in 1922 a book under this name.

court early enunciated the theory of the basic wage, based on the 'normal needs of the average employee, regarded as a human being living in a civilised community'.[1] Compulsory margins for skill or special qualifications were also laid down. The payment of rates higher than the legal minimum is left to bargaining. It is only lately that the court has approved the principle of equal pay for equal work where women are concerned.[2] The court has coercive powers—it is an offence to pay less than the legal minimum wage; the court has power to summon the parties before it for a compulsory conference; it has power to fine for breach of an award, e.g. if there is a strike in defiance of the procedure laid down in a particular award for the settlement of disputes. There has been much controversy over the exercise of the power to fine unions—this is held to interfere with the 'right to strike'. Union secretaries have gone to gaol rather than submit.

In Australia, there is still scope left for the collective agreement— indeed it may become, by consent, an award of the courts. In England, there has been much dispute concerning the legal enforceability of a collective agreement. It was held in the *Ford Motor Company* case[3] that the parties did not intend to enter into legal obligations.

The Donovan Report of 1968[4] and the White Paper of 1969[5] adopt the policy of encouraging collective agreements, and recommend the establishment of a Commission on Industrial Relations, with which collective agreements could be registered if desired. The policy of giving all collective agreements legal force was rejected, but the suggestion was made that section 4 (4) of the Trade Union Act, 1871, should be amended to allow the parties to make such an agreement legally enforceable, should they expressly so declare. The most controversial proposals relate to restrictions on the freedom to resort to strikes, e.g. a compulsory 'conciliation pause' for twenty-eight days. This, however, would not make legal sanctions available for all strikes.

A possible source of industrial injustice may arise out of the expulsion by a professional association or trade union of one of its members; this may involve loss of livelihood. The law gives pro-

---

[1] Op. cit. 7. The original assumption was that the wage should be sufficient for a married man with three children.

[2] And this principle will not be fully implemented for some time.

[3] N. Selwyn, 32 *Mod. L. R.* (1969), 377; *Ford Motor Co.* v. *Amalgamated Union of Engineering and Foundry Workers*, [1969] 1 W.L.R. 339.

[4] Cmnd. 3623.

[5] Cmnd. 3888; see note, 32 *Mod. L. R.* (1969), 420.

tection only if the expulsion is a breach of the rules, or contrary to natural justice. In some cases there are statutes, e.g. with regard to solicitors and doctors. In cases not covered by statute, there is no appeal on questions of fact to the law courts. Where there is a 'closed shop', the union, by controlling access to membership, affects the right of an individual to have access to the labour market.[1] These problems raise issues of fundamental importance for the individual.

Taxation is used by the modern state, not merely to obtain revenue, but to achieve certain economic objectives.[2] A selective employment tax may attempt to transfer labour to industries considered important; tax may be reduced for a manufacturing company if exports are increased; mining dividends may earn a lower tax rate, so as to encourage exploration; graduated land taxes may be used to break up large agricultural estates. Estate duties redistribute wealth. The annual treasurer's budget, therefore, has important economic results. High taxation has undoubtedly led to the proliferation of incorporated companies in the hope of reducing the personal incidence of tax.

4. *The protection of religious, moral, humanitarian, and intellectual values*

Here we enter upon one of the most controversial fields of jurisprudence. The philosophy of a community will determine its laws, but a discussion of the problem of 'law and sin' will demonstrate that certain ethical ends are not easily attained by law. As in the regulation of restrictive trade practices, there are limits to the effective operation of the law. As Starke J. succinctly phrases it: 'moral indignation must not be mistaken for public policy.'[3]

The relationship between Church and State has varied at different times in different countries. Religion is essentially concerned with the mind and character, with worship of a Creator.[4] Law is concerned

---

[1] See O. Kahn-Freund, 33 *Mod. L. R.* (1970), 241. Cf. *Nagle* v. *Feilden*, [1966] 2 Q.B. 633 (C.A.), where the plaintiff had been refused, on the ground of her sex, the grant of a licence to train racehorses. The court held that this was against public policy. *Edwards* v. *Society of Graphical and Allied Trades* (C.A.), [1970] 3 All E.R. 689.

[2] L. C. B. Gower, *Law and Opinion in England in the 20th Century* (ed. Ginsberg), 153, points out that taxation was ignored by Dicey in the first edition of *Law and Opinion*. In the second edition he expressed great alarm at the increase of the standard rate of income tax to one shilling and eightpence.

[3] *Smith* v. *Jenkins*, [1969] V.R. 267.

[4] See the discussion in *R.* v. *Registrar General, ex parte Segerdal* (C.A.), [1970] 3 All E.R. 886, where a scientology 'chapel' was refused registration as a place of religious worship.

with external conduct, for it knows well that no statute can force a man to love his neighbour as himself or prevent him from coveting his neighbour's wealth. The value of religious observances depends on the willing participation of those who engage in them and the crude weapon of legal compulsion can do no more than secure external compliance. Tolerance is increasing, and most modern states penalize a religious sect only if it encourages conduct which is detrimental to the community life. The change in approach may be illustrated by the law of blasphemy. Once such conduct was punished as an offence against religion; today the most determined attacks on Christianity are not illegal, provided the tone of the discussion is not such as to be likely to provoke a breach of the peace.[1] Thus a rule which was once based on a desire to protect religious interests is continued in order to preserve order.[2]

The rules relating to the protection of the institution of marriage and the discouragement of immorality really fall under this head, although they are here considered under 'family interests'.[3] Lord Mansfield is reported to have said that 'the law of England prohibits everything which is *contra bonos mores*'.[4] This statement is neither true, nor is it desirable that it should be true. The common law has been rightly cautious in creating rules designed merely to protect moral interests, for such attempts often defeat the ends which they were designed to attain.[5] The law adopts three different attitudes to moral or ethical rules: firstly, the rule may be so vital that breach of it is made a criminal offence; secondly, the law may not make the act criminal, but may discourage it by any means short of this; thirdly, it may regard the rule as pertaining only to ethics and as not concerning a matter in which the law should be directly interested. The first and third of these approaches explain themselves. The second is illustrated by the maxim *ex dolo malo non oritur actio*;[6] the law may refuse to punish immorality, but may regard as void bargains

---

[1] *Bowman* v. *Secular Society Ltd.*, [1917] A.C. 406.
[2] The wider approach where obscenity is concerned is illustrated by Stable J. in *R.* v. *Martin Secker Warburg, Ltd.*, [1954] 2 All E.R. 683; and see for an extensive judicial discussion of the question *United States* v. *Roth* (1956), 237 F. 2d. 796, per Frank J., pp. 801–27.
[3] *Infra*, § 38.   [4] *Jones* v. *Randall* (1774), 1 Cowp. 37 at 39.
[5] 'It is not for this court to set itself up as a general *censor morum*'; per Latham C.J., *The King* v. *Connare* (1939), 61 C.L.R. 596 at 609. For an instructive report on the difficulties which attend attempts to make the law enforce moral rules, see *Report of the Committee on Homosexual Offences and Prostitution* (1957), Cmd. 247; and cf. *Director of Public Prosecutions* v. *Shaw*, [1962] A.C. 220.
[6] *Alexander* v. *Rayson*, [1946] 1 K.B. 169.

arising out of this consideration. The maxim has also been applied to actions in tort. An interesting decision is that of Crichton J., who held that a widow could not claim damages for loss of support through the negligent killing of her husband, if that support was the result of criminal pursuits and not honest labour.[1] A shipowner who gives a false 'clean' bill of lading cannot recover the damages, for which he was liable to the recipient, from the shipper who gave an indemnity to the shipowner. The court regarded the agreement as being in effect: 'you create a false document and I will reimburse you'.[2] On the other hand, a plaintiff who is injured in a motor accident does not lose his right to recover damages for loss of profit, merely because his garage is in an area confined to housing by zoning regulations;[3] it is otherwise if the plaintiff and defendant were both guilty of illegally using the vehicle which was concerned in the accident.[4]

The Wolfenden Report,[5] and the discussion which it provoked, provided an interesting commentary on the relationship between sin and crime;[6] prostitution, homosexuality, abortion, obscenity, drunkenness, gambling, and drug addiction—all provide work for the criminal law. Indeed, in the U.S., such 'moralistic' offences lead to nearly half of the six million non-traffic arrests a year.[7] Apart from questions of philosophy, any 'overreach' of the criminal law may so hamper police and courts that the more essential work of criminal prevention may be handicapped. Not all sin is crime, nor is all crime sin. Controversy results when we try to decide the extent to which the sanctions of the criminal law should be used to stamp out what are regarded as moral offences.

The attitude of the Wolfenden Committee may be illustrated by the following quotation: 'We are not attempting to abolish prostitution or to make prostitution itself illegal. We do not think that the law ought to try to do so . . . What the law can and should do is to ensure that the streets of London and our big provincial cities should be free from what is offensive and injurious.'[8] With regard to homosexuality, the Committee, by a majority of twelve to one, recommended that homosexual behaviour between consenting adults in

---

[1] *Burns* v. *Edman*, [1970] 1 All E.R. 886.
[2] *Brown Jenkinson & Co. Ltd.* v. *Percy Dalton (London) Ltd.*, [1957] 2 Q.B. 621.
[3] *Mills* v. *Baitis*, [1968] V.R. 583.   [4] *Smith* v. *Jenkins*, [1970] A.L.R. 519.
[5] (1957) Cmnd. 247.   [6] C. L. Ten, 32 *Mod. L. R.* (1969), 648.
[7] N. Morris and G. Hawkins, *The Honest Politician's Guide to Crime Control* (1969).
[8] Thus the recommendation left as criminal the following offences—soliciting, homosexuality with juveniles, etc.

private should no longer be punishable. The law should not try to enforce morals as such, but only attempt to prevent actions which will do harm to others.[1] This recommendation has now been adopted by the legislature.[2]

The question whether abortion should remain a criminal offence has also become a matter of great controversy. *R.* v. *Bourne*[3] held that the burden rested on the Crown to prove that the operation was not done in good faith for the purpose only of preserving the life of the mother. The last phrase was construed widely as including a case where continuation of the pregnancy would make her a physical or mental wreck. The Catholic church regards abortion as akin to murder, and the conflict is whether we should consider the interests of the unborn child, or that of the mother and her family. There was always the possibility that *R.* v. *Bourne* might not be followed, and so the Abortion Act of 1967[4] laid down the law, broadly on the principles of that case, with the additional justification where there was a serious risk that the prospective child would suffer from such physical or mental abnormalities as would be a serious handicap.

The Obscene Publications Act, 1959, was a valiant attempt to reconcile the interest of the community in stamping out obscenity with that of the artist in freedom of expression. Unfortunately, as was perhaps inevitable, the application of the statute places a very heavy burden on the courts.[5] 'The jury must consider on the one hand the number of readers they believe will tend to be depraved and corrupted by the book, the strength of the tendency to deprave and corrupt, and the nature of the depravity and corruption; on the other hand they should assess the strength of the literary, sociological or ethical merit which they consider the book to possess. They should then weigh all these factors and decide whether on balance the publication is proved to be justified as being for the public good.'[6]

If the law protects the right to live, should it also grant the right to die? This raises the problem of suicide and euthanasia. Should suicide be a crime? Clearly one cannot punish the person who

---

[1] It is curious that lesbianism was never regarded as a criminal offence.
[2] Sexual Offences Act, 1967, c. 60.
[3] [1939] 1 K.B. 687; *R.* v. *Davidson*, [1969] V.R. 667.
[4] C. 87. The question of injury to the physical and mental health of the pregnant woman or of any existing child of her marriage are declared to be relevant factors.
[5] C. H. Rolph, *Books in the Dock* (1969).
[6] *R.* v. *Calder & Boyars Ltd.*, [1968] 3 All E.R. 644; G. Zellick, 33 *Mod. L. R.* (1970), 289.

successfully ends his life, but should attempted suicide be visited with a criminal sanction?[1] The early English law treated suicide as felony with a consequential forfeiture of goods and chattels. Now views have changed, and the Suicide Act, 1961,[2] removed the stigma of criminality from self-destruction, though complicity of another person in the suicide is still a criminal offence. The modern view is not that suicide is justifiable, but that the criminal law is not an effective means of dealing with this problem.

Euthanasia still remains a criminal offence. To administer a fatal dose to a suffering patient would be murder—to assist in suicide would attract penalties under the Suicide Act.

Lord Devlin argues strongly[3] that a society possesses a public morality simply because it is a society, and that the criminal law cannot ignore the collective moral judgment of the community. If there is a strong and pervasive feeling that certain conduct is extremely threatening and extremely reprehensible to basic rules of community life, then the sanctions of the criminal law should be applied. 'Immorality for the purpose of the law is what every right-headed person is presumed to consider immoral.'[4] A recognized morality, protected by the criminal law, is as essential to society as a recognized government.

This runs counter to the philosophy of the Wolfenden Committee, and is regarded by E. V. Rostow as 'entirely natural to a common law judge and peculiarly irritating to an academic philosopher'.[5] It is submitted that the crucial test is whether the act is merely revolting (in which case the criminal law should not intervene) or whether it injures society (i.e. persons other than the actor), in which case there is a justification for using the rather crude sanctions of the criminal law. This broadly is the test used by the Wolfenden Committee. It is not easy, of course, to apply any abstract principle to the complex issues of social life—this illustrates again that law is a compromise reached by a particular community, valid only for that time and place.

It is interesting to contrast two dicta: 'There remains in the courts of law a residual power to enforce the supreme and fundamental purpose of the law, to conserve not only the safety and order, but also the moral welfare of the state and . . . it is their duty to guard

---

[1] N. St. John-Stevas, *Life, Death and the Law*, ch. vi.   [2] C. 60.
[3] *The Enforcement of Morals*, 15.   [4] Op. cit. 15.
[5] *Camb. L. J.* (1960), 174 at 177; see also the discussion by the same writer, *The Sovereign Prerogative: the Supreme Court and the Quest for Law*, ch. ii.

against attacks which may be the more insidious because they are novel and unprepared for.'[1] (This dictum raises questions which would need a volume of philosophy to answer. How do we determine the moral welfare of the State?)

Judge Maude, after referring to onduct that was utterly and disgustingly immoral, stated: 'we are not a court of morals.'[2] In a recent case, Lord Diplock suggested that it was not still open to the courts to enlarge the number of categories of purposes which are so contrary to public policy that those who act in concert to achieve them are guilty of criminal conspiracy.[3] Four other Lords agreed with his speech. This suggests that *Shaw*'s case should be confined to situations already covered by previous decisions. 'It is no offence under the law of England to do, or agree with others to do, acts, which though not prohibited by legislation, nor criminal nor tortious at common law, are considered by a judge or by a jury to be calculated to defeat, frustrate or evade the purposes or intention of an Act of Parliament. If it were otherwise, freedom under the law would be but an empty phrase.'[4]

Humanitarian interests are protected by various rules of the criminal law—e.g. the prohibition of slave-trading, cruelty to children or animals. It is the duty of the master of a ship to take reasonable steps to save life after a collision at sea. The difficulty of classifying interests, to which reference has already been made, is shown by the fact that a large proportion of human interests could be placed under the heading of humanitarianism. The possession of economic security and reasonable means of livelihood is pursued largely for the humanitarian reason of preventing want and suffering.

The social need for education is recognized from the very beginning of the community. The initiation of an Australian aborigine into the rites of his tribe is merely the attempt to mould him into a product that will be satisfactory to his peers. The attempt to make all the population literate is a relatively late development. In education, there is always a conflict between the pursuit of learning as such and the demands of practical training. The natural bias towards the practical in those who have to make their own way in the world is

---

[1] *Shaw* v. *Director of Public Prosecutions*, [1962] A.C. 220 per Viscount Simmonds; A. L. Goodhart, 77 *L.Q.R.* (1961), 560.

[2] *R.* v. *Silver*, [1956] 1 All E.R. 716. Actually this decision was overruled in *R.* v. *Thomas*, [1957] 1 W.L.R. 747.

[3] *Director of Public Prosecutions* v. *Bhagwan*, [1970] 3 All E.R. 97.

[4] Per Lord Diplock, same case, at 106.

reinforced today by the need, in the interests of national survival, to create a body of research workers and technical assistants for the purpose of producing new weapons of offence and defence. In some of the newer countries, particularly, the emphasis on vocational and technological training is tending to upset the proper balance of the universities. The excessive concentration of the twentieth century on science and the failure to study adequately the ends of society and the mechanics of government may bring a grim retribution in the years to come.

There is also a conflict between education, the drawing out of the capacities of the human personality and mere propaganda which is designed to produce a standardized man. Education is usually undertaken with the hope of producing a particular type—education without a guiding idea would be rather pointless. But, so long as all education is not controlled by the State, there is a certain degree of experimentation and flexibility.

The demand that education should be compulsory and free inevitably brings in the State—for private munificence can rarely afford the cost. The danger arises of excessive standardization. If local authorities and voluntary bodies are given a share in the responsibility, some variation is inevitable, but if the whole scheme is centrally controlled, then it becomes too rigid. Where there is no established Church, state education is normally secular. This is probably inevitable, but it increases the tendency to concentrate on the material side.

5. Health and racial integrity

Racial integrity is protected by certain rules of the criminal law, e.g. those relating to incest and unnatural offences. Carnal knowledge of a female lunatic is prevented partly because of its possible detrimental effect on race. In many states marriage laws have endeavoured to prevent the intermixture of races, as in the Nazi prohibition of marriages between Aryans and Jews; sterilization of mental defectives is another illustration of the same policy. The prohibition of suicide falls most easily under this head,[1] since the desire of the community to preserve life seems to be the reason why attempted suicide is still

---

[1] C. K. Allen places suicide under the head of race preservation: *Legal Duties*, 303, but see now Suicide Act, 1961, c. 60, discussed *supra*. The suicide of the assured avoids an insurance policy: *Beresford* v. *Royal Insurance Co. Ltd.*, [1938] A.C. 586; A. L. Goodhart, 52 *L.Q.R.* (1936), 575. But that rule of the common law has been varied by legislation in a number of jurisdictions, e.g. Australia, Life Insurance Act, 1945–61, § 120.

punishable in many jurisdictions. It is murder for a doctor to administer an excessive quantity of a drug in order to kill a patient, even though with true humanity, he but hastens the inevitable in order to put an end to suffering. Is it a criminal offence for a doctor merely to withdraw a machine to keep the heart beating, when he knows that death is inevitable and life unendurable? Euthanasia has been used, however, not only to end suffering, but to get rid of mental defectives or even those who are considered socially dangerous.[1]

The importance to the State of the protection of public health is too obvious to need stressing. Preventive medicine and the storage of food has saved mankind from the worst disasters of pestilence and famine. In the West, the increasing prosperity of the individual is linked with a fall in the birth-rate, but the fecundity of the East is already presenting enormous problems.

The nationalization of medicine has provoked an interesting discussion of the reasons why, and the extent to which, the State should interest itself in the provision of health services without cost to the patient. Such a scheme entails some control of the medical profession which runs counter to some of the most rooted beliefs of a profession, the keynote of which has been independence. In Australia the Pharmaceutical Benefits Act was held invalid by a majority of the High Court, partly on the ground that, contrary to the constitution, it involved civil conscription.[2] England has introduced a national health scheme, which has caused great controversy, but it at least avoids the position which exists in Australia that only the very poor (in the public hospitals) or the very rich can receive the best specialist attention. Hospital benefits insurance goes some way for the middle class, but a long illness may show the weakness of the scheme. As the Carnegie Quarterly shows,[3] even the wealth of America leaves many significant gaps in medical care—thus it is now rated fifteenth in the table of infant mortality. The problem is not lack of resources, but rather the system of application of medical skills for the benefit of the poorer sections of the community.

6. Environment

We cannot have an absolute right to an unspoiled environment,[4] for modern industry must at least in some areas destroy rural beauty.

---

[1] Cf. the Nazi use of euthanasia discussed by G. Ziemer, *Education for Death*, cited S. P. Simpson and J. Stone, *Law and Society* (1949).
[2] *British Medical Association* v. *The Commonwealth* (1949), 79 C.L.R. 201.
[3] Vol. xviii, no. 3 (1970).   [4] Lord Wilberforce, 43 *A.L.J.* (1969), 414.

The best that the law can do is to curb the worst excesses of industrialization by town planning.[1] Noise[2] and pollution are two of the greatest offenders—the latter affects air, water, natural growth, and the health of humanity.

The realistic approach is illustrated by a dictum of 1874: 'It would have been wrong, as it seems to me, for this Court in the reign of Henry VI to have interfered with the further use of sea coal in London, because it had been ascertained to their satisfaction . . . that by the reign of Queen Victoria both white and red roses would have ceased to bloom in the Temple Gardens. If some picturesque haven opens its arms to invite the commerce of the world, it is not for this Court to forbid the embrace, although the fruit of it should be the sights and sounds and smells of a common seaport and shipbuilding town which would drive the Dryads and their masters from their ancient solitudes.'[3]

But the advance of technology has brought an increasing number of problems. Writing in 1970, David Sive states: 'The explosion of concern for the environment, at every private and governmental level, is the great political phenomenon of the last twelve months.'[4] Courses in 'environmental law' are appearing in the law schools of the United States. Legal journals contain articles on 'The Persistent Problem of the Persistent Pesticides'.[5] The United States passed a National Environmental Policy Act in 1969 which set up a 'Council on Environmental Quality'. Once one could escape to the unspoilt forest to avoid noise, but today even these are not exempt from the sonic booms of air transport. The modern kitchen is blamed for causing deafness, for an exhaust fan, dishwasher, and garbage disposal unit operating together may reach 100 decibels.[6]

Concerning approval of buildings, there are strict rules in most communities concerning fire precautions, stairways, ceiling height, and safety of structure, but while these may be reasonably policed, no satisfactory method has ever been found for aesthetic control. An ugly building is not only an eyesore, but it may depreciate the value of surrounding property. Aesthetically, the entire character of a village or town may be destroyed by destruction of historic buildings

---

[1] *Infra,* § 118.
[2] D. A. Anthrop, 20 *Univ. of Toronto L. J.* (1970), 1; J. L. Hildebrand, 70 *Col. L. R.* (1970), 652.
[3] Per James L.J., *Salvin* v. *North Brancepeth Coal Co.* (1874), L.R. 9 Ch. 705 at 709.
[4] 70 *Col. L. R.* (1970), 612.   [5] W. H. Rodgers, ibid. 567.
[6] J. L. Hildebrand, ibid. at 666.

and the construction of glass boxes. There is an increasing interest in the preservation of what is good, and the prevention of what will detract from the elegance that already exists. Advertising boards on public highways are frequently subject to regulation on aesthetic grounds.

7. *Control of growth of population*

Each community faces the problem of population density in a given area—there is also the problem of an increase in population in the world as a whole. Famine, flood, disease, and war for centuries kept the human population in check. Malthus considered that lack of food would remain a constant limiting factor. However, his actual forecasts were falsified by the increase of productivity in agriculture. The skills of the medical profession in reducing infantile mortality and prolonging the span of human life are now creating new problems. It took the human race 200,000 years to reach 2,500 million: it will take only thirty years to add another 2,000 million, and experts predict a total of 6,000 million by the end of the century.[1] The population explosion, unless checked by birth-control methods, may be a greater threat to the welfare of humanity than the nuclear bomb.

§38. PRIVATE INTERESTS

The institution of the *ombudsman* in Sweden in 1809 was an interesting experiment to provide a machinery which would enable the individual to submit to a special official any alleged grievances arising as a result of executive action. New Zealand followed in 1962. In 1967 the Prime Minister of the United Kingdom introduced the Parliamentary Commissions Act 'to humanise the administration and to improve relations between Westminster and Whitehall on the one hand and the individual citizen'. The first Parliamentary Commissioner for Administration, Sir Edmund Compton, took office on 1 April 1967.[2] He cannot deal with any matter in respect of which the complainant could apply to a tribunal. The complaint must be referred to the Commissioner by a Member of Parliament and relate to the actions of departments responsible to Parliament which action is alleged to have caused injustice by maladministra-

---

[1] N. St. John-Stevas, *Life, Death and the Law*, 106.
[2] See the article by Sir Edmund Compton, 10 *J. of Society of Public Teachers of Law* (1968), 101. There is a staff of 49.

tion. The latter term is nowhere defined in the Act. There is no power to question the merits of a decision, if maladministration cannot be shown. The Commissioner has no power of executive action, but there is the weapon of a special report to Parliament, if he finds that injustice has been done and that a remedy is refused.

A problem raising similar conflict of interests is that of administrative law in general. How far should the courts control the functioning of administrative tribunals and executive decisions?[1] Do we need a new bill of rights for this 'administrative age', and if so should we turn to Parliament or to the courts, or to both?

The courts are certainly alive to this problem, as can be seen from a dictum of Salmon L.J.:

> I hope that nothing I have said can be taken to mean that I consider that anyone in this country is allowed to shelter behind any kind of *droit administratif*. Indeed I consider that one of the most important functions of our courts is vigilantly to protect the rights of the individual against unlawful encroachments by public officers and by the administration. The courts' powers to this end might well, in my view, be enlarged. Certainly such powers as we possess should be vigorously exercised.[2]

1. *Personal interests*

(i) *Physical protection.* The criminal law[3] and the law of tort[4] contain many rules designed to grant physical protection. 'Save in defence of his own life against unlawful attack, no private citizen may take the life of another even to save his own.'[5] 'No person can license another to commit a crime',[6] and death caused in a duel is murder, even though both parties consented to fight. There is authority for the view that even statutory provisions should be so interpreted that a sane murderer (or his representatives) should not succeed on intestacy to the estate of a man he has murdered.[7] The rules of the sea recognize a duty to attempt to save life.[8] Even in the interests of justice,

---

[1] K. C. Davis, 61 *Col. L. R.* (1961), 201; H. W. R. Wade, 78 *L.Q.R.* (1962), 188.

[2] *Ministry of Housing* v. *Sharp*, [1970] 1 All E.R. 1009 at 1024.

[3] The offences of murder, manslaughter, malicious injury to the person, assault. The punishment of rape and indecent assault is intended to give physical protection in addition to guarding other interests such as morality.

[4] False imprisonment, negligent injury, assault, strict liability for certain physical injuries; e.g. under *Rylands* v. *Fletcher*, the rules relating to chattels dangerous *per se*.

[5] R. O'Sullivan, 1 *Mod. L. R.* (1937), 31.

[6] *R.* v. *Donovan*, [1934] 2 K.B. 498 at 507.

[7] *Re Pitts*, [1931] 1 Ch. 546; *In re Sigsworth*, [1935] Ch. 89.

[8] *Scaramanga* v. *Stamp* (1880), 5 C.P.D. 295 at 304.

Lord Reid considers that a court cannot order an adult to take a blood test against his will, though Lord MacDermott thinks that this can be done in an appropriate case by use of the ancillary jurisdiction, e.g. a stay.[1] Heart transplants require formal procedures to ensure that the donor's death is not accelerated.[2]

(ii) *Freedom of the person.* Slavery is no longer consonant with the temper of our time. 'The growth of the common law was unfavourable to the existence of a class of slaves.'[3] The Universal Declaration of Human Rights states: 'No one shall be held in slavery or servitude: slavery and the slave trade shall be prohibited in all their forms.'[4] Doctrines of public policy avoid contracts which entirely deprive a man of freedom of action and reduce him to the position of *adscriptus glebae*.[5] But a certain measure of surrender of liberty is valid, e.g. a covenant not to associate with certain undesirable persons, or a covenant not to drink to excess.[6]

Other predominant rights claimed by the individual are: freedom from arbitrary arrest, the right to a speedy trial,[7] and the adoption of the maxim *nulla poena sine lege*.[8] The essentials of a fair trial are— an impartial and independent bench,[9] the existence and enforcement of reasonable rules of evidence which protect the accused, the presumption that a person is innocent until he is proved guilty, and the power to know the charge in advance and to employ counsel in defence. The law should treat confessions of criminal conduct with some suspicion. As Mr. Justice Byrne once said: 'The atmosphere of a police station seems to be singularly conducive to confession.'[10]

The antinomy that law must face is to secure protection for these individual claims and yet allow the police sufficient powers to stamp out crime. In times of war the conflict between individual liberty and national security may become particularly acute. It is to the credit of the English judiciary that they have been willing to sound a note of

---

[1] *S. v. S.*, [1970] 3 All E.R. 107.
[2] See in general G. Dworkin, 33 *Mod. L. R.* (1970), 353.
[3] W. S. Holdsworth, *H.E.L.* ii. 202; *Somersell's Case* (1772), 20 St. T. 1.
[4] Art. 4.
[5] *Horwood* v. *Millar's Timber and Trading Co. Ltd.*, [1917] 1 K.B. 305 at 311.
[6] *Trustee of Denny* v. *Denny and Warr*, [1919] 1 K.B. 583.
[7] Here the importance of the writ of habeas corpus is outstanding.
[8] *Infra*, § 83.
[9] *Adan Haji Jama* v. *The King*, [1948] A.C. 225; *Metropolitan Properties (F.G.C.) Ltd.* v. *Lannon*, [1969] 1 Q.B. 577.
[10] Cited G. Gardiner and A. Martin (eds.), *Law Reform Now* (1963), 252.

warning even in the gravest times of national peril. Lord Atkin has trenchantly said:

> In this country, amid the clash of arms, the laws are not silent. They may be changed, but they speak the same language in war as in peace. It has always been one of the pillars of freedom, one of the principles of liberty for which on recent authority we are now fighting, that the judges are no respecters of persons and stand between the subject and any attempted encroachments on his liberty by the executive, alert to see that any coercive action is justified in law.[1]
> The liberty of the subject and the convenience of the police or any other executive authority are not to be weighed in the scales against each other. This case will have served a useful purpose if it enables your Lordships once more to proclaim that a man is not to be deprived of his liberty except in due course and process of law.[2]

The internment of the Japanese on the west coast of America during the Second World War has been described by an American writer as 'the worst blow our liberties have sustained in many years'. The judgments of the Supreme Court in these cases canvass the issues of personal liberty and national security.[3]

How far can the property of an innocent person be held by the police on the ground that it may provide evidence of the commission of a crime by a third party, e.g. my car is stolen and the police suspect that the car was used in carrying out a murder? 'We have to consider, on the one hand, the freedom of the individual. His privacy and his possessions are not to be invaded except for the most compelling reasons. On the other hand, we have to consider the interest of society at large in finding out wrongdoers and repressing crime.'[4] Liberty of the person and conscription (e.g. for service in Vietnam) is an issue that has raised strong emotions in Australia. Even those who accept conscription as necessary for national self-defence may feel that intrusion into an Asian quarrel is not in the national interests of Australia. These are the conflicts of interests which democracy must solve one way or the other.

[1] *Liversidge* v. *Anderson*, [1942] A.C. 206 at 244. This was a dissenting judgment, the majority upholding the view that the courts could not test the reasonableness of the decision of the Home Secretary to detain under Reg. 18B. See also *McEldowney* v. *Forde*, H. Lds., [1969] 2 All E.R. 1039 and 86 *L.Q.R.* (1970), 171.

[2] *Christie* v. *Leachinsky*, [1947] A.C. 573 at 595 per Lord Simonds.

[3] E. V. Rostow, *The Sovereign Prerogative: the Supreme Court and the Quest for Law*, 193 at 194.

[4] Per Lord Denning, *Ghani* v. *Jones*, [1969] 3 W.L.R. 1158; L. H. Leigh, 33 *Mod. L. R.* (1970), 268; D. C. Pearce, 44 *A.L.J.* (1970), 467; *Butler* v. *Board of Trade*, [1970] 3 All E.R. 593.

(iii) *Freedom of the will*. No legal system can guarantee freedom of the will in general—this raises psychological questions and also matters of economic freedom. All that can be done is to invalidate transactions where there has been gross abuse. Physical duress, undue influence, and fraud are elsewhere discussed.[1] So far as economic duress is concerned, the law has wavered between the desire to protect freedom of the will and the desire not to interfere with free competition. In the early part of this century there was much talk of a tort of intimidation. But in all contractual bargaining, save where the parties are of equal economic strength, there is an element of coercion.[2] The result of forty years of litigation from *Allen v. Flood*[3] to *Crofter Hand Woven Harris Tweed Co. Ltd. v. Veitch*[4] is to demonstrate that, provided there is a legitimate objective, no remedy lies even if there is an agreement between two or more, the result of which is economic ruin to the plaintiff.[5] Since protection of business interests is a legitimate objective, economic duress (where no specific tort is committed) would be actionable only in a case of disinterested malevolence. If there is no conspiracy, one individual is entirely free to use his economic power as maliciously as he pleases. This raises the problem of abuse of rights,[6] and also the effect of the Restrictive Trade Practices Act which is discussed in the preceding section.

(iv) *Liberty of thought and speech*. The law can hardly interfere with liberty of thought but only with its expression. Religious liberty logically falls under this head, for true tolerance demands protection for the reasonable expression both of religious and anti-religious views. 'Religious freedom is too sacred a right to be restricted or prohibited without convincing proof that a legitimate interest of the State is in great danger.'[7] Individual freedom of thought and conscience, to hold and change beliefs, is an absolute and sacred right. Everyone has the right, 'either alone, or in community with others and in public or private, to manifest his religion or belief in teaching, practice, worship and observance'.[8] An interesting decision was that of the U.S. Supreme Court in 1968, invalidating a statute of Arkansas

---

[1] *Infra*, § 100.   [3] J. Stone, op. cit. 511.
[2] [1898] A.C. 1.   [4] [1942] A.C. 435.
[5] But legislative attempts to prevent monopolies and to preserve some measure of fair competition are part of modern government, e.g. the Anti-trust laws in the United States of America and the English Restrictive Trade Practices Act, 1956.
[6] *Infra*, § 106.
[7] Per Murphy J., *Prince v. Massachusetts* (1944), 321 U.S. 158 at 175: cited 32 *Cornell L. Q.* (1946), 177 at 201.
[8] Universal Declaration of Human Rights, Art. 18.

which forbade the teaching of evolution in public schools. 'There is and can be no doubt that the First Amendment does not permit the State to require that teaching and learning must be tailored to the principles or prohibitions of any religious sect or dogma.'[1]

Liberty of expression of political and religious views can never become an absolute right—it must be limited by the need for society to protect itself. Indeed tolerance is the virtue of a secure and settled society—when the government is insecure or totally out of touch with the feeling of the community, then free speech may be most necessary, but it is unlikely to be achieved as self-preservation will dominate the views of those in power.

The sect of Jehovah's Witnesses has provided the Supreme Court of United States of America with a unique opportunity to reconcile the principle of religious freedom with the right of society to protect itself against subversive or annoying practices.[2] Can a schoolchild be expelled for refusing to salute the flag, if it is alleged that the objection is based on religious scruple? If with missionary zeal an organized attempt is made to interview every householder, can a town protect itself against such activities, or is any such action protected by a guarantee of the freedom of religion?

The policy of the Official Secrets Act, 1911, is a matter of controversy. It is reasonable to protect information, the disclosure of which would be injurious to national security, but not to protect information merely because it might lead to criticism of a government.[3]

(v) *Liberty of association.* This involves three elements: the right of peaceable assembly, the right to form associations, and the right not to be forced into associations. The right of free association is won only after many battles, as is illustrated by the history of trade union law throughout the nineteenth century. Both Parliament and the courts have changed their view as to the nature of the trade union and the advisability of collective bargaining. In Australia the whole system of industrial arbitration depends on the recognition of the trade union as an essential factor in industrial relations. This is but one example of the struggle for the right of free association. States are notoriously suspicious of organizations of citizens, lest they develop subversive tendencies. An association may become so strong as to threaten the

[1] *Epperson* v. *Arkansas* (1968), 21 L. Ed. 2d. 228.
[2] V. M. Barnett, 32 *Cornell L. Q.* (1946), 177 at 188; R. H. Pear, 12 *Mod. L. R.* (1949), 167, and cf. *Jehovah's Witnesses* v. *The Commonwealth* (1943), 67 C.L.R. 116.
[3] See G. Gardiner and A. Martin (eds.), *Law Reform Now* (1963), 45.

security of the State or the interests of citizens who are outside the association. Too great an accumulation of wealth in the hands of one group may render the political institutions of that society a mere tool of one section.[1] The law is here faced with a delicate balancing of interests as the civil conspiracy cases show.

The theory of communism provides a real dilemma for a democracy. If we believe that an important value of democracy is the right to debate even the basic political creeds, we should hesitate to suppress any organization, however subversive it may be, in the faith that the good sense of the community will ultimately make the right choice. But at what stage does freedom of debate end, and the wrecking of democracy begin? How far can a society legitimately suppress an association if its declared object is to destroy the foundations on which that society is built? No satisfactory theoretical answer can be given. We must balance the danger of the activity of the group against the evil of the suppression, coupled with the recognition that social, as well as religious, doctrine is sometimes spread by martyrdom.

(vi) *Protection of name and privacy.* There is no copyright in the name of an individual in English law: a name is protected only if material interests are affected. If a criminal borrows another's name in order to pass himself off as that person, the law will intervene. If a trader 'passes off' his goods as those of a rival, the law will grant protection to the latter. If a person trades under his own name, the law will not prevent him even if the public is confused because the name of his competitor is the same, unless there is evidence of deliberate intent to 'pass off' his goods as those of the other. The question of trade-names and proprietary marks is so important that much legislation relates to it. For our purpose it is enough to say that the law does not protect the exclusive use of a name unless material interests are at stake.

An extensive literature has grown around the so-called right of privacy,[2] which is not recognized as such in English law, though it has been developed in certain American states. In English law, 'at the first hint of breach of contract, trust, or confidence, the courts seem to

---

[1] S. Timberg, 46 *Col. L. R.* (1946), 533 at 535, claims that in 1907 the U.S. Steel Corporation owned real property equivalent to the areas of Massachusetts, Vermont, and Rhode Island: in 1935 the premium income of the Metropolitan Life Insurance Co. was three times the tax collection of the State of New York.

[2] M. Littman and P. Carter-Ruck, *Privacy and the Law* (1970); S. D. Warren and L. D. Brandeis, 4 *Harv. L. R.* (1890–1), 193; P. H. Winfield, 47 *L.Q.R.* (1931), 23; W. Prosser, 37 *Mich. L. R.* (1939), 874; Note, 37 *Mich. L. R.* 988; R. Pound, 29 *Harv. L. R.* (1916), 640.

be willing to give protection to what is, in reality, privacy',[1] but unless such a reason can be found there is no protection for privacy as such.[2] A lady who pays a photographer to take her photograph can prevent the photographer from selling copies without her consent only because the law reads an implied term into the contract. But there is no general 'right to be left alone'. No man can prevent the press publishing his photograph taken by a journalist, and the most intimate details of private life may be published, provided the sanctions of the law of defamation can be avoided. If the truth of the statement can be proved, a newspaper may publish an account of a forgotten lapse on the part of a now blameless citizen—or so it was at common law, but several jurisdictions by legislation now require the publisher to show public interest as well as truth in defence. Trespass to land is a specific tort, but a broadcasting company may spy on a racecourse from neighbouring land and publish to the world a description of the races, and, even if the race-course proprietor suffers loss through falling attendances, he has no redress.[3] The development of electronic devices for listening in on private conversations, hidden microphones for recording, and telephone tapping have made the problem much more urgent than in the past. A substantial number of American states recognize a common law right of privacy—the right of a private individual to be 'left alone'.[4] The Universal Declaration of Human Rights denounces arbitrary interference with privacy, family, home, or correspondence.[5]

The right to publish letters illustrates the problem that the law must face. The recipient of a letter acquires property in the paper, but it would be anomalous if he could publish the letter without the writer's consent. Hence English law, in order to protect this personal interest, has talked of the writer's property in the composition. Some systems of law also recognize that publication is unlawful without the consent of the addressee.[6] In these cases the law is, in reality, attempting to protect a personal interest and is using the language of property in order to obtain a legal justification. Effective protection of property

---

[1] G. W. Paton, 16 *Can. B. R.* (1938), 433.
[2] The Report of the Committee on the Law of Defamation, Cmd. 7536, 1948, was against a remedy for breach of privacy.
[3] *Victoria Park Racing and Recreation Grounds Co. Ltd.* v. *Taylor* (1937), 58 C.L.R. 479.
[4] For an example see *Mau* v. *Rio Grande Inc.*, 28 F. Supp. 845 (N.D. Cal. 1939), discussed 88 *Univ. of Pa. L. R.* (1940), 374; W. Feinberg, 48 *Col. L. R.* (1948), 713.
[5] Art. 12.
[6] L. F. Vinding Kruse, *The Right of Property*, 136-7.

rights was evolved before that of personal rights, and hence the courts, wishing to protect a personal interest, frequently feign a tinge of property in order to accomplish their end.

(vii) *Protection of the mind and feelings.* 'Mental pain or anxiety the law cannot value and does not pretend to redress when the unlawful act complained of causes that alone.'[1] At one time this doctrine was carried so far that damages were refused even where serious illness resulted from a nervous shock.[2] It was argued that it was too difficult to secure convincing proof of causal connection between the shock and the illness and that 'compensation neurasthenia' was very frequent—the illness lasted until the healing power of an award of damages had been applied. It has been said that in some of the early cases we can almost detect a masculine astonishment that any woman could be so silly as to allow herself to be frightened or shocked into a miscarriage. But the advance of medical science has deprived these arguments of their base, and modern English cases recognize a cause of action for nervous shock.[3] Lord Denning defines this as 'any recognisable psychiatric illness caused by the breach of duty by the defendant'.[4] But even the intentional infliction of mental suffering is not a cause of action in itself, if actual shock does not follow. There is, however, the parasitic element in damages—although mental anxiety or suffering may not be actionable *per se*, once an action lies on other grounds, it may be allowed to inflame the damages.[5] The father who sues for seduction of his daughter seeks in theory damages for loss of service, but if this can be presumed inflated damages may be awarded as a *solatium* for the outrage to the family honour.[6] Spitting in a man's face may cause no actual loss, although heavy damages may be awarded as compensation for the humiliation involved. But there are still many cases in which a person can with impunity, either intentionally or negligently, inflict mental suffering on another.

---

[1] *Lynch* v. *Knight* (1861), 9 H.L.C. 577 at 598.
[2] *Victorian Railways Commissioners* v. *Coultas* (1888), 13 A.C. 222.
[3] i.e. not mere anxiety, but shock which results in physical illness. *Hambrook* v. *Stokes*, [1925] 1 K.B. 141; *Owens* v. *Liverpool Corporation*, [1939] 1 K.B. 394; *Chester* v. *Waverley* (1939), 62 C.L.R. 1; *Bourhill* v. *Young*, [1943] A.C. 92.
[4] *Hinz* v. *Berry*, C.A., [1970] 1 All E.R. 1074.
[5] e.g. at common law in seduction, assault, or an insulting trespass. In general the rules of contract give damages only for financial loss—the most outstanding exception being breach of promise of marriage where the 'parasitic element' is involved. The action for breach of promise of marriage has now been abolished by the Law Reform (Miscellaneous Provisions) Act, 1970.
[6] This action is now abolished by the Act cited in the previous note.

(viii) *Reputation*. A man's reputation is his most treasured possession—hard to win and easy to lose. The dilemma of the law is to protect freedom of speech and yet allow remedies for unjustified personal attacks. In English law the rules are fairly strict—proof that the defendant took the greatest possible care is no defence. The test is not what the writer meant, but what a reasonable reader would infer from his words.[1] This strict rule has been much criticized, particularly by those concerned with freedom of the press. In recent years legislative attempts have been made in England and some other jurisdictions to redress the balance; e.g., by providing for correction and apology as a sufficient remedy in cases of unintentional defamation by newspapers and periodicals.[2] In libel damage is presumed, whereas in slander (save in four cases), actual loss resulting from the statement must be proved. Since many courts regard broadcasting as constituting slander,[3] the result is that words written on a postcard are treated more seriously than an address to thousands over the air. Here 'the law went wrong from the beginning in making the damage and not the insult the cause of action; and this seems the stranger when we have seen that with regard to assault a sounder principle is well established'.[4] However, the legislature has now declared that broadcast words and words spoken during the public performance of a play shall be regarded as being published in permanent form.[5]

On the other hand justification is in civil cases a complete defence at common law. Whatever the motive in publishing the past frailties of a now blameless citizen, there is no redress if what is stated can be proved true. Some parts of the common law world require, in addition to justification, proof that the publication was in the public interest.[6]

Where fair comment is concerned the law allows a greater freedom for artistic criticism than for personal attacks. In the former case Lord Esher suggest that the test is: 'Would any fair man, however prejudiced he may be, however exaggerated or obstinate his views, have said that which this criticism has said of the work which is

---

[1] *Hulton & Co.* v. *Jones*, [1910] A.C. 20; *Hough* v. *London Express Ltd.*, [1940] 2 K.B. 507—except in regard to subordinate disseminating agencies.

[2] England, Defamation Act, 1952 (15 & 16 Geo. VI and 1 Eliz. II, c. 66), s. 4; Tasmania, Defamation Act, 1957, s. 17; New Zealand, Defamation Act, 1954, s. 6.

[3] *Meldrum* v. *A.B.C. Ltd.*, [1932] V.L.R. 425. The Report of the Committee on the Law of Defamation, Cmd. 7536, 1948, recommended that broadcasting should be treated as libel.

[4] F. Pollock, *Torts* (14th ed.), 193. In New South Wales, slander is assimilated to libel.

[5] Defamation Act, 1952, and Theatres Act, 1968, s. 4.

[6] e.g. Queensland, New South Wales.

criticised?'[1] This is a curious idea of a fair man, but it does illustrate the desire of the law to allow latitude to artistic criticism.

(ix) *Equality*. The removal of discrimination on the grounds of race, religion, and sex has been a slow evolution. Racial discrimination caused many controversies in the United States in the 1960s.[2] In Britain the Race Relations Act was passed in 1965, and a Race Relations Board has been set up to investigate and report on cases of racial discrimination.[3] Enoch Powell made the issue one of his principal policy speeches in the general election of 1970. The growing acceptance of the principle of racial equality is shown by the reaction against South Africa and Rhodesia for their advocacy of the doctrine of white supremacy. The problem becomes really serious when a cricket tour by a South African team is cancelled.

The achievement of religious tolerance and of equality of status for women has been a slow evolution, but it is the mark of a developed civilization to remove all discrimination based on religion and sex.

2. *Family interests*

This is a heading which cuts across the analytical divisions of the law, and affects the law of contract, tort, property, succession, guardianship, and crime. In Europe both Church and State helped to mould the rules with the result that marriage, though in one sense a contract based on the free consent of the parties, actually created a status, since the incidents of the relationships are compulsorily imposed by law. Some rights arising from marriage are similar to rights in other parts of the law (e.g. a husband's usufruct over a wife's property);[4] other rights are unique (e.g. those arising out of the relationship of husband and wife, parent and child).[5]

(i) *Husband and wife*. First the law has to decide what is meant by marriage. In most societies one form of sexual union is treated by the law as on a superior plane to others. The classic English definition is that marriage is the 'voluntary union for life of one man and one woman to the exclusion of all others'.[6] Hill J. went so far as to deny that a marriage which took place in Russia was a marriage in the eyes

---

[1] *Merivale* v. *Carson* (1888), 20 Q.B.D. 275 at 281.
[2] See the comment, 84 *Harv. L. R.* (1971), 1109.
[3] See *Ealing London Borough Council* v. *Race Relations Board*, [1970] 3 W.L.R. 921.
[4] The influence of the family on the law of succession is discussed *infra*, § 121.
[5] Lord Penzance, *Hyde* v. *Hyde* (1866), L.R. 1 P. & D. 130 at 133.
[6] For a discussion of reforms in family law, see G. Gardiner and A. Martin (eds.), *Law Reform Now*, ch. vi.

of English law, because divorce was then obtainable at the will of either party. The Court of Appeal pointed out, however, that divorce depends not on the *lex loci celebrationis*, but on the law of the domicil of the husband at the time proceedings commence.[1] The English definition excludes polygamy—the remedies of the matrimonial courts are designed for monogamy alone. But English law recognizes polygamy for some purposes. 'It cannot, I think, be doubted now (notwithstanding some earlier *dicta* by eminent judges) that a Hindu marriage between persons domiciled in India is recognised in our court, that the issue are regarded as legitimate, and that such issue can succeed to property in this country with a possible exception.'[2]

The interest of the community is in a married partnership which treats each party on an equal basis, and imposes only the limitations which the theory of marriage requires. The law has come far from the original approach which treated the wife as a mere chattel under the control of her husband. Originally marriage was seen in terms of contract, dissolution in terms of property, and divorce in terms of a matrimonial offence.[3] But the recognition of the individuality of the married woman has been a slow process. As late as 1891 a husband claimed the right to lock up his wife, and though the claim was rejected, it was surprising what an antiquated view of marriage the legal authorities took.[4] What is equally as important as physical freedom is economic independence. Classical Rome gave to the wife in the upper classes an element of financial independence in the institution of dowry, which the husband was compelled to restore if the marriage was dissolved through his fault. In England, the wife's lack of proprietary capacity was for long a defect in the law. Equity allowed property to be vested in trustees for the wife and the legislature somewhat tardily extended this protection by allowing the wife to hold property at law. The training of women for business and professional life results in economic independence for an increasing number of wives. The wife's right to sue her husband for maintenance and to pledge his credit for necessaries is also an important economic protection. In Russia it is so common for wives to earn their own

---

[1] *Nachimson* v. *Nachimson*, [1930] P. 85, 217.
[2] Per Lord Maugham L.C., *Sinha Peerage Claim*, [1946] 1 All E.R. 348 at 349 (the possible exception related to real estate); G. C. Cheshire, *Private International Law* (6th ed.), 308 et seq.
[3] H. A. Finlay, 43 *A.L.J.* (1969), 602.
[4] *R.* v. *Jackson*, [1891] 1 Q.B. 671.

living that the wife, if she has means, is bound to support a destitute husband.

The law recognizes the unity of married life in the old doctrine that husband and wife are one person. This maxim was never literally true.[1] It may be justified in so far as it attempts to preserve the unity and intimacies of family life, but it may also be used to reduce the wife to a subordinate position. The law of evidence still places the disclosures of husband and wife in a somewhat privileged position— a spouse is not a competent or compellable witness against the other spouse in certain criminal cases, and spouses are not compellable to disclose communications between each other during marriage.[2] On the other hand, in a murder trial the House of Lords held admissible a letter written by the accused to his wife. The wife had not received the letter as it was intercepted before delivery. Viscount Radcliffe dissented.[3]

If, however, the alleged offence was committed against the wife, her evidence is admissible.[4] Ungoed Thomas J. has held that the court, in the exercise of its equitable jurisdiction, will restrain either party to a marriage from committing a breach of confidence arising from the intimacies of married life, even though the parties had been divorced before the action was brought; for there is no need to prove either a contract, or a right of property, since equity can act even if there is no remedy at common law.[5] There is some support for the rule that a husband and wife cannot be guilty of conspiracy together. No action in tort lies between the spouses, save that the wife may sue for protection of her private property. In some jurisdictions, however, changes have been made in this rule; in Victoria, for example, husbands have been given the same right to sue for protection of their private property as was enjoyed by the wife,[6] and some United States jurisdictions have gone even further in removing restrictions against suits in tort between husband and wife.[7]

---

[1] Glanville Williams, 10 *Mod. L. R.* (1947), 16.
[2] Op. cit. at 20. And see *Rumping* v. *D.P.P.*, [1962] 3 All E.R. 256: this apparently applies even to a polygamous marriage: *Mawji* v. *Reginam* (J.C.)., [1957] 1 All E.R. 385, or where a decree of nullity is subsequently granted: *R.* v. *Algar*, [1953] 2 All E.R. 1381.
[3] *Rumping* v. *Director of Public Prosecutions*, [1962] 3 All E.R. 256.
[4] *R.* v. *Verolla*, [1962] 2 All E.R. 426.
[5] *Duchess of Argyll* v. *Duke of Argyll*, [1967] Ch. 302.
[6] Marriage Act, 1958, s. 160.
[7] See W. E. McCurdy, *Torts Between Persons in Domestic Relation*, 43 *Harv. L. R.* (1930), 1030; and the authorities collected by A. C. Jacobs and J. Goebel, *Domestic Relations* (4th ed., 1961), pp. 565–88.

In some American states, a minor child cannot sue a parent in tort on the ground that this introduces 'discord and contention where the laws of nature have established peace and obedience'.[1] Some courts also allow an action to the child against one who entices the father to leave the family.[2] In private international law the domicil of the wife follows that of her husband. A promise between husband and wife is not always actionable, for 'each house is a domain into which the King's writ does not seek to run and to which his officers do not seek to be admitted'.[3] At common law the husband was liable for the torts of his wife, but this did not depend on the doctrine of legal unity, but upon the necessity of finding a defendant who could meet an adverse judgment. Once the wife ceased to lose her chattels on marriage the reason for the old rule ceased and it has now been abolished by legislation in England and many parts of the common law world.

Many public policy rules illustrate the desire of the law to uphold the institution of marriage. A condition attached to a bequest is void if its object is to separate husband and wife;[4] a promise made by a married man to marry another woman is void, but valid if made after a *decree nisi* has been granted, although before it has been made absolute.[5] Once even an agreement to separate was regarded as void; now it is recognized that the parties should be free to end an intolerable situation in a dignified way.

But the law in its desire to strengthen the institution of marriage must not go too far in its attack on sexual intercourse outside the marriage bond. The criminal law regulates certain aspects of sexual behaviour, where special reasons of public policy are concerned— e.g. where there is no consent as in rape, where the female is not competent to consent because of age or lunacy, where there is a close relationship between the parties as in incest, where the offence is unnatural—but immorality *per se* is not now a crime.[6] Nor is it a civil offence unless it causes loss of service to the parent (or one *in loco parentis*) of the girl seduced,[7] or is a breach of a marital right. But

[1] Per Owen J., *Wick* v. *Wick* (1927), 192 Wisc. 260.
[2] *Daily* v. *Parker* (1945), 152 F. (2d) 174; 48 *Mich. L. R.* (1949), 242.
[3] Per Atkin L.J., *Balfour* v. *Balfour*, [1919] 2 K.B. 571 at 579; see also *Hoddinott* v. *Hoddinott*, [1949] 2 K.B. 406, which seems to bear harshly on the wife, whose skill had assisted the husband in winning prizes in football pools.
[4] *Re Thompson*, [1939] 1 All E.R. 681; *Davies* v. *Elmslie*, [1938] 1 K.B. 337.
[5] *Fender* v. *St. John-Mildmay*, [1938] A.C. 1.
[6] But in ecclesiastical law adultery was a punishable offence, and many countries have treated it as a crime. Some still do, e.g. India, Malaya, Illinois (U.S.A.).
[7] This action is now abolished (*infra*).

many rules of public policy are designed to discourage immorality. If a promise is made in respect of past cohabitation, the promise is made for no consideration at all; if a promise is given in respect of future cohabitation, the consideration is unlawful.[1] At one time it was considered that harsh rules concerning illegitimate children would discourage immorality, but objections to gifts by will to illegitimate children on the ground of their being contrary to public policy are 'not quite so strong now as they were a century ago',[2] for it seems unfair to penalize an innocent child. This is now recognized by the Universal Declaration of Human Rights.[3]

The husband has a right to the *consortium* of his wife, and hence in English law an action lies for loss of services if the wife is negligently or intentionally injured or is enticed away. At first the view was that the wife had no corresponding right to her husband's *consortium* and hence no action against a wrongdoer.[4] The support for that view was historical.[5] The legal and social position of the married woman changed so much during the last hundred years, however, and she has so far come to be regarded as her husband's equal and not in any way his servant, that it has been argued strenuously that she should have the same remedies for loss of *consortium* as have been enjoyed by her husband.[6] It was accepted that the wife should have a similar right to her husband to sue for loss of *consortium* brought about by enticement,[7] but the House of Lords held[8] that no action for loss of *consortium* would lie at the suit of a wife where the loss was caused by the negligence of the defendant. The House took the view that the husband's right of action in this case was an historical anomaly and that it should not be extended. Many cases in the various common law jurisdictions illustrate the change in legal approach to the relation of husband and wife. But the ways of meeting the change vary widely. In some, for example, a remedy based on the old law of master and servant has been adapted to meet the view of marriage as a free partnership. In others, the acceptance of the

---

[1] See *Ayerst* v. *Jenkins* (1873), L.R. 16 Eq. 275 at 282–3.
[2] *In re Hyde*, [1932] 1 Ch. 95 at 98.
[3] 'All children, whether born in or out of wedlock, shall enjoy the same social protection', Art. 25 (2).
[4] See the majority decision of the High Court in *Wright* v. *Cedzich* (1930), 43 C.L.R. 493.
[5] P. Brett, *Consortium and Servitium—A History and Some Proposals*, 29 *Aust. L. J.* (1955), 321, 389, 428.
[6] See for example the dissent of Isaacs J. in *Wright* v. *Cedzich* (1930), 43 C.L.R. 493.
[7] *Gray* v. *Gee* (1923), 39 T.L.R. 429; *Place* v. *Searle*, [1932] 2 K.B. 497.
[8] *Best* v. *Samuel Fox & Co. Ltd.*, [1952] A.C. 716.

notion that marriage is a free partnership has led to a rejection of old rules designed to protect the interests of husbands or to allow women to sue for breach of promise to marry.[1]

The rules of divorce vary from those systems which regard the wife as a mere chattel to be dismissed at will, the wife herself having no power to terminate the relationship, to the strictness of the religious doctrine which regards marriage as an indissoluble sacrament and back to the original theory of U.S.S.R. which emphasized that marriage was a contract and should be terminable at the will of either party. It is significant, however, that U.S.S.R. has recently made more difficult the securing of divorce, as the importance of the family unit to society is recognized.

In dealing with divorce the law is faced with the dilemma—if divorce is made too easy, the institution of marriage is weakened; if it is made too difficult, the cost to the happiness of the individual may be great. The general tendency is to recognize that too strict a view does not uphold morality—but there are still states where divorce is unobtainable.[2] English courts take a realistic view, where both parties ask for the exercise of discretion. Simon L.C. stated that in addition to the interests of the children, the interests of the co-respondent, the question of possible reconciliation between husband and wife, there was the interest of the community in maintaining a true balance between respect for the binding sanctity of marriage and the social considerations which make it contrary to public policy to insist on the maintenance of a union which has entirely broken down.[3]

There is thus a complete revolution in the attitude to marriage since the nineteenth century. If marriage is not thought of in terms of property, but in terms of a partnership between persons of equal status, irretrievable breakdown of the relationship should be the test of dissolution rather than sin or matrimonial misconduct. This is the approach adopted by the Divorce Reform Act, 1969.[4]

If the court is bound to stigmatize one party as guilty of misconduct, then parties will contest every fact, for alimony may depend

[1] See the material collected by A. C. Jacobs and J. Goebel, *Domestic Relations* (4th ed., 1961), pp. 492–550. New York has abolished actions for alienation of affections, criminal conversation, seduction, and breach of promise. The U.K. Law Reform (Miscellaneous Provisions) Act, 1970, has abolished actions for breach of promise of marriage, the right to claim damages for adultery, to sue for seduction of a child.

[2] Argentine, Bolivia, Brazil, Chile, Colombia, Eire, Italy (until 1970), Paraguay, and Spain. But other means of dissolution (by way of nullity proceedings) of marriages exist and go some distance towards diminishing the difference.

[3] *Blunt* v. *Blunt*, [1943] A.C. 517.

[4] C. 55: Jennifer Levin, 33 *Mod. L. R.* (1970), 632.

on the respective guilt of the parties. In *Tumath* v. *Tumath*[1] the Court of Appeal took the realistic approach that where the marriage had irretrievably broken down, it could be a waste of public time and money if both parties introduced voluminous evidence as to which party should be granted the decree. Hence if there were further proceedings relating to the financial provisions to be made for maintenance, the court accepted as a corollary that a husband who had not contested every issue of fact in the divorce proceedings was not precluded on the ground of public policy from introducing new evidence which was relevant to the question of the scale of support.[2]

Is the real purpose of marriage the procreation of children? In America an interesting decision held void a condition in a lease that occupation was to be by adults only and refused to allow a married couple to be evicted when a child was born.[3] The Court of Appeal has held that the persistent refusal of one spouse to have intercourse without the use of contraceptives was a wilful refusal to consummate the marriage.[4] The House of Lords, at a later date, refused to accept this view, Lord Jowitt emphasizing that there were other objects for which marriage was instituted than the procreation of children.[5] Many systems now emphasize that the community cannot afford to ignore the effect of marriage on the future of the race and hence demand certificates of health before the parties are allowed to marry.[6]

The legality of birth control and abortion raises questions of the interests which law should protect. In the nineteenth century a book on contraception would have been classified as obscene.[7] Today the opinion of society and the law has changed, as is illustrated by the decision of the House of Lords in *Baxter* v. *Baxter*:[8] 'Control by men and women over the numbers of their children is one of the first conditions of their own and the community's welfare.'[9] In the United States there are differing rules, e.g. in Connecticut it is an offence not only to sell, but also to use, a contraceptive.[10] Among the

---

[1] [1970] 1 All E.R. 111.

[2] *Warren* v. *Warren and Russell*, [1970] 2 All E.R. 189. See the discussion by O. Kahn-Freund of recent legislation on matrimonial property in 33 *Mod. L. R.* (1970), 601: Matrimonial Proceedings and Property Act, 1970.

[3] *LaMont Building Co.* v. *Court* (1946), 66 N.E. (2d) 552, noted 22 *Notre Dame Lawyer* (1946), 131.

[4] *Cowen* v. *Cowen*, [1946] P. 36.   [5] *Baxter* v. *Baxter*, [1947] 2 All E.R. 886.

[6] e.g. Illinois and many other states of the U.S.A. The Nazis introduced such a law in 1935: S. P. Simpson and J. Stone, *Law and Society* (1948).

[7] N. St. John-Stevas, *Life, Death and the Law*, 56 et seq.

[8] [1948] A.C. 274.

[9] Royal Commission on Population (1949), Cmd. 7695, para. 427.

[10] N. St. John-Stevas, op. cit. 64.

christian churches, all take a liberal view save the Roman Catholic and the Orthodox churches.[1] The Lambeth Conference of 1920 condemned contraception, but by 1958 it was approved.

Artificial insemination raises questions to which the answers are still obscure.[2] If the husband provides the semen, it is difficult to suggest that adultery is committed, but in A.I.D. (as it is called), where a third party is the donor, is the wife guilty of adultery? Lord Wheatley in a Scottish case held that it was not adultery even if the husband had not consented[3] (although he considered that it would be a heinous breach of the marriage contract). In 1956 the Royal Commission on Marriage and Divorce recommended that A.I.D. without the husband's consent should be a ground for dissolution of marriage.[4]

Is a child born as a result of A.I.D. legitimate? There is no decisive common law authority; A.I.D. is not publicized, and if the husband consents, no one is likely to raise the point. There is also a strong presumption of legitimacy.

Probably sterilization, except on grounds of medical necessity, is illegal at common law:[5] some American states have statutes providing for the compulsory sterilization of mental defectives,[6] although many of these statutes have been challenged as unconstitutional. Nazi Germany used it as a means of race extermination, and this has caused a wide revulsion against the practice. It was at one time thought that criminality was a biological characteristic, and that a careful use of sterilization would reduce the criminal propensities of the community—but this view is not accepted today.[7]

(ii) *Parent and child.* The age of majority has varied through the years. Historically the young burgess reached full age when he could count money and measure cloth, the young sokeman at 15, and the tenant by knight service at 21. The latter became the age for the whole community.[8] The recommendation of the Latey Committee[9] was that, in view of the increasing education and maturity of the younger generation, the age should be reduced to 18, and this was

[1] Ibid. 72–3.
[2] G. P. R. Tallin, 34 *Can. B.R.* (1956), 1, 166.
[3] *Maclennan* v. *Maclennan* (1958), *Scots Law Times* 12, cited N. St. John-Stevas, *Life, Death and the Law,* 130.
[4] Cmd. 9678, paras. 90, 318; N. St. John-Stevas, op. cit. 133–4.
[5] Lord Denning, *Bravery* v. *Bravery*, [1954] 3 All E.R. 59 at 67–8; quaere if it is to prevent the transmission of a hereditary disease.
[6] N. St. John-Stevas, op. cit. 165.   [7] See *infra,* § 80.
[8] Pollock and Maitland, *History of English Law,* ii. 438.
[9] (1967), Cmd. 3343.

adopted by Parliament in 1969.[1] The interests concerned are set out in this quotation:

> Whatever age may be fixed as the general age of majority, people will still make improvident contracts which they would not have made if they had been more experienced . . . The problem is to foresee whether, if the age of majority is reduced, the scale of improvident contracts made by people of the critical ages, will be too high a price to pay for the freedom of contract and the security of transactions which the reduction would achieve.[2]

Legal systems provide a wide range of types of relationship between parent and child, for, as in the case of husband and wife, civilization, with its increasing emphasis on the value of human personality, tempers the power of the strong out of consideration for the weak. The father's right to expose the new-born babe or to inflict the death penalty has been succeeded by rules which not only protect the life of the child but compel the parent to take active measures for the well-being of his offspring.

As between husband and wife, the former normally exercises the parental power, but, if the parties are divorced, English law requires the court to consider the welfare of the infant as the paramount consideration in deciding to whom custody of the children should be awarded. Thus the right of the parent is tempered by an emphasis on the duty to consider the needs of the child. Most modern systems also provide means by which a father may be forced to contribute to the upkeep of the child, and in extreme cases of cruelty or neglect, the parental power may be destroyed by an order of the court.

An interesting point of custody arose in a Victorian case. A mother claimed that she was given the wrong baby in hospital and brought a writ of habeas corpus to recover the child whom she claimed to be hers. The child was then over three years old. Barry J. held that the evidence was sufficient and granted custody to the applicant.[3] But he emphasized strongly the inappropriateness of the adversary procedure. The other family was quite convinced that no mistake had been made—the Court was not asked to order the exchange of the two babies, but only to deal with the custody of one. Yet if there had been an error, realistically the order of the court should deal with both children. The Full Court reversed this decision on appeal,

[1] Family Law Reform Act, 1969, c. 46.
[2] Report of the Law Reform Commission (N. S. Wales) (1969), L.R.C. 6, p. 8.
[3] *The King* v. *Jenkins*, [1949] A.L.R. 411.

holding that the evidence did not establish the matter as one of practical certainty.[1] This was a high burden of proof, but apparently the justification adopted was that the welfare of the child was paramount and that the court should not lightly remove a child from a home where it was happy. In the exercise of discretion, only the highest degree of proof would justify the court in disregarding other factors relating to the welfare of the child.

If paternity is in issue, a blood test may provide evidence—it cannot be proved by this means who is the father, but it may be confirmed that a person cannot be the father. Whether in particular circumstances the court should order the child to undergo a blood test, is a question of difficulty as is shown by two decisions of the Court of Appeal, in each of which there was a dissent.[2] The judgments show great concern with the welfare of the child. Thus Sachs L.J. considers the danger that the test might prove the child illegitimate, and he realistically emphasizes that the attitude to illegitimacy of the general population must be considered: one must not merely apply the humanitarian thought of the court, the attitude of London, or even that of the legislature and then decide that illegitimacy is really no disadvantage. 'It is a very practical, human question and I say no more than that the onus is on those who seek to assert that the human outlook has changed.'[3] London is not necessarily representative of England, and who can tell what will be the attitude of the child himself to his illegitimacy? These two cases are a striking example of the desire of the courts to get beneath the technical rules to a discussion of the human issues involved.[4]

In an application by four illegitimate children for provision to be made under the Victorian equivalent of the Testator's Family Maintenance Act, Smith J. stated:[5] 'The task of determining what provision a wise and just person in the situation of this father would have made for the four plaintiffs is rendered difficult by the fact that, in this community, attitudes towards persons, whether infants or adults, who have been born out of wedlock, have been changing.'

---

[1] [1949] V.L.R. 277 and 80 C.L.R. 626.

[2] *W.* v. *W.*, [1970] 1 All E.R. 1157, and *S.* v. *McC. and M.*, same volume, 1162. The House of Lords in *S.* v. *S.*, [1970] 3 All E.R. 107, affirmed the second case, but reversed the first.

[3] *S.* v. *McC. and M.*, *supra* at 1167.

[4] Lord Reid in *S.* v. *S.*, [1970] 3 All E.R. at 111, agreed that on average it is still a considerable disadvantage to be illegitimate. Whatever the attitude of the law, the community may be slow to change its views.

[5] *Re Wren (deceased)*, [1970] V.R. 449.

Parental power ends when the child reaches the age of majority. This has varied from the fourteen years of Roman law to the twenty-five years of middle French. Because it was clear that the Roman limit was too low, the praetor developed special protection for those under twenty-five years. Many systems allow a parent to emancipate a child at any age, or on the attainment of a certain age before majority would be achieved. In some countries marriage of an infant ends parental power, but normally the consent of a parent is necessary before such a marriage can take place. Adoption may destroy the power of a natural parent and place the child under the control of another. At common law the power of the parent lasts till the age of twenty-one years is reached. On the other hand, if the child is over sixteen years of age, the court would consult the wishes of the child and might, in the exercise of its discretion, refuse to act in habeas corpus proceedings.[1] By statute, majority is now achieved at the age of eighteen years.[2]

The parent or guardian has a right availing against persons generally that there shall be no unjustifiable interference with the control over the child. This is a right *in rem* on breach of which a remedial right *in personam* arises against the particular wrongdoer. Various rules of English criminal law protect a father's rights over his children, e.g. abduction of a girl under sixteen is a crime. The law of tort compensates a father for any loss of service caused by an injury tortiously inflicted on the child.

There is the question of the power of the parent over property acquired by the child. In Roman law the *paterfamilias* automatically obtained title to everything acquired by those in his power. But the strictness of the law was tempered by the institution of the *peculium* —the *paterfamilias* could grant to the son a sum of money of which the latter had actual control although legal title remained in the father. The rules concerning the *peculium castrense* went even farther—the father had no immediate interest in money earned by the son on military service, although the father took it if the son died without disposing of it by will. The individualism of modern systems allows a child to hold title to all property earned by or given to him, although naturally it is necessary to circumscribe his actual control in his own

---

[1] *Lough* v. *Ward*, [1945] 2 All E.R. 338 at 348. And even where infants of tender years are concerned, the court may interview them to obtain information which will assist in the exercise of the court's discretion: *Ward* v. *Laverty*, [1925] A.C. 101 at 107. *R.* v. *Murdoch ex p. Hoath*, [1940] V.L.R. 61.

[2] *Family Law Reform Act*, 1969, c. 46.

interest. In English law the trust has proved so useful that few legal difficulties arise. But in countries where this device is not used, a 'statutory agent' is set up to act on behalf of the infant who is fatherless.

3. Right to economic benefits

(i) *Property.* This must inevitably be discussed fully in the analytical survey which follows.[1]

(ii) *Right to rely on the representations or promises of others.* This is the sphere of juristic acts, the most important of which is a contract.[2] The tort of deceit furnishes a remedy for a wilfully false statement made with intent that the plaintiff shall act in reliance on it, with the result that he does so act and thereby suffers loss. The wrong of injurious falsehood protects a plaintiff against misrepresentations made concerning him. Deceit lies only if the defendant knew that the statement was false; apart from the rules governing special relationships, there was no action for negligent statements which cause loss.[3] If I repair a motor-car, I owe a duty of care in tort towards subsequent users of the car, but if I report on a company balance-sheet, the Court of Appeal held in 1951 that I am not responsible in tort for loss which results from my negligent statement, provided that I can prove that I honestly believed the statement to be true. The House of Lords overruled this case in 1964,[4] holding that there could be liability for the consequences of a negligent statement where the defendant possesses special skill and ought to know that the other party relies on his statement.

(iii) *Professional activities.* The law begins with a bias towards freedom. 'Ingrained in the personal status of a citizen under our laws was the right to choose for himself whom he would serve and . . . this right of choice constituted the main difference between a servant and a serf.'[5] Article 19 of the Universal Declaration of Human Rights condemns discrimination based on race, sex, language, religion, political or other opinion, property status or national or social origin. A restraint of trade is prima facie against public policy and must be justified within the narrow rules which English law enforces—i.e. the

[1] *Infra*, Ch. XXI.   [2] *Infra*, Ch. XVII.
[3] *Candler* v. *Crane, Christmas & Co.*, [1951] 2 K.B. 164.
[4] *Hedley Byrne & Co. Ltd.* v. *Heller and Partners Ltd.*, [1964] A.C. 465. In this case the defendants had expressly disclaimed responsibility, and so escaped. Cf. also *M.L.C. Assurance Co. Ltd.*, v. *Evatt*, [1971] 1 All E.R. 150.
[5] Per Lord Atkin, *Nokes* v. *Doncaster Amalg. Collieries Ltd.*, [1940] A.C. 1014 at 1026.

restraint must be reasonable from the point of view of the parties and of the public, the burden of proof that the restraint is reasonable in the first sense being on him who desires to enforce it. 'Liberty to trade is not an asset which the law will permit (a man) to barter for money except in special circumstances and within well-recognized limitations.'[1] Where the relationship of master and servant is concerned it is permissible for the master to exact covenants protecting trade secrets and prohibiting solicitation of clients if the servant leaves his present employment, but the law will scrutinize jealously any covenant which unreasonably prevents the servant exercising in a new employment the subjective skill which he acquired in his former post. The master is not entitled to stifle all competition, for the community is interested in the free exercise by every man of his powers. But where a contract is made between the vendor and the purchaser of a business, the law recognizes two significant differences from the law of master and servant: firstly, the servant needs protection because he is in a weak economic position[2] whereas business firms or companies are more likely to be economic equals; secondly, unless the vendor can be prevented from re-entering the same business in the same locality, it will not be possible to obtain an effective price for the sale of the goodwill. Hence where the agreement is between two companies, the court will not be quite so difficult to satisfy that the restraint is reasonable as between the parties. Theoretically it is also necessary to prove a second point—that the restraint is reasonable in the interests of the public, but there are not many cases where the first point was satisfied and the agreement was held invalid on the second.[3] The courts seem to assume that what is reasonable in the interests of the parties is also reasonable so far as the public is concerned.

A decision that breaks new ground is that of *Hivac Ltd.* v. *Park Royal Scientific Instruments Ltd.*[4] The Court of Appeal laid down that in the circumstances there was an implied term in a contract of service that the employee should serve with good faith and fidelity.

---

[1] *Vancouver Malt and Sake Brewing Co.* v. *Vancouver Breweries Ltd.*, [1934] A.C. 181 at 192.

[2] Per Evershed J., *Routh* v. *Jones*, [1947] 1 All E.R. 179 at 184. 'In contracts between a master and servant the latter is necessarily at a disadvantage and . . . there is . . . an obligation on the part of masters to be scrupulous to see that such covenants are framed with precision and care and do not attempt exaction beyond the requirements of propriety.'

[3] *Wyatt* v. *Kreglinger & Fernau*, [1933] 1 K.B. 793 does illustrate the emphasis on public interest.

[4] [1946] 1 All E.R. 350.

Plaintiffs had skilled workmen on their staff and defendants secretly persuaded them to work on Sundays for defendants' benefit. Where ordinary manual work is concerned, what a servant does in his own time is broadly his own affair, but in this case the servants were highly skilled and trained—in effect the defendants were secretly getting the benefit of plaintiffs' training in order to compete with them.

Economic security has been considered under the heading of social interests. This interest includes the right to work,[1] the right to minimum standards of remuneration, unemployment and sickness insurance, provision of reasonable hours of work, reasonable conditions of work, and holidays. The repudiation of *laissez-faire* is illustrated by the fact that articles are written on unfair dismissal and the right to reinstatement.[2] Trade unions and universities must observe the rules of natural justice in expelling a member.[3] If a union is strong enough to enforce a 'closed shop', expulsion of a member may destroy his livelihood.

How far should the State go in providing work in a time of economic stress? Can full employment always be achieved? There is increasing rejection of the iron laws of economics and an increasing realization of the duty of the State to create opportunities for employment, either directly by public works or indirectly by fostering new industries. The philosophy of the depression of the 1930s is now regarded as too quiescent.

4. *Political freedom*

Participation in government is an essential personal right, according to our modern democratic theory. It was Locke's merit to stress that the ruler was under a trust to regard the welfare of his subjects. It is not enough, however, to emphasize that the State exists for the benefit of men and not men for the glory of the State. A doctrine of the philosopher king may easily lead to despotism, however benevolent it may be. The dignity of human personality demands that the individual takes part in the selection of the fundamental policies which are to guide the welfare of the State.

---

[1] Universal Declaration of Human Rights, Art. 23.
[2] Cf. G. de N. Clark, 32 *Mod. L. R.* (1969), 532.
[3] *R.* v. *Senate of the University of Aston,* [1969] 2 All E.R. 964; *Leary* v. *National Union of Vehicle Builders,* [1970] 2 All E.R. 713. For the position of a teacher see *Hannam* v. *Bradford City Council,* C.A., [1970] 2 All E.R. 690.

Only in the Greek city state of moderate size could there be active participation by all citizens in a democratic assembly—and when we praise the Greek state we must remember that the slave was not considered a *persona*. In the modern state the power of the individual can be exercised only indirectly.

There are two aspects of political rights: the right to vote and the right to be elected. High property qualifications may prevent the exercise of the people's will, or the existence of a second chamber elected on a restricted franchise may act as a brake on progress.[1] True democracy, in the sense of an active exercise of political rights by all adult members of the community is a rare phenomenon. It can be achieved only if there is a minimum standard of education and of political insight. Without these factors universal suffrage provides only an instrument on which the demagogue, or strongly organized vested interests, may play. The fact that in Australia voting has been made compulsory provokes cynical reflections on the modern attitude to the rights for which our fathers fought.

Hence while a first and obvious step is to remove the more obvious discriminations, that is only the beginning of the long road to self-government. The philosopher would emphasize that self-government has an individual as well as a social meaning—it is only so far as the individual is willing to show restraint and play the game within the rules that a stable and progressive community can be achieved. For all its faults, it is the glory of the English tradition that it has achieved respect for the law and on the other hand a willingness to change that law as social philosophy develops. What other countries have achieved through revolutions, England achieves by the ballot box.

The desire to place a fundamental law above the dangers of popular change has virtues, but it may easily become anti-democratic if the fundamental rights thus protected are interpreted by a court with its eye on the past rather than the future. This is illustrated by the attitude of the American Supreme Court in the past to social reforms.[2]

The so-called 'right to demonstrate' has provoked much discussion.[3] Opposition to the war in Vietnam or to a tour by South African cricket teams provokes a desire to express dissent by overt action.

---

[1] This is not confined to the Old World. In Victoria (Australia) the upper house until 1950 was elected on a very restricted franchise.

[2] *Supra*, § 33, dealing with the doctrine of natural rights and the interpretation of the XIVth Amendment.

[3] See Note, 86 *L.Q.R.* (1970), 1; D. G. T. Williams, 28 *Camb. L. J.* (1970), 96.

Democratic states recognize the right to demonstrate as such, but a procession may disrupt traffic or provoke violence by those with opposing views. To wave placards attacking racial discrimination is one thing: to dig up a cricket pitch goes beyond freedom to dissent and is a gross interference with property rights.

'Everyone has the right publicly to protest against anything which displeases him and publicly to proclaim his views, whatever they might be. It does not matter whether there is any reasonable basis for his protest or whether his views are sensible or silly.'[1] But such a right does not justify planning a demonstration that disrupts the hearing of a case in the law courts.[2]

[1] Per Salmon L.J., *Morris* v. *Crown Office*, [1970] 1 All E.R. 1079 at 1086.
[2] Same case.

REFERENCES

ABEL-SMITH, B., and STEVENS, R., *Lawyers and the Courts* (1967).
ALLEN, C. K., *Legal Duties*, 249.
CHRISTIE, I. M., *The Liability of Strikers in the Law of Tort* (1967).
DEVLIN, Lord, *The Enforcement of Morals* (1965).
FRIEDMANN, W., *Legal Theory* (1967), Part III.
—— *Law in a Changing Society* (1959).
FULLER, L., *Morality of Law* (1964).
GINSBERG, M. (ed.), *Law and Opinion in England in the 20th Century*.
HART, H. L. A., *Law, Liberty and Morality* (1963).
KEITH, K. J. (ed.), *Essays on Human Rights* (1969).
Law and Contemporary Problems, vol. 31 (1966), no. 2 (Privacy).
O'SULLIVAN, R., 1 *Mod. L. R.* (1937), 27.
PEDRICK, W. D., 20 *Univ. of Toronto L. R.* (1970), 391.
POUND, R., 57 *Harv. L. R.* (1943–4), 1.
Privacy and the Law, a Report by Justice (1970).
ROLPH, C. H., *Books in the Dock* (1969).
ST. JOHN-STEVAS, N., *Life, Death and the Law* (1961).
STONE, J., *Province and Function of Law*, chs. xx, xxi, xxii.
The Jurisprudence of Interests (trans. and ed. M. M. Schoch), 20th Century Legal Philosophy Series, vol. ii (1948).
The Obscenity Laws—A Report by the Working Party set up by a Conference convened by the Chairman of the Arts Council of Great Britain (1969).
WARREN, S. D., and BRANDEIS, L. D., 4 *Harv. L. R.* (1890–1), 193.
WINFIELD, P. H., 47 *L.Q.R.* (1931), 23.
ZANDER, M., *Lawyers and the Public Interest* (1968).
—— (ed.), *What's Wrong with the Law* (1970).

BOOK III

SOURCES OF LAW

VI

THE SOURCES OF LAW

§ 39. MEANING OF THE TERM SOURCE

THE term *sources of law* has many meanings and is a frequent cause of error unless we scrutinize carefully the particular meaning given to it in any particular text. The philosophical school treat under the heading of the source of law some of the deepest problems of legal philosophy. Thus Gurvitch says that the question of the source of law is only one aspect of the general study of the validity of law.[1]

A formal source of law is defined by Salmond as that from which a rule of law derives its force and validity;[2] the material source is that from which is derived the matter, not the validity, of the law. The formal source of the law is the will of the State as manifested in statutes or decisions of the courts. An example of a material source is custom; the rule which the judge fashions into law may be drawn from the life of the community, but what gives it legal force is not the custom but the solemn determination of a court. However, this approach depends upon the particular definition of law which Salmond adopts.[3] If law is regarded as being created by the will of the State, then that is the formal source of law. If law is the command of the sovereign, then the sovereign is the formal source.

But, if we adopt a different definition, we may well reach the conclusion that the formal source is elsewhere. If law is valid because it is the embodiment of natural law or of absolute justice, then the source of law is the ideal we have laid down. If law is valid because it is the product of an inner sense of right, then that sense of right is the source

---

[1] *L'Expérience juridique*, 229.
[2] *Jurisprudence* (9th ed.), § 44. (In the 12th ed., 109, the relevant wording is changed.)
[3] *Supra*, § 23.

of law; this is the view of the historical school. Del Vecchio regards the source of law as being in the nature of man.[1] If law is valid because it is the product of custom, then the habits of the people are the source of law. Writers who adopt these views do not regard the State as the source of law.

The division of sources into formal and material is usually accepted, however difficult the actual application may be. But Dr. Allen has entered a protest:[2] and so many different theories have now been woven around the term 'source' that it is better to use other terminology and to ask: What is the secret of the validity of law? Whence comes the material from which law is fashioned?[3] What are the historical or causal influences which explain why the law is now as it is seen to be?[4]

In the modern state the law is normally created by the formal act of legislation or the decision of a court, or else by the act (whether legislative or judicial) of a subordinate person or group of persons acting within the limits of delegated authority.[5] The material sources are very comprehensive, since they include anything that may be drawn into the process of creation. Thus an English judge may adopt a principle from an ancient Roman text or a modern American case, from a text-book of law or a custom of the community.

It is necessary to remember that the formal validity of law, as seen from within any particular legal system, will be tested by rules of recognition provided by that legal system itself. '. . . when it is said that "statute" is a source of law, the word "source" refers not to mere historical or causal influences but to one of the criteria of legal validity accepted in the legal system in question. Enactment as a statute by a competent legislature is the *reason* why a given statutory rule is valid law and not merely the *cause* of its existence.'[6] It is also necessary to distinguish between a legal system as a whole, and the rules which are said to be law within a particular legal system.

---

[1] *Le Problème des sources* (Inst. int. de phil. du droit), 21.
[2] *Law in the Making* (7th ed.), 1–5.
[3] These questions are discussed above in Chs. IV and V.
[4] H. L. A. Hart, *Concept of Law.*
[5] *Infra*, § 75, for a discussion of the precise distinction between legislation, judicial decision, and administration.
[6] H. L. A. Hart, *Concept of Law*, 246.

VII

CUSTOM

§ 40. Origin and Limits of Custom

The origin of custom is a question that has been little studied until comparatively recent times. Prior to the birth of modern anthropology, the beginnings of the community were sought by abstract speculation and not by field investigation of primitive communities.[1] Savigny in 1814 emphasized the necessity of historical study: Maine wrote brilliantly on primitive communities, being stirred by his knowledge of the East to undertake comparative studies.[2] This stimulated English jurists to a more realistic study. What is amazing is that, although Maine wrote before modern anthropology was created, his work still remains fruitful. Further research has revealed errors both in his appreciation of Roman law and the Eastern communities, but the broad outlines of his contribution remain of real value.

Towards the end of the nineteenth century, anthropology became a field study and our knowledge of primitive man has greatly increased. In this century the work of Malinowski[3] and H. I. Hogbin[4] has shown that the Pacific provides a field for comparative study. The work of D. F. Thomson[5] and T. G. H. Strehlow[6] among the Australian aborigines is based on long residence with the tribes. We are still, however, only on the fringe of the problem. What has been achieved is scientific analysis and a realization that the problem must be attacked after putting away our modern prejudices. It is as yet too early to pronounce dogmatic generalizations concerning the origin of custom and its relationship to law.

Maine's theory of legal evolution was that first came Themistes, the judgments of inspired kings[7]—next came custom which was really created by the judgment, and finally the code which ends spontaneous development and forces the judge to rely on fictions and equity. But the slightest actual investigation of primitive communities proves that

[1] The classical study is that of C. K. Allen, *Law in the Making* (7th ed.), chs. i and ii.
[2] *Ancient Law* (1861); *Early Law and Custom* (1883).
[3] *Argonauts of the Western Pacific*; *Crime and Custom in Savage Society*.
[4] *Law and Order in Polynesia*.
[5] *Economic Structure and the Ceremonial Exchange Cycle in Arnhem Land*.
[6] *Aranda Traditions*.   [7] *Ancient Law*, ch. i.

custom is anterior to kings and courts.[1] Indeed, custom is coeval with the very birth of the community itself.

Habit,[2] sentiment, desire to satisfy public opinion and vanity—these play their part in the primitive community and they have not lost their force in the modern world. But these alone will not solve the problem why custom is followed. Primitive communities naturally must have their criminal law—certain offences must be stamped out. But there is also the equivalent of civil law—though whether we should use that term may be a matter of debate. Any community, however primitive, demands co-operation. It is the recognition of mutual obligation that is the driving force—if one does not fulfil his duty, he is excluded from the community. Religious beliefs also play a part. 'The *kipua* of Ontong Java are believed to punish, not actual breaches of obligation, but failure to reach a socially approved standard of performance.'[3] Collective religious ceremonies help to provide belief in a body of tradition and in the unity of the tribe. Sorcery is often used in an anti-social way, but it is also one of the weapons for enforcing the observance of customs. Supernatural sanctions are often feared by primitive man, but they are not automatic and sometimes a counter magic is available which is believed to avert the consequences of the breach of a tabu.[4] This illustration shows that there is no spontaneous and slavish adherence to the rules of custom, as some writers have thought. The savage is occasionally desirous of escaping his obligations just as is civilized man.

Suicide cannot be called a legal sanction, but it is sometimes the result of outraged public opinion. Malinowski relates that a youth who committed misconduct with a girl denied to him by the rules of exogamy, was so taunted in public for the incest that he put on festive attire and committed a ceremonial suicide by jumping from the top of a palm tree. In this case, in spite of the general horror of incest, public opinion had not been stirred till the youth's rival made accusation and aroused public indignation.[5]

An interesting analysis is that of Llewellyn and Hoebel in dealing with the Cheyenne Indians.[6] Their postulates are that we have three essential elements in any community: the group, the existence of divergent desires within the group, and claims made by some members

---

[1] P. Vinogradoff, *Collected Papers*, ii. 420.
[2] D. F. Thomson, *Economic Structure in Arnhem Land*, 34, stresses the influence of tradition.   [3] H. I. Hogbin, *Law and Order in Polynesia*, 289.
[4] B. Malinowski, *Crime and Custom*, 80-1.   [5] Ibid. 78-9.
[6] *The Cheyenne Way*, ch. x.

against others or against the group. If the group is to remain a community, the resulting problems must be met. The authors rightly emphasize that the terms *custom* and *mores* are not accurate enough to deal with the problem. Firstly, even in a primitive community we soon reach a distinction between what is done and what ought to be done. Secondly, there is sometimes a conflict between the family, the band, the military society, and the tribe. Each may have its own norms which must somehow be reconciled with those of the group. It is not a mere conflict between the individual and society. Thirdly, the word custom sometimes lends a seeming solidity to practices which are still in the way of being established. The two main factors in the dynamics of a legal order, Llewellyn and Hoebel find to be drift and drive, the first an unconscious development, the second a conscious individual demand. It is the latter element that causes the growth of law, for this produces the problems which society must solve.[1] The 'trouble spots' are the source of law, but we get a false view both of ancient and modern law if we concentrate exclusively upon them.[2]

Custom is useful to the lawgiver and codifier in two ways. It provides the material out of which the law can be fashioned—it is too great an intellectual effort to create law *de novo*.[3] Psychologically, it is easier to secure reverence for a code if it claims to be based on customs immemorially observed and this is true even though historically the claim cannot be substantiated. There is inevitably a tendency to adopt the maxim 'whatever is is right'—what has been followed in the past is a safe guide for the future. Bracton and Beaumanoir used the buttress of custom when dealing with the difficulty felt as to the power of a single judge to lay down the law.[4] From time to time individual claimants voice demands which either are not covered by existing rules or run counter to them. The crucial question is how those demands are dealt with in the community. If such a matter is dealt with in a way which establishes a new rule then a new community practice may be germinated.

[1] Borrowing horses without permission was permissible among the Cheyennes if a security was left: but it caused trouble, so a new rule was made by the Elk soldiers prohibiting borrowing without asking (*The Cheyenne Way*, 127–8).

[2] B. Malinowski, *Crime and Custom*, 73, points out that anthropology has been retarded by emphasis on the sensational.

[3] It is not suggested that codes are merely formulations of existing custom—sometimes the driving force is to abrogate old customs, or to choose the custom of one district and apply it to a wider realm. The very incompleteness of some early codes shows that they were not intended to state all the law—they presupposed a mass of accepted customs: W. Seagle, *Quest for Law*, 111.

[4] T. F. T. Plucknett, *Concise History of the Common Law* (4th ed.), 221 n.

Custom is not always based on abstract justice—the obvious example of slavery illustrates this. Savigny's view that custom springs from an inner sense of right cannot be substantiated. It is often asked whether conviction generates practice, or practice conviction.[1] If we emphasize too much the first alternative, this suggests that the community logically faces its problems and devises self-consciously the best rules. This is a false picture—the growth of much custom is not the result of conscious thought, but of tentative practice. When a problem arises—strife between two members of the community—then an answer must be found: but tact, a sense of the merits, and an appreciation of the strength of each faction play a greater part than any desire to find a rule that is logically justifiable. But once a rule is adopted, practice generates conviction. To primitive man as to the child, what has been done is the thing that ought now to be done.

The mark which distinguishes custom in the legal sense from mere convention is the *opinio necessitatis*, the recognition that there is authority behind it.[2] In the modern state the custom, if legally recognized, has behind it the court and an apparatus of coercion. In primitive communities we do not find authority necessarily organized in the institutional sense. We must ask, 'what is the ultimate power in the group to settle conflicts or to prescribe rules'? It may be the old men, the military group, the priests, or merely a general consensus of opinion. But the *opinio necessitatis* can come into existence only when the community in some way throws its force behind the particular rules. No exhaustive study exists of the psychological factors which create the *opinio necessitatis* in the primitive community.

Custom in its early stages is somewhat vague—it can be made into an effective rule of law only if the practice is hardened and made definite. This can occur only by the slow work of the courts, as technical rules are fashioned out of the raw material afforded, or by legislation, since writing inevitably sharpens the vague outlines of custom.

Custom is not necessarily immemorially old. All customs must have begun at some time and Azo regarded a custom as *long* if it was ten years old, *very long* if thirty years, and *ancient* if forty.[3] Custom, therefore, is more flexible than is sometimes supposed. The test of

---

[1] C. K. Allen, *Law in the Making* (7th ed.), 83.

[2] W. Seagle, *Quest for Law*, 33, makes the problem rather too easy when he states that custom is obeyed merely because it is the custom. 'Custom must be conceded to be sovereign if it is to discharge its social function.'

[3] T. F. T. Plucknett, *Concise History of the Common Law* (4th ed.), 291.

immemorial observance which English law now applies to special custom is a mark of modern and not primitive law.

The task of the law is so to adjust behaviour that the group can remain a group and can spend its energies on more vital matters than internal strife.[1] But the more complex society becomes, the less effective is custom: the test of custom is continued observance and customs *ex hypothesi* cannot be suddenly created to meet a new problem. Again, the most effective way to prevent disputes is to lay down rules in advance—custom is useful for situations that have already occurred, but cannot create a rule to deal with a future difficulty.

In Roman law we find little light. There are titles that deal with the topic, but they are very obscure.[2] Nevertheless, there is sufficient discussion to reveal that custom did play a considerable part in the evolution of the law. It was even thought that custom could effectively abolish a statute. Julian is cited by the Digest as approving this view on the ground that it is immaterial whether the people expresses its will tacitly by conduct or by a formal statute.[3] It is unlikely that Justinian regarded this as applying to his own laws. There are some traces in Scots law of the same theory, though it seems to be limited to statutes passed prior to the Union with England.[4]

§ 41. The Common Law Approach

Blackstone distinguished general custom which became the common law from particular custom which affected only a particular class or the members of a particular locality. It was the traditional view of English writers that the common law was but general custom. We cannot literally accept this view in the sense that the judges were a mere instrument for recording rules already established. But the whole course of pleading assumed the vitality of custom. Thus common carriers were first charged on the custom of the realm, until finally it was not thought necessary to plead the custom.[5] But for the establishment of itinerant justices, it is possible that the types of local custom would have been more diversified. These justices did much to create a uniform common law.

---

[1] K. N. Llewellyn and E. A. Hoebel, op. cit. 290.

[2] Dig. 1. 3; C. 8. 52; C. K. Allen, *Law in the Making* (7th ed.), 80 et seq.

[3] Dig. 1. 3. 32. 1; W. W. Buckland and A. D. McNair, *Roman Law and Common Law*, 15.

[4] W. M. Gloag and R. C. Henderson, *Introduction to the Law of Scotland* (2nd ed.), 3–4. The argument was advanced to Neville J. in *Luby* v. *Warwickshire Miners' Association*, [1912] 2 Ch. 371, but rejected.

[5] *Pozzi* v. *Shipton* (1838), 8 Ad. & E. 963.

The mark of special custom is that it is confined to a particular class or a particular locality—it is, therefore, an exception from the general law of the land. The tests for the existence of custom are fully treated by Allen.[1] The following are the most important: (a) the custom must not conflict with any fundamental principle of the common law; (b) the custom must have existed from time immemorial, which by a legal convention is set at 1189; (c) it must have been continuously observed and peaceably enjoyed; (d) it must be certain; (e) it must not conflict with other established customs; (f) finally, it must be reasonable.

Is a custom which satisfies the tests law before it has been adjudicated upon by a court, or does it become law only when it receives the judicial stamp of approval? However we answer, we run into difficulties. If judicial approval is necessary, then a custom which is so universally recognized that it is never questioned cannot be a rule of law. If we state that the decision of a court is unnecessary, then who is to decide on the application of such tests as reasonableness? Those who define law in terms of the sovereign cannot admit any other source of law. But Allen believes that with exceptions which 'do not seriously affect the guiding principle, if a custom is proved in an English court by satisfactory evidence to exist and to be observed, the function of the court is merely to declare the custom operative law. In other words, the custom does not derive its inherent validity from the authority of the court, and the "sanction" of the court is declaratory rather than constitutive.'[2] Most of the tests certainly relate to proof of the existence of the custom, but the last (that of reasonableness) gives to the court a discretion in recognizing the custom.[3] On Allen's own admission, if the court thinks that a custom was unreasonable in its origin, or that today it conflicts with a fundamental principle of the common law or with doctrines of public policy, it must be disregarded.

Lord Cranworth, however, wrote that 'when it is said that a custom is void because it is unreasonable, nothing more is meant than that the unreasonable character of the alleged custom conclusively proves that the usage, even though it may have existed immemorially, must have resulted from accident or indulgence, and not from any right conferred in ancient times on the party setting up the custom'.[4] In

---

[1] *Law in the Making* (7th ed.), ch. ii.   [2] Op. cit. 130.   [3] Op. cit., Appendix.
[4] *Salisbury (Marquis)* v. *Gladstone* (1861), 9 H.L.C. 692 at 701–2. Compare *North and South Trust Co.* v. *Berkeley*, [1971] 1 All E.R. 980, where an alleged custom relating to brokers was held unreasonable.

Wolstanton Ltd. and A.-G. of Duchy of Lancaster v. *Newcastle-under-Lyme Corporation*,[1] the House of Lords held unreasonable an alleged custom for the lord to get minerals beneath the surface of copyhold or customary freehold lands without making compensation for subsidence and damage to buildings, on the ground that the lands of the copyholder might be made practically useless, although he would still be liable to pay rents and perform stipulated services. The custom was of an oppressive character and more probably founded in wrong and usurpation than in the voluntary consent of the copyholders.[2]

It is sometimes suggested that a custom is law before adjudicated upon by a court because, if approved, it will have retrospective effect. But this applies to all judicial decisions on the common law, whether founded on custom or not. If the Court of Appeal lays down a particular doctrine, and ten years later the decision is overruled by the House of Lords, was the doctrine law between those two dates? The usual English view is that it was not. The House of Lords, according to the accepted fiction, merely lays down what is, and always has been, the law. From the point of view of citizens concerned with the practical application of the law by a hierarchy of courts, of course, this can appear to make pure nonsense.[3]

Mercantile law, perhaps, provides one of the most interesting examples of custom. Can a custom of modern origin have effect in changing the law? In *Crouch* v. *Crédit Foncier*,[4] it was decided that a mercantile custom to treat debenture bonds payable to bearer as negotiable instruments was invalid, as it was a custom of recent origin and not of immemorial antiquity. However, in *Goodwin* v. *Robarts*,[5] Cockburn C.J. refused to treat the law merchant as fixed and stereotyped. Salmond himself considered that the first decision represented the most logical view, the second the more convenient. In fact, very little of the law merchant has existed from time immemorial— certainly the concept of negotiability in its full development is more recent than 1189. Are we not dealing in this case with general custom? It is true that the law merchant once applied only to a special class,

---

[1] [1940] A.C. 860.
[2] At 878.
[3] e.g. see *Re Waring (deceased), Westminster Bank Ltd.* v. *Burton-Butler*, [1948] Ch. 221; and note the interesting possibilities raised by a case like *Doyle* v. *Vance* (1880) 6 V.L.R.(L) 87. In that case the full court of the Supreme Court of Victoria held that there could be strict liability for damage caused by a trespassing dog. Inferior courts in Victoria may well be bound to follow that decision, yet it would be overruled if it came before a higher tribunal.
[4] (1873), L.R. 8 Q.B. 374.
[5] (1875), L.R. 10 Ex. 337.

but it is now part of the law of the land.[1] Do the tests of special custom, which derogates from the common law, apply to general customs
(i.e. the common law)? Clearly, the common law in its modern form
has not existed from time immemorial. Indeed, as early as Henry IV,
it was laid down that existence from time immemorial was not necessary for a general custom, *car comen ley de cest realme est comen
custome de realme.*[2]

The problem is best discussed by looking at the history of the law
relating to negotiable instruments. The rules were first evolved by
custom—a special custom applicable only to those trading with merchants abroad. Gradually the same rules were applied to inland bills
in trading transactions, and finally the law was extended to cover all
transactions whether trading or not.[3] We see here the progress from
special custom to the common law itself. Hence the test of immemorial
user is not relevant. 'We cannot think that if a usage is once shewn to
be universal, it is the less entitled to prevail, because it may not have
formed part of the law merchant as previously recognised and adopted
by the Courts.'[4]

Another use of custom in English law is with reference to contract.
It may often be assumed, if there are no specific clauses in the contract to the contrary, that the parties intend to contract on the basis
of the usages of the trade. Thus general usage has been held enough
to create a general lien. 'Everybody knows, that, by the common law
a man may detain the commodity on which he has bestowed labour
or money. But this is a claim of a larger lien, and those who seek to
establish such a lien must shew a course of dealing so general and
uniform that persons must be supposed to form their contracts
tacitly on the understanding that there is such an usage.'[5]

---

[1] H. E. Salt in *Cambridge Legal Essays*, 279, suggests it is a confused analogy to
apply the rules of particular custom to the law merchant.
[2] 2 H. IV. 18 cited F. A. Greer, 9 *L.Q.R.* (1893), 153 at 157.
[3] F. A. Greer, 9 *L.Q.R.* (1893), 167; *Bromwich* v. *Loyd*, 2 Lutw. 1582.
[4] *Goodwin* v. *Robarts* (1875), L.R. 10 Ex. 337 at 356, per Cockburn C.J.
[5] *Bleaden* v. *Hancock* (1829), 4 Car. & P. 152 at 156, per Tindal C.J.

REFERENCES

ALLEN, C. K., *Law in the Making*, chs. i and ii.
CAMERON, J. T., 27 *Mod. L. R.* (1964), 306.
HOGBIN, H. I., *Law and Order in Polynesia.*

VIII

THE JUDICIAL METHOD

§ 42. INTRODUCTION

WHETHER a community lives in rural simplicity or in modern complexity, whether it pins its faith to case law or to a code, the judicial method plays an important part in the development of law. A study of the technique used by judges raises some of the most fundamental problems in jurisprudence, and in the English-speaking world no other part of the theory of law has provoked such a voluminous literature. Both the strength and weakness of the common law are revealed by the case method, but in a short chapter it is only possible to raise those general issues which are of most importance for jurisprudence.

§ 43. LAW, LOGIC, AND SCIENCE

How far can the task of the judge in developing the law be described as scientific? Or is it an art? It is convenient to approach this problem by a consideration of the theory of the logical plenitude of law. In a broad sense this theory means only that a judge cannot refuse to decide a case on the ground that there is no precise authority in point.[1] Electricity may raise new problems for the law of tort, but a court cannot dismiss a plea merely because there are no precedents dealing with this useful but dangerous force. In this particular instance old rules (either of negligence or strict liability) may be adapted to reach a solution; in other cases no existing rule may be applicable. Smart builds a tower so that he can broadcast the races which his neighbour conducts, and Smart's style is so graphic that many people prefer to listen to his commentary than to pay for admission to the race-course. His neighbour sues for the resulting loss.[2] No court is entitled to refuse to adjudicate merely because counsel can cite no authority on 'all fours'. The court may dismiss the plaintiff's request

---

[1] Thus Art. 4 of the French Civil Code lays down that a judge who refuses to decide a case on the ground that the law is silent or obscure is guilty of a denial of justice. This doctrine may be called the prohibition of *non liquet*: H. Lauterpacht, *Function of Law in the International Community*, 60 et seq.

[2] *Victoria Park Racing Co. Ltd.* v. *Taylor* (1937), 58 C.L.R. 479.

for a remedy, but even then a legal answer is given to the problem, for Smart has a legal right to continue the broadcasts. There is a great difference between deciding that there is no legal *answer* to the problem and decreeing that the defendant's conduct creates no right to a legal *remedy*. Understood in this sense, the theory of the logical plenitude of the law states the undeniable truth that law is not a mere collection of detailed rules, but an organic body of principles with an inherent power of growth and adaptation to new circumstances. In truth it does more than that, it does not state but it does assume that law is not only an organic body of principles but is a rational system for the exercise of authority by human beings. The theory then that all questions are capable of being disposed of according to law, even if it may be that the law requires that the precise question be not answered by a court, is not only logically justifiable but historically true; for we cannot conceive of the whole body of the common law descending from heaven and containing, even implicitly, the developed modern distinctions. Had *stare decisis* been interpreted in a narrow fashion as meaning that no decision could be given unless a clear precedent could be discovered, it is clear that our modern common law could not have been created.[1]

But we need only give a slight twist to our doctrine of the logical plenitude of law to make it a narrowing force. If we postulate that all problems can be solved purely by logical deductions from the actual rules in force,[2] we are depriving the law of all power to develop, and the dead hand of the past will crush its growth. An acute critic has shown the difficulties that have arisen in private international law from the tendency to treat certain dogmas as ends in themselves.[3] Law can develop only by perpetually drawing new values and solutions from the life of the community: this is achieved partly through the development of new law and partly through standards and principles which are implicit in particular branches of the law (e.g. reasonableness or public policy).[4]

In the golden age of rationalism men wished to construct a legal system analogous to Euclidean geometry, the basis of which is the assumption of self-evident truths or axioms and the deduction by

[1] The advance of technology provides many new problems for the law. Thus in international law, liability for space craft has become an important issue: see Bin Cheng, *Current Legal Problems* (1970), 216.

[2] This doctrine is sometimes attacked as the 'jurisprudence of conceptions' or 'mechanical jurisprudence'.

[3] W. W. Cook, *The Logical and Legal Bases of Private International Law.*

[4] *Supra*, § 35.

rigorous logic of the whole system from this base. The axioms of justice were to be discovered, and when a particular dispute came before the court for decision, the judges could say: 'Come, let us calculate.' If there was dissent, then the opinion of either the majority or the minority must contain within it a logical fallacy. It needs no argument today to convince the reader that the judicial method is not as simple as this. The difficulty of securing agreement as to the ends of law has already been discussed,[1] and if the ends of law cannot be rigidly determined, the argument for a 'legal geometry' is left without a foundation. Moreover, modern developments have shown that such a view of geometry was incorrect. Euclidean axioms are not 'self-evident' truths but convenient hypotheses, and it is possible to construct a useful and self-consistent geometry on the postulate (*inter alia*) that parallel lines always meet.[2] The practical test is which type of geometry is more suitable for a particular purpose.

The rules of formal logic are invaluable to the courts and the fallacies of an argument may sometimes be most easily exposed by casting it in the form of a syllogism.[3] Moreover, in systematizing the law, deduction from a general principle may serve to show the real source of a rule. But the syllogism is a method of demonstration rather than of discovery. From the two premisses 'All jurists are dull', 'Alfred is a jurist', we can draw the conclusion that 'Alfred is dull'. But the conclusion does not reveal to us any new truth, since it is implicitly contained in the premisses which have been assumed. The syllogism provides us only with a convenient method of stating conclusions which we have already reached.

The attempt to reduce law to a definite number of legal rules and to make the judicial task one of pure deduction alone has led to a reaction. The judge does not always find his general principle ready-made —frequently it may be implicit in a line of cases and the utmost subtlety may be necessary to discover it. Hence the worship of induction has become popular. Instead of starting with a general rule the judge must turn to the relevant cases, discover the general principle implicit in them, and then deduce from it the rule applicable to the case in hand. The outstanding difference between the two methods is

---

[1] *Supra*, § 36.
[2] For example, see the non-Euclidean geometries of N. I. Lobatschewsky and G. F. B. Riemann, discussed by J. H. Poincaré, *Science and Hypothesis*, 35 et seq.
[3] Cf. per Griffith C.J., *Scott* v. *Cawsey*, 5 C.L.R. 132 at 141; Simonds J., *Lewis and Co.* v. *Bell Property Trust*, [1940] 1 Ch. 345 at 350. J. Stone provides the most acute modern survey, *Province and Function of Law*, chs. vi, vii, though it suffers from taking a rather narrow view of logic: F. C. Hutley, 1 *Annual L. R.* (*W. A.*), 172.

in the source of the major premiss—the deductive method assumes it, whereas the inductive sets out to discover it from particular instances.[1] Hence there arises today an emphasis on the logic of discovery, and the drawing of an analogy between the task of the judge and that of the natural scientist. The latter, with a particular knowledge gained by many experiments, frames a provisional hypothesis (which he hopes will describe the facts), and then tests that supposition by making further experiments in order to assess the accuracy of the deduction drawn from it. It is argued that the judge frames a provisional rule to deal with a particular case; in further decisions the formulation of the rule is tested by application to new facts and perhaps it is adapted, modified, or restricted until finally the rule appears as a satisfactory tool of judicial technique. At best, however, this is only an analogy, as can be seen from the discussion of the function of the judge where there is no authority in point.[2] The scientist is seeking to *describe what is*, and objective tests may be used to discover the accuracy of the description. But the judge must *prescribe what ought to be*, and once we introduce the element of value there may be legitimate differences of opinion which cannot be decided by objective experiments.[3] In developing the standard of care to which motor-drivers ought to conform by applying to it the subtleties of the doctrine of contributory negligence, there is no easy test which a judge can use, for he is not trying to describe what motorists actually do, but what in contemplation of law they ought to do. As is shown in the next section, dissent in appellate courts, where there is no binding authority, is frequently due to differing notions as to the interests that the law should protect.

Moreover, a scientist is free to modify any theories which he finds inaccurate—his loyalty is to scientific truth and not to tradition. He is not bound to worship the golden idols of the past if they have feet of clay, but while a judge may not revere he is bound to follow such precedents as are binding upon him.[4] The common law doctrine of binding precedent has prevented final courts from engaging in tentative experiments and from correcting the mistakes of the past.

Thus the law of torts has two broad divisions, liability for negligence

[1] J. Dewey, 10 *Cornell L. Q.* (1924), 17, cited Jerome Hall, *Readings in Jurisprudence*, 343.
[2] *Infra*, § 46.
[3] Cf. J. Dickinson, 29 *Col. L. R.* (1929), 285 at 287–8; H. J. Laski, 2 *Politica* (1936), 115.
[4] *Leon* v. *Casey* (1932), 48 T.L.R. 452 at 455. Judges dislike having to give judgment against the merits on a technical point: *Rentit Ltd.* v. *Duffield*, [1937] 3 All E.R. 117.

and strict liability. In determining the boundary line between the two, the courts have not relied on logical deductions or *elegantia iuris*: the attempt has been rather to base rules on expedience and social custom. One who creates an abnormal risk should be strictly liable for any injury thereby caused. The legal formulation of this broad principle is that strict liability applies where there is an abnormally dangerous user of land.[1] To collect water within a reservoir subjects to strict liability,[2] but to install water-pipes in a house does not.[3] Gas mains in the street or high-tension electric cables are caught by the rule, but domestic electric wiring and gas-pipes are not.[4] Thus the application of this broad legal standard of unnatural user is a nice question of policy rather than the result of deduction from an accepted formula. If we emphasize the fact that 'burning off' an estate is beneficial in a grazing community because it reduces the risk of bush-fires at the peak of the hot season and because it is the best way to produce good pastures, we may (as some Canadian courts have done) regard this as a natural user of land;[5] if we emphasize the danger to others involved even in careful 'burning off' we may apply the doctrine of strict liability (as the Australian High Court has done).[6] In one sense courts are trying to evolve a reasonable hypothesis just as does the scientist, but the nature of the activity of each is fundamentally different.

In the present century the abuses created by attempts to treat the solution of legal questions as if they were theorems in geometry has led to a reaction, and (as is often the case) the reaction has gone too far. Holmes J. epigrammatically pointed out that 'the life of the law has not been logic: it has been experience',[7] and torn from its context[8] this has been used as a justification for the slogan 'trust life

---

[1] *Rylands* v. *Fletcher* (1868), L.R. 3 H.L. 330.

[2] This is a convenient phrase used in the American Restatement—there is actual liability only if damage follows and no particular defence can be proved.

[3] *Rickards* v. *Lothian*, [1913] A.C. 263 at 280–1.

[4] *Collingwood* v. *Home and Colonial Stores Ltd.*, [1936] 3 All E.R. 200.

[5] See J. T. Robinette, 11 *Can. B. R.* (1933), 88 at 99.

[6] *Hazelwood* v. *Webber* (1934), 52 C.L.R. 268. In this case, however, the 'burning off' was done in midsummer.

[7] *The Common Law*, 1. Lord Simonds, *Gilmour* v. *Coats*, [1949] A.C. 426 at 449, emphasizes that the common law approach is so empirical and historical that it is not possible to argue logically from the category of educational trusts to that of religious trusts. 'Moreover, it is not always possible for the law to be logical. It has to evolve practical and workable rules in the light of experience': per Thesiger J., *S.C.M. (U.K.) Ltd.* v. *W. J. Whittall & Son Ltd.*, [1970] 2 All E.R. 417 at 431.

[8] Holmes J. showed a nice sense of the influence of the logical structure of law, and a consideration of his writings reveals his true position. Cf. *Collected Legal Papers*, 167 et seq.

rather than theory'. Gény, Ehrlich, Gmelin, and Pound all show the abuses of a narrow logical method.[1] Ehrlich points to the profound wisdom of German legend which typifies the devil as a sharp dialectician. Some urge that common sense should be made the source of law—for the purely logical approach we should substitute a dynamic or psychological point of view.[2]

But Hoernlé reasonably asks why should logic be blamed.[3] This is due to two causes: firstly, the 'geometrical view' of law was regarded as the typical logical approach; secondly, the Kantian attempt to use a rigid logic of the *a priori* to determine the permanent element of law led to a reaction against logic as such instead of a dislike of this particular method. But the law cannot dispense with a logical method if it is to have any claim at all to rationality. Can we think at all without following the rules of logic? 'Formally, thinking is good or bad according as the conclusion does, or does not, follow from the premisses.'[4] Materially, thinking may be bad because of a narrow or unskilful choice of premisses. Undoubtedly in the past the premisses from which rules have been deduced have been rather narrow, but instead of attacking logic it would be more reasonable to broaden the foundations of the law.[5] Science once suffered from the attempt to deduce rules from so-called self-evident truths, but its great advance came from the recognition that there is a logic of discovery as well as that of the syllogism. The argument really comes to this—that modern authors suggest that the judicial method requires a broader approach. The categories of law are not ends in themselves but tools that should be adapted to serve the purposes of law. To give up logic because of the excesses of a particular method, or to worship irrationality because of the mistakes of the past, would be as wise as to sacrifice our eyes because occasionally we see what is not there.[6] To suggest that the best law can be achieved without a *proper* use of logic is simply nonsense. Moreover, the realist approach tends to underrate the effect of the judge's desire for certainty and a rock of authority on which to base the decision. If there is no actual binding authority,

---

[1] The most accessible source is *Science of Legal Method* (The Modern Legal Philosophy Series), F. Gény, 42, E. Ehrlich, 84, J. G. Gmelin, 92, R. Pound, 208. Review by R. F. A. Hoernlé, 31 *Harv. L. R.* (1918), 807.
[2] K. G. Wurzel, *Science of Legal Method*, 297.
[3] 31 *Harv. L. R.* (1918), 807.
[4] 31 *Harv. L. R.* (1918), 807 at 810.
[5] K. N. Llewellyn, *The Common Law Tradition, Deciding Appeals*.
[6] Morris Cohen, *Law and the Social Order*, 177; F. C. Hutley, 1 *Annual L. R.* (*W. A.*), 172.

logical argument from legal principles helps to lighten the responsibility of decision. It is absurd to suggest that all judges wish to bend the law to their individual whims: what most desire is a reasonable escape from the agony of decision.

§ 44. THE FACTS AND THE LAW

The task of the court in almost all actual litigation is to ascertain the issues in dispute between the parties and to determine those issues usually in favour of one or more of the parties to them and against the others. In the course of ascertaining and determining those issues the court must make such findings as to matters of fact as are relevant to the issues and as are permitted by the evidence adduced by the parties; and further, the court declares the rules or propositions of law which, in the light of the findings of fact and of the issues to be decided, justify the way in which the court resolves the issues. The distinction between fact and law is important in pleading and proof, the functions of judge and jury, appellate procedure, the theory of precedent, and the doctrine of *res judicata*.

At first sight the distinction between fact and law seems a simple one. Whether the fire that burned my neighbour's house started on my property is a question of fact: the rules that determine my liability raise a question of law. Bohlen has defined a fact as something which has happened or existed, including not only physical facts but also states of mind.[1] When did Smith die? Did Jones know of the existence of the lease? These are questions of fact. As opposed to the facts which describe what happened, law deals with the question of what ought to be done about those facts.

It would seem, then, that a court has two distinct processes: firstly to find the facts and then to apply the law. But this is a very superficial analysis, for the discovery of the facts and the law cannot be too sharply divorced. Even for science a fact is not a stubborn entity existing in the outside world, which of itself suggests the hypothesis which will describe it. Just as the relevancy of a particular fact is determined by the hypothesis which the scientist is investigating, so out of the tangled web of human affairs the law must decide what facts are material to the issue. In one sense we do not know what principles

---

[1] 72 *Univ. of Pa. L. R.* (1924), 112. J. B. Thayer writes: 'All enquiries into the truth, the reality, the actuality of things are enquiries into the fact about them': *A Preliminary Treatise of Evidence* (1898), 191. These references are cited by R. E. Paul, 57 *Harv. L. R.* (1944), 753.

of law are applicable until we know the material facts, but what facts are material in a given claim is determined by the framework of principles we call the law. To prove every fact would be futile, and the lawyer is guided in his proof by the particular rules that he thinks are applicable. When the client pours out his troubles to his solicitor, the first step is to discover the legal pigeon-holes in which the facts are to be placed. If the story is one of loss of reputation due to the verbal attack of a neighbour, then the lawyer brings to mind the rules of slander and searches for those facts which the law has declared to be essential to liability. The skill of the lawyer sifts the relevant factors from the mass of detail placed before him.

Moreover, it is not as easy to determine the meaning of the term fact as was suggested above. This has always proved a difficult problem for philosophy; and even in law, which is often content to ignore the problems of metaphysics, there are several uses of the term. Actually we can discover the meaning of the term *fact* only by examining the context in which it is used. Thus a question of fact is sometimes contrasted with a question of law, or a matter of fact with mere matter of opinion.

Firstly, the facts and the law are frequently contrasted. Even in this use there are several different shades of meaning:[1] indeed, 'fact and law are to some extent inextricable'.[2] There is no ultimate definition —much depends on the rules of the particular system in question. The question has been complicated by the division of functions between the judge and the jury. The general doctrine is that the jury must determine the facts and the judge the law. But there are many qualifications to be made before this statement can be accepted as accurate.

(*a*) The judge (in general) is not entitled to leave the case to the jury unless there is some evidence on which a reasonable man could decide for the plaintiff.

(*b*) Some questions of fact are determined by the judge. Presumably the existence of reasonable and probable cause is a question of fact, and yet it is the duty of the judge to decide this point in an action for malicious prosecution.

(*c*) The task of the jury is frequently to give a general verdict, e.g. finding a prisoner guilty of murder or a defendant of negligence.

---

[1] J. W. Salmond, *Jurisprudence* (12th ed.), 10; R. A. Brown, 56 *Harv. L. R.* (1943), 899; P. H. Winfield, 59 *L.Q.R.* (1943), 327.
[2] P. H. Winfield, op. cit. at 341; A. Farnsworth, 62 *L.Q.R.* (1946), 248.

Although the judge lays down the law, the jury must apply it to the facts and reach a conclusion that theoretically is a mixture of law and fact. When a jury decide that a plaintiff is guilty of contributory negligence, they must first determine what a reasonable man would do in the circumstances and then decide whether the particular plaintiff fell short of this test or not. The law is interested, not in the physical world as such, but in facts as seen by the law in relation to its particular frame of reference. It is true that in science also selection must be made, and that what are called facts are frequently the result of the application of a particular standard to a certain part of the material world. Thus we would regard the statement that a book is six inches long as a statement of fact, but, of course, this is discovered only by the application of a particular standard—the foot rule. It may be argued that this is analogous to the testing of human conduct by the criterion of the reasonable man. But there is one real difference— scientists have agreed on the acceptance of rigid standards and any argument concerning the length of a book may be easily tested. Human fallibility may cause error in carrying out difficult experiments, but there is no room for discretion as to what is really meant by the standard of the foot rule. When we analyse the criterion of negligence there is a large area of free play, for not all are agreed as to what action a reasonable man would take in the particular circumstances. Hence there is a blurring of the lines between questions of fact and of law which causes difficulty on appeal, for an appellate court is entirely free to correct an error of law, but is loath to upset a finding of fact by a jury unless it is one that could have been reached by no reasonable body of men. It has been wittily said that an appellate court is guided by its wish to uphold or reverse the particular decision: if it is desired to reverse the decision the court assumes jurisdiction because a point of law is involved; if it is wished to uphold the verdict it is treated as a particular finding of fact.[1] One writer remarks: 'The delusive simplicity of the distinction between questions of law and questions of fact has been found a will of the wisp. . . .'[2] If two persons both wrongly think that a flat is not subject to the Rent Restriction Act because of substantial alteration, is that a mistake of fact or of law? The difficulty of the problem is shown by a division in the Court of Appeal.[3] Denning L.J. distinguishes

---

[1] Cf. *The Heranger*, [1939] A.C. 94 at 101.

[2] N. Isaacs, 22 *Col. L. R.* (1922), 1.

[3] *Solle* v. *Butcher*, [1949] 2 All E.R. 1107; see also *Chandler* v. *Strevett*, [1947] 1 All E.R. 164 at 165.

primary facts (proved by witnesses or documents) from the conclusions or inferences deduced by a process of reasoning from them. If these conclusions can be as well drawn by a layman (properly instructed in the law) as by a lawyer, then they are conclusions of fact for the tribunal of fact: if, however, the conclusion to be drawn from the primary facts requires for its correctness determination by a trained lawyer, the conclusion is one of law, on which an appellate court is as competent to have an opinion as the tribunal of fact.[1] This is perhaps a working test—the difficulty being to determine when the inferences require determination by a trained lawyer. Later cases[2] more carefully limit the role to be played by courts of appeal, but they preserve the distinction between primary facts, and inferences to be drawn from them. The use of another formula does not remove the ambiguity inherent in the distinction between law and fact.

Secondly, fact and opinion are frequently contrasted. Whether a company has been prosperous in the past is a matter of fact, whether it will fulfil the expectations aroused by its prospectus is a matter of opinion. In the criminal law a person can be convicted of false pretences only if the pretence concerns a present state of fact—obtaining money by a promise to marry does not fall within this requirement as the pretence relates only to the future. Again, a witness is instructed that he must speak only of the facts—not give his mere opinions. In general, only one who has qualified as an expert witness can go beyond the facts. A witness in describing a motor-car accident should reveal what he actually saw, not what he imagined to happen. But the line is not easy to draw, as modern psychology and medicine show. The eye really sees very little and we infer the rest from a hasty glance. Even the most honest person finds it difficult to distinguish between what he actually saw just before a collision and the finished theory which his mind weaves out of the few blurred impressions imprinted on his retina. The eye-witness was once regarded as the best evidence—now learned doctors[3] write articles to show how the imperfect human sense may mislead even an impartial bystander with the result that he is quite convinced that he actually saw what did not take place.

---

[1] *British Launderers' Research Association* v. *Borough of Hendon Rating Authority*, [1949] 1 K.B. 462 at 471–2.
[2] *Watt* (or *Thomas*) v. *Thomas*, [1947] A.C. 484; *Benmax* v. *Austin Motor Co. Ltd.*, [1955] A.C. 370.
[3] 'The Credibility of the Eye-witness', by Dr. Hodgson in 7 *Medico-Legal R.* (1939), 108.

However difficult it may be to define the exact difference between law and fact, the distinction itself is fundamental for any legal system. Law consists of the abstract rules which attempt to reduce to order the teeming facts of life. Facts are the raw material on the basis of which the law creates certain rights and duties. We shall later divide facts into acts and events—the former being subject to human control and the latter designating those facts that occur without human intervention.[1]

§ 45. PRECEDENT

A court may be bound by statute or by the decisions of superior courts. In England the courts are imperatively bound by decisions of higher courts in the same hierarchy;[2] the Divisional Court[3] is bound by its own decisions. Single judges of the High Court are not strictly bound by their brother's decisions but they will as an ordinary practice follow them.[4] Decisions of the Judicial Committee of the Privy Council are absolutely binding on many courts in the Commonwealth, but the House of Lords, the Judicial Committee, and many appellate courts in Commonwealth countries reserve liberty to overrule their own decisions.[5]

The position of the Court of Appeal (Civil Division) is probably that it regards itself as bound by its own decisions unless the previous decision was given *per incuriam*, was opposed to a subsequent decision of the House of Lords, or there were previous conflicting decisions of the Court of Appeal.[6] This allows rather more flexibility than might be imagined.[7] Lord Denning thinks that the Court of Appeal should be free to overrule itself,[8] but there is not yet a majority

---

[1] *Infra*, § 67.

[2] The House of Lords regarded itself as bound by its own decisions from 1898 to 1966, when the Lord Chancellor made a statement abrogating the old rule. See J. Stone, 69 *Col. L. R.* (1969), 1163, for a penetrating theoretical analysis of the Lord Chancellor's statement.

[3] *Huddersfield Police Authority* v. *Watson*, [1947] K.B. 842; W. H. D. Winder, 9 *Mod. L. R.* (1946), 257.

[4] e.g. per Devlin J. in *Alma Shipping Co., S.A.* v. *V. M. Salgaoncar E. Irmaos Ltda.*, [1954] 2 Q.B. 94.

[5] But the Judicial Committee and the Appellate Courts in Commonwealth countries who reserve such liberty seem to be loath to overrule their own decisions; see Note, 68 L.Q.R. (1952), 142 and e.g. *Hughes and Vale Proprietary Ltd.* v. *State of New South Wales* (1953), 87 C.L.R. 49 per Dixon J. at p. 70, and *Attorney-General for New South Wales* v. *Perpetual Trustee Co.* (1952), 85 C.L.R. 237 per Dixon J. at pp. 243–4.

[6] *Young* v. *Bristol Aeroplane Co.*, [1944] 1 K.B. 718.

[7] R. N. Gooderson, 10 *Camb. L. J.* (1950), 432.

[8] *Gallie* v. *Lee*, [1969] 1 All E.R. 1062; *Hanning* v. *Maitland*, [1970] 1 All E.R. at 815.

decision of the Court of Appeal to this effect. With regard to the Criminal Division of the Court, the doctrine of *stare aecisis* 'does not apply in its full rigour'.[1]

An interesting point is made by Russell L.J.:[2]

This court is not omniscient in the law, nor are counsel, however eminent. We work under great pressure from the lists, and whilst not always ready to accept a concession on a point of law from the Bar it is not infrequent to do so, and moreover on a point essential to the decision of the appeal, without further investigation. We are attracted by a suggestion that the conceded point of law should be open to argument in another case, provided it is made plain that that should not be made the basis for the further suggestion that where an argument, though put forward, had been only weakly or inexpertly put forward, the point of law should similarly be open; for much uncertainty could thus be undesirably introduced.

The English doctrine of binding precedent differs from that of other systems, but it is a legitimate study for jurisprudence as one development of the judicial method. In most continental countries a long course of decisions may have very high persuasive authority, but no country pays to the single decision the deference of the English common law. Even in America, where the common law system was inherited, the doctrine of precedent is more liberal.[3]

The detailed rules actually adopted in England with respect to the binding nature of case law authority, and the difficulties encountered in their application, have been adequately set out elsewhere[4] and need not be elaborated upon here. The general theory and the recurring problems of theory and practice call for discussion however. Certain basic matters of terminology and of actual practice in the day-to-day work of the courts must be understood at the outset.

When it is said that a case is binding, what is it that binds?[5] It is often said that a previous case is binding only as to its *ratio decidendi*, and the *ratio* is distinguished from *obiter dicta* which do not bind.

---

[1] Per Widgery J., *R. v. Newsome*, [1970] 3 All E.R. 455. In particular a bench of five feels free to overrule a decision of a court of three: see also *R. v. Gould*, [1968] 2 Q.B. 65.

[2] *Joscelyne v. Nissen*, [1970] 1 All E.R. at 1223.

[3] *Univ. of Cincinnati L. R.* (1940), 203–355.

[4] Salmond (12th ed.), 141; C. K. Allen, *Law in the Making*, ch. iv; R. Cross, *Precedent in English Law* (1968). Although the courts sometimes discourage the citation of cases not reported by a barrister, a decision does not cease to be an authority merely because it is not reported in a recognized series: R. E. Megarry, 70 *L.Q.R.* (1954), 246.

[5] A. W. B. Simpson, *The 'Ratio Decidendi' of a Case and the Doctrine of Binding Precedent*, Oxford Essays in Jurisprudence (1961), 125. D. P. Derham, *Precedent and Particular Questions*, 79 *L.Q.R.* (1963), 49.

It is also said that the *ratio decidendi* of a case is the underlying principle or legal reason on which the result of the case depends. This is deceptively simple, as will be seen, and if combined with the proposition that it is only the *ratio decidendi* which has binding effect, then it leads to confusion and error. The classical view was that the *ratio* was the principle of law which the judge declared in his judgment to justify and explain his decision of the case. But it has been objected to that view that the ratio is the principle of law which links the ultimate determination of the case with the essential or material facts of it, and that the statement by the judge may or may not do that, or may be framed too widely or too narrowly.[1]

Ratio decidendi, literally, would refer to the 'reason of decision' or to the 'reason for deciding', but the use of the term to refer to the binding part of a case requires some attention to the actual terminology used in arguments about case law authority, for there has been much confusion. To begin with, *ratio decidendi* is almost always used in contra-distinction to *obiter dictum*. An *obiter dictum*, of course, is always something said by a judge. It is frequently easier to show that something said in a judgment is *obiter* and has no binding authority than it is to demonstrate that something said has binding authority. Clearly something said by a judge about the law in his judgment, which is not part of the course of reasoning leading to the decision of some question or issue presented to him for resolution, has no binding authority however persuasive it may be, and it will be described as an *obiter dictum*.

Other terms in common use must be made clear. The word 'decision' is used to refer to several different things. It is not a technical term of law with one fixed meaning. It may be used to mean the ultimate order the court makes to determine the case and on the strength of which one party or another may seek execution. Frequently it is used to refer to the whole case—instead of saying 'in a previous case', a lawyer may say 'in a previous decision'. Further it is commonly used to refer to the determination of a particular issue, and sometimes, more loosely, to refer to the reason for reaching such a determination. In the following paragraphs 'decision' will be used to refer to the decision of any issue in the course of judicial proceedings; 'order' will be used to refer to the final order made by

---

[1] A. L. Goodhart, 'Determining the *Ratio Decidendi* of a Case', in *Essays in Jurisprudence and the Common Law*, 1; all the American realists and most of the English and American text writers, e.g. J. W. Salmond, C. K. Allen, J. Stone, E. W. Patterson, and previous editions of this work.

the court and binding the parties to the proceedings; and 'judgment' will be used to refer to the reasons given by the judge to explain and justify his order.[1]

In *Re Hallett*[2] Sir George Jessel said: 'The only use of authorities, or decided cases, is the establishment of some principle which the Judge can follow out in deciding the case before him.' And again in *Osborne* v. *Rowlett*[3] he said: 'The only thing in a Judge's decision binding as an authority upon a subsequent Judge is the principle upon which the case was decided.' That kind of general view has been expressed many times by judges and others. It is seen as erroneous the moment the day-to-day practices of the courts are examined, however attractive it may seem and however much flexibility it may produce when made the basis for argument in the highest appellate courts. To understand the way courts actually function from day to day, it is necessary to appreciate the difference between different kinds of authoritative statements of law found in reported cases, and also the difference in practice at different levels of the judicial hierarchy.

First, it simply is not true to say that the only thing binding in a case is the principle upon which it was decided. One case may provide binding authority for many propositions of law. Each judicial decision of a question or issue leading to the determination of the whole case, whether in interlocutory proceedings or at trial, may provide binding authority. Many such decisions will provide precise answers to precise questions. If the same questions arise in subsequent proceedings in a subordinate court, they will bind that court to decide the question in the same way. This invokes the very core notion of a precedent system: that questions ought to be decided today in the same way as they were decided yesterday simply because they were decided that way yesterday. It provides the great bulk of binding authority actually applied by legal practitioners and by trial courts at all levels in their work. It is too frequently ignored in theoretical legal writing, perhaps because its day-to-day use is somewhat humdrum, and perhaps because it does not involve so obviously the

---

[1] For a useful discussion of the use of the various terms in this area see J. L. Montrose, 'Language of, and a Notation for, the Doctrine of Precedent', 2 *Univ. of Western Australia Ann. L. R.* (1952-3), 301, 504. In *R.* v. *Ireland*, [1970] A.L.R. 727, Barwick C.J. treats the judgment as the order of the court. If the judges in an appellate court agree in allowing an appeal, it is irrelevant that their reasons for so doing are conflicting or even contradictory.   [2] (1879), 13 Ch. D. 696 at 712.

[3] (1880), 13 Ch. D. 774 at 785, and see the vigorously expressed views of C. K. Allen, *Law in the Making* (7th ed.), ch. iv.

intriguing intellectual problems with respect to change and development in the law which are encountered when the authority of
principles or of more general propositions of law is in question.

The distinction between the binding nature of a decision on a particular question or issue and the binding nature of a principle 'upon
which the case was decided'[1] runs right through the ordinary work
of the courts, and it may be illustrated quite simply.

The Dog Act, 1958,[2] provides that if any 'horse, cattle or sheep' is
attacked and injured by a dog, the owner of the 'horse, cattle or
sheep' may claim compensation for the injury from the owner of the
dog. Suppose X claims damages from Y because Y's dog has killed
X's pedigree goat. X claims damages on several distinct legal
grounds[3] and for one of them he relies on Section 26 of the Dog Act.
Y argues that he cannot be made liable under Section 26 of that Act
because goats are not included within 'horse, cattle or sheep' for the
purposes of that Section.

Unless the court awards X damages on one of the other grounds
advanced and refrains from deciding the question raised by Y's
argument[4] its decision that goats are, or are not, comprehended by
Section 26 of the Act will be treated as binding by subordinate courts
in that jurisdiction, and so a precise answer to a precise question is
made part of the law. It may be said that this is a mere matter of
statutory interpretation; that the real problems of precedent arise
where the common law is concerned and apart from statute. Two
things need to be said in answer; firstly, that a very large number
indeed of cases raise issues of statutory interpretation and their settlement is an important part of the work of the courts; and secondly,
that there is an infinite number[5] of questions which may be raised
in the course of human disputes and many of those which are not
concerned with statutes, but with the common law alone, may be
answered in just such a black-and-white way. Thus X may make his
claim on the ground, *inter alia*, that Y is strictly liable for his dog's
attack, in the same way that an owner may be liable in cattle trespass.

---

[1] Sir George Jessel (*supra*).

[2] Of the State of Victoria by Section 26.

[3] Under the common law: (*a*) seeking to prove that Y knew of his dog's dangerous
propensities [scienter], (*b*) seeking to prove that Y directed the assault by ordering his
dog to attack the goat [trespass], (*c*) by arguing that Y is strictly liable for the 'trespass'
of his dog, as in cattle trespass—see *Doyle* v. *Vance* (1880), 6. V.L.R. [L] 87.

[4] The various possibilities here are discussed in the article by J. L. Montrose,
'Language of, and a Notation for, the Doctrine of Precedent' (*supra*).

[5] One mathematician has remarked that the number is infinity to the power of
infinity.

If this is a case of first impression, the court may have to decide whether or not the cattle trespass rules apply to dogs. The yes or no answer to that question will prevent argument of it in subsequent cases in courts bound by the decision. This is a strict binding because it prevents consideration by a subordinate court of the reasons given by the higher court for deciding the way it did, however misconceived they may appear to have been, unless they are in clear conflict with some yet higher authority.

Much of the law at rest, as it were, can be seen to be comprised by decisions of that kind. Practitioners' textbooks are full of classified and indexed answers to just such specific questions. But, as has been said already, the number of such questions which may be raised is infinite; and if this were all to the doctrine of precedent the common law would indeed appear as a wilderness of single instances.[1]

Such precise decisions, however, will ordinarily be supported by a course of reasoning which establishes a general proposition of law which the court uses to explain and justify its decision. That proposition may properly be called the *ratio decidendi* of the decision, and it will be binding upon lower courts also, but its binding nature is of a different kind. For example, in the Victorian case of *Armstrong* v. *Hammond*[2] the court had to decide whether or not a private citizen could prosecute an offence under Section 20(3) of the Victorian Police Offences Act, 1957.[3] Section 190 of that Act designated certain officials as competent prosecutors for various purposes under the Act, and it was argued that only those officials could prosecute for an offence under Section 20(3). The full court of the Supreme Court of Victoria held that any member of the public could prosecute. That decision would clearly foreclose any repetition of that objection to a private prosecution under Section 20(3) in any other Victorian court, once Armstrong's case was brought to the court's attention, whatever the merits of the reasons given by the full court for the decision, unless those reasons were clearly inconsistent with authority from some yet higher court in the hierarchy.

The full court's decision was supported by a reason which may be stated as follows: The power of any member of the public to lay an information for an offence of a public nature is not to be taken as denied in the absence of clear and express legislative language.

---

[1] But a rather different wilderness from that conceived of by those who think of single instances as particular facts rather than as particular legal questions or issues.

[2] [1958] V.L.R. 479.

[3] Wilful damage to property.

That proposition is not of mere persuasive authority so far as other courts in Victoria are concerned. It is not an *obiter dictum*.[1] Only a little thought is needed to see that the binding nature of such a proposition is very different from the binding nature of the decision that anyone can prosecute under Section 20(3). The general proposition is binding in the sense that it cannot be questioned or denied, but must be accepted as a valid proposition of law by a subordinate court; but the question whether or not another Section or another Act of Parliament has taken away the general power to prosecute, is a specific question which cannot be answered by simple deduction from the general proposition. It will not just be a matter of 'doing the sums right'. It will require argument, the marshalling of reasons and authorities permitted or comprehended by the legal system, and the exercise of judgment.

The other matter which must be understood is the difference between the treatment of precedent authority at different levels of the judicial hierarchy. Most of the literature is concerned with the work of the appellate courts, and this is perhaps understandable as that work is the most important so far as the development of the written law to be applied by the courts and by practitioners is concerned. The overwhelming majority of actual legal disputes are disposed of, however, without ever reaching an appellate court.

It is basal to the common law system that a common law court will not give a decision unless there is a real dispute before it. Correlatively, it is basal that a judge's declaration of law will only be treated as binding authority when it is a necessary part of a course of reasoning which justifies the decision.[2] Not in all,[3] but in most cases, the issues can only be described by reference to facts as well as law. Immediately problems of language, definition, and classification infect the process and make room for indeterminacy. This is inevitable wherever a process of reasoning involves the application of general propositions to particular[4] situations. It should be expected, therefore, and it is so, that a general proposition of law on which a decision of a particular question depends, whether declared expressly

---

[1] *Deakin* v. *Webb* (1904), 1 C.L.R. 585 at 604–6; *Great Western Ry. Co.* v. *Mostyn*, [1928] A.C. 57.

[2] *Necessary* here in the sense that it is necessary to the course of reasoning—not *necessary* in that the dispute could not have been decided one way or another without it.

[3] Some quite abstract issues of law may be presented, e.g. on originating summons or on demurrer, where there is little room for argument about the relevant facts.

[4] Perhaps, in a complete analysis, unique situations.

by a judge or imputed by an observer by examining the issue and the decision only, may be stated either widely or narrowly—just as the questions presented for decision may vary infinitely in their precision or generality.

It is natural that an appellate court, conscious of its duty to declare the law and perhaps conscious of its role as a law maker, will look more closely to the precise statement of a rule or principle of law in the light of the reasons for it and of its desirable extension or limitation, than will a lower court less conscious of its law-making and law-declaring role and more conscious of the authority of courts which stand above it.

Thus in courts of summary jurisdiction, where the judicial function is not ordinarily carried on by highly qualified and experienced lawyers, and where the pressure of time is great, fine distinctions in answering questions about just what is binding in previous cases are seldom entertained. In these courts, and in other courts of inferior jurisdiction[1] where experienced lawyers sit on the bench but where procedure is simplified and the pressure of time is great, if a superior court has stated the applicable law in a certain way as part of the expressed reasons for coming to a decision in a previous case, then that statement will be treated as law and will be applied as such.

Where superior courts are concerned differences can be observed between the day-to-day work of courts of first instance and the work of courts of appeal—particularly ultimate courts of appeal. Most of the cases which come before courts for trial do not on their face raise disputes about the correct way the applicable law should be stated. They raise disputes about facts and events and about the way admittedly correct statements of law should be applied to resolve issues arising out of such facts and events. This is one of the reasons why busy practitioners who practise before such courts are heard to say they would rather have 'an ounce of fact than a ton of law'.

Judges sitting in superior courts deliver reasoned judgments supporting their decisions and, in cases which seem to be of importance to the law, those judgments will be reported in the law reports. The judge therefore is conscious of the fact that he is taking part in a law-declaring process at least, and he may be taking part in a law-making process. In these circumstances it is to be expected that the

---

[1] For example, County Courts, Courts of General or Quarter Sessions, District Courts, and other courts of intermediate jurisdiction by whatever name they may be called.

authorities will be examined much more closely to discover just what the correct statement of the law is, than is likely in inferior courts. But the tradition of the common law is strong that the judge is not consciously to initiate the making of law; that he has power to do what is required to decide the case before him but no more; that he is to declare faithfully in the light of the authorities what the law is. Further the judge sitting at first instance is greatly influenced by his respect for the courts higher in the judicial hierarchy and for the authority of their actual pronouncements. Consequently, such judges sometimes find themselves committed to what may be the difficult task of reconciling existing authorities, and of making sure that the statement of law to be applied in the case before them is one that is authorized by, and is not denied by, such authorities. A clear dilemma is not frequently presented to such a judge sitting alone. In most cases he will find a previous authority which binds or persuades him with a statement of law which he can apply to the case before him. He is able to say that if that statement is too wide or needs restriction then a court of appeal will correct him if he is wrong in applying it. So long as the statement of law concerned was expressed by the higher court as part of a course of reasoning leading to decision, he will not ordinarily examine whether or not it was stated too widely or too narrowly in the light of the issues and facts in the previous case.[1]

Where a court is invited to examine one of its own judgments, however, and in the higher courts of appeal, and particularly in ultimate courts of appeal, a different approach is evident. The lighter pressure of respect for expressed authority, and the consciousness that what is said to be the law will be accepted as such by lower courts and is not likely to be varied except by legislation, go far to explain the difference. There is a greater readiness to say that the statement of a rule of law expressed in a previous case was too wide or too narrow and was not binding in the form expressed, as not being required by the particular facts or issues in that earlier case.[2]

---

[1] Some celebrated examples of a judge analysing the statements of a court whose decisions bind him are to be found in the reports, e.g. per Scott L.J. in *Haseldine* v. *Daw & Son Ltd.*, [1941] 2 K.B. 343, but these examples serve rather to highlight the ordinary practice than to deny it. R. N. Gooderson, 30 *Can. B. R.* (1952), 892—distinction between *ratio* which a judge thought he was expressing and the *ratio* which a later court thinks he had power to lay down.

[2] e.g. the analysis of *Barwick* v. *English Joint Stock Bank* (1867), L. R. 2 Ex. 259 in *Lloyd* v. *Grace, Smith & Co.*, [1912] A.C. 716, and see *Great Western Ry. Co.* v. *Mostyn* (*owners of S.S.*), [1928] A.C. 57.

It is in these circumstances that the factors producing the indeterminacy of general propositions of law outlined above may be seen
occasionally in full play. The degree of indeterminacy of course
varies infinitely with the variation in precision with which different
propositions of law are stated as well as with the variation in relation
between the nature of the proposition and the facts and issues of the
case which called it forth. Perhaps some of the more general propositions in the law of torts provide the most extreme examples of
indeterminacy. Here words like reasonable, proximate, remote,
direct, and indirect, etc., find their places in propositions of law laid
down by appellate courts and said to be binding upon other courts.[1]

An example often taken to demonstrate the indeterminacy of precedent authority is the case of *Donoghue* v. *Stevenson*.[2] In that case
a point of law was taken on appeal to the House of Lords from the
Second Division of the Court of Session in Scotland.[3] It was common ground that there was no difference between Scots and English
law affecting the point. The facts averred (but at the time of this
appeal, of course, they were not established at any trial) were that
the appellant suffered injury as a result of consuming part of the
contents of a bottle of ginger beer which had been manufactured
by the respondent, and which contained the decomposed remains of
a snail. The following facts were also averred: That the bottle of
ginger beer was purchased for the appellant by a friend in a café;
that the bottle was made of dark opaque glass so that the appellant
had no reason to suspect that it contained anything but pure ginger
beer; that the occupier of the café poured the ginger beer into the
tumbler from which the appellant drank; that, after the appellant
drank some of the ginger beer, her friend who had purchased the
bottle then proceeded to pour the remainder of the contents of the
bottle into the tumbler, at which point the presence of the decomposed snail was discovered; that the ginger beer was manufactured
by the respondent to be sold as a drink to the public; that it was
bottled by the respondent and labelled with a label bearing his name;

---

[1] See J. Stone, *Province and Function of Law*, ch. vii.

[2] [1932] A.C. 562. Another interesting example is *Mutual Life and Citizens' Assurance
Co. Ltd.* v. *Evatt*, [1971] 1 All E.R. 150, where the J.C. distinguished the decision of the
House of Lords in *Hedley, Byrne & Co. Ltd.* v. *Heller & Partners Ltd.*, [1964] A.C. 465.

[3] The Second Division had dismissed the action, holding that the averments disclosed no good cause of action. Procedurally this may be taken as indistinguishable,
for present purposes, from taking a point of law to an appellate court on demurrer, or
appealing against a decision to dismiss a cause of action by striking out a statement of
claim as not disclosing a cause.

that the bottles were, after labelling, sealed with a metal cap by the respondent. As matters of law the appellant averred that it was the duty of the respondent to provide a system of working his business which would not allow snails to get into his ginger beer bottles, and that it was also his duty to provide an efficient system of inspection of the bottles before the ginger beer was filled into them. She averred that he had failed in both these duties, and had so caused the accident.

The respondent objected that those averments did not disclose a cause of action. What he was saying, therefore, was that even if all the facts were accepted as true, including the allegation that the snail got into the bottle as a result of the negligent or careless conduct of the respondent, none the less the respondent owed no duty to the plaintiff and was not liable for the injuries suffered by her. He argued that if the respondent was guilty of a negligent breach of duty, then it was of a duty established by contract and owed only to those who were in contractual relations with him and not to members of the public who were, like the plaintiff, strangers to the contract under which the ginger beer was supplied by him. He sought to establish, on the authority of English cases, that a manufacturer is under no duty to persons with whom he is not in any contractual relation; and that there were only two exceptions to that general proposition: (1) where the article concerned is dangerous *per se* and (2) where the article is dangerous to the knowledge of the manufacturer. The House of Lords, by a majority, decided that the respondent did owe the appellant a duty of the kind asserted by the appellant and remitted the case to Scotland for trial. It can be said with accuracy, therefore, that the House decided that a manufacturer of ginger beer may owe a duty of care to consumers to take care in the manufacture of the article to be sold, but further questions arise when it is asked under just what conditions that duty arises and when may it be said to be broken.

Now here it can be seen that the House of Lords decided some quite specific questions of law and established a general principle. Thus it was decided that a manufacturer may owe duties of care with respect to the condition of his products, not being dangerous *per se* or dangerous to his knowledge, quite apart from the duty created by contract made by him with persons purchasing from him.[1] As a con-

---

[1] Under those contractual duties, of course, strangers to the contract, under established rules of law, could not claim benefits. Only parties to the contract or beneficiaries under some kind of trust created by the contract could do so.

sequence it was also decided that the cases of *Mullen* v. *Barr & Co. Ltd.* and *M'Gowan* v. *Barr & Co. Ltd.*[1] were incorrectly decided and were overruled. But what was the principle established? Clearly it was decided that a manufacturer of ginger beer owed a duty of care to the consumer to take care that the remains of decomposed snails did not get into his bottles which were intended to reach the consumer in the state they left the manufacturer. It would seem absurd to confine that proposition to ginger beer. But is it limited to food-stuffs? Or to things likely to result in danger to life, limb or health?[2] Is it limited to those articles with respect to which there is no *possibility* of intermediate examination by the retailer? Or is it enough that the article will reach the consumer subject to the same defect, there being no commercial *probability* of intermediate examination?[3] Does the now-famous general principle enunciated by Lord Atkin— 'You must take reasonable care to avoid acts or omissions which you can reasonably foresee would be likely to injure your neighbour. Who, then, in law is my neighbour? The answer seems to be, persons who are so closely and directly affected by my act that I ought reasonably to have them in contemplation as being so affected when I am directing my mind to the acts or omissions which are called in question',[4] control in any binding way the answers to those questions?

Many decisions have been necessary to work out the real meaning and proper application of the 'principle'. In truth such a broad proposition provides only a direction for thinking, and the means by which the answers to specific questions, established authoritatively as rules of law, may be explained, classified, grouped together, and made the basis for further thinking in a developing and changing system of law. Between the wide statement of principle and the narrowest rational way of stating the rule applicable to decide the particular issue in *Donoghue* v. *Stevenson* lies a wide area in which authority, considerations of justice, fairness, and of the effective working of the legal system itself, must be subjected to the processes of human reasoning powers and insights, so that new cases as they arise may be decided consistently with established authority and with prevailing notions of justice.

Under the umbrella of a general principle, so to speak, one case

---

[1] [1929] S.C. 461.
[2] See *Old Gate Estates Ltd.* v. *Toplis & Harding & Russell*, [1939] 3 All E.R. 209.
[3] *Grant* v. *A.K.M.*, [1936] A.C. 85.
[4] [1932] A.C. at p. 580.

plots a point on the graph of the law of torts, but to draw the curve of the law we need a series of points. In many important cases there is a statement of principle much broader than is necessary if the precise issues in that case only are to be considered. If the decision is felt to be wrong the principle will be confined to cases raising precisely the same issue; if it is thought correct, the merest *obiter dictum* may have very great weight. A court if it approves the general doctrine expressed in a case, will apply it whether it is bound or not. The rigid determination of what is strictly binding in a previous case is necessary only where a court considers a decision unfortunate, or where there is an apparent conflict of such binding authorities. To suggest narrow limits to what is absolutely binding does not deny the tremendous influence of a broad general principle expressed in a judgment, if the lips that uttered it were worthy of respect—and *a fortiori* if it were uttered from a bench exercising strict authority over the courts subject to its influence.

Where courts are said to be strictly bound by their own decisions, it is perhaps understandable that freedom should be sought in a narrow delimitation of the strictly binding parts of authoritative cases. In Australia, wider theories have been enunciated by the High Court,[1] but since that court can overrule its own decisions, there is no great danger of premature rigidity.[2]

One criticism of a narrow theory of the strictly binding nature of precedent cases is that it may make the law a 'wilderness of single instances',[3] since legal issues and questions are potentially infinite in number and are infinitely various. It is the fear of such a wilderness that has led so many judges and legal writers to assert that cases are useful and authoritative only in so far as they lay down principles.[4] It has already been asserted that that view is misleading, if taken literally. But neither is its converse correct. At the highest level the narrow theory of strictly binding authority, outlined above, has been

---

[1] *Deakin* v. *Webb* (1904), 1 C.L.R. 585 at 605–6.

[2] The High Court is, save in certain constitutional cases, bound by decisions of the Privy Council, and if it adopts a wide theory with respect to the authority of its own judicial pronouncements, it should logically also apply the same theory to decisions of the Privy Council; and in fact an examination of its judgments, it is suggested, reveals that it does so—see, for example, the treatment by a majority of the High Court in *Hughes & Vale Pty. Ltd.* v. *State of New South Wales* (1952), 87 C.L.R. 49 of the Privy Council's recommendations to Her Majesty in *Commonwealth of Australia* v. *Bank of New South Wales*, [1950] A.C. 235, where in strict theory the Privy Council's reasoning on the merits of the case was all *obiter dicta*.

[3] Griffith C.J., *Fraser* v. *Victorian Railways Commissioners* (1909), 8 C.L.R. 54 at 58.

[4] The vigorous assertions of C. K. Allen provide as nice an example as any—*Law in the Making* (7th ed.), 285 et seq.

thrust on English law by the need to distinguish inconvenient cases which there is no power to overrule. So far as the authority of *rationes decidendi*[1] is concerned there is no real danger of the English doctrine of precedent producing mechanical judges. It is impossible to draw a rigid line, *a priori*, between *rationes decidendi* and *obiter dicta*. The English language creates inevitable ambiguities and indeterminacies which are not present in sciences employing rigidly defined terms. There is no trick of method which can determine as a matter of inexorable logic the precise wording of a statement of law which binds, where what is concerned is a general principle providing the reason for a decision. The interpretation of precedent in this sense is an art rather than a science. Further so long as appellate courts render individual judgments flexibility is inevitably preserved, because of the logical impossibility in some cases of discovering a common *ratio*.[2] Lord Reid approves flexibility in final courts, for he points out the danger of single judgments—the true *ratio* appears better from a comparison of two or more statements in different words which are intended to supplement each other.[3] Moreover, even in appellate courts, there are cases where the appropriate precedents are not cited. Thus in *Broome* v. *Cassell & Co.*,[4] the Court of Appeal accused the House of Lords in *Rookes* v. *Barnard*[5] of not considering its own decisions.[6] Incidentally, the Court of Appeal took a very strong view, holding that *Rookes* v. *Barnard* was a decision *per incuriam* and directing lower courts to follow the law existing prior to the decision until the House of Lords had an occasion to reconsider the matter.

There is much wisdom in the speech of Lord Reid:

Whatever views may have prevailed in the last century, I think it is now widely recognised that it is proper for the court in appropriate cases to develop or adapt existing rules of the common law to meet new conditions. I say in appropriate cases because I think we ought to recognise a difference between cases where we are dealing with lawyer's law and cases where we are dealing with matters which directly affect the lives and interests of large sections of the community and which raise issues which are the subject of public controversy and on which laymen are as well able to decide as

---

[1] Here used in the sense of reasons expressed by the judges for their decisions.

[2] J. Stone, *Province and Function of Law*, chs. v and vi; G. W. Paton and G. Sawer, 63 *L.Q.R.* (1947), 461.

[3] *Gallie* v. *Lee*, [1970] 3 W.L.R. 1078 at 1081.   [4] [1971] 2 W.L.R. 853.

[5] [1964] A.C. 1129.

[6] At p. 869. Megarry J., *Hounslow* v. *Twickenham Garden*, [1970] 3 All E.R. at 340, refers to the 'melancholy list' of relevant decisions that were not cited.

are lawyers. On such matters it is not for the courts to proceed on their view of public policy for that would be to encroach on the province of parliament.[1]

In dealing with maintenance and champerty, Danckwerts J. stated: 'A doctrine which was evolved to deal with cases of oppression should not be allowed to become an instrument of oppression, which it must be if humble men are not allowed to combine or to receive contributions to meet a powerful adversary.'[2] Devlin J. (as he then was), while agreeing that this approach is more fitting for appellate than lower courts, thought that if a refusal to recognize obsolescence leads to absurdity, then even a judge in any court should be a reformer.[3] If the court is considering an order for maintenance, it should recognize that 'the law is a living thing, moving with the times and not a creature of dead or moribund ways of thought'.[4] Lord Upjohn said of a decision which has stood (although criticized) since 1877: 'The *Parana*[5] . . . must be regarded as either obsolete, being overtaken by events, or overruled'[6]—surely a compendious way of getting rid of an awkward precedent.

Is the English doctrine, which allows binding authority to a single decision of a higher court, too narrow? The answer tentatively suggested is that, while it leads to confusion if lower courts do not follow decisions of upper courts in the same hierarchy, the House of Lords is well advised to keep power to overrule itself. Indeed, over the last few years, the shackles of precedent are being loosened. R. Cross writes: 'When I wrote the first edition (1960) I believed, as others did at that time, that the English doctrine of precedent was more rigid than it had ever been before. It is now clear that this is no longer so.'[7] Various reasons have been used to justify the doctrine of precedent[8]—that it is adequate proof of custom, that it shows respect for the opinion of one's ancestors, that convenience demands that a question once decided should not be subject to re-argument in every

---

[1] *Pettitt* v. *Pettitt*, [1969] 2 All E.R. at 390.
[2] *Martell* v. *Consett Iron Co. Ltd.*, [1954] 3 All E.R. 339 at 349.
[3] *Winchester* v. *Fleming*, [1957] 3 All E.R. 711.
[4] Per Sachs L.J., *Porter* v. *Porter*, [1969] 3 All E.R .at 644. 'Much water has passed under the bridges since 1929'—per Lord Denning, *Pett* v. *Greyhound Racing*, [1968] 2 W.L.R. at 1476.   [5] (1877), 2 P.D. 118.
[6] *Koufos* v. *Czarnikow*, [1969] 1 A.C. 350.
[7] *Precedent in English Law*, 1968. Cf. Barwick C.J., *Mutual Life and Citizens' Assur. Co. Ltd.* v. *Evatt*, [1968] 42 A.L.J.R. 316: 'The perpetuation of error by an ultimate Court of Appeal is not an indispensable, nor a desirable, feature of a stable system of law grounded on judicial precedent.'
[8] A. L. Goodhart, *Problème des sources du droit positif*, 37.

case in which it arises. All these arguments contain a certain element of truth. Some claim as a virtue of precedent that it leads to certainty: others that flexibility is the chief merit. Clearly a very flexible system can hardly be certain, since no one knows exactly when and where development will take place. It is the eternal difficulty of law to reconcile rule and discretion,[1] and the practical problem is whether the common law achieves a reasonable certainty with some capacity for development. The doctrine of precedent makes against flexibility, although it has not prevented great development, and it leads to certainty[2] save where the cases are so many or so confusing that no clue can be found to the legal maze. An excess of precedents may easily lead to uncertainty unless they are uniform in result, and unless a satisfactory technique exists for discovering relevant cases: sometimes a case may reach the House of Lords before it is discovered that there is a precedent which is binding.[3] In America the increase in the number of reported cases has led to a modification of the doctrine of *stare decisis*—by 1940 the total was nearing the two million mark, and the flood is more than human ingenuity can cope with.[4]

The view that precedent leads to the scientific development of the law is not convincing, for *elegantia iuris* may be secured either with or without a doctrine of binding precedent. Indeed, the doctrine of precedent may mean that unfortunate cases remain to mar logical symmetry. It is also urged that the doctrine has practical advantages —it is true that the case method is closely related to the facts in its development, but precedent is a hindrance since the truly practical method would allow of experiment and an opportunity to correct one's mistakes.[5] Undoubtedly, reversal of a precedent may cause

---

[1] *Infra*, § 47.

[2] J. Frank, *Law and the Modern Mind*, puts forward the realist thesis that the certainty of precedent is only an illusion, *supra*, § 7. See in general Sachs L.J., *Porter* v. *Porter*, [1969] 3 All E.R. at 643; *Koufos* v. *Czarnikow*, [1969] 1 A.C. 350.

[3] *Penrikyber Nav. Colliery Co.* v. *Edwards*, [1933] A.C. 28; *Christie* v. *Leachinsky*, [1947] A.C. 573 at 586; C. K. Allen, 59 *L.Q.R.* (1943), 308.

[4] A. L. Goodhart, *Essays in Jurisprudence and the Common Law*, 50. See the Report of the Cincinnati Conference on the Status of Precedent, 14 *Univ. of Cincinnati L. R.* (1940), 203–355. The growth may be seen in the following figures. From 1790 to 1840 there were 50,000 reported Federal and State decisions; from 1840 to 1890 there were 450,000 new decisions; from 1890 to 1940, 1,500,000; this makes a grand total of 2,000,000 cases. Will the lawyer of the future operate with microfilm and electronic devices? L. O. Kelso, 18 *Rocky Mt. L. R.* (1946), 378.

[5] A. L. Goodhart, *Precedent in English and Continental Law* (Stevens), 25. One of the greatest vices of the English doctrine of precedent is the occasional distinguishing of cases on very narrow grounds. Thus, Evatt J., in *Chester* v. *Waverley Corporation* (1939), 62 C.L.R. 1, distinguished the *Coultas Case* (1888), 13 A.C. 222, on a very narrow ground in order to secure opportunity for the law to develop.

injustice to those who have shaped their conduct in reliance upon it, but this is an argument for extreme care in overruling precedents rather than for a complete denial of the power. Certainly, if a court follows no consistent policy and frequently changes from one view to another, disrespect for the law results, since a chance majority may affect the decision. The great difficulty, of course, is that, whereas a statute may change the law for the future but leave vested rights untouched, a court can change the law only in the very act of applying it to a case, when 'the attorney who drew the will . . . may have acted on the authority of that very decision' which the court is asked to overrule.[1]

It is also claimed that the individual caprice of the judge is controlled by the necessity of following binding precedents: 'it is better to apply the law, which is the wisdom of a great many, than to act on one's individual impression.'[2] The community must be ruled by law and not by men, for then all are equally treated. But should we carry our natural love of equality as an attribute of justice so far as to treat twenty plaintiffs unjustly because one binding case laid down an unjust rule? Is it better to be ultimately right or consistently and persistently wrong?[3] One factor that is of great importance is that the following of precedent is easier in England than in many other countries, firstly, because the system of justice is centralized and there is a comparatively small number of reported cases; secondly, because there is no written constitution which could be made unworkable if cases deciding its interpretation were made binding; and thirdly,

---

[1] *In the Goods of Hallyburton* (1866), L.R. 1 P. & D. 90. See also *The Annefield*, [1971] 1 All E.R. 394, where the C.A. showed reluctance to overrule a decision in commercial law which had not been challenged for fifty years. In America some courts take the step of following the precedent in the case before them, but of announcing that they will not follow it in future. This runs counter to the English view that the courts are limited to declaring what the law is and cannot lay down one rule for the case in question and another for the future.

[2] Per Madden C.J. who, in *Harvey* v. *Ottoway*, [1915] V.L.R. 520 at 525, read an amusing sermon to justices who had refused to follow a decision of the House of Lords on the ground that two old married men could not be taught much on the subject of a husband's liability. 'They, and indeed every one of us, would do well to listen to the House of Lords—a tribunal not only composed of the greatest lawyers, but also the most authoritative, for they speak last. And if it be said that the magistrates here acted on an inspiration springing from the antiquity of their domestic relations, they ought still to remember that the judges of the House of Lords, in addition to being great lawyers, are probably no less old and no less married than themselves, and that acting on the inspiration in question is certain to lead to confusion and appeals and costs in the administration of justice.'

[3] Cf. Isaacs J. in *Aust. Agric. Co.* v. *Federated Engine-Drivers Assocn.* (1913), 17 C.L.R. 261 at 278: 'It is not in my opinion better that the Court should be persistently wrong than that it should be ultimately right.'

because the legislature has absolute power to remedy any particular defect. Where there are many courts, as in America, the conflict of decisions inevitably leads to bolder criticism even of cases that are binding on a particular court. Similarly, some freedom must be retained in the interpretation of a written constitution, for amendment is not easy and a single decision might cause unforeseen practical difficulties.[1] In England the courts have showed such great discretion in overruling persuasive precedents which have been accepted as law by a long course of conduct[2] that there is no reason to suppose that the Court of Appeal would exercise rashly a power to overrule its own decisions.[3]

On the topic of precedent there is a voluminous literature which cannot be discussed; but it is submitted that what is even more important than the theory of the common law technique is the spirit in which it is applied. If the law tends to that love of subtlety for its own sake for which Parke B. was notorious and applies precedents in a rigid and unthinking fashion, then the future is dark, but there are welcome signs that courts are fully alive to their real task.[4] What is even more important than the machinery is the quality of the men who control it.[5]

The English doctrine causes surprise to many foreign lawyers, for on the Continent no single decision even of the highest court is absolutely binding. While there is naturally a strong tendency to follow the doctrine of a line of cases, even then in theory[6] a lower court can

---

[1] Thus the High Court of Australia, the Privy Council, and the U.S. Supreme Court, all of which interpret written constitutions, have retained freedom to overrule their own decisions, and in 1966 the House of Lords adopted a similar policy.

[2] e.g. *Wolstanton Ltd.* v. *Newcastle-under-Lyme*, [1940] A.C. 860; *Lissenden* v. *Bosch Ltd.*, [1940] A.C. 412. Opinion is divided on the merits of the English system. Lord Wright in *The Future of the Common Law*, 81; W. S. Holdsworth, *History of English Law*, xii. 159 and 50 *L.Q.R.* 180; C. K. Allen, *Law in the Making*, ch. iv and 51 *L.Q.R.* 333; H. Goldschmidt, *English Law from the Foreign Standpoint*, 28 et seq. A. L. Goodhart, 50 *L.Q.R.* (1934), 40, 196, and Lord Tomlin (cited 13 *Can. B. R.* (1935), 606) are rather critical. Lord Chorley thinks that one of the main causes of disagreement between the courts in declaring what the law is and the business community in its contention as to what the law ought to be is the doctrine of precedent: 3 *Mod. L. R.* (1940), 272.

[3] This view is supported by Lord Wright, 8 *Camb. L. J.* (1943), 118; 13 *Mod. L. R.* (1950), 23. Lord Cooper deprecates the introduction of the English doctrine into Scotland: 'We are now helpless in its suffocating grasp'—63 *Harv. L. R.* (1950), 472–3.

[4] *Commissioner for Railways (N.S.W.)* v. *Cardy* (1960), 34 A.L.J.R. 134.

[5] K. N. Llewellyn, *The Common Law Tradition: Deciding Appeals.*

[6] M. Ancel, 16 *J. Comp. Leg.* (1934), 1; M. S. Amos and F. P. Walton, *Introduction to French Law*, 7. In practice, however, a long line of decisions is of such high persuasive authority that it is rarely departed from. Individual decisions are rarely cited in judgments, and hence the judge cannot shelter himself behind a particular decision. He must justify his judgment on principle. For Scotland, see J. C. Gardner, *Judicial Precedent in Scots Law.*

depart from such a rule and higher courts reserve liberty to reverse the trend of case law. E. J. Cohn has claimed that the development in Germany of a theory of frustration of contract was greatly assisted by the ability to ignore inconvenient decisions.[1] It is absurd, however, to suggest that cases have no weight, for, as in England, they provide the life blood of the law and there is a more extensive adherence to precedent than English lawyers sometimes suppose.[2] At first sight we might think that the existence of codes provided an explanation of the different views of English and continental law, since a code supplies a core of certainty which England finds in decided cases. But France only enacted her code in 1804, Germany in 1900—moreover, the English doctrine of precedent was fully established only in the eighteenth[3] or nineteenth[4] century. What was decisive was the greater influence on the Continent of Roman law which traditionally put great emphasis on the textbook because of the respect paid to the opinions of the jurists and the fact that Justinian's *Digest* was largely 'Readings from famous Text-Books' (to use a modern tag). As Roman law was regarded as a common law for the Continent, it tended to carry the prestige of the textbook with it. In England, due perhaps to the greater reverence which the Bench enjoyed, lawyers turned to decisions rather than to textbooks for binding authority. Another reason is that England has a centralized hierarchy of courts and a relatively small number of judges and reported decisions. If there are a multitude of Courts of Appeal, it is difficult to make all decisions binding.

It is rare on the Continent to cite decisions of last century or before. 'Surely it is significant that continental lawyers are of opinion that a statute, which expressly orders judicial decisions to be binding, cannot mean that such binding force should be given to decisions so far back as twenty years ago.'[5] English assiduity in searching the early reports and even the Year Books for authority seems very strange to a continental lawyer.[6] But in the 'run of the mill' case 'the last twenty years takes up most of the law into itself'.[7]

---

[1] 28 *J. Comp. Leg.* (1946), 15 at 19.
[2] J. P. Niboyet, 20 *Iowa L. R.* (1935), 416 at 430.
[3] W. S. Holdsworth, *History of English Law*, xii. 146 et seq.
[4] C. K. Allen, *Law in the Making* (7th ed.), 230 et seq.
[5] E. J. Cohn, 5 *Camb. L. J.* (1935), 366 at 370.
[6] C. K. Allen, *Law in the Making* (7th ed.), 230, states that out of 167 cases cited in [1961] K.B., only 5 were older than the nineteenth century. But even making allowance for this, there is a difference of approach between English and continental jurists, for in England nineteenth-century authorities are regarded as modern. Some parts of English law, where there is rapid development, cannot pay great respect to

[*Note 6 cont. and note 7 on facing page.*]

§ 46. SOURCES WHERE THERE IS NO AUTHORITY

Many codes lay down specific instructions as to the sources on which the judge should rely when there is no authority. The Japanese Code relies on custom and in default of that on reason and equity.[1] The Swiss Code lays down that in the last resort the judge should apply the rule which he would establish if he were acting as legislator.[2] When there is no code which provides precise directions as to the sources in the absence of authority, a judge will normally turn to persuasive precedents,[3] textbooks,[4] the use of analogy, and such help as may be afforded by custom or the course of business.

Analogy is a useful weapon but it must be cautiously applied. Mill describes it as follows: 'two things resemble each other in one or more respects: a certain proposition is true of the one; therefore it is true of the other.'[5] The accuracy of the conclusion drawn will depend on the relative importance of the resemblances and the unimportance of the differences between the two things—the situation being analysed from the point of view of the proposition which it is desired to establish. For example, it may be desired to find a rule to apply to electricity, and an analogy is sought in the rules relating to water. Artificial accumulations of water are likely to cause great damage if they escape, and the risk, even with reasonable care on the part of the owner, is greater than that to which an occupier normally subjects a neighbour. Yet analogy can furnish only a guide, not a decisive answer. There are nearly always two conflicting analogies which may be used in law. In life we find almost every degree between actual identity and remote resemblance, and a supporter of an analogy will emphasize the points of resemblance, an opponent will maintain that the differences are crucial. Thus it has been accepted by the courts that although electric wiring in a private house may be a source of danger

---

old precedents. Thus G. C. Cheshire, *Private International Law* (3rd ed.), 479, rejects *Lolley's Case* (1812), 2 Cl. & F. 567 n. as 'too old to be of value'. On the other hand, the C.A. *In re Diplock*, [1948] Ch. 465, canvassed the authorities for 250 years.

[7] Holmes in *Pollock–Holmes Letters*, ii. 20.

[1] N. Sugiyama, *Rec. Gény*, ii. 446.

[2] Art. I. C. Du Pasquier points out (*Introduction à la théorie générale*, 203), that, although the Swiss court uses the classical theories of interpretation, it uses them with a practical sense of what is demanded by the needs of today—it is largely open to the current of ideas represented by *Interessenjurisprudenz*.

[3] Cf. the use made in English courts of Roman law: *Bechervaise* v. *Lewis* (1872), L.R. 7 C.P. 372; *Coggs* v. *Bernard* (1703), 2 Ld. Raym. 909; or of American decisions: *Haynes* v. *Harwood*, [1935] 1 K.B. 146.

[4] *Infra*, § 55.   [5] *A System of Logic* (1879), ii. 88.

similar in kind if not in degree to a high-tension cable, nevertheless there is no unusual risk created by an occupier who has his house fitted with electric light, since such a procedure is the normal practice.[1] Broadcasting has raised many problems. Is the proper analogy libel or slander? Is the owner of the station liable for interpolated remarks, on the analogy of the newspaper? If a defamatory broadcast is heard in forty-eight states, is a separate tort committed in each state?[2]

The advantage of a proper use of analogy is that it enables the new situation to be dealt with by a rule which can be placed in a coherent relation with rules that are already established. It is thus assumed that the law is a consistent body of principles and every attempt is made to keep it as such.

If analogy fails the judge may turn for help to any source.[3] Such material as he discovers will not, of course, be imperatively binding upon him, and he will reach such a conclusion as can best be fitted into the general body of the law. Textbooks may provide an acceptable solution, or there may be borrowing from a kindred system of law—thus American cases may provide useful material for English courts.[4] Even systems whose basis is far removed may be drawn upon, and the Roman storehouse of legal learning has proved of considerable assistance to English jurists.[5]

But in drawing on these aids, a consideration of what is expedient for the community concerned is

the secret root from which the law draws all the juices of life. . . . Every important principle which is developed by litigation is in fact and at bottom the result of more or less definitely understood views of public policy: most generally to be sure . . . the unconscious result of instinctive preferences and

---

[1] *Collingwood* v. *Home and Colonial Stores*, [1936] 3 All E.R. 200. Is a hydroplane a vessel or not? If the question is whether it should be subject to Admiralty jurisdiction while afloat, its resemblance to a vessel is more important than the fact that it can also fly. But, if the question is whether the representatives of a passenger drowned while the hydroplane was afloat on the water can recover under an insurance policy which excepted the perils of flying, the answer is 'No', for the mere fact that it was afloat at the moment did not lessen the risk, since a hydroplane is more likely to capsize than an ordinary vessel. Hence in one case the analogy was applied and in the other was not: *Reinhardt* v. *Newport Flying Service Corp.*, 232 N.Y. 115 and *Wendorff* v. *Missouri State Life Insurance Co.*, 318 Mo. 363, cited J. C. H. Wu, *The Art of Law*, 127–8.

[2] 60 *Harv. L. R.* (1947), 941.

[3] B. N. Cardozo, *The Nature of the Judicial Process*; F. Gény, *Méthode d'interprétation.*

[4] *Haynes* v. *Harwood*, [1935] 1. K.B. 146 at 156.

[5] *Hamps* v. *Darby*, [1948] 2 All E.R. 474. Speaking of Roman law, Pollock and Maitland, *History of English Law*, i. 24, write: 'It came to us soon; it taught us much; and then there was healthy resistance to foreign dogma.'

inarticulate convictions, but none the less traceable to views of public policy in the last analysis.[1]

What is really decisive is the 'inarticulate major premiss', the judge's view as to the reasons and policy which lie behind the law. Pound has pointed out that there are in every system of law not only concepts and a method of applying them but a body of philosophical, political, and ethical ideals as to the end of law which gives direction to its development.[2] Lord Macmillan writes that 'in almost every case, except the very plainest, it would be possible to decide the issue either way with reasonable legal justification' and that, in such cases, ethical considerations operate and ought to operate.[3] No developing system of law can avoid the influence of the general views of the community as to the end that law should pursue. Although developed and consistent theoretical views as to the purpose of law may not always exist,[4] nevertheless there are decisive practical views which sway the court in its choice either between competing analogies or its adoption of the material out of which a new rule is to be fashioned. An analysis of the judicial method thus raises many of the problems which we have already discussed under the heading of natural law.

Whether in the application of a settled rule, or in the creation of new law, we cannot avoid the influence of the personal factor. Lord Wright says of the particular examples which Lord Abinger cited to justify his doctrine of common employment that 'these instances seem to show personal apprehensions rather than any principle'.[5] Scrutton L.J. has confessed to the difficulty of being sure that 'you have put yourself in a thoroughly impartial position between two disputants, one of your own class and one not of your own class'.[6] Sir Ivor Jennings has traced the effect of changes in the personnel of the Judicial Committee on the interpretation of the Canadian Constitution.[7] Lord Buckmaster in the snail case[8] thought it would be

---

[1] O. W. Holmes, *The Common Law*, 35–6.   [2] *36 Harv. L. R.* (1923), 645.
[3] *Law and Other Things*, 48. With respect, it is submitted that this dictum must be confined to cases which come before appellate courts.
[4] *Supra*, § 36; P. H. Winfield, 45 *Harv. L. R.* (1931), 112; R. Pound, 45 *Harv. L. R.* (1931), 136. A. I. Vyshinsky, *Law of the Soviet State*, put it that the class essence of juridical chicanery is obscured by a system of formal interpretation. But the issue is not as simple as that.
[5] *Radcliffe* v. *Ribble Motor Services Ltd.*, [1939] A.C. 215 at 239. On the other hand we must beware of formulating facile explanations: e.g. that the view of the judge is determined solely by economic forces. Few today would deny the great part played by economic factors, but it is idle to suggest that they are a sole or ultimate cause: R. Pound, 53 *Harv. L. R.* (1940), 365; K. Renner, *The Institutions of Private Law and their Social Functions.*   [6] 1 *Camb. L. J.* (1922), 8.
[7] 51 *Harv. L. R.* (1937), 1.   [8] [1932] A.C. 562.

little short of outrageous to make a manufacturer responsible to members of the public for every bottle that issues from his works, whereas Lord Atkin thought that to impose liability for negligence was in accordance with sound common sense. 'A tincture of humanity will stain the law reports until the courts are manned by Robots',[1] and few would prefer the Robots to the humanity of the judge.

§ 47. FIXITY AND DISCRETION

'Almost all of the problems of jurisprudence come down to a fundamental one of rule and discretion, of administration of justice by law and administration of justice by the more or less trained intuition of experienced magistrates.'[2] It has been shown that primitive law tends to be too fluid, but that in the middle period there is too great an emphasis on formality and rigidity. Thereafter many are the devices used to introduce flexibility. One method of extending the scope of the law, the fiction, is discussed above,[3] and legislation, which falls outside the judicial method, is the subject of the next chapter.

If we regard law as a body of rules, we may regard judicial discretion concerning the application of those rules as being outside the law. Thus we might imagine a club with a very strict body of rules, which the committee has power to waive if it so desires. Markby regards the standards applied to the facts by juries as non-legal.[4] But if we emphasize the legal order, such discretion is as much part of it as the rules themselves. Thus the discretion used by the Chancellor in granting injunctions which prevented the plaintiff from securing the fruits of a common law victory may be clearly separated from the rules of common law, but it was a very important part of the English legal order. In truth, discretion is used in two senses—sometimes it means a power to depart from rules, sometimes it means a power of choice within fixed limits set up by law. In this second sense a judge may have discretion as to the sentence he will impose, the upper and sometimes the lower limits being fixed by law. Even an application of the standard of negligence to the facts of a case involves some element of discretion. In truth we can make a clear-cut distinction between the certainty of rules and discretion as to their application,

---

[1] C. H. S. Fifoot, *English Law and its Background*, 249. One writer suggests that we should apply 'job analysis techniques' to the judiciary!
[2] R. Pound, *Philosophy of Law*, 111.
[3] *Supra*, § 15.
[4] *Elements of Law* (5th ed.), 20.

only if we regard law as a set of detailed rules and ignore the elastic nature of general standards and broad principles.[1]

There are two issues which are sometimes confused: How far *is* the law certain? How far *should* the law be certain? The modern realist school has dealt with the first problem by claiming that certainty is in practice only an illusion;[2] presumably their answer to the second would be that, as certainty is impossible to achieve, it is futile to discuss how far it *should* be achieved. Another point which is sometimes overlooked is that certainty and rigidity are not necessarily the same. Certainty really means a possibility of accurate prediction, and although an unchanging system is more certain than a developing one, nevertheless flexibility does not always mean uncertainty,[3] if the direction of development can be clearly foreseen.

There are many abstract arguments in favour of certainty which can be countered by others to show the need for elasticity. The discussion of precedent, which is set out above,[4] illustrates some of the points that arise. Even justice itself demands some certainty, some rule that will diminish the scope of arbitrary caprice and the personal factor. Judges sometimes show themselves impatient of an argument that is founded on justice alone: 'it is very difficult to call upon judges, who may be assumed to know the law, to lay down standards of high-mindedness or honour as to which perfectly honest and honourable persons may take entirely different views.'[5] Absurdity as a legal test has been stigmatized as a very unruly horse.[6] Modern business would be difficult without fixed rules of law by which men could order their conduct. Popular confidence in the courts is shaken if law is regarded as the mere *ipse dixit* of a judge. Moreover, the law is wiser than the individual view of one man.

Thus to secure certainty, qualitative tests are sometimes made quantitative. If universal suffrage is a principle of democracy, it is desirable that a certain maturity of intellect be present before a vote is awarded. But the difficulty of applying such a test, and the multitude of decisions that would be necessary, makes a quantitative test of age easier than a qualitative test of mental development. The same tendency may be seen in the legal definition of infancy, and in the rules concerning the criminal guilt of children. In one sense the test of

---

[1] *Infra*, § 48.   [2] *Supra*, § 7.
[3] H. Goldschmidt, *English Law from the Foreign Standpoint*, 44–5.
[4] *Supra*, § 45.
[5] *In re Wigzell*, [1921] 2 K.B. 835 at 859, per Scrutton L.J.
[6] *Grundt* v. *Great Boulder Pty. Mines Ltd.*, [1948] 1 Ch. 145 at 158, 159–60.

age is purely arbitrary, but it prevents arbitrariness in those who have to apply it.[1] The real test of legal technique is whether it can translate ideals into working doctrines: the theoretically perfect rule is of little use if its application leads to such uncertainty that its object is really defeated. But the eternal difficulty of law is that, while it must translate its broad purpose into rules that can be easily applied, it must never forget that rules are made to serve men and not men to serve rules—hence, on the one hand, the struggle to create definite rules, and, on the other hand, to escape from those rules of the past which have become too definite and are no longer in keeping with modern conditions. Economic conditions change, social philosophies develop, and 'an expanding society demands an expanding common law'.[2] What is considered a charity in 1895 may be held not to be one in 1972.[3]

But, even were the community static, a general rule would sometimes create injustice in a particular case, for law has to operate over such a wide field that it must in formulating its rules ignore particular circumstances. Hence the cry for *aequitas* to reduce the harsh effects of a logical application of *strictum ius*, to individualize the general rule, to humanize the administration of the law. A plea which is technically valid may, if allowed, lead to unjust results. Jones marries in 1927 and is granted a deduction in respect of income tax because he is supporting a wife. In 1930 he obtains a decree of nullity, which renders the marriage void *ab initio*. The taxation authorities claim to reassess him for those three years, since it has now been decided that his wife in fact was not his wife in law. The court was courageous enough in this case to find a legal method of dismissing this rather harsh claim.[4] But in other cases it may be more difficult. Thus if French law regards lack of parental consent as a fatal bar to the validity of the marriage of a French minor, and an English court treats such lack as a mere matter of form[5] if the marriage is celebrated in England, it may be that a lady who marries a French minor in England without the consent of his parents is a wife in England but not in

---

[1] J. Dabin, *Technique de l'élaboration du droit positif*, 122–5; C. Du Pasquier, *Introduction à la théorie générale*, 167–8.

[2] Per McCardie J., *Prager* v. *Blatspiel, Stamp & Heacock Ltd.*, [1924] 1 K.B. 566 at 570. 'The law must keep pace with the times': *Lock* v. *Abercester Ltd.*, [1939] 1 Ch. 861 at 864.

[3] *National Anti-Vivisection Society* v. *I.R.C.*, [1948] A.C. 31.

[4] *Dodworth* v. *Dale*, [1936] 2 K.B. 503.

[5] *Ogden* v. *Ogden*, [1908] P. 46. Quaere whether this case was correct in treating lack of consent as a mere formality: G. C. Cheshire, *Private International Law* (3rd ed.), 288.

France. If the man returns to France, the lady cannot secure a divorce in England as it is not the country of her husband's domicile, and she fails also in France, because a court cannot grant a divorce from a marriage which, according to its own rules, is void *ab initio*. Thus if the English courts refuse to recognize a declaration by the French courts that the marriage is invalid, general rules which are not unreasonable in themselves may produce an absurd result.[1] Hence in 'judge-made law the strict logical position has been departed from time after time in favour of rules of justice and convenience'.[2]

A dislike of the results of *strictum ius* has led to the movement for free law[3] which is popular in many quarters today. This theory takes many forms, ranging from the comparatively mild view that the judge must fill the gaps in the law by relying on his view of reason and public policy to the dangerously wide doctrine that would deprive the law of its logical core of rules and allow each judge to decide every case by relying only on his subjective sense of justice. This last form of the theory is dangerous:

liberty to decide each case as you think right without any regard to principles laid down in previous similar cases would only result in a completely uncertain law in which no citizen would know his rights or liabilities until he knew before what judge his case would come and could guess what view that judge would take on a consideration of the matter without any regard to previous decisions.[4]

But an exaggerated emphasis on rigidity will also lead to unwelcome results: if the courts ignore the practical effects of their decisions, the community will suffer. If the legal system has crystallized too early and allows little scope for development (for example, where law has been cast in the form of a code that is too detailed),[5] the desire for certainty may defeat itself, for warped interpretation will be introduced

---

[1] A decree of nullity by the courts of the country where the husband was domiciled would now be recognized in England: *Galene* v. *Galene*, [1939] P. 237. But in *Chapelle* v. *Chapelle*, [1950] 1 All E.R. 236, Willmer J. refused to recognize a decree of a Maltese court since only the husband was domiciled there and the marriage was treated by the foreign court as void *ab initio*.

[2] *Townley Mill Co.* v. *Oldham Ass. C'tee.*, [1936] 1 K.B. 585 at 613, per Greer L.J.

[3] 'What we are striving for is that the courts may find the right judgment on the merits by practical sense and true comprehension of the facts, instead of the correct legal deduction by the help of scholastic subtleties': E. Fuchs, cited in *Science of Legal Method*, 101. The *Freirechtslehre* is a dangerous theory politically, for these jurists have anticipated in theory what became reality in the administration of justice under National Socialism: the judge is free to apply what he regards as the will of the Leader: see W. Friedmann, *Legal Theory* (5th ed.), 343.

[4] *Hill* v. *Aldershot Corp.*, [1933] 1 K.B. 259 at 263–4, per Scrutton L.J.

[5] For the problem of the interpretation of a code see *infra*, § 52.

and, once jurists begin reading into the text what is not there, differing opinions will soon lead to chaos. It is better frankly to emphasize the influence of the pressure of social interest on the development of the law and to secure a reasonable elasticity. Even where a judge does not admit the need to adapt the law, we sometimes see the employment of what the barbarous language of jurisprudence terms the crypto-sociological method. In plain words, this means only that the judgment on its face expresses a perfect chain of logical reasoning but conceals the real reasons for the decision—the case is decided 'on the merits', and then the court searches feverishly for legal authorities which will justify this result. What can explain the difference of the approach of Lord Abinger in 1837[1] to the doctrine of common employment from that of the House of Lords a century later,[2] save a change in the social philosophy of the community. Lord Abinger merely assumed that his decision was the only possible one, whereas the House of Lords deliberately canvassed the interests at stake. The doctrine of common employment was too firmly entrenched to be abolished by the courts,[3] but a different view of social realities led to its being cut down as far as possible.

Gény's theory of free scientific research[4] should not be confused with the broader doctrines of free law, for Gény would limit his method to cases where definite authority is lacking. Where no help can be found in the sources, Gény advocates a study of the moral conscience and of the social facts in order that a judge may understand the real nature of the problem. In discussing the end of law, it has been pointed out that Gény considers that natural law does provide universal objective principles which will curb arbitrary caprice, but some of the difficulties of this theory have been touched on.[5] The great value of Gény's work is not his philosophical base but rather his detailed analysis of what he terms technique—the methods by which broad principles are translated into working rules of law. The judge has greater freedom than many classical theories of jurisprudence allowed, and it is the theme of much modern work that it

---

[1] *Priestley* v. *Fowler* (1837), 3 M. & W. 1.
[2] *Radcliffe* v. *Ribble*, [1939] A.C. 215. Some writers think that there is something sinister in admitting that judges may be influenced by what they call 'extra-legal' considerations. In truth, no legal system could remain tolerable were this not so, for the policy of the law would be alien to the life of today. The courts take account of changes in social manners and the higher degree of self-control now existing in the face of insult: *Holmes* v. *Director of Public Prosecutions*, [1946] A.C. 588 at 600.
[3] It has now been abolished by statute: Law Reform (Personal Injuries) Act, 1948.
[4] *Science et technique: méthode d'interprétation.*   [5] *Supra*, § 34.

is better frankly to recognize this than to exaggerate the element of certainty in law.

It is rather artificial, however, to argue in abstract terms about the rival methods of certainty and discretion. No system of law has ever achieved absolute certainty, and even the most fluid form of law inevitably tends to create a core of principles and rules. What is more practical is to analyse each particular branch of the law, to discover the degree of fixity and elasticity therein, and to consider the effectiveness of its operation. (*a*) Parts of the law require fairly rigid rules for business convenience, for example, in transfers of property and in commercial law generally.[1] The business man wants to know what is a bill of exchange and what is not, instead of leaving the decision to the discretion of a judge. (*b*) Elsewhere, justice may demand certainty, in order that men may know what conduct will subject them to liability for punishment—thus it is unjust to leave the criminal law so uncertain that crimes are in effect created by the courts with retrospective operation. The maxim *nulla poena sine lege* is accepted by many systems[2]—i.e. the doctrine that a person should be punished only if his conduct is prohibited by a specific rule which is already accepted. England has not actually adopted the maxim. Penal statutes may have retrospective operation. Some common law offences are so wide (e.g. criminal conspiracy and an offence to the public mischief) that it is impossible to determine their exact limits in advance. But the general spirit of the maxim is approved by many English writers. (*c*) In other branches the law must deal with varying types of human conduct which cannot be regulated by the rigid detailed rules that may be appropriate to the definition of a crossed cheque. Thus the law of tort is fluid because of the broad standards which it applies.

But a consideration of the problem of fixity and discretion demands an analysis of the method by which law is expressed. There is a vast gulf between the elasticity of a general principle such as public policy and the rigidity of a detailed rule that a killing is murder only (*inter alia*) if the death follows within a year and a day. This entails a discussion of principles, standards, concepts, and rules.

---

[1] R. Pound, *Philosophy of Law*, 137 et seq. This particular statement has been attacked by the realist school on the ground that the certainty in the law of property is only an illusion. It is true that absolute certainty is rarely attainable in human affairs, but there is relatively more definiteness in the law of property than in tort. In most cases it is fairly easy to say what is a properly drawn cheque, but it is not always easy to determine whether particular facts constitute negligence. On the other hand, rigid and static rules may easily become inconvenient when new business practices are developed: see R. S. T. Chorley, 3 *Mod. L. R.* (1940), 272.   [2] *Infra*, § 83.

§ 48. Principles, Standards, Concepts, and Rules

Modern juristic analysis shows law operating through four distinct categories—principles, standards, concepts, and rules.[1] It is a *principle* of public policy that those who exercise a public calling should not take an unfair advantage of their position. One formulation of this principle is the *rule* that a common carrier must not charge more than a reasonable rate. This rule contains within itself a *concept* (common carrier) and also a *standard* (reasonable rate).[2]

A principle is the broad reason which lies at the base of a rule of law: it has not exhausted itself in giving birth to that particular rule but is still fertile. Principles, the means by which the law lives, grows, and develops, demonstrate that law is not a mere collection of rules. Through the medium of the principle, law can draw nourishment from the views of the community, for the *ratio legis* is wide and, in deducing from it a particular rule, regard may be paid to the circumstances to which the rule is to be applied. A legal principle should be capable of accurate expression, for there is a vast difference between reasonable elasticity and confused statement. The most accurate expression of a principle may still leave its application to particular circumstances in doubt, but that is a characteristic inherent in the nature of all principles. The marks of an efficient legal principle are that it should give cohesion to a particular branch of the law by capably explaining the relevant cases:[3] it must be suited to the practical needs and ethical requirements of that particular community and be elastic enough to afford opportunities for development in the rules that are based upon it. There are, of course, disadvantages in leaving the law expressed only in terms of a fluid principle, for the law may be too indefinite, and hence it is the task of the judge to decide when it is better to secure certainty by laying down a rule.

Legal rules are precepts laying down a definite consequence as the results of certain facts—for example, the rule that a will is invalid unless attested by two witnesses.[4] They provide 'patterns for definite situations'. Legal rules are sometimes born from principles—sometimes even the greatest legal ingenuity cannot discover the reason

---

[1] J. Dickinson, *Administrative Justice and the Supremacy of Law*, 128; R. Pound, *Philosophy of Law*, 115–43; A. Al-Sanhoury, *Rec. Gény*, ii. 144.

[2] This illustration is borrowed from J. Dickinson, op. cit.

[3] Or the majority of them. In some instances it is naturally impossible to explain anomalies.

[4] R. Pound, 7 *Tulane L. R.* (1933), 475; cited J. Hall, *Readings in Jurisprudence*, 661.

which lies behind a particular rule. A legal rule operates by means of concepts and standards. When within the rule there is a standard, then elasticity is retained—thus the rule that 'a driver on the highway must exercise reasonable care to prevent injury to others' is elastic, for the standard of reasonable care may be applied to the ancient chariot or a modern car. On the other hand, the rule that no damages will lie at common law for the death of a human being[1] is rigid, for it contains no standard, and it is difficult to discover the principle which lies behind it. Such rules are 'infructuous'—they are not agencies of development, but static rules applied only when the courts are bound to follow them.[2] A man can be convicted of murder or manslaughter only if the death follows within a certain time after his act: had the courts laid down the standard of a reasonable time, that would have allowed the law to take notice of improvements in medical knowledge, but, since the detailed rule was applied that death must follow within a year and a day, all elasticity was lost.[3]

The term 'concept' has many meanings, but broadly a concept is an abstraction from particular things, or events etc., forming a general notion. It is man-made and serves to aid thought as in the organization of the infinite particularity of things into classes. For the purpose of jurisprudence, concepts may be defined as those 'categories of classification'[4] which are rigidly determined as a matter of law. In one sense both *negligence* and *necessaries* are legal concepts, for each is a definite category of legal thought. But, as it is desired to analyse the element of fluidity in law, these two terms are treated as standards, for each depends on an idea of what is reasonable, and once this element is introduced, there is room for honest differences of opinion; what is reasonable care or reasonably necessary can be determined only by applying a wide standard to the facts. A concept for our purposes is a category that is so rigidly defined that its application is definite—for example, a document is either a bill of exchange or it is not, for the formal requirements are laid down by the law in a detailed fashion.

Concepts may be built up out of perceptions of fact—thus the idea of a motor-car is not a picture of any particular car, but conveys the notion of the class of car. Other concepts may be created of more abstract factors—e.g. corporate personality is a concept that is the

---

[1] *Baker* v. *Bolton* (1808), 1 Camp. 493.
[2] Cf. per Slesser L.J., *Flint* v. *Lovell*, [1935] 1 K.B. 354.
[3] *R.* v. *Dyson*, [1908] 2 K.B. 454.
[4] J. Dickinson, *Administrative Justice and the Supremacy of Law*, 136.

result of a long process of development. The more abstract the concept, the greater the play that may be made with it—the notion of the *estate* enabled the lawyer to introduce many subtleties and to carve out future interests in a way that would have been difficult if the land itself had been the object of thought. The intellectual maturity of a legal system may be tested by the degree of abstract generality it achieves in its concepts.[1]

Many concepts fail in their true purpose because they cannot be adequately defined. Thus the category of chattels dangerous *per se* is determined as a matter of law, but, as no precise definition of the class can be given, it would be more convenient (instead of seeking to label chattels by a consideration of their abstract qualities) to leave the law in the form of a fluid standard which could be applied and adapted to the circumstances of each particular case. Thus a loaded gun is not always dangerous, and the attempt of courts to classify chattels according to their abstract qualities has ended in confusion.[2] The concept serves best where there are relatively fixed 'counters' the definition of which can be rigidly determined, as in the law dealing with bills of exchange.

In comparison with the elastic principle and the adaptable standard, concepts thus give a *relative* certainty to law, but it is ridiculous to expect that even a concept can remain absolutely definite and static, for concepts are tools of thought, and the end which the thinker has in mind will determine his use of terms. Thus a child who has received no actual permission to enter may be removed from the category of trespassers to that of licensees, if the law of tort can grant a remedy by spelling out an implied licence because of the occupier's failure to eject on previous occasions.[3] Practical considerations have strained the accurate use of language. It was once considered that a legal concept was a substantive reality with a fixed and definite meaning discoverable by analysis. Today we adopt a more functional view—a concept is a tool of thought which we use to deal with certain situations and its development is guided as much by a desire to do justice in the individual case as by any *a priori* logic which deals with the

---

[1] H. Goldschmidt, *English Law from the Foreign Standpoint*, 21, suggests that English law is rather deficient in general conceptions: thus there is a tendency for each statute to set up its own definitions.

[2] W. T. S. Stallybrass, 3 *Camb. L. J.* (1929), 385–9.

[3] *Cooke* v. *Midland G. W. Rly.*, [1909] A.C. 229; cf. *Gough* v. *National Coal Board*, [1954] 1 Q.B. 191; see for Australia, *Commissioner of Railways (N.S.W.)* v. *Cardy* (1960), 34 A.L.J.R. 134. Changes were brought about in England by the Occupiers' Liability Act, 1957 (5 & 6 Eliz. II, ch. 31).

'inherent properties' of a concept.[1] We would expect to be able to say whether growing corn was realty or personalty, but it has been held that a sale of growing corn is not a sale of land within the Statute of Frauds, and also that it is not personalty so far as the laws of execution are concerned.[2] It might be thought that such a concept as marriage was rigidly defined, but a person may be married for one purpose and not for another. If a husband obtains a decree that his marriage was void *ab initio*, he is still entitled to rebates of income tax for the period while the marriage was subsisting,[3] but if a husband leaves money to his wife, so long as she does not remarry, a marriage afterwards avoided *ab initio* is ignored.[4] A daughter who had been married, and then obtained a decree of nullity, is unmarried for the purposes of the Inheritance (Family Provisions) Act.[5] The progressive development in the meaning of concepts is emphasized by two decisions of the Judicial Committee in the same year. In the first it was admitted that it was difficult to define piracy, since history shows so much development,[6] and in the second it was pointed out that the concept of *poena* in Roman-Dutch law has widened, for 'that law is a virile living system of law, ever seeking, as every such system must, to adapt itself consistently with its inherent basic principles to deal effectively with the increasing complexities of modern organised society'.[7] A railway ticket has been held to be property in the sense that it can be stolen, and also not property because it lacks the element of transferability.[8] The motive of economy of thought often leads to the extension of the meaning of a concept, so that a new situation may be dealt with by an old rule instead of creating a new doctrine. Thus we do find some flexibility even in concepts, especially if we take the law over a long period; but, compared with the broadness of a principle or the elasticity of a standard, concepts represent comparatively fixed counters of legal thought.

It is not always easy to determine whether a previous line of cases has laid down a detailed rule of law or merely applied a wide standard to particular facts. Thus in *Nordenfelt* v. *Maxim Nordenfelt*

---

[1] As J. C. H. Wu puts it, many now reject the *a priori* subject–predicate analysis and prefer the *a posteriori* antecedent consequent: *The Art of Law*, 124. See also an interesting paper by Zechariah Chafee jun., 41 *Col. L. R.* (1941), 381.
[2] E. R. Latty, 34 *Mich. L. R.* (1936), 597 at 605.
[3] *Dodworth* v. *Dale*, [1936] 2 K.B. 503.
[4] *In re Dewhirst*, [1948] Ch. 198.
[5] *Re Rodwell (deceased)*, [1969] 3 All E.R. 1363.
[6] *In re Piracy Iure Gentium*, [1934] A.C. 586 at 600.
[7] *Pearl Assur. Co.* v. *Govt. of Union of S.A.*, [1934] A.C. 570 at 579.
[8] C. R. Noyes, *The Institution of Property*, 381.

Guns and Amn. Co.,[1] the real issue before the court was whether the rule concerning restraint of trade was rigid (that general restraints are always bad) or whether it contained within itself a standard (that the restraint must be reasonable in the interests of the parties and of the public). There are various factors that are useful in reaching a conclusion. Firstly, history may furnish a guide—the treatment of the rule in question by judges in the past. 'When a rule has become inveterate from the earliest time . . . it would be legislation pure and simple were we to disturb it.'[2] Secondly, conditions may have so changed that it becomes almost unthinkable to enforce what appears to be a definite rule of law. Thirdly, the actual language in which the rule is expressed will throw light on the question. If in case after case the rule has been laid down in the same detailed terminology, it is difficult to escape the conclusion that it has crystallized into a definite rule of law. But the ultimate view held as to the purpose of law will naturally influence its interpretation and development. There are those who glory in the strong decision which upholds the technical consistency of the law even at the cost of injustice, and those who regard the rules of law as subject to the moulding influence of the principles which originally fashioned them.[3] In some parts of the law creative activity has greater scope than in others, but the distinction between static and dynamic interpretation is just as useful in considering case law as in dealing with a written constitution. The reforming mind attempts, if possible, to get behind the detailed rules of the law to the broad principles which lie behind them.[4] Where certainty is necessary, detailed rules and definite concepts are needed. Some parts of the law, for example the law relating to property and to commercial transactions, demand certainty almost above all else; and there is much to be said for requiring certainty in the criminal law.[5] If fluidity is desired, the principle or the standard should be used as the medium of legal expression.

A practical problem illustrates the issues that arise. Can a secular

[1] [1894] A.C. 535.

[2] Per Earl Loreburn, *Admiralty Commissioners* v. *S.S. Amerika*, [1917] A.C. 38 at 41. And see per Lord Porter: 'I do not think it possible to say that a change in the outlook of the public, however great, must immediately be followed by a change in the law of this country.' *Best* v. *Samuel Fox & Co. Ltd.*, [1952] A.C. 716 at 727.

[3] *Prager* v. *Blatspiel, Stamp & Heacock Ltd.*, [1924] 1 K.B. 566 at 570 per McCardie J.; per Cockburn C.J., *Wason* v. *Walter* (1868), L.R. 4 Q.B. 73 at 93; *In the Matter of Davy*, [1935] P. 1.

[4] Equity had its great creative period: it has now become relatively rigid.

[5] Cf. *R.* v. *Newland*, [1954] 1 Q.B. 158; and *Shaw* v. *D.P.P.*, [1961] 2 All E.R. 446, [1962] A.C. 220, and per Lord Simonds at 452–3.

society, one of whose objects is to deny the truth of the supernatural element in religion, lawfully take property by bequest? Is it a rule that 'Christianity is part of the law of England'? Lord Finlay thought that such a doctrine had been laid down by previous cases, but the majority looked behind what was apparently a rule to the wider principle that behaviour which tended to cause a breach of the peace or to endanger society is illegal. Today society is more tolerant and a reasoned denial of the truths of religion is not likely to provoke violence. Hence the maxim that Christianity was part of the law of England may once have been a fairly accurate summary of the application of the principle that acts dangerous to society should be regarded as illegal— but it was held by the House of Lords not to be a rule of law, and, conditions having changed, the same principle would now allow gifts to a secular society.[1]

Public policy illustrates the varying degrees of definiteness which the law may assume. In itself, public policy is a principle, the broadness and fluidity of which may be seen in the variety of cases professing to have been decided under it. But sometimes a rule that was originally based on public policy has become so crystallized that only a statute can alter it, e.g. the rule against perpetuities. In other cases, there may be an apparent rule, but courts will go behind the rule to see whether the reason for it applies in the particular case. It is accepted that public policy prohibits an alien enemy suing in time of war, but, if he is a member of a British partnership, and sues merely as a co-plaintiff in order that the partnership may be wound up, does that remove the mischief? Lord Atkinson and Lord Sumner thought that the court should not go behind the detailed rule, but the majority considered that the rule was still subject to the dominant reasons of policy which created it,[2] and, as the particular evils, which the prohibition of suits by enemy aliens was designed to avoid, would not arise in this case, there was no object in preventing the action being brought.

---

[1] *Bowman* v. *Secular Society Ltd.*, [1917] A.C. 406. Cf. *Bourne* v. *Keane*, [1919] A.C. 815; W. S. Holdsworth, *History of English Law*, viii. 402–20. But these cases illustrate again the different situations at different points in the judicial hierarchy. There can be little doubt that the maxim would have been applied as law (with differing consequences at different times it is true) at any time in the eighteenth or nineteenth centuries— see *Briggs* v. *Hartley* (1850), 19 L.J. (Ch.) 416; *Cowan* v. *Milbourn* (1867), L.R. 2 Ex. 230; *De Costa* v. *De Paz* 2 Swanst. 487, note (2), 532; and *In re Bedford Charity* 2 Swanst. 470, 522, 527.

[2] *Rodriguez* v. *Speyer*, [1919] A.C. 59.

REFERENCES

ALLEN, C. K., *Law in the Making*, chs. iii, iv.
BARWICK, G., 'Precedent in the Southern Hemisphere', 5 *Israel L. R.* (1970), 1.
CARDOZO, B. N., *The Nature of the Judicial Process.*
—— *Paradoxes of Legal Science.*
CECIL, HENRY, *The English Judge* (1970).
COHN, E. J., 5 *Camb. L. J.* (1935), 366.
CROSS, R., *Precedent in English Law* (1968).
DICKINSON, J., *Administrative Justice and the Supremacy of Law*, 128.
—— 29 *Col. L. R.* (1929), 113, 285.
FRIEDMANN, W., *Legal Theory*, Part VI.
GOODHART, A. L., 50 *L.Q.R.* (1934), 40, 196.
HART, H. L. A., *The Concept of Law.*
HOLDSWORTH, W. S., 50 *L.Q.R.* (1934), 180.
LAUTERPACHT, H., *Function of Law in the International Community*, 60 et seq.
LEVI, E. H., *An Introduction to Legal Reasoning.*
LLEWELLYN, K. N., *The Common Law Tradition: Deciding Appeals.*
LLOYD, D., *Public Policy* (1953).
MONTROSE, J. L., 'The Language of, and a Notation for, the Doctrine of Precedent', 2 *W. A. Annual L. R.* 301, 504.
PATON, G. W., and SAWER, G., 63 *L.Q.R.* (1947), 461.
POUND, R., 36 *Harv. L. R.* (1923), 641, 940.
—— 53 *Harv. L. R.* (1940), 365.
—— *Philosophy of Law*, 100–43.
Report of Cincinnati Conference on the Status of Judicial Precedent, 14 *Univ. of Cincinnati L. R.* (1940), 203–355.
ROSTOW, E. V., *The Sovereign Prerogative: The Supreme Court and the Quest for Law* (1962).
Science of Legal Method (Modern Legal Philosophy Series).
STONE, J., *Province and Function of Law*, chs. vi, vii.
WINFIELD, P. H., 45 *Harv. L. R.* (1931), 112.
—— 59 *L.Q.R.* (1943), 327.

IX

STATUTES AND CODES

§ 49. COMPARISON OF CASE LAW AND STATUTE

IT has often been claimed that the method of developing law by
statute has inherent advantages over any system which leaves it to the
judges to create new law. Firstly, it is said that a statute is abrogative
and can sweep away inconvenient rules, whereas, while a precedent
may constitute the law for the future, the judge is imperatively bound
by such rules as the legislature or higher courts may have laid down.
If the judge is, in one sense, a law-maker, it must be remembered that
this power of creation is limited by his duty to apply the law as laid
down by the legislature or by previous judicial authority. His most
obvious creative role, therefore, is seen when he must fill a gap existing
in the legal system. Hence, when unjust rules exist, a legislature may
sweep them away, whereas a judge must follow binding authority
which is in point, however much he may dislike the rule which it lays
down.

Secondly, a statute can lay down the law in advance, whereas case
law is sometimes created only at the actual time of application. A
statute can change the law for the future, leaving vested rights untouched, whereas if an English appellate court wishes to overrule
a line of persuasive precedents it can do so only by making the change
retrospective, thus (perhaps) upsetting the expectations of a party
who reasonably relied on the previous authorities.[1] But these statements need some qualification. A reading of the law reports gives
a false view of the fluidity of case law, for (at least in theory) only
cases of definite legal importance are reported. Moreover, new points
may arise under statute just as under case law. But, even admitting
these qualifications, it remains true that there is no method whereby
the courts can lay down law for the future save in the decision of
a specific dispute.

[1] In America, however, a court may apply its previous precedents, but at the same
time announce that it will apply a different rule to subsequent transactions: *Gt. N.
Rly.* v. *Sunburst Oil and Refining Co.* (1932), 287 U.S. 358; E. W. Patterson, 88 *Univ.
of Pa. L. R.* (1939), 156 at 158; *Moliter* v. *Kaneland Community School District* (1959),
18 Ill. (2d) 11, 163 N.E. (2d) 89; B. H. Levy, *Realist Jurisprudence and Prospective
Overruling* (1960), 109 *U. of Pa. L. R.* 1.

The greater creative power of the legislature is frequently justified by the traditional doctrine of the separation of powers[1]—that it is for the legislature to change the law, to decide awkward questions of social policy, and to live amid the dust of party politics; whereas the court, untouched by strife, is to apply the law with Olympian calm, secure in the belief that if injustice is done, or if the law is obsolete, a kindly legislature will take the necessary steps for reform. But even statutes themselves, when obsolete, need new legislation to reform them, for statutes do not lose force through desuetude.[2] Hence the makers of codes have sometimes attempted to confine the courts to their task of applying law, but no legislature has had the necessary time or zeal to decide all doubtful points and, whether they wish it or not, courts have been forced to develop the law in some degree.[3]

It is sometimes alleged that statute law is superior, in that the rules are logically arranged and may easily be discovered, whereas the quest for a common law principle entails a long search through multitudinous reports and, even when the cases bearing on the issue have been isolated, it may still be difficult to reconcile them. This defect of form is inherent in the very nature of case law, however lawyers may try to minimize it by the use of digests and textbooks as a guide to the law.[4] But logical and concise arrangement of the rules is not necessarily a merit of statute law, though it is a mark of a well-drafted code. When, as in England, statute provides a gloss or amendment of the common law, then we may find the utmost disorder in the statute book. Lawyers who are used to a code, or even a general consolidation, are amazed that England should be content with the chaotic arrangement of her statute book. Similarly, even a particular statute may sometimes be described as a 'thing of shreds and patches', 'a kind of statutory Joseph's coat'.[5]

Another suggested advantage of statute law is greater certainty, since the rule is laid down in categorical language, whereas in dealing

---

[1] *Infra*, § 75.

[2] *A.G.* v. *Prince Ernest Augustus of Hanover*, [1957] A.C. 436.

[3] *Infra*, § 52, for a reference to the French experiment of obliging the courts to refer gaps in the law to the legislature.

[4] In *Worthy* v. *Lloyd*, [1939] 2 K.B. 612, two cases were cited from the *Estates Gazette Digest*. In *Gibson* v. *S. American Stores*, [1949] 2 All E.R. 985, the C.A. followed a decision of their own, given in 1935, of which no report existed at all. In 1953 Somervell, Denning, and Romer LL.J. stated that they were not willing to permit citation of reports which were not made by members of the Bar; and Denning L.J. said there were enough cases that could be cited apart from those in the *Estates Gazette*, *Birtwistle* v. *Tweedale*, [1953] 2 All E.R. 1598, [1954] 1 W.L.R. 190.

[5] Per Rich J., *The King* v. *The Federal Commissioner of Taxation*; *Ex Parte Sir Kelso King* (1930), 43 C.L.R. 569 at 574.

with a judgment it may be extraordinarily difficult to discover the *ratio decidendi*. But difficulties of interpretation are not confined to case law, and in some reports over half of the cases are concerned with statutory interpretation.[1] Lord Buckmaster wrote of a taxing act:

I do not pretend that the opinion I hold rests on any firm logical foundation. Logic is out of place in these questions and the embarrassment that I feel is increased with the knowledge that my views are not shared by other members of the House. . . . It is not easy to penetrate the tangled confusion of these Acts of Parliament, and though we have entered the labyrinth together, we have unfortunately found exit by different paths.[2]

Austin considers that statute law is superior because it is made after due deliberation, whereas judicial law, owing to the practical exigencies of disposing of a crowded list, is made in haste. But there is nothing essential about this distinction. The modern 'end of session' rush in Parliament creates law at a greater speed than any court would dare to attempt, even at the end of term.[3] An appellate court may take long to consider a judgment, though fortunately today there are none as cautious as Lord Eldon, who pondered for years over a particular decision.[4] It is also claimed by some that judge-made law may be the result of the whim of an individual, whereas a statute must pass the scrutiny of a body of men. There is some truth in this, but a legislature under a wave of political opinion may be as partial as any one man could be.

Such are some of the suggested advantages of statute. A recent study by a committee of the Statute Law Society[5] suggests the following defects, which were based on a questionnaire sent to nearly 5,000 'users' of statutes:

(*a*) It is difficult to find out when a statute comes into force— sometimes part of an Act is proclaimed, while other sections are left for the future.

---

[1] Workmen's compensation, taxation, industrial regulation, and traffic control account for a surprisingly large number of decided cases.

[2] *G. W. Rly.* v. *Bater*, [1922] 2 A.C. 1 at 11.

[3] Griffith C.J. once refused to follow a case on the ground that it was 'briefly, and I regret to say, insufficiently argued and considered on the last day of the Sydney Sittings. . . . The arguments which now commend themselves to me as conclusive did not then find entrance to my mind': *Duncan* v. *State of Queensland* (1916), 22 C.L.R. 556 at 582. Curiously enough, *Duncan's Case* itself was later overruled in *McArthur Ltd.* v. *State of Queensland* (1920), 28 C.L.R. 530.

[4] W. S. Holdsworth, *History of English Law*, i. 437–8.

[5] *Statute Law Deficiencies* (1970).

(*b*) A statute is drafted with two purposes in mind. It must fit into the legislative procedures and be so designed as to favour the political chance of its passing into law: it is also a legal instrument once it is affirmed. The requirements of the first purpose sometimes derogate from the efficiency of the statute as a binding rule. To meet opposition a 'formula' may be devised which is intentionally obscure. The politician's insistence on haste causes much difficulty for the draftsman.

(*c*) The same subject may be dealt with in many Acts, e.g. there are 179 national Acts and 220 local Acts dealing with building operations. As far as possible, there should be one Act for each particular topic and that Act should deal with that topic alone.

(*d*) It is almost impracticable for the practitioner to keep his statute law up to date. The official indexes are inadequate. Scarman J. writes[1] that taking the 32 volumes of the Statutes Revised, up to 31 December 1965 over 9,000 pages (out of a total of 26,000) had been cancelled. This amounted to over one-third of the material. On the pages which remain there are amendments and annotations slips. Periodic consolidation is one answer to this problem: another is the use of computers to discover the ruling section.

(*e*) Because of the strict attitude taken by the courts to the interpretation of statutes, excessive detail is inserted in the draft, with highly complicated schedules.

(*f*) Legislation by reference is an easy political way of securing the passing of an Act, but it causes great difficulty in interpretation, as it frequently sacrifices simplicity and clarity.[2]

(*g*) The secrecy surrounding the initial stages of a bill prevents full consultation with professional experts outside the Department.

Sometimes obsolete statutes cause difficulty. 'I find it incredible that the law (on charities) is still derived from the preamble to the Statute of Elizabeth, long since repealed and long since out of date and in modern times applied by analogy on analogy on analogy. It is time this branch of the law was reconsidered, rationalised and modernised.'[3]

Now the merits traditionally ascribed to case law fall to be considered. It is said that case law has within itself an organic principle

---

[1] *Law Reform*, 50–1. In the five years ending on 31 December 1968 there were nearly 400 statutes and 10,000 statutory instruments enacted.
[2] Per Salmon L.J., *R.* v. *Goswami*, [1969] 1 Q.B. 453 at 461.
[3] Per Foster J., *Council of Law Reporting* v. *A.G.*, [1971] 1 All E.R. 436 at 448.

of growth and therefore that it can be adapted to new situations, whereas the statute lays down a detailed rule which will be rigidly applied to certain circumstances and will remain inflexible however much conditions may change. If reform is desired, a new statute is passed, and hence the statute book becomes a disjointed series of particular rules, whereas, since case law contains broad principles, it is more of a consistent whole. The periodic swing in political parties means that the policies of statute law change rather too rapidly as the sessions progress. But the accuracy of this distinction depends on the particular types of statute and case law which we are considering. There is no *a priori* reason why a statute should not lay down broad principles which are sufficiently elastic to be made the foundation of a developing body of law—on the other hand, case law, if great skill is not used, may easily become a 'wilderness of single instances'.

Again, case law is said to be more practical, since it is developed only after studying carefully the precise facts to which it is to be applied, whereas the legislature lays down an abstract rule the precise effect of which may be the opposite of that desired. This is frequently true, but it is sometimes impossible for a court to foretell the practical effects of a particular decision. Thus, in public policy cases, no evidence is given as to what is for the public benefit, and a judge must use his knowledge of the world as best he may;[1] on the other hand, a legislature may set up a commission to carry out the most detailed factual investigation of local circumstances and of the experience in other countries of the effects of the suggested rule. Both case law and statute may be exceedingly practical or exceedingly remote from the currents of life. The only advantage of case law in this respect is that it proceeds one step at a time, whereas a statute is usually rather more ambitious in its aim.

But it is rather futile to discuss the question in the abstract, for no country today is faced with a choice between pure statute law and pure case law. No code has ever been successful in preventing the growth of a body of judge-made law; no case system has ever functioned so well that the legislature or some other authority has not been forced to intervene.[2] The practical question today is the degree

---

[1] Cf. Lord Haldane, *Rodriguez* v. *Speyer*, [1919] A.C. 59 at 79: 'It was certainly the opinions of men of the world, as distinguished from opinions based on legal learning, which guided this House to its conclusion in that appeal.' The reference is to *Egerton* v. *Brownlow* (1853), 4 H.L.C. 1.

[2] Thus in the law of tort, the legislature intervened when case law became confused on such subjects as contributory negligence, defamation, occupier's liability, limitation of actions, and personal injuries.

to which freedom should be left to the judge. This question can be determined only by a consideration of all the circumstances in a particular country, for it is dangerous to codify until the law has reached a certain stage of development.

The criticisms discussed above may suggest that English law is but a chaos of particular rules. As the courts increasingly turn out new precedents, and the legislature drafts additional statutes, how is a working knowledge of the law to be gained? The sections which follow indicate some of the answers to this problem. Consolidation and codification deal with the accumulated mass of statutory law: institutions for the purpose of initiating law reform are set up in many countries. The digest and the textbook attempt to provide a clue to the maze of precedent.

§ 50. CONSOLIDATION

Consolidation is the combination in a single measure of all the statutes relating to a given subject-matter and is distinct from codification in that the latter systematizes case law as well as statutes. Thus the Partnership Act and the Sale of Goods Act are really codes in that both case law and statute are arranged in a harmonious whole. There is some confusion in the meaning of the terms consolidation and codification in many English books, but the orthodox view makes this clear distinction between the two.[1]

Consolidation does not primarily aim at amendment, but rather at making accessible the *statute* law on a given point. But if there are, for example, 132 statutes dealing with perjury,[2] it is clearly inadvisable to be content with paste-and-scissors work. Hence amendment is usually necessary in some degree. The great advantage of consolidation is that it renders the statute law easier to handle. Thus Victoria[3] has consolidated the whole of her statute law on four occasions, in 1890, 1915, 1928, and 1958, eight volumes being sufficient on the last occasion. In England the task of consolidation

---

[1] Thus C. E. Odgers, *The Construction of Deeds and Statutes* (2nd ed.), 226, seems to recognize no distinction. 'Consolidating acts are acts to comprehend in one statute the provisions contained in a number of statutes and which codify the law on some subject as far as they go.' The illustration given is the Bills of Exchange Act, 1882, which according to the distinction drawn in the text is a code. Lord Watson in 1895 referred to a consolidation as a code, *Administrator-General of Bengal* v. *Prem Lal Mullick* (1895), L.R. 22 I.A. 107 at 116. Cf. per Chitty J., *Re Budgett*, [1894] 2 Ch. 557 at 561.

[2] As in England in 1913.   [3] Australia.

is proceeding slowly,[1] but an attempt to consolidate all the statute law would, doubtless, be regarded as grandiose.

Even if the words are not changed, the actual effect of re-enacting a section in a consolidating statute may be great, since the consolidation, like any other statute, speaks from the date on which it comes into force.[2] Thus, unless there are saving clauses, by-laws made under the old act will lapse, since Parliament has repealed the section under which the power to create them was exercised. It is true that the re-enacted section will give the same power to make by-laws, but a power given in 1938 will not, without express words, validate by-laws made before that date.[3]

But the general intention lying behind a consolidation has two practical effects on the theory of interpretation: firstly, in cases where the meaning is doubtful, it is presumed, in the absence of evidence to the contrary, that the consolidation did not intend to change the law;[4] secondly, respect is still paid to prior decisions interpreting a section which is drawn into the consolidation.[5] The majority view supports these two presumptions, although, of course, they must give way before any clear evidence that the intent of the consolidation was otherwise. Since many amendments are made in the course of consolidation, each particular case must be examined on its merits. In a code there is no presumption against an intent to change the law, and cases decided before the code was enacted are no authority for its interpretation, although they may be examined to throw light on the previous state of the law.[6]

---

[1] From 1870 to 1934 there were over 100 consolidation bills—see W. M. Graham-Harrison, *J. Soc. Public Teachers of Law* (1935), 9 at 24. From 1935 to 1960 there were 90 consolidation acts passed.

[2] Hence it is wrong to speak of a consolidation as a declaratory act, for: (1) most consolidations introduce some changes; (2) even where there is no change in the language, the re-enacting of a section may lead to unforeseen results, as the new section now speaks from a different date.

[3] *Martin* v. *Trigg*, [1931] A.L.R. 34. Cf. M. Chalmers, cited W. M. Graham-Harrison, op. cit., at 22: 'The language of an old Act can hardly be introduced into a new Act without alteration. I was looking the other day at a clause in a Consolidation Bill. If the words of the original section had been reproduced, five important changes in the existing law would have been made, including the re-establishment of the three old common law courts at Westminster.'

[4] Per Romer L.J., *Swan* v. *Pure Ice Company*, [1935] 2 K.B. 265 at 274; *Nolan* v. *Clifford* (1904), 1 C.L.R. 429 at 447; *Re Warren*, [1939] 1 Ch. 684.

[5] This has been laid down in many cases: *Smith* v. *Baker*, [1891] A.C. 325 at 349; but Lord Watson, *Administrator-General of Bengal* v. *Prem Lal Mullick* (1895), L.R. 22 I.A. 107 at 116, referred to it as a singular proposition which had neither reason nor authority to commend it.

[6] *Bank of England* v. *Vagliano Bros.*, [1891] A.C. 107 at 144–5, which dealt with the interpretation of the Bills of Exchange Act which is really a code.

§ 51. Statutory Interpretation in England

The manner in which an Englishman interprets statutes has recently come in for much criticism—'the common lawyer is at his worst when confronted with a legislative text'.[1] The skill that has been trained, not to accept the words of a judgment at their face value, but to search for the spirit of the decision, seems to desert him when he turns to the consideration of statutory texts. We cannot cavil much at the theoretical canons of construction, though a few are rather narrow and suggest, as Pollock has stated, an underlying assumption that all parliamentary interference is evil *per se*.[2] But the rules are wide enough to afford justification for the most diverse interpretations, and what is decisive is the spirit in which they are used.

Pound has pointed out that statutes might be received fully into the body of the law as affording, not only a narrow rule, but a principle from which to reason, to be extended if necessary by analogy just as are the rules of common law; or courts might confine the statute to the cases with which it directly deals, but give a broad interpretation to the words used; finally, a narrow and rigid construction might be applied. The learned author suggests that the last is the typical common law approach.[3]

There are three fundamental rules suggested in the English cases: firstly, the literal rule that, if the meaning of a section is plain, it is to be applied whatever the result; the 'golden rule' that the words should be given their ordinary sense unless that would lead to some absurdity or inconsistency with the rest of the instrument;[4] and the 'mischief rule' which emphasizes the general policy of the statute and the evil at which it was directed.[5] Judges frequently disagree as to whether a section is plain or not, and, even where it is agreed that the meaning is plain, each may differ from the other as to what that plain meaning is. The doctrine that the intent of Parliament should be followed does not take us very far, for it is agreed that the subjective intention of Parliament cannot be considered, and that the intent must be gathered from the statute itself.[6]

---

[1] R. Pound, *Future of the Common Law*, 18.
[2] *Essays in Jurisprudence and Ethics*, 85. See also M. Radin, 43 *Harv. L. R.* (1930), 863; J. M. Landis, 43 *Harv. L. R.* (1930), 886; D. J. Llewelyn Davies, 35 *Col. L. R.* (1935), 519; R. A. Eastwood, *J. Soc. Public Teachers of Law* (1935), 1; W. M. Graham-Harrison, op. cit. 9.   [3] 21 *Harv. L. R.* (1908), 385.
[4] Cf. *Grey* v. *Pearson* (1857), 6 H.L.C. 61 at 106.
[5] J. Willis, 'Statute Interpretation in a Nutshell', 16 *Can. B. R.* (1938), 1.
[6] *Sussex Peerage Claim* (1844), 11 Cl. & F. 85 at 143.

Many of the presumptions used in construction are not unreasonable. Thus we should not expect Parliament to interfere with a fundamental common law rule (for example, to take property away without compensation, or to impose criminal liability where there is no *mens rea*) except by clear words bringing about those results.[1] But an improper use of these presumptions may go far to defeat the purpose of an act. 'I venture respectfully to think that the view of the Court of Appeal illustrates a tendency common in construing an Act which changes the law, that is, to minimise or neutralise its operation by introducing notions taken from or inspired by the old law which the words of the Act were intended to abrogate and did abrogate.'[2] When an individualist common law is modified by collectivist legislation, we sometimes see an unsympathetic construction. Thus the real basis of housing legislation is a sacrifice of private rights of ownership in order to make possible a planned attack on the problem of the provision of suitable accommodation—hence an over-emphasis on the presumption against interference with the private rights of the landowner sometimes in the past led to a defeat of the real purpose of an Act.[3] Pennsylvania has attempted to overcome rigid interpretation by a Statutory Construction Act which abolishes the rule that statutes in derogation of the common law are to be strictly construed.[4]

The most marked difference from continental methods of interpretation is the greater tendency in England to the literal approach.[5] Thus, where an Act stated that bills of sale should be attested by a solicitor and that the attestation should assert that the solicitor had explained the nature of the instrument to the grantor before execution, it was held that it did not matter whether in fact the solicitor had given an explanation so long as the attestation asserted that he had done so.[6] But it is wrong to consider that English judges always

---

[1] 'But who, that is acquainted with the difficulty of new modelling any branch of our statute laws (though relating both to roads or to parish settlements) will conceive it ever feasible to alter any fundamental point of common law, with all its appendages and consequents, and set up another rule in its stead?' Blackstone, *Commentaries*, iii. 267. 'Would it be within the capacity of a Parliamentary Draftsman to frame, for example, a provision replacing a deep-rooted legal doctrine with a new one?' Sir Owen Dixon, *The Common Law as an Ultimate Constitutional Foundation*, 31 *Aust. L. J.*, (1957), 241.

[2] Per Lord Wright, *Rose* v. *Ford*, [1937] A.C. 826 at 846.

[3] W. I. Jennings, 49 *Harv. L. R.* (1936), 426: 'What (administrative lawyers) ask is not that judges shall pervert legislation in favour of a "bureaucracy", but that they shall not interpret it against public policy in the interests of private property' (pat. 454).

[4] 43 *Dickinson L. R.* (1938–9), 236.

[5] M. S. Amos, 5 *Camb. L. J.* (1934), 163.

[6] *Ex. p. National Mercantile Bank* (1880), 15 Ch. D. 42, cited M. S. Amos, op. cit. 167.

construe statutes narrowly, for there are many examples of a liberal interpretation.[1] The rules hunt in pairs—the court may not fill a *casus omissus*, but it must attempt to find a construction which will not defeat entirely the intention of the Act. The court must accept a meaning which is plain, but, if possible, the section should be so interpreted as not to lead to unjust results. If a person keeps strictly within the letter he may offend against the spirit of an Act with impunity, but on the other hand the court will not allow an Act to be evaded by shift or contrivance.[2] Hence a court can build on that rule which it considers best suited to the merits of a particular problem— but a difference of approach between various courts will be manifest, as is also the case in the interpretation of a written constitution.

There are welcome signs that a pedantic use of technical rules is falling into disfavour. Lord du Parcq thought it worth while to emphasize the truism that the best way of finding out the meaning of a statute is to read it and see what it means.[3] Denning L.J. deprecates the old-fashioned tendency to belabour the draftsman and points out that it is beyond human reason to foresee all contingencies and beyond the resources of language to achieve absolute clarity—the judge must work constructively by drawing the conclusion which fits the policy of the Act.[4] 'We do not now in this court stick to the letter of a statute. We go by its true intent. We fill in the gaps.'[5] Logic plays its part, but interpretation is really a creative art and it has been persuasively argued that the approach should differ according to the type of statute in question.[6] A constitution and a criminal code may both be statutes, but it is dangerous not to take account of the

---

[1] Cf. *Miller* v. *Hilton*, [1937] A.L.R. 298: 'No person shall on any controlled route drive any vehicle or cause any vehicle to be driven for the purpose of carrying etc.' If the regulation is literally read, a person who causes is liable only if he is on the controlled route himself, but this so obviously is a drafting slip that the High Court of Australia refused to read the statute in this way. See also *In re Allen, Craig & Co. (London) Ltd.*, [1934] Ch. 483; *Anstee* v. *Jennings*, [1935] V.L.R. 144; *Day* v. *Simpson* (1865), 34 L.J.M.C. 149. Contrast for a narrower interpretation *Moore* v. *Tweedale*, [1935] 2 K.B. 163; *Inland Revenue Commissioners* v. *Duke of Westminster*, [1936] A.C. 1. 'Simplicity and common sense are . . . qualities which must be applied with caution in the construction of a taxing statute': per Megarry J., *Roberts* v. *Granada T.V. Rental Ltd.*, [1970] 2 All E.R. 764 at 771–2.

[2] Compare *Samuel* v. *Adelaide Club*, [1934] 2 K.B. 69 with *Milne* v. *Commissioner of Police for City of London*, [1940] A.C. 1.

[3] *Cutler* v. *Wandsworth Stadium Ltd.*, [1949] A.C. 398 at 410.

[4] *Seaford Court Estates Ltd.* v. *Asher*, [1949] 2 K.B. 481 at 499; D. Lloyd, *Current Legal Problems* (1948), 89.

[5] *Ministry of Housing* v. *Sharp*, [1970] 1 All E.R. 1009 at 1015; Cross L.J. at 1034. See also *R.* v. *Bonner*, [1970] 2 All E.R. 97, which emphasizes that the object of the Theft Act was to get rid of the subtleties and absurdities of the previous law.

[6] W. Friedmann, 26 *Can. B. R.* (1948), 1277.

difference between them.[1] 'How long can we assume that the statute provides a complete set of answers?'[2]

Many of the narrowing presumptions of the English doctrine of interpretation would not be applied on the Continent. In England statutes are a gloss written around the common law, and hence we can regard the common law as primary except in so far as it is specifically altered by legislation. On the Continent the influence of the work of Justinian led lawyers to regard enacted law as the primary type,[3] and today, of course, the real foundation of the law of Western Europe is found in the codes. Hence the continental statutes are more broadly drafted and more sympathetically applied. In England statutes are not extended by analogy, although in earlier times the doctrine of the equity of a statute led to a treatment that was similar to that applied to English case law today.[4]

Thus a vicious circle has been created. The interpretation in the past has tended to be so literal that the draftsman is forced to be very specific; and the method of drafting is so detailed that the broad interpretation given to the French Code is rendered difficult, if not impossible.[5] If present English methods of interpretation and drafting were continued, it would be a tragedy if a code were instituted. The continental draftsman 'whether of a will, of articles of association, or of a law, does not regard himself as a general disposing his troops for a frontal attack upon a hostile position, but as one who is bringing up reinforcements to an ally. A nod is as good as a wink to a friendly court.'[6] It is hardly fair to put the blame on the draftsman, as is sometimes done.[7] The doctrine of precedent has increased the difficulties of the situation, for a comparatively short section may

---

[1] J. Bentham, *Limits of Jurisprudence Defined*, 253, cynically states that interpretation is called strict when it is what the legislator really intended and liberal when you apply to him an intention he did not possess because he failed to appreciate the problem.

[2] Harry Bloom, 33 *Mod. L. R.* (1970), 197.

[3] M. S. Amos, 5 *Camb. L. J.* (1934), 163 at 173.

[4] W. S. Holdsworth, *Sources and Literature*, 46; T. F. T. Plucknett, *Statutes and their Interpretation in the Fourteenth Century*, 72 et seq.

[5] Cf. T. F. T. Plucknett, in *Rec. Lambert*, i. 434. M. S. Amos instances § 3 of the Wills Act, 1837, as 'a good example of the frenzy of caution to which at that time draftsmen were driven by the reign of judicial terror under which they lived. If the judges could not be relied on to help, by occasionally taking something for granted, the only course to take, so it seemed, was to endeavour to enumerate every possible case': 5 *Camb. L. J.* (1934), 169.   [6] M. S. Amos, ibid. 175.

[7] But sometimes we find unconscious humour in a statute: see § 1 (2) of 24 & 25 Geo. V, c. 21: '. . . if an animal appears . . . to be unbroken or untrained it shall lie on the defendant to prove that the animal is in fact broken or trained.' Scrutton L.J., *Roe* v. *Russell*, [1928] 2 K.B. 117, regretted that he could not order the costs to be paid by the draftsmen and the members of the legislature at 130.

soon be overlaid with a mass of binding case law which is difficult to harmonize. Goddard L.J. has stated:

I cannot help thinking if those words had to be construed by somebody who did not labour under the considerable disadvantage of having at his elbow a copy of the Workmen's Compensation Reports and the various text-books on the subject, he would have no difficulty is saying that 'suitable' meant 'suitable' and that work which involved danger to the eyes was not suitable work for a one-eyed man.[1]

Another difference between English and continental methods of approach is that in England very little use is made of 'preparatory work'. Thus reports of debates in Parliament are not admissible as evidence of the policy of a statute,[2] and a report of a royal commission can be used only to show the state of the law before the Act was passed.[3] Sometimes this rule has led to a result the opposite of that which Parliament really intended,[4] and there are some signs that the rigid exclusionary rule may be weakened a little.[5] A dictatorship sets simpler problems for the draftsman. In 1938 a pithy German statute imposed a contribution of one million reichsmarks on the Jews. 'All necessary implementing regulations shall be issued by the Minister of Finance in agreement with the Minister of the Reich concerned.' No English draftsman could be so concise.[6]

§ 52. CODIFICATION

A general movement towards codification marked the nineteenth century.[7] It is sometimes said that the predominant motive for codifi-

---

[1] *Hoe and Co.* v. *Dirs*, [1941] 1 K.B. 34 at 42.

[2] They have been cited in Australia (*Engineers' Case* (1920), 28 C.L.R. 129 at 147) and by the J.C. with the discreet omission of inverted commas or reference (see 48 L.Q.R. (1932), 145), but the general rule now is that it is not permissible to refer to them: P. B. Maxwell, *Interpretation of Statutes* (10th ed.), 25–8.

[3] Per Lord Wright, *Assam Railways and Trading Co. Ltd.* v. *Inland Revenue Commissioners*, [1935] A.C. 445 at 457–9.

[4] *Ellerman Lines Ltd.* v. *Murray*, [1931] A.C. 126. Lord Halsbury has said that the person least qualified to interpret a statute is the person responsible for its drafting, for he is likely to confuse his actual intention with the effect of the language which he employed: *Hilder* v. *Dexter*, [1902] A.C. 474 at 477; C. B. Nutting, 20 *Boston Univ. L. R.* (1940), 601.

[5] See per Sholl J. in *T. M. Burke Pty. Ltd.* v. *City of Horsham*, [1958] V.R. 209 at 216; and G. Barwick, *Divining the Legislative Intent*, 35 *Aust. L. J.* (1961), 197.

[6] S. P. Simpson and J. Stone, *Law and Society*, 1987.

[7] 1804, the French Civil Code; 1811, Austria; 1838, Holland; 1844, Serbia; 1864, Rumania; 1865, Italy; 1889, Spain; 1900, Germany; 1907, Switzerland. The French Code was also taken as a model for Argentina, Bolivia, Chile, Colombia, Costa Rica, Ecuador, Guatemala, Haiti, Honduras, Louisiana, Mexico, Montenegro, Peru, Portugal, Quebec, Salvador, San Domingo, Uruguay, and Venezuela: R. Pound, *Outlines of Jurisprudence* (1943), 136.

cation was a desire to render the law certain, but this, at least in the case of France and Germany, was really overshadowed by the desire to replace the differing laws of the various provinces or states by a system that was national and unified.[1] Two types of countries tend to adopt codes: those with well-developed systems where the possibility of further development is remote for the moment: those with undeveloped systems which cannot grapple with new economic problems.

Nevertheless, many codifiers emphasize that one of their aims is to make the law simple and accessible, logically arranged and harmonious, certain and definite. Both Justinian and Napoleon thought that the law would remain clear until the commentators started to explain it. In the first flush of enthusiasm it was said in France that all the problems of law had been solved and that every case could be decided by deduction from the provisions of the code. Bugnet said: 'Je ne connais pas le droit civil, je n'enseigne que le code Napoléon.'[2] Hence a purely logical method of interpretation was adopted. Liard writes that law is only the *loi écrite* and that the work of the judge should be as exact as that of the geometrician who by deduction draws from his axioms the answer to all possible problems.[3] The writers who took this view are known as the exegetical school, since all the emphasis was put on the interpretation of the written law.[4]

But no code can be all-sufficient. The doctrine of the logical plenitude of law is a useful one,[5] but if jurists think that a limited number of sections in a code include all the law that there is, the problem becomes increasingly difficult as the decades roll by. No draftsman can altogether avoid such flaws as ambiguity, obscurity, or conflict of sections, and even if he could, new problems arise which could not possibly have been foreseen and new social philosophies become popular which are out of keeping with the basis on which the code is built.

In the long run, the real test of a code is the measure of flexibility which it has allowed the law. It was the early French scheme that the

---

[1] In France there were 60 general systems of law and 300 particular systems before 1789. W. Simons in *Law, a Century of Progress*, i. 84, says that when he was a judge in Thuringia there were 13 different systems dealing with property of married persons within his *Landgericht*.   [2] Cited F. Gény, *Méthode*, i. 30.
[3] Cited ibid. 54. See also J. Bonnecase, *La Pensée juridique française de 1804 à l'heure présente* (1933), i. 522, where he discusses *l'école de l'exégèse*.
[4] The school emphasized the intention of the legislature as the primary source of law, and thus regarded it as omnipotent. But, as in the case of Austin (*supra*, § 4), they also thought that there were fundamental and absolute principles which could be made the basis of jurisprudence.   [5] *Supra*, § 43.

courts should merely apply the law; if points of obscurity did un-accountably arise, the judges might refer them to the legislature, and when a conflict of decisions revealed a gap in the law, such reference was obligatory.[1] But the scheme proved unwieldy, for the long delays were injurious to suitors and it was soon abolished without regrets. It also proved to be increasingly difficult to regard the code as containing the answer to every possible problem, especially as the passing of the years brought new difficulties which could not have been foreseen when the code was drafted. If the legislator has not directed his mind to a specific point, there will always be differences of opinion when the argument by analogy is used, and if the most likely answer leads to unjust results, it is difficult not to succumb to the temptation to use a 'perverse logic'. In England, where a statute clearly does not deal with a specific point, there is the reservoir of common law principles which may be drawn upon, but if in France the theory was adopted that *all* the law was contained within the code, it is easy to see the problem that arose. In many cases the traditional method of interpretation did not lead to certainty, for, where there was a gap in the law, opinions differed as to what the legislature would have enacted had the particular problem been present to their minds. Moreover, the code was based on a somewhat narrow individualism and upheld the interests of the middle classes—consequently the rising tide of collectivism and an increasing concern for the welfare of the labourer have created difficulties for any theory of literal interpretation.

As a reaction to the exegetical school there arose a dangerously wide theory of interpretation that the jurist should not attempt to discover the intention of the legislator, but should treat the code as having a life of its own—the text should not be *interpreted*, but rather *adapted* to the changing world of modern times. That interpretation is best which most successfully warps the text to suit the needs of the present hour.[2] When the increasing number of accidents caused by the motor-car led jurists to desire a stricter theory of liability which could be applied to the driver it was necessary to find a peg in the code on which such a doctrine could be hung. This was difficult, for the traditional interpretation of the relevant articles founded liability for delict on fault and fault alone. Saleilles and Josserand advocated that

---

[1] F. Gény, *Méthode*, i. 78–9. A. I. Vyshinsky considered that difficult questions of statutory interpretation should be dealt with only by somebody responsible to the legislature: *Law of the Soviet State*, 339.

[2] Cf. the dictum of M. J. Percerou, cited F. Gény, *Méthode*, i. 262.

strict liability should be the lot of the driver, but each based it on a different section.[1] Gény approved the result, but not the particular means by which it was reached, for the torturing of the text leads to a dangerous arbitrariness, since once the process begins of reading into the codes what is not there, how are limits to be set to this method, and how is the content of the new rules to be determined?

Gény prefers to restore the code to a place of respect, and argues that the judge must interpret it as faithfully as possible by attempting to discover the real meaning of the words in which it is expressed, as is done in the construction of contracts or wills. But he would rigidly confine the code to the precise circumstances with which it deals, and, where a problem arises on which the code, honestly construed, throws no light, he argues that the judge, instead of reaching a conclusion by a fanciful use of analogy, should fill the gap by free scientific research —free because the formal authorities do not bind, and scientific because it places itself on a solid base of objective truth. The topic has already been discussed.[2] But the importance of Gény's approach, so far as the code is concerned, is that he recognizes that the code does not contain all the law.[3] Hence, even where codification is adopted, the search for new law must proceed, and in France there has been on many points greater flexibility than in England during the last generation. Hence it is superficial to consider that a code makes inevitably for rigidity, for all depends on the method of its drafting and the manner of its interpretation.

§ 53. THE GROWING IMPORTANCE OF STATUTE LAW

There is still a tendency in English legal education to treat statute law too lightly. For this there are several reasons: first, the common

---

[1] L. Josserand based it on 1384. 1, which enacted that a person is responsible for damage caused by things in his custody. R. Saleilles boldly reinterpreted 1382, putting the notion of cause in place of that of fault. The French courts finally adopted a theory of presumption of fault, which could be rebutted only by showing that the cause of the accident was external to the car.

[2] F. Gény, Méthode, ii. 78. It is rather difficult to translate Gény's word *scientifique*, for it has a special meaning in his work which it derives from its opposition to *technique*. *Science* is the study which scrutinizes the *donné*, the objective realities which lie at the base of law, as opposed to *technique*, the intellectual elaboration wherein the jurist has certain powers of construction within the limits set by the *donné*. 'Scientific' is not an adequate translation, for science in English suggests a concern with empirical facts.

[3] J. Bonnecase, *La Pensée juridique française*, ii. 27: 'La loi n'est plus le droit, mais bien l'expression plus ou moins parfaite du droit.'

law is the basis and must be understood before a statute becomes intelligible: secondly, common law is, in general, more interesting to teach: thirdly, statutes may be more ephemeral—especially during a war there is a vast quantity of legislation most of which disappears. Consequently, the student receives an intensive drill in the mechanics of precedent and the methods of searching for authority and not enough emphasis is placed on the technique of drafting statutes and the problems of their interpretation.

This attitude is reflected in the character of the books available. It is true that drafting is an art to be learnt rather than an abstract study to be lectured on, but not nearly enough has been done to assist the student. There are the pioneer efforts of Bentham, the works of Sir Henry Thring,[1] of Sir Courtenay Ilbert,[2] and an excellent paper by Sir William Graham-Harrison.[3] It is also significant that the parliamentary draftsman's office was not established till 1869—this led to an improvement in the style of statutes and greater uniformity in drafting. Many of the works on interpretation collect dicta instead of coming to grips with the real problems of drafting and interpretation. If the lawyer has no appreciation of the real problems, it will deprive him of the power to understand statutes. 'The best Act you can have is a repealing Act: the only good Act is a dead Act'—these words were written flippantly, but they do describe the attitude of some writers.

The importance of statute is emphasized by the spread of codification on the Continent, and the increasing bulk of the statute book in England. The common law is historically based on individualism, and the increasing popularity of collectivist measures (such as the nationalization of mines, railways, or the provision of free medical services) requires extensive statutory interference with the fundamental doctrines of the common law. A new Duguit is needed to write on the Transformation of Private Law. It is a delicate task to work out a new balance between common law and statute and only the fullest knowledge of the technique of the drafting and interpretation of statutes will succeed in retaining some consistency in English law as a whole. The greater the use of statute, the more skilful must be our technique.[4]

---

[1] *Practical Legislation* (1877).
[2] *The Mechanics of Law Making* (1914); *Legislative Methods and Forms* (1901).
[3] *J. Soc. of Public Teachers of Law* (1935), 9.
[4] H. R. Hahlo writes of the dangers of a code for England: 30 *Mod. L. R.* (1967), 241. For a reply see M. R. Topping, 33 *Mod. L. R.* (1970), 170.

§ 54. Law Reform

It is clear that any far-reaching study of law reform requires a choice between the ultimate ends that law should pursue. An adequate discussion of the choices that face a modern community would require several volumes, and lengthy excursions into the fields of politics, economics, and sociology.[1]

But even without trenching on controversial issues there is room for much reform in cutting out the inconvenient relics of the past and amending rules which, whatever may once have been the case, are now for the benefit of none. Law reform is an urgent need of all countries, and on the whole the lawyer has not played the part that would be expected (although the cynic may say that the lawyer's apathy was natural). If we may adopt Gény's terminology, there is within the realm of technique much room for improvement without changing the basic principles on which a legal system is based. The mode in which the law is expressed, its clarity and ease of application, the simplicity of procedure and the cost of litigation—all these demand the serious study of the lawyer. In this sphere jurisprudence should indeed be a creative study by focusing attention on such parts of the law as do not achieve the purpose for which they were designed. The Crown Proceedings Act, 1947, is a good example of what reform should do. The Act not only improved the substantive law, by granting fuller remedies to the subject, but it also swept away many old procedural forms (e.g. Latin and English informations) and replaced them by simpler rules. Another illustration is the Theft Act, 1968, which made a heroic attempt to remove useless subtleties from the old law.[2]

An interesting development is the use of the royal commission or special committee appointed to investigate thoroughly the matter in question, and to make suggestions for legislation based on a detailed consideration of all the evidence that is available. This enables the legislative body to build on a more secure foundation, especially where the experience of other countries has been available for analysis. But the royal commission is specially appointed for each particular project, and hence it cannot serve as a permanent impetus to law

---

[1] One of the greatest English law reformers was Jeremy Bentham: W. S. Holdsworth, 28 *Calif. L. R.* (1940), 568; *Jeremy Bentham and the Law* (ed. G. W. Keeton and G. Schwarzenberger).

[2] The Report of the Criminal Law Revision Committee, which was the basis of the Act, took seven years to prepare.

reform. A significant experiment in England was the appointment in 1934 of a Lord Chancellor's Law Revision Committee. The personnel was composed of judges, practising and academic lawyers, and thus a representative opinion was ensured. Although the committee is limited to reporting on the topics referred to it by the Lord Chancellor, much useful work has already been done, and several statutory changes have resulted.[1] The Law Reform Committee was set up by Lord Simonds in 1952, and produced eleven reports.[2]

The appointment of the Law Commission in 1965[3] was hailed by Lord Chorley and G. Dworkin as a landmark in the history of English law.[4] The function of the Commission was breath-taking in its scope: 'to take and keep under review all the law . . . with a view to its systematic development and reform.'[5] Five full-time members were appointed: some criticism was evoked on the ground that membership should not be confined to lawyers. The Chairman, Scarman J., points out that the Commission has independence, deriving its existence not from a Cabinet decision, but from a statute.[6] The Commission is required to submit to the Lord Chancellor from time to time programmes for the reform of different parts of the law, but the Lord Chancellor is bound only to lay before Parliament those schemes which meet with his approval. The Commission has a 'close and confidential relationship with the Government machine'.[7] It can take the initiative, and also act in an advisory capacity to government departments: for example, a paper was prepared for the Lord Chancellor on the proposal for the reform of the divorce law. The fact that the Commission received 632 proposals for law reform soon after its inception shows that there is much public interest in its operation. Consolidation is one of the subjects stressed in the Act, as is the repeal of inoperative statutes. Both these methods will reduce greatly the sheer volume of statute law. Its published programme includes the preparation of a series of codifying enactments

[1] e.g. Law Reform (Married Women and Tortfeasors) Act, 1935, 25 & 26 Geo. V, c. 30; Law Reform (Miscellaneous Provisions) Act, 1934, 24 & 25 Geo. V, c. 41; Limitation Act, 1939, 2 & 3 Geo. VI, c. 21; Law Reform (Contributory Negligence) Act, 1945, 8 & 9 Geo. VI, c. 28; Law Reform (Enforcement of Contracts) Act, 1954 (2 & 3 Eliz. II, c. 34); Variations of Trust Act, 1958 (6 & 7 Eliz. II, c. 53); Occupiers, Liability Act, 1957 (5 & 6 Eliz. II, c. 31).
[2] For an interesting survey see 24 *Mod. L. R.* (1961), 1–143. In addition a Private International Law Committee was set up in 1952, and a Criminal Law Revision Committee in 1959.
[3] Law Commissions Act, 1965.   [4] 28 *Mod. L. R.* (1965), 675.
[5] § 3.   [6] 10 *J. Soc. of Public Teachers of Law* (1968), 91.
[7] The Chairman, op. cit. 94.

relating to contract, landlord and tenant, family law, and criminal law.

Scarman J. states that it is 'high time that legal education took full account of the truth about legal reality and abandoned the fiction that our law is to be found in the law reports . . . Our law has been set, since the middle of the nineteenth century, upon a course that takes it away from the law reports and towards the statute book.'[1] 'The true work of the Law Commission is therefore, in my submission, to help Parliament and the courts to maintain in a changing world that capacity for development which has always been a feature of the common law, and is the secret of its survival over the centuries.'[1]

'We think that we are justified in treating as axiomatic the proposition that much of our English law is out of date and some of it shockingly so. The fact that this view is shared by the overwhelming part of the legal profession is significant; for taken as a whole, no profession could be more conservative.'[2]

The major difficulty is to secure a close relationship between the courts, the commission, and the legislature. Many pages of the law reports bear testimony to the desire of the Bench for reform. It is a most unpleasant task for a judge to give a decision that he knows to be unjust because the weight of authority is compelling. The judicial complaint, however, is often buried in the reports and no action follows. In many countries the judges are empowered as a body to make suggestions for the reform of the law, but for various reasons few changes can be ascribed to this source. If there is lacking a channel between the courts and the legislature, there may also be little co-operation between the legislature and a law revision committee. It is of little practical use to draw up new bills if they are to be stored in the pigeon-holes of an administrative department. Legislatures are busy with their own projects and are traditionally shy of long bills relating to matters which are not of immediate political interest. Hence 'education' of the legislature is just as necessary as intensive research by the reformer. One of the advantages of a permanent body for law revision is that it has the opportunity of gaining, by its record of service, the respect of the legislature.[3]

---

[1] Ibid. 99.

[2] Gerald Gardiner and Andrew Martin (eds.), *Law Reform Now*, 1.

[3] e.g. the Law Institute in the State of Louisiana, U.S.A. This will also presumably apply to the Law Commission in U.K. In Australia, there are active Law Reform Commissions in Queensland and N.S. Wales, and a Chief Justice's Law Reform Committee in Victoria.

Another aim of law reform is to secure unification of law. This problem is particularly acute in federations. America with fifty states and Australia with six appreciate the inconvenience of diversity in state statutes. Australia has six bodies of law relating to commercial transactions. Even when English statutes are adopted, sometimes each State introduces small amendments. As between the nations, it is clear that trade is hampered by differences in commercial law. Since 1851, much enthusiasm has been spent on projects for the unification of law, but progress has been slow.[1] One difficulty is the cleavage between Anglo-American and continental systems: a second, national pride: a third, that of persuading legislatures to devote sufficient time to the topic.

[1] H. C. Gutteridge, *Comparative Law*, ch. xi.

REFERENCES

ALLEN, C. K., *Law in the Making* (1964), ch. vi.
AMOS, M. S., 5 *Camb. L. J.* (1934), 163.
FRIEDMANN, W., 26 *Can. B. R.* (1948), 1277.
GARDINER, G., and MARTIN, A. (eds.), *Law Reform Now* (1963).
GÉNY, F., *Méthode d'interprétation et sources en droit privé positif.*
GRAHAM-HARRISON, W. M., *J. Soc. Public Teachers of Law* (1935), 9.
HOLDSWORTH, W. S., 28 *Calif. L. R.* (1940), 568.
POUND, R., 21 *Harv. L. R.* (1908), 383.
SAWER, G., 20 *Univ. of Toronto L. J.* (1970), 183.
Statute Law Deficiencies, Report by a Committee of the Statute Law Society (1970).
STONE, J. F., and PETTEE, G. S., 54 *Harv. L. R.* (1940), 221.
WILLIS, J., 16 *Can. B. R.* (1938), 1.

X

JURISTIC WRITINGS AND PROFESSIONAL OPINION

§ 55. THE INFLUENCE OF JURISTIC WRITINGS AND PROFESSIONAL OPINION

JURISTIC writings and professional opinion have played a part in legal evolution that should not be ignored. If it is a question whether a persuasive precedent should be followed, a court may be swayed by the opinion of the profession concerning the correctness of that decision, by the 'press' which it has received in the law reviews, or by the views expressed in the leading textbooks.[1]

In England a humbler place is afforded to the textbook than in most systems of law. 'There is everywhere a sort of competition between the judiciary and the scientific jurists. When one of these groups is endowed with all the official power and the other is restricted to private activity, as is the case in England in respect to the Bench and the theorists, there can be little doubt as to the result of the contention.'[2] But it must not be supposed that the textbook has had no influence in English law. In the early period the dearth of authority led men to turn to such books as there were, and the work of Bracton did much to shape the foundations of English law. It was at one time thought that Bracton had foisted on his contemporaries a second-hand version of Roman law as an English textbook, but further investigation[3] has shown that Bracton searched for and gave English authority where it existed and used Roman law only to provide the

---

[1] Thus in discussing whether it should follow *Hurst* v. *Picture Theatres Ltd.*, [1915] 1 K.B. 1, the High Court of Australia discussed adverse criticisms and defences of the decision by Holdsworth, Miles, Denis Browne, Cheshire, Hanbury, Gale, Winfield, Pollock, Geldart, Salmond, Smith's Leading Cases: *Cowell* v. *Rosehill Racecourse Co. Ltd.* (1937), 56 C.L.R. 605. '*Communis opinio* is evidence of what the law is': per Lord Goddard, *R.* v. *St. Edmundsbury and Ipswich Diocese*, [1947] K.B. 263.

[2] H. Goldschmidt, *English Law from the Foreign Standpoint*, 71–2. But nevertheless 'so soon as there is a legal profession, professional opinion is among the most powerful of the sources that shape the law. . . . In Edward the First's day it is impossible to uphold a writ which "all the serjeants" condemn and often enough to the mediaeval law reporter, the "opinion of the serjeants" seems as weighty as any judgment': F. Pollock and F. W. Maitland, *History of English Law*, i. 196.

[3] *Bracton and Azo* (Selden Society, ed. F. W. Maitland).

general structure and to fill the gaps left by the decisions of the King's Courts. The five great names of Glanvil, Bracton, Littleton, Coke, and Blackstone demonstrate the debt that English law owes to her text writers. Bracton laid the foundations, borrowing from Roman law what was necessary to create a system with a reasonable flexibility and sufficient coherence to withstand the later assaults of Roman law. Littleton gave a scientific account of the theory that lay behind the decisions on real property and his 'glory is that he proved that English law could form a legal system independent of the Roman law'.[1] Coke, versed in the ancient learning, provided a bridge between medieval and modern law, and finally Blackstone, with a genius for comprehensiveness, reduced to an ordered system and ornamented with a literary style the diverse sources of English law.

After the days of Coke the growth of law reports meant that decisive authority could be found for an increasing number of problems, and as the reports became more accurate there was greater reliance upon them. But if at this period there was a tendency for law reports to kill the textbook, the very increase of reports resurrected it as a guide to the luxuriant chaos of case law. In the days of Bracton the textbook was important because there were so few precedents; today it is valued because there are so many. But textbooks remain only persuasive authorities, although it must be stressed that the five great books of English law have such high prestige as statements of the law of their day that there is only a thin line between the degree of their authority and that of a case of the same period.[2]

Lord Eldon once remarked that a writer who had held no judicial situation could not properly be cited as an authority.[3] This view has been gradually modified, and it became the convention that the works of dead authors could be cited—not, of course, as binding authorities, but only as expert evidence as to the state of the law. Thus Lord Wright paid a graceful tribute to Pollock's *Law of Torts*, 'fortunately not a work of authority'[4]—the point being that the learned author was still adorning the literature of the law. But there is not a great practical difference between adopting the argument of a living author

---

[1] H. Lévy-Ullmann, *The English Legal Tradition*, 142.
[2] Humphreys J. said in *R.* v. *Sandbach*, [1935] 2 K.B. 192 at 197: 'It is too late, in 1935, to attempt to show that Blackstone was wrong.'
[3] *Johnes* v. *Johnes* (1814), 3 Dow 1 at 15; but he continued that it would be flattery even of a judge to say that he knew as much law as Serjeant Williams.
[4] *Nicholls* v. *Ely Beet Sugar Factory Ltd.*, [1936] 1 Ch. 343 at 349. In one report the force of this remark was lost and the remark was reported as 'unfortunately not a work of authority': 154 L.T. at 533.

without citing him as authority (which was permissible) and citing his work as authority or as an expert opinion of what the law is (which was not), and in modern times the number of citations of the work of living authors has increased and is increasing. This is due mainly to an improvement in the quality of text-books and to the growth in the quality and quantity of contributions to legal learning appearing in the periodical literature. The excellence of the work of Glanvil, Bracton, Littleton, Coke, and Blackstone must not blind us to the fact that their work covers a span of five centuries, and there were few other books of the same quality. In the last seventy years many books have been written by barristers who afterwards achieved fame on the Bench, and the universities have aroused a greater interest in the literature of English law. To take an example from private inter-national law, Dicey's work[1] exercised a great formative influence, and Cheshire's more recent textbook[2] has achieved repute within a remarkably short time of its appearance. The classic texts of Pollock and Salmond on the law of tort were cited in numerous cases even before the deaths of these authors. In *Bradford* v. *Symondson*[3] the judgment turned almost entirely on a discussion of the books of leading writers on insurance.[4] The work of the conveyancers and real property lawyers has exerted a tremendous influence.[5] Lord Wright said of Sir Frederick Pollock: 'This at least is clear that he has vindicated to this generation the vital importance of extra-judicial writing.'[6] Moreover, we note a surprising increase in the citation of articles from periodicals.[7] In *Haynes* v. *Harwood*[8] the Court of

[1] *Conflict of Laws* (1st ed., 1896, 7th ed., 1958).
[2] *Private International Law* (1st ed., 1935, 7th ed., 1965).
[3] (1881), 7 Q.B.D. at 462–3.
[4] In *China* v. *Harrow U.D.C.*, [1954] 1 Q.B. 178 at 183, Lord Goddard C.J. said: '... not only is there no authority on this question, but there is no *communis opinio* among text writers.'
[5] e.g. H. W. Challis on *Real Property*, cited by Byrne J., *In re Hollis's Hospital and Hague's Contract*, [1899] 2 Ch. 540 at 551. See C. K. Allen, *Law in the Making* (4th ed.), 240. In *Shenton* v. *Tyler*, [1939] 1 Ch. 620, Greene M.R. cited the works on Evidence of Gilbert, Peake, Starkie, Best, Greenleaf, Taylor, Wigmore, Wills, Stephen, Phipson, Cockle; Halsbury's *Laws of England*, Lush on *Husband and Wife*. In addition, Luxmoore L.J. cited Holdsworth, *History of English Law*.
[6] (1937), 53 *L.Q.R.* 151.
[7] The High Court of Australia has shown great industry in exploring articles in periodicals: see *Cowell* v. *Rosehill Racecourse Co. Ltd.* (1937), 56 C.L.R. 605, where articles from the *L.Q.R.* by Geldart, Miles, Pollock, and Winfield were cited: *Thomas* v. *The King* (1937), 59 C.L.R. 279, cited the *Camb. L. J.* and *L.Q.R.*; *Davis* v. *Bunn* (1936), 56 C.L.R. 246, cited the *Can. B. R.*; *Chester* v. *Waverley* (1939), 62 C.L.R. 1, cited the *Camb. L. J.*, *Harv. L. R.*, and the *Can. B. R.* In *Gold* v. *Essex C.C.*, [1942] 2 K.B. 293, great reliance was placed on an article by Goodhart.
[8] [1935] 1 K.B. 146. Cf. G. V. Nicholls, *Can. B. R.* (1950), 422.

Appeal adopted as the basis of their decision a conclusion reached by Professor Goodhart in an article in the *Cambridge Law Journal*, and this is not an isolated instance of the influence of legal reviews.[1]

An interesting account of the part played by the textbook in the development of American law is given by Roscoe Pound.[2] His view is that doctrinal writing has had more influence in America than in England, especially in the formative era. Even today that influence is not waning, for the lists of courts are congested, authorities are many, and there is a natural temptation to turn to any textbook which states the law clearly and definitely.[3] The American *Restatement of the Law* is an interesting modern example of co-operation between Bench, the practising profession, and the law teacher. The mass of decisions given in fifty-one jurisdictions makes it impossible for the practitioner to keep abreast of the law. Hence the American Law Institute, recognizing that the law was becoming uncertain, set up machinery to enable the law to be restated in short sections. An acknowledged authority was appointed as reporter for each subject, and given the assistance of a council of advisers consisting of judges, practitioners, and university teachers. After passing the scrutiny of these advisers, the work was submitted to the Law Institute for its approval. The *Restatement* is neither a textbook nor a digest, for no authorities are cited: the law is stated in black-letter sections to which comment and illustrations are attached. Nor can it be called a code, for it has no authority, save that gained by its prestige. But it is an interesting example of co-operative effort by the legal profession and the twenty-seven volumes already published have exercised great influence in the courts,[4] and even the Privy Council is not immune.[5]

In Roman law the textbook occupied a much higher place. There was no official bench in the early period, and the jurist secured the prestige which in England is accorded to the judge. The Law of Citations of A.D. 426 recognized the work of five jurists as the main source of Roman law, and the *Digest* of Justinian was largely a series of readings from famous textbooks. When, at the time of the Renaissance, the reception of Roman law was stimulated, it was to the *Digest* that men turned. The great teachers of Roman law achieved international fame, and Roman law was regarded almost as the *ius commune* of Western Europe. Many countries employed lay judges

---

[1] Cf. *Re Cleadon Trust Ltd.*, [1939] Ch. 286.
[2] *The Formative Era of American Law* (1938), ch. iv.   [3] Ibid. 165.
[4] *The Restatement in the Courts* (American Law Institute).
[5] See *Mutual Life and Citizens' Assurance Co. Ltd.* v. *Evatt*, [1971] 1 All E.R. 150.

and there was little or no systematic instruction given in the native customary law. Hence when an expert class was needed, it was the doctors of Roman law who were called upon, with the result that the influence of Roman law increased, and correspondingly the textbooks gained greater prestige.

The French Code was largely indebted to the work of the great jurists Domat and Pothier who had begun the task of fusing the Roman rules of the south and the Germanic customs of the north. Even today in Europe some of the outstanding teachers of law are more fortunate than the highest judges in their reputation, prestige, and emoluments.[1]

In international law the textbook is still an important source, and must remain so until there is a greater body of case law. 'Vattel', said Sir William Scott, 'is here to be considered not as a lawyer merely delivering an opinion, but as a witness asserting the fact—the fact that such is the existing practice of modern Europe.'[2]

Can we trace any characteristics of English law which are due to the humbler place occupied by the textbook? It is difficult to answer, because it is hard to separate from this problem the results which are due to the doctrine of binding precedent and, indeed, to the particular English temperament. Would the doctrine of binding precedent have become established had the textbook enjoyed greater prestige? One result of the reliance on cases is that English law is very practical and related to the concrete facts of life. On the other hand, there is a dearth of general principles and in some cases a lack of general terms. Moreover, since a single decision may be binding, most branches of the law are disfigured by somewhat narrow distinctions between particular cases. But it is impossible to say whether the attitude towards the textbook is a cause or itself a result of more significant factors.

§ 56. THE FUNCTION OF THE TEXTBOOK

The textbook attempts to universalize, to reduce to an ordered unity, and to discover the deeper principles that underlie particular decisions. There are works which are mere collections of cases strung together in narrative fashion, but while these have their use as convenient repositories of the relevant decisions, they are not textbooks

---

[1] M. S. Amos and F. P. Walton, *Introduction to French Law*, 8–9.
[2] *The Maria* (1799), 1 C. Rob. 340 at 363; *R. v. Keyn* (1876), 2 Ex. D. 63 at 69.

in the true sense of that word. The speculative and generalizing mind of an expert views particular decisions in their proper perspective and discovers principles which are latent in a line of cases. Under the English system, which treats even a single decision of a higher court as binding, there must be a perpetual struggle to prevent law becoming a mere collection of specific decisions and to search for unifying principles. As one judge has remarked, paying a sincere tribute to the function of the textbook: 'I think the law as to damages still awaits a scientific statement which will probably be made when there is a completely satisfactory textbook upon the subject.'[1]

The textbook may be necessary for teaching, but its influence goes farther. Ehrlich suggests that Roman law owed its great systematic completeness and perfection of form to the teaching activities of the jurists.[2] Maitland remarked that taught law is tough law, and thereby he was referring not to the sufferings of students but to the strength given to a system when it is systematically expounded. Roman law had greater influence on the Continent than in England largely because the teaching of the universities was confined to Roman law alone and the native systems were rather despised, whereas in England, even if the earlier universities concentrated mainly on Roman law, the Inns of Court established a learned tradition for the common law. Teaching requires that the law should be, as far as possible, reduced to a systematic order—hence the search for principle which can afford the *ratio legis* lying behind a particular part of the law. If the reason for a particular rule can be explained, then it is remembered more easily and the teacher tries to discover broad principles that are only implicit in the law. Thus the early textbooks of the law of tort attempted to organize the subject on the principle of 'no liability without fault'. The generalization may have been premature, but it aided in transforming the law from a collection of forms of actions into a body of principles—although it must be confessed that the law of tort is still notoriously difficult for those who demand logic, order, and system.

Text books were naturally influenced by the prevailing theory of law. In the eighteenth century natural law was drawn upon in order to fill the gaps of the law, and in this way new principles were introduced and law was brought into closer touch with moral theories. To many persons today natural law seems a mere empty figment, but the

---

[1] Per Atkin L.J., *The Susquehanna*, [1925] P. 196 at 210.
[2] *Fundamental Principles of the Sociology of Law* (trans. W. L. Moll), 269.

text-writer, in his search for reason, drew largely on the experience of other systems and thus filled with a practical content the philosophic theory borrowed from the past. Kent and Story in America treated comparative law as declaratory of natural law.[1] In the nineteenth century in England the analytical school was predominant, and the attempt to organize and explain the mass of cases on the basis of logical principles gave to English law strength and cohesion. Today it is realized that the analytical school tended to subordinate everything to *elegantia iuris*, and textbooks are exercising more independence of thought and are criticizing rules on the basis of their social effects.

But the text-writer has a much narrower creative function than the judge, for he holds no official position. His first task is to expound the law that is and to correlate the various rules. But there must inevitably be some discussion of the basis of law. The main dispute today is the degree of independence which a textbook should show. Should it merely record and explain or should it aim at being creative? Is it limited to analysing the decisions of the court, or should it adopt a critical approach in the hope of developing the law? The English analytical school treated the decided case with great reverence: on the other hand, Duguit wished to abolish all outworn concepts, and the modern realist school in America speaks of the 'transcendental nonsense' involved in certain legal theories.[2] The best means of approach is a *via media*. It is of little use for a textbook to write of an ideal law of tort under the pretext of discussing English law; on the other hand, merely to record decisions is an abdication of function. The limits of freedom left to a text-writer are narrow, but within these there should be an attempt to create. An interesting technique is that of Cheshire,[3] who in dealing with each topic concerning private international law first discusses what the theory of the law should be, and then deals with the actual decisions. This allows a textbook to be a faithful record of the law that is, while pointing the way to further reform by providing a critical commentary of the cases that have been decided.

[1] R. Pound, *The Formative Era of American Law*, 147.
[2] F. S. Cohen, 35 *Col. L. R.* (1935), 809.   [3] *Private International Law.*

REFERENCES

AMOS, M. S., and WALTON, F. P., *Introduction to French Law*, 8-9.
LÉVY-ULLMANN, H., *The English Legal Tradition*, ch. v.
POUND, R., *The Formative Era of American Law*, ch. iv.

BOOK IV

THE TECHNIQUE OF
THE LAW

XI

CLASSIFICATION

§ 57. THE PURPOSE OF CLASSIFICATION

WITHIN a legal system, classification has two objects: firstly, the creation of a logical structure that will enable the rules of the law to be so interrelated and so effectively and concisely stated that they may be more easily grasped, applied, and developed;[1] secondly, in order to enable lawyers to find their law. The second purpose may be achieved by a very rough and ready classification—provided it be understood, it perhaps matters not if it is unscientific. Thus an alphabetical classification may have little logical merit but be quite useful to enable the practitioner to find the necessary rule. Even the crudest alphabetical arrangement, however, requires the choice of concepts round which particular rules may be grouped: e.g. bailment, book debts, negligence.

For jurisprudence the problem is more difficult. If we confine ourselves to English law, a classification may be achieved which will be more or less generally acceptable. But legal systems differ not only in their rules but also in their methods of classifying these rules. It was once thought that it would be possible to 'discover' a universal classification within which all systems could be placed. It is now recognized that many distinctions claimed by jurists to be fundamental were merely the pigeon-holes created by the medieval carpenter out of Roman materials.[2]

[1] R. Pound, 37 *Harv. L. R.* (1924), 933 at 944.
[2] And it is easy to exaggerate the influence of pure classical Roman law—much of what is adopted is the product of the civilians who adapted Roman law to the needs of western Europe from the sixteenth century onwards.

English law has proved remarkably stubborn to the classifier with a Romanist bias. Thus the trust (in the view of some writers) spoils the dichotomy between rights *in rem* and rights *in personam*. Bracton cannot make up his mind whether *novel disseisin* is an *actio in rem* or *in personam*.[1] 'The too impatient student who looks down upon mediaeval law from the sublime heights of "general jurisprudence" will say that most of our English actions are mixed, many of them very mixed.'[2] Even today it is not always an easy matter to determine what is a 'criminal cause or matter',[3] and the boundary between tort, contract, and quasi-contract is rather blurred.[4] Again the tort of seduction, which in essence protects the family honour, is historically an action for loss of service. In feudalism there is hardly any distinction between public and private law—jurisdiction, even kingship, is largely regarded as property.[5]

The problem of characterization in private international law illustrates this difficulty. Breach of a promise to marry falls under the heading of contract in English law and delict in French law. If a promise to marry is made in France and broken in England, how are we to classify the action? If we treat the action as contract it will be governed by its proper law: if we treat it as tort then presumably the law of the place of the wrongful act must be considered. Is the French doctrine of community of property between husband and wife part of the matrimonial law (governed by the law of the domicil of the parties at marriage) or part of the testamentary law (governed by the law of the domicil at death)? Does the English Statute of Frauds relate to substance or procedure? The former is governed by the proper law of the contract which in a given case may be French, but if the action is brought in England, procedural points will be governed by English law.

To apply English law to every point would cause injustice. There are no universal principles of classification. A start must be made somewhere in the process of analysis. Hence the first step is primary classification which is normally carried out according to the rules of English law. Having classified the problem as one of contract or tort, the next step is to find the 'connecting factor' (such as domicil or the proper law of a contract) which will point to a particular foreign system of law. The next step is to apply the appropriate foreign law.

---

[1] F. Pollock and F. W. Maitland, *History of English Law*, ii. 568.
[2] Ibid. 570.   [3] C. K. Allen, *Legal Duties*, 230.
[4] P. H. Winfield, *Province of the Law of Tort*.
[5] F. Pollock and F. W. Maitland, op. cit. i. 209.

These few sentences cannot do justice to the complexity of the problems that arise and there are keen disputes as to the rules of characterization and their theoretical basis. But the rules of private international law would be much simpler if a universally agreed system of classification existed.[1]

§ 58. POSSIBLE METHODS OF CLASSIFICATION

For a particular system an historical classification of law by its sources may be extremely useful—thus in England an appreciation of the development of common law and equity is essential. But such tests are of little use for a general juristic classification, since the accidents of history will largely determine what law was created by a specific source in each country.

Holland adopted the method of classifying law on the basis of rights, using as his first division the distinction between rights *in rem* and *in personam*.[2] The major difficulty of this approach is that equity creates rights which can only with difficulty be fitted under either head and that many legal relationships give rise to both types of rights— thus a contract creates rights *in personam* as between the parties, but each party to the agreement has also a right *in rem* against persons in general that they should not knowingly induce breach of contract. Holland also separates sharply antecedent rights (which exist independently of wrongdoing) and remedial rights[3] (created by some particular injury).

Some jurists expect to achieve a universal classification, a 'generalized comparative anatomy' under which all the legal systems of the world could be organized, but the greater the knowledge we obtain of other systems, the smaller does this hope become.[4] Each legal system is stubbornly individual in some respects. Nevertheless, the analysis of legal concepts provides the most useful means of approach. Thus, to understand the working of the legal mind we must analyse its development of categories such as legal personality, obligation, liability, crime, contract, tort, property, ownership, possession. No claim need be made that all such concepts are universally present in

---

[1] A. H. Robertson, *Characterization in the Conflict of Laws*; G. C. Cheshire, Private International Law (7th ed.), 40.   [2] *Infra*, § 65.
[3] *Infra*, § 65. This division has been attacked by certain realists on the ground that the so-called antecedent rights do not exist at all—there is no right to reputation but only a power to sue, if that reputation be attacked. This point is discussed in the next section.   [4] R. Pound, 50 *Harv. L. R.* (1937), 565.

legal systems. The law has certain problems to solve in its endeavour to discover a reasoned basis for compromising the disputes of the community. It must develop a certain minimum technique, e.g. in deciding what persons will be recognized, in what cases constraint will be applied, what rights to enjoy portions of the material world will be recognized. A legal system might exist without a clear notion of legal personality, but, since this concept is vital in mature systems, it would be ridiculous for jurisprudence to ignore it, even if it could not logically be proved to be an *a priori* necessity.

The major difficulty is to strike a happy mean between treating of the pure form of the law and making jurisprudence an outline study of English and Roman law. It is reasonable for one writing for English students to draw much (if not most) of the illustrative material from English law; but the material must be used because it throws light on jurisprudence and not merely to explain English law. In the teaching of geology or botany, emphasis will be placed on local characteristics, but in each case these are related to the general principles of the science. Probably one of the best short descriptions of jurisprudence is the theory of the legal method. One of the favourite legal methods is the development of concepts or categories in terms of which particular legal rules are expressed. Hence the concept of contract is important, even if it is not universal (Roman law never had a general theory of contract), because it illustrates a method by which a particular problem is solved. Even if many modern systems of law abolished the concept of contract, it would still rightfully hold a place in jurisprudence, for in the history of the law it has played an important part. An analysis on the basis of concepts enables us more easily to understand the history of the law than if we build our analysis purely on rights.

But any purely analytical survey must be supplemented by a functional approach, which shows the actual working of these concepts in the world both in the past and today. Some have so exaggerated the importance of the functional approach that they advocate teaching the law on the basis of 'typical factual situations' rather than by analysing the conceptual basis of the law.[1] Thus instead of teaching the law of contract or of tort, these writers would approach the problems from the situation of an actual motor accident, and bring in the concepts of law by an analysis of the facts. Political relations, or family relations, could also be used as a basis. As a supplementary

---

[1] J. Hall, *Readings in Jurisprudence*, 618.

method of teaching, this is quite useful, for it demonstrates that the problems of actual practice do not come labelled as contract or tort, but represent a cross-section of life which may raise difficulties in many fields of law. But the defect of using 'factual situations' as the primary approach to law is that at some point the student must be grounded in the judicially accepted meaning of words such as contract, tort, property. Unless this teaching precedes a study of particular situations, it is a mere matter of chance where an analysis of contract is to be found. Moreover, unless the meaning (say of contract) is systematically discussed at some point, there must be much repetition under the different heads.

The same difficulty of arrangement seems fatal to any adoption of interests as a primary classification. Thus an examination of the interest of association entails a discussion of corporations and groups —under one head we must discuss legal personality, contract, tort, the trust deed, co-ownership, and the injunction. Again a person's interest in his bodily freedom is protected by the criminal law, the law of torts, and doctrines of public policy. What are sometimes called the 'rights of personality' are protected by doctrines belonging to public and private law, and a full discussion would cut right across the analytical division.

It therefore seems preferable to analyse fundamental legal concepts in the traditional manner, but to apply functional tests to the working of each legal category. If two corporations contract with each other, the law may regard each as capable of protecting its own interests, but when a workman contracts with his employer, it may be thought necessary to protect the welfare of the economically weaker party. Analytically the two contracts are the same, but functionally the law has distinguished between them. Once we understand the nature of contract, we can easily study its working in the world today, but we can hardly appreciate the scope of contract without a previous grounding in analysis.

Codification clearly is difficult unless there be an adequate analysis of the law. Firstly, the rules must be distributed among the various codes—civil, criminal, procedural, etc.; secondly, the whole process is simplified by creating a General Part which contains a definition of all the concepts which bear on more than one division of the classification adopted. To approach the matter scientifically there should be a general part discussing the concepts common to all the codes and also a general part for each specific code. This clearly saves much repetition and also helps to ensure a uniform use of legal concepts.[1] An adequately organized general part would provide very useful material for jurisprudence. The arrangement of the actual codes leaves, however, much to be desired, and not as much help can be obtained from them as one would expect.

§ 59. THE ARRANGEMENT ADOPTED

Firstly, there is the distinction between international law and the law of the State, but this has already been discussed.[2] Within the law of the State there is a fundamental division between public and private law.[3] Public law is normally divided into constitutional, administrative, and criminal law, but there is less certainty concerning the appropriate heads of private law. Indeed we find in actual codes almost every possible principle of arrangement.[4] Primitive codes are frequently based on external similarity of subject-matter rather than an analysis of the rules of law—thus having mentioned a rule relating to women, the codifier considers this a useful point at which to collect other rules relating to that sex. The classical Roman analysis is a threefold division of the law relating to persons, to things, and to actions, but this scheme is not carried out very logically. The law of actions is today called the law of procedure, but the distinction between procedural and substantive rights applies not only to private law but to public law as well. The Roman law of things covers both the law of obligations and of property. In the law of persons we do not find (as we would expect) a discussion of the notion of legal personality and the effect of a restriction of capacity on legal right, but rather a mere collection of different types of status, the legal effect of membership of a status being only incidentally mentioned, if it is referred to at all.

The modern orthodox approach is as follows:

(a) The law of persons—a discussion of the nature of legal personality and of the effect of restricted capacity on legal right.

---

[1] A. Kocourek, cited J. Hall, *Readings in Jurisprudence*, 636. For a summary of the classification of typical codes, see R. Pound, *Outlines of Jurisprudence* (1943), 163.
[2] *Supra*, § 21.   [3] *Infra*, Ch. XIV.
[4] From the purely logical point of view the French Code suffers from serious defects. Thus there is no adequate attempt to separate the general part from the special part, e.g. to discover the nature of a juristic act we must turn to the law of contract. The German Code is in this order: *General Principles*: Persons, Things, Legal Transactions, Computation of Time, Prescription, Exercise of Rights; *Special Part*: Law of Obligations, Law of Things, Family Law, Law of Inheritance. The Swiss Code: Law of Persons, Family Law, Law of Inheritance, Law of Things, Law of Obligations. For a discussion see R. Pound, 37 *Harv. L. R.* (1924), 933.

(b) The law of obligations—obligations being classified as arising from (1) contract, (2) quasi-contract, (3) tort or delict, (4) quasi-delict.

(c) The law of property.

From a juristic angle this classification is not satisfactory. Firstly, there are many systems which do not know of such concepts as quasi-contract or quasi-delict, which depend merely on the historical accidents of particular systems. The only logical division is between rights created directly by the law and rights created by the consent of another—or, to look at the same question from the angle of duty, to distinguish between duties imposed on a person against his will and duties which he freely accepts. Delict, quasi-delict, and quasi-contract deal with duties imposed by the law; contract concerns duties voluntarily incurred. Logically, therefore, quasi-contract is akin to delict, although English legal history has related it to contract.[1]

Secondly, the classification is not exhaustive. In common speech, obligation is merely a synonym for legal duty, but in jurisprudence it is confined to that part of the law which creates rights *in personam*. Thus the Romans distinguished between *dominium* which creates rights *in rem*, and *obligatio* which gives rise to mere rights *in personam*.[2] If obligation is confined to rights *in personam*, and if the classification of persons, property, and obligations is meant to be exhaustive, wherein are the general duties of tort to be placed? What the traditional classification implies is that obligations arise (*inter alia*) from the making of a contract or the commission of a tort. But this has always proved confusing, for what is analogous to the commission of a tort is the breaking, not the making, of a contract. The significant contrast between tort and contract is that in the former case rights *in rem* are created by the law and bind persons generally, whereas in contract rights *in personam* are acquired by consent and bind only a specific person or persons. Hence it is useful to distinguish those rights which exist independently of wrongdoing (antecedent or primary rights) and those which come into existence only because another has committed a wrong (remedial or secondary rights).[3] Thus I have a primary right granted by the law that I shall not be defamed; if Jones libels me, I have a secondary right to recover

---

[1] *Infra*, §§ 108, 109.
[2] The Roman definition of *obligatio* was: 'iuris vinculum, quo necessitate adstringimur alicuius solvendae rei, secundum nostrae civitatis iura': *Inst.* 3. 13.
[3] *Infra*, § 65.

damages. I have a primary right that Brown shall fulfil the contract that he made with me—this right arises out of Brown's consent to incur the corresponding duty. If Brown breaks the contract, I have a secondary right to secure damages.[1] The traditional divisions of the law of obligations rather tend to obscure this distinction.

A further difficulty also arises. The general duty to fulfil a contract may be placed under the heading of obligation, because the contract creates only rights *in personam*. But the general duties of tort are *in rem* and so cannot be placed under obligation if we confine it to rights *in personam*. If this be so, many of the general duties of tort seem to fall outside the division of persons, obligations, and property. Some solve this difficulty by denying that primary rights really exist—there is no right not to be defamed, but only a right to a remedy if one is defamed; there is no right that another shall fulfil his contract, but only a right to sue for damages if he does not. Thus Holmes suggests that at common law a person does not promise to keep his contract, but is liable to pay damages if the promised event does not come to pass.[2] This approach, however, is inconvenient and seems to suggest a lack of proportion. The primary rights are the foundation on which the structure of remedies is built. It may be true that, at certain periods, the law rather narrowly places undue emphasis on procedural rights and tends to say that where there is no remedy there is no right. But the struggle of law is ever to reverse this proposition and to create remedies where primary rights have been infringed. Moreover, it is inconvenient to treat ownership not as creating a right *in rem* but merely incidentally in dealing with remedies. Again, in some cases the law will directly enforce the primary duty as by ordering Brown to fulfil his contract or by preventing Robinson from defaming Smith as he threatens to do. All these considerations show the importance of recognizing the existence of primary rights.

What is quite illogical is to recognize that there is a primary right where contract is concerned, but to fail to appreciate this in tort. If we recognize that all the general duties of tort cannot be fitted into the heading of persons, obligations, and property, then it seems that another approach is necessary. The remedy in tort is ancillary to the primary right that others shall obey the prescriptions of the law, just as the remedy in contract is ancillary to the primary right that the other party shall carry out his promise.

---

[1] Or in certain cases Brown may be forced by an injunction to carry out his promise.
[2] *The Common Law*, 298, criticized W. W. Buckland, 8 *Camb. L. J.* (1944), 247.

Obligation should be sharply distinguished from liability. Obligation relates to what a person ought to do because there is a duty laid upon him: liability to what he must do because he has failed to do what he ought. We do not say that a prisoner ought to serve the sentence pronounced upon him—the law will see to it that he must. If a person refuses to meet a judgment debt, he is liable to have his property seized.

It is, therefore, more convenient to avoid the use of the term 'obligation' as one of the major heads. Instead we distinguish between rights created directly by the law, and rights created by consent. These are primary rights breach of which gives rise to a remedial right.

The basis adopted for the remainder of this work is as follows:

1. Rights and duties.
2. Titles, acts, and events.
3. Public law.
4. Private law:
   (*a*) The concept of legal personality.
   (*b*) Rights created by a juristic act.
   (*c*) Rights directly created by law.
   (*d*) Remedial rights.
   (*e*) Extinction of rights.
   (*f*) The concept of property.
   (*g*) The concept of possession.
5. The law of procedure.

§ 60. SUBORDINATE CLASSIFICATIONS

Family Law is not treated as a separate heading in the analytical survey, but many points relating to it arise in the law of personality and of property. A short attempt was made to draw the rules together under the heading *Family Interests*.[1] The law of succession and inheritance is historically grounded in the rules relating to the family, but in modern times the rules have in part broken free and succession is most conveniently treated under the law of property.

Private International Law. A case which falls to be decided in England may contain a foreign element. If a Spaniard assaults a German in a Parisian night-club, can an action be brought in England if the parties subsequently arrive there? If a contract, made by correspondence between an American living in Italy and a Peru-

---

[1] *Supra,* § 38.

vian residing in Germany, is to be performed in France, what law should be applied? It would be unjust for English courts to apply purely English rules to a contract made and to be performed abroad. The mere fact that the defendant is served with a writ when on a visit to England does not necessarily make it reasonable to apply English law to the transaction. There is, therefore, in every mature system of law a set of rules dealing with cases that have a foreign element. There are three broad questions to be answered: firstly, in what circumstances are the courts of England competent to deal with cases that have a foreign element? Secondly, if the English courts are competent, what law should be applied to the transaction in question? Thirdly, in what circumstances will a foreign judgment be regarded as decisive in English courts or as enforceable by action in England?[1]

The typical English view is that conflict of laws is part of the common law. Pillet thinks that, since the rules deal with the conditions under which one state will give effect within its territory to the rules of another state, there is no essential difference in the nature of public or private law.[2] The rules, so to speak, prescribe the competence of the courts of each nation to deal with specific disputes—in other words, conflict of laws deals with the application of the law in space. If there were a universal set of rules applied by the courts of every country, this view would be correct, but as the English doctrines of conflict of laws differ materially from those of any other country, it is absurd to compare conflict of laws with international law. English and French jurists may differ as to the precise principles that should be applied to a blockade, but the dispute would concern the meaning of international law itself, for both would agree that there cannot be one international law for England and another for France; whereas there may easily be one set of rules for conflict of laws applied in England and another in France. It is true that there are certain principles which underlie the various systems of conflict of laws in the several countries; but we may also discover principles common both to the French and German law of contract, and the law of contract is universally admitted to belong to municipal law alone. It is also true that in certain cases the International Court of Justice may be asked to decide a question dealing with conflict of laws. England may bind herself by treaty with France to adopt a particular rule in dealing with French cases: in rare instances there may be a rule of international

---

[1] G. C. Cheshire, *Private International Law* (7th ed.), 3.
[2] *Traité pratique du droit international privé*, 20; J. G. Starke, 52 *L.Q.R.* (1936), 395.

law which determines the question; but, in general, conflict of laws is part of the municipal law of each state.[1]

Why should one country take notice of the laws of another? Dicey[2] supported the theory of vested rights. If I obtain a right by the law of Patagonia, that right should be recognized in England, if no reasons of policy forbid. This theory, however, begs the question, for sometimes we do not know what law is to govern a transaction till the English rules for choice of law are applied. In truth, English courts can only apply English law. A right does not exist *in vacuo*, and, torn from the system to which it belongs, it changes its nature. English rules are decisive on questions of procedure, public policy, application of statutes, and choice of law. But, in appropriate cases, where English rules point to a particular system of law, our courts will enforce a right as alike in content to the foreign right in question as is permitted by the nature of our system and its particular views of policy.[3] If a father could sue his daughter for maintenance according to the law of Ruritania, he could not enforce his right against his daughter while they were both in England even if he were still domiciled in Ruritania. Some foreign rights have no counterparts in our system and are, as it were, indigestible.

Private international law is a subject that throws much light on jurisprudence. The application of laws in space, the characterization of situations, the analysis of the nature of a right, the conflicting rules of the various systems which may be brought into play—all these are part and parcel of a subject in which academic theories may lead to important practical results.[4]

The connecting factors which assist in the choice of a particular law are of several kinds. In the law of persons, half the world stresses the element of domicil, half that of nationality. The main defect of domicil is that it is sometimes difficult to ascertain what the domicil is. Nationality is not a useful test for the British Commonwealth, as a common nationality may cover many different systems of law. The domicil of origin of a legitimate child is the domicil of his father at the time of birth, of an illegitimate that of his mother. Domicil may be changed by a person *sui iuris*, provided there is an actual removal to a new country, with intent to make it a permanent home.

Commercial Law is another cross-division that is rapidly growing

---

[1] See Judgment No. 14 of the P.C.I.J.—the case of the Serbian loans cited J. G. Starke, 52 *L.Q.R.* (1936), 395 at 400. [2] *Conflict of Laws* (7th ed.), 11.
[3] W. W. Cook, *Logical and Legal Bases of the Conflict of Laws*, 20 et seq.
[4] The theory of *renvoi* alone is one that would have delighted medieval logicians.

in importance today. Many countries have separate codes for commercial and civil law.[1] From the juristic point of view it is difficult to frame a precise test which will distinguish an 'act of commerce', and normally the problem is solved by a mere enumeration of particular acts which are declared to be acts of commerce. Commercial law cuts across both the law of obligations and the law of property. Thus from one point of view a bill of exchange is a contract, yet functionally it is property. A bill of lading is partially a receipt for the bailment of a specific object and possesses the quality of being 'negotiable', so that in some ways it may come to represent the goods: it is also a document which contains a contract for the carriage of the goods.

The course of business provides many of the detailed rules of law, and many foreign jurists make a special study of *droit économique*.[2] Thus the law merchant of the Middle Ages was not created by the State, but developed autonomously and was 'received' into legal systems long after the merchants had developed it. The recent growth of state regulation of industry and the creation of public utilities owned by the State have led to the intrusion of public law into the realm of commerce. Although for purposes of exposition it may be useful to isolate commercial law, jurisprudence must strive to distribute it under the various heads.

Industrial Law is another cross-division which is assuming increasing practical importance. In the days of *laissez-faire*, this realm was left to the free play of the rules of contract, tort, and property. Today the State cannot tolerate industrial anarchy and a growing body of law regulates the wage contract, conditions of work, holiday pay, and even sometimes the right of dismissal. Australia has ambitiously set up courts to try to create, in the words of Higgins, 'a new province of law and order'. This experiment has not fully justified the hopes of an earlier generation, but the arbitration and conciliation procedure has averted many strikes and raised the general standards of livelihood. This is but another example of the increasing complexity of the problems with which law attempts to deal in the twentieth century.[3]

---

[1] e.g. France: M. S. Amos and F. P. Walton, *Introduction to French Law* (2nd ed. 1963), 339–40.

[2] Or *Wirtschaftsrecht* as the Germans call it. See H. Goldschmidt, *English Law from the Foreign Standpoint*, 90; F. de Király, *Rec. Gény*, iii. 111; H. Sinzheimer, *Le Problème des sources*, 73.

[3] Many other subordinate classifications have appeared and are appearing in response to the increasing complexities of practice and changes in the aims and methods of legal education.

§ 61. LEGAL PERSONALITY—AN INTRODUCTORY NOTE

Before embarking upon a discussion of the matters classified above[1] it is desirable to point out that most of the matters to be discussed involve not tangible things which exist in the world around us independently of man, but intangible things created in one way or another by man for his purposes as a social animal. Notions and concepts like rights and duties, juristic acts, remedial rights, property, or possession, although they may be concerned with tangible things in one way or another, are not themselves tangible things but represent or stand for or serve or describe certain relationships. If Adam were the only animal on earth he would not need to conceive the notion of ownership. It is not until a question of *meum* or *tuum* arises that notions of ownership or property need to be considered. It is difficult to conceive of rights or duties except as going to the relationships between persons.

If by persons we meant always human beings, then perhaps there would not need to be much discussion about legal personality. It is clear, however, that the law creates not only its own rules for determining the relationships between persons but its own rules for determining what entities shall be recognized as persons for the purposes of the law. For the purposes of the law an idol, a trade union, or a 'one man' commercial company may be recognized as persons for the purposes of legal relationships, distinct from any human beings connected with them.[2]

This being so, it would perhaps be logical to discuss the concept of legal personality at the outset when embarking upon a discussion of the techniques of the law. Legal personality has been placed later for treatment, however, partly because it is traditional to treat it as a question arising within the area of private law, and partly because the matters discussed under the heading of public law are either, as with the State, matters requiring special treatment on their own so far as the notion of legal personality is concerned, or, as with crimes, matters which have traditionally concerned themselves with human beings, if not to the exclusion of other kinds of legal persons, at least very nearly to their exclusion.

[1] §§ 59–60 *supra*.
[2] The relevant cases are discussed *infra*, Ch. XVI.

REFERENCES

HALL, J., *Readings in Jurisprudence*, ch. xiv.
—— *Some Basic Questions Regarding Legal Classification for Professional and Scientific Purposes* (1953), 5 J. Legal. Ed. 329.
JOLOWICZ, J. A. (ed.), *The Division and Classification of the Law* (1970).
POUND, R., 37 *Harv. L. R.* (1924), 933.
ROBERTSON, A. H., 52 *Harv. L. R.* (1939), 747.

XII

RIGHTS AND DUTIES

§ 62. ANALYSIS OF A RIGHT

THE noun *right* is one that has many meanings. A common dictionary definition of it is that it means the standard of permitted action within a certain sphere.[1] Until we are clear about the sphere of which we are speaking, however, it is absurd to argue whether a particular act is right or not. If a Frenchman and an Englishman are arguing about the length of a path, they would not be so stupid as to use different standards (metres and yards) without attempting to adopt common units for the purpose of solving the dispute—but in the sphere of Jurisprudence we sometimes find bitter disputes because of reckless ambiguity in the use of the term 'right'.

Within a particular system of ethics we discover whether a particular action is right by asking whether it is consonant with the general principles on which the system is based. Christianity may supply yet other standards, or we may judge an action by the positive morality of a given community. A theory of natural law may be made the basis for the deduction of natural rights which (it is argued) inhere in every human being by virtue of his personality and are inalienable and imprescriptable.[2] From all these uses of the term there must be distinguished a *legal* right, of which the test is a simple one—is the right recognized and protected by the legal system itself? Thus a person may have a legal right to do an act which is unethical and opposed to the standards of positive morality. But to draw a distinction between legal rights and other rights is not to suggest that the law is unreceptive to the general conception of right which exists in a community, for the ethical views and positive morality of a given community naturally influence the law in its determination of the conduct which it will protect and of the actions which it will prohibit. '*Rights* spring from *right*. Principles of liability, in the last analysis, must be derived from the moral sense of the community.'[3]

The term 'right-duty' covers several legal relations, each with its distinct characteristics.[4] For the moment it is sufficient to emphasize

---

[1] *Shorter Oxford English Dictionary.*   [2] *Supra,* § 33.
[3] C. K. Allen, *Legal Duties,* 111.   [4] *Infra,* § 63.

that there are four elements in every legal right: (1) the holder of the right; (2) the act or forbearance to which the right relates; (3) the *res* concerned (the object[1] of the right); (4) the person bound by the duty.[2] Every right, therefore, involves a relationship between two or more legal persons, and only legal persons can be bound by duties or be the holders of legal rights.[3] Rights and duties are correlatives, that is, we cannot have a right without a corresponding duty or a duty without a corresponding right. When we speak of a right we are really referring to a right-duty relationship between two persons, and to suppose that one can exist without the other is just as meaningless as to suppose that a relationship can exist between father and son unless both father and son have existed.[4] Some examples will make this clear. If Jones owes Smith five pounds, then Smith has a right that Jones should do an act (pay) relating to a *res* (the money). If Brown owns Blackacre, then Brown has a right to exclude persons generally from the object of the right—the land. Persons generally are under a duty to refrain from trespassing.

As used in this analysis, the term *res* is very wide, and covers much more than material things. Thus Robinson has a right that others shall not unjustifiably defame him—here the object of the right is that intangible but valuable possession, a good reputation. Can a person ever be the object of a right? There is no doubt that a human person may be a *res*, as we can see in the case of slavery which treated a man as mere property. But the slave was not a legal person and could neither possess rights nor be bound by duties. A more difficult question arises if we ask whether a *legal* person may be the object of a right. Austin suggests that since a master has an action against anyone who knowingly induces the servant to break his contract, or against anyone who negligently injures the servant so that he cannot perform his duties, the servant is the object[5] of the right. But the object is the services of the servant rather than the servant himself. Similarly, the rights which a father possesses that no one shall interfere with his control over his children relate not to the child as a *res* but rather to the custody and guardianship of the children.

Turning to another problem in the definition of rights, there are

---

[1] Austin calls the *res* the 'subject' of the right (*Jurisprudence*, Lect. XVI), but this introduces confusion and 'object' seems a more convenient term.

[2] T. E. Holland, *Jurisprudence*, ch. viii.

[3] Legal personality is defined below: see Ch. XVI.

[4] A possible exception to the doctrine that no duty can exist without a corresponding right is the conception of absolute duties, but this is discussed *infra*, § 64.

[5] *Jurisprudence*, i. 368.

three elements that must be considered. A right is legal because it is protected (or at least recognized) by a legal system—hence the criterion of enforceability must be discussed. The holder of a right exercises his will in a certain way, and that will is directed to the satisfaction of a certain interest. Each of these elements—protection, will, and interest—is essential to a true description of a right, but many disputes have arisen because of a false emphasis either on the will which is exercised or on the interest desired. Thus some define right in terms of will, and others in terms of interest alone. Each of these elements now falls to be discussed.

(a) The Protection afforded by the State

As has been said, the characteristic mark of a legal right is its recognition by a legal system. If the right is challenged, will the State enforce it, or grant damages for any failure to carry out the corresponding duty; or in some other way recognize the right and attach legal consequences to interferences with it? In the case of a right which is recognized *only* by morality or ethics, the law will grant no remedy. Enforceability by legal process has, therefore, sometimes been said to be the *sine qua non* of a legal right. Three qualifications must, however, be made to this statement, for enforcement is only the most obvious mark of recognition.

Firstly, the law will not always enforce a right, but may grant the injured party only a remedy in damages.

Secondly, there are certain rights, sometimes called imperfect rights, which the law recognizes but will not enforce directly. Thus a statute-barred debt cannot be recovered in a court of law, but for certain purposes the existence of the debt has legal significance. If the debtor pays the money, he cannot later sue to recover it as money paid without consideration; and the imperfect right has the faculty of becoming perfect if the debtor makes an acknowledgement of the debt from which there can be inferred a promise to pay. But there is no real difficulty in this case; if we use terms which are discussed below,[1] the creditor has no claim for the money, the debtor has liberty to pay if he so desires, but no claim to recover the money once he has paid it, as the 'natural obligation' prevents him from bringing an action for money had and received. The law has really cut down the creditor's rights to the receipt of a voluntary payment, although

---

[1] *Infra*, § 63.

in certain circumstances (e.g. a promise to pay) the imperfect right may become perfect.

Thirdly, in some systems courts of justice do not control an adequate machinery for enforcement. Thus in international law there is no power in the court to enforce its decree. Hence, ultimately, the answer to the question whether the essence of a legal right lies in its enforceability will depend on our definition of law. Dicey distinguished between constitutional conventions and laws, the test of the latter being that they will be enforced by the courts, whereas the conventions will not.[1] Many constitutional lawyers point out, however, that if we apply rigorously the test of enforcement in a court of law, we are left with too narrow a view of constitutional law.[2]

Because of the difficulties which sometimes arise in the enforcement of particular rights, it is better to define a legal right in terms of recognition and protection by the legal order.[3] This does not unduly narrow the meaning of legal right. Thus an international court would recognize any rights granted by international law and would protect them so far as it could, even although there was no machinery for direct enforcement. The element of enforceability is important in questions of jurisdiction and private international law. The principle of effectiveness must be considered, since it is absurd for a court to make a decree that is futile. An English court will not make a decree concerning the title to immovables situated abroad and even if a defendant is subject to the English jurisdiction, equity will not order him to do an act illegal by the law of the country where it is to be performed.

(b) The Element of Will

Many uphold the will theory on the ground that the very purpose of the law is to grant the widest possible means of self-expression—the maximum of individual self-assertion. Rights, therefore, are inherent attributes of the human will. This theory was extended by the doctrine of natural rights, which declared that there were certain spheres of personal life with which the State could not legally interfere. This is based on a confusion of what is and what ought to be. There are certain rights which it is desirable that the law should protect, but that does not prove that they are protected by the law nor

---

[1] *Law of the Constitution* (8th ed.), 23.
[2] W. I. Jennings, *The Law and the Constitution* (3rd ed.), 314.
[3] e.g. J. W. Salmond, *Jurisprudence* (12th ed.), 217: 'A right is an interest protected by rules of right.'

that any law which interferes with them is void. But we must not rush to the other extreme and think of the law as creating rights out of nothing. After all, the law exists to compromise the conflicting desires of society, and some partisans of the will theory merely say that the law should protect the individual will as far as possible.

Holmes defines a legal right as 'nothing but a permission to exercise certain natural powers and upon certain conditions to obtain protection, restitution, or compensation by the aid of the public force'.[1] This is not quite exact, for some rights or claims[2] consist not of a liberty to do something but of an ability to force others to perform an act. In some cases the law, as Holmes says, does merely protect the natural powers. Jones may garden or sleep, make love or quarrel upon his own plot of ground—and one who interferes with these activities does so at his peril unless he can justify his act. Here the law adds nothing except protection. But when the State grants me power to dispose of my property by will, it is not merely protecting my natural activities, for, once dead, I cannot actually distribute my property. This is a realm where the law does not merely protect the natural powers of individuals, but grants a power by virtue of which a declaration of intent will operate after death.[3]

Duguit's attack on the traditional concept of subjective right is really based on his opposition to the notion that right depends upon will. The traditional theory of right he conceives as being based on the metaphysical idea of two wills being face to face with one another, one of which in the particular relationship is superior to the other.[4] Will (he argues) is not the essential element in law or in the right which flows from it, for the real basis of law lies in the objective fact of social solidarity. The emphasis on will is anti-social, for it suggests that man is in conflict with his fellows, instead of emphasizing that man is bound by duties created by the fact of social solidarity. Society creates duties for every man, but no right save that of always doing his duty. Duguit's paradox is a useful antidote to the excessive individualism of some of the theories of natural law, but truth lies in a *via media* between the two extremes. It is true that man can realize an effective life only in society, but that does not mean more than that his rights must be adjusted to those of his fellows. The individual will may be directed to social or anti-social ends, but the will is the 'mainspring'

---

[1] *The Common Law*, 214.   [2] *Infra*, § 63.
[3] *Infra*, § 63, for a discussion of the difference between a liberty and a power.
[4] C. K. Allen, *Legal Duties*, 156; O. Ionescu, *Archives de phil. du droit* (1932, 1–2), 269.

of the individual personality, and for the law to attempt to create a system which ignored the wills of individuals would be futile. The aim of the law is not primarily to create a new life for society and new desires for men, but rather to regulate such life and such desires as already exist. Will may be an essential element in many attempts to analyse the conception of legal right, but it is not the only element. As we shall see, it is artificial to divorce will from interest.

(c) The Element of Interest

The main argument of those who hold that interest and not will is the fundamental basis of right is that persons may have rights, although they have no wills: a baby one day old, an irrational idiot, a corporation, or a foundation cannot be regarded as having wills, but undoubtedly the law grants to such persons legal rights. Yet in all these cases there is a will operative, for the law sets up a guardian to protect the rights of the child, a committee in the case of the lunatic, and it imputes to the corporation or foundation the acts of human beings to whom power to bind the artificial entity has been granted. Nékám is so impressed by this division of will and interest that he suggests that we should always distinguish between the subject of rights and the administrator of those rights.[1] The passive capacity to be the subject of rights may belong to any entity to which the law chooses to grant this privilege. The administrator must be a human person with an actual will. In the case of the normal adult, the subject of the rights is also the administrator, but this power may be taken away, for example in the case of the prodigal or the lunatic. On the other hand, if the law grants legal rights to an idol, then there must be a separation, since the idol has no will to guard its interests. Nékám suggests that it is only a coincidence that in the majority of cases the subject administers his own rights—but surely this is allowing exceptional cases to have undue weight.

Ihering attacked the will theory because he thought that the purpose of law was not to protect individual assertion but certain interests. He therefore defined rights as legally protected interests.[2] These interests or values are not created by the State for they already exist in the life of the community, and the State merely chooses such as it will protect.

In truth it is an exaggeration to set interest and will too much in

---

[1] *The Personality Conception of the Legal Entity*, 29; H. A. J. Ford, *Unincorporated Non-profit Associations*; L. C. Webb (ed.), *Legal Personality and Political Pluralism.*
[2] *Geist des römischen Rechts*, iii. 332; F. Hallis, *Corporate Personality*, 169.

opposition to each other. 'The essence of legal right seems to me to be not legally guaranteed power by itself, nor legally protected interest by itself, but the legally guaranteed power to realize an interest.'[1] The human will does not operate *in vacuo* but desires certain ends, and interests are but objects of human desire.[2] An interest is a claim or want of an individual or a group of individuals which that individual or group wishes to satisfy. And the law grants rights not to the human will as an end in itself, but to a human will that is pursuing ends of which the legal system approves. The vigour with which this problem has been debated is due, not so much to an academic interest in the nature of a right, as to the theories of law and the State which are built on any particular theory of the nature of a right. If a legal right consists merely of a protected will, how are we to reconcile the conflicting wills of men save by postulating a superior will which can overcome all opposition? It is hard to reconcile wills if we do not consider also the ends which mankind strives to reach. If we define rights as interests, it is easier to effect a reconciliation on paper, since true interests do not always conflict; but such an approach often leads to abstract solutions which neglect the fact that men are not entirely rational in their behaviour or choice of ends. Again, the will theory may easily lead to the doctrine that, since the purpose of law is to protect individual self-assertion, there should be as little interference with freedom as possible: the interest theory may be exaggerated so as to destroy liberty in favour of forcing men to seek what they should desire.[3] A true theory of the State can be based only on a proper analysis of a legal right that gives due scope to the elements both of interest and of will. Frequently the law allows me to exercise my own will; in other cases my will may be restricted in order to serve what are deemed to be my higher interests or the needs of others. A lunatic or a prodigal is not always allowed to effect his own desires. But there is danger in assuming that the law can in every case dictate to man wherein his interests lie.

§ 63. Claim, Liberty, Power, Immunity

Salmond[4] pointed out long ago that the term 'right-duty' was very overworked and was frequently used for relationships which were not

---

[1] C. K. Allen, *Legal Duties*, 183. Cf. G. Jellinek: 'a right is the will-power of man applied to a utility or interest recognized and protected by a legal system': *System der subjectiven öffentlichen Rechte* (2nd ed.), 44; cf. F. Hallis, *Corporate Personality*, 191.
[2] *Restatement of the Law of Torts*, i. § 1.
[3] Cf. N. S. Timasheff, *Sociology of Law*, 333–4.
[4] *Jurisprudence* (9th ed.), 299. (See 12th ed., ch. vii.)

in reality the same, thus causing confusion in legal argument. Hohfeld carried the analysis farther,[1] and his work has been developed by other writers. Hence an attempt has been made to analyse the right-duty relationship (in its broad sense) into its component parts, and the table set out below is the result of the work of Hohfeld, although some changes of terminology have been made. At first the tendency was to regard this analysis as too academic, but it has had increasing influence—for example, it has been adopted by the American *Restatement of the Law*. The table provides an interesting test of the accuracy of legal thought and, though there are defects which have been exposed by the subtle insight of Kocourek,[2] it repays study.

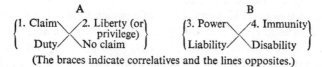

(The braces indicate correlatives and the lines opposite.)

In the claim-duty[3] relationship the emphasis is on what I may force another to do, or to refrain from doing. I have a claim against Jones for five pounds and he is under a duty to pay it. Claim and duty are correlatives in the sense that one cannot exist without the other. Under the second head, liberty represents what I can do for myself, free of the possibility of legal interference by others.[4] I have liberty to breathe, to walk in my own fields, to play golf on my private links. Here no precise relationship to others is in question, save that the law will protect my liberty if others interfere with its exercise. But it is more accurate to say that I have a liberty to play than that I have a claim, for I may exercise my liberty without affecting others, whereas my claim can be enforced only by coercing another to act or forbear. If the table is examined, it will be seen that liberty is the opposite of duty. Logically, therefore (it is argued), the correlative of liberty should be the opposite of claim. But there is no word in English which expresses the lack of a claim and therefore the rather barbarous 'no-claim' has been suggested.

---

[1] *Fundamental Legal Conceptions*, R. Pound, 50 *Harv. L. R.* (1937), 572; M. Radin, 51 *Harv. L. R.* (1938), 1141; G. W. Goble, 35 *Col. L. R.* (1935), 535.
[2] *Jural Relations*.
[3] W. N. Hohfeld used the term 'right-duty'. But since 'right' is here used in a somewhat narrower sense than is customary, it seems advisable to use another term in order to prevent confusion.
[4] It is *legal* interference by others that is emphasized. There are few situations where a person is entirely free from the risk of illegal force—but if the law be broken, a remedy normally lies.

One of the difficulties of the table is the desire to retain formal symmetry, and this forces us to link together liberty and privilege. The usual distinction is that liberty covers those acts that are primarily lawful for all, whereas privilege[1] covers those that are prima facie unlawful but allowable in certain circumstances to all, or else to a limited number of persons. The *Restatement of the Law of Property* defines a privilege as a legal freedom on the part of one person as against another to do a given act or a legal freedom not to do a certain act. Thus, where qualified privilege arises, a person has a privilege to make defamatory statements concerning another, provided he makes an honest use of the occasion; the person defamed has 'no-claim' to prevent him.

A power is an 'ability on the part of a person to produce a change in a given legal relation by doing or not doing a given act'.[2] In one sense, I have a liberty to make a will, since persons generally are under a duty not to interfere with the free exercise of my power. But the question which arises under this third head is not my liberty to inscribe certain words on paper, but the effect which those words will have on the distribution of my property. The notion of a power of appointment is familiar, and, by its exercise, the legal rights of another may be affected by the receipt of the property in question. The table generalizes the notion of power in this sense and uses it to cover all ability to affect the legal relations of others.

There is no convenient word to express the correlative of power. The term 'liability' (which is used) certainly conveys the sense of being affected by the exercise of the power, but it suggests something disadvantageous which one would seek to avoid. Hohfeld generalizes the term so as to cover a chance of being benefited as well as of suffering loss. Thus Jones has power to make a will and his children are liable to benefit. The State has power to punish a criminal and he is liable to suffer the penalty.[3]

An immunity is 'a freedom on the part of one person against having a given legal relation altered by a given act or omission on the part of another person'. A judge is immune from having to pay damages for

---

[1] This term has many meanings in English usage: A. Kocourek, *Jural Relations*, 8. (1) It may mean immunity, e.g. the privilege of a Member of Parliament from arrest; (2) it may mean power, e.g. the privilege of the recaption of chattels; (3) it may mean privilege in the sense set out in the text: W. E. Hearn, *Legal Duties and Rights*, 172.

[2] *Restatement of the Law of Property*, § 3.

[3] A. H. Campbell, 7 *Camb. L. J.* (1940), 206 at 209, points out that in one sense Hohfeld's table is incomplete, because I am under a liability to have my legal position changed by an *event* beyond human control as well as by the act of another.

defamation because of anything he has said in the course of a trial. The correlative is disability. It may be noted that, just as in the case of the first half of the table, there are opposites in the second. Thus disability is the opposite of power, and immunity the opposite of liability. If a legislature passes an unconstitutional statute, that is not a breach of duty for which the State can be sued in damages— the statute is merely a nullity. Thus we cannot say that a fruit-grower has a claim that the legislature should not pass an unconstitutional statute, for that would imply that the legislature was bound by a duty, since a claim cannot exist without a duty. But the grower is legally immune from interference by a statute that is not within the powers of the legislature.

Thus a trustee has power to convey the legal title of the trust property to a purchaser, but he has no privilege to do so in breach of trust. If he does act in defiance of the trust deed, the purchaser, pro- vided he gives value in good faith and with no notice of the equitable claim, takes a good title, since the trustee has power to convey it. But if the beneficiary learns in time of the prospective breach of trust, he has a claim which can be made effective, for the court, if appealed to, will enforce the duty lying on the trustee to carry out the terms of the trust. This is an example which is dealt with more clearly by the use of Hohfeld's terms than by attempting to force the term 'right-duty' to express every shade of the relationship. Again a royal commission may have liberty to carry on an inquiry in the sense that no one can prevent its functioning, but no claim which imposes on witnesses a duty to answer questions.[1] A judge has power to try a prisoner who is liable to be affected by his decision; the Crown has a claim that the judge shall perform his work and the judge is bound by a duty. An owner of a mine asks for an injunction against union leaders who are attempting to induce his employees to join a union. The employer has a liberty to employ non-union labour, but this is not necessarily a claim which will impose a corresponding duty on union leaders not to attempt to persuade the employees to join the union.[2]

One value of the table is that it emphasizes that a particular legal relationship may give rise not to a single right and duty relationship but to a bundle of claims, liberties, immunities, and powers. Thus if A and B make a contract, each has a claim against the other that the contract shall be fulfilled. If A breaks the contract, B has power to

---

[1] Cf. *A.-G. of Australia* v. *Colonial Sugar Refining Co. Ltd.*, [1914] A.C. 237.
[2] W. W. Cook, in *Lectures on Legal Topics*, v. 5, 335 at 339.

sue for damages and to enforce execution. Both A and B have a claim against persons generally that they shall not knowingly induce breach of the contract.

The most accurate and subtle analysis of legal rights has been carried out by Kocourek,[1] but it is impossible to expound his scheme within the limits available. A high algebra for the law may conduce to clarity but it cannot be concisely explained. His glossary covers over seventeen pages, and the first two terms are 'abnormal concatenation' and 'abnormal intercalation'.[2] It is not easy to explain such a term as 'heterophylaxis' in a few words. Nevertheless, where it has been possible to do so, his ideas have been drawn upon, and, for those who can master the terminology, there is much value in his work.

§ 64. ABSOLUTE AND RELATIVE DUTIES

Austin distinguished between absolute and relative duties. In the latter case we have the normal relationship of a right held by one person to a duty owed by another—this is exemplified by the normal jural relationship between subjects. But Austin claimed that there was also a class of absolute duties to which no corresponding rights attached. An analysis of this type of duty throws interesting light on the nature of law itself.

There were four kinds of such absolute duties according to Austin's analysis:

(a) duties not regarding persons (e.g. those owed to God and the lower animals);

(b) duties owed to persons indefinitely (e.g. towards the community);

(c) self-regarding duties;

(d) duties owed to the sovereign.[3]

The first type create no difficulty—they are not, in fact, legal duties at all. Man's relation to his Creator is a matter of religion and not of law: if the legal system protects certain religious duties with a sanction, then that duty is part of the law and amenable to the same analysis as other legal duties. If I must attend church or pay a fine, then the criminal law is brought into play. So far as duties towards animals are concerned, I have no legal duty towards them. If the law prohibits

---

[1] *Jural Relations* (2nd ed.).   [3] Op. cit. 427.
[2] *Jurisprudence*, i. 400; C. K. Allen, *Legal Duties*, 156.

cruelty, then I may owe a duty to the State; so far as the law of tort is concerned, I may owe a duty to the owner of the dog. But I cannot owe a legal duty to something that is not a legal person.

It is difficult to know what Austin meant by duties owed to persons indefinitely: I have a general duty not to defame my neighbours, but this duty is merely the correlative of the right inhering in each member of the community. The 'general duty' towards the community breaks up into a mass of duties towards each particular individual.

As for self-regarding duties, there cannot be a legal duty owed to oneself. The duty not to commit suicide is not a duty I owe to myself but is part of the criminal law and subject to the same analysis as any other duty of the criminal law.[1] This point cannot be discussed without considering Austin's last point—duties owed to the sovereign.

The State should be regarded as a legal person.[2] But, even if this is granted, Austin would deny that there can be a legal relationship between sovereign and subject, on the ground that a right-duty relationship can exist between two persons only if there is above them a political superior who will enforce the obligation. The sovereign, *ex hypothesi*, has no superior, and hence may change the law whenever he desires. From a realistic point of view it must be admitted that in practice a legal right against the State is not as effective as one against a fellow citizen.[3] In a dictatorship, where one person is the supreme lawgiver, administrator, and judge, it may smack of hypocrisy to say that a subject has a legal right against one who may retrospectively change the content of the law as he pleases and give judgment in his own favour. If the State has absolute power to change the law, formal limits *ex hypothesi* cannot be set to its ability to change the rules in its own interest.

This argument thus leads to the rejection of the notion that there can be a right-duty relationship between the subject and the State.

---

[1] If the suicide be successful, more difficult problems arise, for by committing suicide the individual has destroyed his legal personality. If the penalty is dishonour of the body, a realistic analysis shows only that the State has power to prevent the executors disposing of the body in the normal way; if the penalty is confiscation of goods, the State has power to prevent the beneficiaries from receiving the goods and the beneficiaries are liable to be affected. There seems to be no need to suggest, as A. Kocourek does, that we must postulate that the legal personality survives the death, even for an instant: *Jural Relations*, 296–7.

[2] *Infra*, § 77. 'The State is surely as capable of possessing a right as is the Corporation of London': T. E. Holland, *Jurisprudence* (10th ed.), 126.

[3] Until 1947, the Crown was not liable in tort in England. Even now that the Crown Proceedings Act has changed the rule, the Crown still possesses advantages in litigation, e.g. concerning discovery and the periods of limitation. In Victoria, the Crown was not made liable in tort until 1955 (Crown Proceedings Act, 1955).

This means that an investor has no legal right to interest on funds lent to the government. It was natural, therefore, for Austin to maintain the converse of this proposition—that when the State imposes a duty on a subject, it is a misuse of language to say that the State has a corresponding legal right. The State has physical power, and since no superior binds it, to say it has only a legal right, is to understate the position, for the exercise of a legal right is regulated, whereas the power of the sovereign is not.

This approach is logical enough if Austin's definitions are accepted as premises, but it is more convenient to regard the State as bound by law until the law is changed. If the example of the dictatorship seems to show that there is certain realism in Austin's approach, the example of the modern democratic federation shows that the power to change the law may be so circumscribed (at least where the constitution is concerned) that for practical purposes the subject is protected. This topic raises the issue of the relationship between law and the State,[1] and the theory adopted concerning absolute duties will depend on the more fundamental question of the nature of the State.

Austin's thesis is generally rejected in modern times, but Dr. Allen has given it powerful support.[2] He defines right as legally guaranteed power to realize an interest.

The power and the interest embodied in legal right are essentially the attributes of an individual, in his relation to other individuals. If right be regarded as *mere* power, no doubt the state has the 'right' to punish anything or to order anything. . . . And similarly if legal right be regarded as *mere* interest or social advantage, then . . . doubtless all legal right is ultimately the interest of the community.[3]

The learned writer denies that the duties imposed by the criminal law have any true counterpart in legal right. It is admitted that the community is too nebulous a body in which to place legal rights. But is it not too narrow to suggest that legal rights are essentially the attributes of individuals? Corporations have rights and are bound by duties—is not the State the supreme juristic person? Is not the counterpart of the duty imposed by the criminal law the claim of the State that its prescription shall be obeyed? If the criminal law is broken, then the State has power to punish and the wrongdoer is liable to be punished.

---

[1] *Infra*, § 76.   [2] *Legal Duties*, 183 et seq.
[3] Op. cit. 185–6.

The State has power to impose taxation on the community, and once taxation is imposed the State has a claim against each specific person subject to the impost and that person is under a duty to pay. It is true, of course, that the State frequently has power to change the rules at any moment. Acts that are innocent may be retrospectively declared criminal; a special statute may double John Smith's income-tax assessment after he has received it. This, however, relates to Austin's point that the sovereign cannot be bound by law. But if we admit, as Dr. Allen does, that an investor in the public funds may have legal rights against the State,[1] it seems illogical to regard the duties of the criminal law as absolute.

It is submitted, therefore, that Austin's list of absolute duties can be reduced to one head—duties owed to the sovereign. These are of a special nature because of the particular powers possessed by the State as a legal *persona*. Whether we regard the relationship between sovereign and subject as one of law will depend on our theory of the State. But convenience demands that we treat the State as a legal person bound by law until it is altered.

§ 65. Classification of Legal Rights

1. *Perfect and Imperfect Rights*

These have already been discussed.[2]

2. *Antecedent and Remedial Rights*

Some rights exist for their own sake before any wrongful act has been committed. Thus Jones has a right against persons generally that his reputation shall not be unjustifiably attacked. If Brown breaks his duty in this respect, then Jones has a remedial right to secure damages.[3] Some modern writers would ignore antecedent rights altogether on the ground that, looked at realistically, there is no such thing as a right to reputation, but only a claim to damages if one's fair name is unjustifiably impugned.[4] This raises the whole question whether law is only the realm of constraint. Does law end where liberties begin? It is rather narrow to confine law to litigation or even to threats of proceedings, and it is convenient to retain the notion of

---

[1] Op. cit. 190.　　　　　　　　　　　　　　　　　[2] *Supra*, § 62.
[3] T. E. Holland, *Jurisprudence* (10th ed.), 141. Remedial rights should not be confused with the narrower sphere of the law of procedure: *infra*, Ch. XXIII.
[4] Sometimes called the monist theory: A. Kocourek, 20 *Col. L. R.* (1920), 394.

a legal duty (e.g. not to defame) even if the only remedy be damages for non-fulfilment of it. We uphold the existence of antecedent rights for three reasons: firstly, the language of the law becomes difficult if we ignore such antecedent rights as a right to property, a right to reputation; secondly, law does not exist only to provide constraint but also to create the conditions under which community life is possible and to increase the powers of men;[1] thirdly, some antecedent rights may be specifically enforced—for example, specific performance of a contract may be ordered. In these cases the court normally has a discretion whether it will grant specific performance or not, and it seems surprising to say that Jones has a legal claim against Brown that he shall fulfil his contract only if the court will exercise its discretion in his favour. Again it is said that a husband owes a duty of care to his wife even though she has no remedial right to sue him in tort: this antecedent right is not a mere fiction as she can sue her husband's employer if the husband injures her negligently while in the course of his employment.[2] The mere existence of a legal duty is frequently sufficient to secure its fulfilment. It seems too narrow to confuse the law, the rules on the basis of which the life of the community is carried on, with the remedies which are provided for the comparatively rare number of cases of breach of legal duty.

3. *Rights* in rem *and Rights* in personam

These terms have caused confusion to readers who cannot resist the temptation to translate them literally as a right to a thing and a right against a person. The Romans distinguished between an *actio in rem*, an action brought to recover a specific *res*, and an *actio in personam* which was a claim against a specific person. There was in Roman law a clear-cut distinction between *dominium*, title which availed against the world, and *obligatio* which bound only the parties to the agreement. An action *in personam* was one for the enforcement of an *obligatio*. *Mancipatio* was the typical conveyance and it transferred title alone. For a conveyance to contain covenants would have seemed to the Romans inelegant. If the parties wished to make a collateral agreement, it would be in a separate document. The covenant

---

[1] W. W. Buckland and A. D. McNair, *Roman Law and Common Law*, 265: 'It is difficult to see how one can infringe a right *in rem* unless there is such a thing.'

[2] *Broom* v. *Morgan*, [1953] 1 Q.B. 597; cf. *Schubert* v. *August Schubert Wagon Company*, 249 N.Y. 253, 164 N.E. 42 (1928); and *Riegger* v. *Bruton Brewing Company* 16. A, (2d), 99 (Md. 1940), 25 *Marquette L. Rev.* (1941), 169.

would create a right *in personam* alone—it would not be a right running with the land which could bind persons generally.[1]

The modern terms right *in rem* and right *in personam* have been generalized, somewhat inaccurately, from Roman sources. The typical modern example of a right *in rem* is that of the owner of land against persons generally that they shall not interfere with his rights of ownership. A typical example of a right *in personam* is that arising between the parties to a contract. A right *in rem*, since it relates to a greater number of persons, is more secure—indeed, it is somewhat arrogantly defined as a right availing against the world, although the usual definition is now more limited and describes it as availing against persons generally.[2] On the other hand, a right *in personam* binds only either a particular person or persons. If I buy a motor-car and obtain title, I have a right *in rem* which is effective in that a purported sale by another of the car without my consent is of no avail; if I merely make a contract to buy a particular car in six months time, and the vendor sells in breach of contract, the sale is valid. The contract would bind only the parties to it, and its effect was to promise me a right *in rem* in the future, not actually to transfer one at the moment.

This analysis shows that all rights concern two persons, a *res*, and an act or forbearance. But in a right *in rem* the relation to the *res* seems more prominent (thus it is Jones's special relationship to Blackacre that creates rights availing against persons generally); whereas in rights *in personam* attention is attracted to the particular relationship between definite parties which gave rise to the obligation.[3] To avoid the cumbersome repetition of *in personam* and *in rem* the adjectives 'real' and 'personal' are sometimes used, but, however clearly the meaning may be explained, there is always confusion in the mind of the English student because of the fundamental distinction between real and personal *property*. Historically there was at first no *actio in rem* for the recovery of personal chattels, since judgment was given in the alternative that the defendant either return the chattel or pay its value as damages, but the owner of land could recover it by action. In the critical period, when English terminology was becoming fixed, the tenant had a mere right *in personam* against the landlord—if the landlord sold the property and the purchaser ejected the tenant, the latter was confined to an action for breach of contract against the

---

[1] W. W. Buckland and A. D. McNair, *Roman Law and Common Law*, 92.
[2] J. Austin, i. 370; B. Windscheid, *Pandekten* (9th ed.), § 41; A. Kocourek, *Jural Relations* (2nd ed.), 189.
[3] J. W. Salmond, *Jurisprudence* (12th ed.), 235.

landlord. Hence a leasehold interest was regarded as *personal* property, since the tenant had no *actio in rem*;[1] and since the owner of land could specifically recover it, such an interest was held to relate to *real* property. This, however, is a usage peculiar to English law.

A right *in rem* need not relate to a tangible *res*. Thus a right that one's reputation should not be unjustifiably attacked is today described as a right *in rem*, since it is a right that avails against persons generally. This shows how far the conception has developed from the Roman notion of *actio in rem*, for one who sues to protect his reputation is not asking for judgment for a specific *res*. It should also be noticed that on breach of a right *in rem*, a right *in personam* arises against the aggressor. Most rights *in rem* are negative; it is difficult to conceive of a positive claim against persons generally since the persons on whom the active duty would fall would be so numerous. But there is no *a priori* reason why a positive claim should not lie against every member of a given community.[2] Rights *in personam* may also be either positive (requiring a specific act) or negative (requiring a forbearance).

The distinction between rights *in rem* and rights *in personam* is a useful one, although analysis shows that no adequate definition has yet been discovered. Firstly, a right *in rem* is not a single right but merely a convenient short expression for a bundle of as many rights as there are persons bound by the duty.[3] What causes these rights to be linked together is the fact that they are fundamentally similar in content. Thus I have a right availing against persons generally that they shall not trespass on Blackacre—although there may be many duties, the content is in each case the same. This consideration leads Hohfeld to define a right *in rem* as 'one of a large class of fundamentally similar yet separate rights, actual and potential, residing in a single person (or single group of persons) but availing respectively against persons constituting a very large and indefinite class of people'.[4] A right *in personam* is 'a unique right residing in a person (or group of persons) and availing against a single person (or single group of persons): or else it is one of a *few* fundamentally similar, yet separate, rights availing respectively against a few definite persons'.[5]

---

[1] 'English law for six centuries and more will have to rue this youthful flirtation with Romanism': F. Pollock and F. W. Maitland, *History of English Law*, ii. 114.
[2] A. H. Campbell, 7 *Camb. L. J.* (1940), 206 at 212–14: 'most real rights are negative, but positive real rights are not inconceivable, and some examples are actually found.'
[3] A. Kocourek, *Jural Relations*, 198; W. N. Hohfeld, *Fundamental Legal Conceptions*.
[4] He uses the term 'multital claim' for right *in rem*: op. cit. 72.
[5] A *paucital* claim in W. N. Hohfeld's terminology.

Secondly, from a logical point of view the distinction is defective in that no clear line can be drawn between the limits of 'persons generally' and 'particular person or persons'.[1] If a landowner grants the right to cross his land to every person except to B, what is the nature of the landowner's right against B? According to the traditional definition the right would be *in personam*, because it did not avail against persons generally. Yet, before the landowner granted a right to all of the community except B, the claim against B would be *in rem*, and why should it change its character merely because of an agreement made between the landowner and persons other than B? The answer is that if the only distinction between rights *in rem* and rights *in personam* is the number of persons bound by the duty, then such an agreement does change the nature of the right against B. But suppose that the landowner each day makes agreements with a hundred members of the community imposing a duty to pay for the privilege of crossing the land and continues this practice until he has treated with every member of the community save B, what is the precise point at which the right *in personam* arising out of contracts of this type becomes a right *in rem*, because of the fact that similar duties are owed by a great number of people? This example shows that the distinction is not a very logical one. Kocourek's own solution is that a right *in rem* is one of which the essential investitive facts do not serve directly to identify the person who owes the duty. According to this test, the landowner's rights against those members of the community to whom he has granted privileges arise out of a contract which serves specifically to identify the parties to the relationship (i.e. they would be *in personam*). The right against B would remain *in rem* on this test, even if he were the only person who did not have a privilege to cross the land, since the right arose from ownership of the land, and this title would not specifically identify B as being bound by a duty.

Thirdly, the dichotomy does not suit the peculiarities of every system. English law stubbornly resists Roman classification, and the fact that the right of a beneficiary under a trust cannot easily be placed either under the one head or the other raises doubts in the minds of some writers as to the accuracy of any dogma that all rights are either *in rem* or *in personam*. It is frequently argued that the beneficiary's right is not *in rem*, because it does not avail against a bona-fide purchaser for value without notice and that it is not merely a right *in personam* against the trustee, because of the extensive

---

[1] A. Kocourek, *Jural Relations*, 198–201.

powers of following the trust property.[1] But if we admit that a right is not *in rem* merely because it may be defeated by a particular class of purchaser, that argument would apply not only to the beneficiaries' rights under a trust, but also to the whole class of negotiable instruments. Have I no right *in rem* to my money, because one who receives it for value and in good faith obtains a title superior to mine even though it was originally taken from me by a thief? Hence some writers regard the right of the beneficiary to the trust property as being *in rem*. If so, the existence in English law of the trust would not prevent the division of rights into the two classes (*in rem* and *in personam*) from being exhaustive. However, as Hanbury points out,[2] the immunity of the bona-fide purchaser for value and of the holder in due course of a bill of exchange, have a totally different origin, the former being the logical result of equitable theory which will not touch a person whose conscience is unscathed, whereas the latter is demanded by the exigencies of commerce.

The phrase *ius ad rem* is sometimes used. 'I have a *ius ad rem* when I have a right that some other right shall be transferred to me.'[3] This is merely a specific claim against a particular person, and hence it is not as effective as one which avails against persons generally. If Jones agrees to sell me a book next December, I have a claim against him for performance of the contract, but that claim, in most systems of law, will not be effective against one who purchases in good faith in November.

4. *Proprietary and Personal Rights*

Property is an extraordinarily ambiguous term,[4] and the adjective 'proprietary' conveys the same confusion. Personal rights can be defined only as the residuary rights which remain after proprietary rights have been subtracted. We cannot say that personal rights are those which are necessary for the development of the human personality, for many would think that certain rights over property were necessary for a true self-expression. Some have suggested that personal rights are those which cannot be transferred or have no money value. But neither of these tests will suit English law. Choses

---

[1] F. W. Maitland, *Equity* (1936), 23; W. W. Cook, B. Ames, and T. Lewin call the beneficiary's right one *in personam*. A. W. Scott, 17 *Col. L. R.* (1917), 269, suggests that it is a right *in rem* and is supported by P. H. Winfield, *Province of the Law of Tort*, 112. F. Pollock, 28 *L.Q.R.* (1912), 297, would treat trust as a head *sui generis*. H. G. Hanbury, *Modern Equity* (5th ed.), 505–7.   [2] 63 *L.Q.R.* (1947), 115.
[3] J. W. Salmond, *Jurisprudence* (12th ed.), 238.   [4] *Infra*, Ch. XXI.

in action were regarded as creating proprietary rights even before
they were transferable, and equity treats as a proprietary right
a member's share in the assets of a club to which he belongs, yet his
share cannot be transferred to another or sold for value. A pension
may be inalienable and yet none the less property. The goodwill of
a medical practice in England, under the National Health Service Act,
1946, may exist as an asset and yet be non-transferable.[1] It is true
that most 'personal' rights cannot be transferred (for example, the
right to physical integrity), but it does not follow that all proprietary
rights can be transferred. In English law the distinction has achieved
a certain practical importance because of the dictum that equity
will act only to protect rights of property. The protection against
financial and material loss developed more speedily than the protection of rights concerning more intangible things. The backwardness
of the law in protecting personal rights is due partly to the emphasis
placed on the necessity of showing financial loss, partly to the desire
to discourage a flood of litigation, partly to difficulties of proof.
Damage to a car is easy to demonstrate and the resulting loss may be
easily calculated: it may be difficult to prove that nervous shock
resulted from an accident, or to assess damages that would be equitable.[2] Thus there has been an increasing tendency, when at last it was
desired to protect a particular personal right, to attempt to discover
an element of property on which protection could be based. If a girl
be seduced, the father cannot sue for the outrage to the family
honour, but he can sue for loss of service, and incidentally in an
appropriate case claim exemplary damages.[3] If a writer wishes to
prevent the publication of his love letters by a faithless recipient, he
pleads property in the letters.[4] If a lecturer wishes to prohibit publication of a lecture delivered only to a limited class, he claims property
in his composition.[5] If a broadcasting company arranges to spy on
the land of a race-course owner so as to broadcast to the community
the happenings on the race-course, the owner has no remedy, even if
he can show financial loss due to falling attendances, as he has no
property in the spectacle.[6] But in different branches of English law

---

[1] *Whitehill* v. *Bradford*, [1952] 1 Ch. 236; 68 *L.Q.R.* (1952), 145.
[2] R. Pound, in *Selected Essays on the Law of Torts*, 108–9; 29 *Harv. L. R.* (1916),
670; *Social Control through Law*, 60.
[3] *Irwin* v. *Dearman* (1809), 11 East. 23. This action is now abolished.
[4] *Gee* v. *Pritchard* (1818), 2 Swans. 402; *Pope* v. *Curl* (1741), 2 Atk. 342.
[5] *Caird* v. *Sime* (1887), 12 App. Cas. 326.
[6] *Victoria Park Racing and Recreation Grounds Co. Ltd.* v. *Taylor* (1937), 58 C.L.R.
479; G. W. Paton, 16 *Can. B. R.* (1938), 425 at 435.

we find that different meanings are given to the term 'proprietary right'. Some dicta go so far as to speak of 'property in reputation' and thus deprive the term of any consistent meaning.[1]

In America the term is also of practical importance because of constitutional provisions for the protection of property. A monumental work[2] which discusses the term in all its meanings leaves us at first with the depressing feeling that law is crudely unscientific in its use of terminology, then with the reflection that law is a subtle art which will find its way by devious means to the result desired in the particular case.

Salmond concludes that the essential nature of the distinction is that proprietary rights are valuable, whereas personal are not—'the former are the elements of a man's wealth, the latter are merely elements in his well-being'.[3] There may be a guiding principle lying behind these words, but it is not one that can precisely be applied. A man's right to his reputation may be very valuable—the loss of reputation may mean that of livelihood. The right to physical integrity is a personal one, yet health is a valuable asset in the sense that economic welfare may depend on it. Value is a difficult term to define unless we adopt the test of exchange value, and we have seen that not all proprietary rights can be exchanged. The vital thing to grasp at the outset is that proprietary rights, like all other rights, involve legal relationships between legal persons, and cannot be explained by reference to relationships between human beings and things. Some of our legal terminology springs from times when that was not generally understood and confusion has been made easy.[4]

The most important proprietary rights are discussed below.[5] Here we may note that an important division of proprietary rights is into *ius in re propria* and *ius in re aliena*.

Ius in re propria and *in re aliena*. Salmond defines a *ius in re aliena* or encumbrance as one 'which limits or derogates from some more general right belonging to some other person in respect of the same subject matter. All others are *iura in re propria*'.[6] Austin confines the latter right to ownership and describes a *ius in re aliena* as a fraction or particle of ownership which is held by another than the owner of

---

[1] Malins V.C. in *Dixon* v. *Holden* (1869), L.R. 7 Eq. 488 at 499.
[2] C. R. Noyes, *The Institution of Property*.
[3] Op. cit. 239.
[4] F. S. Cohen, *Dialogue on Private Property*, 9 *Rutger's L. R.* (1954), 357.
[5] *Infra*, Ch. XXI.
[6] *Jurisprudence* (12th ed.), 241.

the *res* concerned.[1] The precise nature of the distinction is, however, best discussed in connection with the analysis of ownership and of property.[2] The problem is now much more complex than in the days when land, cattle, and other material things formed the subject-matter of property. The growth in importance of the company share and the negotiable instrument renders it necessary to examine the position afresh.

5. Vested and Contingent Rights

The satisfaction of rights is always subject to contingency in one sense. Smith may owe me £100 and may be able to meet the debt, but, before he pays it, he may be involved in some financial disaster. The distinction between vested and contingent rights, however, is based on another notion, but unfortunately terminology is not consistent in the various systems of law, and it is difficult to secure a broad definition.[3] Much feudal learning was built around the English distinction between vested and contingent remainders, but the details of any one system are not a proper study for general jurisprudence.

Every right arises from a title.[4] When all the investitive facts which are necessary to create the right have occurred, the right is vested; when part of the investitive facts have occurred, the right is contingent until the happening of all the facts on which the title depends. This is a simple distinction. But, unfortunately, the word 'vested' is used in two senses. Firstly, an interest may be vested *in possession*, when there is a right to present enjoyment, e.g. when I own and occupy Blackacre. But an interest may be vested, even where it does not carry a right to immediate possession, if it does confer a fixed right of taking possession in the future. Since all the investitive facts which are necessary to create the right have occurred, the right is vested in interest, even though actual enjoyment be postponed to a definite time in the future. If a grant is made to B in fee simple, he takes a vested interest in possession. If a grant is made to A for life, remainder to B, then according to English terminology B takes a vested estate in remainder. From one point of view, B's title is not complete until A has died, but two factors are regarded as important. Although it is uncertain when A will die, he must die at some time, and even if B dies first, B's heirs will take. Hence B has a definite interest which cannot be defeated;

---

[1] *Jurisprudence*, ii. 847.   [2] *Infra*, § 116.
[3] See J. Austin, Lect. LIII.   [4] *Infra*, § 67.

moreover, it is an interest which he can alienate at once, for it has a present money value. But if the grant is to B for life, and if C survives B, to C in fee simple, C has a contingent interest only, because it is uncertain whether he will survive B. A grant to D at twenty-one is contingent, because until D reaches that age, it is uncertain whether the condition will ever be fulfilled.

A mere *spes successionis* must be distinguished from a contingent right. If Matilda has nursed her invalid friend for thirty years, she may have every hope of succeeding to the property, but she has no right. The title necessary would be a valid will. If such a will leaves the property to Matilda on condition that she marries, she then has a right which will become effective on satisfaction of the condition.

In the civil law a legacy was vested if it was payable at a future time certain to arrive and the legatee had a transmissible right, contingent if it depended on an event which might never happen, in which case the legatee had no right which he could transfer until the condition was satisfied.

6. Legal and Equitable Rights

This classification depends on the division between common law and equity which is peculiar to English history. The problems that arise are elsewhere discussed.[1]

§ 66. The Creation and Extinction of Rights

When a person claims a right he must show a title thereto. In a broad sense all rights flow from the law, since it is only through the protection of the law that a legal right gains its efficacy. Sometimes, however, a right may be granted directly by the law without the consent of the person bound, e.g. the general rights of the law of tort. Jurisprudence frequently refers to these rights as arising *ex lege*. Other rights are created by consent through a juristic act, or else from the happening of a particular event, e.g. a river may by accretion add to the land of Jones. The points are discussed in the next chapter.

The problem of extinction of rights is more easily discussed after the methods of creation have been sketched.[2]

---

[1] *Supra*, § 15.   [2] § 112.

REFERENCES

ALLEN, C. K., *Legal Duties*, 156.

COOK, W. W., in *Lectures on Legal Topics, Assoc. of Bar of N.Y.* v. 5, 335.

HART, H. L. A., *The Ascription of Responsibility and Rights* (1949), Aristotelian Society Proceedings, vol. xlix.

HOHFELD, W. N., *Fundamental Legal Conceptions*.

KOCOUREK, A., *Jural Relations*.

POUND, R., in *Selected Essays on the Law of Torts*, 87.

—— 29 *Harv. L. R.* (1916), 640.

ROSS, A., *On Law and Justice*, chs. v, vi, and vii.

XIII

TITLES, ACTS, EVENTS

§ 67. TITLES OR OPERATIVE FACTS

'EVERY right is a consequence attached by the law to one or more facts which the law defines, and wherever the law gives any one special rights not shared by the body of the people, it does so on the ground that certain special facts, not true of the rest of the world, are true of him.'[1] A person claims rights, then, because of some particular title or fact.

Some rights arise *ex lege*, in the sense that they are directly conferred by the law, as when a statute gives to the Sunshine Trust a monopoly of the sale of oil. Jurisprudence interprets the term 'title' in a broad sense and treats the existence of this statute as the title of the particular rights claimed by the trust. In practice, it is impossible for the law to confer every right directly, for law has to operate over a wide field and is bound to generalize in order to achieve economy of thought and time; therefore certain particular situations of fact are specified by the law as giving rise to certain rights and duties. Thus when a child is born there is no need for a statute to be passed defining the reciprocal rights and duties of parent and child, for in such a typical relationship the general duties are laid down by the law. The technique of the law is to create a chain of legal rights and duties spreading from the normal relationships of life. Thus the duties of a user of the highway towards others upon it are laid down by the law of tort, and the fact of negligent driving causing damage to another is a title creating a right of compensation in that other. The juristic use of the word 'title' is wider than its common use: the word is generalized to cover any fact or combination of facts which creates rights and duties.

Bentham criticizes the word 'title' because, while it denotes the facts which give rise to the creation of right, it does not denote those which destroy a right. He proposes to call every fact by which a right or duty is created or destroyed a dispositive fact—he further divides those dispositive facts into investitive which create rights and duties, and

[1] O. W. Holmes, *The Common Law*, 214.

divestitive which destroy them.[1] Title, however, has a well-accepted meaning, and Bentham's terminology has not succeeded in maintaining itself. It must be remembered that the same facts which give rise to rights in A may destroy rights in B—for example, a river may by changing its course add to A's land and subtract from B's.

Facts may be divided into acts and events. In one sense acts are events, but for the purpose of jurisprudence it is convenient to distinguish between them. A change in a legal relation may take place because of the occurrence of a particular fact: if that fact is under the control of human agency, then there has occurred an act which has produced certain consequences; if that fact is independent of human intervention, we may describe it as an event.[2]

Thousands of events and acts may and do occur without affecting the legal relations of any person, but the law lays down that certain acts and events will have a particular influence on legal relations. Thus a river may gradually deposit accretions on A's land and wear away the bank on B's side. In this case an *event* independently of human activity has added to and subtracted from the area of particular estates. If a hunter kills a lion, by his own *act* he has created new rights with respect to the lion.

Theoretically the same analysis should be applicable to all acts, whether they be lawful or unlawful.[3] But for practical reasons we find that the law has adopted a slightly varying approach, on the one hand to wrongful acts which create either criminal or tortious liability, on the other hand to juristic acts[4] which are carried out subject to the rules of law with the express purpose of creating, altering, destroying, or transferring rights. In the first case, the law emphasizes that certain physical acts will lead to the imposition of liability against the will of the actor. If you do this, you will be punished (crime) or forced to pay compensation (tort). Under the second head, the law emphasizes the element of power—if you do this act according to the legal requirements, a certain series of rights (or duties) will accrue to you. Logically in both cases the law is adding a legal result to certain manifestations of the human will. In both cases there is conduct in the

---

1 J. Bentham subdivides further the investitive facts into collative (which confer rights) and impositive (which confer duties); and divestitive facts into destructive (which end rights) and exonerative (which release from duties). See J. Austin, Lect. LV.

2 F. Pollock, *First Book of Jurisprudence* (4th ed.), 142.

3 A. Kocourek, *Jural Relations* (2nd ed.), 270.

4 For example, the question of capacity is approached from a different angle in the case of juristic and criminal acts.

physical world and legal results which are attached by the law to that conduct. The making of a contract requires physical acts, just as does the murder of Jones. But in practice there is more emphasis on the physical side in cases of crime and on the element of legal power in making a contract.

§ 68. AN ACT AS THE BASIS OF LIABILITY IN CRIME AND TORT

Does an act require to be manifested in the external world? Is thinking an act? In one sense it is a form of action so arduous that it is indulged in by few people. Some distinguish between internal and external acts,[1] but this terminology is confusing, and it is better to regard the so-called internal acts as states of mind and to define an act 'as any muscular or glandular change which results from motor nerve impulse'.[2] There are many views today as to the nature of human action, one extreme being the old metaphysical theory of an entity called will with absolute freedom to determine the destiny of each human being, the other consisting of the modern determinist theory that our physical make-up and our environment determine almost exclusively our action in any particular event. The typical modern view lies between these two doctrines. The amazing changes that may be caused in a human personality by diseased functioning of the ductless glands shows that human action is rather less free than man's conceit had believed. 'A drop of iodine stands between most of us and insanity.' On the other hand, if the importance of physical influences in determining men's actions is increasingly realized, the influence of mental factors on the health of the body is also recognized. Medicine, psycho-analysis, and psychiatry are opening new doors and the law will gradually be forced to reconsider the theories on which its analysis of an act is based, although it is as yet premature to seek in the new learning for definite and accepted hypotheses which can be made the basis of a new legal approach.[3]

In ordinary speech, while we distinguish between an act and its consequences, the line is drawn very crudely, for some of the consequences of an act are frequently included in the act itself. The average man would say that Jones's act was that of killing Brown; but if we

---

[1] A. Kocourek, op. cit. 277.
[2] H. C. Warren and L. Carmichael, *Elements of Human Psychology*, 419.
[3] *Infra*, § 82.

confine act to its strict sense of muscular change, then Jones's act was merely to exert certain pressure on the trigger, the flight of the bullet to its objective and the death of Brown being consequences of that act. For purposes of analysis, the strict use of terms is necessary.[1]

In the typical legal analysis of an act, there are the following factors to be considered:[2]

(a) A certain psychic awareness sometimes called volition. The legal analysis was founded on the old assumptions that there is a will and that it is largely, if not entirely, free. Certain actions the law would clearly regard as involuntary (for example, sleep-walking)[3] but, unless a man's conduct falls within certain narrow categories, it is assumed that his act was voluntary. In many legal systems there is little psychological analysis of the nature of volition, and hence there is a certain crudity in the legal approach.

(b) The motive with which the act was done.

(c) The intent. The average man considers that he has no difficulty in distinguishing between motive and intention, but it is not easy to discover a precise criterion.[4] Literally motive is that which moves a person to a course of action. Thus A and B each intend to commit a murder, A desiring to save his country from a tyrant, B wishing to acquire money. Some writers, however, would regard the motive as ulterior intention.[5] Thus A's immediate intention is to murder, but his ulterior intention is to save his country. This approach is confusing. The law, when it considers A's conduct, asks: did he mean to murder (intention)? and why did he murder? The law cuts the inquiry short at the particular act which it is investigating. If we take a person's conduct as a whole, we see that in an ordered life many actions are but stepping-stones to others, but the law cuts short the

---

[1] For a different view, see A. Kocourek, op. cit., ch. xvi. The *Restatement of the Law of Torts*, § 2, says that the term 'act' is used in the Restatement 'to denote an external manifestation of the actor's will and does not include any of its results, even the most direct, immediate and intended'.

[2] A valuable discussion is that of H. L. A. Hart, *Punishment and Responsibility*, ch. iv. See also *R.* v. *Payne*, [1970] Qd. R. 260, which treats the act of the prisoner as that of pulling the trigger, the resulting death being a consequence of that act.

[3] Thus the *Restatement of the Law of Torts*, Comment, § 2: 'There cannot be an act without volition.'

[4] For a short survey, see G. J. Stokes, *Encyclopædia of Religion and Ethics*, viii. 859.

[5] e.g. J. W. Salmond, op. cit., § 90. For a discussion of Salmond's view, see J. Hall, *General Principles of Criminal Law*, 149 et seq. T. A. Cowan, 97 *Univ. of Pa. L. R.* (1949), 502, criticizes the separation of intent and motive.

sequence by investigating one particular act. To Bentham the intention covers all the contemplated origins of the act, both those for the sake of which and those in spite of which we do it. The motive covers only the former. In the complicated web of life there are few actions which are 'sheer profit', and we must balance the advantages and disadvantages of a particular course of action. I may desire a gold cup offered to the winner of a certain race, and count the training loss— in such a case the motive for my entry is the gold cup. Or I may enjoy running for its own sake—then my motive is the interest in running; or I may hate running, and have no love for cups, but appreciate the increased fitness which running brings—in this case my motive is a desire for health. Morality considers both motive and intent: the law normally disregards motive in civil cases: in criminal cases, proof of motive may be practically important as leading to an inference of guilt, but evil motive is not essential to liability. A good motive is no defence, though it may be considered in regard to punishment.

(*d*) The circumstances in which the act was done.
(*e*) The consequences which result from the act.

Holmes regards intent as made up of two factors: foresight that certain consequences will follow from an act, and the wish for those consequences which determines the act.[1] To judge a person's action from the subjective point of view, we must know what were the circumstances as they appeared to him at the time of action and what were the consequences which he expected to follow. If we see a person fire into a bush and discover that the shot has killed someone, it is vital in a court of morals to know whether the actor knew the circumstance that a human being was in the bush. To press a trigger may be laudable, careless, or unethical, according to the circumstances known to the actor. One who runs his sword through a curtain and kills a man may prove as an extenuating circumstance that, although he knew there was a person behind the curtain, he thought that he was a felon about to attack him. Similarly, to judge an action ethically, we must understand the consequences which an actor appreciated as likely or possible. A child who, pretending to be a physician, administers a dose of poison to his brother is blameworthy, if at all, only for touching that which does not belong to him, for he does not appreciate that

---

[1] *The Common Law*, 53. O. W. Holmes actually describes the last clause as 'the wish for those consequences working as a *motive* which induces the act', but this use of the term 'motive' seems to introduce unnecessary confusion.

death is a likely consequence. From a purely subjective point of view[1] we could distinguish between:

i. *Action*

(a) Intention[2] where the particular consequences which result from the act are foreseen and desired. A consequence may be intended, although the chance of its happening is very remote. Smith, a crack shot, may shoot at his enemy from such a distance as to render it very unlikely that he will be successful, but if he does succeed in killing him, the consequence is intended. On the other hand, a consequence may be almost inevitable and yet not intended. A doctor may undertake an operation although it is almost certain to cause death, because surgery provides the only chance of removing a dangerous growth which will inevitably be fatal. A general may order his troops to attack a strongly fortified post although he knows that it is inevitable that thousands will be killed. Intent does not necessarily involve expectation and expectation does not necessarily involve intent.[3]

(b) Recklessness where the actor foresees the consequences, but cares not whether they result from his act.[4]

(c) Rashness where the actor foresees possible consequences, but foolishly thinks they will not occur as a result of his act.

(d) Heedlessness where a person acts without bothering to advert to the possible consequences.

ii. *Inaction*

(e) Forbearance—the intentional refraining from an action.

(f) An omission to carry out an act because it is not realized that there is a legal duty to act.

But no legal system adopts such a subjective approach, for there is a tendency to use external tests, although the actual degree to which this

---

[1] J. Austin, Lects. XIX, XX; W. E. Hearn, *Legal Duties and Rights*, 104–5.

[2] 'Wilful' is a word which should be avoided because of its ambiguity. 'Wilful is not a term of art and is often used as meaning no more than a high degree of carelessness or recklessness. It is not necessarily limited in its use to intentional or deliberate wrongdoing': per Lord Wright, *Caswell* v. *Powell Duffryn Assoc. Collieries*, [1940] A.C. 152 at 177. Talbot J. uses it as synonymous with intentional, *Wheeler* v. *New Merton Mills Ltd.*, [1933] 2 K.B. 669 at 677.

[3] J. W. Salmond, *Jurisprudence* (12th ed.), § 89. See G. Marston, 'Contemporaneity of Act and Intention in Crime', 86 *L.Q.R.* (1970), 208.

[4] There is dispute as to the meaning of recklessness, as is shown in the decision of the C.A. in *Herrington* v. *British Railways Board*, [1971] 1 All E.R. 897: is recklessness more akin to intent or to gross negligence? The view stated in the text is more logical.

is carried differs from one system to another. The law may compel men of full age to know at their peril the teachings of experience, and may treat them as having foreseen the consequences which a reasonable man would foresee. Thus in the law of tort the law sets up the standard of the reasonable man and, instead of delving into the mind of the defendant, asks what would a reasonable man have done in those circumstances. Failure to act up to this criterion is termed 'negligence'.[1] If we examine the subjective analysis set out above, we see that negligence includes acts as well as omissions, and that certain examples of recklessness, rashness, heedlessness, and forbearance would be covered by the comprehensive test of failure to conduct oneself as would a reasonable man. In the older books of English law there is a distinction between gross and simple negligence, but in the general law of tort today, 'gross negligence has no more effect than negligence without an opprobrious epithet'.[2] In the law of gratuitous bailment, the concept of gross negligence has striven hard to maintain itself. Roman law did distinguish between different degrees of care, but the terms used indicated 'courses of conduct, not states of mind'.[3] *Culpa levis* was failure to take the care which a *bonus paterfamilias* would take; *culpa levis in concreto*, the failure to show the care which that particular person exercised in his own affairs; *culpa lata* the failure to take the obvious precautions that any ordinary man would take; and finally *dolus* entered the realm of intentional wrongdoing.

Since in the civil law the object is not to punish a wrongdoer but to award compensation to one who has suffered injury, the adoption of an external test may easily be justified. In the criminal law it is necessary to take more account of the guilty mind of the wrongdoer, if punishment is not to be unjustly inflicted. But we shall see that even here the law has in some measure adopted an external test, and in certain cases there need be no *mens rea* at all.[4]

Malice is a most unfortunate term and it has many different meanings in English law:

(*a*) in murder it merely means that there is present one of the various forms of *mens rea* necessary to constitute the crime;

---

[1] *Infra*, § 105.
[2] Per Lord Wright, *Caswell* v. *Powell Duffryn Assoc. Collieries*, [1940] A.C. 152 at 175.
[3] W. W. Buckland, *The Main Institutions of Roman Private Law*, 300.
[4] *Infra*, § 82.

(b) in certain statutory offences it means that there must be either an intention to cause results of the particular kind prohibited by the statute, or at least a recklessness which cares not whether the prohibited consequence occurs or not;

(c) sometimes the word is otiose, a pleading relic, as in the allegation that defendant maliciously defamed the plaintiff, since even proof that there was no malice is not a defence;

(d) sometimes the word means spite or actual ill will or other improper motive, for example malice in this sense may be proved to rebut a defence of qualified privilege in defamation;

(e) sometimes, as in the phrase *malitia supplet aetatem*, it means that the act was done with the knowledge of its nature.

An interesting case from New Guinea is that of *Timbu Kolian* v. *R*.[1] The prisoner quarrelled with his wife and left the hut to secure peace. She followed him, continuing her tirade. He picked up a stick and gave his wife a blow which would not be likely to cause an adult a significant injury. By the law of the Territory of New Guinea, it was unlawful for a husband to beat his wife. The wife was carrying her baby—it was dark and the prisoner did not see the child which died from the effect of the blow. Three judges held that under the Criminal Code the act of killing occurred independently of the exercise of his will, and three held that the act of the prisoner was an event which occurred by accident. Had the act been likely to kill the wife, the decision would have been otherwise.

How far is automatism a defence?[2] It has been defined as involuntary action performed in a state of unconsciousness not amounting to insanity. Theoretically the defence is that no act in the legal sense took place at all—the plea is that there was no volition or psychic awareness.[3]

§ 69. JURISTIC ACTS

By juristic acts legal persons create, modify, or destroy rights and duties and thereby affect legal relations between legal persons. Some writers term these manifestations of the human will acts in the law.[4]

---

[1] [1969] A.L.R. 143.

[2] *Bratty* v. *A.-G. for Northern Ireland*, [1961] 3 W.L.R. 965.

[3] N. Morris and C. Howard, *Studies in Criminal Law*, 62. The onus of proof differs from the position in a defence of insanity. The accused must show a proper foundation for the plea of automatism; it is a question of law for the judge whether there is evidence to go to the jury, but if the jury are in doubt, they should acquit. See *R*. v. *Joyce*, [1970] S.A.S.R. 184.

[4] The *Rechtsgeschäfte* of German law, *actes juridiques* of French law.

Here the question is whether a person within the framework of the law has been successful in creating rights and duties. There are four elements of a juristic act:

(a) The Will

The actor must direct his will to the end in question. The main emphasis under this head is on those factors which may prevent the free functioning of the will of the actor.[1] Thus duress by a third party may exercise such effective pressure that the will is overborne, for example by a threat to prosecute a near relative.[2] Fraud may create such a false situation that the will is not effectively directed to the true state of affairs. One party may have such a predominant influence over the other that what is termed 'undue influence' results. 'No court has ever attempted to define undue influence',[3] but 'the principle applies to every case where influence is acquired and abused, where confidence is reposed and betrayed'.[4] A mistake by C caused either by the conduct of the other party or C's own carelessness may raise difficult problems for the law. But this issue is best discussed under the law of contracts.[5]

(b) The Expression of the Will or Declaration of Intention[6]

The will must be expressed or made manifest. It is true that in some cases 'silence is consent', but this is only because the situation calls for action, if consent by remaining silent is not to be inferred. Thus a meeting may remain quiescent when the chairman says: 'If no one speaks against this proposal, I will take it that you all agree that this course of action is approved.'

The expression of the will may be either formal or informal.

The law may lay down that in order to effect a particular result the will must be expressed in a formal way and that, if the precise form

---

[1] *Vices de la volonté* of French law: M. S. Amos and F. P. Walton, *Introduction to French Law* (2nd ed.), 21.

[2] Cf. *Kaufman v. Gerson*, [1904] 1 K.B. 591. For a case of marriage declared void because of fear not caused by other party, see *Szechter v. Szechter*, [1970] 3 All E.R. 905; for a case of a foreign divorce declared void because of duress, see *Meyer v. Meyer*, [1971] 1 All E.R. 378.

[3] Per Lindley L.J., *Allcard v. Skinner* (1887), 36 Ch. D. 145 at 183; *Re Craig*, [1970] 2 W.L.R. 1219.

[4] Per Lord Kingsdown, *Smith v. Kay* (1859), 7 H.L.C. 750 at 779. See W. H. D. Winder, 3 *Mod. L. R.* (1939), 97.

[5] *Infra*, § 100.

[6] The *Willenserklärung* of German law. For a historical note on the juristic act in Roman law, see H. Lévy-Bruhl, *Archives de phil. du droit* (1939, 1-2), 75.

is not carried out, the juristic act will have no effect. The required form may be signed writing attested by two witnesses. A transfer of *res mancipi* in Roman law required the oral repetition by the parties of set words and the carrying out of certain gestures.

In other cases the law cares not how the will be expressed, so long as its expression is clear and unambiguous. A nod in an auction room may be accepted by the hammer of the auctioneer. Law is at first very fluid, but then it passes through a stage of technicality where there are set forms for most legal transactions. In the modern world the tendency is to abolish formal requirements, save where they are useful for particular reasons. Thus the form of a will is strictly laid down in order that clear evidence of the testator's wishes may be available, and to make forgery more difficult.

In a unilateral act it may not be necessary to publish the intention at once, provided that clear evidence of it be put in writing. Thus the contents of a will may remain secret until the death of the testator. In a bilateral act (one which is the result of an agreement between two or more parties) it is clear that the will of each must be communicated to the other. An offer to sell certain shares may be made by Jones in Paris, to Smith in London, and accepted by the latter by telegram. At what moment is the contract made? When the offer is accepted? When the telegram is sent? When the telegram is received? Or when the telegram is read? The rules of each system may vary, but the needs of business demand definite rules upon this point.[1]

(c) *Power to Bring About the Legal Result Desired*

A juristic act can be effective only if the actor is empowered by the law to act in this way. The term 'capacity' is frequently used in this connection, but it is preferable to use *power*, in the sense in which that word is defined above.[2] Thus a minor in English law had at common law no power to make a binding contract save for necessaries —a statutory company can make valid contracts only within the ambit of the powers bestowed upon it.[3] From the physical angle, an infant may perform similar acts when he buys on credit jewellery and food, but in the one case the law will not hold him bound and in the other it will force him to pay on the ground that food is a necessary commodity.

---

[1] *Infra*, § 97; E. J. Schuster, *Principles of German Law*, 86–7.   [2] *Supra*, § 63.
[3] The doctrine of *ultra vires* is now being reconsidered.

(d) Material Validity

The object which it is desired to achieve must not be prohibited by the law. An agreement to pay a certain sum as the price of the vote of a member of the House of Commons would be invalid on the grounds of public policy. In one sense such a prohibition may be put under the head of power, since it may be said that no member of the community has power to create a valid agreement contrary to public policy. But it is convenient for some purposes to distinguish between power and material validity. If only a limited class is prevented from attaining a particular result, that falls most easily under the head of variations of power. If everyone in the community is prohibited from achieving a particular result, then it is easier to class it under the head of material invalidity. Thus the topic of infants' contracts falls under power, whereas the rules nullifying certain contracts on the ground of public policy relate to material invalidity.

A defect may make a juristic act either void or voidable. If the defect is such that the act is devoid of the legal results contemplated, then the act is said to be void.[1] A void act is sometimes said to be a nullity in law, but this is not strictly so, as an act void in its primary intent may nevertheless have an effect in another way.[2] Thus the Infants Relief Act, 1874, declared that certain contracts shall be absolutely void. Yet there is authority for the view that the property in the goods passes to the infant[3] and possibly the infant can enforce the contract if he desires.[4] In systems which even in regard to chattels distinguish clearly between the contract of sale and the conveyance, the distinction is easier to draw. The contract of sale of a chattel may be entirely void, but the conveyance may be valid until it is rescinded. In English law where the mistake of a party to a contract is so fundamental that the contract is avoided, so is the conveyance. Thus if a rogue obtains goods on credit under circumstances which are held to make the contract entirely void, the rogue obtains no title—hence an innocent third party to whom he sells the goods also obtains no title.[5] On the other hand, a voidable transaction is

---

[1] W. Markby, *Elements of Law* (6th ed.), 143. *Lewis* v. *Averay*, [1971] 3 All E.R. 807.
[2] E. J. Cohn, 64 *L.Q.R.* (1948), 324 at 325–6; F. Pollock, *First Book of Jurisprudence* (4th ed.), 165.
[3] *Pearce* v. *Brain*, [1929] 2 K.B. 310, see now, Family Law Reform Act, 1969.
[4] G. C. Cheshire and C. H. S. Fifoot, *Law of Contract* (5th ed.), 342–4. Also if the infant has paid for the goods, he cannot recover the money.
[5] It has been suggested that where one of two innocent parties must, under present law, suffer as the result of the fraud of a third, the rule should be adopted that the loss

valid for all purposes, until steps are taken to avoid it. If a marriage, because of failure to comply with some rule of law, is entirely void, theoretically, no judgment of a court is necessary to declare it so.[1] If the marriage is merely voidable, it remains valid until a court avoids it at the instance of one of the parties to the marriage.[2] If a contract is voidable only, it cannot be avoided so as to prejudice a third party who has in the interim honestly and for value acquired an interest in the *res* which is the subject-matter of the contract.

§ 70. TYPES OF JURISTIC ACTS

A juristic act may be unilateral or bilateral. A unilateral act, as the adjective implies, is one in which the will of only one party is operative, for example a testamentary disposition. A bilateral act is the result of an agreement between two or more parties. It is preferable to use the word 'agreement' in a broad sense rather than to confine it to one specific type of agreement such as a contract. Contract may be one of the most important forms of agreement, but the possible types of agreement are numerous. Gareis defines an agreement as 'a declared concurrence of will of two or more persons whereby a change in their legal spheres is intended'.[3] We should distinguish between the agreement itself and the obligations to which it gives rise. Agreements may create, transfer, or extinguish rights. The problems that arise can most easily be discussed in connection with the law of contract.

Another meaning sometimes given to the terms 'unilateral' and 'bilateral' is based not on a study of the means by which the agreement is made but of what remains to be done by the parties. If the agreement binds both parties by a duty, it is said to be bilateral, but if only one party has an active duty, it is unilateral.[4] This, however, is not the sense in which the term is used in this work.

---

should be divided: see G. Gardiner and A. Martin (eds.), *Law Reform Now*, 156. Thus in tort where there is negligence on both sides, the loss may be divided in proportion to fault.

[1] For practical purposes a judgment may be desirable, e.g. if the parties are not agreed that the marriage is void or if one of them wishes to marry again, and to place on record the nature of the first 'marriage'.

[2] If a marriage is merely voidable, then the 'wife', even after a declaration of nullity, remains an incompetent witness against her 'husband' for crimes (e.g. forgery) committed during coverture—*R. v. Algar*, [1954] 1 Q.B. 279; *contra*—where the marriage was void *ab initio*.

[3] *Science of Law* (trans. A. Kocourek), 162.

[4] J. W. Salmond, *Jurisprudence* (12th ed.), 336.

§ 71. ACTS OF THE LAW

A juristic act is thus the result of a voluntary manifestation of the will and is sometimes described as an act in the law (i.e. an act done within the legal framework).[1] In these cases the law makes the human will effective. But the law may also bind a person against his will, e.g. there is a general duty not to defame others, a liability to pay compensation if a court so orders. Some writers put such examples under the heading of acts of the law, contrasting this term with juristic acts which are acts *within* the law. This distinction between duties voluntarily incurred and duties imposed by the law is a fundamental one.

§ 72. REPRESENTATION IN A JURISTIC ACT

A declaration of intention may be made either by A in person or by another acting as agent on his behalf. The agent is more than a mere messenger—a servant who conveys a letter from A accepting an offer made by B is not an agent. In English usage the term 'agent' is used very widely,[2] sometimes almost being coextensive with employment, but strictly the term should be confined to employment for the purpose of bringing the employer into legal relation with a third party. Representation first develops in connection with persons of restricted capacity. A baby a few days old may have much wealth and yet he is clearly physically incapable of performing a juristic act—hence the device of appointing a guardian or tutor to represent the will of the infant and to take effective steps for the protection of his property. Nowadays the guiding principle behind the restriction of the legal powers of certain classes of human persons is that of protection. It is in the best interests of an infant (or minor as termed by the Family Law Reform Act, 1969)[3] to deprive him of some of the powers which an adult possesses. But in early law guardianship frequently was a right and not a duty. The guardian was he who would succeed, if the ward died intestate, the maxim being *ubi beneficium successionis ibi onus tutelae*: thus he had a direct interest in restricting the powers of the infant. The wardship of feudal times protected the interests of the lord, and the ward might find that the utmost had been ruthlessly extracted from his estate during his

---

[1] But cf. H. L. A. Hart, *The Ascription of Responsibility and Rights*, vol. xlix, Aristotelian Society Proceedings (1949).
[2] Thus an independent contractor is sometimes called an agent.
[3] This Act reduced the age of minority from 21 to 18 years.

minority and that he was then forced to pay a fine for the privilege of succeeding. We see an illustration of the fact that tutorship was regarded as a right in the rules concerning the age at which tutorship ceased at Rome. Since a male could found a family at the age of fourteen years, the nearest agnate then lost interest in the *spes successionis*, and tutorship ceased.

But by the time of the Republic the newer conception of tutorship as a duty imposed in the interest of the ward was accepted. Stringent rules were enforced to ensure that the tutor acted fairly, and, instead of being a right, tutorship became an onerous duty which the law in some circumstances would enforce even on an unwilling person in the absence of proof of one of the specified 'excuses'.

At Rome males between the ages of fourteen and twenty-five were so protected by the power of the praetor to annul transactions that were disadvantageous to them that they found it difficult to enter into any legal negotiations at all. Hence arose the custom of obtaining the opinion of a temporary adviser that the transaction was a fair one. A form of curatorship gradually arose, not so much to protect the minor as the third party, by providing evidence which would make it more difficult to annul the transaction.[1]

Lunatics were given a curator, partly in their own interests, partly in the interests of the family in order to prevent the dissipation of the property. The curatorship of prodigals illustrates an institution that is foreign to the individualistic common law. It was strongly felt in Rome that property was held, not for individual satisfaction alone, but for the benefit of the family, and a *paterfamilias* who extravagantly squandered his patrimony might find that his powers of administration and alienation were curtailed by the appointment of a curator who would ensure that the family property was preserved. Some continental systems have adopted this institution from Roman law.[2]

In English law the powers of a guardian are somewhat vague and there is no clearly developed theory of agency by which the guardian can exercise the will of the infant. This lack has been made tolerable by the institution of the trust, since, if there is property concerned, it would normally be invested in trustees for the benefit of the infant—and being legal owners of the trust property, the trustees would have full powers of administration.

---

[1] The later development of *cura minoris* is discussed by W. W. Buckland, *The Main Institutions of Roman Private Law*, 84.   [2] e.g. French and German law.

These forms of agency are sometimes called tutorial representation, or to use the language of modern codes, the guardian is the statutory agent of the ward. From such tutorial representation, which arises because of the restricted powers that pertain to certain forms of status, we must distinguish that form of agency which arises because of business convenience. An agent (in this sense) is one who acts as a conduit pipe through which legal relations flow from his principal to another. Agency is created by a juristic act by which one person (the principal) gives to another (the agent) the power to do something for and in the name of the principal so as to bind the latter directly. If the agent acts within the terms of his authority and contracts in the name of an existing principal, then, in general, the agent is not personally liable on the contract.

The germ of agency in the business sense may be found in the particular organization of the Roman family. The *paterfamilias* by a rule of law acquired the ownership of property received by his children, for they were in his power. The slave was not a legal person, and since he was in the possession of his master, it was natural to say that the master possessed what was held by the slave. The slave could be used to acquire possession if the master gave a specific order.[1] There was a tendency to use the slave more and more as a means for the acquisition of property and the administration of business. So far as the master and slave *inter se* were concerned there was no real problem. One was a legal person and the other was a chattel; one had complete legal power over the other. But where third parties were concerned, it was necessary to develop rules stating precisely the master's liability on contracts made by the slaves: especially was this essential when it became usual to set a slave up in business with a particular sum of money (the *peculium*) as capital. The detailed Roman rules cannot here be discussed. All that can be said is that a maxim which gave extraordinary protection to the master—slaves can make the master's position better, but not worse—was gradually modified on grounds of business convenience. The master became liable in *solidum* if he ordered a particular transaction, and the *peculium* itself became liable to execution for contracts made in connection with it.

So long as these principles were confined to the bonds of the family no difficulty arose—as was the case in early law. But if a master freed a slave and set him in charge of a particular business,

---

[1] *Infra*, § 123.

should not the same rules apply, even though the manager was no longer a slave? Thus there was a gradual extension of the master's liability in contract and a recognition that even a free procurator might be used as a means of acquiring possession or title.

But Roman law provided no explicit theory of agency. 'As to transactions by sons and slaves, we must keep clear of the notion of representation, apart at any rate from authorised alienations.'[1] The extension of these rules to free persons made it impossible to seek the explanation in terms of the peculiar structure of the family, but Roman law never quite reached a coherent doctrine.[2] Perhaps the nearest approach to modern doctrine was the theory of mandate. Caesar might give a mandate to Antony to buy a certain estate from Cleopatra. But in reality, when Antony carried out the request there were two transactions, one between Caesar and Antony, one between Antony and Cleopatra. This was no mere academic point, for Antony himself was liable to Cleopatra for the purchase price; and strictly Cleopatra could not directly sue Caesar. The praetor, however, allowed an *actio institoria* against one who appointed a man to contract in relation to a business, and if we can accept a text of Papinian, such an action might lie even where the mandate was for a single transaction.[3] Caesar could sue only by taking an assignment of Antony's rights against Cleopatra. *Obligatio* could not be assigned, but a mandate could be given to Caesar to sue on Antony's claim. These clumsy devices conclusively show that Roman law had not achieved the simplicity of a working theory of agency.

Holmes maintains that modern law is based on the fiction that within the scope of the agency principal and agent are one, and that the starting-point is still the *patria potestas* of ancient Rome.[4] However true that may be, modern law has travelled far along the road, and agency is now a most important conception of commercial law. In the case of master and servant, the former is extensively liable for the negligence and even the wilful frauds of the servant in the course of employment, and it was inevitable that this should affect the liability of those who employed agents who were not technically servants. Identification of the principal and agent sometimes, however, led to absurd results. An agent honestly makes a statement which he believes to be true; the principal knows facts which render

[1] W. W. Buckland, *Main Institutions of Roman Private Law*, 161.
[2] Ibid. 167.
[3] W. W. Buckland, *Textbook of Roman Law* (2nd ed.), 519.
[4] *Select Essays in Anglo-American History*, iii. 368 et seq.

the statement false, but is unaware that the agent has made the statement. To hold the principal to the agent's representations in an action for breach of contract may be reasonable—but common sense, as well as the law, recoils from allowing an action for fraud, although if we identify the principal and agent, that is a logical result.[1]

It has been said that agency normally arises from a juristic act. In some cases agency of necessity may arise—the agent may exercise a power which has not specifically been bestowed. Thus a wife left without means of support may pledge her husband's credit for necessaries. In such a case the wife need not show that this power has been granted by the husband, for it flows directly from the marriage relationship itself. Possibly the development of this rule was helped by the early tendency to treat a wife as a mere servant, or the later identification of husband and wife as one person at law.[2] But the doctrine of agency by necessity is not confined to the family. The master of a ship may, if circumstances render it imperative, pledge his employer's credit. A carrier may have authority to effect a sale if the goods are perishable and action is necessary to avert a total loss.

§ 73. ASSIGNMENT

Where a chose in possession is concerned, e.g. Blackacre which A owns and possesses, A may transfer to another either all or some of the rights which A possesses. Thus A may surrender possession but retain ownership, surrender both ownership and possession, or transfer title but remain in possession with the consent of the new owner. Such cases are discussed in the chapter on property.[3]

Where a contract is concerned, A may wish to transfer to C the rights which A has to a performance of the agreement by B. This raises more difficult questions which are discussed below.[4] In early systems the notion of obligation was intensely personal, and it was inconceivable that it could be transferred, but modern business convenience has demanded a modification of these rules.[5] In England

---

[1] Cf. *Anglo-Scottish Beet Sugar Corp. Ltd.* v. *Spalding Urban District Council*, [1937] 2 K.B. 607 at 625. 'I cannot myself see how a principal can be held liable for fraud when there has been no element of fraud either on the part of himself or on the part of anyone for whose acts he is responsible': per Atkinson J. and see *Armstrong* v. *Strain*, [1952] 1 K.B. 232 and discussion of that case in 68 *L.Q.R.* (1952) at 148–50.

[2] O. W. Holmes, op. cit.　　　　　　　　　　　　[3] *Infra*, Ch. XXI.

[4] *Infra*, § 114, 'Chose in action'.

[5] If A wishes to transfer to another his liability to B, A can do so only with B's consent and only if A can find another who is willing to assume liability. This is really a case of *novation*, i.e. the destruction of the old agreement by creating a new one: *infra*, § 112.

the common law courts did not at first recognize the assignment of a benefit under a contract, but equity would permit it in certain cases and force the assignor to allow the use of his name if an action to enforce the contract at common law became necessary. The common law kept to its theory that choses in action were not assignable, and thus any action must proceed in the name of the assignor. In 1873 the Judicature Act simplified the problem, but to discuss the detailed provisions is not in point. There are, however, certain types of right which cannot be transferred: the assignment of a mere right to sue for damages in tort would have infringed the rules of maintenance and champerty before these relics of the past were abolished.[1] A right to personal services cannot be transferred without the consent of the person bound.[2] Assignment has proved a useful device for modern commerce, but unfortunately English law has not dealt with the problem comprehensively and has created a statutory patchwork quilt of particular enactments dealing with specific problems.

[1] Criminal Law Act, 1967, c. 58, s. 13.
[2] *Nokes* v. *Doncaster Collieries Ltd.*, [1940] A.C. 1014.

REFERENCES

AUSTIN, J., *Jurisprudence*, Lectures XIX, XX, LV.
HOLMES, O. W., *The Common Law*, chs. ii, iii.
POLLOCK, F., *First Book of Jurisprudence*, Part I, ch. vi.

BOOK V

PUBLIC LAW

XIV

LAW AND THE STATE

§ 74. DISTINCTION BETWEEN PUBLIC AND PRIVATE LAW

AUSTIN and Kelsen consider that most jurists exaggerate the importance of the distinction between public and private law. Austin[1] thought that the main mark of public law was the 'peculiarity' of one of the persons to the relationship (the State), and hence that it was most conveniently treated under that branch of the law which dealt with variations in legal capacity—the law of persons. To Kelsen public as well as private law is merely the 'individualization' of a general norm. The ultimate effect of law is to impose constraint on individuals, and an obligation may be imposed either by the order of an administrator, the passing of a statute, the judgment of a court, or the making of a contract. The power to make a contract will depend on the civil code, just as the power of a judge to sentence a convicted criminal will depend on the criminal code, or an administrative act on a particular statute. In making a contract I 'execute' the civil law, just as an administrator does in ordering a ruinous house to be pulled down. Thus all these methods of creating obligations represent law-making within the limits imposed by a superior norm. The only real distinction between public and private law is that in the latter an individual may co-operate in the law-making process (for example, by signing a contract), but in public law he may be bound by a norm in the creation of which he plays no part. But even in private law a duty may be imposed against a person's will, e.g. in quasi-contract.

Why is Kelsen so eager to attack the traditional distinction between public and private law? In part it arises from his view that

[1] *Jurisprudence*, ii. 748.

the developed legal order and the State are the same thing,[1] but in addition he emphasizes that, if the sphere of public law is magnified, it may suggest that the rule of law is one thing for the monarch and another for the subject. One traditional view was that private law deals with co-ordination and the relation between equals, whereas public law is the realm of political domination;[2] but Kelsen maintains that the rule of law has exactly the same scope in the two fields— private law created by contract may be just as much a realm of domination as any constitutional power. What is private law but the particular legal form which corresponds to the economic order of that community? A capitalist society will have one form of private law, a communist another. Kelsen thus desires to show that there is not between public and private law the great gulf which the traditional theory emphasizes.

His analysis follows rigorously from his premises, but does it reveal more than the rather obvious truth that the foundation both of private and public law lies in the legal order itself?[3] If we postulate an initial premiss[4] as the basis of that order, then the power of Parliament to change the law may be traced to that basic norm, just as can my power to make a binding contract. If there is a legal system, every legal exercise of power must be related thereto. But when we come to apply Kelsen's analysis to the functioning of actual states, we see that his abstract theory of norms gives a false impression. It is difficult to appreciate the real nature of the State without considering, not only the abstract rules, but the organs to which certain powers are given. Yet when Carré de Malberg[5] mildly protested that Kelsen's theories could not easily be fitted to the constitutional structure of France, Weyr[6] replied: 'So much the worse for French law'—his argument being that the truth of juristic theories can be determined only by rigorous logical argument, not by examining the historical antecedents of particular systems. This is somewhat high ground even for a 'pure science' of law to take.

The real crux of the matter is whether we should regard a private individual who makes a contract as sharing in the law-making power given by the legal order. Kelsen answers in the affirmative—the ultimate effect of law is to impose constraint on individuals, and general norms are executed by the creation of the rights and the duties which

---

[1] *Infra,* § 76.   [2] *Annales de l'Institut de droit comparé* (1936), ii. 44–5.
[3] E. Riezler in *Rec. Lambert,* iii. 117.   [4] *Supra,* § 5.
[5] *Confrontation de la théorie de la formation du droit par degrés.*
[6] *Revue internationale de la théorie du droit,* viii. 235.

flow from a contract. Within the sphere of the law, Brown and Robinson sign a contract and create a norm which will be enforced, if necessary, by the constraint of the law. But it appears paradoxical to regard the private citizen as a law-making organ. Some differences, which according to abstract logic may seem only differences in degree, are so great as to be in reality differences of kind. Within the state machinery there is a broad distinction between the sovereign power of a legislature to create new law and the limited power of the administrator or the judge whose task is primarily to apply the law that exists. It is true, of course, that the judge and the administrator may have a limited power of creation, and that it is difficult to define precisely the distinction between legislation, administration, and the judicial process[1]—but the distinction is of practical importance in most systems of law. As contrasted with these powers, the private citizen has a limited capacity only to use such rules of law as are created by other forces. The citizen has power to create rights and duties within the framework of the law, but cannot modify the rules themselves. Traditionally, jurisprudence distinguishes between the law and the rights and duties created under that law. It seems more reasonable, therefore, to admit the importance of the peculiar character of the State by recognizing a fundamental division between public and private law.[2]

Nevertheless, this distinction has not always been clearly marked. Until the State itself has developed, public law is a mere embryo. Even in the days of feudalism there is much confusion; for no clear line can be drawn between the private and public capacities of the king. Jurisdiction, office, and even kingship are looked upon as property—indeed public law might almost be regarded as 'a mere appendix' to the law of real property so far as the feudal ideal is realized.[3]

How then should the sphere of public law be defined? Holland adopts the simple test of the nature of the parties to the relationship in question—if one of the parties is the State, the relationship belongs to public law.[4] In the days of *laissez-faire* such a criterion would not give too great a scope to public law; but today, with the entry of

---

[1] *Infra*, § 75.
[2] For much the same reasons it is inadvisable to treat the State only under the heading of the law of persons. To consider the powers of the State in connection with the status of married women, infants, and lunatics seems to suggest a lack of proportion.
[3] F. Pollock and F. W. Maitland, *History of English Law*, i. 209.
[4] *Jurisprudence* (13th ed.), 128.

the State into the business world, we find that the sphere of private law is diminishing. In a community where the ideal of state socialism was realized, public law would cover all the instruments of production. Hence modern jurists seek a narrower criterion.[1] The test of private and public interest is not sufficiently precise—the whole doctrine of public policy depends on a concept of public interest, yet much of it undoubtedly belongs to private law. Another theory we have already mentioned—that public law is the realm of domination, private law that of co-ordination—one treats of ruler and subject, the other of the relations of equals. There is some truth in this test, but it is not sufficiently precise. Others ask whether there is an authoritarian character in that particular activity of the State.[2] Salmond seems to have propounded the most useful definition: 'public law . . . is not the *whole* of the law that is applicable to the state in its relations with its subjects, but only those parts of it which are different from the private law concerning the subjects of the state and their relations to each other.'[3] Private law is thus the residue of the law after we subtract public law. This approach seems to involve fewer assumptions as to the nature and quality of state activity than any other. If the State sets up a state-owned monopoly in order to sell tobacco, then the rules governing the institution of the monopoly belong to public law, but if a contract for the sale of tobacco may be enforced against the monopoly in the normal way, then such a contract belongs to private law.[4]

The normal divisions of public law are constitutional and administrative law. Constitutional law deals with the ultimate questions of the distribution of legal power and of the functions of the organs of the State. In a wide sense, it includes administrative law, but it is convenient to consider as a unit for many purposes the rules which determine the organization, powers, and duties of administrative authorities. Criminal law, the infliction of punishment directly by the organs of the State, is also usually regarded as falling under the head of public law. Some would say that civil procedure should also be placed in this section, since these rules regulate the activities of courts which are mere agencies of the State; but civil procedure is so linked with the enforcement of private rights that it is more convenient to regard it as belonging both to public and private law.

---

[1] E. Riezler in *Rec. Lambert*, iii. 117. It is said that there are seventeen different theories.   [2] Sometimes called the *Subjektstheorie*.
[3] *Jurisprudence* (10th ed.), 506. (This discussion does not appear in the 12th edition of Salmond's work.)   [4] E. Riezler, op. cit. 132.

One of the most marked features of the present age is the growing importance of public law. Today one of the first points to be examined in any commercial enterprise is the incidence of taxation on various methods of controlling the industry. In a factory we must consider collective agreements as to wages, regulations as to lighting and safety precautions—there may even be an appeal to an industrial board against a dismissal by the master. Price control may affect the market. 'It is today impossible and misleading to study the functioning of the property norm in isolation from public law.'[1]

§ 75. THE SEPARATION OF POWERS

Although in political theory much has been made of the vital importance of the separation of powers, it is extraordinarily difficult to define precisely each particular power.[2] In an ideal state we might imagine a legislature which had supreme and exclusive power to lay down general rules for the future without reference to particular cases; courts whose sole function was to make binding orders to settle disputes between individuals which were brought before them by applying these rules to the facts which were found to exist; an administrative body which carried on the business of government by issuing particular orders or making decisions of policy within the narrow confines of rules of law that it could not change. The legislature makes, the executive executes, and the judiciary construes the law.

The political usefulness of a separation of powers is clearly recognized today,[3] but the major juristic difficulty is to discover any clear definitions of the legislative, administrative, and judicial process which can be related to the functioning of actual states.[4] Many of the suggested tests break down under critical analysis, and hence there has arisen a school of jurists who deny that any clear distinction

---

[1] O. Kahn-Freund, K. Renner's *The Institutions of Private Law*, 38.

[2] The distinction was known in theory to the ancient Greeks. But it was not recognized by feudalism. In some cases there has been a confusion between separation of powers as a political postulate and as a legal principle: see W. Ebenstein, *Wisconsin L. R.* (1938), 287 at 290.

[3] In most countries. In a dictatorship the notion of checks and balances is anathema. A. I. Vyshinsky, *Law of the Soviet State*, 497–8, claims that in the Socialist State, protection of the interests of the State is also protection of the interests of the citizens, but he admits that there must be power to destroy without pity the enemies of the State.

[4] H. Kelsen, *Allgemeine Staatslehre*; Carré de Malberg, *Théorie générale de l'État*; W. I. Jennings, *The Law and the Constitution*, Appendix 1.

can be drawn. Duguit regards the conception of a single sovereign with three powers as a metaphysical conception analogous to the theological doctrine of the Trinity.[1]

What, then, are the tasks of a court, a legislature, an administrative official? The orthodox view was that each performed a different function in the legal order; the modern approach is that whatever broad classification is adopted, no sharp lines can be drawn *a priori* which will enable all governmental functions to be assigned by logic alone to one category or another. Convenience and history have dictated in each particular country the parcelling out of a certain subject-matter to each category.

Courts and Legislature

'The most obvious function of Parliament is to enact general laws';[2] that of the court is to make binding and enforceable orders applying the existing law to disputes before it. The French jurists at the beginning of the nineteenth century believed that, if the courts created new law, they were usurping the province of the legislature. Hence it was laid down that, where the text of the code was silent or obscure, the courts might refer points of difficulty to the legislature, and, where a gap in the law was revealed, such reference was compulsory. But the experiment failed completely, for the legislature had neither the time, the energy, nor the capacity to deal with the task,[3] and there were few regrets when the system was abolished. In fact courts must make law in the course of deciding disputes—did they not do so, the law would soon become intolerable. But to admit that courts make law does not mean that they have full powers of legislation. A court is bound by such authority as exists (whether it be statute or precedent), and its creative power is called into play only within the limits set by that authority.[4] A court may, however, be created to deal with an entirely new field, e.g. the determination of a compulsory basic wage. Such a function may be more like those accepted as proper to legislative bodies, although the procedure

---

[1] *Traité de droit constitutionnel* (1928), ii. 669; W. Ebenstein, *Wisconsin L. R.* (1938), 291; cf. W. I. Jennings, *The Law and the Constitution* (3rd ed.), 262.
[2] Ibid. 263.
[3] F. Gény, *Méthode d'interprétation*, i. 78–9; B. A. Wortley in *Modern Theories of Law*, 142. A. I. Vyshinsky also believes that interpretation of statutes should be controlled by a body subject to the legislature. But he rejects the doctrine of separation of powers: *Law of the Soviet State*, 339.
[4] *Supra*, §§ 45, 46.

adopted is that employed by bodies accepted as strictly judicial in character.[1]

If the courts encroach on the sphere of creation, Parliaments also sometimes trespass on the judicial sphere. Legislation may be enacted for the settlement of a particular dispute, or a statute may convict and sentence a particular prisoner, as when Parliament made provision for the boiling of the Bishop of Rochester's cook.[2] Moreover, even if we were to admit that Parliament could lay down only *general rules*, it would be impossible to frame a test of generality which could be applied with precision. Under the English system the courts recognize that Parliament is competent to change the law in any way it pleases. No statute can be attacked on the ground that it trespasses on a field reserved to another organ of the State. In countries where there is a written constitution the precise distinction between legislative, judicial, and administrative powers may be of great practical importance, for the exercise of each power may be surrounded by safeguarding conditions. In a federal system where powers are divided between co-ordinate governments and where disputes as to the limits of constitutional powers have to be resolved by courts, the distinction between judicial and other powers may be vital to the maintenance of the constitution itself.[3] But English constitutional theory, being based on the dogma of the supremacy of Parliament, can ignore these difficulties.

Legislation and Administration

In theory we can draw a clear line between power to create rules of law and power to put those rules into effect in the appropriate circumstances. But the delegation of limited legislative authority to administrators has obscured the theoretical division. It is becoming increasingly difficult for a legislature to deal with the detailed complexities of the modern regulation of social life, and, whether we like it or not, delegation of power has come to stay, for Parliament has neither the time nor the desire to take the full burden upon itself. Again, Parliament may be incompetent to understand the technical issues involved and may prefer to leave the working out of a broad statutory principle to an expert body. Some legislative schemes are

---

[1] O. Kahn-Freund, 11 *Mod. L. R.* (1948), 269; *The Queen* v. *Kirby ex. p. The Boilermakers Society*, [1957] A.C. 288 (*The Boilermakers Case*).
[2] 22 Hen. VIII, c. 9, cited Committee on Ministers' Powers, 1932, Cmd. 4060, 21.
[3] See e.g. *The Boilermakers Case* (*supra*) in the High Court of Australia (1956), 94 C.L.R. 254 and in the Privy Council, [1957] A.C. 288.

frankly experimental, and Parliament is sometimes persuaded to grant to a Minister power to make minor amendments in order to carry out the purpose of the Act so as to obviate the necessity of using parliamentary procedure. Flexibility, speed, expert knowledge —these are all in point when the convenience of delegated legislative power is concerned. Thus we obtain what the optimists call government by the expert and the pessimists term control by the dead hand of bureaucracy.[1]

But there is one fundamental limit to bureaucracy under the English system. The King in Parliament has supreme power to change the law—the administrator can act only within the limits of the power that is delegated to him. Hence an administrator can 'legislate' on a particular topic only where he can show a surrender of that power to him.

The Courts and the Administrative Process

It is not easy to define the judicial function with any exactitude. The Committee on Ministers' Powers wrote that

a true judicial decision presupposes an existing dispute between two or more parties and then involves four requisites:

1. the presentation (not necessarily orally) of their case by parties to the dispute;
2. if the dispute between them is a question of fact, the ascertainment of the fact by means of evidence adduced by the parties . . .
3. if the dispute between them is a question of law, the submission of legal arguments by the parties; and
4. a decision which disposes of the whole matter by a finding upon the facts in dispute and an application of the law of the land to the facts so found, including, where required, a ruling upon any disputed question of law.[2]

The Committee regard a quasi-judicial decision as one which presupposes an existing dispute and the first two factors set out above, but which does not necessarily involve the third and never involves the fourth—the authority is left free to act by reference to considerations of policy. Yet further removed is the 'pure' act of administration. Shall Australia buy her aeroplanes in England or manufacture

---

[1] For a pithy mis-statement, see A. I. Vyshinsky, *Law of the Soviet State*, 367: 'There is no bureaucracy in the U.S.S.R.'

[2] Committee on Ministers' Powers, 1932, Cmd. 4060, 73. An unkind critic has suggested that this Report 'did more to emphasise the primitive state of political science in England than to solve any constitutional problems': B. Abel-Smith and Robert Stevens, *Lawyers and the Courts*, 120.

them herself? The only relevant statute may create a power to spend a certain sum in the purchase of aeroplanes. In making the decision, the administrator has a discretion that is almost entirely unfettered—there is no legal duty to hear the claims of Australian manufacturers, or to buy the aeroplanes where they are cheapest or best. The grounds of policy on which the administrator decides are left to his own judgment.[1]

These classifications, as Sir Ivor Jennings has shown, cannot be regarded as entirely satisfactory, because reliable criteria for allocating any particular function are not provided.[2] The following difficulties emerge:

(a) Courts sometimes find that there is no clear authority on the point in question and hence must create law in the very act of applying it.

(b) Merely because the courts decide according to law, we cannot assume that they exercise no discretion or are not concerned with broad issues of policy.[3] A decision whether a particular contract is against public policy involves (if there is no authority) an analysis of the interests at stake. If a petitioner in an undefended divorce suit confesses that he has been guilty of adultery and asks the court to exercise its discretion in his favour and to grant a divorce because of his wife's misconduct, are we not coming very close to the administrative process? The discretion of the court must be exercised in accordance with such rules of law as exist, but that is also true of the administrator.[4]

(c) The problem has been made even more difficult in England because of the fact that certain courts exercise what are logically administrative functions, and the rising tide of collectivism has caused executive bodies to encroach on the functions of the courts.[5]

---

[1] 'The Minister, acting in his administrative capacity, is governed by considerations of expediency only . . . no principle of natural justice . . . has any place in that kind of administration': per Henn Collins J., *Miller* v. *Minister of Health*, [1946] 1 K.B. 626 at 628.

[2] W. I. Jennings, *The Law and the Constitution* (4th ed.), 220; W. A. Robson, *Justice and Administrative Law* (2nd ed.), 350.

[3] *Sorrell* v. *Smith*, [1925] A.C. 700, required a very close analysis of matters of policy, for the law was so confused that it afforded no clear guidance.

[4] Of course, as an accumulation of such cases is dealt with by the courts, precedents are established which sometimes crystallize the broad lines of policy by laying down detailed rules of law. But, in some of these cases, the courts explicitly refuse to fetter their discretion. An administrator does not create binding precedents by following a certain line of policy, although there is a natural tendency to develop a consistent practice. See W. A. Robson, op. cit. 294.

[5] *Administrative Tribunals at Work*, ed. R. S. W. Pollard.

Hence the test of the name by which the tribunal is called has ceased to be of service and there has been a feverish search for a true principle which can differentiate between the judicial and the administrative process. There are tribunals with the trapping of courts which do not really possess judicial power; there are administrative bodies which exercise functions which seem to satisfy all suggested tests of the judicial process. In order to secure a wide operation for the writs of prohibition and *certiorari* (which lie only against inferior *courts*), there is a tendency to extend the meaning of the term 'court' rather far and the phrase 'to act judicially' comes almost to mean the decision after proper investigation of any matter relating to the rights and liabilities of a subject. On the other hand, when it is a question whether a tribunal has the advantage of immunity from actions for defamation, a much stricter view has been taken, and the test is whether there is power to make a binding and enforceable order—that is, an order disobedience to which is punishable, or which is enforceable by execution without further legal proceedings. Thus if we are asked whether a particular body is a court or not, we must reply, 'a court for what purpose?'[1] Willis suggests that in Canada the courts have given up attempting to find a logical distinction and in effect ask, 'Is this tribunal doing something which in 1867 was done exclusively by a Superior Court Judge?'[2]

In Australia it has been necessary to find a working test for another purpose. By the Constitution of the Commonwealth, judicial power may be vested only in courts and the tenure of the judges must be for life, subject to the powers of removal given in § 72. Hence a long line of cases deals with the attempt to find a criterion. If an administrative board is set up to deal with objections by taxpayers, or to deal with the wages of women, is judicial power being exercised?[3] A court martial seems to fall under any test that might be proposed, but the High Court has held that the composition of a court martial is not governed by these sections of the Constitution.[4] The simplest test is the power of enforcement: 'to erect a tribunal into a "Court"

---

[1] *R.* v. *L.C.C.*, [1931] 2 K.B. 215; *Re Ashby*, [1934] 3 D.L.R. 565 (Ont.); *R.* v. *Woodhouse*, [1906] 2 K.B. 501 at 535; *Shell Company of Australia* v. *Federal Commissioner of Taxation*, [1931] A.C. 275; *R.* v. *Electricity Commissioners*, [1924] 1 K.B. 171 at 194.

[2] 53 *Harv. L. R.* (1939), 269; W. I. Jennings, 49 *Harv. L. R.* (1936), 426 at 429; D. M. Gordon, 49 *L.Q.R.* (1933), 94; J. Willis, 1 *Univ. of Toronto L. J.* (1935), 53; E. R. Hopkins, 17 *Can. B. R.* (1939), 619; *Toronto Corporation* v. *York Corporation*, [1938] A.C. 415.

[3] See the incisive survey by G. Sawer, 1 *Annual L. R. (W. A.)* (1948), 29.

[4] *R.* v. *Bevan* (1942), 66 C.L.R. 452; *R.* v. *Cox* (1945), 71 C.L.R. 1.

or "jurisdiction" . . . the essential element is that it should have power, by its *determination* within jurisdiction, to impose liability or affect rights.'[1] Australian cases have been summed up in the following propositions. Firstly, there must be the decision of a dispute by officers authorized by law; secondly, the dispute must be decided by reference to a pre-existing rule or standard;[2] thirdly, an interpretative decision is judicial only if it satisfies at least one of the following tests: (*a*) there is power to enforce the decision by execution; (*b*) the decision is conclusive and binding; (*c*) the constitution, procedure, and powers of the tribunal are such as to indicate that Parliament intended that the tribunal should exercise judicial power.[3] The difficulty of applying these tests is shown by the strong dissent in *Rola Co. (Aust.) Pty. Ltd.* v. *Commonwealth.*[4]

Quasi-judicial is a term that is also not easily definable. In the United States, the phrase often covers judicial decisions taken by an administrative agency—the test is the nature of the tribunal rather than what it is doing. In England quasi-judicial belongs to the administrative category and is used to cover situations where the administrator is bound by law to observe certain forms and possibly hold a public hearing but where he is a free agent in reaching the final decision. If the rules are broken, the determination may be set aside, but it is not sufficient to show that the administration is biased in favour of a certain policy, or that the evidence points to a different conclusion.[5] Yet in *Franklin* v. *Minister of Town and Country Planning,*[6] the House of Lords treated such functions of the Minister as purely administrative, although previous cases had regarded them as quasi-judicial.

The growth of administrative law seems to be inevitable, but there are many writers who point out the possible dangers involved. Pound goes so far as to say that 'the pre-supposition of administrative absolutism is that of every form of autocracy. . . . The corollary of the proposition that men are not competent to manage the details of their private affairs is that they are not competent to manage public affairs. In the end administrative absolutism must stand upon a

---

[1] *R.* v. *Local Government Board*, [1902] 2 I.R. 349 at 373.
[2] This seems to depend on the theory that the rules of the common law are clear, but that the only difficulty is to find out what they are.   [3] G. Sawer, op. cit.
[4] (1944), 69 C.L.R. 185, and also by such cases as: *The Queen* v. *Davison* (1954), 90 C.L.R. 353; *The Queen* v. *Spicer ex. p. Aust. Builders' Labourers' Federation* (1957), 100 C.L.R. 277; *The Queen* v. *Spicer ex. p. Waterside Workers' Federation of Australia* (1957), 100 C.L.R. 312. *R.* v. *Trade Practices Tribunal*, [1970] A.L.R. 449.
[5] H. W. R. Wade, 10 *Camb. L. J.* (1949), 216.   [6] [1948] A.C. 87.

political absolutism.'[1] This is somewhat exaggerated, but it is true that the division of powers supplies a useful system of checks and balances. If the same administrative body makes the regulations, prosecutes the offender, acts as a court, and inflicts the sanction, there is less chance of impartiality than if the case comes before an independent tribunal. To consider in detail this most controversial topic of modern law is beyond our scope; suffice it to say that administrative law has come to stay,[2] and that the only practicable reform is to secure such safeguards as will adequately protect the liberty and property of the subject. It is natural that Fascist or Soviet states demand executive freedom and scorn any doctrine of separation of powers.[3] The liberal state 'is derided as atomistic, negative, pluralist, mechanistic; the nation state is extolled as integrating, dialectic, organic'.[4] The problem before the democracies is to secure machinery for rapid and effective executive action, and at the same time to preserve those essential liberties which are necessary for the development of human personality. The courts of law have manifested great independence in protecting the subject and, however valid may be the reasons for referring certain matters to the decision of administrative bodies, we must see that checks on arbitrary action are imposed either through judicial review or the creation of a new system of administrative courts. On the other hand, if the jurisdiction of the courts is to be preserved, speed of trial and cheapness of cost are factors that must not be ignored.

In the United States there has been much controversy over the working of administrative tribunals and after an exhaustive inquiry the Federal Administrative Procedure Act was passed in 1946 as an attempt to destroy the worst evils without trammelling administrative necessities. There is a case for separation of function within an agency, if it is given power both to make regulations and to impose penalties. The administrative court should be independent and distinct from the part of the agency that determines policy and creates law.[5]

---

[1] *West Virg. L. Q.* (1938–9), 205 at 219; see also R. Pound, *The Task of the Law* (1944). For a reply see H. J. Morgenthau, 57 *Harv. L. R.* (1944), 922. For an English analysis, see C. K. Allen, *Law and Orders*.

[2] See e.g. K. C. Davis's major work in four volumes, *Administrative Law Treatise* (1958); B. Schwartz, *Introduction to Administrative Law* (1958); G. Sawer, *The Separation of Powers in Australian Federalism*, 35 *A.L.J.* (1961), 177.

[3] J. W. Jones, *Historical Introduction to the Theory of Law*, 280; A. I. Vyshinsky, *Law of the Soviet State*.

[4] J. W. Jones, op. cit. 283.   [5] K. C. Davis, 61 *Harv. L. R.* (1948), 389.

Thus no test for distinguishing between the three powers of government is at once intellectually satisfying and functionally useful. However, there are sound political reasons for preserving some separation. Sir Ivor Jennings suggests that the major principles of policy should be laid down by Parliament and that in general law should be administered in contested cases by courts staffed with an independent judiciary employing a technique and procedure which gives some guarantee of justice. But the precise determination of the subject-matter attributed to each function can be determined only by convenience and policy, not by logic. 'The safeguard against bureaucracy and tyranny lies not in a precise delineation of functions, but in democratic control through an elected House of Commons in which the Party system makes criticism open and effective'.[1]

§ 76. LAW AND THE STATE

There are three ways of constructing a theory of the State: we may examine the actual functioning of the State (as in political science), or the ideal of what a state ought to be (as in political philosophy), or the theoretical basis of the lawyer's approach to the State. The last method (the so-called juristic theory of the State) is not meant to present a complete picture of the actual working of a state, but rather the theoretical conceptions around which the doctrines of the law are built. In particular, the juristic theory of the State deals with the relationship of law and the State, or (to put the same problem in another way) it asks the question whether public law is really law. Can a subject have legal rights against the State?

There are three main juristic theories of the relationship between the State and the law which can tersely be expressed thus: the State is superior to and creates law; law precedes the State and binds it when it comes into existence; law and the State are the same thing looked at from different points of view.[2]

---

[1] W. I. Jennings, op. cit. 284. Even A. I. Vyshinsky emphasizes the importance of the independence of the judiciary: *Law of the Soviet State*, 505. H. Kelsen suggests that logically a pure democratic theory requires that both courts and executive should be subject to parliament: *General Theory of Law*, 282. Courts may, of course, be resistant to new social experiments and eviscerate statutes, but no human institution will ever be beyond the risk of error.

[2] G. Gurvitch, *L'Expérience juridique*, 213. Lon L. Fuller compares analytical jurisprudence with its theories of law, the State, and the sovereign to theology with its doctrine of the Trinity: *The Law in Quest of Itself*, 41; R. Pound, 57 *Harv. L. R.* (1944), 1193·

(a)

The first theory is illustrated by the work of Austin, who defines law as the command of the sovereign. But when Austin attempts to define sovereignty and the State he adopts a practical test. Firstly there must be a political society of 'considerable' numbers, and a superior in that society who is habitually obeyed by the bulk of the members of that community and who is not in the habit of obedience to another superior.[1] Within this community, the superior has a sovereign power to lay down the law. The relation between subject and sovereign is therefore one of power: the sovereign can have no legal rights against his subjects nor can he be bound by legal duties, for a legal relationship can exist between two parties only when there is above them a sovereign who will enforce the rule of law. Hence constitutional law must be divided into two parts: as against the sovereign body as a whole, constitutional law is mere positive morality enforced by moral sanctions alone; but it may be regarded as positive law in so far as it binds particular members of the sovereign body.[2] Collectively considered, the sovereign is above the law, but a member of the House of Commons is individually bound by an Act of Parliament though he is a member of the body which creates the law. If the sovereign consists of only one person, constitutional law is only positive morality. Rules of the game can hardly be considered to bind a person who can change them at any minute, though it is true that, if he is always changing the rules to suit himself, he may find it difficult to persuade the others to play with him. The word 'unconstitutional',[3] Austin points out, is often merely a vague term of disapprobation, since the conduct criticized may involve no actual breach of the law.

The lawyer's view of sovereignty is based on practical considerations rather than on any theory of values—'the English sovereign is merely the "person" who has the last word in a particular connection'.[4] The fact that there is in England an omnicompetent legislature and a strong centralized organization of justice which recognizes the power of Parliament has obviated the necessity of

---

[1] *Jurisprudence*, Lect. VI. It is difficult to say precisely what is the smallest community which could be rightfully regarded as a state. In practice the doctrines of international law are usually invoked to determine whether a particular society is a state or not.

[2] J. Austin, *Jurisprudence*, i. 267.   [3] As used in England.

[4] J. W. Salmond, *Jurisprudence* (9th ed.), 689. (This passage is rewritten in the 12th ed.)

theoretical debates since the settlement of 1689. The particular problem of the relationship of Church and State, which has produced so many theories of sovereignty, was settled in England at a fairly early date. To an English lawyer the concept of the sovereignty of Parliament merely means that the courts will recognize as law rules made by Parliament in the form of legislation.[1]

But it is not easy to find out who has the 'last word' in a federation. The legislature is bound by the constitution, and in most cases a court has power to decide whether a particular statute is constitutional or not. Hence the court is the ultimate authority in one sense; but only in a narrow sense because, firstly, the power of the court is purely negative, since it can reject but not initiate legislation, and, secondly, the electorate normally has the ultimate power of amending the constitution.

But there is no need for any *one* person or body to have the 'last word' on every point. So long as the system provides a method of settling the law on each particular issue, it matters not in theory how many 'authorities' there may be, provided there be some practical means of resolving conflicts. The legal theory of the State becomes increasingly difficult the more this ultimate power is divided, but that does not prove that in practice it cannot be divided. The constitutional law of an absolute dictatorship is simple: 'whatever pleases the emperor has the force of law'; and in England it is comparatively easy, since the legally unrestricted power of the King in Parliament prevents deadlocks arising from a division of powers. But in a federation constitutional difficulties may prevent effective action, for powers may be so divided that a particular reform can be achieved only by the co-operation of the states and the central authority: indeed, there may be some powers which cannot be exercised even by this co-operation.[2] The difficulties of waging modern war have made this point apparent in every federation.[3]

How far can a sovereign parliament place legal limits on its future exercise of the power to create law? The past has shown that statutes which were declared to be immutable have been changed, and

---

[1] W. I. Jennings, op. cit. 143.

[2] Thus § 92 of the Australian Commonwealth Constitution declares that trade, commerce, and intercourse between the states shall be absolutely free. This binds the Commonwealth as well as the states and prevents legislation on marketing from becoming effective.

[3] E. S. Corwin, *Total War and the Constitution* (1947); D. P. Derham, *The Defence Power*; ch. vi of *Essays on the Australian Constitution* (2nd ed. 1961), ed. R. Else-Mitchell.

probably if the Imperial Parliament repealed § 4 of the Statute of Westminster (which restricts the right of the Imperial Parliament to legislate for the Dominions without their request and consent), the English courts would treat the repeal as lawful. This, however, is academic theorizing, for the Statute of Westminster really created a new basic norm for the Empire. It is doubtful if Dominion courts would recognize the validity of such a repeal.[1] If a statute grants 'Dominion status' to Scotland and Wales, presumably in theory a subsequent statute could repeal the former grant. If Parliament cannot bind its successors, this is the only logical answer, however unrealistic it may be politically. If a statute granted true independence, the answer might well be different. Where parliaments are not sovereign, it is possible to evolve a technique whereby a statute can be protected from simple repeal[2]—thus a referendum may be required before the statute can be altered.[3]

Should constitutional conventions be regarded as law? If we adopt as the test of a rule of law whether it will be applied by a court, many of these conventions are not law, for they could not be made the subject-matter of an action.[4] If we are considering the juristic theory of the State, an answer would depend on the facts. If the convention was so wrapped up with the functioning of the State that the ultimate power could not be described faithfully save by reference to it, then such a convention would be law, or, more accurately, part of the essential premiss on which the legal order was built.[5]

As a postulate to explain the working of a legal order the concept of sovereignty has its uses. But the term is used with so many conflicting meanings and so easily stirs the emotions that it is better for jurisprudence to forgo its use. The 'initial premiss' is a better and more neutral phrase: there is no need for jurisprudence to postulate sovereignty in the sense of power that is unlimited, illimitable and indivisible. These qualities are not *a priori* necessary, but depend

---

[1] W. I. Jennings, op. cit. 145, discusses the problem. Cf. Dixon C.J.: 'The Act of 1956 (Copyright) contains no declaration that the Commonwealth of Australia has requested or consented to the enactment thereof. The repeal, therefore, of the Act of 1911, which is effected by the Act of 1956, does not because of s. 4 of the Statute of Westminster, 1931 . . . extend to Australia': *Copyright Owners Reproduction Society Ltd.* v. *E.M.I. (Aust.) Pty. Ltd.*, (1958) 100 C.L.R. 597 at 604.

[2] *Harris* v. *Dönges*, [1952] 1 T.L.R. 1245.

[3] *A.-G. for N.S.W.* v. *Trethowan*, [1932] A.C. 526.

[4] W. I. Jennings, op. cit. 99–100.

[5] Constitutional law is obligatory because it is recognized that, if the rules are not obeyed, the society will come to an end: A. L. Goodhart, *Interpretations of Modern Legal Philosophies*, 293.

only on particular political theories, as is demonstrated by a study of the functioning of actual states. The basis of law is a legal order, the presuppositions of which are accepted by the community as determining the methods by which law is to be created, and those presuppositions will vary from one community to another.

This legal conception of the initial hypothesis does not pretend to explain the real nature of politics or the art of government. If England were ruled by a Fascist Council of Three, whose demands Parliament obeyed, the King in Parliament would still be the formal means used to change the law. But from the moment the Fascist Council directly imposed its will on the courts, and was accepted by the community as having power to create law, a new legal order with a new initial premiss would have been created. And it may be that the purely juristic theory is not sufficient for all the purposes of jurisprudence. But the fact that to understand the real functioning of the law of contract we must go beyond Anson's analysis does not absolve us from understanding the propositions that the learned author lays down. And in the same way it is indispensable to have a knowledge of the legal forms through which the law approaches the problem of government.

Thus the theory of sovereignty has been of service as a formal theory, but some writers go farther and seek to justify sovereignty as a moral necessity instead of as a convenient hypothesis. For example, Hegelianism treats the State as a supreme moral end—being a value in itself it is not bound by the rules of ethics that apply to individual men.[1] Only in the State can man attain true self-realization; and since the will of the State represents the real will of the individuals, the State thus includes the entire hierarchy of social life. This theory 'grants to state absolutism the virtue of moral truth'.[2] 'The state is the divine idea as it exists on earth.'[3] This doctrine has been carried farther by the Nazi and Fascist conceptions which regard law as but the will of the Leader. To attempt to bind the State (these engaging theorists tell us) is to commit treason at the bidding of out-moded liberal ideas, which, striving to protect the liberty of the subject, strike at the welfare of all. This doctrine is more understandable (if less palatable) when we appreciate that the totality deserving of consideration consists only of those whose political heart is in the right place.

[1] For the philosophic issues that lie behind the Hegelian theory of the State, see B. Bosanquet, *Philosophical Theory of the State*; F. Hallis, *Corporate Personality*, 61 et seq. But as W. Friedmann shows, *Legal Theory* (4th ed.), 354, finally the Nazis turn to Nietzsche rather than Hegel.
[2] F. Hallis, *Corporate Personality*, 68.   [3] Hegel, *Philosophie des Rechts*, 349.

In Russia there are traces of the same theory. 'Despotism is . . . not merely tolerated by Soviet jurists and publicists: it is an essential element in their conception of the social order of their time and place.'[1] These doctrines treat law as an instrument of executive action, not as a check upon it: law is a weapon to achieve the ends of state policy, not a chain to hamper the executive.[2]

This approach is far removed from that of Austin and Kelsen. Austin said only that, if law was the command of the sovereign, you could not in theory bind that sovereign. Kelsen makes no ethical plea but argues that logically we must accept some source of power as the formal basis of the legal order. Hegelianism, on the other hand, claims that ethically the State is an end in itself, and that the individual has claims only as a unit in the absolute of the State.

This grant of ethical justification to a formal theory of 'the last word' has led to a revolt, not only against Hegelianism, but also against formal theories such as those of Austin and Kelsen. This leads to the next view of the relation of the State and the law.

(b)

The second theory regards law as more fundamental than, and as anterior to, the State. Hence law may bind the State. Some turn to the medieval solution of natural law—the sovereign has absolute power over positive law, but is bound by *ius naturale*. In the Middle Ages even a royal justice such as Bracton could 'fearlessly proclaim' that the king was bound by law.[3] We cannot impose on the Middle Ages an Hegelian theory of the State, for the Church still exercised over the State an undefined control. Moreover, the baronage claimed vague rights of judging the king in his own court, although there were no effective means of bringing this about save by revolution. Modern constitutional theories may attempt to bind the government by the creation of a higher law which can be amended only by referendum. Declarations of rights may be inserted in constitutions to place certain interests beyond the reach of arbitrary interference by chance majorities.[4]

---

[1] J. W. Jones, *Historical Introduction to the Theory of Law*, 278.
[2] Op. cit. Contrast the approach of Greene M.R. in *Kawasaki v. Bantham S.S. Co.*, [1939] 1 All E.R. 819 at 822: 'I do not myself find the fear of the embarrassment of the executive a very attractive basis upon which to build a rule of English law. . . .'
[3] F. Pollock and F. W. Maitland, *History of English Law*, i. 160.
[4] Such an approach really strengthens H. Kelsen's argument that the problem should be looked at, not as a conflict between law and government, but on the basis of the postulates of the legal order.

Ihering considered that law in the full sense was achieved only when it bound both ruler and ruled. But, as Ihering regards the State as the maker of law, we may well ask how the creator may be bound by the creature of his fancy? Ihering solved the problem by what is really a political argument: law is the intelligent policy of power, and it is easier to govern if the State voluntarily submits to the law it has created. This is merely an argument of expediency—we can do everything with bayonets but sit on them—and, while it undoubtedly contains much truth, it is of little service to juristic theory.

Jellinek develops this doctrine into a theory of autolimitation—the State is the creator of law, but voluntarily submits to it. But if the State is bound only because of its own consent, why cannot that consent be withdrawn at any time? A more radical attack is made on the problem by Krabbe and Duguit, both of whom deny that the State creates law. Once we postulate that law is created by a source other than the State, it is easy to see how the State can be bound. Krabbe places the source of law in the subjective sense of right in the community[1]—he is not merely making the obvious point that the moral ideas of a community are reflected in the legal system under which it lives; he goes further and asserts that the State cannot make law. He abruptly asserts that any statute which is opposed to the majority sense of right is not law.[2] Hence the legislature, executive, and the judiciary are but subordinate instruments through which the community expresses its sense of values. Krabbe thus treats as the source of law an instinctive sense of right—he rejects all definitions which emphasize the general will of the community for he fears that once law is made to depend on will, an attempt will be made to invoke the superior will of a sovereign with power to crush the discordant individual wills of the community.

But there are many faults in Krabbe's theory. How can a sense of right be effective unless men are willing to put their wills at the service of the ends they desire? Moreover, Krabbe uses the term 'law' in a sense very different from that of the lawyer—his theory would be true only if the judge could ignore all statutes and precedents and base his decisions purely on what he conceived to be the sense of right of the majority of the community. Thus he says that a statute

---

[1] *The Modern Idea of the State.*
[2] It is difficult to justify majority rule save as a convenient political expedient—it is preferable to count heads rather than to break them. But H. Krabbe holds that any rule possesses a higher value if approved by the majority.

ceases to be law when it is no longer acceptable, that constitutional provisions are void if they require a majority of more than half the electors before amendment can be made. From this angle a statute and a decision of a court are but experiments—either would create a rule of law only if and when that rule is accepted by the community. Although the ethical basis of Krabbe is far removed from the positivism of Duguit, in essence they both take the same view of the relationship of the State and law. Rules derived from the fact of solidarity bind the State, writes Duguit; there is no such thing as sovereignty, for the State is merely a convenient term for the organization of such public services as the dictates of solidarity demand.

Accordingly, to these theories public law is positive law in every sense of the word. It binds the ruler who lacks power to change the law by his mere volition. Hence law is not organized power, as in Fascist theories, but rather a check on the arbitrary exercise of power by the executive. Krabbe emphasizes the hackneyed dictum that there should be a government of laws and not of men,[1] but he employs the term 'law' in a sense very different from that of the normal use. It has been reiterated again and again in this work that law is a result of the social forces of the community, but the acceptance of this doctrine does not lead to Krabbe's result that some statutes are not law. The lesson of legal history is that law functions best if adequate organs are set up to create, declare, and enforce it— law cannot be left to be determined only by a vague sense of right. Efficiency demands that power be placed at the service of law and that institutions be set up to draw the boundaries of legal rules as sharply as possible. We can best secure the effective protection of the subject, not by denying power to the State nor by inventing paradoxical theories of law, but by spreading the basis of political power among as many members of the community as possible through a wide franchise. The ultimate sanctions of 'constitutional law' as against the ruling body are extra-legal—'revolution, active, and passive resistance and the pressure of public opinion'.[2]

In English writing, the same problem has been discussed under the heading of *the rule of law*. Dicey found three meanings in this

[1] T. I. Cook, 30 *Calif. L. R.* (1942), 151.

[2] P. Vinogradoff, *Historical Jurisprudence*, i. 120. See also W. I. Jennings, *The Law and the Constitution* (3rd ed.), 314: 'The constitution of a country, whatever it be, rests upon acquiescence.' This does not, of course, mean that an active minority in a country may not control power to such an extent that few are willing to revolt. Again a conquering horde may hold a smaller community in subjugation.

phrase: firstly, the supremacy of regular law over arbitrary power; secondly, equality before the law in the sense that officials must obey it and are subject to the jurisdiction of the ordinary courts; thirdly, the fact that the law of the constitution is the result of decisions of the courts as to the rights of private individuals.[1] These are undoubtedly the characteristics of the English legal system, but they result from the political struggles of the past and are not logical deductions from a rule of law.[2] For law may have a varying content; it may protect the subject against despotism or give the most ruthless power to a tyrant. It is not enough for the democrat to demand a rule of law—everything depends on the nature of that law. Every legal order which functions has a rule of law; this applies to a Nazi state as well as a democracy. What democratic liberals desire is that the powers of government should be restrained so as to protect as far as possible the 'personal freedoms'— this is a noble ideal, but not one that is necessarily secured by a rule of law.[3]

There is, however, a growing movement among Western nations, and others influenced by them, to achieve more than that and attach a more specific and demanding meaning to the phrase 'rule of law'. The nineteenth-century movements for constitutional reform, based in the main on eighteenth-century thinking, did not proceed on any Diceyan kind of notions about the rule of law. They sought to fetter governmental powers by laws which would protect individual human values. It is seen today that economic questions must be solved before such ideas can be implemented fully: that men must eat before they can enjoy freedom from tyranny.[4] Further there has been a growing school of thought, often based on revived 'natural law' notions, which seeks to find in the concept of law itself fundamental aspects requiring limits to be placed upon the exercise of power by governments of whatever kind.[5]

[1] *Law of the Constitution* (8th ed.), ch. iv.
[2] W. I. Jennings, *The Law and the Constitution*, Appendix II.
[3] Note the interesting argument of Dixon J. (as he then was) in 51 *L.Q.R.* (1935), 590. In English legal history three conceptions have been struggling for mastery—the supremacy of the law which was owed to the Middle Ages, the supremacy of the Crown symbolized in the Divine Right of Kings, and finally the supremacy of Parliament established by the revolution settlement. Today, if we take the Commonwealth as a whole, the Crown is the symbol of unity, and 'thus in the end we return to a conception of the supremacy of the Crown'.
[4] See the many recent publications of the International Commission of Jurists, and in particular the *'Declaration of Delhi'* on the Rule of Law.
[5] See e.g. Lon L. Fuller, *Positivism and Fidelity to Law—A Reply to Professor Hart*, 71 *Harv. L. R.* (1958), 630.

(c)

Kelsen illustrates the third type of theory that law and the State are really the same. The State is only the legal order looked at from another point of view. Human individuals alone can act, and legal force is imputed to their behaviour only if it is in accordance with a rule of law. Just as men personified world forces and created a deity, so the jurist has personified the hierarchy of norms and created a state.[1] When we think of the abstract rules, we speak of the law: when we consider the institutions which those rules create, we speak of the State. But the practical importance of Kelsen's approach is that he emphasizes that law is a more fundamental notion than that of the State. While it is true that law cannot exist without a legal order, that order may take forms other than that of the State. Hence the theory is wider, and therefore more acceptable, than that of Austin. A legal order may be created in the international sphere even though no super-state is set up.

The three theories relating to the relationship of law and the State have now been discussed. Logically, each may be defended, but, if we examine actual states, we discover that no one solution will apply to all. Just as law may serve many purposes, so the relationship between law and the State may vary.[2] It is possible to conceive of a state which recognizes a fundamental law, which it is beyond the power of any authority to alter. Such a legal order might prove impracticable as conditions changed, but an unalterable fundamental law is not beyond the bounds of imagination. At the other extreme a sovereign parliament may have no limits whatever on its exercise of legislative powers.

What are the essential marks of the State? Salmond defined the State as an association of human beings established for the attainment of human ends, two of which are primary and essential—war and the administration of justice. These two purposes Salmond regarded as partaking of the same quality—the maintenance of right by the exercise of force: hence he regarded a state as a society organized so as to use force to maintain peace and justice within a given territory.[3] But in what way can we show that the functions

---

[1] 'It can be said that the state creates the law, but this means only that the law regulates its own creation': H. Kelsen, 55 *Harv. L. R.* (1941), 65.

[2] E. Bodenheimer, *Jurisprudence*, 57.

[3] *Jurisprudence* (10th ed.), 129–30. J. W. Salmond, in order to take this point, argued that only a *just* war can be regarded as an essential form of state activity. Salmond's own view is seen in 9th ed. 165. This discussion does not appear in the 12th ed.

chosen by Salmond are more essential than any other activities of the State?[1] The theory of *laissez-faire* would curtail the State's sphere of operation, just as modern collectivist conceptions would increase it. If a permanent international order were set up, it may be that war would entirely disappear—however pessimistic we may be, we cannot prove *a priori* that the carrying on of war will always be a function of the State.

From the purely juristic angle, many say that what distinguishes the State is the fact that legally it cannot, without its own consent, be deprived of its power to rule. Kelsen,[2] on the hypothesis that international law is supreme, suggests that the national legal order can be defined as 'a relatively centralized coercive order whose territorial, personal, and temporal spheres of validity are determined by international law and whose material sphere of validity is limited by international law only'. A corporation may set up its own legal order, but it is subject to the overriding power of the State. If a powerful corporation within a state sets up a legal order which defies the State, nevertheless the State (at least in formal theory) remains supreme, until its legal order is overthrown and a new basis for law set up: in other words, until revolution has taken place. As we have said, constitutions have an extra-legal origin and the jurist can only accept that which has been created by the wars and struggles of the past. The normal marks of a state are a fixed territory, population, and competence to rule which is not derived from another state.[3] Groups existing within the State may not have been created by the State, but the extent of their legal power depends on what is granted by the law. Kantorowicz, therefore, defines the State as a juristic person endowed with the right to impose its will on the inhabitants of a given territory, of which right it cannot by law be deprived without its own consent.[4]

§ 77. THE STATE AS A LEGAL PERSON

The State has been regarded by some as the greatest corporation known to the law, by others as mere machinery or as one aspect of

---

[1] H. Kantorowicz, 12 *Economica* (1932), 5.

[2] *General Theory of Law and State*, 351.

[3] Many emphasize the originality and the non-delegated character of the State's competence to rule. It may be that this theory has a theological counterpart, but it is none the less true that, for juristic theory, the State created itself. The tests of international law are an independent government, a sufficient degree of internal stability to give effective government, and a defined territory: H. Lauterpacht, *Recognition in International Law*, 26.   [4] 12 *Economica* (1932), 12.

the legal order. The wealth of learning and the subtle argument that has been applied to the notion of corporate personality[1] has almost buried the problem of the nature of the entity which we described as the State. In modern systems the State can be seen as a legal person endowed with such powers as the legal system which supports it provides. These may vary from absolute power to impose its will on the inhabitants of a given territory, to much more limited powers as in federations like those of the United States of America and the Commonwealth of Australia. It is always necessary to distinguish 'states' and 'sovereigns' seen from the international point of view from the aspect they wear when seen from within a legal system as the principal legal person in that system.

In the history of English law we find much confusion. English lawyers were not good at abstract theory: 'they liked their persons to be real.' Nearly all that is said of the king in the Year Books is strictly true of a man.[2] When it became necessary to find a legal theory for the State, the notion of the *corporation sole* was borrowed from ecclesiastical law and the king was '*parsonified*'.[3] But neither in the case of the parson nor in that of the king was a clear-cut separation made between the artificial *corporation sole* and the natural man who occupied the office.[4] It is 'idle optimism to seek logic in constitutional law'.[5] When a king died, instead of the law assuming that the artificial *corporation sole* continued, there was a curious hesitancy. All delegation ceased, litigation ended and must be begun again, military commissions terminated. 'When on a demise of the Crown we see all the wheels of the State stopping or even running backwards, it seems an idle jest to say that the King never dies.'[6] When George III wished to buy some land for his private use, a special Act had to be passed to allow him to hold it as a man and not a King.[7] The most obvious difficulties were gradually dealt with by statute and today the theory of the *corporation sole* is

---

[1] *Infra*, Ch. XVI.
[2] F. W. Maitland, *Collected Papers*, iii. 246–7.   [3] Ibid. 245.
[4] There were various reasons why it was felt dangerous politically to apply a logical doctrine of separation, and curiously enough the confusion was supported by both monarchists and anti-monarchists: see W. S. Holdsworth, *History of English Law*, ix. 4–7. 'Even in Bracton's day the number of legal ideas is very small and public law has hardly an idea of its own': F. Pollock and F. W. Maitland, *History of English Law*, i. 511. G. W. Keeton, *Elementary Principles of Jurisprudence* (2nd ed.), 152, gives an excellent historical survey.
[5] R. R. Sholl, 3 *Aust. L. J.* (1929), 6 at 9.
[6] Maitland, *Collected Papers*, iii. 253.
[7] Ibid. 252 referring to 39 & 40 Geo. III, c. 88.

well understood. But history has still left us a legacy of theoretical difficulties.[1]

The expansion of the British Empire and the grant of self-government to the Dominions raised many problems for juristic theory. Within Australia, the Crown acts both in right of the Commonwealth and of the States, and Griffith C.J. suggested that in this sense the Crown should be regarded not as one but as several juristic persons.[2] Later cases, however, adopted the view that the Crown is one and indivisible, but that its legislative, judicial, and executive power is exercised by different agents in different localities.[3] To evolve a general theory that explains that amazing self-contradiction, the British Commonwealth, is more than most scholars attempt. The Commonwealth of Australia, which has a separate international legal personality as a member of the United Nations, is (at least where prerogative rights are concerned) a mere agent of an indivisible Crown.[4] In practice, however, the Commonwealth of Australia and the States are separate legal personalities whatever the theory may be. The question whether a suit should be brought against the Crown in right of one dominion, possession, or jurisdiction rather than another depends on the treasury out of which the claim put in suit is to be satisfied.[5] The Constitution of Australia, in effect, treats Commonwealth and States as separate juristic entities, although it has not incorporated them. 'The principle that the Crown is one and indivisible is very important and significant from a political point of view. But, when stated as a legal principle, it tends to dissolve into verbally impressive mysticism. It is of little assistance in a practical system of law where a Commonwealth can sue a State. . . .'[6]

The doctrine of the indivisibility of the Crown throughout the British Commonwealth gives rise to practical difficulties. Can New

---

[1] Sometimes the Crown is used as a term to denote any act of the *corporation sole*: at other times, however, the *Crown* is used to refer to acts of ministers, and the *King* kept for acts of the monarch in person. The Crown Proceedings Act, 1947, 10 & 11 Geo. VI, c. 44, s. 40, refers to 'His Majesty in His private capacity'.

[2] *Municipal Council of Sydney* v. *The Commonwealth* (1904), 1 C.L.R. 208 at 231.

[3] *Amalgamated Society of Engineers* v. *Adelaide Steamship Co.* (1920), 28 C.L.R. 129 at 152.

[4] At least where prerogative rights are concerned 'the Crown is to be considered as one and indivisible throughout the Empire and not to be considered as a quasi-corporate head of several distinct bodies political': per Strong J., *R.* v. *Bank of Nova Scotia*, 11 S.C.R. 17. See W. Harrison Moore, 20 *L.Q.R.* (1904), 357.

[5] *A.-G.* v. *Gt. S. & W. Rly. Co. of Ireland*, [1925] A.C. 754; *Faithorn* v. *Territory of Papua* (1938), 60 C.L.R. 772.

[6] Per Latham C.J., *Minister for Works* v. *Gulson* (1944), 69 C.L.R. 338 at 350; *R.* v. *Dalgety & Co. Ltd.* (1944), 69 C.L.R. 18.

Zealand claim priority for a Crown debt (e.g. income tax) in an action in Canada? How do we rank priority between Commonwealth and States in Australia?[1] A reference to the Crown in a State statute does not bind the Crown in right of the Commonwealth.[2] In England there is now statutory recognition of the phrase 'belonging to His Majesty in right of the Government in the United Kingdom'.[3] In fact each part of the British Commonwealth must be treated as a separate legal *persona*. In spite of historical theory, the Crown is now a symbol of free association of nations each with individual and international personality.

In international law the State is a legal person. Since there is no super-state at whose magic touch personality may be conferred, such law as there is concerns the recognition of a new State by its equals. Recognition is sometimes withheld for political reasons, but should be given as soon as the new order shows a reasonable promise of permanence and of stable government. Recognition, as the term implies, is not creation but an acknowledgement of facts that already exist—in other words, in international law it is a question of fact whether legal personality exists.[4] The United Nations has legal personality.

The application of the doctrine of the *corporation sole* to the State has not proved a very convenient technique for English law. The superior advantage of the analogy of the corporation aggregate is that it emphasizes that subjects are also members of the State. The *corporation sole* is a convenient conception, only if the powers are exercised by one human personality at a time. Since the powers of government are often widely distributed, the organization of the State can best be understood if we think of the analogy of powers shared between the members and directors of a corporation; the memorandum and articles of association of the State are to be found in the fundamental presuppositions of the legal order which may be expressed in a written constitution or unwritten. If to any organ of the State there is given an unlimited power to create law, then logically we cannot bind by law powers that by definition are unlimited. Protection of the subject can be found only in a

---

[1] *Federal Commissioner of Taxation* v. *Official Liquidator of E. O. Farley Ltd.* (1940), 63 C.L.R. 278.

[2] *City of Essendon* v. *Criterion Theatres Ltd.*, [1947] A.L.R. 270.

[3] Crown Proceedings Act, 1947, § 38.

[4] H. Kelsen, 35 *Amer. J. Int. Law* (1941), 605; H. Lauterpacht, *Recognition in International Law*.

distribution of powers, but even this will fail unless there be a strong public opinion which will express itself in cases where power is abused by the ruling body.

If the State is a legal person, how far is it, and how far should it be, liable to actions brought by citizens? The formal theory of sovereignty considered that suit against a sovereign was a contradiction in terms: in England the maxim, 'The King can do no wrong', was thought to provide a practical bar. Modern Fascist jurists think that the grant of any rights to the subject as against the State is a relic of obsolete ideas, since the judge is above private law and his only duty is to execute the will of the Leader.[1] Some Russian writers argue that rights of property should never be placed above the welfare of all. At the end of last century in France the dogma of sovereignty was so emphasized that a theory that the State should be liable for wrong was thought anomalous. But if, as is the case in democratic countries, we do desire to make the State liable to suit, there is no *a priori* reason why this should not be done. If there is a written constitution, then it may make the State liable both in contract and in tort—in such a case amendment of the constitution would be necessary to remove this protection of the subject. In England an Act makes the Crown liable in tort,[2] although it would alway be possible for Parliament to repeal it: the State is bound only so long as it consents to be bound. In France one of the most interesting developments in the field of administrative law is the working out of a definite theory of state responsibility. Duguit perhaps goes too far when he states that the doctrine of sovereignty must give way to one of social service, but a distinct change of approach is visible since the beginning of this century. Certainly, the problem of state responsibility is today much more acute than in the days of *laissez-faire*, for the activities of officials are now much more likely to infringe the rights of individuals.

The conflict between the ancient and the modern conceptions of the State may be seen in the argument whether the Crown can be criminally liable. If we put the emphasis on the old feudal conceptions, there is something ludicrous in the Crown condemning itself to pay a fine to itself: if we consider the modern collectivist state, there is much to be said for the view that the sanctions of the criminal

---

[1] R. Hoehn in *Rec. Lambert*, iii. 240.

[2] Crown Proceedings Act, 1947. The Commonwealth of Australia and all of the states subject the Crown to liability in tort. In U.S. the Federal Tort Claims Act, 1946, imposed liability.

law should be available against government departments.[1] If the Crown may make itself liable in civil cases, why not in criminal?[2] Many modern statutory offences are administrative in character and the object is not financial punishment but rather to police the rules by way of the stigma of conviction.[3]

[1] *Cain* v. *Doyle* (1946), 72 C.L.R. 409, discussed W. Friedmann, 13 *Mod. L. R.* (1950), 24.

[2] 'A penal sanction does not seem an impossibility especially when, as in this case, the judicial authority may order that portion of the penalty be paid to the employee': per Starke J., same case, at 421. The statute in question related to preference to ex-servicemen.

[3] W. Friedmann, op. cit. 35.

REFERENCES

Committee on Ministers' Powers, 1932, Cmd. 4060.
DICEY, A. V., *The Law of the Constitution.*
DIXON (Justice), 51 *L.Q.R.* (1935), 590.
FRIEDMANN, W., *Legal Theory* (5th ed.), ch. xxix.
JENNINGS, W. I., *The Law and the Constitution.*
JONES, J. W., *Historical Introduction to the Theory of Law*, ch. v.
KANTOROWICZ, H., 12 *Economica* (1932), 1.
MAITLAND, F. W., *Coll. Legal Papers*, iii. 210–70.
POUND, R., 57 *Harv. L. R.* (1944), 1193.
ROBSON, W. A., *Justice and the Administrative Law* (2nd ed.).
SIEGHART, MARGUERITE, *Government by Decree.*
TROTABAS, L., *J. Comp. Leg.* xii. 44 and 213, and xiii. 56.
WILLIS, J., 53 *Harv. L. R.* (1939), 251.

XV

CRIMINAL LAW

§ 78. INTRODUCTION

To determine whether criminal law should properly be placed under the heading of public law it is necessary to consider what are the characteristic marks of a crime. Criminal law may be easily distinguished from most branches of private law, but it is very closely related to the law of tort. It is impossible to use the type of act as a test, since the same act may well be both a crime and tort. If Fagin takes John's watch, then that is both the tort of conversion and the crime of larceny. *Furtum* in Roman law was a wrong which gave a right to compensation to the injured owner, but the thief could alternatively be punished criminally.[1]

One suggested distinction is that crime is a breach of public law and tort a breach of private law. But this does not aid us, for to know whether a particular wrong falls under public law we must first decide whether it is a crime. Another test is that the criminal law requires *mens rea*, whereas in tort there may be absolute liability. But not all crimes require *mens rea*.

In English law the formulation of the distinction has been made more difficult by the course of legal evolution. One juristic freak, the action by the common informer, defied all logical classification. The object was punishment, but the penalty went into the pocket of the informer.[2] We shall first examine the formal differences. Kenny defines crimes as 'wrongs whose sanction is punitive, and is no way remissible by any private person, but is remissible by the Crown alone, if remissible at all'.[3] Firstly, the Crown has control over proceedings—a plaintiff in tort may compromise an action at any stage and the Crown cannot interfere, whereas in crime, even though a private prosecutor wishes to discontinue, the Crown may continue the proceedings. Moreover, the Crown has the right to pardon,[4]

---

[1] Clearly all acts which constitute torts do not subject to criminal liability; nor does every crime give a right of action in tort, for many crimes protect a public rather than a private interest, e.g. treason. See C. S. Kenny, *Criminal Law*, ch. i.

[2] The procedure was abolished by the Common Informers Act, 1951.

[3] *Criminal Law* (15th ed.), 16. The treatment is changed in the 19th ed.: see p. 5.

[4] There are exceptions to the power of pardon: see C. S. Kenny, op. cit. (19th ed.), 634.

whether the private prosecutor be agreeable or not, whereas in tort the plaintiff has the sole right to compromise proceedings. Secondly, a crime involves liability to punishment.[1] Although the prisoner suffers, the private individual who has been wronged does not benefit in a material sense.[2] The essence of a civil action is that a plaintiff sues to protect his own rights—either to secure performance or to recover compensation. Exemplary damages may introduce a punitive element, but the inflated damages go to the wronged individual and not to the State. Imprisonment for debt belongs to the civil law, but its object is not to punish but rather to coerce the debtor and, when the debt is paid, release follows.

In considering the material elements of crime, Dr. Allen stresses intrinsic wrongfulness and social expediency as two of the most important factors which have led to the designation of certain conduct as criminal.[3] Jerome Hall finds the distinguishing mark of a crime in social harm involving moral culpability. This is a factor which cannot be disregarded in studying the evolution of the criminal law, but it is not true that this is the only point to be considered.[4] Cutting across this notion of intrinsic wrongfulness are what have been called the 'public welfare' offences, which involve no moral delinquency, but are intended to secure the effective regulation of conduct in the public interest. Thus no moral slur is cast on a person who is convicted of driving a motor car without showing a rear light, nor is it necessary to prove that the defendant knew that his lamp was not alight. Criminal law may have originally been intended to keep the peace—today it also is used to enforce traffic regulations,[5] the selling of pure food, the keeping of a dustbin of an appropriate pattern, the

---

[1] C. K. Allen, *Legal Duties*, 220 at 231. P. H. Winfield defines a crime as 'a wrong the sanction of which involves punishment: and punishment signifies death, penal servitude, whipping, fine, imprisonment (but not, as a rule, non-coercive imprisonment) or some other evil which, when once liability to it has been decreed, is not avoidable by any act of the party offending': *Province of the Law of Tort*, 200. Punishment is personal to the offender, and the courts will not entertain an action against another for indemnity: *Askey* v. *Golden Wine Co. Ltd.*, [1948] 2 All E.R. 35 at 38.

[2] It is true that in certain cases a court may have a power after conviction of the prisoner to award restitution of stolen goods to the true owner, but this function is given to criminal courts merely for administrative convenience.

[3] *Legal Duties*, 237: naturally these cannot be used as a formal test. Many acts which are intrinsically wrong are not crimes, and many crimes do not consist of acts which are intrinsically wrong: see C. S. Kenny, op. cit. 8 et seq.

[4] *General Principles of Criminal Law*, 213. From this premiss the learned writer draws the conclusion that no conduct which is merely negligent should involve criminal liability (p. 239). To apply this doctrine to Anglo-American law would force us to deny that 'public welfare offences' were crimes.

[5] In England and in the U.S.A. over 60 per cent of the total offences are concerned with violation of the traffic law.

duty to vote at a parliamentary election.[1] In these cases proof of *mens rea* would make the task of the Crown too difficult: moreover, no injustice is done in imposing a light fine even on a person who is morally innocent. The danger is that these offences may be confused with 'true crimes' where the penalty is serious and there is a real stigma attached to conviction.[2] It is in recognition of the fact that some crimes involve no moral wrongdoing that certain countries which prohibit the entry of convicted criminals limit the operation of the rule to such crimes as involve moral turpitude.

Historically the general test of a crime is the degree of activity of the community. Thus if a wrong is regarded as primarily a matter of compensation as between individuals, it is a private delict. If the community itself takes steps to punish the offender, it is a public delict. The test is—if the victim does nothing or is compensated, will the community act? Hence, historically, intrinsic wrongfulness and social expediency are the tests which each community applies— but wide are the variations between the opinions of primitive men and the world of today. Moreover, we must add the pragmatic test that the community must consider that the wrong can be satisfactorily dealt with by punishment. It is wrongful to think evil of one's neighbour, to covet, to plan a seduction—but the law, in general, confines its attention to conduct.

Dr. Allen distinguished between 'public' and 'private' crimes in the sense that some offences primarily injure specific persons and only secondarily the public interest, while others directly injure the public interest and affect individuals only remotely.[3] There is a broad distinction along these lines, but differences naturally arise in the application of any such test. The learned author finds that out of 331 indictable English offences 203 are public wrongs and 128 private wrongs.

In crime, therefore, we find that the normal marks are that the State has power to control the procedure, to remit the penalty, or to inflict punishment. Many crimes also are wrongs against particular individuals only indirectly if at all. Thus we see that special rules apply because the State is one of the parties to the relationship— there is the power of the State to punish and the liability of the prisoner to be affected. Hence criminal law is correctly placed under the heading of public law.

---

[1] In Australia voting is compulsory in certain cases.   [2] *Infra*, § 82.
[3] *Legal Duties*, 249.

The criminal law is an interesting field in which to test the tenets of functional jurisprudence. The determination of what conduct should be termed criminal illustrates the relationship between law and morals; the imposition of strict liability in some cases shows the demands of social convenience; the analysis of *mens rea* reveals a serious lack of a logical approach; the imposition of prohibition in the United States shows that there are effective limits to the criminal law in action; the relative failure of the law to decrease the extent of crime shows how much more research is necessary before there can be increased detection and improved methods of 'treatment' of those convicted. Functional jurisprudence cannot proceed faster than the social sciences in solving these problems.[1]

§ 79. Theories of Punishment

Crime is man's second fear. A third of the people of America are afraid to walk alone at night in their communities.[2] Moreover, the intensity of the problem is increasing. In 1901, 80,962 crimes were recorded by the police in the United Kingdom: by 1965 the figure had risen to 1,133,382.[3] Even allowing for the growth of population and for the greater efficiency of the police force in recording crime, the increase is staggering. In the United States, taking 1940 as an index number of 100, the index rose to 165 by 1952.

There are many theories concerning the justification of punishment, but only typical approaches to this problem can be dealt with here. It is clear that the philosophy of punishment will affect the actual standards of liability laid down by the law. If punishment is based on an ethical desire to make men better, then a subjective theory of liability should be adopted. If punishment is designed to protect society from certain acts, then punishment may be inflicted where there is no moral guilt.

Is punishment an end in itself or a means to an end? Some theories look to the past—e.g. those that emphasize either the need to take vengeance on the wrongdoer or the necessity for expiation or retribution. The preventive theory concentrates on the prisoner, but seeks to prevent him offending again in the future. The reformative theory sees in the readjustment of the prisoner to the demands of society

---

[1] The problem of the relationship of crime and sin is discussed *supra*, § 37 (4).
[2] N. Morris and G. Hawkins, *The Honest Politician's Guide to Crime Control*, ix.
[3] McClintock and Avison, *Crime in England and Wales*, 23.

the greatest need of the criminal law. The deterrent theory emphasizes the necessity for protecting society, for so treating the prisoner that others will be deterred from breaking the law.[1] No system of law adheres entirely to any one theory. Even primitive law, apparently based on vengeance, is also built on the hope of deterring others. A successful reform of the prisoner will prevent him from offending again. On the other hand, the easiest way to prevent a prisoner from offending again is to hang him, but this can scarcely be called a reformative method.

The theories of expiation depend on moral doctrines which go beyond the limits of the law. It is not suggested that criminal law can or should be entirely divorced from the moral views of a particular community, but ethics must take a more subjective viewpoint than is possible for the law. Many ethical wrongs are not crimes at all and, conversely, the State often condemns acts which are free of ethical guilt.[2] It is not the task of the State to punish sin, but only to adopt measures against certain social dangers. Any attempt to enforce an ethical code in its entirety by the crude compulsion of the criminal law is foredoomed to failure. The more that science examines the mainsprings of human action, the more forcibly do we feel the strength of Christ's maxim, 'Judge not that ye be not judged'. If expiation be the reason for punishment, then a prisoner should be convicted only where he is ethically responsible for the act. Whether the will be free or not, it is now recognized that environment, heredity, and physical factors play a greater part in the urge to crime than our forefathers dreamed of.[3] How much of our administration of criminal law would stand an ethical searchlight? Clearly law must act to protect society, but it should not claim too lofty a justification for acts the reason for which is necessity rather than morality.[4]

Some forms of the retributive theory emphasize that punishment should be inflicted not merely in order to attain certain ends, but

---

[1] Cf. the sentence in *R*. v. *Blake*, [1961] 45 Cr. App. Rep. 292 at 298: 'This sentence had a threefold purpose. It was intended to be punitive, it was designed and calculated to deter others, and it was meant to be a safeguard to this country'—per Hilbery J. in considering an appeal in a spying case. There was a decrease in drunken driving cases after the new legislation in 1967.

[2] Ignorance of the law is no excuse. Some statutory crimes do not require *mens rea*. It is no defence that the accused considered it his moral duty to perform the act.

[3] *Infra*, § 80.

[4] Jerome Hall strongly attacks this utilitarian approach. He considers that punishment should be based only on moral culpability—this would exclude liability for negligence: *General Principles of Criminal Law*, 239.

solely because the prisoner has committed a crime. If an island community was about to dissolve, its duty (so it is said) would be first to execute the convicted murderers in prison. The retributive theory is not, of course, the narrow theory of vengeance, but rather the doctrine that the wrong done by the prisoner can be negated only by the infliction of the appropriate punishment. The community as a whole places emphasis on the retributive theory, at least where certain crimes are concerned; a feeling of outrage demands satisfaction and, if the penalty imposed by the courts is not considered sufficiently harsh, there is a danger of lynch law. But 'the fuller becomes our insight into the springs of human conduct, the more impossible does it become to maintain this antiquated doctrine (of retribution)'.[1] Modern criminal law must seek another basis, whatever may be the view of religion or morality.

Today the usual legal approach is utilitarian, for it is recognized that the law cannot attempt to carry out all the dictates of religion or morality, but can enforce only that minimum standard of conduct without which social life would be impossible. The law must certainly protect society, and its rules cannot, of course, be determined without reference to moral values. But the object of the criminal law is not to reform men's hearts but to stamp out courses of conduct which either offend the minimum ethic or are socially inexpedient. Punishment must be directed both to deterring others from breaking the law and to readjusting the attitude of the offender to the demands of social life. Norval Morris writes that every criminal law system except one 'has deterrence as its primary and essential characteristic'.[2] But even a utilitarian approach does not mean that we can ignore the inner springs of human conduct, for punishment based on a real understanding of the mind of the particular criminal is more likely to be effective than that which metes out the same punishment for the same acts irrespective of the individual's character.

The tendency in the past has been to emphasize the *wrongful act*

---

[1] W. P. McDougall, *Social Psychology*, 12. Cf. Sir Samuel Hoare, introducing the Criminal Justice Bill, 342 *H.C. Debates* 282 (29 Nov. 1938), where he points out that he is trying to approach these problems principally 'from the angles of prevention and reformation. In a scheme of this kind there is no place for the remnants of a period that looked at the treatment of crime principally from the angles of retribution. I am therefore proposing to sweep away the remnants of former dispensations, now little more than the stage properties of Victorian melodrama: penal servitude, hard labour, ticket-of-leave, the name criminal lunatic.'

[2] 33 *Univ. of Chicago L. R.* (1966), 631. The exception is Greenland.

of the prisoner, and to assume that the traditional methods of treatment achieve good results. Seventy years ago Holmes J. asked: 'What have we better than a blind guess to show that the criminal law in its present form does more good than harm?'[1] Today skilled workers are examining the problem in an endeavour to discover the real effect of different methods of punishment. Modern criminology considers that the *personality* of the offender is as important as his *act* and emphasizes that the wrongdoer is not only a criminal to be punished but a patient to be treated.[2] The cry is for individualization of the penalty, not to let the punishment fit the crime, but the personality of the criminal.

Thus it is argued that the real test of criminality should be the extent to which the prisoner is endangering society, his act being treated as an index to his personality rather than as that alone which is deserving of punishment.[3] Some cases graphically show the weakness of our present methods. Thus in 1937, a man was convicted of rape. He was a psychopath, but not insane. After serving a sentence of five years, he was convicted of molesting two young girls. He was released after one year and then committed rape and murder, for which he was electrocuted.[4] If we fully applied the test of the danger of the personality of the prisoner, it would change the principles on which the severity of the punishment is calculated, for a relatively innocuous act may be done by one who is in fact a danger to society, whereas a serious crime may be committed by one who is unlikely to repeat the wrong. If we put all the emphasis on the likelihood of the prisoner's offending again, we would reach results very different from those of the orthodox system which grades penalties merely by a consideration of the act that was done and the harm that resulted. In the case of a lawyer or a doctor the real punishment is not the imprisonment, but his exclusion from the professional brotherhood, and, even without imprisonment, he is less likely to offend again than one who suffers no such loss. Ferri suggests that no doctor would fix rigidly in advance a patient's stay in hospital—his stay is

---

[1] (1897) in *Collected Legal Papers*, 188.

[2] In the medical sense treatment covers both cure and precautions against infection. Few today are likely to ignore the necessity for the treatment of the prisoner to be such as to deter others from following the example of the prisoner. Cf. P. Vinogradoff, *Historical Jurisprudence*, i. 59. *R.* v. *Ford*, [1969] 1 W.L.R. 1703, is an interesting case. Two accused pleaded guilty to the same offence. One was regarded as incorrigible and was sentenced to twelve months: the other was given a longer sentence in the hope that there would be time for reform. On appeal the longer sentence was reduced to twelve months. Cf. T. B. Hadden, 23 *Camb. L. J.* (1965), 117.

[3] S. Glueck, *Crime and Justice*, 214–15.   [4] 18 *Univ. of Cin. L. R.* (1949), 167.

determined by the time it takes to effect a cure.[1] Similarly he urges that the legal provisions for the treatment of criminals should be flexible enough to take into account the prisoner's response to treatment, or, in other words, the speed with which his reformation takes place. Baroness Wootton[2] has carried the modern theory furthest, in her thesis that the court should be confined to determining the facts and that punishment (or rather treatment) should be determined by a panel of experts who, as in the case of a doctor and a sick patient, could vary the treatment according to the progress of the prisoner.

There are several factors to be considered in assessing the practicability of such an approach. Firstly, it is not always easy to determine by a prisoner's conduct, when subject to observation, how he will behave when he is released. Secondly, there is the problem of the protection of individual liberties. In the case of disease, we are willing to enforce quarantine if necessary, but, save for such instances as leprosy, the periods of isolation are relatively short. Imprisonment raises more serious issues concerning private rights—thus liberalism feels that the power of the State to curb the liberty of wrongdoers must be curtailed and hence supports the rigid fixing of the maximum limits of punishment in each case. If an offender is incorrigible, should he be permanently detained, even if his only crime be larceny? The safeguarding of the liberty of the subject by stating in advance the maximum penalties involved in certain breaches of the law has its advantages.[3] C. S. Lewis has shown the danger of divorcing the criminal law entirely from morality.[4] The concept of danger to society, divorced from moral guilt, may lead to authoritarian interference with human liberty. The community would not tolerate deterrence as being the sole determinant of punishment. At a time of social fear, a judge may award a heavy sentence to a spy,[5] without raising resentment in the community—but it is otherwise with regard to more common offences. Illegal

---

[1] See *Relazione sul progetto preliminare di codice penale italiano* (1921); S. Glueck, 41 *Harv. L. R.* (1928), 453 at 469. See also a translation by J. I. Kelly and J. Lisle of Enrico Ferri's *Criminal Sociology* (1917). The Soviet theory also emphasizes that the social danger of the act should be the most important consideration—in this case, of course, the social danger being considered from the point of view of the proletariat: see J. Zelitch, *Soviet Administration of Criminal Law*, 366.   [2] 76 *L.Q.R.* (1960), 224.

[3] *Infra*, § 83, for the effect of the maxim *nulla poena sine lege.*

[4] *The Humanitarian Theory of Punishment*, 3 *Twentieth Century* (1949), 5; (1953) 6 *Res Judicatae*, 224, but see N. Morris and D. Buckle, *The Humanitarian Theory of Punishment, a Reply* (1953) 6 *Res Judicatae*, 231, and J. J. C. Smart (1954) 6 *Res Judicatae*, 368; C. S. Lewis (1954) 6 *Res Judicatae*, 519; H. L. A. Hart, *Changing Conceptions*, 205; P. Brett, *An Enquiry into Criminal Guilt*, 74.

[5] *R.* v. *Blake*, [1961] 3 All E.R. 125.

parking of motor cars would be much diminished if the penalty was the confiscation of the car, but no society of motor car owners would tolerate such a law.[1] Thirdly, the law treats an attempt as deserving of less punishment than a completed crime. Yet, if the consummation of the crime is prevented by causes beyond the control of the prisoner, an attempt reveals that the prisoner is as much a social danger as if the crime had been completed. But so imbued are we with the notion that the punishment must bear some measure to the injury caused, that, at first sight, it would seem unjust to treat an attempt as severely as a completed crime.[2] Fourthly, in addition to social danger, we must also consider moral blameworthiness. There are cases where it is expedient to create crimes which do not require *mens rea*, but these exceptions should be strictly limited. Unless the average man feels that there is an element of blame attachable to the offence, then it may become 'respectable' to be convicted and the criminal law may lose one of its deterrents. It may be necessary to have objective standards, but, if these are not related to the habits of the ordinary citizen, the standard set will probably be too high. Even from an objective standpoint it is necessary to consider *mens rea*, for a prisoner who commits a dangerous act accidentally is on the whole less likely to repeat his conduct than is one who acted intentionally. Fifthly, we can carry the theory too far. If a person commits a murder under extraordinary psychological stress which is most unlikely to recur, then that murderer is hardly a future danger to society. But few would suggest that punishment should therefore be waived. Lastly, it must be remembered that in an imperfect world the law must provide an outlet for that resentment which arises against the perpetrator of certain outrages. If modern schemes are to be successfully applied, then a cautious and tentative beginning must be made with crimes that do not arouse too much public indignation.[3] But even in these cases we must remember that the treatment should not only readjust the prisoner, but be such as to deter others. If it were proved that all tendency to steal could be removed by a grant of £20,000, would that 'treatment' encourage or discourage *others* from committing larceny? Psycho-analysis has shown that even the law-abiding citizen is helped in the struggle against his anti-social desires by the spectacle of others being punished for doing that which he

---

[1] H. L. A. Hart, *Punishment and Responsibility*, 76.
[2] See the discussion by Rupert Cross, 81 *L.Q.R.* (1965), 205.
[3] J. Hall, *Theft, Law and Society*, 293, 298. The author suggests petty larceny as a useful field for experimentation.

consciously or unconsciously desires to do.[1] There is thus a conflict in each case between the needs of a particular prisoner and the social interest in enforcing the law. What may be the best treatment for a criminal may conflict with the necessity of deterring others.[2] Moreover, the 'social danger' school should be modest, for our methods of treatment do not yet win the success which they should. Until we can be more exact in methods of treatment, we should not divorce the criminal law too far from community standards.[3] The real problem is therefore to combine the deterrent and reformative theories in due proportions. The expense of research into proper methods and of experimental treatment will be high—but what is the cost of crime to the community? To readjust a prisoner so that he may play a useful part in social life is in the long run a cheaper method than that of periodical sentences or life imprisonment.

Among lawyers, the deterrent theory was, until recently, the most popular, and much scorn was sometimes poured on the 'weak' or 'sentimental' approach of those who advocate reform. It is true that some reformative theories are marked by lack of realism, by sentiment, and show no evidence of contact with the criminal classes, but the modern approach to criminology is as coldly scientific as it can be. The criminal is a danger both to society and to himself, and the criminologist urges only that the most scientific methods be used to remove this danger.[4] Few modern writers fail to recognize the need to deter others. On the other hand, to regard deterrence as the sole end of the criminal law is a confession either of defeatism or of cynicism.

One of the best deterrents is that a wrongdoer's chance of discovery and conviction is fairly high. The percentage of crime 'cleared up' in England is estimated by McClintock and Avison[5] as follows:

Year	Percentage	Year	Percentage
1938	50·1	1955	48·7
1945	41·3	1964	39·6
1954	49·2	1965	39·2

[1] F. Alexander and H. Staub, *The Criminal, the Judge and the Public.*

[2] F. B. Sayre, 43 *Harv. L. R.* (1930), 689 at 720; Barbara Wootton, *Social Science and Social Pathology* (1959), 336.

[3] N. Morris and Howard, *Studies in Criminal Law,* 168.

[4] Thus Dr. R. D. Gillespie writes that in so far as the psychiatrist forgets society, he is ceasing to be a psychiatrist, and lapsing into sentimentalism: 7 *Medico-Legal and Crim. R.* (1939), 153 at 154.

[5] *Crime in England and Wales,* 93. Such figures cannot be entirely relied on, for some alleged crimes reported to the police may not have taken place, and there may be many

The detection rate varies for different offences, from 95 per cent for homicide to 25 per cent for larcenies. Where there is an 'even chance' of escaping conviction, many may be willing to take the risk who would not do so if punishment followed as certainly as night follows day.

Russia divides crime into two classes: minor crimes and those which strike at the safety of the State or are the result of *bourgeois* motives. Those guilty of offences of the latter description are harshly treated, and Russian jurists scornfully dismiss as out-moded liberalism any guarantee to the prisoner of rights which might conflict with the safety of the State. Thus trial by jury is distrusted, as a jury might not always decide in accordance with the general directions of state policy. But those who are guilty of minor crimes are tried in the People's Court, and the treatment in prison is built on modern reformative methods. Many persons are placed in open or semi-open camps: in some cases prisoners are placed in labour communes, with a village life which is as much as possible like that of free men.[1] There is little prison stigma and, since many prisoners receive a technical training, they have, on release, no difficulty in securing employment. But the accessible data are not yet full enough to make a final assessment of the result—such literature as is available shows very diverse pictures. This is clearly brought out by the analysis of Zile who points out that American writers on Soviet law have by and large tended to find what they wanted to find.[2]

But the real problems of punishment cannot be finally disposed of until the question of the causes of crime has been discussed.[3]

§ 80. THE CAUSES OF CRIME

The question 'What is the cause of crime?' has been called a non-question. We do not look for a cause of all disease, we analyse the cause of each specific disease.

Criminology is a fairly new science and is in a rapid state of development. Moreover, it is a 'parasitic' science and its conclusions

crimes which for various reasons are not reported to the police at all. For an examination of the method by which criminal statistics are compiled, see L. Radzinowicz, 56 *L.Q.R.* (1940), 483; see C. H. Rolph, *Common Sense about Crime and Punishment* (1961), ch. ii; Barbara Wootton, *Social Science and Social Pathology* (1959), 21–2.

[1] See D. N. Pritt, in *Twelve Studies in Soviet Russia* (ed. M. I. Cole), 145.
[2] Z. L. Zile, 70 *Col. L. R.* (1970), 194.
[3] The same crime may be committed by very different types. Thus the receiver of stolen goods may be one who buys cheaply for his own use and has never offended before, or one who makes a profession of the practice. For a functional study of the problems of larceny and receiving, see Jerome Hall, *Theft, Law and Society*.

are dependent on the further development of psychology, psychiatry, and sociology. Much more research is necessary before a criminologist can draw sound conclusions. Indeed, the apparently chaotic list of what are alleged to be causal factors does not at the moment provide much assistance in the prevention of crime. It is not quite true to say that statistics can be found to prove anything, but it is alarming to see the conflict between different statistical studies of causative factors.[1] This is strongly borne out by even a casual reading of Sutherland and Cressey's work.[2] One great problem is that criminal statistics, being collected on different bases, are not really comparable as between one country and another: and even within one country, methods of collection have varied over the years. Moreover, our study of the criminal classes is limited to those convicted—those who escape arrest are not known as criminals—and, as Baroness Wootton points out, in much research work there is a devastating lack of precision in the terms used.[3]

The acts termed criminal by the law have nothing (or little) in common save that a statute or the common law has prohibited them —crimes vary from deliberate murder to not having a dustbin of the appropriate pattern. Hence we need to break the subject up into its component factors, for the incoherent mass of the criminal law cannot be dealt with as a whole from the angle of causation.

(a) Physical Causes

Lombroso believed that criminality was closely related to the possession of certain physical qualities. From his examination of prisoners he believed that certain physical characteristics revealed a tendency to crime in their possessor and that, if several of these characteristics were found in one person, he belonged to a criminal type.[4] Crime was an atavistic phenomenon. Dr. Goring, however, subjected these conclusions to a detailed examination,[5] correlating his results with statistics obtained from the non-criminal population, and he found greater physical differences between the English and the Scottish than between convicts and observers of the law. He concluded that there is no such thing as a 'physical criminal type'. The most recent detailed examination of the biological characteristics

---

[1] Morris and Hawkins, *The Honest Politician's Guide to Crime Control* (1969), 241.
[2] *Principles of Criminology* (1955).
[3] *Social Science and Social Pathology*, 170.
[4] *Criminal Man* (ed. G. L. Ferrero).   [5] *The English Convict.*

of criminals is that of Hooton,[1] who devoted twelve years to tabulating and measuring 17,000 American cases. The criminals were divided into racial stocks and the conclusions were checked by comparative samples taken from the non-criminal population. The conclusion was that, while there was no evidence to support the conclusion of Lombroso that the criminal is in general a primitive man at odds with society, nevertheless the criminal was, on the whole, poorer in physique and organic adaptability. Hence the result of the statistics collected is only that the more numerous and accentuated are the signs of organic inferiority in any individual, the more likely he is to indulge in crime. This is far removed from any doctrine that our physical characteristics inevitably predispose us to crime, for Hooton recognizes that sociological, as well as biological, factors play their part. Moreover, the criminal in custody is largely drawn from the lower economic strata in which the position is unfavourable for physical development. Females have a lower rate of criminality than males. If we accept Hooton's thesis, it should follow that females are biologically superior to males.

While it is impossible to find general physical characteristics which mark all the criminal population, nevertheless, in an individual case, a physical condition may be a contributory cause of crime. Medical research on the ductless glands reveals what tremendous changes in personality may take place because of their disordered functioning. It is, however, rash to conclude from a few striking cases either that character is solely determined by physical causes, or that such cases represent more than a small percentage of the criminal population. But it is reasonable to admit that, where the cause of crime can be demonstrated to be due to physical disease, a hospital and not a prison should be the answer of the law.[2]

Age and sex, however, are physical characteristics, and the influence of these is reflected in the statistics. For some years, the most dangerous age bracket for males was thirteen to fourteen years, and for females fifteen to seventeen, but by 1965, the age was fourteen for both sexes.[3] In the United Kingdom, over half of those convicted of

---

[1] *The American Criminal; Crime and the Man.* Cf. W. Norwood East, 30 *Minn. L. R.* (1946), 435. Serious criticisms have been made of the statistical techniques used by Hooton. His control groups were rather small and were not a random sample.

[2] Compare the case of males with an extra γ chromosome—R. G. Fox, 2 *Aust. and N.Z. J. of Criminology* (1969), 5. Exaggerated claims have been made for the causative effect of the extra chromosome in inducing crime, and more research is necessary before dogmatism is justified.

[3] Barbara Wootton, *Crime and the Criminal Law*, 10.

indictable offences are under twenty-one years.[1] The chances of a person being convicted drop after the age bracket of greatest criminality.

With regard to sex, Baroness Wootton points out that no serious attempt has been made to explain why the ratio of male criminality to female is 8:1.[2] In countries where the female is not emancipated, the ratio of feminine crime is exceedingly slight.[3]

It has often been argued that race is a cause of crime. To the native born American it was a convenient hypothesis that immigrants were responsible for a large proportion of crime. The figures show, however, that while the first generation of immigrants tend to follow the pattern of criminal behaviour of the country they have left, their contribution to the criminal problem is lower than that of the local born: the children of the migrants begin to adopt the American criminal pattern, and by the third generation, there is no significant statistical difference between the grandchildren of the immigrant and the local population.[4]

Crime rates of the negro are high, but this does not necessarily demonstrate biological causation. If the figures are analysed, the rates vary from one district to another, and are lower as educational status rises. Depressed economic environment at least plays some part.

(b) Mental Factors

There have been many rash assumptions made as to the influence of mental weakness. 'Enthusiasm not uncommonly outruns discretion and it would be a great misfortune if the psychiatric approach to crime became discredited by irresponsible exponents unaware, perhaps, of the complexity of the problems involved.'[5] Before the war many investigators maintained that weak intelligence was one of the major causes of crime, but recent researches have shown that there is less difference between the criminal class and the general population than was formerly believed.[6]

[1] Op. cit.   [2] Op. cit. 6.
[3] The proportion in Algiers is alleged to be 2,744 males to 1 female.
[4] E. H. Sutherland and D. R. Cressey, *Principles of Criminology* (1955), ch. viii.
[5] W. N. East and W. H. de B. Hubert, *The Psychological Treatment of Crime*, 157.
[6] R. H. Gault, *Criminology*, 123. East and Hubert, op. cit. 7, think that the 'normal group would include at least 80 per cent of offenders'. 'More recent psychological evidence has conclusively demonstrated that inferior mentality is neither the specific cause nor the outstanding factor in crime and delinquency': J. C. Coleman, cited Sutherland and Cressey, op. cit. 120. Even if a high percentage of delinquent children come from the ranks of the mentally defective, the real cause is the failure to adjust to school or society.

It must not be supposed, however, that the work of the psychiatrist is limited to those with a low level of intelligence. Possession of the highest intellectual power is no guarantee against crime. Mental conflict, a neurosis, or an unconscious feeling of guilt may lead astray one with a high intelligence quotient. Where certain types of personality are concerned, ordinary methods of punishment may well fail, unless psychotherapy removes the mental factors which are the real cause of the delinquency. The psychopath, for example, may not be insane as the law defines that term, but may benefit greatly from understanding treatment. The psychologist would be the first to admit that society must be protected from such persons and that in many cases there may be little prospect of successful treatment.[1] But a wider power to order psychiatric treatment would add to, and not diminish, the effectiveness of the law. The practical difficulty is to discover a method which will isolate the cases in which such treatment will be useful, for to order psychological examination of all offenders would be impracticable. But great advances are now being made, as knowledge of the working of the human mind increases. Without accepting the views of determinism, it is clear that the will is not as free as was once thought—a bad environment or wrong handling may predispose to crime. Moreover, the line between the sane and the insane is not as clear cut as the law supposes, and even if we adopt an air of cautious reserve towards some of the more startling claims of the psycho-analyst, it must be admitted that there are many cases where ordinary punishment will not protect society and will not 'cure' the offender.[2]

Insanity. The legal test of insanity is still based on the advice which was given by the judges to the House of Lords in 1843.[3] English law puts all the emphasis on the cognitive factor: did the prisoner understand the nature and quality of his act? If he did, did he know that what he was doing was wrong? If a prisoner's act falls outside these tests, it matters not how weak or diseased the will may

---

[1] East and Hubert, op. cit., *Mental Abnormality and Crime* (ed. Radzinowicz).
[2] Dr. D. Carroll in 8 *Medico-Legal and Crim. R.* (1940), 182. See A. A. Bartholomew, 'The Forensic Psychiatrist's Place in Correction', 3 *Aust. and N.Z. J. of Crim.* (1970), 83.
[3] *R. v. M'Naghten* (1843), 10 Cl. & F. 200; H. Barnes, 8 *Camb. L. J.* (1944), 300; L. A. Tulin, 32 *Col. L. R.* (1932), 933. Dr. R. D. Gillespie has described the rules from the angle of a psychiatrist as 'both theoretically fantastic and practically unacceptable'—7 *Medico-Legal and Crim. R.* (1939), 153 at 159; Sir Roland Burrows, K.C., has retorted that some doctors commit themselves to definitions of insanity which would make it almost impossible to find a really sane person—op. cit. 163. For a spirited defence of the *M'Naghten* rules, see J. Hall, *General Principles of Criminal Law*, ch. xiv.

be—thus irresistible impulse is no defence.[1] Many judges have urged that the more powerful the influence, the more certain should be the punishment. 'If an influence be so powerful as to be termed irresistible, so much the more reason is there why we should not withdraw any of the safeguards tending to counteract it', said Bramwell B.[2] Similarly Lord Hewart referred to the fantastic and subversive theory of uncontrollable impulse.[3] Yet many psychiatrists recognize that one under the control of an irresistible impulse is not really responsible for what he is doing. The High Court of Australia has suggested that, where there is evidence of uncontrollable impulse, it should be carefully explained to the jury, as it may provide reason for inferring lack of capacity to understand the nature of an act or to know that it was wrong.[4] This would be an effective way of broadening the spirit of the M'Naghten rules. Many are rightly dubious of the wisdom of leaving the decision of such an issue as irresistible impulse to a jury; but this argument really shows that the jury is not a fit body to determine the question of sanity rather than that the doctrine of insanity should be narrowed for the benefit of laymen. The Queensland Criminal Code recognizes as a defence both the cognitive and the conative aspects—incapacity to control as well as incapacity to understand are relevant.[5]

If a person suffers from insane delusions, the law adopts a simple but rather quaint test—provided that the act would be innocent if the delusion represented a true state of facts, then the prisoner escapes. If the act would be a crime, even if the delusion pictures reality, then the prisoner is guilty. The absurdity of this test is that it assumes that a man's mind may be divided up into separate compartments, and that a delusion may exist in one, while the other compartments are perfectly sane.[6] What is really significant is the unhealthy state of mind which allows an insane delusion to flourish—the connection between the delusion and the act may be quite irrational but nevertheless exist.

---

[1] *A.-G. for South Australia* v. *Brown*, [1960] 1 All E.R. 734, and see the note of this case and of the Australian developments by P. Brett, in 23 *Mod. L. R.* (1960), 545.

[2] *R.* v. *Haynes* (1859), 1 F. & F. 666 at 667.

[3] *R.* v. *Kopsch* (1925), 19 Cr. App. Rep. 50.

[4] *Sodeman* v. *R.* (1936), 55 C.L.R. 192: per Latham C.J. at 203–4; per Dixon J. at 214–15; per Evatt J. at 227. Actually statistics show that the jury must treat the rules in a broad fashion. Thus in England, of 77 persons arrested for murder, 27 were convicted, 16 found guilty but insane, 15 were found insane on arraignment: *Home Office Criminal Statistics* (1948), Cmd. 7428.   [5] § 27.

[6] As J. F. Stephen puts it, the prisoner is treated as a sane man under a mistake of fact for which he is not to blame: *H.C.L.* ii. 157.

The doctrine of 'diminished responsibility' was introduced by the Homicide Act of 1957. When capital punishment was in force, this provided an alleviation of penalty, when it could be shown that the accused suffered from such an abnormality of mind as to substantially impair his mental responsibility for his act. Lady Wootton has incisively examined the case law in this respect.[1] The rules of insanity were difficult to apply,[2] but to ask the jury to rule on diminished responsibility was to give to them a question which even the experts found unanswerable. She takes the heroic step of suggesting that the concept of responsibility should be allowed to wither away. Courts would be concerned with finding the prisoner guilty of the prohibited act. Questions of insanity, diminished responsibility, and moral guilt would be considered only after conviction and be relevant to treatment only. This is further discussed below.[3]

It may be noted here, however, that if the criminal law is entirely divorced from moral values and if mental health is regarded merely as adjustment to community demands, then deviant liberals under Hitler's regime were fit subjects for criminal treatment.[4] Is mental health to be determined by the psychiatrist without any thought of moral values?

(c) Regionalism and Economic Causes

Crime rates vary, not only from one nation to another, but also are normally higher in urban than in rural areas. The United States has a fire-arms homicide rate of 2·7 per 100,000 persons, whereas that of the United Kingdom is 0·05 per cent.[5] In many countries there is a greater crime ratio in the large towns than in rural areas. Thus per 100,000 of the population London had a rate in 1965 of 3,378 and the small counties 1,719.[6] If we take a particular city and draw a series of concentric circles based on the centre, crime rates decrease as we

---

[1] 76 L.Q.R. (1960), 224.
[2] Barbara Wootton points out that, for all its faults, the M'Naghten rule could be more easily applied than any doctrine of an impaired will: *Social Science and Social Pathology*, 233.
[3] § 81. S. H. Kadish, 26 *Camb. L. J.* (1968) at 285, reads Barbara Wootton's proposal as abolishing *mens rea* in the widest sense (the mental element required for a particular crime), but this is questionable, as she states: 'I am not, of course, arguing that all crimes should immediately be transferred into the strict liability category. To do so would in some cases involve formidable problems of definition—as, for instance, in that of larceny': *Crime and the Criminal Law*, 56–7.
[4] Barbara Wootton, *Social Science and Social Pathology*, 221.
[5] Morris and Hawkins, 10 *Midway* (1969).
[6] McClintock and Avison, *Crime in England and Wales*, 74.

get to the periphery.[1] Criminality rates may sometimes be linked to slum areas, but we find also in new communities, e.g. Housing Commission development with high rise flats, that the incidence of crime is higher than in the normal suburb. The type of community is thus important, as much criminality is behaviour learned from associates.

Statistics are not yet complete enough to discover any precise relationship between poverty and crime. Indigence may afford a contributing cause. A millionaire, who is not abnormal mentally, is not likely to steal a hundred pounds, whereas one pressed by hunger has strong motives to do so. But there are crimes other than those against property and to these the wealthy as well as the poor may be tempted. Glueck writes that in the juvenile delinquent group 68 per cent of the families were in 'marginal economic circumstances', and in the adult criminal group 56 per cent of the families.[2] But these figures would need to be tested by comparison with other data, e.g. the proportion of families in the whole population that lived in such poor conditions and reliable comparative figures are not yet available.[3] At least it may be said that it is now recognized that the attack on the problem of crime must be accompanied by an attempt to raise the general standard of life both in a material and an intellectual sense. If we confine our attention to indictable offences, then nine out of every ten criminals are convicted for an offence against property. This does not, of course, show that poverty was a factor in each of these cases, but it illustrates the great concern of the law with the protection of property. Whenever an economic depression occurs, the number of criminal offences increases.

(d) Alcoholism

While we cannot accept the easy answer that consumption of alcohol is *the* cause of crime, a study in Victoria showed that out of 1,836 prisoners sentenced to imprisonment for three months or more, 17·6 per cent were chronic alcoholics and 25·8 per cent were under the influence—a total of 43 per cent.[4]

---

[1] Ibid. 138.

[2] *Crime and Justice*, 189.

[3] In England in 1965, out of 1·1 million indictable crimes known to the police, 95·8 per cent related to offences against property: McClintock and Avison, *Crime in England and Wales*, 36.

[4] A. Bartholomew, 1 *Aust. and N.Z. J. of Crim.* (1968), 70.

(e) Conclusion

It is impossible to regard crime as the result of any one cause. Crime is the result of character, but what is character? Is it mainly a resultant of heredity or of environment or do both play an equal role? The theory of evolution is more easily understood if we accept the view that parents transmit to their children the characteristics which they have acquired, but no conclusive biological evidence has yet been produced to justify this doctrine. In the human sphere especially it is difficult to distinguish what is due to heredity from what is the result of the environment in the early years of life, for in the normal case the parents determine the environment for the child. Moreover, there is sometimes great diversity in the characteristics of children of the same parents. Biology and psychology are only on the fringe of the problem of the inheritance of acquired characteristics and of the formation of character.[1]

What can be dogmatically stated is that, whatever is the precise role of the genetic factor, environment frequently predisposes to a criminal life. Maladjustment to society may easily follow from the wrong treatment of children by parents. No successful attack can be made on the problem of crime if the evils which threaten home life are not removed. But this is an issue which goes to the roots of the community life. Just as general health is necessary to the individual to make him strong enough to ward off disease, so a sound life in the body politic is the best preventive of crime. Poverty which makes home life miserable, friction between the parents which makes it intolerable, both influence adversely the children exposed to it. The most fruitful course for the community to pursue is to ensure as far as possible that the influences which surround the young are such as to adjust them to community life. But the statistics do not allow us to put forward any simple theory of causation of crime or any miraculous method of lessening its incidence.

§ 81. Modes of Punishment

A set punishment for a particular crime will not operate with equal effectiveness if the causes which led the first offender to break the law are different from those which induce the second offender.

---

[1] Interesting work has been done concerning the records of 'identical twins': J. Lange, *Crime as Destiny*, trans. Charlotte Haldane.

The more savage modes of punishment have gradually been abolished—physical torture is now happily rare. Few modern codes emphasize corporal punishment as a general sanction. In England corporal punishment is abolished save for those guilty of serious prison offences while serving their punishment.[1] In the last case, further imprisonment is not an effective deterrent to one who has already been sentenced for life. In the other cases, there is great difference of opinion. Is corporal punishment the effective deterrent it is claimed to be? Does it brutalize the prisoner?[2]

There has been a gradual decrease in the number of offences for which the penalty is death. In the time of George III there were at least 220 capital offences.[3] The agitation for reform was assisted by the bankers who realized that the sentence for forgery made it too difficult to secure a conviction.[4] Today a growing number urge that capital punishment should be entirely abolished, although some still support it as the appropriate penalty for murder and treason. In England, capital punishment was abolished in 1965 for an experimental period of five years,[5] and this was made permanent in 1970. In America it has recently been argued that the death penalty is unconstitutional as a cruel and unusual punishment.[6]

It is now realized that, if public opinion regards the punishment as out of all proportion to the nature of the offence, the law defeats its own object, since even the courts may encourage evasion of the law. There is no need to recall the pious perjury of juries—thus Joseph Court was indicted for stealing goods valued at £300 and the jury found him guilty of larceny of goods to the value of 39 shillings in order that the conviction should not carry with it the penalty of death.[7] The frequent spectacle of executions brutalizes a community, and pickpockets plied their trade under the shadow of the gallows during an execution which was intended to be a dread warning to malefactors.

---

[1] Prison Act, 1952. 15 & 16 Geo. V and 1 Eliz. II, c. 52, § 54 and Schedule 4.

[2] See *Report of the Departmental Committee on Corporal Punishment* (1938), Cmd. 5684, reviewed 2 *Mod. L. R.* (1938), 54; *Corporal Punishment: Report of the Advisory Committee on the Treatment of Offenders* (1960), Cmd. 1213; J. W. J. Edwards, *Corporal Punishment in Northern Ireland* (1956), *Crim. L. R.* 814; C. H. Rolph, *Common Sense about Crime and Punishment* (1961), ch. viii.

[3] L. Radzinowicz, *History of English Criminal Law*, 3–5.

[4] Ibid. 592.

[5] Murder (Abolition of Death Penalty) Act, 1965: see also the Home Office publication, *Murder 1957–1968*.

[6] A. J. Goldberg and A. M. Dershowitz, 83 *Harv. L. R.* (1970), 1773.

[7] J. Hall, *Theft, Law and Society*, 97.

Imprisonment of offenders, if enough offenders are caught and convicted, undoubtedly has a deterrent effect on many others, but it is impossible to be satisfied with the actual results to the criminal himself. McClemens J. has written: 'As each year passes, . . . I become more convinced of the sterile and crimogenic qualities of imprisonment.'[1] To quote an understatement by Sir Alexander Paterson: 'I gravely doubt whether an average man can serve more than ten continuous years in prison without deterioration.'[2] The percentage of persistent offenders is a sad commentary on the effectiveness of a prison sentence. In the U.S.A. the Wickersham Commission writes that it would not be surprised to learn that 60 per cent of the persons received in prison are recidivists.[3] Although a large proportion of 'first-timers' are not convicted again, 'the probability of relapse increases with the number of previous sentences, and a substantial part of the prison population consists of a "stage army" of individuals who pass through the prison again and again'.[4]

There is, however, a welcome recognition of the need to individualize the penalty—not to let the punishment fit the crime, but the particular criminal.[5] Although the staple sanctions are still fine, imprisonment, and death, much research is being carried out and English penal policy over the last few years has been very 'bold, consistent and experimental'.[6] There is decreasing faith in the efficacy of imprisonment as a satisfactory method for all cases. Out of 100 punishments, the year 1900 shows 49 of incarceration, but by 1959 the figure had dropped to 14; in 1900 there were 17 cases of conditional releases, whereas in 1959 this method was used in 43

---

[1] 43 *A.L.J.* (1969), 358.

[2] *Memorandum to the Select Committee on Capital Punishment, 1930.*

[3] The *Report of the Persistent Offenders Committee* (1932), Cmd. 4090, states that in 1930, of the 39,000 sentences of imprisonment, 28,000 were imposed on persons who had previously been found guilty of offences: cited L. W. Fox, *The Modern English Prison*, 167. At 206, however, Fox points out that to get a true picture it is necessary to separate out the convictions for drunkenness which enormously raise the total of recidivists. Ignoring drunkards, in 1931, 51 per cent of the men and 47 per cent of the women were known to have been in prison before. In 1955, 35,000 recidivists came before the English courts; in 1965, the figure had risen to 90,000: McClintock and Avison, *Crime in England and Wales*, 247.

[4] 1932, Cmd. 4090. For a comparative survey see N. S. Timasheff, 30 *J. of Crim. Law and Crimin.* (1939), 455; G. K. Brown, 23 *Can. B. R.* (1945), 630; N. Morris, *The Habitual Criminal.*

[5] An interesting study of the sympathetic attitude of the courts to immigrants who may not fully understand the British way of life is that of F. O. Shyllon, 34 *Mod. L. R.* (1971), 135.

[6] L. Radzinowicz, 3 *Mod. L. R.* (1939), 127 and 75 *L.Q.R.* (1959), 381; *Penal Reform in England* (eds. L. Radzinowicz and J. W. C. Turner).

cases. Whipping fell from 7 to 0·2 per cent,[1] and by 1948 it had been abolished save for prison offences.

In the case of all offenders dealt with in the higher courts in 1965, 40 per cent were imprisoned, 20 per cent were sent for Borstal training to a detention centre or an approved school, 5 per cent were conditionally discharged, 17 per cent placed on probation, and 15 per cent fined.[2] 'The prison population has been thinned out by at least three quarters: from 145,000 before the First World War to 35,000.'[3]

It is hasty to say that, since the use of imprisonment is receding and the incidence of crime is increasing, the first fact is the cause of the second. 'A penal philosophy based on principles of reformation does not appear to have a direct connection with the upward trend in crime. Reformative measures, even today, are applied to only a small proportion of offenders found guilty.'[4]

One thing that has reduced the incidence of imprisonment is that it is generally recognized that the short prison sentence has many disadvantages and few counterbalancing benefits. The stigma of prison life causes loss of self-respect, the influence of other prisoners may corrupt what good there is, and the period is not long enough for the prison authorities to follow any constructive policy aimed at reform.[5] It is true that classification of prisoners attempts to avoid the worst results of moral pollution, but even the extensive schemes of modern prison administration cannot secure complete success. In 1948 this was recognized by extending the power to fine even to cases of felony.[6]

Yet, until more data are available, the imposition of sentences can depend only on the 'merest empiricism'.[7] The common law reliance on judge and jury has secured an impartial tribunal for the determination of the guilt of the prisoners, but it does not necessarily follow that this method should be used for the decision of the separate question of the type of treatment which should be applied to the prisoner. Glueck suggests that the trial judge should be aided in his deliberations on sentence by a board consisting of a psychiatrist or

[1] L. Radzinowicz, 55 L.Q.R. (1939), 273.
[2] The percentages have been rounded off: McClintock and Avison, *Crime in England and Wales*, 258.
[3] L. Radzinowicz, 75 L.Q.R. (1959) at 397.
[4] McClintock and Avison, op. cit. 60.
[5] 'The grim and costly cycle of law enforcement provides temporary alleviation without effecting a cure': *Victorian Report on Penal Establishments*, 5129/49.
[6] Criminal Justice Act, 1948, § 13: the power is in lieu of, or in addition to, any other punishment laid down.
[7] Dr. R. D. Gillespie, 7 *Medico-Legal and Crim. R.* (1939), 153 at 155.

psychologist and a sociologist or educational expert who would consider not only the individual needs of the prisoner but also the general interests of society.[1] Most modern systems, however, tend to leave the judge to his traditional methods but to require him to fix minimum and maximum limits to the sentence imposed, and so to leave room for discretion to be exercised by an expert board with power to determine the particulars of the correctional process whether by use of 'parole' or otherwise. Baroness Wootton suggests that the court should be confined to determining the facts, and that treatment of the convicted should be determined by a panel of experts.[2] Interesting comments on this proposal are made by Barry J., a judge with over twenty years' experience.[3]

Discharge is a method that is increasingly used. In England the court has power to discharge without penalty, if after considering all the circumstances it is felt to be expedient to do so. As an alternative, the court may discharge the defendant conditionally subject to his committing no offence for the next twelve months. If the prisoner commits no further offence during the set period he escapes punishment; but if he commits another crime, he also renders himself liable to a sanction for the first. In addition to being 'bound over', the prisoner may be placed under the care of a probation officer for three years. If the officer is skilled and energetic, and possesses the necessary understanding of human nature, he may be able to exercise a decisive influence by finding the prisoner a post and giving him warning of unfortunate associations before they are a cause of relapse.[4] There is power to fine for breach of a probation order

---

[1] *Crime and Justice*, 225–6. For examples of discrepancies in sentences in the U.S.A., see M. F. McGuire and A. Holtzoff, 20 *Boston Univ. L. R.* (1940), 423: for violation of the liquor laws during 1935, the average sentence of imprisonment imposed by one judge was 815 days, the average sentence imposed by another was 40 days. H. Mannheim, *The Dilemma of Penal Reform*, ch. vi; N. Morris, *Sentencing Convicted Criminals* (1953), 27 *A.L.J.* 186; H. E. Lane, *Illogical Variations in Sentences of Felons Committed to Massachusetts State Prison* (1941), 32 *J. Crim. Law and Criminology*, 171; Winifred A. Elkin, *The English Penal System*, 270–1; P. W. Tappan, *Crime, Justice and Correction* (1960), 441–6, 453–5; E. Green, *Judicial Attitudes in Sentencing*.

[2] *Supra*, § 80. The growing interest in the problem of sentencing is shown by the fact that the Vinerian Professor chose 'Paradoxes in Prison Sentences' as the title of his inaugural lecture: Rupert Cross, 81 *L.Q.R.* (1965), 205.

[3] *The Courts and Criminal Punishment* (1969), 41.

[4] Dr. East points out that of 2,311 people placed on probation, 70 per cent had not committed an indictable offence within 3 years: 8 *Medico-Legal and Crim. R.* (1940), 196. *Practical Results and Financial Aspects of Adult Probation in Selected Countries* (U.N. Department of Social Affairs, N.Y. 1954); M. Grünhut, *Probation and Related Measures* (1951); *The Results of Probation*, ed. L. Radzinowicz (1958)—this report of the Cambridge Department of Criminal Science gives 73·8 per cent success for adults and 62·4 per cent success for juveniles.

in addition to the sanction of being sentenced for the original offence.

Parole is conditional release from prison. In some states in America when a prisoner is approaching the end of the minimum sentence imposed, the prisoner automatically comes before a Board of Parole which has the power to release him under certain conditions. The prisoner, if released, is placed under the control of a parole officer whose function it is to afford such help as may be necessary or possible. In some cases the system has worked well, the main criticism being that too often parole boards are amenable to political pressure.

Corrective training and preventive detention are devised to afford protection to society from habitual offenders and to assure longer periods for reformative treatment. If a person not less than twenty-one years of age is convicted on indictment of an offence punishable with imprisonment for a term of two years or more and has been convicted since the age of seventeen on two previous occasions of offences punishable with such a sentence, the court may pass a sentence of corrective training. If the offender is over thirty and it is a fourth offence,[1] then the sentence may be preventive detention from five to fourteen years.[2]

Clinics may be necessary for the treatment of those who are guilty of certain sexual offences, e.g. in cases of indecent exposure imprisonment is rarely successful. Illinois has made it compulsory to refer all psychopathic criminal sexual offenders to a board of psychiatrists for examination and report,[3] and there is a growing use of the psychiatrist in progressive countries.[4] By the Criminal Justice Act, 1948, the court, in making a probation order, may require that the defendant shall submit for a period not exceeding twelve months to treatment by a duly qualified medical practitioner with a view to the improvement of the offender's mental condition.[5] The order may compel treatment as a resident patient. A court of summary jurisdiction may remand a convicted person in order to enable a medical report to be given on his mental condition.[6] In the hope of increasing the chance of successful treatment, criminal lunatic asylums are now to be called Broadmoor institutions and a criminal lunatic is to be termed a Broadmoor patient.[7] These

---

[1] The offences specified are those that create liability to imprisonment for two years or more.
[2] Criminal Justice Act, 1948, § 21. [3] 39 *Col. L. R.* (1939), 534.
[4] D. Carroll, 8 *Medico-Legal and Crim. R.* (1940), 182; L. S. Selling, 30 *Minn. L. R.* (1946), 416. [5] § 4. [6] § 26. [7] § 62.

changes may seem to some a mere matter of terminology but it is an important symptom of the revolutionary change that has taken place in the attitude of society towards the problem of the prevention of crime.

Juveniles. It is perhaps in the treatment of juvenile delinquents that the greatest strides have been made in the twentieth century. The importance of the problem is shown by the fact that in 1961 half of those found guilty of indictable offences were under twenty-one years of age.[1] The institution of juvenile courts introduced a new approach.[2] In America these courts frequently have psychiatrists attached to them, in order to deal with cases where the real cause of crime seems to be some maladjustment to society. If the juvenile delinquent can be examined at an early age, there is more chance of employing effective methods. Thus home influence, a nagging mother, the desire of the physically inferior to 'show off', favouritism shown by the parents to another child, lack of means of self-expression—any of these may be causes predisposing to crime. It is not suggested that all cases of juvenile delinquency are easily solved—the psychiatrist would be the first to admit that in many cases there is little prospect of success. But the results in more favourable cases justify the attempt to prevent youth from embarking on a life of crime.[3]

If we are to avoid sending juveniles to prison, other institutions must be created. As early as 1908 Borstal institutions were set up for those between the ages of 16 and 21 years, the object being to give mental, moral, physical, and industrial training of a strenuous kind.[4] The emphasis is put, not on repression, but on building up self-respect and self-reliance; as in other cases, what is really conclusive is not the system but the personality of those who control it. In 1929, 71 per cent of the lads whose first experience of institutional treatment was that of Borstal showed the success of the system; but of those who had already endured a prison sentence before entering Borstal only 55 per cent were made into satisfactory citizens.[5] These figures seemed to show the danger of prison for the young

---

[1] Barbara Wootton, *Crime and the Criminal Law*, 10.

[2] L. Page, *Crime and the Community*, 225 et seq.

[3] This is clearly recognized by the courts. Thus only 19 per cent of males convicted in England and Wales under the age of 21 of indictable offences were sentenced to imprisonment: of those over 21 the percentage is 70: 1948, Cmd. 7428. These figures are for courts higher than magistrates' courts.

[4] *Young Offenders Committee* (1927), Cmd. 2831, 95, cited L. W. Fox, *The Modern English Prison*, 181; see also S. Barman, *The English Borstal System*.

[5] Cited L. W. Fox, op. cit. 194; L. Page, *Crime and the Community*, 235.

offender, and a satisfactory measure of success for the Borstal method where it can operate on youths who are not already embittered by a prison sentence.[1]

The Criminal Justice Acts, 1948 and 1961, and the Homicide Act, 1957, pay particular attention to the punishment of juveniles. Sentence of death shall not be pronounced or recorded, if the prisoner was at the time of the offence under the age of eighteen years.[2] Courts of summary jurisdiction, of assize and of quarter sessions, cannot sentence to imprisonment a person under seventeen years.[3] This is subject to the overriding principle that no court shall sentence to imprisonment any person under twenty-one years unless it is of opinion that no other method of punishment is appropriate. Power is given to issue an Order in Council prohibiting courts of summary jurisdiction from imprisoning any person under twenty-one years of age. Where a person under twenty-one years is remanded or committed for trial, if under fourteen he shall be sent not to prison but to a remand home: if over fourteen and under seventeen, he shall be sent to a remand home unless the court certifies that he is of too unruly a disposition: if over seventeen he shall be sent to a remand centre if one is available.[4] All these measures show a laudable desire to save the juvenile from the contamination of imprisonment. As alternatives to prisons, detention centres are created for those between fourteen and twenty-one.[5] For those over seventeen the maximum period is six months if certain other conditions are satisfied; for others the maximum is three months. A milder penalty is to order the offender to be present at an 'attendance centre'. The hours of attendance are to be arranged so as not to interfere with school or working hours. It is a method by which the leisure of the offender is used for reformative treatment.[6]

Although it is not a 'punishment', the use of the caution by the police is a useful technique—this requires much tact and judgment in police circles. In 1965 nearly 28,000 cautions were given.[7]

[1] H. Mannheim and L. T. Wilkins, *Prediction Methods in Relation to Borstal Training* (1955, London, H.M.S.O.), 110–13; but the 'open' Borstals seem to have a better record than the closed; Winifred A. Elkin, *The English Penal System* (1957), 267, 273.

[2] § 9 (3) of the Homicide Act, 1957.

[3] § 17 of Criminal Justice Act, 1948, as amended by § 2 (2) of Criminal Justice Act, 1961.

[4] § 27 of Criminal Justice Act, 1948.

[5] § 4 of Criminal Justice Act, 1961.

[6] § 19 of Criminal Justice Act, 1948, as amended by the 1961 Act.

[7] McClintock and Avison, *Crime in England and Wales*, 155. The practice is mainly confined to juveniles.

The most satisfactory way to deal with the problem of crime is to take such preventive measures as are possible. One of the greatest achievements of the medical profession has been the preventive measures which have so greatly reduced the incidence of plagues which once were allowed periodically to ravage the community. An increase in the social services and a raising of the standard of life will help to prevent the ravages of those crimes the cause of which is economic. The making of life more interesting will do something to remove the motives of those who seek in crime satisfaction for that love of adventure which a 'respectable' life fails to give. The treatment by psychiatrists of those schoolchildren with an unsatisfactory adjustment to society may reduce the number of potential criminals. Preventive measures are expensive, but so is the cost of crime to the community. It has been estimated that in the years following the 1939–45 war, crime detection required an outlay for Britain of £24,000,000 a year.[1] But though these methods may help, we cannot hope to destroy crime any more than we hope to destroy disease. A weak character will fall in moments of great stress or temptation, and the most that can be done is to treat such cases in an enlightened and scientific manner, as a doctor does the sick. But the fundamental difference is that sickness is its own deterrent, whereas the law must not only 'cure' a criminal, but also deter others from pursuing a course which will result in ill-gotten profit.

§ 82. ANALYSIS OF CRIMINAL LIABILITY

The general maxim to which lip-service is paid is *actus non facit reum nisi mens sit rea.* On this basis the law requires both a wrongful act and a guilty mind. Few systems apply the maxim in a sense which would require ethical guilt. Thus ignorance of the law is, in general, no defence,[2] and the highest motive is not a justification for an infraction of the law.

German criminal law is much more developed than English law

---

[1] H. T. F. Rhodes, *The Criminals we Deserve.* In Canada it has been estimated that 188 recidivists cost the State four and a half million dollars: S. K. Jaffary, 27 *Can. B. R.* (1949), 1021.

[2] Most systems of law adopt this doctrine. An exception is the Ethiopian Penal Code issued in 1941. Penalties are remitted to some extent in favour of the weak and forgetful who are unable to keep on remembering the law, the poor man who is unable to know the law, and the foreigner who has never heard of it: even the countryman (who does not know the Amharic language) is not forgotten: 8 *J. of Crim. L.* (1944), 318. Cf. the Roman law doctrine of persons *permissum est ius ignorare.*

on its theoretical side and distinguishes various forms of *mens rea*.[1] First there is a fundamental distinction between *Vorsatz* (*dolus*) and *Fahrlässigkeit* (*culpa*). *Mens rea* requires both a will directed to a certain end and knowledge as to the consequences that will follow from a particular act.[2] Concrete examples will make the German approach clearer. A wishes to shoot B and sees him so far away that he thinks it is almost impossible to hit him. Nevertheless A attempts the shot and kills B. A is guilty of the gravest form of *mens rea* (so long as he realized that there was any possibility of causing death), for he deliberately intended the result and he desired it for itself.[3] If the prisoner reluctantly intends to kill his friend in order to marry the friend's wife and adopts means which he knows must bring about death, this may be described as *dolus directus*. Here knowledge of consequences is stronger than in the first instance, but the element of will is weaker since the death is not desired for itself. To English law, this distinction seems rather unnecessary. In the latter case the prisoner desires to bring about the death—why should the law worry as to the motives which led a wrongdoer to achieve this particular act? Few commit a crime for its own sake, but for other ends, and although the reason for which a crime is committed may be important in the case of treatment, nevertheless, so far as liability is concerned, is it necessary to distinguish between those who knowingly commit a breach of the criminal law?[4] A third degree of *mens rea* in German law is sometimes called *dolus eventualis*. For example, A has carnal knowledge of a girl not yet sixteen years of age: he is ignorant of her age, but is not willing to allow the possibility that she is under sixteen to deter him. On the other hand, if A wrongly came to the conclusion that she was sixteen, and so thought he was within the law, the Germans would term this conscious negligence—that is, the actor recognized the possibility that the act was wrongful, but committed it only because he thought it was lawful. It would be unconscious negligence if the actor did not realize at all that his act was wrongful. It is naturally rather difficult to draw a clear line between *dolus eventualis* and conscious negligence, for in both the prisoner is in a state of doubt. It is hard to say after the event whether he was willing to run the risk of his belief being unfounded.

---

[1] H. Mannheim, 17 *J. Comp. Leg.* (1935), 82, 236, to whose treatment the following paragraph is indebted.
[2] *Supra*, § 68.   [3] *Absicht.*
[4] This, at any rate, is the practical approach of the common lawyer; but German writers regard the English theory of *mens rea* as very undeveloped.

In English law, if the prisoner believed that the girl was over sixteen, that would be regarded as a mistake of fact; but the precise effect of this particular error upon the existence of *mens rea* has caused great dispute.[1]

One of the theoretical difficulties of German law is that the doctrine of *mens rea* is based on will, and yet negligence is treated as a form of *mens rea*. In criminal matters a subjective theory of negligence is, on the whole, adopted. There is normally, however, a lighter punishment if the *mens rea* consists of negligence alone, and for some crimes the graver forms of *mens rea* are essential.

In English law the test is rather more external. Firstly, the exact degree of subjective guilt required varies in the different offences and it would perhaps be more exact to talk of *mentes reae* than of *mens rea*.[2] Secondly, in some crimes the test of *mens rea* is objective and not subjective. Thirdly, there is an increasing number of crimes where *mens rea* is not required. To illustrate the first point, in bigamy it is a defence that the prisoner honestly thought her husband was dead,[3] whereas in a charge of abducting a girl under the age of sixteen, an honest and reasonable belief that the girl was over sixteen is no defence.[4] Lord Esher (then Brett J.), dissenting, thought that *mens rea* required an intent to commit a criminal offence, but the majority decision was that in this particular case such an intent was unnecessary. Some judges considered that an intent to commit a tort was sufficient, others that it was sufficient if the prisoner intended to commit a moral wrong even though he believed that he was not breaking the law.

Now let us discuss the second point—the use of an objective test. A court can judge the state of a man's mind only by making inferences from his conduct. We have already analysed intent into foresight of consequences and a desire to bring them about. Holdsworth writes: 'we must adopt an external standard in adjudicating upon the weight of evidence adduced to prove or disprove *mens rea*. That, of course, does not mean that the law bases criminal liability upon non-

---

[1] Cf. *R. v. Prince* (1875), L.R. 2 C.C.R. 154: this was a case of abduction and not of carnal knowledge.

[2] J. F. Stephen, *H.C.L.* ii. 95. But see J. W. C. Turner, 6 *Camb. L. J.* (1936), 31 at 38, and G. Williams, *Criminal Law, The General Part* (2nd ed.), chs. ii–v.

[3] *R. v. Tolson* (1889), 23 Q.B.D. 168; *R. v. Bonnor*, [1957] V.R. 227; *R. v. Broughton*, [1953] V.L.R. 572; and N. Morris, *The Burden of Proof in Bigamy* (1955), 18 *Mod. L. R.* 452, and cf. the prevailing rule in the U.S.A. as to strict liability for bigamy, see R. A. Anderson, *Wharton's Criminal Law and Procedure* (1957), vol. ii, §§ 705 and 720.

[4] *R. v. Prince* (1875), L.R. 2 C.C.R. 154.

compliance with an external standard. So to argue is to confuse the evidence for a proposition with the proposition proved by that evidence.'[1] Moreover, even if the circumstances are not such as to prove intent, a confession may make the prisoner liable—in this case the law does consider subjective factors.[2] In most crimes there is not any great difficulty. Larceny requires an intent permanently to deprive the owner of the chattel, and whatever may be the reasonable inference from the prisoner's conduct, if he can prove that he only wished to borrow the chattel, the offence is not committed. Rape or burglary cannot be accidentally or negligently committed —the very definition requires a subjective intent.[3] In *R.* v. *Steane*,[4] Lord Goddard emphasized that, where a particular intent is a necessary ingredient of an offence, the intent may be proved by the Crown by an external standard: but this may be rebutted by the prisoner by evidence of his real intent. Since the onus of proof is on the Crown, the jury must acquit if they are in doubt. In murder and manslaughter, however, the problem is more complicated. Thus in murder it is not necessary that the prisoner should actually desire that death should be a result of his act: if he foresees death as a likely consequence of his act he is liable. But the law goes farther than holding a man guilty for mere foresight without desire, for it may ask what would a reasonable man have foreseen had he been in the position of the prisoner? Once this criterion is applied, we may go far from a purely subjective test. 'Unlawful homicide with malice aforethought' may seem to define subjective requirements, but the 'arbitrary symbol'[5] of malice may be satisfied by proof that the prisoner intended only to hurt, but by means intrinsically likely to kill,[6] or even intended to do an act intrinsically likely to kill although with no purpose of inflicting any hurt at all. Turner considers that, with two exceptions,[7] in murder the jury must be satisfied that the prisoner foresaw that his conduct might cause the death of some

---

[1] *History of English Law*, iii. 374.

[2] J. Hall, *General Principles of Criminal Law*, 220–1.

[3] J. W. C. Turner, 6 *Camb. L. J.* (1936). 31 at 39: 'No one could reasonably contend that a man, in a fit of inadvertence, could make himself guilty of the following crimes ... arson, burglary, larceny, rape, robbery, perjury, breaking prison, conspiracy; or of incitement or attempt.'   [4] [1947] 1 All E.R. 813.

[5] C. S. Kenny, *Criminal Law* (15th ed.), 153. If A, intending to kill, aims a pistol at B but kills C, he is in English law guilty of the murder of C. In German law the killing of C is only regarded as a killing due to negligence—one that lacks the graver forms of *mens rea*. This illustrates the differences in approach between the two systems.

[6] Cf. *R.* v. *Halloway* (1628), Cro. Car. 131.

[7] Death caused in resisting arrest by an officer of justice and death caused in the commission of a felony involving violence.

person,[1] but many of the cases seem to be in conflict with this. It is true that in *Woolmington* v. *Director of Public Prosecutions*,[2] the Lord Chancellor said that throughout the web of the English criminal law one golden thread is always to be seen—that the Crown must prove the prisoner's guilt which includes 'malice'. But the defence in this case was that the gun went off by accident and the court merely decided that it was not enough for the Crown to prove the killing and then leave to the prisoner the onus of proving as a defence the events that led to the firing of the gun. 'Malice may be implied where death occurs as the result of a voluntary act of the accused which is intentional and unprovoked'—this quotation is from the judgment which is sometimes supposed to reject the objective test. The real issue was whether there was a voluntary act—not what malice should the law assume where an act is intentionally done. But the case is important as being another defence of the prisoner against a presumption that the act was voluntary. It has been held that if A does a voluntary act which is intrinsically likely to kill or to cause grievous bodily harm, it matters not whether he foresaw the possibility of serious injury. The law requires a man to know at his peril the teachings of common experience, and he is deemed to foresee that which a reasonable man would foresee.[3] This decision has been severely criticized,[4] and has been rejected by the High Court of Australia,[5] and now the legislature has intervened to undo the mischief.[6]

English law does not distinguish between different degrees of murder, but certain American states have set a neat problem for the courts in their definition of the degrees of homicide. It is homicide in the first degree if the prisoner acted from a deliberate or premeditated design, in the second degree if there was a design to kill, but without deliberation or premeditation. How long does premeditation take? Is it enough to deliberate as one pulls the trigger? Some courts have answered in the affirmative in spite of the apparent desire of the statute to distinguish between planned killings and hasty acts.[7]

---

[1] *Camb. L. J.* (1936), 31 at 53.   [2] [1935] A.C. 462 at 481.
[3] *Director of Public Prosecutions* v. *Smith*, [1961] A.C. 290.
[4] G. Williams, *Constructive Malice Revived* (1960), 23 *M.L.R.* 605; (1961), 77 *L.Q.R.* 1 (note); and J. L. Travers and N. Morris, *Imputed Intent in Murder* (1961), 35 *Aust. L. J.* 154.
[5] In *Parker* v. *Queen*, [1963] A.L.R. 524, Sir Owen Dixon C.J., stated that *Smith's Case* should not be used as authority in Australia at all.
[6] Criminal Justice Act, 1967, s. 8.
[7] J. K. Knudson, 24 *Washington Univ. L. Q.* (1939), 305.

The exact degree of *mens rea* required for manslaughter has also been a subject for dispute. It is recognized that for manslaughter it is sufficient to prove criminal negligence without intent.[1] In tort, the test is the conduct of a reasonable man, but criminal liability requires some greater degree of negligence which is difficult to define precisely. Turner suggests that the prosecution must prove (in addition to the *actus reus*) that the prisoner was 'indifferent or reckless as to the obvious risk of bodily harm to which his conduct was exposing someone'.[2] Elsewhere he states that it must be shown that the prisoner foresaw that his conduct might cause physical harm to someone.[3] The confusion in the cases has arisen from a defect in analysis. Theoretically, recklessness is no more a degree of negligence than is intent. The analysis of recklessness should emphasize awareness of increasing the danger as contrasted with negligence which stresses mere inadvertence. To treat recklessness merely as gross negligence inevitably leads to theoretical difficulties.[4] Holmes, however, concludes that the law adopts a purely external test and finds one difference between murder and manslaughter to be the degree of danger shown by experience to attach to the act in the given state of facts.[5] 'In such cases the *mens rea,* or actual wickedness of the party, is wholly unnecessary and all reference to the state of his consciousness is misleading if it means anything more than that the circumstances in connection with which the tendency of his act is judged are the circumstances known to him.'[6] And the law may even assume that a man knows the facts which a reasonable man in his position should know. But Holmes's theory cannot today be accepted with any confidence.

The old rule that death, caused accidentally in the commission of a felony, is murder was indefensible. But juries show a well-rooted dislike of such constructive murders, and in this particular instance

---

[1] See the decision of J.C. in *Palmer* v. *Reginam,* [1971] 1 All E.R. 1077. In 'voluntary manslaughter'—killing which is not murder only because there is provocation—the test is objective in the sense that the provocation must be such as would have deprived a reasonable man of self-control, but subjective in the sense that, if the prisoner is of superior character and did not lose his self-control, it is no defence that the reasonable man would have done so: J. Hall, *General Principles of Criminal Law,* 185.

[2] 5 *Camb. L. J.* (1933), 61 at 70–1.

[3] 6 *Camb. L. J.* (1936), 31 at 50.

[4] J. Hall, op. cit. 232, and see G. Williams, *Criminal Law, The General Part* (2nd ed.), 54; and cf. *R.* v. *Bates,* [1952] 2 All E.R. 842.

[5] *The Common Law,* 59.

[6] Op. cit. 75, and Holmes's view was adopted by the House of Lords in *D.P.P.* v. *Smith,* [1961] A.C. 290 at 327; but see *R.* v. *Jakac,* [1961] V.R. 367, and the criticisms noted in footnote p. 384 *supra.*

the law itself has been modified.[1] A juryman still hesitates to convict a motorist of manslaughter, even in the most flagrant cases, because he unconsciously feels there is no broad gulf between himself and the motorist in the dock. There is thus a conflict between the theory of the law and its application by juries, which causes much confusion. Instead of reforming the law, the typical English solution was to create new offences with which motorists might be charged, but from the theoretical angle of the definition of *mens rea*, these have only added to the difficulties.[2] Neither in the case of murder nor of manslaughter can the present English theory of *mens rea* be regarded as satisfactory.[3] It is generally argued that strict rules will protect society, but if these rules are not honestly applied by juries, then there is a divorce between the theory and practice of the law which is full of danger.

The defence of mistake is objectively treated, as it must be proved that the mistake was a reasonable one.[4] A purely subjective theory would recognize necessity as a defence, but this plea is rigidly limited.[5]

The third point was that there is an increasing number of crimes which are defined without reference to subjective guilt—indeed some writers speak of the 'eclipse of *mens rea*'.[6] The growing tendency to use the sanctions of the criminal law as a means of social regulation has led to the creation of many new offences, the penalty for the breach of which is slight and involves no moral stigma. To secure effective enforcement, the Crown need prove only the wrongful act, and the disadvantage of inflicting a fine on a morally innocent defendant is more than counterbalanced by the social gain in securing the observance of certain minimum requirements. In England

---

[1] See now Homicide Act, 1957. Even before this, the rule was limited to such felonious acts as involve violence to an unwilling victim: A. L. Turner, 1 *Annual L. R.* (*W. A.*) (1949), 295.

[2] Various standards may be applied to the conduct of a motorist: (a) Civil negligence—the failure to use the care which would be used by a reasonable man. (b) The criminal offence of driving without due care and attention. How far does this differ (if at all) from the civil standard of lack of reasonable care? (c) The criminal offence of driving dangerously or recklessly. (d) Manslaughter (criminal negligence). Surely if the prisoner causes death by driving recklessly, he has sufficient *mens rea* for manslaughter? P. Dean, 53 *L.Q.R.* (1937), 380; J. W. C. Turner, 5 *Camb. L. J.* (1933), 61; *R.* v. *Stringer*, [1933], 49 T.L.R. 189; *Andrews* v. *Director of Public Prosecutions*, [1937] A.C. 576.

[3] G. Williams, *Criminal Law, The General Part* (2nd ed.), chs. ii–v.

[4] J. Hall, op. cit. 333.

[5] Ibid., ch. xii.

[6] e.g. W. T. S. Stallybrass, 52 *L.Q.R.* (1936), 60. Cf. also F. B. Sayre, 33 *Col. L. R.* (1933), 55.

over half of those convicted of offences are guilty of breaches of traffic laws.[1] But, while we may agree with this approach, it would be unfortunate if the increasing number of such regulatory measures should prejudice the case where the more serious crimes are concerned.[2] Some suggest that to impose a heavy penalty and the stigma of conviction on a person whose conduct has been reasonable brings the law itself into disrepute. But this approach can be exaggerated: the attitude towards rape is hardly likely to be affected by prosecutions under the Pure Foods Act. This problem has arisen mainly with regard to the interpretation of statutory offences where there is no specific reference to *mens rea*. *R*. v. *Tolson*[3] represented a liberal approach, but in recent cases there is an increasing tendency to say that, at least where modern statutes are concerned, omission of any reference to *mens rea* must be presumed to be intentional. Some modern English cases take a very strict view,[4] but the High Court of Australia approves a wider interpretation, Dixon C.J. considering that the absence of a specific reference to *mens rea* does no more than change the onus of proof: instead of the Crown having to prove *mens rea*, it is assumed unless the prisoner can prove his innocence.[5] Generally speaking, this means that honest and reasonable belief by the defendant in facts which, if true, would have made his act an innocent one, will provide a defence, unless a clear legislative intent to the contrary is discovered.[6]

§ 83. NULLA POENA SINE LEGE

This maxim really involves four different notions: that the categories of the criminal law should be determined by general rules; that a person should not be punished unless his act is a breach of these rules; that penal statutes should be strictly construed; that

---

[1] In 1936, 60 per cent were found guilty of traffic offences: ten years later the petrol shortage reduced the percentage to 50.

[2] F. B. Sayre in *Harvard Legal Essays*, 408.

[3] (1889), 23 Q.B.D. 168.

[4] e.g. *Chajutin* v. *Whitehead*, [1938] 1 K.B. 506.

[5] *Maher* v. *Musson* (1934), 52 C.L.R. 100 at 105; see also *Thomas* v. *R*. (1937), 59 C.L.R. 279, where the High Court refused to follow *R*. v. *Wheat*, [1921] 2 K.B. 119. Cf. *R*. v. *Dolman*, [1949] 1 All E.R. 813, and see also *Proudman* v. *Dayman* (1941), 67 C.L.R. 536 and *Bergin* v. *Stack* (1953), 88 C.L.R. 248, where the views accepted by Australian courts are adequately explained. In *R*. v. *Gould*, [1968] 1 All E.R. 849 (C.A. Criminal Division) it was considered that *R*. v. *Wheat* was wrongly decided and that *Thomas* v. *R*. should be followed.

[6] See *Proudman* v. *Dayman* and *Bergin* v. *Stack* (*supra*); *Mens Rea in Statutory Offences* (1958), 74 *L.Q.R.* 342.

penal laws should not have a retrospective operation.[1] It is based on the elementary notion of justice that the criminal law should be as fixed and as certain as possible in order that men may know in advance what conduct is criminal. It is felt to be unfair to punish a man for conduct which was not criminal at the time when the act was done—what is demanded is a rule of law as opposed to the caprice of an official.

English law has not specifically adopted the principle. Thus new crimes may be created by statutes with retrospective operation. Theoretically, a statute could delegate to officials the power to declare certain acts criminal and to decide whether or not particular individuals should be punished for committing the acts.[2] Some crimes are defined so broadly that it is not always possible to say in advance how the law will be applied, e.g. criminal conspiracy or offence to the public mischief. But the principle is accepted as a desirable one by most English writers, as can be seen from the criticism of the rather wide formulation in *R.* v. *Manley*[3] of the crime known as an offence to the public mischief,[4] and of the crime of conspiring to corrupt public morals as established in *Shaw* v. *D.P.P.*[5]

The doctrine of *nulla poena sine lege* is regarded in many countries as a vital protection of the subject. Russia, however, rejected the doctrine as a bourgeois relic and the law of 28 June 1935 abrogated it

---

[1] J. Hall, op. cit., ch. ii; M. Ancel in *Annales de l'Institut de droit comparé* (1936), ii. 245. The principle is recognized, e.g. by the French, Belgian, Jugoslav, Portuguese, Italian, Swiss, Chinese, Chilean, Polish, Colombian, and Uruguayan codes. Nazi Germany was an exception (law of 28 June 1935). S. Glaser, 24 *J. Comp. Leg.* (1942), 29.

[2] In a unitary system on the English model, though, the courts will read such Acts strictly. In federal systems, however, and where there are written constitutions imposing limits on legislative powers the position may well be different even when there is no express constitutional denial of such delegation; see e.g. *The Communist Party Case* (1951), 83 C.L.R. 1; *The Boilermakers' Case* (1956), 94 C.L.R. 254; and *Commissioner of Taxation* v. *Brown* (1958), 100 C.L.R. 32, per Dixon C.J. at 40.

[3] [1933] 1 K.B. 529.

[4] Cf. W. T. S. Stallybrass, 49 *L.Q.R.* (1933), 183. On the other hand, W. S. Holdsworth, 37 *L.Q.R.* (1921), 462 at 467, supports the doctrine of elasticity, as the criminal law should have a power of development. Cf. Evatt J. in *R.* v. *Weaver* (1931), 45 C.L.R. 321. The question of the width of the power of the courts to exploit 'elasticity' in the criminal law without the aid of the legislature remains a live one. In *R.* v. *Newland*, [1954] 1 Q.B. 158, Lord Goddard C.J. emphasized the need for caution and made some critical comments on *R.* v. *Manley* (*supra*); that decision may be justifiable but the dicta are too wide, see *R.* v. *Todd*, [1957] S.A.S.R. 305; *Joshua* v. *R.*, [1955] A.C. 121; [1958] C.L.R. 522-3; A. L. Goodhart, *The Shaw Case: The Law and Public Morals* (1961), 77 *L.Q.R.* 560; J. E. Hall Williams, *The Ladies' Directory and Criminal Conspiracy, The Judge as Custos Morum* (1961), 24 *M.L.R.* 626.

[5] [1961] 2 W.L.R. 897; [1961] 2 All E.R. 446; and see *R.* v. *Quinn*, [1961] 3 W.L.R. 611. See, however, *D.P.P.* v. *Bhagwan*, [1970] 3 All E.R. 97 (H. Lds.) which suggests that criminal conspiracy and offence to the public mischief should be confined to cases already established by the law: see Note, 34 *Mod. L. R.* (1971), 81.

in Germany.[1] The theory of the totalitarian state is that the judge is charged with the duty of protecting the new régime—liberal or democratic scruples as to the rights of the prisoner should not be allowed to hinder the effective execution of state policy. In other words, *nulla poena sine lege* is rewritten so as to read *nullum crimen sine poena.* The old Japanese criminal code stated that only the magistrates should be allowed to peruse it—this takes away the effective protection of the maxim as it makes the law inaccessible.[2]

At first, in Russia, great use was made of analogy to fill the gaps in the criminal law which became, from the point of view of the subject, dangerously elastic, but as the Soviet moved farther from the Revolution the advantages of certainty and predictability in the criminal law were recognized.

The doctrine of *nulla poena* would at first sight seem to require a very rigid criminal law and a severe pruning of the discretion allowed to the court in determining sentence. This would run counter to the theory that the act should be regarded merely as an index to the social danger of the prisoner, and that punishment should be determined by the progress of the prisoner rather than laid down in advance. But we cannot hope to achieve progress by limiting too rigidly the discretion which exists as to penalty. *Nulla poena sine lege* should be adopted strictly so far as we are concerned with the determination of the limits of criminal conduct—but power must be left to a skilled sentencing body to adjust the penalty to the individual offender, although it may be necessary to set maximum limits to possible sentences for each type of crime in order to prevent arbitrariness. Here law must delicately compromise the liberty of the individual with the demands of society, remembering that it is in the individual's own interest that he should be cured and that society demands a policy that will stamp out, as far as possible, breach of the criminal law.

---

[1] Any person who commits an act which the law declares to be punishable or which is deserving of penalty according to the fundamental conception of a penal law and sound popular feeling shall be punished. If no penal section applies to the case in question, the act shall be punished under the law which applies most nearly to the act.

[2] L. C. Green, *Current Legal Problems* (1948), 188.

REFERENCES

ALLEN, C. K., *Legal Duties*, 221.
BARNES, H. E., and TEETERS, N. K., *New Horizons in Criminology.*
BARRY, J. V., *The Courts and Criminal Punishment* (1969).

BLOM-COOPER, L., *The Hanging Question* (1969).
COWIE, J. and VALERIE, *Delinquency in Girls* (1968).
DEVLIN, K., *Sentencing Offenders in Magistrates' Courts* (1970).
EAST, W. N., and HUBERT, W. H. de B., *The Psychological Treatment of Crime.*
FOX, L. W., *The Modern English Prison.*
GAULT, R. H., *Criminology.*
GLUECK, S., *Crime and Justice.*
—— *One Thousand Juvenile Delinquents.*
GREEN, E., *Judicial Attitudes in Sentencing* (1961).
HALL, JEROME, *Theft, Law and Society.*
—— 47 *Yale L. J.* 165.
HART, H. L. A., *Punishment and Responsibility* (1968).
HOLMES, O. W., *The Common Law,* Lecture II.
HOOTON, E. A., *Crime and the Man.*
McCLINTOCK, F. H., and AVISON, N. H., *Crime in England and Wales* (1968).
MANNHEIM, H., *Social Aspects of Crime in England between the Wars.*
—— *War and Crime.*
—— *The Dilemma of Penal Reform.*
—— 17 *J. Comp. Leg.* (1935), 82, 236.
MORRIS, N., and HAWKINS, G., *The Honest Politician's Guide to Crime Control* (1969).
MULLINS, C., *Crime and Psychology.*
—— *Why Crime?*
Penal Reform in England (ed. L. Radzinowicz and J. W. C. Turner).
RADZINOWICZ, L., *History of English Criminal Law.*
SAYRE, F. B., 33 *Col. L. R.* (1933), 55.
STALLYBRASS, W. T. S., 52 *L.Q.R.* (1936), 60.
SUTHERLAND, E. H., and CRESSEY, D. R., *Principles of Criminology* (1955).
TAPPAN, P. W., *Crime, Justice and Correction* (1960).
The Challenge of Crime in a Free Society (A Report by the President's Commission on Law Enforcement), (1967).
TURNER, J. W. C., 5 *Camb. L. J.* (1933), 61 and vol. 6 (1936), 31.
WALKER, N., *Crime and Punishment in Britain* (1965).
—— *Sentencing in a Rational Society* (1969).
WILLIAMS, G., *The Criminal Law, The General Part* (2nd ed.), (1961).
WOOTTON, BARBARA, *Social Science and Social Pathology* (1959).
—— *Crime and the Criminal Law* (1963).

BOOK VI

PRIVATE LAW

XVI

THE CONCEPT OF LEGAL PERSONALITY

84. INTRODUCTION

THE orthodox approach is to divide private law into three parts: the law of persons, the law of obligations, and the law of property. There is, however, much debate as to what parts of the law should be treated within the law of persons, and it seems better to describe this division by the more specific heading, 'the concept of legal personality'.

§ 85. THE NATURE OF LEGAL PERSONALITY

It has already been asserted[1] that legal personality is an artificial creation of the law. Legal persons are all entities capable of being right-and-duty-bearing units—all entities recognized by the law as capable of being parties to a legal relationship. Salmond said: 'So far as legal theory is concerned, a person is any being whom the law regards as capable of rights and duties. Any being that is so capable is a person, whether a human being or not, and no being that is not so capable is a person, even though he be a man.'[2]

And yet a little later Salmond said: 'A legal person is any subject matter other than a human being to which the law attributes personality. This extension, for good and sufficient reasons, of the conception of personality beyond the class of human beings is one of the most noteworthy feats of the legal imagination . . .'[3] Here are the seeds of confusion. In one passage *person* refers to anything recognized by the law as capable of bearing rights and duties whether

---

[1] § 61 (*supra*).   [2] *Jurisprudence*, 12th ed., 299.   [3] Op. cit. 305.

human or not, in the other human beings are *persons* with *personality* but non-human beings may be *legal persons*. The problems which this kind of confusion have caused will be discussed more fully when the nature of corporate personality is considered; but it is desirable to remove some of the confusion, arising out of the mere use of the word *person*, at the outset.

It is perhaps unfortunate that the same words, *person* and *personality*, have been used both in a legal and philosophical sense. The Latin *persona* was, it appears, the equivalent of the Greek *prosopon*, which originally referred to the mask worn by the actor to represent the god, the hero, etc. impersonated in a play. It came to mean the part played by the actor, and was extended to refer to the part played by a human being in legal proceedings, for example, as a *pater-familias*.[1] It was not difficult to confuse the part played with the player playing it, especially as the use of the word was extended to cover all sorts of publicly recognized offices or capacities.

This is only part of the story, however. In classical times there was much to dissuade the adoption of a view which would confuse human beings and legal persons in one notion, for the law clearly contemplated human beings who were not legal persons—as in some systems of slavery or alienage.[2] The more lasting confusion grew from the attempts of the early Christian theologians to grapple with the doctrine of the Trinity in the light of Greek (principally Aristotelian) metaphysics, and later, in the dark ages, from the Christians' failure to enjoy or to understand that light. By the sixth century Boethius was able to define *persona* as the individuality of a rational being, and the primary use of the word referred to as the part played was obscured. The ambiguity and confusion produced is with us yet.

The concept of human personality is difficult to define and has become a storm centre of intellectual controversy; many of the matters in dispute have been transferred to the legal field. The first essential to any clearer understanding of the nature of legal personality

---

[1] It is not proposed to conduct an exhaustive inquiry into the use and development of these words, but to give an outline only: see C. C. J. Webb, *God and Personality*, Lecture II; P. W. Duff, *Personality in Roman Private Law*, ch. i; H. C. Dowdall, *Special Article and Correspondence on the Word 'Person'* (reprinted from *The Times Literary Supplement*), The Shenval Press (1948); F. Hallis, *Corporate Personality*, Introduction, xix–xxi; and A. Nékám, *The Personality Conception of the Legal Entity*, particularly ch.iii.

[2] Some light is thrown on the problem by attempting to answer the question—addressed to a man reduced to utter slavery—'when you lost your legal personality, what was it you lost?'

is to distinguish it sharply from personality in the sense which refers to the rational individuality of a human being.[1] Human beings do not necessarily possess legal personality; thus in early systems slaves were regarded as mere chattels and aliens were not permitted to bring suit in the courts. Many human beings may possess a restricted legal personality, such as infants and lunatics. Legal personality may be granted to entities other than individual human beings, e.g. a group of human beings, a fund, an idol. Twenty men may form a corporation which may sue and be sued in the corporate name. An idol[2] may be regarded as a legal *persona* in itself, or a particular fund may be incorporated. It is clear that neither the idol nor the fund can carry out the activities incidental to litigation or other activities incidental to the carrying on of legal relationships, e.g., the signing of a contract; and, of necessity, the law recognizes certain human agents as representatives of the idol or of the fund. The acts of such agents, however (within limits set by the law and when they are acting as such), are imputed to the legal *persona* of the idol,[3] and are not the juristic acts of the human agents themselves. This is no mere academic distinction, for it is the legal *persona* of the idol that is bound to the legal relationships created, not that of the agent. Legal personality then refers to the particular device by which the law creates or recognizes units to which it ascribes certain powers and capacities.

To argue whether such legal devices are artificial or real is a waste of time which we avoid when we are discussing the legal concepts of contract or of tort. The law says that such an agreement will be a contract and that from that fact certain legal consequences will flow. Similarly it says that certain things shall be units for the purposes of the law, and that such units shall possess the capacity of being parties to the claim-duty and power-liability relationships. It might be absurd, but not impossible, for the law to award legal personality to trees, sticks, or stones.[4] Hence, from the juristic angle,

---

[1] H. Kelsen, *Annales de l'Institu de droit comparé* (1936), ii. 26–7; A. Nékám, *The Personality Conception of the Legal Entity*, 48–9.

[2] See *Pramatha Nath Mullick* v. *Pradyumna Kumar Mullick*, [1925] L.R. 52 Ind. App. 245, discussed by P. W. Duff, 3 *Camb. L. J.* (1927), 42.

[3] As it was put in the Indian case cited *supra*: 'The will of the idol in regard to location must be respected.' Normally this will would be interpreted by the guardian, but the law would interfere if the guardian did not act in the interests of the idol, that is, presumably, after consulting the interests of the worshippers.

[4] Animals have been regarded as legal personalities in some systems. In Germany, during the Middle Ages, a cock was tried for contumacious crowing, and, in 1508 in Provence, the caterpillars of Contes were condemned for ravaging the fields; G. W. Keeton, *The Elementary Principles of Jurisprudence* (2nd ed.), 149.

the legal personality awarded to John Smith is of the same essential nature as that awarded to a corporation, an idol, or a fund.

All legal systems no doubt are concerned with the control and organization of relations between human beings by means of general rules. So soon as there is any system, any organization, with a logic of its own, just so soon must there be some constants, some reference points given, on which to base the logic of the system. Just as the concept 'one' in arithmetic is essential to the logical system developed and yet is not one something (e.g. one apple, or one orange, etc.), so a legal system must be provided with a basic unit before full legal relationships can be devised which will serve the primary purpose of organizing the social facts. The legal person is the unit or entity adopted. For the logic of the system it is just as much a pure concept as 'one' is in arithmetic. It is just as independent from a human being as 'one' is from an apple. It is unfortunate perhaps that we use the same word 'personality' to indicate that an entity is recognized by the law as a legal person and also to indicate the differences in the capacities of legal persons. It might have been better to speak of legal entities[1] to indicate that something has been recognized as what we refer to as a legal person, and to reserve the phrase 'legal personality' to indicate differences in capacities between legal entities.[2]

Although various changes in terminology have been suggested from time to time, none has been adopted universally. It is therefore necessary to be careful to distinguish between those occasions when we use the words 'legal personality' to refer to the fact that some entity has been recognized as a legal person from those occasions when we are really talking about the differing legal personalities of entities whose recognition as legal persons is assumed. But that of course does not mean that the problems, philosophical or otherwise, about human personality which have been so much in dispute in the past are irrelevant so far as the law is concerned. The entities which receive recognition as legal persons differ greatly. John Smith is a human being with certain physical and mental powers, a corporation is a product of rules which recognize a group of human beings

---

[1] A. Nékám would abolish the term 'legal personality' altogether and speak of the legal entity. He attempts to show that there are no essential characteristics of corporations as such and that no single criterion is in any sense typical of corporate existence (p. 110).

[2] A. Kocourek makes the distinction clear by referring to mere existence as a legal person as 'personateness': *Jural Relations* (2nd ed.), 291–2.

or perhaps a succession of human beings as an entity for legal purposes and it can act only through agents; an idol or a fund are entities with no life and no physical powers of decision or action, and their interests can be protected only by agents set up for that purpose. The law must of course take account of such differences by adapting its rules to the nature of the entities concerned, and by making special rules to meet special cases.

Where human beings are concerned, the nature of human personality may be vital, not merely to the question of whether or not humans should be recognized as legal persons, but for questions as to the rules which shall govern their legal rights, duties, liabilities, powers, capacities, etc. They may be vital to other questions also. As Professor Hart has pointed out: 'In all legal systems we have occasion not only to pick out units but to *re-identify* a given unit over stretches of time. Is this man who is sued the same person as he who smashed the plaintiff's windows? Is this company the same company as guaranteed the tenant's rent ten years ago? To answer the second we use criteria of identity which have no use apart from law.'[1] To answer the first, of course, we draw upon notions about human beings which do not depend on the law for their value. The mere recognition of legal persons, as such, remains a basic juristic device by which the organizing of rights and duties is made possible.

§ 86. NATURAL PERSONS

In ancient systems not all human beings were granted legal personality. The case of the slave is too well known to need stressing. A monk who enters a monastery is regarded in some systems as being 'civilly dead' and his property is distributed just as if death had in fact taken place.[2] In modern times it is normal to grant legal personality to all living within the territory of the State.

Most systems lay down the rule that, in cases where legal personality is granted to human beings, personality begins at birth and ends with death.

In the case of birth most systems require complete extrusion from the mother's body—the child in the womb is not a legal personality and can have no rights. For some purposes, however, the maxim

---

[1] (1959–60) 5 & 6 *Aust. J. of Politics and History*, 246.
[2] In New York a person imprisoned for life is by statute regarded as civilly dead: *Brooklyn L. R.* (1949), 70.

nasciturus pro iam nato habetur takes effect. In the civil law the fiction was invented that in all matters affecting its interests the unborn child *in utero* should be regarded as already born, but English law applies this fiction only for the purpose of enabling the child if it is born to take a benefit.[1] It is thought reasonable that a child who has lost his father should not be further penalized by losing any interest which he would have secured had he been alive at his father's death.

In English law it is still doubtful whether an infant born alive can recover for injuries inflicted before birth.[2] To prove in fact a causal link between the negligence and the particular injury may well be difficult, but, if this hurdle can be surmounted, there seems to be no conclusive reason why recovery should be denied.[3] The law relating to child killing is too intricate for survey in short terms.[4] A child must be completely born alive before the rules of murder will protect it, for murder is the killing of a reasonable person in being. If, however, the prisoner intentionally inflicts serious injury on a child in the womb, and the child is born alive and then dies from the injuries, this is murder.[5] But these rules, even when coupled with the prohibition of abortion, left too many opportunities for child destruction.[6] For example, if a child was killed during the process of birth it was not murder at common law,[7] since the whole body of the child must be extruded before it becomes a person.

If birth is necessary to create rights, so death, in general, ends rights. In English law to 'libel the dead is not an offence known to our law: the dead have no rights and can suffer no wrongs'.[8] It is, however, a misdemeanour to publish defamatory words of a deceased person, if it be done with intent to bring scandal on his family and to

---

[1] *Elliot* v. *Joicey (Lord)*, [1935] A.C. 209 at 238 et seq.

[2] Salmond, *Torts* (14th ed.), 622, and 4 *Univ. of Toronto L. J.* (1942), 278. Recovery was denied in the Irish case, *Walker* v. *G. N. Rly. of Ireland* (1890), 28 L.R. (Ir.) 69: and many American cases deny a remedy. See *Smith* v. *Luckhardt* (1939), 19 N.E. (2d) 446, discussed 87 *Univ. of Pa. L. R.* (1939), 1016; contra *Stemmer* v. *Kline* (1940), 17 A. (2d) 58; 45 *Dickinson L. R.* (1941), 238, and *Williams* v. *The Marion Rapid Transit Co.* (1949), 87 N.E. (2d) 334. Recovery has been allowed in Canada: *Montreal Tramways* v. *Leveille*, [1933] 4 D.L.R. 337; and since 1949 an increasing number of courts in the United States of America have allowed recovery; see Prosser, *Torts* (2nd ed.), 174–5. In Victoria, recovery is allowed: *Watt* v. *Rama* (1971, as yet unreported).

[3] Salmond, *Torts* (14th ed.), 622.

[4] S. C. Atkinson, 20 *L.Q.R.* (1904), 134; D. Seaborne Davies, 1 *Mod. L. R.* (1937), 203, 269.

[5] D. S. Davies, op. cit. 209.   [6] Ibid. 218.

[7] But now see the Infant Life (Preservation) Act, 1929, 19 & 20 Geo. V, c. 34.

[8] Per Stephen J., *R.* v. *Ensor* (1887), 3 T.L.R. 366. For America see *Rose* v. *Daily Mirror Inc.* (1940), 20 N.Y.S. (2d) 315; 40 *Col. L. R.* (1940), 1267. In N.S. Wales a plaintiff can sue in respect of any imputations on any members of his family, living or dead, if they affect his reputation or livelihood: Defamation Act, 1958, s. 5.

provoke them to a breach of the peace.[1] The law must tread warily, for, as Lord Kincairney has cynically remarked, 'about the half of history consists of what might be called defamation of the dead'.[2] In Roman law an heir could sue for *iniuria* if an insult was offered to the body of the deceased at the funeral. But this was in some ways a direct insult to the heir himself.[3] French law grants a civil remedy to relatives, even when there is no specific intent to attack them, if they can prove either material or moral damages resulting from untrue statements concerning the dead.[4] The problem which every system must face is to protect serious studies in history while striking at the salacious gossip written only to pander to lower tastes.

The effect of death on causes of action already subsisting in tort represents a very confused chapter of English law. The maxim *actio personalis moritur cum persona* has darkened counsel, and 'like some other Latin maxims which have been invented or adopted by our law, we should have missed nothing if it had never found its way there'.[5] The common law rule was that if I commit a tort against you and either of us dies, the liability is extinguished. This doctrine was made tolerable only by a series of exceptions, and it was largely swept away in England in 1934.[6] French law, in general, allows both the claim of the deceased and his liability to pass to his legal successors,[7] but there are difficulties when the claim is based on injury to the person or to the reputation of the deceased.

Another question is whether the infliction of death is a cause of action in tort. A master may sue for loss of the services of a domestic because Jones has, intentionally or negligently, so injured the servant that she cannot perform her work, but at common law[8] it was cheaper for Jones, instead of maiming, to kill, for in that case no action lay.[9] Thus loss resulting to third parties by the infliction of death is not a tort, nor is the infliction of death a tort against the person killed. The Fatal Accidents Act, 1846, provides a remedy for certain dependants in cases where the breadwinner has been killed. French law has no need of any specific statute, since the

---

[1] Hawkins P.C. 1, 542; F. P. Walton, 9 *J. Comp. Leg.* (1927), 1.
[2] *Broom* v. *Ritchie* (1905), 6 Fraser 942, cited F. P. Walton, op. cit. 2.
[3] Cf. Paul, *Dig.* 47, 10. 27: an action for *iniuria* lies if the statue of one's father is stoned.   [4] See F. P. Walton, 9 *J. Comp. Leg.* (1927), 1 at 10–11.
[5] P. H. Winfield, *Textbook of the Law of Tort* (8th ed.), 605.
[6] Law Reform (Miscellaneous Provisions) Act, 1934, 24 & 25 Geo. V, c. 41.
[7] F. P. Walton, 18 *J. Comp. Leg.* (1936), 40 at 51.
[8] Leaving aside the possibility of criminal liability.
[9] The rule in *Baker* v. *Bolton* (1808), 1 Camp. 493.

general principles of the code are wide enough to cover loss to A arising from the negligent killing of B by the defendant.[1] The English rule that the infliction of death is not a tort to the person killed has been partially evaded by the grant of an action for loss of expectation of life which can be brought by the representative.[2] In French law many writers support the view that there is a transmissible action for instantaneous death, but this is still a matter of dispute.[3]

Kocourek suggests that if the infliction of death is regarded as a tort to the person killed (as it is in some American states), then we can explain this only by postulating that the legal *persona* survives death, for, since the wrongful act is that of causing *death*, the act is not complete until the victim is no longer living and, if at that moment legal personality ceases, no wrong has been done to any *persona*.[4] This is reminiscent of the famous argument in *Hales's Case* that a man who committed suicide did not commit a felony during his life, for the felony was completed only when death resulted, and then of course he no longer existed.[5] It may possibly be that in some systems a man's estate is liable for defamatory matter in his will, although it was published only after he was no longer in being.[6] If a child may recover compensation for injuries negligently inflicted before birth, should we say that the legal *persona* precedes the physical birth?[7] If it is convenient to do so, there is no conclusive theoretical reason why the law should not adopt some such theory as Kocourek suggests. But it is the express theory of most systems that legal personality begins at birth and ends at death, however difficult it may be to reconcile this with some of the actual rules in force.

§ 87. STATUS

Status is a word which has no very precise connotation. Salmond[8] gives four meanings:

(*a*) legal condition of any kind, whether personal or proprietary;

---

[1] F. P. Walton, op. cit. 53.
[2] *Rose* v. *Ford*, [1937] A.C. 826; cf. *Benham* v. *Gambling*, [1941] A.C. 157.
[3] F. P. Walton, op. cit. 53.   [4] *Jural Relations*, 296.
[5] *Hales* v. *Petit*, 1 Plowden 253. An American case allowed recovery for nervous shock against deceased's estate when suicide was committed in a friend's kitchen: *Blakeley* v. *Shortal's Estate* (Iowa, 1945), 20 N.W. (2d) 28; 32 *Cornell L. Q.* (1946), 297.   [6] 53 *Scot. L. R.* (1937), 145; *contra* 97 *Univ. of Pa. L. R.* (1948), 289.
[7] A. Kocourek, op. cit. 298. Legal personality could not be held to continue indefinitely after death without upsetting many rules of law, e.g. that the dead have no rights. Indeed, Kocourek's theory would raise more difficulties than it solves.
[8] *Jurisprudence* (12th ed.), 240.

(b) personal legal condition, excluding proprietary relations;

(c) personal capacities and incapacities as opposed to other elements of personal status;[1]

(d) compulsory as opposed to conventional legal position.

Austin[2] agrees that the term cannot be used with exactness, but thinks that when for ease of exposition it is useful to separate a complex of rights and duties, of capacities and incapacities which specifically affect a narrow class, it is convenient to designate that complex by the term *status*.

Very many factors may lead to the creation of a status. Thus sex, minority, and marriage are bound up with the problem of the family; illegitimacy shows the lack of proper family ties; mental or bodily defect may lead to special treatment by the law. Caste, official position, or profession may create certain privileges or disabilities. Criminality may destroy liberty, or bankruptcy may divest of property. Foreign nationality, race, or colour may cause the law to distinguish a group.[3]

One of the best analyses is that of Allen.[4] Status may be described as the fact or condition of membership of a group of which the powers are determined extrinsically by law, status affecting not merely one particular relationship, but being a condition affecting generally though in varying degree a member's claims and powers. The nature of this definition will be clearer as the various points involved are discussed. Status is not merely a basis for classification, but a matter of great political, legal, and social importance.

Firstly, status arises from membership of a class and the powers of that class are determined extrinsically by law, not by agreement between the parties.[5] There is no power for a member to vary the conditions imposed by law, for example, the rules relating to the status of marriage are conclusively fixed.

Secondly, while an infant has no choice whether he will enter the status of infancy or not, it is not always the case that members of a status are compulsorily placed within that group by law. Thus

---

[1] 'Status is in the main a matter of personal capacity': per Scott L.J., *Re Luck's Settlement Trusts*, [1940] Ch. 864 at 889.

[2] *Jurisprudence*, ii. 687.

[3] Other possibilities are civil death, heresy, slavery. But the latter hardly creates a status, for the slave is not really a *persona* at all. Prodigality may create a status, but some regard the prodigal as only another instance of the feeble-minded.

[4] *Legal Duties*, 28. And see R. H. Graveson, *Status in the Common Law* (1953).

[5] 'Status is in every case the creature of substantive law': per Scott L.J. in *Re Luck's Settlement Trusts*, [1940] Ch. at 890.

Phyllis cannot be forced into the status of a married woman against her will, but if she does marry, the law attaches to that status certain incidents which cannot be varied by the consent of the parties. Thus she became at common law immune from actions in tort brought against her by her husband: she has a claim to support from her husband, and in cases of necessity a power to pledge his credit. The status of marriage cannot be ended merely by the wish of the parties. Graveson suggests that the will of the party may affect the beginning or the end of status, but never both.[1] Marriage illustrates freedom at the beginning, and the control of law at the dissolution, of the status. An ambassador can be made such only by act of the State, but presumably he can destroy his status by resignation.

Thirdly, Maine emphasizes that status normally arises today because of a defect in judgment of the members of the class in question.[2] This statement is not universally true. Historically, status is due not to a desire to protect the weak, but rather to exploit them, as has already been seen in discussing the evolution of the law of guardianship.[3] Today many typical cases of status do reflect a desire to protect certain classes against their own weaknesses,[4] but this is not the only cause for the singling out of a certain class for special treatment. Ambassadors may suffer from occasional defects of judgment, but that is not the reason why the law places them in a special status.

Fourthly, membership of a status does not always result in restricted power. In the case of an infant or a lunatic, legal power is restricted, but an ambassador has increased privileges because he belongs to that particular class. It should not be thought that status creates only incapacities.

Fifthly, not all groups give rise to a status. Clearly membership of the group must affect a person's legal relations, or at least his power to enter legal relations. There is no status of the blue-eyed or of bridge-players, for although both of these groups may be regarded as forming a class, that class has no precise legal significance.[5] It is not enough even to confine the term to groups based on a classification of legal relations; thus it is inaccurate to speak of the status of trustees or of bankers. The test is that status is a condition which affects generally, although in varying degree, a person's claims,

[1] 10 *Mod. L. R.* (1947), 80 at 81.   [2] *Ancient Law* (ed. F. Pollock), 173.
[3] *Supra*, § 72.   [4] L. Josserand, *Évolutions et Actualités*, 159.
[5] C. K. Allen, *Legal Duties*, 43.

liberties, powers, and immunities. In the case of a trustee, there are particular powers relating to the trust property and particular duties owed to the beneficiary of the trust. But the fact that a man is a trustee does not affect his general powers. The particular rights and duties of a trustee spring from one particular title (the trust) and extend no farther. But an infant suffers from a lack of contractual power which affected at common law not only one contract or relationship but all his contracts save those which relate to necessaries. Holland asks: 'does the peculiarity of the personality arise from anything unconnected with the nature of the act itself which the person of inherence can enforce against the person of incidence?'[1] I am a mortgagee because of one particular transaction and that does not affect my other legal relations. If Smith is a lunatic so found, his power entirely disappears and thus he can perform no juristic acts. It is easy to draw the line between these two extremes, but it is not easy to determine the exact limits of the requirement that membership must affect *generally* a person's claims and powers. Does a decree of judicial separation affect status?[2]

Allen distinguishes between status which is a condition, capacity which is a power to acquire and exercise rights, and the rights themselves which are acquired by the exercise of that capacity.[3] Using the terminology of Hohfeld, we would say that status is the condition of being a member of a particular group, which membership affects generally claims, liberties, power, and immunities. In private international law it is only reasonable for English law to recognize a status which may be imposed by French law on a Frenchman, but English courts may refuse to recognize as effective in England some of the claims or powers which arise from that status. As Scott L.J. puts it: 'The general principle of status is that, when created by the law of one country, it is or ought to be judicially recognized as being the case everywhere, all the world over',[5] and only for imperative reasons of public policy should the law refuse to allow in England the normal results that flow from a foreign status. Thus if a child is legitimate by his personal law, he should be

---

[1] *Jurisprudence* (10th ed.), 136.
[2] The majority of the High Court of Australia held that such a decree did not affect the status of the parties, but only the incidents thereof: *Ford* v. *Ford*, [1947] A.L.R. 181.
[3] *Legal Duties*, 47.
[4] Cf. *Re Selot's Trust*, [1902] 1 Ch. 488, where the court refused to recognize the incapacity which in French law flowed from the status of a prodigal.
[5] *Re Luck's Settlement Trusts*, [1940] 1 Ch. 864 at 891; see also *Salvesen* v. *Administrator of Austrian Property*, [1927] A.C. 641.

regarded as legitimate the world over,[1] but English law may refuse to recognize the status of slavery, or the status of a wife where the marriage is incestuous by English law, although valid by the law of the country where the marriage took place.

One of Maine's most famous epigrams is that 'the movement of the progressive societies has hitherto been a movement from status to contract'.[2] When we contrast the difficulty in early communities of rising above the level which birth imposed and the comparative freedom of social movement in the modern world, there seems much historical justification for Maine's thesis. The law has abolished many of the lower grades of society, and the tendency is to confine the creation of status to those cases where there is special justification. What were once the lower ranks begin to enjoy many of the privileges of their 'betters'.[3] The evolution of the rules relating to married women represents an increasing power to contract, and the long-continued *patria potestas* of Roman law is now, for most systems, merely an historical curiosity.

But there are grave dangers involved in treating Maine's epigrammatic generalization as a universal law of legal history. Some neo-Hegelians regard contract as *the* legal category in which the free will of the individual has full play, and hence urge that its scope not only is increasing, but ought to be increased in the interests of human liberty.[4] Yet it may be necessary to restrict freedom of contract in order to give real freedom and protection to economically weaker classes,[5] and interference with freedom of contract has been so general that it is sometimes suggested that the conception of status is winning back some of its ancient importance.[6] In some countries the details of employment for particular industries are so fixed by law that

---

[1] But according to the decision of the C.A. cited in the preceding note, there are exceptions to this rule. The dissenting judgment of Scott L.J. seems more reasonable: G. C. Cheshire, *Private International Law* (8th ed.), 442.

[2] *Ancient Law* (ed. Pollock), 174.

[3] Once the age of majority varied according to the class of the person concerned. Thus the mercantile community required only ability to count and weigh, the sokeman must achieve the age of fifteen years and the knight twenty-one: Pollock and Maitland, *History of English Law*, ii. 436. Again the rules evolved by equity to protect the property of wealthy wives were gradually extended by statute for the protection of all.

[4] R. Pound, *Interpretations of Legal History*, 54–61. R. H. Graveson, 4 *Mod. L. R.* (1941), 261, suggests that the dictum is not readily applicable to the common law—the foundation of feudalism was agreement.

[5] *Infra*, § 99.

[6] Cf. P. Vinogradoff, *Collected Papers*, ii. 230 et seq. L. Josserand, *Évolutions et Actualités*, 167, speaks of *les nouveaux faibles*. It should be pointed out that Maine expressly guarded himself, for he stated that the progress has *hitherto* been from status to contract.

there is little scope for free discussion by the parties. But, even where wages, hours, and conditions of labour are rigidly laid down by arbitration courts, is it accurate to say that the workman enjoys a status? Is it not rather a legal determination of the conditions of one particular contract than a condition which affects capacity generally? Apart from the labour contract, does the fact that a person is a workman in a regulated industry affect generally his claims or powers? In one sense, marriage is a contract the terms of which are fixed by law, but the powers of a wife[1] may be affected generally— that is, not only in relation to her husband, but in relation to third parties as well. On the other hand, the wage contract affects only the relationship of employer and employed. It is, of course, a question of degree and it is not inconceivable that marriage may cease to create a status, whereas in a Socialist state the worker may enjoy particular powers merely because he is such. The ambiguity of the term 'status' is such that dogmatic assumptions are unwarranted, and, even on Allen's test, it is a question of degree whether the modification of powers and claims is sufficiently general to justify an assumption that a status has been created.

§ 88. Evolution of the Notion of Corporate Personality

In mature systems of law the doctrine of corporate personality is fully developed and a clear-cut distinction is made between the individuals who compose a corporation and the corporation itself. This can be illustrated by contrasting a company having limited liability with a partnership. A shareholder may retain his millions while his company goes bankrupt, but a partner must answer to his last penny for the debts of the firm. A man may become in effect his own preferred creditor by taking debentures from a company of which he holds all the shares but six; and as a result creditors of the firm can recover only after the debentures have been satisfied.[2] If we postulate that the company has a legal *persona* distinct from that of the shareholders or directors, it is difficult to attack the logic of this distinction, whatever may be said of its practical effects. Conversely,

---

[1] In modern communities the powers of a husband are not 'affected generally' because he is married. Yet it is common to speak of a married man (or even a bachelor) or a woman as enjoying a particular status. This illustrates the wider use of the term, which really deprives it of all significance for jurisprudence.

[2] *Salomon* v. *Salomon and Co.*, [1897] A.C. 22.

the acts of two separate departments of a company are in law the act of the same person.[1] If a group of miners wish to co-operate in order to secure cheap delivery of coal from the colliery at which they work, they must be careful as to the legal forms they use. If they create an incorporated company to organize the transport, a carrier's licence must be secured, since the company is carrying goods for hire or reward; but if they merely form an association, then each member is regarded as part owner of the vehicles and co-owners do not carry their own goods for hire or reward merely because they contribute to the running expenses. The formation of a company introduces a new legal *persona* which owns vehicles and receives money for carrying coal that does not belong to it.[2] In modern law there is thus a clear-cut distinction between the personality of the company and the personalities of its members. The company may engage in juristic acts, sue, and be sued. Though all the members change overnight, indeed, even if they all die, the company remains the same legal *persona*. But this conception of corporate personality is achieved but slowly.

The first group to evolve is based on the family, but no doctrine of group personality is necessary. At Rome the family retained a very strong organization, but no theoretical difficulty arose as its powers were centred in a human *paterfamilias*. Religious and ecclesiastical grouping provides another unifying element, and we also have the manifold agencies of government such as the counties, hundreds, and boroughs of English law.[3] Economic associations such as the merchant guilds create another organization of the community. But it is futile to expect to find answers to problems phrased in modern language concerning corporate personality, for they were not asked by the early lawyer. We have already seen that the State in England reached a high degree of organization on the very inadequate theory that the State was the king and the king a corporation sole.[4] Duff's analysis of the rules of Roman law reveals how long is the road to a fully developed conception of human personality.[5] *Persona* was not always used in the sense of legal personality, and there are 'hundreds of passages where *homo* could be substituted for *persona* without any apparent change in the sense'.[6] If we find a lack of analysis where

---

[1] *Harrod's Ltd.* v. *Lemon*, [1931] 2 K.B. 157; *Dunlop Rubber Co. Ltd.* v. *W. B. Haigh and Son*, [1937] 1 K.B. 347.   [2] *Wurzel* v. *Houghton*, [1937] 1 K.B. 380.
[3] Pollock and Maitland, *History of English Law*, i. 469. The delictual responsibility of medieval corporations is discussed by W. Ullmann, 64 *L.Q.R.* (1948), 77.
[4] *Supra*, § 77.   [5] *Personality in Roman Private Law.*   [6] Ibid. 5.

the individual is concerned, it is not surprising that 'the Republican lawyers did not get beyond the first rudiments of that very abstract and artificial conception, corporate personality'.[1] *Collegia, societates publicanorum*, the *hereditas iacens*, municipalities, and charities raised awkward questions, but, although a practical solution was reached, there was a 'very slender foundation of abstract legal theory'.[2] Thus Paul thought that 'municipes per se nihil possidere possunt, quia universi consentire non possunt'.[3] Who owned the property donated to *collegia*?[4] These questions cannot be answered —indeed it 'is highly improbable that (the lawyers) ever asked, or were asked the question'.[5] Gradually, by means of representatives, 'colleges' can perform many juristic acts, but the jurists give no clear analysis.

In English law there were in the thirteenth and fourteenth centuries numerous active groups such as countries, boroughs, hundreds, manors, merchant guilds, trading guilds, chantries, deans and chapters, monasteries, and societies of lawyers.[6] Some of these groups were 'dissolved into their component parts'[6] before they became corporations, others followed a gradual development to legal personality. When Bracton wrote, the notion of corporate personality was not clearly understood, and the evolution was comparatively slow.[7] The inimitable touch of Maitland has enlivened the story of the corporation sole, and we see there the great difficulty that exists in securing a clear distinction between the rights of the natural man and the rights of the corporation sole which he represents.[8] The corporation sole was a useful device for the holding of title to Church land, but, although logic would require us to recognize that the artificial corporation sole can survive the death of the natural man, medieval lawyers thought that the freehold was in abeyance if the benefice was vacant. A Statute of Limitations speaks of a corporation sole or his predecessor.[9] A parson cannot make a lease to the corporation sole, for he cannot be both lessor and lessee. 'The ecclesiastical corporation sole is no "juristic person"; he or it is either natural man or juristic abortion.'[10] The same confusion is seen in the law relating to corporations aggregate. Even when theoretical ideas are accepted,

---

[1] Op. cit. 129.   [2] Op. cit. 236.   [3] *Dig.* 41. 2. 1. 22.
[4] Op. cit. 133.   [5] Op. cit. 134.
[6] Holdsworth, *History of English Law*, iii. 469.
[7] Op. cit. 482.
[8] *Collected Papers*, iii. 210; G. W. Keeton, *Elementary Principles of Jurisprudence* (2nd ed.), 152.
[9] 3 & 4 Will. IV, c. 27, § 29; F. W. Maitland, op. cit. 240.   [10] Op. cit. 243.

there is naturally great difficulty in applying them to particular cases. In the fifteenth century it was felt that a corporation could not sue one of its members, for this was really a case of a man suing himself.[1]

By the time of Coke it was laid down that a corporation could be created either by the common law, by authority of Parliament, by royal charter, or by prescription—but some 'lawful authority of incorporation' there must be.[2] Corporations played a large part in the development of the British Empire, but the 'South Sea Bubble' of 1720 caused a general feeling of mistrust, and it was not until the nineteenth century that incorporation could be easily secured by trading bodies.[3] Modern commerce would be impossible without the convenient device of the limited liability company. By 1914 there were 65,000 registered companies in England, but within forty years the number increased to 331,000.[4]

§ 89. TYPES OF INCORPORATION

In English law there are two main types, the corporation aggregate and the *corporation sole*. The former 'is an incorporated *group* of co-existing persons, and a *corporation sole* is an incorporated *series* of successive persons'.[5] The joint-stock company illustrates the first, the ecclesiastical *corporation sole* (the parson) the second.[6] But the courts have not treated a *corporation sole* as a conception akin to that of the corporation aggregate, and have restricted its powers considerably.[7]

Continental law does not recognize the *corporation sole*, although property may be assigned to the successive holders of a particular office, but the device of *separatio bonorum* is regarded as sufficient.[8] There are two forms of juristic persons which are recognized by continental law but unknown to English law. Firstly there is the *hereditas iacens* which in Roman law was said not to be, but to resemble, a person.[9] Between the death of the *paterfamilias* and the entry of the heir there might be a long gap. In English law the institution of the personal representative ensures that there will be someone immediately responsible for the administration of the estate, but in

---

[1] Holdsworth, op. cit. v. 280–1.   [2] Op. cit. ix. 46.
[3] B. C. Hunt, *Development of the Business Corporation in England, 1800–1867.*
[4] L. C. B. Gower, *Law and Opinion in England in the 20th Century* (ed. M. Ginsberg), 144–5.   [5] J. W. Salmond, *Jurisprudence* (12th ed.), 308.
[6] *Supra*, § 77, for a discussion of the Crown as a *corporation sole.*
[7] G. W. Keeton, op. cit. 162.   [8] M. Wolff, 54 *L.Q.R.* (1938), 494.
[9] *Dig.* 46. 1. 22. P. W. Duff discusses many of these texts, op. cit. 19, 162.

Roman law the heir was the administrator, and until he had 'entered'
on the inheritance there was no legal person who could give validity
to the acts of slaves belonging to the inheritance. How was this problem to be solved? The first Roman view was that the *hereditas iacens*
represented the person of the deceased; but a second view held that
it was supported by the *persona* of the heir, his entry having a retrospective effect; a third view was that there was no owner and that the
hereditas itself must 'own itself'. This last theory can be made intelligible only by treating the *hereditas* as a legal *persona*. The second
form of juristic person is the incorporated foundation which in
English law is usually based on a trust, but which in the absence of
this device can satisfactorily function only if it is personified. In
French law the *fondation* has been defined as *l'affectation perpétuelle
d'un fonds à un but déterminé*.[1] Legal personality may be acquired
by presidential decree if the purpose is one which is in the public
interest. In some systems the personification of a fund may be obtained
with a minimum of formalities.

§ 90. THEORIES OF THE NATURE OF CORPORATE PERSONALITY

In this part of jurisprudence we see an interesting conflict between
philosophic theories as to the nature of corporate personality and
the insurgent demand of economic forces for a further recognition
of those forms of organization which seem so essential to modern
life. The grant of legal personality is clearly within the gift of the
State, for it may be refused to natural persons. In the case of the
natural person, however, it is clear that the law grants legal personality to a physical entity existing in space and possessing what (for
lack of a better term) we describe as human personality. While
philosophy may find difficulty in analysing or describing the real
nature of human personality, few of us doubt that we exist, and we
compensate for our defective analysis by an intuitive understanding
of our own nature which, however inadequate it may be, at least
gives a substratum on which to build.

We have already seen that, so far as legal personality is concerned,
there is no very significant difference between that granted to human
beings and that granted to non-human beings such as groups or

---

[1] L. Michoud, *Théorie de la personnalité morale* (3rd ed.), 1, § 76, cited M. S. Amos
and F. P. Walton, *Introduction to French Law*, 50. For analogous provisions of German
law, see *BGB*. 80.

other entities.[1] There are vital differences, however, between a human being on the one hand and a group of human beings or an idol or some other entity on the other. A question which has often been asked is: 'When the law grants legal personality to a group, what is the nature of the entity which is thus recognized?' as though the answer to that question will resolve the problems relating to the nature of legal personality and, in particular, to the nature of corporate personality. If for no other reason, it will not resolve those problems because it is impossible to discover a common *essence* which unifies all the entities on which legal personality is conferred.

For that and for other reasons it may seem outside the range of jurisprudence to discuss that question. It is desirable to do so, however, for the following reasons: Firstly, philosophic (or what are alleged to be philosophic) views as to the nature of groups have not remained in the rare air of the universities, but have been put forward as justifications for working rules of law. Thus the fiction theory was used by some to restrict the power of corporations, and the realist theory as a basis for the argument that the road to legal personality should be made as easy as possible and that the widest powers should be given. In countries where incorporation was difficult and the device of trustees was not available[2] many philosophical arguments were introduced into jurisprudence. The doctrine of natural rights was that a human being possessed certain inherent rights by virtue of his personality as an individual.[3] When it was desired to protect the interests of groups, it seemed an obvious approach to prove that a group possessed a real personality from which sprang certain inherent rights. Some of the realist theories might be paraphrased as the doctrine of 'natural rights for groups'. A second reason for the study of the theories that have been developed to answer the question posed is that many of the purely legal problems arising in connection with groups and associations cannot be fully understood without some acquaintance with the nature of the entities which have enjoyed legal personality. A third is that to do so provides an opportunity to

---

[1] Cf. A. Kocourek, *Jural Relations* (2nd ed.), 57.

[2] Cf. Maitland, introduction to Gierke's *Political Theories of the Middle Age*, xxx–xxxi. The fiction theory gave the prince the right to keep the corporate form 'under lock and key . . . but . . . what for the civilians was a question of life and death was often in England a question of mere convenience and expense, so wide was that blessed back-stair. The trust deed might be long; the lawyer's bill might be longer . . . but the organized group could live and prosper, and be all the more autonomous because it fell under no solemn legal rubric'. The law of France after the Revolution settlement has been parodied as a command by the State: 'Thou shalt have no other associations but me': J. Bonnecase, *La Pensée juridique française*, i. 272.   [3] *Supra*, § 33.

illustrate the kind of thinking[1] attributed in outline to Oxford lawyers in the early part of this work[2] and to suggest that some of the most puzzling problems for the legal theorist may be elucidated by it.

At the outset a warning is necessary. Jurisprudence has been much confused by amateurish excursions into the closely defended realms of philosophy. Moreover, there have been so many theories[3] and so many variations even in doctrines that fight under the same banner, that we must beware of exaggerating the role that theory has played. With a little skill (and a lack of scruple) we can reach almost any practical result from any particular theory, so complicated are the issues that arise. Both the fiction and the realist theories have been upheld for the same purpose and each for opposed ends.[4] Thus some regard the doctrine of *ultra vires* as a deduction from the fiction theory;[5] Pollock thinks it a rule of constitutional limitations based on convenience.[6] Duff suggests that 'like most English cases and most Roman texts, *Salomon* v. *Salomon & Co*.[7] can be reconciled with any theory, but is authority for none'.[8] Any penetrating analysis shows that, while theories have provided shells for the attack, the decision as to where the ammunition was to be fired has been the result of the economic and social desires of those who used the artillery.

Most of the theories which have received support suffer from the common defect that they have attempted to answer the question posed above. It has already been pointed out that many legal words are not names for things but are 'systematic' words[9] in that their meaning can only be elucidated by looking to see how they are in fact used and then by looking to the rules by which it is possible to say whether their use is part of a valid proposition of law or not. Thus it should be clear that if we take three statements such as 'Smith is a legal person', 'Krupps is a legal person for the purposes of the law of Massachusetts', and 'Corporations are legal persons', there is little profit in taking 'Smith', 'Krupps', and 'Corporations', to search them for the common essence which will identify them as legal persons. The only common factor may be that they are all, within some existing

---

[1] Not yet adopted by the courts, it is true.   [2] *Supra*, § 4.
[3] There are said to be sixteen: M. Wolff, 54 *L.Q.R.* (1938), 496.
[4] E. R. Latty, 34 *Mich. L. R.* (1936), 597 at 621; A. Nékám, *The Personality Conception of the Legal Entity*, 60.   [5] F. Hallis, *Corporate Personality*, xlv–xlvi.
[6] *Essays in the Law*, 156–7.   [7] [1897] A.C. 22.
[8] *Personality in Roman Private Law*, 215.   [9] See § 4, *supra*.

legal system, treated in accordance with the rules of that system as units for that system's method. The term 'legal person' in each of the statements cannot be elucidated by examining the natures of Smith, Krupps, etc., but only by referring to the legal system, and its rules which enable the statement to be true or untrue and thereby give the term meaning.[1] The best-known theories which have been debated in the past either attempted the infinitely difficult task of searching the entities concerned for a common essence or, assuming there was none, attributed the transposition, by an act of authority, of personality from the human model to the non-human entity by a fictional process. What are those theories?

The Fiction Theory. This theory has appeared in many forms and has been put to many uses. Some of its exponents have sought to trace it to Ulpian or at the latest to Pope Innocent IV. In its modern form it owes more to the work of Savigny than to any other jurist. Briefly, his theory started from a proposition like this: 'Besides men or "natural persons" the law knows as "subjects" of proprietary rights certain fictitious, artificial or juristic persons; as one species of this class it knows the corporation. We must carefully sunder this ideal person from those natural persons who are called its members.'[2] Long before, of course, Coke had referred to corporations as 'invisible, immortal, and resting only in intendment and consideration of the law',[3] and Blackstone was careful to describe corporations as 'artificial persons'.[4] In 1819 Marshall C.J. defined a corporation as 'an artificial being, invisible, intangible, and existing only in contemplation of law'.[5] In contrast, of course, a human being is real, tangible, existing quite apart from the contemplation of the law, and possessed of 'personality'.

Salmond said that the group has 'reality' or existence, but that it has no real personality in the philosophic sense. When the law grants legal personality to John Smith it is granting legal power to a real

---

[1] This approach is fully explained by Professor H. L. A. Hart, *Definition and Theory in Jurisprudence*, 70 *L.Q.R.* (1954), 37.

[2] F. W. Maitland, in the introduction to his translation of Gierke's *Political Theories of the Middle Age*, xx.

[3] Sutton's Hospital Case, 10 Co. Rep. 1 (*a*) 32.

[4] 1 Bl. Com. 467–8.

[5] *Dartmouth College* v. *Woodward*, 4 Wheat. 518 at p. 636. In *Rolloswin Investments Ltd.* v. *Chromolit Portugal*, [1970] 1 W.L.R. 912, it was held that a corporation was not a person within the meaning of the Sunday Observance Act, 1677, as limited liability companies were then unknown, and anyway, a corporation could not attend divine service. But surely the persons who signed the contract on behalf of the corporation could have attended church?

will: when it does so to Sunshine Limited, it is granting legal personality to an entity that has no mind and no will—in short, no real
personality.[1] When Lord Shaw said of an idol which had legal
personality that its will had to be realized, 'it is hard to doubt that
there is fiction in the air'.[2] In such a case the law imagined that the
idol was capable of exercising its will and performing acts, and imputed to it the acts of certain agents. Salmond's argument was that
the same analysis applies to the group.

The chief interest of the fiction theory, however, is the series of
deductions drawn from it. Not being a 'real' person, the corporation
cannot have any 'personality' of its own; it has no will, no mind, no
ability to act. It can have only so much as the law imputes to it by a
fiction—as though it were a real person. But most rules of law were
expressed with human beings in mind and they contain words like
'wilfully', 'intentionally', 'doing', 'acting', 'fraudulently', etc. all
too frequently. One deduction drawn from the fictional nature of a
corporation was that, as a corporation has only a fictional will imputed by the law, it could only will lawful things. By definition therefore it could not make itself liable for certain kinds of legal wrongs—
certainly it could not commit a crime involving any mental element.
Other deductions can be imagined easily and many were accepted or
at least argued. The practical effects often shock the conscience and
the reason, and many of them which were at one time accepted have
been avoided by various devices. Some illustrations of the practical
effects of these doctrines are discussed below.[3]

The Concession Theory is bound up with and sometimes confused
with the fiction theory. So far as it maintains that the law is the only
source from which legal personality may flow, it states a truism.
Whatever we may think the law should do, few would maintain that
legal personality can be secured otherwise than by compliance with

---

[1] *Jurisprudence* (9th ed.), 417–18, 433. This discussion does not appear in later
editions.
[2] P. W. Duff, *Personality in Roman Private Law*, 212. The reference is to *Pramatha
Nath Mullick* v. *Pradyumna Kumar Mullick*, [1925], L.R. 52 Ind. App. 245.
[3] See § 91. There is great diversity among the different adherents of the fiction theory
as to its precise formulation and the practical deductions that should be drawn from
it. M. Wolff, 54 *L.Q.R.* (1938), 505 et seq., discusses some of the suggested defects
of the fiction theory: it has been accused (*a*) of being incompatible with the conception
of subjective rights; (*b*) of leading to dangerous political results, e.g. confiscation of the
property of these *personae fictae*; (*c*) of being opposed to the doctrine of free association.
Wolff himself supports a fairly broad view of the fiction theory. These notes do scant
justice to Savigny's theories and arguments, which were developed with great skill and
detail, but for present purposes it is sufficient to indicate some of the difficulties which
flowed from theories such as this.

the conditions laid down by the legal order.[1] If we regard this theory as laying down the sociological truth that all group *life* (as apart from the mere grant of *legal* personality) is created by the State, then it is clearly both mischievous and erroneous. The main cause of complaint is that the reader is so often uncertain which form of the theory is meant.

The Bracket Theory[2] rests on the proposition that only human beings can have interests and rights, and that a corporation is only a legal device or formula which will enable very complex jural relations to be comprehended more simply.[3] A, B, and C form a company, and, as it is inconvenient to refer always to all of them, a bracket is placed around them to which a name is given—but, in order to understand the real position, we must remove the bracket. One value of this theory is that it emphasizes that it may be necessary to look behind the entity recognized by the law to discover the real state of affairs if that is desired.[4] It is true that most (though not all)[5] groups exist to further the interests of individual men—if the entity is an economic one, its aim is to promote the interests of members, if it is a philanthropic or charitable one, the interests of others. But while, as objective observers from outside a legal system we may regard legal personality as merely a device of the law, it is to deny the law itself to say that the only legal relations which are fixed and certain are those which are discovered by removing 'the brackets' of the corporation, for example, and analysing the relations of all the human beings involved. New and separate entities are recognized as units in the legal system by that system itself and such recognition makes possible a clear distinction between the property, rights, and duties of the legal person, on the one hand, and of the individual human beings which may be involved in the make-up of that legal person, on the other.

[1] The right to associate should be distinguished from the question of the grant of legal personality to such associations as exist. (*a*) The law may prohibit all associations or the forming of organized groups, for any purpose or for particular purposes which are specified. (*b*) The law may give a wide liberty of association for lawful ends, but refuse legal personality. (*c*) The law may grant liberty of association and grant legal personality to some groups and not to others. (*d*) Legal personality may be regarded as a matter of fact to be achieved by a certain degree of inner unity and organization. Even in this sense, however, it is granted by the law, since the law lays down the conditions which create legal personality.
[2] Otherwise the Symbolist Theory of Ihering.
[3] R. Ihering, *Geist des römischen Rechts*, i. 202.
[4] M. Wolff, 54 *L.Q.R.* (1938), 497.
[5] A group might be set up to prevent cruelty to animals. In a broad sense the cultivation of humanitarianism is a human interest, but it might be argued that the protection of the interests of the individual members was not the real purpose of the group.

One can hardly make a contract with a bracket.[1] It is socially and economically false, as well as legally untrue, to say that only individual men can be the bearers of legal rights. Further, the deductions that may be drawn from this theory have been rejected repeatedly by courts in common law jurisdictions on both sides of the Atlantic. The academic puzzle of generalizing the conditions under which a court may 'pierce the veil of incorporation' would not have presented itself had they not been so rejected.[2]

The 'group concept' has led to many difficulties. A typical organization is a finance company which raises the capital, a holding company which determines policy, and finally a host of subsidiary companies, some wholly owned by the holding company and some partly owned. Sometimes there is a tendency to treat the whole 'empire' as one unit and to transfer money from one company to another, just as a man might transfer his change from a waistcoat to a trouser pocket. Thus the finance company may lend money to a subsidiary in difficulties, without taking security. This ignores the fact that each unit is a legal entity, with its own shareholders and creditors. It is unfair to those who invest in the finance company to have its assets dissipated to help another unit. Where there are overlapping boards of directors, public policy demands that each director considers the interest of the company on the board of which he is sitting at the moment. The 'group' has no legal personality, and while it may have a broad financial policy and have a certain unity from the business angle, the rights and obligations of each incorporated company must be kept distinct so far as the law is concerned. The publication of consolidated accounts sometimes makes it difficult for the shareholder in a subsidiary to understand the true position. There were two spectacular crashes in Victoria in the 1960s which underlined the importance of not allowing the group concept to overshadow the legal position which must treat each incorporated company as a separate legal personality.[3]

Kelsen[4] adopts the purely formal approach, which is adopted as the basis for the present discussion, and argues that there is in essence no difference between the *legal* personality of a company and that

---

[1] Unless that bracket has been recognized by the legal system as a legal person.

[2] See e.g. I. M. Wormser, *The Disregard of the Corporate Fiction and Allied Corporation Problems* (1927).

[3] The reference is to the collapse of the Korman and Reid Murray groups; see e.g. Parliamentary Papers—Victoria 7859/66.

[4] *Annales de l'Institut de droit comparé* (1936), ii. 26–7.

of an individual. Personality, in the legal sense, is only a technical personification of a complex of norms, a focal point of imputation which gives a unity to certain complexes of rights and duties. More or less arbitrarily, the law individualizes certain parts of the legal order and establishes a certain unity in the rights and obligations pertaining to it, but this is only a technical means of securing facility of procedure, for all that is real consists of the rights of human individuals. This (he submits) is the only approach for a pure science of law and has the advantage of ending the tiresome and futile arguments concerning the psychological and philosophical nature of group personality. The analysis is sound and essential to the understanding of the legal problems that arise, but it goes too far to argue that jurisprudence must be limited to an understanding of the legal logic involved once the recognition of legal personality is accepted for what it is. If light is to be thrown on the actual problems which arise for solution, students of jurisprudence must have some understanding of the nature of the facts and hence of the different kinds of entities which may be made the subject of claims that they be recognized as legal persons.[1] It is, however, essential not to confuse the two matters for study—the logic of the law once recognition is achieved, and the legislative problem of when and why recognition should be granted.

The Realist Theory. It has long been common to apply the analogy of the organism to a group. John of Salisbury in the twelfth century designated the prince as the head, the senate as the heart, the praesides and the judges as the ears, eyes, and tongue, the tax collectors as the intestines, and the workers as the feet.[2] But it is hardly necessary to emphasize the rather fanciful extravagance of these physical comparisons. The modern realist theory builds on an analysis of human personality, and regards group personality as in essence possessing the same characteristics. Gierke speaks of the group as having a real mind, a real will, and a real power of action.[3] What then is the essence of human personality? 'By a person we mean a rational individual, or if we prefer to put it so, a concrete individual mind.'[4] There are two elements in personality, a rational element and what (for lack of a better term) may be described as individuality.

---

[1] See *Legal Personality and Political Pluralism.* L. C. Webb (ed.), 1958.
[2] Cited M. Wolff, 54 *L.Q.R.* (1938), 498–9.
[3] F. W. Maitland's introduction to Gierke's *Political Theories of the Middle Age*; F. Hallis, *Corporate Personality*, 137, 146; Sobie Mogi, *Otto von Gierke*; W. M. Geldart. 27 *L.Q.R.* (1911), 90.   [4] C. C. J. Webb, *God and Personality*, 89.

If the power of the reason to organize experience and to direct action is emphasized as the sole essential mark of personality, we may plausibly argue that a group is a person. The same reason, which (we flatter ourselves) directs our individual lives, may be seen in the life of the group working in the service of those ends which the group desires. In a very real sense we may speak of the honour of Great Britain or the purposes of her foreign policy. But there is also in human personality an 'irrational surd'[1]—a feeling of individuality, of self-consciousness, an 'experience centre' which organizes experience, not only on the basis of abstract reason, but on the foundation of personal experience. Each individual has a continuity of experience: when he wakes in the morning he has (or should have) no difficulty in knowing who he is or in picking up the threads of his individual life. Attempts have been made to discover a collective consciousness or experience centre for the group, but they have not been particularly successful. We do find in the group a sense of the warmth and intimacy which belong to self-consciousness; there is, as Hauriou maintains, a communion between the members of the group which directly affects their actions;[2] but all the bold and interesting metaphors of the institutionalists fail to demonstrate that the inner unity of the group exists otherwise than in the minds of the members who compose it. It is difficult to accept the arguments brought forward to prove that there is a psychological continuity in the group mind similar to that of the individual—stripped of their eloquent verbiage, many of the arguments seem rather threadbare.[3] However interesting this line of thought, it is impossible to do justice to it in a general textbook.

The realistic theory or the institutional doctrine may be more easily applied to certain groups than to others. There may be very real analogies to human personality in the life of a nation, a group, or a university, but a one-man company or a foundation seems worlds removed. 'It has often struck me that morally there is most personality where legally there is none. A man thinks of his club as a living being, honourable as well as honest, while the joint-stock company is

---

[1] Ibid. 111. 'Thus to the generalizing reason . . . personality is, as it were, a surd: it can at best be represented by a series of characteristics which can never be completed, so as to constitute *that very person* and not merely *a person of just that kind*.'

[2] *Cahiers de la Nouvelle Journée,* no. 4, p. 10; A. Desqueyrat, *L'Institution, le droit objectif et la technique positive,* 15.

[3] M. Hauriou considers that the dynamic will of the institution brings together past, present, and future in an indissoluble unity: J. T. Delos, *Archives de phil. du droit* (1931, 1–2), 97.

only a sort of machine into which he puts money and out of which he draws dividends.'[1] There is something rather ludicrous in treating joint-stock companies as bearers of 'natural rights' so that it is *contra bonos mores* for one company to agree to become a mere tool of another—yet so it has been decided in Germany, apparently in reliance on the realist theory.[2] Wolff asks whether a promise by a company to dissolve itself would be unenforceable as being a promise to commit *felo de se*.[3] Thurman Arnold has humorously shown the curious results that follow from the tendency to treat great industrial combines as real persons whose liberty and dignity must be defended. Constitutional provisions designed to protect the personal rights of the American citizen were pressed into service to protect the freedom of huge enterprises which tyrannized over the consumer.[4] Freedom of the great industries from restraint 'was dramatized as individual freedom. . . . So long as men instinctively thought of these great institutions as individuals, the emotional analogies of home and freedom and all the other trappings of "rugged individualism" became their most potent protection.'[5] The lesson is that, while analogies are useful servants, they warp our thought ruthlessly if they become masters of our intellectual processes and are applied without rigorous scrutiny.

Some have said that Maitland accepted the realist theory. It is true that he explained Gierke's theories to English readers and that he showed the difficulties in the fiction theory. It is not true, however, that he wholly accepted, or preached the total acceptance, of that theory.[6] It is much more true to say that Pollock and Dicey accepted the realist theory.[7] Maitland sums up Gierke's theories by saying: 'Our German fellowship is no fiction, no symbol, no piece of the State's machinery, no collective name for individuals, but a living organism and a real person, with body members and a will of its own. Itself can will, itself can act; it wills and acts by the men who are its organs as a man wills and acts by brain, mouth, and hand; it is a

---

[1] F. W. Maitland, *Collected Papers*, iii. 383.

[2] *Reichsgericht, Zivilsachen*, 82, 313, cited M. Wolff, 54 *L.Q.R.* (1938), 494 at 501. Lord Maugham shows a clear understanding of the absurdity of this approach, in dealing with clogs on the equity of redemption. There is less likelihood of a company being oppressed than there is in the case of the individual: *Knightsbridge Estates Trust Ltd.* v. *Byrne*, [1940] A.C. 613 at 623.

[3] Op. cit. 501.

[4] *The Folklore of Capitalism*, ch. viii.

[5] Ibid. 190.

[6] See H. L. A. Hart, *Definition and Theory in Jurisprudence*, 70 *L.Q.R.* (1954) at 51.

[7] P. W. Duff, *Personality in Roman Private Law*, 216.

gesamtperson, and its will is a *gesamtwille*; it is a group-person, and its will is a group will.'[1]

The Purpose Theory.[2] The name goes a long way to explain this theory. It rests on the same initial premiss as the symbolist theory: that really only human beings are persons. But the law protects certain purposes as well as the interests of individual beings. 'The property supposed to be owned by juristic persons does not belong to anybody: Gaius is strictly accurate in calling it *res nullius*. But it does "belong for" a purpose, and that is the essential fact about it.'[3] All juristic or artificial (or non-human) persons then, are merely legal devices for protecting or giving effect to some real purpose. There is much truth in this, of course, as an observation of social fact. The continuing real theme that seems to be of importance in many charitable corporations or in many associations which have been recognized as legal persons for some purpose or another, such as trade unions,[4] is the continuing fund concerned and the purposes for which it is established. An examination of the nature of such funds and their purposes, however, tells us nothing about the legal device and that is the main purpose of the present enquiry.

Conclusion. Some of the theories, when the proper modifications are made, approach very closely to each other. Thus Hallis's form of the realist theory is that the conception of corporate personality is neither more nor less than a juristic reality—which leaves aside awkward questions of psychology and philosophy.[5] Wolff would modify the fiction theory: 'if all juristic persons are treated as if they have wills of their own and are capable of acting it makes no material difference whether you say "they *are* real animate beings with wills of their own, and so on" or whether you say "some of them may be and some certainly are not, but the law treats them all as if they were".'[6] The English lawyer often flatters himself that abstract speculation has not played an undue part in the decision of cases, but the same claim has been made for continental law.[7] As has already been suggested,

[1] In his introduction to his translation of Gierke's *Political Theories of the Middle Age*, xxvi.

[2] This theory has been developed recently as the 'kitty' theory by S. Stoljar, 'The Corporate Theories of Frederick William Maitland', in *Legal Personality and Political Pluralism*, and as the 'fund' theory by H. A. J. Ford in *Unincorporated Non-profit Associations* (1959).   [3] Duff, ibid., 220.

[4] See *Bonsor* v. *Musicians' Union*, [1956] A.C. 104; *Williams* v. *Hursey* (1960), 103 C.L.R. 30; R. M. Martin, 'Legal Personality and the Trade Union', in *Legal Personality and Political Pluralism*.

[5] *Corporate Personality*, 240.   [6] 54 *L.Q.R.* (1938) at 510–11.

[7] M. Wolff, ibid. 521. Cf. the summary by M. S. Amos and F. P. Walton, *Introduction to French Law*, 45, of the theory of M. Planiol and G. Ripert.

any one theory may lead to absurd results if not wisely applied. The practical object which the realist theory seeks to achieve is to secure freedom for the group and a just recognition of its claims. But this may be more easily achieved by an appeal to social necessities than by buttressing a theory with rather questionable philosophical arguments. The law is wise to treat corporations as far as possible as if they were natural men.[1] But it can hardly be claimed that legal personality should be automatically achieved as soon as a group develops a certain stage of organization—if only for convenience, the law demands compliance with certain formalities as a condition of the grant of legal personality. It would be burdensome if the law had to investigate the real development of each group before it could determine whether it possessed legal personality.[2]

It should be pointed out that the phrase, 'a realist approach', has two different meanings. Firstly, there is the theory of Gierke that the group has a real mind and a real will; secondly, the doctrine of realism that practical considerations and convenience, rather than any theory, determine the solution of practical problems. A realist approach in the second sense may call for refusal to apply Gierke's theory, say, to a one-man company.

It has been suggested that, while the first task of a jurist is to understand analytically the role played by the notion of legal personality in the logic of the law, he cannot stop there. Because of the ambiguities of the word 'person' and the confusion inherent in the various theories of legal personality, the wrong questions have been asked in the process of resolving many problems concerning legal personality. The jurist must seek to ask the right questions and to distinguish between those which go to the formal logic of a legal system and those which go to the assimilation and evaluation of facts which the legal

---

[1] 'If the law allows men to form permanently organised groups, those groups will be for common opinion right-and-duty bearing units; and if the lawgiver will not openly treat them as such he will misrepresent, or, as the French say, he will "denature" the facts: in other words, he will make a mess and call it law': F. W. Maitland, *Collected Papers*, iii. 341.

[2] Some legal systems have recognized that legal personality may exist without direct grant from the State. Roman-Dutch law has recognized the personality of a building society formed before the Companies Acts were passed, even although the company had never been expressly incorporated; see *Morison* v. *Standard Building Society*, [1932] A.D. 229, discussed by D. Lloyd, *Law of Unincorporated Associations* (1938), 11–14. In some American states there is a doctrine of *de facto* corporations, but it has a fairly narrow application. French law recognizes *la demi-personnalité* in some cases: D. Lloyd, op. cit. 222. H. J. Laski, 29 *Harv. L. R.* (1916), 404 at 424, argues that the distinction between corporations and voluntary associations should be abolished, but this would lead to uncertainty whether the group was so developed that it should be treated as a legal person.

system seems to organize. The jurist cuts himself off from life itself and from communication with other workers in the field if he limits himself to the first task. It is suggested therefore that he should seek to separate the questions which ask whether or not an entity *has been* or *is* recognized by the rules of a particular legal system as a legal person for the purposes of legal reasoning[1] and, if so, just what kind of legal personality the rules of that legal system establish for it, from questions which ask whether or not a given entity *should be* recognized as a legal person within a legal system whose rules do not clearly answer the question and, if yes, then just what kind of personality *should be* accorded to that entity within that legal system.[2] Questions of the former kind are proper for courts to decide and are commonly undertaken by courts whereas questions of the latter kind are, within the traditions of common law courts, properly for legislatures to decide and in this modern day are usually decided by legislatures. Courts, however, from time to time, must face such questions and they do so with an uneasiness which reveals their reluctance to tread within the legislative field.[3]

§ 91. SOME PRACTICAL PROBLEMS

If we examine English writing we find the utmost diversity as to which theory best explains decided cases. Some advocates say English law has adopted the fiction theory,[4] others the realist,[5] while Holdsworth considers that no theory has been adopted save that the corporation should be treated as far as possible like a natural man—practical considerations, rather than the logic of theory, being the guiding force.[6] This clash of views represents the real difficulties that arise in translating any general theory into practical rules of law.

English law makes a clear-cut distinction between a company and the individuals who happen to compose it.[7] To take an example: a particular company had only two shareholders, who were also the directors. By the articles the directors' fees were to be determined by

---

[1] i.e. is to have the capacity to enter legal relations.

[2] See D. P. Derham, 'Theories of Legal Personality', in *Legal Personality and Political Pluralism* (1958).

[3] Contrast *Salomon* v. *Salomon & Co.*, [1897] A.C. 22 and *Lee* v. *Lee's Air Farming Ltd.*, [1961] A.C. 12; [1960] 3 All E.R. 420, with *Bonsor* v. *Musicians' Union*, [1956] A.C. 104; and see the discussion by Fullagar J. in *Williams* v. *Hursey* (1960), 103 C.L.R. 30, 52–70.   [4] e.g. F. Hallis, *Corporate Personality*, xli.

[5] e.g. Lord Wright in *The Future of the Common Law* (Harvard Tercentenary), 74. Cf. F. Pollock, *Essays in the Law*, 179.

[6] *History of English Law*, ix. 52.   [7] Ibid. 71.

a meeting of shareholders and the two men (as shareholders) voted to the directors practically all the profits, the object being to secure a lower rate of income tax, since directors' fees are (in legal theory) the result of personal exertion. It was held that the validity of this procedure could not be attacked in liquidation proceedings, however unreal the distinction between the powers of the directors and the shareholders might be on the facts of the particular case.[1]

The problem becomes more involved when a parent corporation begins to create subsidiaries controlled by the parent body. If a railway company is prohibited from carrying goods manufactured by itself, can it transport goods manufactured by a subsidiary which has been set up to evade the law? If a company promises not to engage in a certain business within a particular town can it legally set up a subsidiary to carry on that business? In America the problem has been hotly debated whether the court is entitled to 'pierce the veil of the corporate entity' and examine the reality beneath.[2] Where a corporation has been created to escape an obligation in contract or tort, to perpetrate a fraud, to evade a statute, to hinder or delay creditors, or to obtain property free of equities, some courts will treat the corporation as a mere agent either of the shareholders or of the parent corporation, as the case may be. The solution of this problem when to 'pierce the veil' is dictated by practical needs, and the only theory which can be usefully applied is a realism which holds, not that corporations are real persons, but that they should be treated as such save where there are imperative reasons to the contrary.[3]

Early English cases, even if the fiction theory was not expressly

[1] *In re Eutrope*, [1932] V.L.R. 453.

[2] G. F. Canfield, 17 *Col. L. R.* (1917), 128; I. M. Wormser, *Disregard of the Corporate Fiction and Allied Corporation Problems* (1927); E. R. Latty, 34 *Mich. L. R.* (1936), 597; 21 *Iowa L. R.* (1936), 630. For an English discussion see *Smith, Stone & Knight Ltd.* v. *Birmingham Corp.*, [1939] 4 All E.R. 116; O. Kahn-Freund, 7 *Mod. L. R.* (1944), 54; L. C. B. Gower, *Modern Company Law* (2nd ed.), ch. x. In 1926 Cardozo J. said: 'The whole problem of the relation between parent and subsidiary corporations is one that is still involved in the mists of metaphor. Metaphors in law are to be carefully watched, for starting as devices to liberate thought, they often end by enslaving it': *Berkey* v. *Third Avenue Railway*, 244 N.Y. 84 at p. 94—cited by B. F. Cataido, *Limited Liability with One-Man Companies and Subsidiary Corporations* (1953), 18 *Law and Contemporary Problems*, 472 at 498.

[3] Realism in the sense that the actual facts must be examined and the decision based on a shrewd appreciation of the substance of the matter. But such an approach does tend to lead to inconsistency in the decisions. The law must also balance the advantages of a definite, if rather narrow theory, with the rather too great fluidity that is achieved by an approach governed by expediency. Section 35 of the Transport Act, 1947, 10 & 11 Geo. VI, c. 49, is realistic enough to take account of, and define, a 'holding company'.

adopted, show a tendency to regard a corporation as possessing only
a fictitious will. Thus it was argued that a will which was imputed by
law could not be directed to criminal activities, for the fictitious will
was imputed only for the pursuit of lawful ends. The development
of case law shows an increasing tendency to overcome the theoretical
difficulties involved, and to hold corporations liable for certain
crimes, but how far this evolution will go is still uncertain.[1] The
first difficulty is that of punishment.[2] If the only possible sentence
is imprisonment or death, then it is futile to indict a corporation. In
Tasmania the Criminal Code lays down maximum penalties only
and leaves the court free to impose a lower sentence of imprisonment
or a fine if it desires. Under such a code, no difficulty arises about
punishment. The second difficulty is that a corporation can act only
through agents and that there is a presumption against imputing the
mens rea of the agent to the principal. One escape from this doctrine
is to treat acts of the primary representatives of the company as the
act of the company itself.[3] This is the approach of German law.
Where common employment was concerned, English law did not
treat the directors as being fellow servants with an inferior employee.[4]
In *D.P.P.* v. *Kent & Sussex Contractors Ltd.*,[5] the charge was that
returns, known to be false, were sent in by the transport manager
for the purpose of obtaining petrol. Lord Caldecote held that the
company 'by the only people who could act or think for it' had
committed the offence.[6] *Moore* v. *Bresler Ltd.*[7] goes beyond this
doctrine. Here the acts were not authorized by the directors but by
the secretary of the company who was also a branch manager, and
the branch sales manager. Moreover, these officers intended to
defraud the company itself. Lord Caldecote thought it sufficient that
the men were important officials of the company acting within their
authority. This increases greatly the area of criminal liability of
corporations and seems to blur the distinction between the primary
representatives and mere servants: in the case of the latter, the

---

[1] R. S. Welsh, 62 *L.Q.R.* (1946), 345—an authoritative survey; L. H. Leigh, *The
Criminal Responsibility of Corporations in English Law* (1969).
[2] Procedural difficulties concerning indictment of corporations were overcome by
§ 38 of Criminal Justice Act, 1925.
[3] C. R. N. Winn, 3 *Camb. L. J.* (1929), 398.
[4] *Fanton* v. *Denville*, [1932] 2 K.B. 309 at 329.   [5] [1944] K.B. 146.
[6] Approved by C.C.A., *R.* v. *I.C.R. Haulage Ltd.*, [1944] K.B. 551. See also *Tesco
Supermarkets Ltd.* v. *Nattrass*, [1971] 2 Al. E.R. 127. Lord Reid points out at 132 that
the person who acts for the company is not its *alter ego*, but is the company itself.
Other servants are the agents of the company.
[7] [1944] 2 All E.R. 515.

corporation should not be vicariously liable in crime (in the absence of statutory direction), whatever may be the position in tort. The conclusion of Welsh[1] is that a corporation can be indicted and that whether the criminal act of an agent can be regarded as the act of the company itself must depend upon 'the nature of the charge, the relative position of the officer or agent, and the other relevant facts and circumstances of the case'.[2]

In the law of contract there was a curious distinction between common law and statutory corporations. The former may bind themselves in the same way as a natural person, though if the provisions of the charter are not observed, the Crown may proceed by *scire facias*: the latter may make contracts only within the limits of the memorandum of association.[3] This last rule seems to have some affinities with the fiction theory, since the power of the company is limited by the terms of the grant of personality. But we do not argue that because an infant's powers are restricted, therefore a special theory of personality should be applied to him. Moreover, the doctrine of *ultra vires* was not fully developed until the nineteenth century and in the leading case five judges were on the losing side:[4] the dispute concerned the detailed provisions of the Companies Act of 1862 and not the general theory of corporation law. In England there has been recent criticism of the *ultra vires* rule, and foreign observers regard it as strange that the company should be able to evade the performance of an agreement by the plea that it acted beyond its powers. In fact, however, the rule is becoming of less practical importance because the memorandum and articles are now drafted so widely that it is difficult to bring the doctrine of *ultra vires* into play.[5] Where it can be relied upon, however, it should be noted that it works to prevent a company binding itself by contract beyond its powers; it does not work to prevent a company receiving due

---

[1] Op. cit.

[2] Cited from *R.* v. *I.C.R. Haulage Ltd., supra* at 559. In *Lennard's Carrying Co. Ltd.* v. *Asiatic Petroleum Company Ltd.*, [1915] A.C. 705 at 713, Lord Haldane points out that the active and directing will of the company must be sought in the person of somebody who is really the directing mind and will of the corporation, 'the very ego and centre of the personality of the corporation'.

[3] W. S. Holdsworth, *History of English Law*, ix. 59–61.

[4] Including the astute Blackburn J.: *Ashbury Railway Carriage and Iron Co.* v. *Riche*, L.R. (1875), 7 H.L. 653. In the Court of Exchequer two out of three judges found for the plaintiff; in the Exchequer Chamber the six judges were equally divided; the House of Lords unanimously found for the defendants.

[5] The Cohen Committee on Company Law Amendment advised in 1945 that the *ultra vires* rule should be abolished. Australia has modified the rule in the Uniform Companies Acts passed by the several states.

consideration for performance of a contract which went beyond its powers—at least that seems the better view.[1]

In the law of tort, after some hesitation, metaphysical difficulties were avoided by adopting the simple principle that a corporation was liable for the acts of its servants in the course of employment. As late as 1886, however, Lord Bramwell thought that a corporation was not liable for any tort in which proof of malice was an essential element,[2] but the tide was too strong.[3] Once the doctrine of master and servant is applied, there is no reason why the malice of the servant (if it be in the course of employment) should not be imputed to the master. The old problem, however, has raised its head with regard to torts committed during the carrying out of an undertaking which is *ultra vires* of the corporation. The strict view is that if a tram company has no power to run buses, then any bus drivers engaged are not in law the servants of the company and therefore the company is not liable for their torts.[4] Even approval of all the shareholders and directors of the company's entrance into the field of bus transport is of no avail, since the question is one of lack of legal power. But although logically unassailable,[5] this doctrine has been rejected by the overwhelming weight of American authority.[6] English law is still uncertain, but there is support for a practical approach which emphasizes the injustice to the victim if he is denied a remedy. In effect, the acts of the directors in their official capacity should be regarded as the acts of the company—at least so far as liability in tort is concerned.[7]

---

[1] *In the Matter of K.L. Tractors Ltd.* (1961), 34 Aust.L.J.R. 481 (in the High Court of Australia); and see L. C. B. Gower, *Modern Company Law* (3rd ed.) at 95.

[2] *Abrath* v. *N.E. Rly.* (1886), 11 A.C. 247. Sometimes the judgment is called a dissenting one. Strictly there was unanimity in dismissing the appeal, but Lord Bramwell was the only one to make this specific point.

[3] See *Citizens Life Assurance* v. *Brown*, [1904] A.C. 423.

[4] A. L. Goodhart, *Essays in Jurisprudence and the Common Law*, 91.

[5] P. H. Winfield's argument in *Text-Book of the Law of Tort* (4th ed.), 107, does not touch Goodhart's main point, which is that the company cannot act beyond its power. At the most, an order of the directors would make them personally liable, ratification by the shareholders might make them jointly responsible, but no act can give power to a company to engage a servant when that power is refused by law. In the 6th ed. of Winfield's *Text-Book*, the editor (T. Ellis Lewis) argues that questions of power are irrelevant when a company expressly authorizes a tort. He asserts that a company is also liable for the torts of a servant acting within the scope of his employment but not otherwise, and that the whole ground is covered by those two propositions.

[6] F. V. Harper, *Law of Torts*, 654. See also the Cohen Committee Report, 1945, Cmd. 6659 and the Jenkins Committee Report, 1962, Cmd. 1749.

[7] J. W. Salmond, *Torts* (15th ed.), 571; *Campbell* v. *Paddington Corp.*, [1911] 1 K.B. 869; L. C. B. Gower, op. cit. 95.

The recognition of foreign corporations raises several interesting questions. If we apply the concession theory logically, then a French company has no legal personality in England, unless it is specifically granted personality by English law—and strictly there would be two legal persons, one governed by French and one by English law. But common sense and convenience have dictated the recognition of the personality of foreign companies.[1] In this respect a corporation has indeed been treated as far as possible like a natural man, but this has been due to the practical needs of business—not to deductions from any particular theory. Since a Russian company trades in England as a *persona* created by Russian law, it follows that if the company be dissolved in Russia, this is equivalent to laying an axe at the roots, and the English branches fall with the Russian tree.[2] How the English branches are to be wound up has provided an interesting problem, but apparently a section of the Companies' Act[3] allows the company to be brought to life in order that it may die a second time, secure in the knowledge that justice has been done.[4] There were great logical difficulties involved in such a view,[5] but the practical viewpoint of English law may be seen in Lord Macmillan's quip that a legal system which allowed John Doe and Richard Roe (who never existed at all) to sue could suffer with equanimity 'the apparition, at the bidding of the Legislature, of a dissolved company as a plaintiff'.[6]

If we rail at English law for its easy worship of convenience, we can see in American law the effects of the worship of an obsolete theory. Taney C.J. laid down that a company had no existence outside the boundaries of the state which had incorporated it.[7]

---

[1] E. H. Young, 22 *L.Q.R.* (1906), 178; A. Farnsworth, *The Residence and Domicil of Corporations.*

[2] *Russian and English Bank* v. *Baring Bros.*, [1932] 1 Ch. 435 at 440; *Lazard Bros. & Co.* v. *Midland Bank*, [1933] A.C. 289 at 297.

[3] § 338 of the Companies' Act, 1929.

[4] *Russian and English Bank* v. *Baring Bros.*, [1936] A.C. 405; the question of what effect the revival of the company has upon acts done during the interregnum creates problems—see *Re Banque des Marchands de Moscou*, [1958] Ch. 182; and see the interesting note on the practical difficulties arising out of the revivification of a dissolved foreign corporation by M. Mann, 15 *Mod. L. R.* (1952), 479.

[5] See the dissenting judgment of Lord Russell. Lord Maugham states that, if there is a legal entity bearing the name of the Russian and English Bank, 'it must be a different corporation existing by English law . . . possessing assets, if any, only within the British jurisdiction, and apparently it must be a quasi-trading corporation without statutes, or charter or articles of association . . .' (same case at 442).

[6] Same case at 438.

[7] *Bank of Augusta* v. *Earle* (1839), 13 Pet. 519; G. C. Henderson, *The Position of Foreign Corporations in American Constitutional Law*, 48.

Theoretically, therefore, a company could neither sue nor be sued in a foreign state. The practical evils which resulted have been largely remedied by fictions, but to the English lawyer the chief impression left by American writing is the complexity of American law and the simplicity of the English doctrine of recognition. Facts exact a penalty when the theory of the law is too rigid.

The residence of corporations raises many interesting problems. In determining liability for income tax, English law uses a realist test—where are the head and brains of the company situated?[1] For the purpose of determining enemy character the court looks to the actual control, and not the place of registration.[2] So far as domicil is concerned, the law adopts the analogy of birth in the case of the individual and asks where the company is registered. But, unlike the individual, the company has no power to change its domicil:[3] if it dissolves and is incorporated in another country, it is technically a new person.

The purpose of this cursory survey is to illustrate the practical problems that arise and to show how impossible it is to regard any one theory as affording an easy answer. Two more illustrations may complete the story. If land is bound by a restrictive covenant that title shall not be transferred to a coloured person or persons, is it a breach of covenant to convey the land to a corporation consisting entirely of negroes?[4] In many continental systems a donor can revoke a gift for ingratitude. Can a company be guilty of this graceless trait?[5] How far is the law to go in allowing to corporations the emotions and characteristics of *homo sapiens*? Can one company deal oppressively with another?[6] It is submitted that the tendency will be increasingly to impute to the company the acts and mental states of those who in effect control it.

---

[1] *De Beers Consol. Mines Ltd.* v. *Howe*, [1906] A.C. 455; but a company may apparently have two residences—*Swedish Centra. Rly. Co.* v. *Thompson*, [1925] A.C. 495; A. Farnsworth, *The Residence and Domicil of Corporations*; and see *Union Corporation Ltd.* v. *Inland Revenue Commissioners*, [1953] A.C. 482 and *Unit Construction Co. Ltd.* v. *Bullock*, [1960] A.C. 351.

[2] *Daimler Co. Ltd.* v. *Continental Tyre and Rubber Co. Ltd.*, [1916] 2 A.C. 307; R. E. L. Vaughan Williams and M. Chrussachi, 49 *L.Q.R.* (1933), 334; *Sovfracht V/o* v. *Van Udens Scheepvaart*, [1943] A.C. 203.

[3] *Gasque* v. *Commissioners of Inland Revenue*, [1940] 2 K.B. 80.

[4] *People's Pleasure Park Co.* v. *Rohieder*, [1909] 61 S.E. 794.

[5] M. Wolff, 54 *L.Q.R.* (1938) at 515.

[6] *Scottish Co-operative Wholesale Society Ltd.* v. *Meyer*, [1958] 3 All E.R. 66.

§92. ASSOCIATIONS

In English law, although there is no doctrine of 'semi-personality', many of the advantages of corporate life may be secure even without the gift of legal personality by the State.[1] The law of contract, of agency, and of co-ownership allow the members' club to flourish by the skilful use of legal devices that have been developed for other purposes. Thus if a subscription be paid, and the parties intend to enter into legal relations, the rules of the club become the terms of a contract between them.[2] If a member is wrongfully expelled, then, since the expulsion is void, it is doubtful whether damages can be recovered at common law;[3] but if a right of property is involved, equity will grant an injunction restraining members of the committee, or officers of the club, from taking any steps to prevent the member from enjoying the amenities of club life.[4] It is very difficult to define clearly what is meant by that right of property which must exist before equity will lend its aid. If the members hold the property of the club in co-ownership, then the case is clear. (But it may be noted in passing that it is a very special form of co-ownership, for the co-owners are a changing body of persons, a member's share is not alienable, neither can it be seized by his creditors nor transmitted on death—it is merely the right to enjoy the club property so long as he is a member and to share in the distribution of the property if the club be dissolved during his membership.[5] On resignation all rights disappear, and there is no power for a member to demand a

[1] D. Lloyd, *Law of Unincorporated Associations*.

[2] But the High Court of Australia has held that the payment of a subscription to the Australian Labour Party did not create a contract, since the parties did not intend to enter into legal relations: *Cameron* v. *Hogan* (1934), 51 C.L.R. 358.

[3] Halsbury, *Laws of England* (2nd ed.), iv. 494; *Cameron* v. *Hogan supra* at 372; *Edgar and Walker* v. *Meade* (1916), 23 C.L.R. 29 at 43; in *Wood* v. *Woad* (1874) L.R. 9 Ex. 190, the majority considered that an award of damages should not be made.

[4] An expulsion is wrongful if the rules of the club have not been observed, or if there is a violation of the principles of natural justice: *Maclean* v. *Workers' Union*, [1929] 1 Ch. 602 at 625; or if the committee has wrongly interpreted their powers: *Lee* v. *Showmen's Guild of Great Britain*, [1952] 2 Q.B. 329.

[5] The New Zealand Supreme Court held that a plaintiff had a remedy for wrongful expulsion although the golf club concerned had no beneficial interest in land or chattels. The plaintiff's property right was said to be his right to compete in golfing fixtures. North J. held that the refusal to accept his entry for golf fixtures was nearly enough related to a right of property. *Millar* v. *Smith* (1953), N.Z. L. R. 1049; and see H. A. J. Ford, *Expulsion from Associations*, 1 Sydney L. R. (1954), 186: 'the property and contract concepts appear from recent English decisions to be fictions behind which the courts have looked to real problems'; and see the same author and the cases he has collected in *Unincorporated Non-profit Associations* (1959)—a most valuable monograph on the problems of associations generally.

dissolution.) Another example of a right of property would be
that of a clergyman not to be expelled from a church community;[1]
but it is doubtful if an ordinary member of a church could sue for
wrongful expulsion—in whatever way the Church property was held,
it would probably be regarded as impressed with a religious trust, and
not as being held beneficially by the members.

Sometimes, instead of holding the property in co-ownership,
members may prefer to vest the property in trustees on such terms
as seem suitable. Hence the 'hedge of trustees' has been a convenient
protection behind which the corporate life may flourish. In British
communities great use is made of these devices, and powerful
churches, trade unions, clubs, and stock exchanges may be only
voluntary associations in the eyes of the law. Sometimes the rules
of the club may be so drawn as to make amendment (e.g. raising of
the subscription) impossible;[2] sometimes the trust deed may be so
narrowly drawn that the will of the majority of the members of
a church is made impotent. Thus one result of the *Free Church Case*[3]
was that twenty-six congregations were granted 1,104 churches, and
an immediate Act of Parliament was necessary to remove the
anomaly. Severe strictures have been cast on the law for its treatment
of a living organism as being rigidly bound by the original contract
or trust deed. 'The moment the religious body begins to act as though
it had any inherent life, it is liable to be hauled up in the courts and
to be condemned as having acted *ultra vires*.'[4] 'The dead hand
of the law fell with a resounding slap upon the living body of the
church.'[5] Was the Free Church a dead branch and not a living
tree?[6] But is not the criticism misdirected? Founders may draw
the contract or the trust deed as narrowly or as widely as they please:
if they choose to identify the trust with a certain theological doctrine,

---

[1] The reference, of course, is to a church which is not incorporated: *Macqueen* v.
Frackelton (1909), 8 C.L.R. 673. A member's club which bought liquor and sold it
to members was not caught by the older Licensing Acts, since the liquor was already
held by the members and the transaction was not in reality a sale: *Graff* v. *Evans* (1882),
8 Q.B.D. 373.

[2] *Harington* v. *Sendall*, [1903] 1 Ch. 921. But see *Re Conveyances dated June 13*,
(C.A.) [1969] 3 All E.R. 1175. By a majority the members of a club agreed to transfer
the property to a newly-constituted body. There was no power given in the Rules for
amendment. The Court of Appeal upheld the transactions, holding that since the
majority vote, there had been no opposition and therefore there was implied unanimity
(*sed quaere*).

[3] *General Assembly of the Free Church of Scotland* v. *Overtoun*, [1904] A.C. 515.

[4] J. N. Figgis, *Churches in the Modern State*, 43.

[5] Maitland, cited F. Hallis, *Corporate Personality*, lvii.

[6] Per Lord Macnaghten [1904] A.C. at 631. See also F. Hallis, op. c.t. lvii.

are the courts to have liberty to impose new conditions?[1] Many powerful bodies in England have, at one time or another, been content to exist as voluntary groups, and if group life were as harshly treated by the law as some suggest, the easy method of incorporation would have been adopted.[2] If properly drawn, either the form of contract or of the trust deed may supply reasonable opportunity for growth and development in the life of the group.

Indeed, it might be suggested that associations are the spoilt darlings of English law, especially when we consider the difficulties that beset the path of the hardy adventurer who would seek to make the funds of the association liable in contract or in tort. This protection of associations is not the result of any conscious policy but rather an accidental result of the application of ordinary well-known principles which work well in other fields. It is trite law that an association cannot be sued in its own name, for it has no legal personality. Hence an action lies in contract only against members who have bound themselves personally or who can be treated as principals under the ordinary rules of agency. And the law assumes that, in the case of the ordinary club, there is no implied authority in the committee to pledge the credit of members.[3] If a contract is expressed to be made between two football clubs (both being not incorporated), does the contract bind only the members at the time the contract was made? If so, in a contract intended to operate for twenty years, there may be few of the original members left, when a breach takes place.[4] If the contract was meant to bind the members of the club from time to time, no such contractual obligation can be created. Trustees who sign a lease on behalf of a club must take care, for, while they have a lien on any existing club property for reimbursement of any expenses properly incurred, there is no right of recourse against the individual members.[5] It is difficult to show that the members are liable in tort for the acts of a secretary or a servant,

---

[1] The fact that the powers of the Methodist Conference were drafted widely allowed Megarry J. to give a flexible operation to the power of the Church to enter into union: *Barker* v. *O'Gorman*, [1970] 3 All E.R. 314.
[2] Lloyd's was not incorporated till 1871. The Inns of Court are not incorporated. Many churches prefer to be voluntary associations or to create a corporation only for the purpose of holding trust moneys and property.
[3] J. Wertheimer, *Law Relating to Clubs*, ch. iii; D. Lloyd, 12 *Mod. L. R.* (1949), 409.
[4] See the interesting discussion by Gowans J. in two Victorian cases relating to football clubs: *Banfield* v. *Wells-Eicke*, [1970] V.R. 481 and *Carlton Cricket and Football Social Club* v. *Joseph*, [1970] V.R. 487.
[5] *Wise* v. *Perpetual Trustee*, [1903] A.C. 139, criticized T. C. Williams, 19 *L.Q.R.* (1903), 386.

though members of the committee may be, of course, made personally liable for torts committed by them as committee members.[1] It is not easy to generalize in simple terms, however. A representative action has been allowed against all members of a club (not only the committee) to enable a cleaner injured in the club to recover[2] and yet members of an association have been held not liable for the tortious acts of officials of the association unless they have authorized those acts.[3]

Cases decided concerning trade unions at one time gave rise to the notion that a representative action could be readily used against associations. Although the various statutes which legalized the trade union expressly stopped short of endowing it with legal personality, the *Taff Vale Case*[4] nevertheless held that a union could be sued in a representative action and its funds made liable in tort; but recent cases have emphasized that this decision depends rather on the particular statutes concerned than on any general principles relating to associations. In most cases it is difficult to show that all the members have a 'common interest' within the meaning of Order XVI, r. 9. Thus in *Barker* v. *Allanson*,[5] the plaintiff wished to recover for goods supplied to an association, but at the time the action was brought only 19 members out of a present membership of 841 had belonged to the association when the goods were supplied. Thus the majority could claim that they neither authorized nor ratified the contract in question. 'Judgment against representative defendants means judgment against each individual person covered by the representation',[6] and it is clear that it is only rarely that an action lies against every member of a club. Hence liability is normally confined either to the person who made the contract or to the committee if they can be proved to be principals: if a third party makes a contract with the association, without appreciating that it has no legal personality, then the committee or directors are liable in person.[7]

---

[1] *Brown* v. *Lewis* (1896), 12 T.L.R. 455; *Bradley Egg Farm Ltd.* v. *Clifford*, [1943] 2 All E.R. 378; *Prole* v. *Allen*, [1950] 1 All E.R. 476.

[2] *Campbell* v. *Thompson*, [1953] 1 Q.B. 445.

[3] *Baker* v. *Jones*, [1954] 2 All E.R. 553; and see H. A. J. Ford, *Unincorporated Nonprofit Associations*, for a full discussion of the relations involved in circumstances like these. [4] *Taff Vale Rly.* v. *Amal. Soc. of Rly. Servants*, [1901] A.C. 426.

[5] [1937] 1 K.B. 463.

[6] Same case at 475 per Scott L.J.; *Ideal Films* v. *Richards*, [1927] 1 K.B. 374; *Walker* v. *Sur*, [1914] 2 K.B. 930; *Hardie & Lane Ltd.* v. *Chiltern*, [1928] 1 K.B. 663 and at 696, 698, 701. Megarry J. allowed a wider theory of representation, where the action was brought to determine who the office-bearers were, on the ground that all members were interested in determining the legal position, although their views differed on the question of who the officers were: *John* v. *Rees*, [1969] 2 All E.R. 274.

[7] *Bradley Egg Farm* v. *Clifford*, [1943] 2 All E.R. 378.

Some suggest that, to avoid these difficulties, legal personality should be awarded to groups which reach a certain state of inner unity, but the resulting doubt whether a particular group possessed legal personality or not might well make the position worse instead of better. Associations may, in English law, obtain the gift of personality fairly easily, and third parties who wish to contract with a group can protect themselves by making the contract bind individual members of substance. There is no easy way, however, of guaranteeing satisfaction to those who sue in tort. To overcome difficulties of litigation French law at one stage recognized what has been termed *la demi-personnalité*.[1] An action could be brought by representation, in the English sense, but this was apparently confined to institutions formed in the public interest which possessed *une individualité véritable*.[2] Doubts naturally arose as to what privileges this 'half-personality' conferred,[3] and also as to what groups had achieved it, and the experiment cannot be regarded as having justified itself. In England a statute can create a *tertium quid*—an entity that is not a corporation and yet can sue and be sued.[4]

In *Bonsor* v. *Musicians' Union*[5] the question presented to the House of Lords was whether or not a member of a trade union could obtain damages for wrongful expulsion from the union. In the *Taff Vale Case*[6] their Lordships had held that a trade union could be sued in its own name, by non-members, to prevent a tortious act. But that decision had not clearly established the trade union as a legal person. In *Kelly* v. *National Society of Operative Printers' Assistants*[7] the Court of Appeal had held that a member of a trade union could not sue the union or its officers for wrongful expulsion, for the union had no independent legal existence and the officers were the agents of all the members including the plaintiff. In *Bonsor's Case* the House of Lords held that the plaintiff could sue the union and could recover

---

[1] G. Baudry-Lacantinerie, *Traité de droit civil* (3rd ed.), i. 354. In 1901 the acquisition of legal personality was made easier in France and the *société non-déclarée* was expressly deprived of legal personality.

[2] See appendix to D. Lloyd, *The Law of Unincorporated Associations*, 219.

[3] In English law the Minister of Health may be a corporation for the purpose of holding land, but not for the purpose of being sued. Cf. *Gilleghan* v. *Minister of Health*, [1932] 1 Ch. 86.

[4] *National Union of General and Municipal Workers* v. *Gillian and Others*, [1946] K.B. 81. Scott L.J. admitted that the trade union was not a corporation, but treated it as a *persona juridica*, which must mean a 'semi-personality'. In *Chaff and Hay Acquisition Committee* v. *Hemphill & Sons Pty. Ltd.* (1947), 74 C.L.R. 375, the High Court held that a statutory committee could be sued, though the statute had not created it a corporation.

[5] [1956] A.C. 104.   [6] *Supra.*   [7] (1915), 84 L.J.K.B. 2236.

damages out of the union's funds. The union was not 'incorporated' under any statute. A minority of their Lordships faced the question squarely and held that the union was a legal person ('a distinct legal entity') which had broken its contract and could be sued. The remainder of their Lordships approached the matter more indirectly. They took the view that the union was an unincorporated association (which it clearly was in one sense of those words) and had no independent juristic existence.[1] The whole House, none the less, achieved the result that the union could be sued in its own name and that judgment could be satisfied out of the union's assets.[2]

It is clear that there may be groups of people which look like mere voluntary associations at first glance, which none the less are recognized as legal entities by the law for some purposes. In the English common law tradition, however, the question whether or not they have been recognized as legal entities by the law (or quasi-corporations, as they are sometimes called) will usually be treated as one of statutory interpretation, on the assumption that it is the legislature alone that can create such entities.[3] It is submitted that the questions outlined in Section 90 above are the proper jurisprudential ones to ask when problems like these are encountered, however, for it is clear that courts cannot always avoid playing a substantive part in the creation or initial recognition of entities as legal persons.

REFERENCES

ALLEN, C. K., *Legal Duties*, 28.
DUFF, P. W., *Personality in Roman Private Law*.
FARNSWORTH, A., *The Residence and Domicil of Corporations*.
FORD, H. A. J., *Unincorporated Non-profit Associations* (1959).
GOODHART, A. L., *Essays in Jurisprudence*, 91.
GRAVESON, R. H., *Status in the Common Law* (1953).
HALLIS, F., *Corporate Personality*.
HENDERSON, G. C., *The Position of Foreign Corporations in American Constitutional Law*.
LLOYD, D., *Law of Unincorporated Associations*.
MAINE, H., *Ancient Law* (ed. Pollock, 1924), Note L.

[1] Lord Keith, it is true, was somewhat doubtful and at one point said it would not be wrong to call the union a legal entity—the House of five, therefore, could be said to have been equally divided on that point.
[2] And see the case of *Williams* v. *Hursey*, in the High Court of Australia (1960), 103 C.L.R. 30; and in particular the judgment of Fullagar J. in that case.
[3] See *Williams* v. *Hursey* (*supra*). Incorporation may, of course, be also created by a royal charter. See also K. W. Wedderburn, 28 *Mod. L. R.* (1965), 62.

MAITLAND, F. W., *Collected Papers*, iii. 210, 321.
NÉKÁM. A., *The Personality Conception of the Legal Entity*.
POLLOCK, F., *Essays in the Law*, 151.
POUND, R., *Interpretations of Legal History*, 54–61.
WALTON, F. P., 9 *J. Comp. Leg.* (1927), 1.
WEBB, L. C. (ed.), *Legal Personality and Political Pluralism* (1958).
WELSH, R. S., 62 *L.Q.R.* (1946), 345.
WOLFF, M., 54 *L.Q.R.* (1938), 494.

XVII

RIGHTS CREATED BY
A JURISTIC ACT

§ 93. INTRODUCTION

THE nature of a juristic act has already been discussed.[1] Rights are created either by consent or by the direct gift of the law. In this chapter we are concerned with the manner in which parties may themselves create rights.

A juristic act may be the expression of the will of one party alone—a unilateral act, as it is frequently called. An example is the testament, where the will of one party alone is operative. Or the juristic act may be the result of agreement between two or more parties, as in the case of a contract. It is convenient to discuss first the notion of agreement.

§ 94. RIGHTS CREATED BY AGREEMENT

Agreement has been defined as the expression by two or more persons communicated each to the other (or others) of a common intention to affect the legal relations between them.

Anson finds five essential elements in an agreement.[2]

(*a*) There must be at least two parties.

(*b*) All the parties must have a distinct common intention.

(*c*) Each must communicate his intention to the others concerned.

(*d*) The common intention must be to affect legal relations. The legal sense of agreement is much narrower than the popular usage. If I agree to play bridge with the Browns, this is assumed not to be an agreement which will be recognized by the law, since I would not ordinarily be intending to enter into legal relations. Such a promise belongs to the social and not to the legal sphere.

(*e*) The legal relations intended to be affected must be those of the parties. An appellate court of three judges may affect the legal

---

[1] *Supra*, § 69.
[2] *Law of Contract* (16th ed.), 2 (this passage does not appear in the 23rd ed.); see also G. H. Trietel, *The Law of Contract* (3rd ed.), ch. ii.

relations of an appellant when the court 'agrees' to reverse the judgment of a lower court, but this is not an agreement in the sense in which the word is used in jurisprudence.

Agreement is thus the result of a bilateral juristic act, and the analysis already given of a juristic act can be applied—there must be a free expression of the will, by parties who have capacity, concerning an object which is not illegal.[1]

Agreement is a generic term which includes the species contract. All contracts are agreements, but not all agreements are contracts. Salmond divides agreements into four broad classes:

1. Contracts: creating rights *in personam*.
2. Grants: creating rights of any other kind.
3. Assignments: transferring rights.
4. Releases: extinguishing rights.[2]

The orthodox definition of a contract is that it is an agreement the express purpose of which is the creation and definition of rights *in personam* between the parties.[3] The emphasis is that a contract creates rights which are valid only as between the parties, and that these rights are brought into being by the agreement itself. The Romans distinguished very clearly between a conveyance, a transfer of *dominium* with its attendant rights *in rem*, and a contract which created only rights *in personam*. Hence a contract of sale did not pass the property and a separate transaction was necessary for this purpose. If the vendor wished to limit the use to which the land sold could be put, he could bind the purchaser by a contract, but this would not create rights which could be enforced against a subsequent purchaser. Contract creating *obligatio* was one thing, *dominium* creating rights which bound persons generally was another. In English law, the contract for sale of chattels may itself transfer the property and hence our categories are not so clear cut.[4] Also covenants may be made to 'run with the land', i.e. given an effect *in rem*.

Salmond confines contracts to those which *create* rights: there is no *a priori* reason why a contract, in addition to creating rights, should not also assign or release them. Indeed a normal way of transferring rights is by novation which originally is the substitution of a new contract for the old one. I can release my rights by contract, just as I can thereby create new rights.

[1] *Supra*, § 69.   [2] *Jurisprudence* (12th ed.), 339.
[3] Ibid. 338; J. W. Salmond and J. Williams, *Contracts*, 10.   [4] *Infra*, § 98.

An even more fundamental point has been stressed, that it is better not to define contract in terms of agreement.[1] The law will sometimes enforce a contract even although there may be no real subjective agreement.[2] English law holds a person to the inferences which a reasonable man is likely to draw from his behaviour, and if Brown's conduct presents all the external phenomena of agreement, then the law may declare that a contract is created, even although it is later proved that Brown had no subjective desire to contract. It is argued that it is somewhat clumsy to begin by defining contract in terms of agreement and then to point out that the law will sometimes impute to a man an intention which he does not possess, if the other contracting party was reasonably entitled to infer the intention from his acts.[3] These critics prefer to regard a contract as an actionable promise.[4] Thus the American Restatement defines a contract as 'a promise or a set of promises for the breach of which the law gives a remedy, or the performance of which it in some way recognizes as a duty'.[5]

But does this carry us very much farther? In the ordinary sense of the word, a promise is just as subjective as an agreement. In a court of ethics, a man is held to a promise only if he intended to promise and only in the sense in which the promise was honourably meant.[6] Whatever definition of contract be used, the jurist must face the difficulty that, in order to protect others, the law will sometimes infer either an agreement or a promise, even although the party did not subjectively intend to bind himself. Moreover, all systems do not go as far as English law in adopting an external approach, and for jurisprudence a definition of contract in terms of agreement seems to be the most suitable.

In such a contract as barter with its simultaneous exchange of one product for another, there is no need for any theory of enforceable agreement, for nothing remains to be done by either party. Once, however, the law begins to recognize that a promise may create an obligation, it must face the problem of the terms on which it will force parties to fulfil their engagements. The English analysis of contract explains it as the acceptance by one party of an offer made

---

[1] R. M. Jackson, 53 *L.Q.R.* (1937), 525.
[2] See the discussion of the rules concerning mistake, *infra*, §§ 97, 100.
[3] R. M. Jackson, op. cit. 535.   [4] W. R. Anson, *Contracts* (23rd ed.), 23.
[5] F. Pollock, *Contracts* (13th ed.), 1: 'a promise or set of promises which the law will enforce'.
[6] R. M. Jackson, 53 *L.Q.R.* (1937) at 535, states that promise suggests an objective aspect, agreement a subjective. But is this so?

by the other.[1] The offer which becomes the basis of the contract may take various forms:

(*a*) I may offer a promise in return for your promise. (This is sometimes called a bilateral contract since both parties are bound to do something in the future, but this use of the word must be distinguished from the other sense which defines a bilateral juristic act as one which is the result of agreement between two parties. In this latter sense all contracts are bilateral.) Example: I promise to pay £5 in return for your promise to transfer to me your golf-clubs.

(*b*) I may offer a promise in return for your act. (This is sometimes called a unilateral contract, as only one party is bound to perform a duty in the future. In the sense referred to earlier no contract can be unilateral, since it is the result of agreement.) Example: You accept my offer to pay £5 next month by handing over your clubs now.

(*c*) Sometimes it is suggested that in a cash sale—threepence for your newspaper—there is really no promise, but only an offer of an act for an act. Once the coins and the newspaper have changed hands, neither party is bound by any outstanding duty and hence it is argued that this transaction falls outside the definition of contract as actionable promise.[2] The orthodox analysis, however, is that this is a case of an offer of a *promise* to pay threepence for delivery of the newspaper—although the promise is quickly discharged.

Another difficulty is to distinguish between those agreements which are true contracts and those which lead to the creation of a status. Salmond and Winfield[3] find the test of a contract in the freedom of the parties not only to create the relationship but also to define it by the terms of the agreement between them—if they are merely limited to entering into a relationship, the terms of which are compulsorily determined by the law, then it is a case of status. But this test is far too broad. If the law compulsorily fixes all the terms on which electric light can be supplied to a consumer, that does not mean that the consumer has a particular status—the agreement between the supplier and the consumer remains a contract even although neither can vary the terms. The test of status is that membership must affect generally a person's claims and powers and not only one particular relationship.[4] This seems the only possible way of distinguishing between contract and status. On this test, marriage creates a status, for the

---

[1] P. H. Winfield, 55 *L.Q.R.* (1939), 499.
[2] M. Ferson, 31 *Cornell L. Q.* (1945), 105 at 113.
[3] *Contracts*, 8.   [4] *Supra*, § 87.

claims and powers of husband and wife are generally affected by their entry into the marriage relation—whereas the legal results which flow from signing a contract with an electricity supply company are limited to the particular legal relationship in question.

There are several minor points of confusion in terminology. Frequently contract is used both for the actual agreement and also for the obligations to which it gives rise. Strictly contract should be used only in the first sense and we should not speak of assigning a contract, but rather of the rights and duties which arise out of it. Again contract is frequently regarded as an enforceable agreement, yet the term void contract is not unknown. If we adopt the test suggested, a void contract is a contradiction in terms—yet it is a useful phrase, especially if we remember that a void contract is not entirely devoid of legal result.[1]

Taking all these points into consideration, we may define a contract as an agreement which will be recognized by the law as effective in creating, transferring, or extinguishing rights *in personam*.

§ 95. EVOLUTION OF THE CONCEPT OF CONTRACT

Theories of the origin of contract are sometimes bound up with economic doctrines that society has passed through the three stages of barter, money, and credit. Credit depends essentially on ability to rely on the promises of others and thus can flourish only where there is a fully developed law of contract.[2] It is, as yet, too early to attempt to show a universal law of evolution, for not all societies have passed through the same order of progress.[3] But it may be regarded as established that each group tends to develop contracts suited to its own particular economic organization, and, while any attempt at premature generalization must be deprecated, it is useful to contrast the nature of contract at various stages, since this throws into relief the real nature of our modern agreements.

The great advantage of contract in modern law is that the law will enforce certain agreements and thus men may rely on others carrying out their engagements. Probably the first step in the evolution of contract is ceremonial exchange—tradition demands that a gift be reciprocated in due course.[4] In barter or the sale of a slave for cash

---

[1] *Supra*, § 69, W. R. Anson, op. cit. 7.
[2] H. Cairns, *Law and the Social Sciences*, 82.
[3] Cairns, op. cit. 83. A. S. Diamond, *Primitive Law*, chs. xxxii–xxxiv.
[4] D. F. Thomson, *Economic Structure and Ceremonial Exchange in Arnhem Land.*

there is no need for any theory, since, the agreement being fully executed, there are no outstanding obligations to be performed in the future—indeed in primitive law the rights of the parties arise from the transfer of the possession of the chattels rather than from any doctrine of the effect of agreement.

'Credit barter' or loan takes us a little farther—a *res* is delivered to another in return for a promise that another *res* of greater value shall be restored at some time in the future. In some communities the sole sanction for these agreements is the fear of ostracism. Apart from the community, primitive man is helpless, and if a native does not fulfil his obligations, he knows that in the future no other man will help him.[1] But parties soon desire a more effective sanction than the mere fear of economic boycott. A hostage may be demanded as security for the performance of what is promised.[2] But the emphasis is not on any notion of legal duty, but rather on the physical liability of the hostage who will be punished if the obligation is not fulfilled. It is the physical possession of the hostage that creates rights in the creditor, rather than the promise of the debtor. Perhaps the germ of contract arises when a person may make his own body liable in the event of default—but the penalty at first is physical slavery and not execution against any goods that the debtor may possess.[3] The loan of money is of such frequent occurrence that it is soon surrounded with special rules. Indeed, there is a tendency to novate other agreements into fictitious loans in order to secure the advantage of the effective process that has been developed.[4] Many arrangements on credit must have been necessary where wergild was concerned. The Franks first required hostages to be given—later a wand could be delivered to the creditor who would hand it to the person who was willing to stand as surety. Finally, the debtor could make himself his own pledge by accepting the wand.[5] Even today we can speak of 'pledging our faith'. In the thirteenth century in England, in order to save the trouble of suing for debt, a vigilant creditor got his judgment first and then lent the money.[6]

When certain transactions are recognized as binding, the early

---

[1] B. Malinowski, *Crime and Custom*, 58.
[2] Where money is borrowed, we may perhaps regard the hostage as being exchanged for the money.
[3] For the controversy concerning *nexum* see H. F. Jolowicz, *Hist. Introd. to Roman Law*, 166.
[4] Cf. the Roman contract *literis*.
[5] Pollock and Maitland, *History of English Law*, ii. 185.
[6] Op. cit. 201–2.

emphasis on the formal nature[1] of the contract leads to the following results: firstly, obligation can be created only by the observance of certain forms, since there is no theory that mere agreement may create rights and duties; secondly, the real question is whether the particular form was carried out, and hence questions of good faith and fraud, or even duress, are sometimes treated as irrelevant. Moreover, these contracts are unilateral in the sense that there are duties to be performed by one party alone.

Roman law later developed certain 'consensual' contracts that depended, not on any particular form, but merely on the agreement of the parties. The notion of good faith was emphasized and it was clearly recognized that the contract was bilateral, not only in the sense that it arose out of the agreement of two or more minds, but also in the sense that it might impose executory obligations on two or more parties. Roman law, however, stopped short of any general theory of contract, for the number of 'consensual' contracts was strictly limited. In modern times some systems adopt a broad theory that all agreements are actionable where the parties intend to enter into legal relations. But the exact limits of such a doctrine are discussed in the next section.

§ 96. CAUSA AND CONSIDERATION

The law is naturally hesitant about enforcing all agreements. Is it to compel Jones to keep his promise to play bridge with the Browns whom he detests or to grant damages to Mrs. Robinson because her husband failed to buy the exclusive model which he promised in a rash moment? Roman law had no difficulty, since only a limited number of agreements were enforceable. But in modern systems, since the theory of contract is wider, we must ask: are agreements enforceable because they are agreements, or must there be some additional factor?[2] There are three possible courses. The law may either (a) enforce all agreements; (b) enforce all agreements where the parties intend to enter into legal relations and the agreement is not contrary to law; or (c) require some additional element such as form or consideration.

---

[1] It cannot be proved that all formal contracts arose first: Pollock and Maitland, op. cit. 182–4.
[2] Lord Wright, *Legal Essays and Addresses*, 289. A series of articles on the problem of consideration will be found in vols. 41 and 42 of the *Col. L. R.* (1941–2).

Nearly all systems require particular types of contract to be in a set form, either because they are of special importance or because experience has shown that, to prevent fraud, clear evidence of the terms is necessary. English law requires some contracts to be by deed, others to be in writing, while yet others may be verbal. Contrary to the widespread notion that 'it's not binding because there is nothing in writing', in many cases a verbal agreement is enough. But if the contract be not by deed, English law differs from other modern systems in requiring consideration which may be defined as something done, forborne, or suffered, or promised to be done, forborne or suffered by the promisee in respect of the promise of the other party.[1] Unless there is this *quid pro quo* for the promise, there is no consideration. Several studies have pointed out the narrowing effect that this doctrine has on English law. A promise to keep an offer open is not enforceable unless there be consideration which moves from the promisee.[2] Such a common business arrangement as a banker's commercial credit can only with difficulty (if at all) be fitted into the narrow doctrine of consideration.[3] If I promise to accept £800 in full settlement of a debt of £1,000, the promise to forgo £200 is not binding, since there is no consideration for it—but if I accept £800 and a box of matches, the latter may be consideration for a promise to forgo £200, for, while consideration must be of some value, it need not be adequate.[4] Lord Wright refers to the English emphasis on consideration as a 'mere encumbrance',[5] and the Law Revision Committee confesses that 'there is much to be said for its abolition',[6] for it allows 'the most cynical disregard of promises solemnly undertaken'.[7]

---

[1] Anson, op. cit. 80 et seq.

[2] *Sixth Interim Report of the Law Revision Committee* (1937), Cmd. 5449.

[3] A. G. Davis, 52 *L.Q.R.* (1936), 225. Cheshire and Fifoot, *Law of Contract* (7th ed.), 408.

[4] *Sibree* v. *Tripp* (1846), 15 M. & W. 23, lays down that the giving of a negotiable instrument for a lesser sum is consideration for a promise to forgo the balance; and see *Hirachand Punamchand* v. *Temple*, [1911] 2 K.B. 330.

[5] *Legal Essays and Addresses*, 323. Elsewhere Lord Wright refers to it as 'riddled with illogicality, fiction and anomaly': 55 *L.Q.R.* (1939), 189 at 202. Denning L.J. (1952), 15 *Mod. L.R.* 1, and F. Bennion (1953), 16 *Mod. L.R.* 441.

[6] But the Committee did not recommend its abolition, but contented themselves with proposals which would remove the most striking injustices. This report has not been implemented by legislation. See the valuable critical contributions by C. T. Hamson, *The Reform of Consideration* (1938), 54 L.Q.R. 233; and K. O. Shatwell, *The Doctrine of Consideration in Modern Law*, 1 *Sydney L. R.* (1955), 289.

[7] 1 *Mod. L. R.* (1937), 97 at 100, referring to *Dunlop* v. *Selfridge*, [1915] A.C. 847; and see G. W. Paton, in 25 *Can. B. R.* (1947), 123, and Denning L.J. (dissenting) in *Candler* v. *Crane Christmas & Co. Ltd.*, [1951] 2 K.B. 164.

Moreover, consideration will not serve as a universal test, for deeds
are enforceable where there is no consideration and some agreements, where there is consideration, are not enforceable because the
parties did not intend to enter into legal relations. A husband's
promise to buy his wife a new hat does not create legal relations,
even if a consideration could be spelled out, nor does the acceptance
of an invitation to dinner.[1] Collective contracts (agreements between
unions and employers) have been held not to be legally enforceable,
as there was no intention to create legal obligations.[2]

Denning J. (as he then was), although he admitted that the courts
would not allow an action for breach of promise without consideration, thought that such a promise, made with intent that the other
party should rely upon it, could operate as a defence.[3] 'The logical
consequence no doubt is that a promise to accept a smaller sum in
discharge of a larger sum, if acted upon, is binding notwithstanding
the absence of consideration: and if the fusion of law and equity
leads to this result, so much the better.'[4] This is a courageous view.[5]

French and Roman-Dutch law have adopted the theory of *causa*.
But the doctrine has become so broad that it is almost true to say that
any agreement for a lawful object is valid, if the parties seriously
intend to enter into legal relations.[6] The meaning of *causa* appears
'from Grotius' expression of "reasonable cause". There must be
a reason for a contract, a rational motive for it, whether that motive is
benevolence, friendship, or other proper feeling, or, on the other hand,
of a commercial or business nature. In other words, the agreement

---

[1] Per Atkin L.J., *Balfour* v. *Balfour*, [1919] 2 K.B. 571 at 578; aliter if the parties are
about to separate: *Merritt* v. *Merritt*, [1970] 2 All E.R. 760; cf. mother and daughter,
Jones v. *Padavatton*, [1969] 2 All E.R. 616; agreements where the parties state that no
legal obligation is to be incurred, *Jones* v. *Vernon's Pools Ltd.*, [1938] 2 All E.R. 626.
An intent to enter into legal relations may, however, be inferred from conduct: *Upton*
v. *Powell*, [1942] 1 All E.R. 220; R. Tuck, 21 *Can. B. R.* (1943), 123, discusses this case,
arguing that there is no need for an intention to contract; and see Cheshire and Fifoot,
Law of Contract (6th ed.), ch. iii, where the view that intention to create legal relations
is an independent element in the common law of contract is reasserted.
[2] *Ford Motor Co. Ltd.* v. *Amalgamated Union of Engineering and Foundry Workers*,
[1969] 2 All E.R. 481. See B. A. Hepple, 28 *Camb. L. J.* (1970), 122; N. Selwyn, 32
Mod. L. R. (1969), 377.
[3] *Central London Property Trust Ltd.* v. *High Trees House Ltd.*, [1947] 1 K.B. 130.
[4] Same case at 135; Cheshire and Fifoot, 63 *L.Q.R.* (1947), 283.
[5] But now see *Combe* v. *Combe*, [1951] 2 K.B. 215, and *Tool Metal Manufacturing
Co. Ltd.* v. *Tungsten Electric Co. Ltd.*, [1955] 2 All E.R. 657; Cheshire and Fifoot,
Law of Contract (7th ed.), 83–7; L. A. Sheridan, *High Trees in New Zealand* (1958),
21 *Mod. L.R.* 185–6. It seems clear that the doctrine of the *High Trees* case is confined
to defences in the nature of 'equitable estoppel'. See Ld. Hodson, *Emmanuel Ayodeji
Ajayi* v. *B. T. Briscoe* (*Nigeria*) *Ltd.*, [1964] 3 All E.R. 556.
[6] R. W. Lee suggests that in Roman-Dutch law *causa* means little more than that
contracts must be seriously made: *Introduction to Roman-Dutch Law*, 232, 429.

must be a deliberate, serious act, not one that is irrational or motiveless.'[1] But great battles still rage as to the true definition of *causa*[2] and some definitions are so broad that they would include all agreements seriously made, for no one but a lunatic would make a contract that is entirely irrational and motiveless. The orthodox theory of French law is that the cause of an obligation is the immediate end which the party has in view.[3] In this sense cause should be distinguished both from the object of the contract and the motive which moves each of the parties. The object is what is owed (money, golf-clubs), the cause tells us why it is owed (gift, sale, legacy). The cause, which is objective, must also be distinguished from the motive which is subjective—thus in sale each purchaser shares the common desire to acquire the goods which are the subject-matter of the contract, but the reason for the purchase varies from one individual to another. In reaching agreement neither party is directly concerned with the motive of the other.

But in making these distinctions difficulties arise. In a real contract the cause is said to be the delivery of the *res*. But here we are using the term not to express the immediate end of the party, but the element which makes the contract binding. The phrase means that a real contract legally comes into existence only when the *res* is actually delivered. The confusion between cause and motive is particularly marked. In *donatio* the cause is the intention to make a gift—it is possible to say that the motive (the reason why I intend to make a gift) is irrelevant, but it is natural for the two aspects to become intertwined. When we come to illegality of cause, the position is even more difficult. A lets a house to B for an agreed rent—here the cause is clear. But suppose B's motive is to use the house as a brothel and that A knows this. Logically the law may refuse to enforce the contract on grounds of policy, but there is no illegality of cause— cause is invariable and objective and there is a genuine hire. Yet the French courts treat the contract as void on the ground of illegality of cause, which naturally introduces much confusion between cause and motive. English law reaches the same result, but on the ground that the object of the contract is unlawful. Hiring a brougham or leasing a flat is a lawful transaction, but, if the hirer or lessor knows

---

[1] G. T. Morice, cited in *Jayawickreme* v. *Amarasuriya*, [1918] A.C. 869 at 876.

[2] Buckland and McNair, *Roman Law and Common Law*, 173 et seq.; S. G. Vesey-Fitzgerald, 14 *J. Comp. Leg.* (1932), 1 at 13; F. P. Walton, 41 *L.Q.R.* (1925), 306; Holdsworth, *History of English Law*, viii. 42 et seq.

[3] F. P. Walton, 41 *L.Q.R.* (1925), 306, to which this paragraph is indebted.

that the *res* is to be put to an immoral use, he cannot enforce the contract.[1] Further, the width of the notion of *causa* has led to the introduction of procedural safeguards, such as the requirement of a notarial deed where an agreement benefits one party at the expense of another and there is no obviously acceptable reason for the benefit. Sometimes the rigidity of such procedural safeguards can be just as irksome as any doctrine of consideration as found in English law.

It is significant, therefore, to find that many French lawyers attack the notion of cause as being confusing. The simpler doctrine is that *conventio* without more is *contractus*, provided that the agreement concerns a lawful subject-matter, and that the parties intend to enter into legal relations. Many modern codes have built an efficient theory of contract on such a basis, the doctrine of cause being rejected as an unnecessary complication.[2] The very variety of the uses of the term cause militates against clarity. The lesson of modern times is that society demands a wide theory of contract and the Law Revision Committee in England has recommended legislative change in order to avoid some of the worst results of the narrowing effect of the English theory of consideration.[3] Two of the Committee's suggestions illustrate this point of view—that an agreement should be enforceable if the offer or promise has been made in writing (even if there is no consideration), and that a promise should be actionable if the promisor knows or reasonably should know that it will be relied on by the promisee and the latter alters his position to his detriment in reliance upon it.[4] These and the other changes suggested would reduce consideration to being merely one of the methods by which the existence of a contract could be shown, and would bring English law somewhat nearer to the broader theories of the Continent.

The more radical changes, however, which would bring such a result about have not been adopted. This is not merely because inertia tends to make law reform difficult, but because there are good reasons for viewing the committee's recommendations for change with great caution. On the one hand the committee's reliance upon writing as a test for enforceability of a contract seems to be somewhat

---

[1] *Pearce* v. *Brooks* (1866), L.R. 1 Ex. 213; *Upfill* v. *Wright*, [1911] 1 K.B. 506.
[2] e.g. the German Civil Code. For a defence of 'cause', see H. Newman, 30 *Can. B. R.* (1952), 662.
[3] *Sixth Interim Report* (1937), Cmd. 5449.
[4] This view is supported by Denning J., *Central London Property Trusts Ltd.* v. *High Trees House Ltd.*, [1947] 1 K.B. at 135.

ingenuous in this day and age, and on the other, the committee's treatment of consideration as mere evidence of intention to enter legal
relations tends to ignore the 'bargain' basis of much of the English
law of contract. It may well be that other kinds of agreements than
those seen to be 'bargains' ought to be enforced by the law, but this
does not necessarily mean that consideration should be viewed as
nothing more than evidence of an intention to enter legal relations.[1]

§97. THEORIES OF THE NATURE OF A CONTRACT

(a) The Will Theory

This doctrine sees the reason for the enforcement of a contract in
the fact that the wills of the two parties have reached agreement. The
will is 'inherently worthy of respect',[2] and this is recognized by the
law in its theory of contract. Some write legal history in a neo-
Hegelian fashion which pictures the slow evolution of the Idea
of Freedom—since contract is the legal category which gives the
greatest means of self-expression, its sphere is not only increasing,
but ought to be increased. The dictum 'status to contract' becomes
not merely a convenient generalization of certain aspects of legal
history but an eternal principle the onward march of which cannot
and should not be stayed.[3]

Thus it is argued that, unless the real will of the parties is *ad idem*,
no contract should be binding. A secret mental reservation should be
a bar to enforcement, since the test is the real will and not the will
as declared. Apparently the will theory was so popular in Germany
that it was thought necessary to declare specifically in the code that
a secret mental reservation should not affect the validity of a declaration of intention.[4]

It is impossible to apply strictly the theory that the law can take
account only of the real will of the parties. Firstly, what is in a
person's mind can be proved only from his own evidence, or by
inferences from his conduct. To accept a person's word allows too
easy a method of escape for perjurers, while, if the intent is inferred
from conduct, there is a tendency to assume that a man intends the

---

[1] See C. J. Hamson, *The Reform of Consideration* (1938), 54 *L.Q.R.* 233; K. O.
Shatwell, *The Doctrine of Consideration in Modern Law*, 1 *Sydney L. R.* (1955), 289;
Sir Owen Dixon, *Concerning Judicial Method*, 29 *Aust. L. J.* (1956), 468.
[2] M. Cohen, *Law and the Social Order*, 92.
[3] The increasing tendency to restrict freedom of contract is discussed below, §99.
[4] *BGB.* Art. 116; E. J. Schuster, *German Civil Law*, 93.

reasonable consequences of his act. Secondly, when it is a question of the interpretation of a contract, the most difficult problems arise when the parties did not direct their wills to some particular contingency, or when each interpreted the agreement in a different way. To avoid every contract where precise subjective agreement on every detail could not be shown would interfere too greatly with business demands. The courts give to an agreement the meaning it reasonably bears—not the view taken by one party of its interpretation.

Thirdly, for convenience, the law demands definite rules with regard to the time that an offer is accepted, if the parties are corresponding by post. In English law a contract is made when a letter of acceptance is posted, but an offer can be revoked only when the revocation is communicated to the offeree. It may happen that Jones reads an offer and posts his acceptance after Brown has sent a telegram revoking the offer, but, so long as Jones posts the letter before he receives the telegram, the contract is valid, although the real wills of the parties were not *ad idem* at any particular moment.[1] Actually there are many theories which the law might adopt. There is the declaration theory that the contract is formed at the moment the offeree declares his acceptance of the offer, whether the offeror knows of it or not; the expedition theory that the contract is made when the acceptor posts the acceptance; the reception theory, that the decisive moment is the receipt of the acceptance, whether it is read or not; and finally the information theory that the contract is binding only when the letter of acceptance is actually read.[2] But for any particular system it is more convenient to have fixed and definite rules than to rely too greatly on subjective tests. Further, it should be noted that convenience demands a high degree of certainty in this matter because the time of acceptance will usually fix also the place of acceptance and hence in many cases the law which governs the contract. Modern means of communication raise new problems in the application of old principles. Thus communications by telephones and teleprinters are assimilated to the rules governing negotiations

---

[1] It may be, in English law, that if I post an acceptance and then telegraph revoking it, so that the telegram reaches the offeror before he receives the letter, I am nevertheless bound; P. H. Winfield, 55 *L.Q.R.* (1939), 499 at 512; Cheshire and Fifoot, *The Law of Contract* (6th ed.), 42–3. There is no English decision which finally settles the point, but such persuasive decisions as there are go in the other direction: *Dunmore (Countess)* v. *Alexander* (1830), 9 Sh. (Ct. of Sess.) 190; *Wenkheim* v. *Arndt* (N.Z.), 1 J.R. 73; *Dick* v. *United States* (1949), 82 Fed. Supp. 326; and see C. L. Pannam, *Postal Regulation 289 and An Acceptance of an Offer by Post* (1960), 2 M.U.L.R. 388.

[2] Amos and Walton, *Introduction to French Law*, 153; P. H. Winfield, op. cit. at 506–7.

between two persons face to face and acceptance is incomplete until received by the offeror.[1]

Fourthly, the will theory leads to such a subjective view of mistake that the security of transactions is thereby imperilled. Where the mistake is due to A's carelessness and the other contracting party is unaware of A's error, the real wills of the parties cannot be regarded as *ad idem*, but to avoid the contract would frequently be very unjust. Modern law tends to take rather a narrow view of the kinds of mistake which will avoid a contract.[2] Even German law, which was strongly influenced by the will theory, has been compelled to modify it in practice.[3]

(b) The Injurious Reliance Theory

In sharp contrast to the will theory is what Pound has termed the 'injurious reliance theory' which puts the emphasis, not on the real will of the parties, but on the expectations reasonably aroused by the conduct of each.[4] The emphasis is on conduct rather than on states of mind, the reason for enforcement is security rather than any mystical union of wills. Ethics may require fulfilment of a promise only in the sense in which it was honestly meant, but the law does in certain cases hold men to their acts or representations even when these acts or representations do not faithfully represent their intention.[5]

It is not enough, when a claim for rectification is made, to show that the parties intended a different result—that would lead to uncertainty. Rectification can be claimed, however, where the parties show that the *agreement* was otherwise than as expressed.[6] In dealing with estoppel by conduct, the question may be how letters would be reasonably interpreted by those to whom they were addressed.[7]

---

[1] See *Entores Limited* v. *Miles Far East Corporation*, [1955] 2 Q.B. 327; but cf. the position in the United States of America where, although the Restatement assimilates acceptance by telephone to oral acceptance between parties in the presence of each other (Contracts, § 65), it has been held in several jurisdictions that the place where a contract made by telephone is completed is the place where the offeree speaks the words of acceptance into the telephone—see Corbin *On Contracts* (1963), vol. 1, § 79.

[2] *Infra*, § 100.

[3] E. J. Schuster, *German Civil Law*, 92.

[4] R. Pound, *Introduction to the Philosophy of Law*, 269; M. Cohen, 46 *Harv. L. R.* (1933), 533 at 578; T. E. Holland, *Jurisprudence* (10th ed.), 253.

[5] L. Duguit, in *Progress of Continental Law in the Nineteenth Century*, 104; F. Gény, *Science et Technique*, iii. 80.

[6] Russell L.J., *Joscelyne* v. *Nissen*, [1970] 1 All E.R. at 1221.

[7] *Woodhouse* v. *Nigerian Produce*, [1970] 2 All E.R. 124.

Such an approach has two practical results: firstly, there is an external attitude towards mistake, a tendency to regard unilateral error as insufficient to avoid a contract at least if that mistake was neither known to, nor induced by, the other party;[1] secondly, there is an attack on any theory (such as that of consideration) which would defeat the expectations of the business man by rather technical rules.

But the injurious reliance theory is at best only an approach, for it has not been fully worked out. Firstly, the law of contracts is not created by deductions from a particular theory, but by the pressure of practical needs on the legal structure bequeathed by history. The views of lawyers change, and in every legal system we find legacies from the past that conflict with modern views. Hence, even if it be useful to study the theories that underlie the law of contract, we cannot expect to find a consistent approach in any one system of law. Thus no legal system regards mere reliance on the promise of another as sufficient. Both English and continental law require an intention to affect legal relations, and in England there is the further requirement that there must be either consideration or deed. Secondly, in most systems, if a contract is created, there is no need to prove injurious reliance. A promise by deed to give a donation is binding even although the recipient has not altered his position for the worse by relying upon it. Thirdly, the term 'security' has not been thoroughly analysed. Demogue, dealing with transfer of title, distinguishes between static and dynamic security.[2] Static security protects the rights of owners and prefers to sacrifice, if necessary, the rights of bona fide purchasers for value. Dynamic security results from the desire to facilitate transactions and to overrule some of the inconvenient consequences of the maxim, *nemo dat quod non habet*. With regard to the transfer of land, the traditional English approach has been to protect the interests of the owner even at the cost of rendering transactions slow and cumbersome, although legislation has lately somewhat simplified the problem. With regard to personal property, the intrusions of dynamic security were more far reaching. Rules concerning negotiable instruments, the Factors' Act of 1889, and certain provisions of the Sale of Goods Act may lead to the title of the true owner being defeated without his own consent. The security of which Pound speaks is somewhat analogous to dynamic security in that it facilitates the speed of transactions. But Demogue is analysing the problem from the angle of the owner of property, Pound from

---

[1] *Infra*, § 100.   [2] In *Modern French Legal Philosophy*, 418.

the approach of a contracting party who wishes to know if he may rely on the conduct of another. Security, in terms of the injurious reliance theory, can mean only ability to rely on expectations reasonably aroused by the conduct of another.

There are many other theories suggested as bases for the law of contract. Thus it is argued that a promise has inherent moral force and should be recognized by the law, and that without the adoption of the maxim *pacta sunt servanda* society could not exist. Ethically, however, it is doubtful whether all promises should be kept (e.g. a promise to commit murder) and no legal system enforces all promises as such. Historically, however, the maxim *pacta custodiantur* was important, since it was laid down by the Church courts as a general principle to be followed, and provided a theoretical justification for the attempt to create a broad principle in place of the list of specific enforceable agreements which was provided by Roman law.[1]

§ 98. SALE AND HIRE-PURCHASE

A contract of sale is one whereby the seller transfers, or agrees to transfer, the property in a *res* to the buyer for a money consideration called the price. Gift is a transfer, but there is no price. In barter, one *res* is exchanged for another—neither *res* can be regarded as the price and hence the transaction is not sale. The emphasis on price means that sale can arise only when money is in use, or when some commodity plays the part that money plays in modern life.[2]

There are two aspects of sale which must be kept distinct. Firstly, a sale results from a contract between the parties. Hence the modern conception of sale can arise only after the law of contract has reached maturity. It is familiar law that a contract creates rights only in the parties thereto. A contract between A and B, by which A agrees to sell a chattel to B on 2 January next, does not prevent A from

---

[1] For Holmes's 'risk theory', see *The Common Law*, 298; R. Pound, *Philosophy of Law*, ch. vi. But it has been held that an executor is not entitled to break a contract merely because it will be more advantageous to the estate to pay damages than to carry out the agreement: *Ahmed Angullia Bin Hadjee* v. *Estate and Trust Agencies (1927) Ltd.*, [1938] A.C. 624. A commentator in 55 *L.Q.R.* (1939), 1, suggests that this is additional proof that Holmes's view cannot be supported. W. W. Buckland, 8 *Camb. L. J.* (1944), 247, illustrates by telling examples the weaknesses of Holmes's theory, and concludes that it cannot be squared either with English or with Roman law. F. Pollock, *Holmes-Pollock Letters*, i. 80, asks, if it is not a wrong to break a contract, why it should be a tort to induce breach of contract. On the other hand, where performance is impossible, there is an increasing tendency to regard contract in terms of assumption of risk.

[2] A comparative survey is that of F. de Zulueta, *The Roman Law of Sale.*

conveying a good title to C by sale and delivery on 1 January. The only remedy of B at common law is an action for breach of contract. However, B's right may be protected firstly by equity, which regards the purchaser as the equitable owner, and secondly by legislation, e.g. with regard to land, it may be enacted that if the contract of sale is registered, it is effective against third parties. In such a case the agreement is more than a contract as it affects the right *in rem* to the land.

Secondly, there is involved in sale a delivery or conveyance. This is a transfer of the right *in rem*. In the law of real property a conveyance is necessary and perhaps registration with the Registrar of Titles. In the case of personal property, however, the title may pass by the contract, even before delivery to the purchaser has occurred. Hence in the English law of personal property the categories of contract and conveyance of title are to some extent fused: whereas in Roman law a sharp distinction was retained: title did not pass until the *emptio* was *perfecta*, delivery was made, and either the price was paid or credit specifically given.

In English law, *res perit domino*, i.e. the general principle is that if the *res* is destroyed without any fault on the part of anyone, it is the owner for the time being who must bear the loss. Hence in asking when the risk passes from vendor to purchaser, we must ask when title passed. From the practical point of view Roman law reached the same business result. The risk passed when the contract was perfect[1] but, as title did not pass till conveyance was made, the Romans could not base their theory of risk on the passing of the title.[2] It perhaps illustrates the necessities of commerce that the doctrine of the passing of the risk should be the same in systems theoretically divergent.

In early Roman law there was no need for any special rule to protect the seller's right to the price, for (as stated above) title did not pass till the price was paid. The seller, therefore, retained an action *in rem*.[3] In English law as title could pass by the contract, special rules were devised, e.g. the vendor's lien and the right of stoppage in transit. Whatever the theory of a legal system, the interests that demand protection have a root similarity.

---

[1] Paul, 18. 6. 8. pr. 'Sale is perfect if the identity, quality and quantity of the thing are ascertained and also the price and if the sale is absolute' (translation of F. de Zulueta, op. cit. 115).

[2] This was at least law in Justinian's time—see F. de Zulueta, op. cit. 33.

[3] In later Roman law, title could pass before payment, if credit was specifically given.

In English law the seller impliedly warrants that he has a title which he can convey. In Roman law, in the absence of fraud, I could lawfully sell a *res* belonging to another, e.g. if I thought I could secure title from him before delivery took place. As this provided an opportunity for fraud the following qualifications must be added: (*a*) as the contract of sale required good faith, one guilty of fraud had no remedy; (*b*) it was customary for the vendor to stipulate that he would pay damages if the purchaser was evicted; (*c*) later this *stipulatio* was held to be implied in the nature of sale itself.

Hire-purchase is a comparatively modern phenomenon. It was devised to protect the vendor in cases of sale where long-term credit was given. If title passes immediately to the purchaser, then the vendor suffers two disadvantages: (*a*) the *res* may be seized by the purchaser's creditors; (*b*) the purchaser has power to convey a good title on resale. In order to secure the advantages of retaining title, the vendor uses the device of hire-purchase whereby he delivers the goods to the hirer upon terms that the hirer is to pay a fixed periodical rental, but has in addition an option of purchasing the goods by paying the total amount of the agreed hire at any time or of returning them before the total amount is paid.[1] The hirer is not a person who has agreed to buy—otherwise the Factors Act may apply and allow a purchaser in good faith from the hirer to secure a good title. Analytically, a hire-purchase agreement creates a bailment plus an option to purchase—it is neither pure bailment nor pure contract. If it were pure bailment, any act by the bailee inconsistent with the terms of the bailment would terminate the bailment—but it has been held that, if the hire-purchaser wrongfully sells to X, and X is sued by the owner, the measure of damages is not the value of the *res* but the value of the unpaid instalments. Hence the hire-purchaser has an interest in the *res* which he can transfer.[2] However, it is difficult to give a precise name to the proprietary interest of the hire-purchaser. It is clearly not the legal title, for the whole object of hire-purchase is to prevent title passing till the instalments are paid: it is not an equitable interest.[3]

Hire-purchase is a very modern development in commercial life, and surely it is a commonplace in commercial law that if one finds commercial men inventing new methods of business and using documents which

---

[1] A. Dean, *Hire-purchase Law in Australia* (2nd ed.), 1.
[2] *Whiteley Ltd.* v. *Hilt*, [1918] 2 K.B. 808; *Belsize Motor Co.* v. *Cox*, [1914] 1 K.B. 244.   [3] Dean, op. cit. 5.

are, perhaps, unfamiliar at the time when they are first brought into use, but which are invented to meet the requirements of a particular time or peculiar circumstances, the law has to be moulded and developed to meet the commercial developments which are taking place.[1]

Another difficulty that arose in a transaction which combined elements both of hire and sale was that of the implied conditions—were the rules of sale or hire to be applied? The Court of Appeal held that the statutory warranties of sale were to be applied,[2] but the Victorian Supreme Court rejected that view as a contract of sale requires an agreement to buy, whereas the hirer has an option to reject.[3] Does the letter of the chattel imply that he is owner at the time the contract of hire-purchase is made, or is he bound only to show title when the hire-purchaser exercises the option to buy? Goddard J. adopted the first alternative, but the Legislature the second.[4]

In many cases of hire-purchase, the customer consults a car dealer, and finance is provided by a separate company. The customer thinks he has made a contract with the dealer, whereas the contract is really between the customer and the finance company. Hence there is difficulty in suing the finance company because of representations made by the dealer. Usually, there is a minimum payment which requires the customer, if he wishes to return the goods, to bring his payments to a certain total. The difficulty in applying the law can be seen by a consideration of *Bridge* v. *Campbell Discount Co. Ltd.*[5] One view is that if the finance company exercises an option to annul the contract because of breach of terms, then the minimum-payment clause may be held to be a penalty and no damages would be allowed beyond those actually suffered: however, if the customer exercises an option to return the goods, he is bound to the full extent by the minimum-payment clause. Lord Denning points out that this view penalizes the honest hirer who, realizing he cannot meet the monthly payments, immediately gives notice to the finance company. In

---

[1] Per Goddard J., *Karflex Ltd.* v. *Poole*, [1933] 2 K.B. 251 at 263–4.

[2] *Felston Tile Co. Ltd.* v. *Winget Ltd.*, [1936] 3 A.l E.R. 473. In *Warman* v. *Southern Counties Car Finance Corporation Ltd.*, [1949] 2 K.B. 576, a distinction was drawn between hire-purchase agreements and credit sale agreements which pass title before instalment payments are completed and to which therefore the Sale of Goods Act applies. The Hire-Purchase Acts of 1938 and 1954 apply to both types of transaction below certain stated prices. See also *R.* v. *R. W. Proffitt Ltd.*, [1954] 2 Q.B. 35.

[3] *Woods' Radio Exchange* v. *Marriott*, [1939] A.L.R. 409. And see *Rendell* v. *Associated Finance Pty. Ltd.*, [1957] V.R. 604.

[4] Hire-Purchase Act, 1938, c. 53, s. 8.

[5] [1962] 1 All E.R. 385.

view of the conflict of opinion in *Bridge's case* the law must be regarded as uncertain.

Inevitably when one party dictates the terms of the contract and the customer frequently signs a document which he does not really understand, it is not possible for the courts to remedy the injustices which are thereby caused. The magnitude of the problem is illustrated by the fact that in March 1970, £1,273,000,000 was owed under instalment credit transactions.[1] Accordingly the legislature, by a series of Acts, protected the position of the hire-purchaser.[2] However, it is difficult, even with careful drafting, to envisage all the cases of hardship which might ensue, and there is much to be said for a statutory provision in Victoria which gives power to reopen a transaction where it appears to the court to be harsh and unconscionable.[3]

§99. MODERN DEVELOPMENTS

In view of modern conditions we can no longer say that the sphere of individual self-assertion is increasing and ought to be increased. For various reasons the law has interfered seriously with contractual liberty, sometimes in the interests of the economically weaker party, sometimes in the hope of regulating an industry in order to protect it from foreign competition. Apart from the law, we sometimes see that powerful suppliers may require a customer to contract on dictated terms or not at all; lastly, for reasons of convenience certain types of contract are standardized in the interests of all concerned.[4] The abstract legal theory of a contract as an agreement arrived at through discussion and negotiation must be supplemented by a realistic study of its actual operation in the world today.[5] Some French writers speak humorously of unilateral contracts or *contrats d'adhésion*, where the will of one party is confined to choosing whether or not to

[1] See 11 *J. Soc. Public Teachers of Law* (1970), 113.
[2] Notably in 1938, 1964, and 1965.
[3] Hire-Purchase Act, 1959, s. 24 (1).
[4] O. Prausnitz, *Standardisation of Commercial Contracts*, 52 *Harv. L. R.* (1939), 700.
[5] Cf. R. A. Eastwood and B. A. Wortley, *J. Soc. Public Teachers of Law* (1938), 23; L. Josserand, *Rec. Gény*, ii. 333; G. Ripert, *Rec. Gény*, ii. 347; L. Duguit, *Les Transformations générales du droit privé*. The *Columbia L. R.*, July 1943, is devoted to the problem of 'Compulsory Contracts in Theory and Practice'. Nearly every industry has worked out standard contracts which purchasers must accept. Some American writers have adopted the French terminology and write of 'adhesion contracts'; see e.g. A. E. Ehrenzweig, *Adhesion Contracts in the Conflict of Laws* (1953), 53 *Col. L. R.* 1072; and many studies of such contracts in particular fields have been made, e.g. F. Kessler, *Automobile Dealer Franchises: Vertical Integration by Contract* (1957), 66 *Yale L. J.* 1135.

sign on the dotted line a contract entirely dictated by the other.[1] Where one party is strong enough to dictate the terms, the State is frequently forced to intervene in order to prevent abuse of power. Thus the series of Hire-Purchase Acts introduced many compulsory conditions protecting the weaker party.

Is public law in its invasion of private law removing contract from its pedestal? It is significant that an article should discuss 'Administrative Law and the Teaching of the Law of Contract'.[2] The theory of the autonomy of the will may be saved by saying that after all a person has still a choice whether to enter into contractual relations or not, but, while legal freedom may exist, economic and social necessities are frequently all-compelling. Whether the increasing regulation of contract by the State is advisable or not is a question of economics and social philosophy; but, when writers attack modern tendencies on the ground that freedom of contract is an *a priori* principle deducible from the nature of man as a reasonable being, we may reply with Kelsen that this is politics masquerading as jurisprudence, the ideology of vested interests deemed useful as a weapon against collectivism.[3] Few today would deny that freedom in theory may be the reverse in practice, and what is at first sight an interference with the liberty of one may give greater freedom to many. Society is interested in the means of living rather than in abstract freedom of will. If modern social movements are a regression, then let us attack them after a real analysis of the problem, not by citing superficial generalizations wrapped in naïve philosophy. Whatever our attitude to modern developments, regulation of particular contracts is now becoming so usual that we must take it into account in considering the function of contract in the world today.[4] Indeed, the State not only regulates the terms of contracts not yet made, but occasionally interferes with vested rights resulting from contracts already in being. Thus a moratorium statute may suspend a creditor's rights: a Farmers' Debt Adjustment Act may reduce the liabilities of the man on the land. There is a great divorce between contract as it is taught in the classical textbooks and contract as it actually operates in the world today.[5]

---

[1] See the analysis by W. D. Slawson, 84 *Harv. L. R.* (1971), 529. He claims that 'standard form contracts' probably account for ninety-nine per cent of all the contracts now made. It is impossible to check this figure.

[2] R. A. Eastwood and B. A. Wortley, *J. Soc. Public Teachers of Law* (1938), 23.

[3] *Annales de l'Institut de droit comparé* (1936), ii. 30.

[4] e.g. Hire-Purchase Acts (*supra*); Rent Restriction Acts; Acts affecting employer-employee relations, such as Factory and Shops Acts and so on.

[5] For a suggested list of reforms in the law of contract, see G. Gardiner and A. Martin (eds.), *Law Reform Now*, ch. iv.

It is frequently stated that public law is the realm of political domination, while private law is that of co-ordination or co-operation between equals. Kelsen does not regard the distinction between public and private law as in any sense fundamental, and he emphatically states that contract may play as great a part in the realm of control as public law.[1] Private law is only the particular juridical form which corresponds to the economic order of that society. To Kelsen, law may be made either by a parliament, a judge, or a private citizen: a contract 'executes' a superior norm, and creates a binding obligation for the parties, and therefore, although he may not realize it, Brown in signing a contract is making law. The more usual view is that, instead of treating Brown as one of the law-making organs of the State, it is simpler to say that the formation of a contract is one of the facts to which the law attaches certain legal consequences. The social service State increasingly uses the private law conception of contract in the achievement of its ends. Thus the setting up of state instrumentalities means firstly an increasing number of contracts with private individuals, and also between the various public corporations themselves. The former raise interesting questions of administrative law[2] and in the latter questions of public policy may lead to interference with the economic relations between the two bodies. Contract is thus today nearly as important in public as it is in private law.

Another illustration of modern developments is the collective contract made between a union of workers and an employers' federation in order to regulate the general conditions of the industry. In practice, even if not in theory, such agreements frequently bring about a *modus vivendi* which affects not only the original contracting parties but also future employers or workers.[3] But, in the absence of legislation, it is difficult to enforce such agreements by judicial process.[4] In Australia the machinery of the Arbitration Court provides a method of formal recognition, and in the United States an Act of 1947 made such agreements specifically enforceable.

A further problem concerns the rights of third parties. The logic of the Roman and the common law was that only the parties to a contract could claim rights under it. Modern developments are

---

[1] *Annales de l'Institut de droit comparé* (1936), ii. 45.
[2] Cf. *Smith v. River Douglas Catchment Board*, [1949] 2 K.B. 500, with *East Suffolk Rivers Catchment Board v. Kent*, [1941] A.C. 74.
[3] J. Dickinson, 43 *Col. L. R.* (1943), 688.
[4] B. A. Hepple, 28 *Camb. L. J.* (1970), 122; *Ford Motor Co. Ltd. v. Amalgamated Union of Engineering and Foundry Workers*, [1969] 2 All E.R. 481. See *supra*, § 37 (economic interests).

giving increasing importance to the *stipulation pour autrui*,[1] in which, illogical as it may seem, C may enforce a right given to him by an agreement between A and B. A clear and concise examination of the problem is made by the Law Revision Committee.[2] 'The Common Law of England stands alone among modern systems of law in its rigid adherence to the view that a contract should not confer any rights on a stranger to the contract, even though the sole object may be to benefit him.'[3] There are some statutory exceptions based on the needs of commerce and, in certain circumstances, the promisee may be regarded as a trustee for the third party. But the exact limits of this equitable exception are not very clear. In *Lloyd's* v. *Harper*[4] a father promised the committee at Lloyd's that he would guarantee the son's engagements. It was held that the committee could enforce this promise for the benefit of those with whom the son had entered into business relations. Lloyd's were treated as trustees for the benefit of all those with whom the son entered into contracts of insurance. On the other hand, if an insurance company promises B to cover the liability not only of B while he drives his car but also of any driver whom B allows to use the car, B is not a trustee of the benefit of the contract for the 'permitted driver'.[5] This decision created such difficulties that legislation was introduced to cover insurance of motor drivers.[6] The Law Revision Committee suggested that the law should be modified: 'Where a contract by its express terms purports to confer a benefit directly on a third party, the third party shall be entitled to enforce the provision in his own name, provided that the promisor shall be entitled to raise as against the third party any defence that would have been valid against the promisee.' Denning L.J. approves of such an amendment: indeed, he thinks that the principle denying rights to a third party is not nearly as fundamental as it was supposed to be.[7] Thus modern law is more concerned in securing serviceable rules than in adhering closely to the logical analyses of the past. Lord Reid,[8] after approving of the amendment suggested by the Law Revision Committee, stated that if one had to

---

[1] The French Code forbids it in principle, but the courts have extended the limited exceptions allowed in the text: Art. 1119 et seq.; German law, *BGB*. Art. 328 (i).
[2] *Sixth Interim Report* (1937), Cmd. 5449; Glanville Williams, 7 *Mod. L. R.* (1944), 123; A. M. Finlay, *Contracts for the Benefit of Third Persons*.
[3] Op. cit. 25.   [4] (1880), 16 Ch. D. 290.
[5] *Vandepitte* v. *Preferred Accident Insur. Corp. of New York*, [1933] A.C. 70.
[6] Road Traffic Act, 1930, 20 & 21 Geo. V, c. 43, s. 36 (4).
[7] *Smith* v. *River Douglas Catchment Board*, [1949] 2 K.B. 500 at 514.
[8] *Beswick* v. *Beswick*, [1968] A.C. at 72 and *Olsson* v. *Dyson*, [1969] A.L.R. 443.

contemplate a further long period of Parliamentary procrastination, the House of Lords might find it necessary to deal with the matter. In the case in question, justice could be done without upsetting the old rule.

§ 100. MISTAKE, MISREPRESENTATION, DURESS

These 'vices of the will' have already been mentioned in the analysis of a juristic act,[1] but it is useful to discuss them at somewhat greater length, because the view which a legal system takes towards these questions reveals its unconscious theory of the nature of contract.

In a formal contract, mistake is sometimes regarded by primitive law as irrelevant. The binding element is sought in the sacred ritual and not in the intention of the parties.[2] In consensual contracts the will of the parties is all important, and the question naturally arises whether a person should be bound if his will has been influenced by mistake. The texts of Roman law are not easy to decipher, nor is it always possible to reconcile them.[3] We find rules which emphasize that mistake avoids a contract where the error is of such a kind as to exclude the hypothesis of real consent,[4] and by contrast Paul's dictum that mistake due to carelessness is of no avail.[5] But it is safe to say that Roman law gave a far wider operation to the doctrine of mistake than English law—in many cases a unilateral error, unknown to the other party, being sufficient to avoid the contract. German law also takes a fairly subjective view. It distinguishes clearly between a mistake by one party in the expression of his intention, and cases where relief is sought because the declarant was under a mistaken assumption as to certain facts and would not have made the declaration had the truth been known.[6] There are extensive powers of avoidance in each case.[7] A declaration of intention may be avoided by the declarant on the ground of a mistake in its tenor, if it may be assumed that he would not have made it had he known the true facts; an error as to such characteristics of the other party, or the subject-

---

[1] *Supra*, § 69.

[2] In later Roman law the *exceptio doli* could be pleaded even in the case of formal contracts.

[3] J. B. Moyle, *Contract of Sale in the Civil Law*, ch. vi.

[4] Ibid. 51. In *Dig*. 18. 1. 9–11 presumably a unilateral mistake is enough. In 18. 1. 14 Ulpian asks what is the rule if *both* are mistaken. In a textbook this contrast would be decisive, but the method of compilation of the *Digest* renders such a contrast less effective.   [5] *Dig*. 18. 1. 15. 1.

[6] See E. J. Schuster, *Principles of German Law*, 94–5.   [7] *BGB*. Art. 119.

matter of a transaction, as are deemed essential in ordinary inter-course, has the same effect. But the party to whom the declaration was made may recover damages for loss suffered by reason of having acted on the faith of the validity of the declaration, if he was excusably ignorant of the ground of avoidance.[1] This last rule shows a recogni-tion of the necessity to protect the rights of the other contracting party.

In English law the emphasis on *consensus ad idem* seems to suggest a subjective theory, but the development of the principle of estoppel has led to a more external theory in practice. Mistake may be classi-fied as follows:

1. Real consensus, but error *in verbis*. No problem arises here, save the terms on which a court will rectify a written document so as to give expression to the real will of the parties.
2. Common mistake, i.e. where both parties make the same mistake.[2]
3. Where the parties mistake each other. Each is mistaken as to the other's intention though each is ignorant that a mistake exists. (This is sometimes called mutual mistake, but this term is likely to confuse.)
4. Unilateral mistake, i.e. where one of the parties alone is under a misapprehension. In such a case the mistake may have been caused by, or known to, or reasonably should have been known to, the other party.
5. Documents mistakenly signed as the result of fraud.

The doctrine of common mistake does not have a wide operation—indeed, Cheshire and Fifoot think that in practice no mistake will be regarded as sufficiently fundamental unless it affects the existence of the subject-matter of the contract.[3] Whatever is the precise effect of *Bell* v. *Lever Bros. Ltd.*,[4] the case at least shows a disinclination to avoid contracts, save in special circumstances. In a case of mutual

---

[1] *BGB*. Art. 122. 'Error is a cause of nullity of the agreement only when it is as to the substance itself of the thing which is the object of the agreement': C.C., Art. 1110. Amos and Walton, *Introduction to French Law*, 155–6.

[2] See Cheshire and Fifoot, *Law of Contract* (7th ed.), 193.

[3] But even where it does, it may not go to void the contract entirely. It may be possible to spell out a promise by one party that the subject matter of the contract in fact existed as in *McRae* v. *Commonwealth Disposals Commission* (1951), 84 C.L.R. 377.

[4] [1932] A.C. 161. See P. A. Landon, 51 *L.Q.R.* (1935), 650; 52 *L.Q.R.* (1936), 478; T. H. Tylor, 52 *L.Q.R.* (1936), 27; H. W. R. Wade, 7 *Camb. L. J.* (1941), 361; see also Denning L.J., *Solle* v. *Butcher*, [1949] 2 All E.R. 1107 at 1119, and in *Frederick E. Rose (London) Ltd.* v. *William H. Pim, Jnr., & Co. Ltd.*, [1953] 2 Q.B. 450 at 460.

mistake the contract is not necessarily void, for the test of intention is objective: 'the concern of the Court has been to implement, not the actual expectations of each party, for that indeed would be impossible, but the sense of the promise objectively considered'.[1]

The injurious reliance theory would ignore unilateral mistake unless it was known to, or should have been known to, the other party. A is not justified in relying on an agreement if he knows that the other party is labouring under a mistake. The doctrine of estoppel has the practical result that 'whatever a man's real intention may be [if] he so conducts himself that a reasonable man would believe that he was assenting to the terms proposed by the other party, and that other party upon that belief enters into the contract with him, the man thus conducting himself would be equally bound, as if he had intended to agree to the other party's terms'.[2] Unilateral mistake is, in general, not sufficient,[3] for we must not 'open the door to perjury and destroy the security of contracts'.[4] Thus estoppel may 'intervene at various points to supplement the lack of consensus'.[5] On the other hand, the court may refuse to grant damages for breach of contract, if the plaintiff had snapped at an offer which he knew was made in error.[6] This is not unjust, for where the unilateral error is known to, or innocently caused by the other party, there is no sacrifice of security in avoiding the contract if the error is sufficiently important.[7] If Dick, thinking that the lady is Dorothy, proposes to Phyllis in the shadows, and Phyllis accepts, believing that she is the lady of his heart, presumably a valid contract is made if the lady was reasonable in thinking that the offer was meant for her, for the test is not what Dick meant, but what could reasonably be inferred from his conduct.[8] Mistake can affect the operation of a contract only if it concerns the terms of the contract: error affecting the motives leading to the contract is irrelevant.

[1] Cheshire and Fifoot (2nd ed.), 145; and see their 7th ed., 194; C. Grunfeld, 13 *Mod. L. R.* (1950), 50, provides a general analysis of the problem. See also *Magee* v. *Pennine Insurance Co. Ltd.* (C.A.), [1969] 2 Q.B. 507.
[2] Per Blackburn J., *Smith* v. *Hughes* (1871), L.R. 6 Q.B. 597 at 607.
[3] Unless *non est factum* can be pleaded.
[4] Per Kekewich J., *Van Praagh* v. *Everidge*, [1902] 2 Ch. 266 at 272.
[5] J. D. I. Hughes, 54 *L.Q.R.* (1938), 370 at 371; see also 375.
[6] *Hartog* v. *Colin and Shields*, [1939] 3 All E.R. 566: Singleton J. held that there was no binding contract as the acceptor was aware of the offeror's mistake; *A. Roberts & Co. Ltd.* v. *Leicestershire County Council*, [1961] 2 All E.R. 545.
[7] Cf. *Scriven Bros. & Co.* v. *Hindley & Co.*, [1913] 3 K.B. 564.
[8] See J. D. I. Hughes, op. cit. 380; A. L. Goodhart, 57 *L.Q.R.* (1941), 228; *Ingram & Ors* v. *Little*, [1960] 3 All E.R. 332 and *Fawcett* v. *Star Car Sales Ltd.*, [1960] N.Z. L.R. 406.

There are thus evident marks in English law of an objective attitude towards the question of mistake.

It is beyond question that when a court has a contract before it, it does not in general attempt to examine the state of mind of the parties. To do so would indeed be an impossible task wherever the interpretation of the contract was in dispute. . . . The law therefore is necessarily driven to proceed on the basis of the external manifestations of the parties, words, written or spoken, or other overt acts.[1]

But we must remember that the external method is not only more convenient, but also that in most cases it actually does give effect to the will of the parties. And we must not ride the objective theory to death, for it represents an approach rather than a theory which attempts to explain everything.

Although English law is fairly strict in defining the cases in which it will give relief on the ground of mistake, in those instances which have satisfied the test the contract is entirely avoided. This is wider than French law which confined the party labouring even under an error *in substantia* to an action for rescission—in other words, the contract is only voidable.[2] The English rule had the effect that, if the contract is avoided, a third party may not secure title to goods he has bought. As between two innocent parties, the person whose carelessness contributed to the mistake should suffer, rather than the careful buyer. The doctrine of estoppel by carelessness could have developed, but the courts have 'relegated the doctrine to the background and have condoned the negligence of the first party to the detriment of the innocent trader'.[3]

Now, however, the House of Lords in *Saunders* v. *Anglia Building Society*[4] has overruled the decision criticized above.[5] Their Lordships discussed in great detail the scope of the old doctrine of *non est factum*, which allowed the plea if the signer was mistaken as to the nature of the document, as opposed to its contents. The Court of Appeal[6] pointed out that the doctrine of *non est factum* was reasonable when many of the population were illiterate, but that today it was a dangerous anachronism. The House of Lords affirmed the actual decision of the Court of Appeal, but the speeches left somewhat more

---

[1] Lord Wright, 55 *L.Q.R.* (1939), 189 at 197. Cf. T. H. Tylor, 11 *Mod. L. R.* (1948), 257.   [2] C.C., Art. 1110 et seq.
[3] Cheshire and Fifoot, op. cit. (7th ed.), 220.   [4] [1970] 3 All E.R. 961.
[5] *Carlisle and Cumberland Banking Company* v. *Bragg*, [1911] 1 K.B. 489.
[6] Sub nom. *Gallie* v. *Lee*, [1969] 2 Ch. 17.

scope to the doctrine of *non est factum* than did the dicta of the Court of Appeal. The Lords rejected the old distinction between the character of the document and its contents. Lord Reid pointed out that the doctrine of *non est factum* must be kept within narrow limits 'if it is not to shake the confidence of those who habitually and rightly rely on signatures when there is no obvious reason to doubt their validity'.[1] However, the doctrine is still left standing: 'to eliminate it altogether would, in my opinion, deprive the courts of what may be, doubtless on sufficiently rare occasions, an instrument of justice'.[2] Perhaps what is left of *non est factum* relies on a subjective test,[3] but the person pleading the defence must show that he was not careless in signing.

Misrepresentation

Misrepresentation may be fraudulent or innocent. Where one party has been guilty of fraud there are no merits in his claim to enforce the agreement thus obtained. The injured party has the remedy of the tort of deceit, if he suffers loss by relying on representations known to be false.[4] The common law ignored innocent misrepresentation, unless the representation formed part of the contract, in which case an action for damages lay.[5] Equity adopted a broader approach, allowing an action for rescission in appropriate circumstances.

Duress

In Roman law the *actio quod metus causa* gave extensive protection. It operated *in rem*, since even an innocent third party might be forced to restore what he had gained as a result of duress by another. The threats must be of bodily hurt, of enslavement, of a capital charge, or of an attack on chastity. At common law duress might make a contract voidable, but the limits of duress were as in Roman law rather narrow. Actual or threatened violence or imprisonment was necessary. Doctrines, other than that of duress, may, however, be called into play. Thus it may be against public policy to enforce

---

[1] At 963.   [2] Per Lord Wilberforce at 972.
[3] Per Lord Pearson at 980.   [4] *Derry* v. *Peak* (1889), 14 A.C. 337.
[5] See also Misrepresentation Act, 1967, s. 2 (1), which imposes liability unless the person making the representation proves that he had reasonable grounds to believe it and did believe it at the time of making the contract. S. 3 restricts the operation of any clause excluding liability for misrepresentation.

a contract obtained by extreme moral pressure;[1] or the equitable doctrine of undue influence may be in point.

In ordinary cases each party to a bargain must take care of his own interest, and it will not be presumed that undue advantage or contrivance has been resorted to on either side; but in the case of the 'expectant heir', or of persons under pressure without adequate protection, and in the case of dealings with uneducated ignorant persons, the burthen of showing the fairness of the transaction is thrown on the person who seeks to obtain the benefit of the contract.[2]

§ 101. UNILATERAL JURISTIC ACTS

In the interests of clarity is should again be pointed out that there are two uses of the term 'unilateral'. In the strict sense of jurisprudence, a unilateral juristic act is one in which the will of only one party is operative:[3] a bilateral act is one which is the result of agreement between two or more persons. In the second sense a contract (which is clearly a bilateral act) is described as unilateral if it imposes an executory duty on one party alone. It is the first sense with which we are here concerned.

A last will and testament is an example of a unilateral act, for the disposition of property may be determined by the testator alone—there is no need for two minds to be *ad idem*. A gift by deed is also a unilateral act. It is true that the will and the gift may fail of their intended effect if the beneficiaries refuse to accept, for even a present cannot be forced on a man against his will. But a gift by deed is a binding juristic act even before it comes to the knowledge of the beneficiary.[4]

In another type of unilateral act the transaction can be made fully effective even against the active dissent of the party affected. The forfeiture of a lease for breach of covenant falls under this head, since the landlord may terminate the tenant's rights in spite of the latter's active opposition. Such action by the landlord may, however, be regarded as a remedial right.

German law instances the constitution of an incorporated foundation and the offer of a reward as unilateral acts. In English law the

---

[1] *Kaufman* v. *Gerson*, [1904] 1 K.B. 591; or a marriage to escape fear of arrest in a communist country: *H.* v. *H.*, [1953] 2 All E.R. 1229.
[2] *O'Rorke* v. *Bolingbroke* (1877), 2 A.C. 814 at 823; *Zamet* v. *Hyman* (C.A.), [1961] 3 All E.R. 933; *Re Craig (deceased)*, [1970] 2 All E.R. 390.
[3] Salmond, *Jurisprudence* (12th ed.), 334.
[4] *Xenos* v. *Wickham* (1867), L.R. 2 H.L. 296.

first transaction would normally be effected by drawing up a trust deed; the second would be treated as an offer which would become a contract if and when it was accepted by someone who performed the service required.[1]

[1] According to English theory, a person can sue for a reward only if he knew of the offer before he performed the act requested: *R. v. Clarke* (1927), 40 C.L.R. 227, and Cheshire and Fifoot, op. cit. 44.

REFERENCES

COHEN, M. R., 46 *Harv. L. R.* (1933), 553.

DAVIS, A. G., 52 *L.Q.R.* (1936), 225.

EASTWOOD, R. A., and WORTLEY, B. A., *J. Soc. of Public Teachers of Law* (1938), 23.

HOLMES, O. W., *The Common Law*, 298.

HUGHES, J. D. I., 54 *L.Q.R.* (1938), 370.

JACKSON, R. M., 53 *L.Q.R.* (1937), 525.

POUND, R., *Philosophy of Law*, 236.

WALTON, F. P., 41 *L.Q.R.* (1925), 306.

WINFIELD, P. H., 55 *L.Q.R.* (1939), 499.

XVIII

RIGHTS DIRECTLY CREATED BY LAW

§ 102. INTRODUCTION

THE rights of contract arise directly from a juristic act. Other rights
are granted by the law, whether the person bound by the duty
consents or not. The American Restatement contrasts three broad
branches—contract, tort, and restitution.[1] In contract the underlying
postulate is that a person shall obtain what was freely promised, in
tort that a person has a right not to be harmed by an unlawful act;
in restitution that a person has a right to have restored to him
a benefit gained at his expense by another, if the retention of that
benefit would be unjust. Since both in tort and restitution the rights
do not arise from consent but are granted by the law, there will
naturally be some overlapping of the boundaries in actual systems.[2]

§ 103. DELICT

The simplest definition of a tort in English law is that it is a civil
wrong which infringes a right *in rem* and is remediable by an action
for damages, but historical considerations render it difficult to discover any form of words both accurate and concise. Some definitions
tell us what a tort is not, but leave us in doubt as to what it is.
Professor Winfield states that 'tortious liability arises from the breach
of a duty primarily fixed by the law: this duty is toward persons
generally and its breach is redressible by an action for unliquidated
damages'.[3]

In Roman law delict was merely a generic term covering actions
for *furtum, rapina, damnum iniuria datum* and *iniuria*. In French
law (and indeed in most modern codes) the definition may easily be
framed in terms of broad principle. 'A delict is an unlawful act
infringing the right of another and causing damage, such act being

[1] W. A. Seavey and A. W. Scott, 54 *L.Q.R.* (1938), 29.
[2] Winfield, *Province of the Law of Tort*, ch. vii.
[3] *Text-Book of the Law of Tort* (8th ed.), 2. For other definitions see Winfield,
Province of the Law of Tort, ch. xii; Salmond, *Torts* (14th ed.), 15; Buckland and
McNair, *Roman Law and Common Law*, 263.

imputable to its author, and not constituting the fulfilment of some legal obligation on his part, or the exercise of a right. And the act must be done knowingly, and with the intent to cause injury.'[1]

The term 'quasi-delict' was invented in Roman law to cover cases of liability where, although there was neither intention nor fault, liability was imposed on grounds of expediency, e.g. a householder was liable if something was thrown from his dwelling and injured a passer-by. The obvious difficulty of discovering the actual perpetrator would have meant in practice the frequent denial of a remedy in the absence of some such rule. In French writing 'delict' is confined to intentional injury and 'quasi-delict' is used to cover injury caused by negligence.[2] In English law there is no such distinction, the term 'tort' covering both intentional and negligent injury as well as strict liability.

§ 104. Purpose of the Law of Delict

The purpose of the law of delict is to protect certain rights which relate to person, property, and reputation, and to provide compensation or redress for any wrongs which infringe them. The essential mark of the criminal law is punishment inflicted by the State, that of delict redress to a wronged plaintiff. But the emphasis on compensation has only lately been made clear. The Roman law of delict tended to exaggerate the penal element and is more akin to the approach of the criminal law than is the English law of tort.[3] Thus in *furtum* the thief was liable, not only to an action for the recovery of the property, but also to fourfold damages for *furtum manifestum* or double for *furtum non manifestum*. In the *Lex Aquilia* damages were calculated on a very favourable basis to the owner, and double damages lay if one who unreasonably denied liability lost the action.[4] The *furiosus* and the *infans* escaped liability, as it was felt unjust to punish where fault was absent. This is far removed from the approach of the English law of tort, which has no general defence of minority:[5] how

[1] Aubry and Rau, *Cours de droit civil français* (5th ed.), vi. 337.

[2] The French Code does not in its articles refer to this distinction, but the chapter heading includes delicts and quasi-delicts. This distinction has been worked out by writers and decided cases. See Aubry and Rau, op. cit. 363.

[3] Buckland and McNair, op. cit. 267–9. Thus under the *Lex Aquilia* if there were several wrongdoers each was liable for the full penalty and the fact that one had paid in no way released the others: *Dig.* 9. 2. 11. 2.   [4] Gaius, *Dig.* 9. 2. 2. 1.

[5] Presumably the term *infancy* will now be changed to *minority*—see the Practice Direction, [1970] 2 All E.R. 280, arising as a result of the Family Law Reform Act, 1969, which reduced the age of minority from 21 to 18 years.

far, if at all, lunacy is a defence is still a question open to argument in
the higher courts of appeal.[1]

The law faces a difficult task in determining the level of compensation, when a plaintiff is so injured that he has lost everything but life
itself. 'Juries are set the task of weighing the imponderable and
predicting the unforeseeable', as is pointed out in an incisive judgment by Barry J.[2]

The emphasis on compensation, instead of fault, has been encouraged by the practice of insurance. If an industry involves a
dangerous activity it may be reasonable to impose strict liability:
insurance really means that the consumers of the product will ultimately pay the insurance premiums and it is more just to spread the
risk in this way than to leave it entirely on a plaintiff. Sometimes
insurance is optional and taken out for particular risks: sometimes
it is compulsory for one class of risk, as in the case of Workers'
Compensation or third party risks where motor driving is concerned.
Finally, we may have a comprehensive and compulsory scheme of
social insurance covering such risks as unemployment, accident, and
illness. Clearly the last must ultimately have some effect on the law
of tort and point was given to this in England by the passing in 1946
of the National Insurance Act, the National Insurance (Industrial
Injuries) Act, and the National Health Service Act.[3] Was it reasonable to allow a person to recover both his social insurance benefits and
damages at common law? A special Departmental Committee produced an interesting report which throws light on the views held by
various sections of the community concerning the ultimate ends of the

---

[1] A child may be in a favourable position as defendant, e.g. if negligence must be
proved it must be shown that the child did not exercise the care that was reasonable
for a child of that age. There is modern English authority on lunacy as a defence, and
also authority from other common law jurisdictions, but the detailed rules relating to
such a defence have yet to be worked out by the highest appellate courts. In *Morriss* v.
Marsden (1952), 1 All E.R. 925, it was held that insanity is no defence to a civil action for
damages for assault unless the defendant neither knew the nature of the act committed
nor formed an intention to commit it. It was thought to be immaterial to ask whether
or not he knew what he did to be wrong. In Canadian cases such as *Tindale* v. *Tindale*
(1950), 4 D.L.R. 363 and *Phillips* v. *Soloway* (1956), 6 D.L.R. (2nd) 570, the defence
was accepted as being a good one if the defendant literally did not know what he
was doing. In New Zealand as early as 1900 it was held that lunacy is not a defence
to a claim for intentional injury: *Donaghy* v. *Brennan* (1900), 19 N.Z.L.R. 289. It
may be that with greater emphasis being given in modern times to the aspect of compensation rather than fault in the area of torts, severe limits upon the defence of
lunacy in torts may be justified—see Denning L.J. in *White* v. *White*, [1950] P. 39
at 58–9.
[2] *Tzouvelis* v. *Victorian Railways Commissioners*, [1968] V.R. 112 at 120.
[3] W. Friedmann, 63 *Harv. L. R.* (1949), 241.

common law.[1] The Law Reform (Personal Injuries) Act, 1948,[2] adopted a compromise by which there is deducted from any damages recovered for loss of earnings or profits arising from personal injuries one-half of the value of the rights to insurance over five years from the time of the cause of action.[3] This is based on the fact that damages in tort are on a higher scale than the limited insurance benefits. The question of the deductibility of other collateral benefits in personal injury cases has also provided much judicial disagreement. When income tax was small the question did not arise whether compensation for loss of earnings should be reduced to take account of tax which would have been paid, if the earnings had been received. Now it is a relevant deduction.[4]

For the present the law of tort survives these charges. No doubt this is partly because social insurance is not the only purpose of the law of torts; awards of damages may operate as sanctions to support standards of care.[5] Moreover, there are many torts which social insurance will not affect, e.g. defamation, seduction, injurious falsehood, conversion, malicious prosecution, some injuries to property. Friedmann suggests that the width of the statutory schemes of insurance has led to a judicial tendency to be conservative in the interpretation and extension of common law doctrines.[6] It is yet rather early to draw definite conclusions. It is clear, however, that the modern view of tort is that its aim is to provide a reasonable adjustment of risk in society, as is illustrated by the dictum of Holmes J.: 'Be the exceptions more or less numerous, the general purpose of the law of torts is to secure a man indemnity against certain forms of harm to person, reputation or estate, at the hands of his neighbours, not because they are wrong, but because they are harms.'[7]

---

[1] 1946, Cmd. 6860; and the case law in the last ten years or so reveals strikingly divergent views about the effects, not only of insurance and superannuation schemes, but of the statutory background of modern taxation systems on the traditional law of torts—see *British Transport Commission* v. *Gourley*, [1956] A.C. 185; *West Suffolk County Council* v. *W. Rought Ltd.*, [1957] A.C. 403; *Judd* v. *Board of Governors of the Hammersmith, West London and St. Mark's Hospitals*, [1960] 1 All E.R. 607; *Lister* v. *Romford Ice and Cold Storage Co. Ltd.*, [1957] 1 All E.R. 125.

[2] 11 & 12 Geo. VI, c. 41.

[3] The formula is a detailed one, too long for exact reproduction: § 2 (1). A functional survey of the overlapping of the various systems of insurance, compensation, and tort is given by Atiyah, *Accidents, Compensation and the Law* (1970), ch. xviii.

[4] P. S. Atiyah, 32 *Mod. L. R.* (1969), 397.

[5] Even in the Soviet systems this is emphasized: see J. Hazard, 65 *Harv. L. R.* (1952), 545 at 577–8.

[6] 63 *Harv. L. R.* (1949), 241 at 258, instancing *Adams* v. *Naylor*, [1946] A.C. 543, and *Read* v. *J. Lyons & Co. Ltd.*, [1947] A.C. 156.

[7] *The Common Law*, 144.

But the persistent emphasis of the so-called moral theory that there should be no liability in the absence of intent or negligence shows that old ideas die hard.

§ 105. STANDARDS OF CARE

The question of standards of care is important, since it determines how far the protection of the rights of the plaintiff is to be carried. Does his right to freedom from harm extend only to intentional injury, or does it extend to negligent injury, or is strict liability imposed on the defendant? In Roman law the problem was fairly simple. Firstly, there was no general principle of liability, since there was only a limited number of actionable wrongs. Just as the Romans developed no general theory of contract, so they developed no doctrine of delict as such. In the cases where liability was recognized there must either be wrongful intent (as in *furtum*, *rapina*, or *iniuria*) or negligence (as under the *Lex Aquilia*). The emphasis on fault was so strong that the heading of quasi-delict was invented to cover anomalous cases. 'Roman classical law was not far removed from absolute application of the rule: no liability without fault.'[1]

In French law a broad principle of liability was laid down in the code,[2] and nothing is known of specific torts as these are understood in English law.[3] The traditional interpretation of the code founded liability on fault although there were a few exceptions.[4] There is, therefore, no great difficulty in stating the general principle which lies at the base of the law and the example of France has been followed by many modern systems.[5] This tendency to create a general principle of liability based on fault unified the law.

English law is founded on the rather narrow forms of action, and broad generalizations concerning its early history are full of danger. But the rapid development of *case*, where liability was founded on fault, led to the rationalization of part of the law, and it was inevitable that attempts should be made to construct a coherent system out of the particular instances of specific wrongs. The principle of no liability without fault was peculiarly suited to the nineteenth century.

---

[1] W. W. Buckland, *The Main Institutions of Roman Private Law*, 327.
[2] C.C., Arts. 1382, 1383; F. P. Walton, 49 *L.Q.R.* (1933), 70.
[3] Amos and Walton, *Introduction to French Law*, 215.
[4] There were certain cases of vicarious responsibility, and fault was presumed where damage was caused by the fall of a building or by animals.
[5] e.g. *BGB*. 823, 826; Italian C.C., 1151; Swiss Code, 41. Cf. F. P. Walton, 49 *L.Q.R.* (1933), 78.

It was regarded as a moral theory, since the innocent actor escaped. It encouraged free activity, instead of cramping it by the imposition of strict liability. The doctrine could thus be linked with the currents of individualism and the theory of *laissez-faire*. Moreover, the standard of negligence was an elastic one that could be applied without difficulty to very different situations. Hence arose a tendency to write the history of tort as an evolution from the un-moral theory of acting at one's peril to the ethical theory that liability should be imposed only on those who acted unreasonably.[1]

To those nineteenth-century writers who argued this way, the decision in 1868 of *Rylands* v. *Fletcher*,[2] with its emphasis on strict liability, came as an unwelcome surprise. Salmond refused to accept the principle in its entirety,[3] Pollock accepted it only under protest,[4] and it was prophesied that the decision would be rapidly eaten away by exceptions. But strict liability became established and this century has seen a surprising elasticity in the doctrine of *Rylands' Case*. If we regard the law of torts as a penal instrument, then it may seem unjust to punish where there has been no fault; but once the emphasis is placed on compensation, it is clear that it is not unjust to cast the risk of essentially dangerous conduct on the person who pursues it.[5] Instead of *Rylands' Case* being crippled by exceptions, many watched with mingled fear and admiration its triumphant progress. A principle that began with water flowing from a reservoir and extends to caravan dwellers 'escaping' from a brickfield[6] must at least be alive. The courts have retained elasticity by refusing to make a closed list of the substances to which *Rylands' Case* applies and have imposed strict liability wherever the plaintiff had been subjected to excessive risk. Thus electric cables or gas mains in the street are within the principle, but not electric wiring or gas pipes in a private house, for the latter are both normal and necessary.[7] The test of natural user of land is really more suited to a stable community than a developing one, but the courts are careful not to deter development by a too harsh imposition of strict liability.[8] In truth, the modern doctrine of strict liability requires a delicate balancing of interests: the court

---

[1] Cf. J. B. Ames, 22 *Harv. L. R.* (1908), 99.   [2] L.R. 3 H.L. 330.
[3] Preface to *Torts*, 5th ed.
[4] 25 *L.Q.R.* (1909), 317 at 321; E. R. Thayer, 29 *Harv. L. R.* (1916), 801 at 814.
[5] R. Pound, 27 *Harv. L. R.* (1914), 195 at 233.
[6] *A.-G.* v. *Corke*, [1933] 1 Ch. 89, criticized W. S. Holdsworth, 49 *L.Q.R.* (1933), 158. For an analysis of the cases see W. T. S. Stallybrass, 3 *Camb. L. J.* (1929), 376 at 382.
[7] *Collingwood* v. *Home and Colonial Stores*, [1936] 3 All E.R. 200.
[8] W. Friedmann, 1 *Mod. L. R.* (1937), 39 at 52.

must consider not only the danger inherent in a course of conduct, but also whether that conduct is abnormal or usual, whether it is beneficial to the community or pursued only for individual ends. The rank growths of individualism are being checked by new doctrines of social value. The question is often put in the form—who can best bear the loss?

The modern extension of the field of strict liability is an interesting illustration of the adaptation of case law to new situations and new social philosophies.[1] We see illustrations of the same approach in Workmen's Compensation Acts and in Air Navigation Acts.[2] Nor is the principle confined to England alone. The increasing casualties caused by the motor car have aroused a greater interest in doctrines of strict liability. In America the very diversity of solutions shows that the law is driven, not by deductive logic, but by the pressing need to find an answer to a social problem.[3] The argument is that the motorist introduces a danger for his own pleasure or profit; moreover, he is better able to bear the loss since he can protect himself by a small insurance premium and thus spread the risks of traffic over motor users; why should he not bear the loss? In France, by rather dubious methods of interpretation, the theory was adopted that a motorist should be presumed to be at fault. But though the courts thus pay lip-service to fault, there is, in reality, an imposition of strict liability (*risque créé*), for the presumption can be rebutted only by proof of a cause exterior both to the car and the driver.[4] In administrative law we see traces of the same doctrine of *risque créé*. Thus it is significant that a country which placed such emphasis on fault should see the necessity of modifying its rules in this way. It is therefore clear that in modern times there is not merely one principle of liability, there are at least two. In English law, a check to the development of strict liability has been given by the speeches in *Read* v. *J. Lyons & Co. Ltd.*[5] The actual decision was that as there was no escape, no liability could be imposed. But what was more significant was the deliberate refusal to attempt to rationalize the law or to place

---

[1] There were, of course, precedents. Indeed, medieval liability may well have been strict, but the re-enunciation of the principle in *Rylands* v. *Fletcher* (*supra*) in 1868 was all-important.

[2] See A. D. McNair, *Law of the Air*, chs. i and iii, and the Act of 1936, 26 Geo. V and 1 Ed. VIII, c. 44.

[3] 32 *Col. L. R.* (1932), 785.

[4] L. Josserand, *Évolutions et Actualités*, 52 et seq.; F. Gény, *Méthode*, ii. 174–5; Amos and Walton, *Introduction to French Law*, 262; Deák, 79 *Univ. of Pa. L. R.* (1931), 271. [5] [1947] A.C. 156.

it on a broad basis.[1] Counsel had attempted to persuade both the Court of Appeal and the House of Lords that, just as doctrines of negligence have been brought together within a broad principle, so the various doctrines of strict liability should be freed from their historical origins and based on a doctrine that abnormally dangerous conduct involves strict liability. This invitation was decisively rejected. The result of the decision is that the historical differences between *Rylands* v. *Fletcher*, liability for fire, dangerous chattels, and savage animals will probably remain in the law of tort.[2] The instances of strict liability, therefore, remain in separate pigeon-holes.

An analysis of standards of care produces the following result:

(*a*) *Strict liability*

While it is not accurate to say that defendant acts at his peril, nevertheless there is no need to prove negligence, and defendant can rebut a prima facie liability only by bringing himself within one of the rather narrow defences. The actual rules depend on historical considerations, but the broad justification is that it is reasonable to cast the risk of essentially dangerous conduct on him who pursues it.

(*b*) *Vicarious liability*

The liability of a master for the acts of his servant depends on the fact that the servant is rarely worth 'powder and shot' and it is not unfair that he who takes the profit should have the risk of loss. At common law the husband was liable for the torts of his wife because he got title to his wife's chattels, but a changing law of property has led to his exemption.[3]

(*c*) *Liability for negligence*

Negligence is used in two senses in English law. Used narrowly it means unreasonable conduct, the failure to act up to the standard which would be set by the reasonable man. In a wider sense it is the name of an independent tort and includes the notions of duty, breach of duty (unreasonable conduct), causation, and damage.[4] The standard

---

[1] 'Your Lordships are not called upon to rationalize the law of England': per Lord Macmillan, at 175.   [2] G. W. Paton, 23 *A.L.J.* (1949), 158.

[3] Law Reform (Married Women and Tortfeasors) Act, 1935, 25 & 26 Geo. V, c. 30. The liability of an employer for certain torts of an independent contractor depends on various considerations. The law is now too fluid to be expressed briefly.

[4] Per Lord Wright, *Lochgelly Iron and Coal Co.* v. *M'Mullan*, [1934] A.C. 1 at 25.

is not subjective, for the court asks: 'what would a reasonable man have done after considering the circumstances that he ought to have known and the consequences that should have been foreseen?' Yet English law is not entirely objective in its approach. Thus a child of tender years is expected to use only the care reasonable for a child of that age. If a person holds himself out as possessing special skill, he will be judged by a higher standard. A point that has been little discussed is that of the physically infirm. If I am congenitally clumsy and yet drive a motor car, the existence of my physical defects is no defence, for my negligence really consists in the attempt to drive the car. But if we can reasonably expect forbearance from driving, we can hardly hope that the physically infirm will refrain from using the highway. Where contributory negligence is pleaded there is authority for the view that one who is deaf or has defective vision should not be judged by the standard of the physically sound.[1] Is a blind man who falls into a hole in the footpath, negligently created by the defendant, to be debarred on the ground that a man with sight could have seen it?[2]

(d) Liability only where a specific subjective element is present

There are some cases where liability is imposed only where a specific subjective element can be proved, e.g. a predominant intent to injure in the case of civil conspiracy, intention in the case of assault or in inducing breach of contract, malice in defamation where qualified privilege applies.

(e) Damnum sine iniuria

Lastly, there are cases of *damnum sine iniuria*. In some circumstances I may intentionally cause injury and not be liable; or escape in spite of unreasonable conduct which causes damage.

We may now approach the question whether there is a general doctrine of liability in English law. Much controversial writing exists, but the answer seems clear. There are broad principles of liability which the courts have applied to particular circumstances. There are decisions which exempt from liability on the ground that there is no

---

[1] *Daly* v. *Liverpool Corp.*, [1939] 2 All E.R. 142.
[2] *Restatement, Torts*, § 289, and W. L. Prosser, *Torts*, § 36, suggest the test is the reasonable care of a blind man; G. B. Weisiger, 24 *N. Car. L. R.* (1945–6), 187; G. W. Paton, 23 *A.L.J.* (1949) at 161–2.

duty. Between the two 'is a stretch of disputed territory, with the Courts as an unbiased boundary commission'.[1] Whatever may be the case in the future, it is not yet possible to say that he who causes harm is prima facie liable unless it can be justified or excused. English law has rationalized the doctrine of negligence, but much work is necessary before the whole law of tort is welded into a uniform and rational body of principles. This branch of law is far from static: it is not so much a collection of specific injuries as a reservoir of principles which have been applied with limitations which are sometimes rather arbitrary because of historical accidents. I can still intentionally injure my neighbour in many ways without being subjected to liability. The law is being slowly extended, and it may be that in time general theories of liability can be confidently set forth—but that time is not yet. When it does come there will not be one principle of liability but several based on the inherent risk involved in the conduct which is complained of.[2] Few would deny that all unjustifiable harm should be actionable, but, while such a philosophy may be behind the law, to suggest it as a working explanation of the cases seems premature.

Causation

The legal treatment of the problem of causation is an interesting one. Both in science and philosophy, cause has proved difficult to define. But the law is interested in tracing physical phenomena only in so far as they show the responsibility of a particular human being. I drop a burning match on a hot day and as a result Brown's house, which is two miles away, is burnt. The physical contributory causes are many—the dryness of the vegetation, a hot wind taking the fire in that particular direction, the absence of fire-breaks around the house. The law concentrates on my responsibility for starting a chain of causation. It is clear, therefore, that the problem must be dealt with on broad common-sense lines rather than by any scientific analysis that is too subtle. Law exists to be applied, and the best of rules

---

[1] G. L. Williams, 7 *Camb. L. J.* (1939), 131. 'It has been contended that if damage is caused to any person by the act of any other person an action will lie unless the second person is able to justify his action. Many cases show that there is no such principle in the law': per Latham C.J. in *Victoria Park Racing and Recreation Grounds Co. Ltd.* v. *Taylor* (1937), 58 C.L.R. 479 at 493.

[2] Pollock affirmed the existence of a general principle, *Torts*, ch. ii (but in the 15th ed. his editor is against him, 41–6): opponents are Salmond, *Torts*; Jenks, 14 *J. Comp. Leg.* (1932), 207 at 209; Goodhart, 2 *Mod. L. R.* (1937), 1. Glanville Williams mediates, 7 *Camb. L. J.* (1939), 111. Winfield in the first edition of his *Text-Book of the Law of Tort* adopted the first view, see discussion (8th ed.), 10.

on paper may prove so difficult to apply that expense and injustice result. Hence the law asks: 'Was the conduct of the defendant a substantial factor in bringing about the final result?' Again, once a cause is set in motion, its results may be infinite. Thus the loss of Brown's ship, because of a collision caused by the negligent navigation of another ship, may force Brown into bankruptcy, deprive his sons of their professional education, lead to his wife's suicide through worry, and the loss of a marriage by his daughter. 'The law cannot take account of everything that follows a wrongful act. . . . In the varied web of affairs, the law must abstract some consequences as relevant, not perhaps on grounds of pure logic but simply for practical reasons.'[1] At bottom the problem is one of balancing interests—how far is the protection of the plaintiff to be carried?[2] Hence an act is the 'legal cause' of a consequence only if the law considers that liability should be imposed for that consequence. Hence 'legal cause' can be analysed only by examining the cases in which liability has been imposed. 'Direct cause' has no easily expressed meaning as it is used in law—it is a phrase that is a rationalization of concrete decisions.[3] The law would be simpler if some decisions were expressed in this way: 'undoubtedly in a physical sense the defendant's act was the direct cause of plaintiff's damage, but we consider for reasons of policy that it is inexpedient to impose liability.'[4] 'How wide the sphere of the duty of care in negligence is to be laid depends ultimately upon the courts' assessment of the demands of society for protection against the carelessness of others.'[5]

[1] Per Lord Wright, *The Edison*, [1933] A.C. 449 at 460.

[2] If a defendant negligently severs an electricity cable, can a plaintiff recover for loss of production? See *S.C.M. (U.K.) Ltd.* v. *Whittall & Son Ltd.*, [1970] 3 W.L.R. 694. Lord Denning: 'In actions for negligence when the plaintiff has suffered no damage to his person or property, but has only sustained economic loss, the law does not usually permit him to recover that loss. The reason lies in public policy.'

[3] L. Green, *Rationale of Proximate Cause*; H. L. A. Hart and A. M. Honoré, *Causation in the Law* (1959); Thesiger J., *S.C.M. (U.K.) Ltd.* v. *Whittall & Son Ltd.*, [1970] 1 W.L.R. 1017.

[4] Compare *Cattle* v. *Stockton Waterworks Co.* (1875), L.R. 10 Q.B. 453. It seems likely that the rule in *Re Polemis*, [1921] 3 K.B. 560 can now be laid to rest even in England. It certainly can be in all those jurisdictions which recognize the Privy Council as authoritative—see *Overseas Tankship (U.K.) Limited* v. *Morts Dock and Engineering Co. Ltd. (The Wagon Mound)* (1961), 2 W.L.R. 126 (P.C.); A. L. Goodhart, *Obituary: Re Polemis*, 77 L.Q.R. (1961), 175; G. Williams, *The Risk Principle*, 77 L.Q.R. (1961), 179.

[5] Per Lord Pearce, *Hedley Byrne & Co. Ltd.* v. *Heller & Partners Ltd.*, [1964] A.C. at 536. See also the decision of the J.C. in *Mutual Life and Citizens' Assur. Co. Ltd.* v. *Evatt*, [1971] 1 All E.R. 150, where the court split three to two in determining the boundaries of the duty of care.

§ 106. ABUSE OF RIGHTS

Strictly, the phrase 'abuse of rights' is not very elegant; how can the law denounce as illegal the exercise of a right which is granted by the law? The notion lying behind the doctrine is, however, that rights are created for a certain purpose and that a right ceases to be such if it is exercised for an end foreign to that for which it was given. Many modern codes recognize this principle,[1] but the greatest difficulty is to determine its real limits. Sometimes a purely subjective test is used—the intent to injure—but this can be proved only in the clearest cases. Another solution is to deduce the intent from the circumstances.[2] Josserand has made a lengthy examination of the problem[3] and he distinguished between three classes of rights: firstly, there are absolute rights on the exercise of which there is no check (for example, the right of cutting overhanging branches); relative rights which can be exercised only to protect some lawful interest; and altruistic rights the exercise of which is governed by the necessity of considering the interests of those who will be affected (e.g. the rights of a guardian over his ward). In short, Josserand pleads for the further *moralisation du droit*[4] by increasing the number of rights which can be exercised only to gratify a legitimate interest. To carry the doctrine to its logical end we should have to dethrone the individualist theory of rights and use as a test the measure by which that particular exercise was useful to the community.[5] An individualist theory of property renders it difficult to carry very far any doctrine of abuse of rights.

Yet most systems of law have curbed to some extent the abuses of exaggerated individualism. Thus ownership, defined by the French Code as the right to enjoy and dispose of things in the most absolute manner,[6] has been greatly cut down. The building of structures (such

---

[1] *BGB*. Art. 226: 'The exercise of a right is forbidden, if it can have no other purpose than to harm some other person.' (826 aims at the suppression of acts which are *contra bonos mores*.) Swiss C.C. 2: 'The law does not protect the manifest abuse of a right.' Chinese Code: 'A right cannot be exercised for the main purpose of causing injury to another.' Soviet Code, 1923: 'Civil rights are protected by the law, except in those cases in which they are exercised in a sense contrary to their economic and social purpose.' The Polish Code of 1934, Art. 135, speaks of an act 'going beyond the limits fixed by good faith, or by the end for which the right was conferred'. French law has no specific article, but the doctrine is accepted that abuse of rights is fault under C.C., Art. 1382. The Permanent Court of International Justice referred to the doctrine twice with approval: H. C. Gutteridge, *Comparative Law* (2nd ed.), 68.

[2] H. C. Gutteridge, 5 *Camb. L. J.* (1933), 22.

[3] *De l'esprit des droits et de leur relativité* (1927); *Évolutions et Actualités*, chs. iv, v.

[4] *De l'esprit des droits et de leur relativité* (1927), 91.

[5] Cf. L. Josserand, ibid. 73; W. Friedmann, 21 *Can. B. R.* (1943), 369.

[6] Art. 544. The article adds the necessary qualification: 'provided they are not used in a way prohibited by law or regulations.'

as false chimneys) for the purpose of blocking a neighbour's view, and the tapping of underground water solely to prevent a neighbour's use of it, are actionable. Even a refusal to enter into contract may lead to responsibility, if the law disapproves of the motive, for example, if an employer refuses to engage any union labour. The Russian Code regards as unlawful the exercise of acts contrary to their social or economic purpose. Ultimately, therefore, the dispute concerning abuse of rights is a conflict between the individualist view which would give as much freedom of self-assertion as possible and the collectivist view that would examine the exercise of rights from the angle of the community as a whole. So far, all legal systems have been fairly cautious in developing theories of abuse of rights.

In English law there are traces of the view: 'Keep within the law, and you may gratify your malice to your heart's content.'[1] But there are cases where rights are qualified, i.e. protected only if they are exercised for the purpose for which they are given. A combination of two or more has a qualified right to injure Smith, provided the intention is to protect a legitimate interest and not to gratify a 'disinterested malevolence'.[2] Where qualified privilege is raised as a defence to defamation, only an honest use of the occasion is protected.[3] The law of nuisance depends on a compromise between the interests of neighbours, and a proved intention to annoy may create liability for what would otherwise be covered by the principle of mutual forbearance.[4] Some U.S. cases have gone even farther. 'Spite fences' are not protected—'the right to use one's property for the sole purpose of injuring others is not one of the immediate and indestructible rights of ownership'.[5] Some jurisdictions give a remedy on facts analogous to *Bradford* v. *Pickles*.[6]

Gutteridge concludes that, while the doctrine of abuse of rights is recognized in most continental systems, there is little attempt to give a definite content to the theory.[7] The main difficulty is to discover

---

[1] C. K. Allen, *Legal Duties*, 96, referring to *Mayor of Bradford* v. *Pickles*, [1895] A.C. 587 at 598.

[2] *Sorrell* v. *Smith*, [1925] A.C. 700; *Crofter Hand Woven Harris Tweed Co. Ltd.* v. *Veitch*, [1942] A.C. 435.   [3] *Watt* v. *Longsdon*, [1930] 1 K.B. 130.

[4] *Hollywood Silver Fox Farm* v. *Emmett*, [1936] 2 K.B. 468; criticized by Holdsworth, 53 *L.Q.R.* (1937), 1, and approved by Goodhart, 52 *L.Q.R.* (1936), 461, and 53 *L.Q.R.* (1937), 3.

[5] *Barger* v. *Barringer* (1909), 151 N. Car. 433; *Restatement, Torts*, § 829: *contra Cohen* v. *Perrino* (1947), 355 Pa. 461. Quebec allows a remedy: 25 *Can. B. R.* (1947), 512.

[6] [1895] A.C. 587. Cf. *Barclay* v. *Abraham* (1903), 121 Iowa 619; *Wyandot Club* v. *Sells* (1896), 4 Dec. 254, 3 Ohio N.P. 210.

[7] 5 *Camb. L. J.* (1933), 22 at 42.

a formulation that will neither be too narrow nor too wide. Undoubtedly there should be a remedy if the *sole* purpose of the exercise of a right was to injure another. But, as the conspiracy cases show, it is but rarely that 'disinterested malevolence' can be shown, for usually some interest of the actor can be pleaded as the object of the act. Even Mr. Pickles could claim that he drained the percolating water in order to encourage the corporation to buy his land. Clearly, if we put the emphasis on the purpose for which the right was given, much accurate analysis would be necessary before the application of the law was clear. Care is needed not to phrase the doctrine too widely, lest excessive scope be given to the vexatious litigant to interfere unduly with the freedom of his neighbour.

Legislation is active in preventing abuse of certain rights. Town planning laws prohibit conduct by the individual which would be socially inexpedient: industrial laws prevent abuse of economic power, and patent legislation[1] stresses that the right of the owner is not the only factor to be considered—in theory at least the legal rights of the owner are created and protected primarily to ensure that new inventions shall be encouraged and their benefits made available to the community generally.

§ 107. FUNCTIONAL ANALYSIS

So far we have discussed the law of delict purely from the standpoint of the care required of the defendant. A functional analysis would ask—how far are these rules successful in achieving their end (so far as they may be said to have an end)?

Firstly, greater merit both from the theoretical and the practical approach can be claimed for those systems which base liability in tort on a broad principle or principles. It is theoretically more satisfying to have general principles of liability, just as the modern law of contract with its theory of actionable agreement is superior to the undeveloped Roman law. General principles of liability allow a coherent body of law to be developed in a more consistent fashion than if the law is confined in too many pigeon-holes. The Roman and English emphasis on specific delicts or torts leaves gaps in the law and there are various anomalies which can be justified by history alone. In English law one may be as careless as one pleases without

---

[1] Patents Act, 1949, e.g. compulsory licences (§ 37).

being subject to liability unless there is a duty to take care.[1] It being a question of law for the court to determine when a duty exists, this concept could have been used to introduce uniformity into the law, instead of leaving the question at large to the jury.[2] But an examination of the cases shows that the results of the emphasis on duty are rather surprising. Why should a manufacturer, when there is no commercial probability of intermediate examination, owe a duty of care to the ultimate consumer,[3] and the liability of a builder who puts up a defective ceiling be limited to those who have entered into contractual relations with him?[4] Realistically, the explanation is that the latter problem was decided in 1906,[5] the former in 1932, when the tendency to increase liability was stronger. The influence of the ghosts of the past is still important. It is true that within the individual forms of action there has been much rationalization, but this indirectly has had a confusing result. Rules that were once narrow and absolutely distinct have been extended until in practice there is much overlapping between the specific torts.[6] The law of negligence is fairly coherent, but in strict liability the exact relationship of the various rules to each other is still a matter of dispute. It has been said that the rules relating to liability for fire and to responsibility for damage done by savage animals are but instances of the rule in *Rylands' Case*,[7] yet there are many practical differences,[8] which were emphasized by the Lords in *Read* v. *J. Lyons & Co. Ltd.*[9] Any part of the law is fascinating while it is in a fluid state, but the time has come to rationalize all the rules of strict liability and remove detailed differences in particular cases which cannot be justified. One of the defects of case law is that it tends to create too many minute distinctions; in that part of the law of torts relating to the responsibility of an occupier to those who enter on his premises the English courts developed a variety of categories of those who enter as of right, those who enter under contract, invitees, licensees, and trespassers. Much learning surrounded the precise distinction between the duty of care owed in each of those cases, and not infrequently the rules proved too subtle and courts were led into error. The Occupier's Liability

[1] P. H. Winfield, 34 *Col. L. R.* (1934), 41.
[2] L. Green, *Law, a Century of Progress*, iii. 34 at 50–1.
[3] *Donoghue* v. *Stevenson*, [1932] A.C. 562, as explained in subsequent cases.
[4] *Otto* v. *Bolton*, [1936] 2 K.B. 46; P. H. Winfield, 52 *L.Q.R.* (1936), 313.
[5] *Cavalier* v. *Pope*, [1906] A.C. 428.
[6] W. Friedmann, 1 *Mod. L. R.* (1937), 63.
[7] (1868), L.R. 3 H.L. 330.
[8] G. W. Paton, 23 *A.L.J.* (1949), 158 at 167.   [9] [1947] A.C. 156.

Act, 1957,[1] was an attempt to provide broader rules and to obliterate unnecessary distinctions. Similarly, the law relating to liability for animals is complex and, in many ways, obsolete.[2] It is suggested that the kind of work exemplified by the Act of 1957 should be followed in other common law jurisdictions where it has not yet been attempted; and that similar work should be pursued with respect to other categories of liability where diverse rules as to strictness of liability still obtain.

On the other hand, the English reliance on case law has made the doctrine of tort very practical, and foreign lawyers emphasize that it is frequently possible in English law to find a speedy answer to a concrete problem which the general principles of a code leave in doubt.

Secondly, in most modern systems there is a tendency gradually to extend the field of liability. This is partly due to the growing acceptance of the doctrine that the object of tort is to compensate the plaintiff for injury and not to punish the defendant for his wrong.[3] This has caused a frame of mind which will apply strict liability more extensively than did our ancestors a century ago. The spread of insurance has enabled us to contemplate with equanimity the imposition of damages on a substantial scale and has tended to make the courts concentrate more on the woes of the plaintiff than the protection of the defendant.[4] The desire to favour a poor plaintiff is perhaps carried farthest in Soviet Russia, which lays down that if there is no specific duty broken, the court may consider the financial standing of the parties.[5]

The emphasis on compensation may be illustrated by modern developments of the law of contributory negligence. The penal theory requires that if the plaintiff's fault has contributed to the accident, he should be denied redress, for it is unjust to punish the defendant for what was caused in part by the fault of the claimant. But courts

---

[1] 5 & 6 Eliz. II, c. 31. Even where legislatures do not act there is still possibility of improvement by skilful work by the highest appellate courts—cf. *Thomson* v. *Cremin*, [1953] 2 All E.R. 1185 and *Commissioner for Railways (N.S.W.)* v. *Cardy* (1960), 34 *Aust. L.J.R.* 134.

[2] See the Report of the Law Commission, no. 13—a somewhat disappointingly conservative recommendation: 31 *Mod. L. R.* (1968), 683.

[3] See G. Williams, *The Aims of the Law of Tort* (1951), 4 *Current Legal Problems*, 137.

[4] See the judgment of Lord Denning in *Launchbury* v. *Morgans*, [1971] 1 All E.R. 642, where a majority of the C.A. treated the husband, on a 'pub crawl', as the agent of the wife who owned the car. Lord Denning said the wife was probably insured and so the plaintiffs could get redress.

[5] S. P. Simpson and J. Stone, *Law and Society*, 2008.

naturally dislike refusing a remedy to a pedestrian (whose fault may have been as small as his injury was grave) and allowing a negligent motorist (who may have suffered no loss) to escape, and this attitude has led to many refinements which today make this part of the law a despair to the teacher and a terror to the litigant. The reasonable theory is that of comparative negligence and this has been adopted by many foreign countries. In England, the Law Reform (Contributory Negligence) Act, 1945,[1] has modified the defence of contributory negligence by providing that

> where any person suffers damage, as the result partly of his own fault and partly of the fault of any other person or persons, a claim in respect of that damage shall not be defeated by reason of the fault of the person suffering the damage, but the damages recoverable in respect thereof shall be reduced to such extent as the court thinks just and equitable, having regard to the claimant's share in the responsibility for the damage.

This statute introduced a much-needed reform, as it was universally admitted that the law of contributory negligence was too harsh, and attempts to avoid a harsh doctrine make the law too complicated. But immediately controversy arose and authority was provided by the courts for the following propositions: (a) the doctrine of *Davies* v. *Mann*[2] and that of the last clear chance are one and the same;[3] (b) the doctrines are distinct;[4] (c) the doctrine of the last clear chance was dead before the Act of 1945;[5] (d) the doctrine is still in force after the Act;[6] (e) the Act substantially modifies a living rule of the last clear chance.[7] The moral it that it is difficult to avoid the effects of a stubborn doctrine of the common law.

All writers seem to be agreed that, regarded from the functional point of view, the law relating to personal injuries should be reformed: inevitably opinions differ as to the form which the reform should take. The necessity of proving negligence in motor car accident cases has often been criticized. Australia has suffered more casualties from the motor car than the total of dead and injured in the Boer War and

---

[1] 8 & 9 Geo. VI, c. 28; and the Australian states, for example, have made similar legislative reforms.   [2] (1842), 10 M. & W. 546.
[3] Denning L.J., *Davies* v. *Swan Motor Co.* (*Swansea*) *Ltd.*, [1949] 2 K.B. 291 at 324.
[4] Evershed L.J., same case at 317.
[5] Law Revision Committee, Eighth Report (1939), Cmd. 6032, Denning L.J., same case at 321; Lord Wright, 13 *Mod. L. R.* (1950), 2; and see *Alford* v. *Magee* (1952), 85 C.L.R. 437.
[6] W. T. S. Stallybrass, Salmond, *Torts* (10th ed.), preface; Asquith L.J., *Henley* v. *Cameron* (1949), 65 T.L.R. 17 at 20; A. L. Goodhart, 65 *L.Q.R.* (1949), 237.
[7] Glanville Williams, 9 *Mod. L. R.* (1946), 105.

two world conflagrations.[1] A Royal Commission in New Zealand[2] has recommended the abolition of the common law rules applying to actions for personal injuries, and the enactment of a compulsory state insurance scheme which would cover all injuries by weekly payments and require no proof of fault in the defendant. This proposal runs counter to many vested interests. Private insurance companies would lose a source of profit: the legal profession would suffer by the disappearance of this type of action from the courts, and many plaintiffs prefer the chance of substantial damages to the solid reality of smaller weekly compensation.

Even, however, if the common law is retained, there are serious difficulties. Many plaintiffs will lose their actions; some who win may not be able to recover from a poor defendant; various factors lead to long delay before judgment is given. The plaintiff is not encouraged to speed his suit, until he knows the extent of his injuries. Damages must be recovered in one action once and for all. The court is faced with the difficulty of weighing 'medical imponderables'. Also, is it permissible to consider inflation and the effect of income tax in determining the award of damages? In *Thurston* v. *Todd*,[3] Asprey J. regretted that he was not empowered to deal with the case by awarding damages on a periodical basis, subject to review when the real extent of the injuries was ascertainable. Otherwise there is a serious risk of injustice to one party or the other.

The Law Reform Commission of New South Wales in a Working Paper[4] realized that there are two advantages in the rule of 'once for all': it saves the legal costs of periodic revision, and there is a therapeutic value in the award of a final sum for compensation.[5] However, South Australia[6] has passed a statute which empowers the Supreme Court to enter a declaratory judgment on the issues of liability and to postpone the assessment of damages (with a normal maximum period of postponement of four years) until the medical prognosis has become reasonably clear. In the meantime, appropriate periodic payments may be ordered. The New South Wales Commission approves this approach provided that it is confined to cases where the Court on the evidence is unable to reach a decision with reasonable confidence.

---

[1] Sir John Barry, 31 *A.L.J.* (1964), 339.
[2] *Compensation for Personal Injury in New Zealand* (*The Woodhouse Report*), 1967.
[3] 83 W.N. (N.S.W.), Pt. i. 335.   [4] 1969 (not printed).
[5] An improvement in health can no longer reduce his claim, so he may well recover if he can.   [6] 1967, no. 21.

Atiyah considers exhaustively whether the object of the law of tort should be general deterrence or an efficient distribution of loss.[1] Even if the law of tort does provide some element of deterrence (in spite of the fact that liability is frequently covered by insurance), it is an expensive process. Atiyah calculates that nearly half of the insurance premiums paid by motorists disappear in administrative and legal costs. The relevant cost in distributing social security payments is ten per cent. Atiyah concludes that there is virtual unanimity in condemning the existing tort system, but much less agreement about what to put in its place.[2]

Thirdly, there is an increasing tendency to give protection to personal rights, even if there is no injury to property in the strict sense of the word. The negligent infliction of nervous shock is now recognized as a cause of action in English law,[3] and damages may be awarded for loss of expectation of life.[4] This last example is rather interesting, for the infliction of death is not a tort in English law—logically, therefore, there should be no action for the loss of ten years of life. But the courts frankly admitted the anomalous nature of the rule which denies a cause of action when death is negligently inflicted and refused to extend the doctrine farther than was required by a narrow view of the theory of precedent. In many continental systems offensive invasion of the privacy of another is an actionable wrong; English law has refused to recognize such a tort,[5] although in particular cases what is in essence a right of privacy may be protected by the use of other rules. Further examples show that English law is still backward in its protection of some personal rights. The law of slander is based on damage rather than insult; recovery for seduction at common law required proof of loss of service;[6] in some jurisdictions truth is still a complete defence to those who publish the youthful lapse of a grave and now blameless citizen, and only in criminal libel must it also be shown that the publication was in the public interest. Yet where juries are concerned 'a soiled reputation seems assured of more liberal assuagement than a compound fracture',[7]

---

[1] *Accidents, Compensation and the Law.*   [2] Ibid. 603.

[3] *Hambrook* v. *Stokes*, [1925] 1 K.B. 141; *Bourhill* v. *Young*, [1943] A.C. 92.

[4] *Rose* v. *Ford* [1937] A.C. 826; and see D. Kemp and M. Kemp, *The Quantum of Damages in Personal Injury Claims* (1954), ch. ix.

[5] Cf. *Victoria Park Racing Co. Ltd.* v. *Taylor* (1937), 58 C.L.R. 479.

[6] This action is now abolished by statute: Law Reform (Misc. Prov.) Act, 1970, c. 33.

[7] Per MacKinnon L.J., *Groom* v. *Crocker*, [1939] 1 K.B. 194 at 231. 'I can well imagine the other Mr. Groom saying to the plaintiff: "You have all the luck, I had my skull fractured and I only get £900. But because someone said you fractured it,

and this is an index of the modern realization of the importance of the protection of personal rights.

§ 108. Quasi-contract

It is impossible to define accurately the nature of quasi-contract, for it originated as a heterogeneous collection of actions which could not easily be fitted under the heading of delict or contract.[1] The term really means that a man in certain cases is bound as if he had made a contract, but, as the obligation is frequently enforced in circumstances in which it is clear that no contract was intended, the term is a source of confusion. It is desirable that a more appropriate nomenclature should become established—such as 'unjust enrichment' or 'restitution'.[2] From the standpoint of jurisprudence, many quasi-contracts are analogous to delict rather than to contract; for in contract the duty is incurred by the free consent of the party, whereas in delict and most quasi-contracts the duty is laid down by the law.

Roman law instances such cases as the following: *negotiorum gestio*,[3] the liability of a guardian to his ward, the relation between common owners who were not partners and the *condictio indebiti*.[4] This *condictio* is a particular remedy for certain types of unjust enrichment, but Justinian did not include analogous examples under his heading of quasi-contract. Thus we do not find in Roman law a broad principle that unjust enrichment should be restored; it can be said only that there were several remedies which covered part of the ground.

The French Code defines quasi-contract[5] (not very elegantly) but instances only two specific cases—*negotiorum gestio* and unjust enrichment. The textbooks and courts have, however, developed a broad principle of unjust enrichment which is discussed in the next section. In English law the traditional classification of the forms of action has had rather a narrowing effect. The remedy of *indebitatus assumpsit* was extended to cover cases of a contract implied in

you get £1,000. And it was only said to my solicitors, who would not believe it for a moment."'
[1] P. H. Winfield, *Province of the Law of Tort*, ch. vii.
[2] W. A. Seavey and A. W. Scott, 54 *L.Q.R.* (1938) at 38–9.
[3] A *gestor* who in an emergency looked after the affairs of an absent citizen without his authority could recover his expenses in certain cases.
[4] *Inst.* 3. 27: a claim for the return of money paid in error.
[5] C.C., Art. 1371.

law.[1] Lord Mansfield attempted to rescue this branch of the law from the 'marsh of technicality into which it was sinking'[2] and laid down a broad doctrine depending on natural justice and equity, the conception of *aequum et bonum*.[3] This attempt has been sharply criticized, partly because of the confusion between equity and common law, partly on the ground that these vague tests are not a very precise guide.[4] But is the fiction of the implied contract of any real assistance in determining what after all is a question of policy? Historically the doctrine was useful as it enabled *assumpsit* to be extended to a new situation. But how seriously should we take these fictions today? Is the fiction which was once progressive now to be used to hamper the law?[5] Winfield is courageous enough to define quasi-contract without any reference to an implied contract—'liability not exclusively referable to any other head of the law, imposed upon a particular person to pay money to another particular person on the ground of unjust benefit'.[6]

In considering the actual rules of English law, firstly, we note that there is no remedy for *negotiorum gestio*, on the ground that 'liabilities are not to be forced upon persons behind their backs'[7]— American law has been here rather more liberal.[8] Secondly, some cases which are treated as quasi-contracts are not really such.[9] Among the true cases Winfield instances (*inter alia*) total failure of

---

[1] The contract implied by law must be distinguished from a contract tacitly made by conduct. If I board a tram, a real contract is made: if I refuse to restore money paid in error, the law imposes on me an obligation to restore. Winfield, *Province of the Law of Tort*, ch. vii; R. M. Jackson, *History of Quasi-contract*.

[2] Winfield, *Province of the Law of Tort*, 127.

[3] *Moses* v. *Macferlan* (1760), 2 Burr. 1005.

[4] *Sinclair* v. *Brougham*, [1914] A.C. 398; *Baylis* v. *The Bishop of London*, [1913] 1 Ch. 127; *Holt* v. *Markman*, [1923] 1 K.B. 504 at 513, where Scrutton L.J. said that the history of this action is one of 'well-meaning sloppiness of thought'. Cf. C. K. Allen's retort, 54 *L.Q.R.* (1938), 201 at 205: 'It is strange that to some even of the most acute legal minds the law seems to be most "sloppy" when it is most sensible.'

[5] Lord Wright, 6 *Camb. L. J.* (1938), 305 at 325–6. Is the law prevented from implying a fictitious contract in circumstances in which a real contract could not have been made, e.g. because it was *ultra vires*? But a lunatic cannot make a real contract and yet may be bound in quasi-contract. An American writer refers to the argument based on *ultra vires* as a heresy which happily does not exist in America: E. S. Thurston, 45 *Mich. L. R.* (1947), 935 at 941. On the other hand, Lord Radcliffe emphasizes that quasi-contract should not be so extended as to evade the law: *Boissevain* v. *Weil*, [1950] 1 All E.R. 728 at 734.

[6] *Province of the Law of Tort*, 119.

[7] *Falcke* v. *Scottish Imperial Insurance Co.* (1886), 34 Ch. D. 234 at 248; *Re Cleadon Trust Ltd.*, [1939] Ch. 286. Friedmann regards this as demonstrating the individualism of the common law: 21 *Can. B. R.* (1943), 369.

[8] *Restatement of the Law of Restitution*, §§ 114 et seq.

[9] e.g. Contracts of record (judgments and recognizances), duties arising from a public calling or profession: Winfield, *Province of the Law of Tort*, 149.

consideration, money paid under mistake, the liability of a husband for his wife's necessaries, contribution, and the liability of a lunatic or drunkard for necessaries.[1] If a minor buys food on credit this may be a case of quasi-contract, for the minor is not bound by his promise to pay a certain price, but he is required to pay a reasonable price on the ground that otherwise he would be unjustly enriched.[2] But some executory contracts will be enforced against a minor[3]—here the law does not demand the restitution of an undeserved benefit but rather enforces a real contract made by the minor.[4] Hence it is not accurate to say that in all cases a minor's liability for necessaries is quasi-contractual.

§ 109. UNJUST ENRICHMENT

The doctrines which fall under the head of quasi-contract are really founded on a broad principle that unjust enrichment should not be retained at the expense of one who has suffered. In some systems, however, the actual rules of quasi-contract are rather limited, and the broader doctrine has been called into play to supplement the law. In French law the principle is known by the name of *actio de in rem verso*,[5] which 'is founded on the principle of equity which forbids one man to enrich himself at the expense of another'. It applies in every case in which, 'the estate of one person being enriched without lawful cause at the expense of another person, the latter, in order to obtain what is due to him, does not enjoy the benefit of any action based on contract, quasi-contract, delict or quasi-delict'.[6]

Some of the more recent codes contain a general article providing that unjust benefit must be returned.[7] The *Restatement of the Law of Restitution* provides interesting material, as it attempts to get

[1] *In re Rhodes* (1890), 44 Ch. D. 94. This matter is now dealt with by statute: Sale of Goods Act, 1893, § 2.
[2] Fletcher Moulton L.J., *Nash* v. *Inman*, [1908] 2 K.B. 1 at 8–9.
[3] *Roberts* v. *Gray*, [1913] 1 K.B. 520; Anson, *Contract* (23rd ed.), 200.
[4] 'As at present advised I find difficulty in acceding to the view that there is nothing that can properly be called a valid contract on the part of an infant—that all that can be inferred is an obligation on his part, which is improperly termed a contract, to repay money spent in supplying necessaries': per Lord Hanworth M.R., in *Doyle* v. *White City Stadium*, [1935] 1 K.B. 110 at 123. P. A. Landon, 51 *L.Q.R.* (1935), 270, and Cheshire and Fifoot, *Law of Contract* (2nd ed. 296–7) are rather critical of this dictum.
[5] This action has a different operation from the Roman remedy.
[6] Cited Amos and Walton, *Introduction to French Law*, 206.
[7] Polish Code (Art. 123); C.C. of Japan (Art. 703); Soviet Russia (Arts. 399–402); BGB. Art. 812; Swiss Federal Code of Obligations (Art. 62); Chinese Code (Art. 179). See H. C. Gutteridge and R. J. A. David, 5 *Camb. L. J.* (1934), 204 at 209, and L. Josserand, *Évolutions et Actualités*, 152.

behind the forms of action and the historical divisions between law and equity to the real principles on which this part of the law is based. Quasi-contract provides many examples of restitution, but we see others in equity, e.g. the doctrine of the constructive trust. This last phrase is defined in the *Restatement* in a very broad fashion as denoting cases where a person holding title to property is under an equitable duty to convey it to another on the ground that he would be unjustly enriched if he were permitted to retain it.[1] This is rather a wider definition than would be given by an English lawyer. The *Restatement*, therefore, treats under the subject 'Restitution' both legal and equitable remedies.[2]

If our law were to be logically arranged it would be necessary to consider whether some remedies which now fall under tort should not be placed under the head of 'Restitution': e.g. replevin, detinue, and trover. The lesson to be gathered from the study of any living system is that it is impossible to force the growth of living forms into rigid classifications. But the jurist should attempt to correlate as far as possible those branches of the law which depend on the same principles or give analogous remedies.

The question how far English law has adopted the principle of unjust enrichment is a matter of great dispute. Lord Wright[3] pleads for a complete resurvey of this branch of the law, arguing that the fiction of the implied contract is now otiose, and that the basis of the law should be restitution where it is unreasonable and unjust for the defendant to retain the benefit which he has received. It would, of course, be necessary to evolve detailed and definite rules, but if these are based on an intelligible principle, then the law can be developed in a more coherent fashion than if it rests on the insecure basis of an obsolete fiction. The theory of the implied contract still has supporters,[4] but it really only pushes the difficulty a stage farther back, for we still have to ask when it is just and reasonable for the law to imply such a contract.[5]

---

[1] § 160.

[2] Cf. P. H. Winfield, 54 *L.Q.R.* (1938), 529 at 532: 'It may be a dreadful shock to the pure common lawyer and to the pure equity lawyer to find themselves compelled to embrace each other, but it is high time that they should realize that there is but one principle in this branch of the system.' The application of the term 'Restitution' has the approval of Lord Wright: *Fibrosa Spólka Akcyjna* v. *Fairbairn Lawson Combe Barbour Ltd.*, [1943] A.C. 32.

[3] In *The Future of the Common Law*, 94; *Legal Essays and Addresses*, 1 at 33.

[4] D. W. Logan, 2 *Mod. L. R.*, 153 at 158, sums up the authorities.

[5] Anson, op. cit. 620.

REFERENCES

ALLEN, C. K., *Legal Duties*, 95.

ATIYAH, P. S., *Accidents, Compensation and the Law* (1970).

FLEMING, J., *The Law of Torts* (2nd ed.), (1960).

GOODHART, A. L., 2 *Mod. L. R.* (1938), 1.

GUTTERIDGE, H. C., 5 *Camb. L. J.* (1933), 22.

HOLMES, O. W., *The Common Law*, Lectures III, IV.

SEAVEY, W. A., and SCOTT, A. W., 54 *L.Q.R.* (1938), 29.

WILLIAMS, G., *The Aims of the Law of Tort* (1951), 4 *Current Legal Problems*, 137.

WINFIELD, P. H., *Province of the Law of Tort*, ch. vii, and 54 *L.Q.R.* (1938), 529.

XIX

REMEDIAL RIGHTS

§ 110. INTRODUCTION

REMEDIAL rights arise from the infringement of a primary right, whether that right is created by a juristic act or directly by law. Thus the breach of a contract is an unlawful act which breaks a duty which has been voluntarily incurred; the commission of a tort is an unlawful act which is the breach of a duty laid down by law. In this chapter we consider the various types of remedial rights which the law will allow.

§ 111. TYPES OF REMEDIAL RIGHTS

(a) Self-help

The early method of enforcing rights was by self-help,[1] but law can operate effectively only when it masters the natural desire of man to 'take the law into his own hands'. The great need for any primitive system is to secure order and to protect the weak against the lawless activities of the strong. Pollock and Maitland suggest that the law in the thirteenth century kept up its courage by bold words: 'it will prohibit utterly what it cannot regulate.'[2] Now that the courts are strong enough to deal with even the most recalcitrant subject, the law allows 'an amount of quiet self-help that would have shocked Bracton',[3] and the rights of recaption of chattels, self-defence, distress for rent, distress damage feasant and abatement of nuisance illustrate methods by which a person may still take active steps to remedy a wrong without setting in operation any process of a court. But the law zealously guards against any abuse of these remedies—for example, Lord Atkinson has said:

the abatement of a nuisance is a remedy which the law does not favour. . . . 'The security of lives and property may sometimes require so speedy a remedy as not to allow time to call on the person on whose property the mischief has arisen, to remedy it. In such cases an individual would be

---

[1] *Supra*, §§ 13 and 14.　　　　　[2] *History of English Law*, ii. 572.
[3] Op. cit.

justified in abating a nuisance from omission without notice. In all other cases of such nuisances, persons should not take the law into their own hands, but . . . appeal to a court of justice.'[1]

(b) Legal Process

I. *Declaratory judgment.* In most cases a person can enforce his rights only by the use of the appropriate legal process. Sometimes the mere declaration that the right exists may be all that a plaintiff requires, for his opponent may be quite willing to carry out such legal duties as a court may declare binding. Hence the *declaratory* judgment has become quite important in modern times. It would be ridiculous if the court, in effect, said that the only way to determine whether the suspect was a mushroom or a toadstool was to eat it[2]— that is, that I must first run the risk of breaking the law before I can ask the court what the precise legal position is. The declaratory judgment must be distinguished from the moot case and the advisory opinion. Courts are too busy to solve problems that are not related to the conflicting interests of two parties actually before the court, and the answering of moot problems would be dangerous, for those whose interests were affected might not have the opportunity of presenting an argument. A declaratory judgment is the result of an action between two parties arising out of a dispute as to their legal rights, and the sole significant difference from an ordinary action is that the plaintiff merely asks for a declaration of rights and not for the execution of any legal process. But such a judgment is binding between the parties in any future litigation arising out of the same facts.[3]

II. *Prevention.* If I discover that you are about to break a legal duty owing to me, the most effective protection that the law can give is to act before the threatened wrong takes place. Medicine has no monopoly of the maxim that prevention is better than cure. Before the court had developed an effective process, the parties themselves attempted to secure the observance of agreements by requiring, at the time the agreement was made, either the surrender of a hostage,

---

[1] *Lagan Navigation Co.* v. *Lambeg Bleaching Co.*, [1927] A.C. 226 at 244–5.
[2] E. M. Borchard, 31 *Col. L. R.* (1931), 561 at 589.
[3] W. I. Jennings, 41 *Yale L. J.* (1932), 407; and see *Barnard* v. *National Dock Labour Board*, [1953] 1 All E.R. 1113; *Vine* v. *National Dock Labour Board*, [1957] A.C. 488; *Pyx Granite Co. Ltd.* v. *The Ministry of Housing and Local Government*, [1960] A.C. 260; S. A. De Smith, *The Province of the Declaratory Judgment Re-determined* (1958), 21 *Mod. L. R.* 401; J. G. Borrie, *The Advantages of the Declaratory Judgment in Administrative Law* (1955), 18 *Mod. L. R.* 138; J. D. B. Mitchell, *The Flexible Constitution* in 1960 *Public Law*, 332.

or of a chattel, as security. Modern law has the more convenient remedy of the injunction by which the court will order the defendant to carry out a positive duty or refrain from committing a particular wrong. If I discover that you are about to defame me in a novel which is in the hands of your publishers, I can attempt to prevent the publication of the novel and thus to protect my reputation before it is ruined.

III. *The enforced performance of a primary right.* Thus the law may prevent an injury before it actually takes place. If a primary right has already been broken, in some circumstances the law will give redress by enforcing the primary right so far as that is possible. If Jones's building interferes with Brown's ancient lights, an English court may compel Jones to remove the building. If Robinson has not carried out his contract, specific performance may be decreed, i.e. he will be ordered to carry out its terms on pain of being guilty of contempt of court. The common law was defective in that it possessed no adequate machinery for these purposes, but the power of the Chancellor provided an effective machinery through the use of the injunction. Equitable remedies cannot, however, be secured as of right, but only if the court considers that damages would not be an effective remedy and that it is equitable to make a decree.[1] In French law a defendant could be ordered to deliver *certa res* or a sum of money, but only in rare cases could any other act be ordered. *Nemo praecise cogi potest ad factum.* But the convenience of a wide protection of primary rights is shown by the efforts of French law to introduce indirectly a power that was not given directly by the Code. By what is termed an *astreinte* the defendant is ordered to pay a certain sum as damages for every day that elapses before the duty is fulfilled, the amount of the sum being determined by a desire, not to compensate the plaintiff, but to conquer the obstinacy of the defendant.[2]

In some cases it is physically impossible for the law to enforce the performance of a primary right—no legal process can restore to a wife her breadwinner, if he has been killed by the defendant's negligent act. In such instances the law must be content with awarding damages, not because they are considered adequate, but because there is no other course open.

---

[1] *Hutton* v. *Watling*, [1947] 2 All E.R. 641 at 645; *Charrington* v. *Simons & Co. Ltd.*, [1970] 2 All E.R. 257.
[2] Amos and Walton, *Introduction to French Law*, 186; G. F. Krassa, 21 *Can. B. R.* (1943), 337.

In other cases the law refuses a grant of specific performance on grounds of policy. It would obviously be impolitic to force a lady to carry out a promise to marry, if she was unwilling to do so. Whatever was once the case, a husband cannot now by English law imprison his wife to secure her obedience to his commands,[1] nor will the court force a wife to return to her husband against her will. It is needless to emphasize that the court will not enforce agreements which it regards as *contra bonos mores*. Contracts for personal services also present many difficulties. If an opera singer has bound herself to appear only in Brown's theatre, the law may prohibit her from accepting a better offer from Jones, but to compel the lady to sing against her will might lead to fantastic results. Specific performance may be refused where undue hardship would be caused to the defendant.

IV. *Damages*. It has been said that no part of English law is so uncertain and so confused as that relating to damages.[2] This is due partly to the inherent difficulty of doing justice to both parties. Sentiment leads us to compensate the plaintiff for all loss, impartiality to remember that, especially where there is no fault, too great a burden should not be placed on the defendant. Partly the confusion is due to our lack of basic theories in tort, partly because the law of damages is surprisingly modern and has not yet been thoroughly worked out. The fact that there has been so much dispute whether there is any difference between contract and tort in the rule relating to remoteness of damage is surely significant.[3]

There are several varieties of damages. The amount awarded may be such as to indicate that 'the Court has formed a very low opinion of the plaintiff's bare legal claim, or that his conduct was such that he deserved, at any rate morally, what the defendant did to him'.[4] These are termed *contemptuous* damages. What are called *nominal* damages do not necessarily indicate that the court has any scorn for the plaintiff's case.[5] Trespass to land is actionable *per se*, i.e. without proof that any actual damage has been done; an owner may sue a trespasser for nominal damages merely as a warning to others. The most common type of damages is *compensatory*—in this case the aim is to grant such compensation as seems a fair recompense.

---

[1] *R. v. Jackson*, [1891] 1 Q.B. 671.
[2] Cf. Atkin L.J. (as he then was) in *The Susquehanna*, [1925] P. 196 at 210.
[3] A. L. Goodhart, 2 *Univ. of Toronto L. J.* (1937), 1.
[4] Winfield, *Text-Book of the Law of Tort* (6th ed.), 180.
[5] Damages are not necessarily nominal because they are small. I may sue for compensation for damage estimated at five shillings—if I recover, this would be compensatory damages.

Difficult problems arise which cannot be solved by any *a priori* theory. If damages are given for loss of expectation of life, it is clearly impossible accurately to assess in money the value of ten, twenty, or thirty years of existence.[1] No damages can adequately compensate for loss of health in a motor-car accident. Just as in problems of causation the lines cannot be drawn with logical accuracy, so in assessing damages the law attempts a reasonable compromise, arbitrarily but necessarily regarding certain types of damage as too remote. It is, perhaps, inevitable that the cases are hard to reconcile. If you convert my goods, should I receive the actual value of the goods or in addition the profit which I have lost on a contract of resale which I have already made? This simple question is not easy to answer on the cases as they stand.[2] The Court of Chancery by Lord Cairns's Act, 1858, was given power to award damages in lieu of an injunction, where damages would be an adequate remedy. If the wrong has not yet taken place, how are the damages to be ascertained? This raises the problem of *anticipatory* damages.[3]

Finally, damages may be *exemplary* or vindictive. Just as in contemptuous damages the court, considering the plaintiff's moral conduct, reduces the amount payable, so in the case of exemplary damages the conduct of the defendant is scrutinized and made a ground for inflating damages.[4] An insulting assault, such as spitting in a man's face, or a wanton trespass in order to disturb a garden party, may be visited with very heavy damages, although no financial loss can be proved.[5] In seduction the action is technically for loss of services, but actually exemplary damages are allowed as a *solatium* for the outrage to the family honour. In contract, the only case in which exemplary damages can be obtained is that of breach of promise to marry.[6] Since the decision of the House of Lords in

[1] Compare the varying figures awarded for loss of expectation of life ranging from £90 awarded for a child of three years who was killed, £1,500 for a child of eight years, to £1,000 for a girl in her twenties. The House of Lords has now decreed that damages should be set at a much lower figure, *Benham* v. *Gambling*, [1941] A.C. 157.
[2] *The Arpad*, [1934] P. 189; A. L. Goodhart, 2 *Univ. of Toronto L. J.* (1937), 1; and see *Hall & Co. Ltd.* v. *Pearlberg*, [1956] 1 All E.R. 297; *Heskell* v. *Continental Express*, [1950] 1 All E.R. 1033 at 1049; G. W. Paton, *The Measure of Damages in Detinue and Conversion*, 22 Aust. L. J. (1949), 406.
[3] *Leeds Industrial Co-operative Society Ltd.* v. *Slack*, [1924] A.C. 851.
[4] Winfield, op. cit. 182.
[5] *Merest* v. *Harvey* (1814), 5 Taunt. 442; *Loudon* v. *Ryder*, [1953] 2 Q.B. 202; *Williams* v. *Settle*, [1960] 2 All E.R. 806.
[6] In the United States of America many states have prohibited, actions for breach of promise to marry. For U.K., see Law Reform (Misc. Provisions) Act, 1970.

Rookes v. *Barnard*,[1] the doctrine of exemplary damages has been somewhat cut down, but the High Court of Australia has refused to follow this decision.[2] However, in *Broome* v. *Cassell & Co. Ltd.*,[3] the Court of Appeal, somewhat boldly, decided that the decision of the Lords was *per incuriam*, as it ignored previous decisions of the House, and it was not until 1966 that the Lords took power to over-rule their own decisions.

The facts of the case in the Court of Appeal show that in certain circumstances the courts should have power to award exemplary damages, e.g. for deliberate or reckless defamation.

Exemplary damages are often regarded as frankly punitive, in that the defendant is forced to do more than make compensation for the loss he has caused. But if we regard the law as protecting not only financial interests but also certain rights of personality, then exemplary damages can be regarded as compensation for a wanton outrage—an *iniuria* in the Roman sense.

Purely penal damages are recoverable in English law only in that curious anomaly, the action by the common informer. In order to supplement the weak enforcement of the law, certain statutes laid down that pecuniary penalties could be recovered by anyone who cared to sue the doers of certain prohibited acts.[4] In Roman law, however, the damages in delict were frequently calculated on a penal basis. Thus in *furtum*, the owner not only had an action for the recovery of goods, but could recover a penalty of twice or fourfold the value according to whether the *furtum* was *non manifestum* or *manifestum*.

Another distinction in the law of damages is that some wrongs are actionable *per se* (such as trespass to land or libel) and others are actionable only on proof of actual loss (such as civil conspiracy). Not all forms of 'damage' are recognized as sufficiently important by the law to justify a cause of action which requires proof of actual damage —thus the law does not attempt to give a remedy for mental pain and suffering *per se*. But once there is a cause of action on other grounds, what Street aptly calls 'parasitic damage'[5] may be allowed

---

[1] [1964] A.C. 1129.

[2] *Australian Consolidated Press* v. *Uren*, [1969] 1 A.C. 590. The Privy Council upheld the right of the High Court to adopt its own rule.　　　　　[3] [1971] 2 W.L.R. 853.

[4] Cf. the revival of the Sunday Observance Act, 1871, which made liable to penalties those who sold seats, or advertised the selling of seats, for performances on Sunday: *Orpen* v. *New Empire Ltd.* (1931), 48 T.L.R. 8. This Act was repealed by the Statute Law (Repeals) Act, 1969.

[5] *Foundations of Legal Liability*, i. 461; H. Street, *The Law of Torts* (4th ed.) (1968) at 455.

to swell the compensation. The disgrace, anguish, and wounded feelings of a father at his daughter's seduction are not a cause of action *per se*: but if loss of service be proved, such factors may increase the damages.[1]

[1] This action is now abolished—see Law Reform (Miscellaneous Provisions) Act, 1970.

XX

EXTINCTION OF RIGHTS

§ 112. Extinction of Rights

THERE are many ways in which rights may be extinguished. In some systems of law this question is discussed in relation to each type of right,[1] but this approach, however necessary in dealing with the minutiae of any one system, is inappropriate for jurisprudence. The only possible method is to treat together the general causes of extinction of rights. Rights may be extinguished by performance of the duty, consent, the exercise of a power by one party without the consent of the other, impossibility of performance, frustration, the operation of law or prescription.[2]

1. *Performance may be actual or substituted*

Dealing first with the former, it is clear that if the right is to one specific act or forbearance or a limited number of acts or forbearances, then compliance with the duty extinguishes the right, for it has served its purpose and has no longer a reason for continuing. If Jones pays me the five pounds that he owes me, that destroys my right to demand the money. But the extinction of the right does not mean that the position is the same as if the right had never existed, for, if it afterwards appears that owing to a mistake of fact my claim to the money was not valid at the moment when it was paid, then Jones may be able to recover it.

But if the right is to a series of acts or forbearances, then performance of the first act of the series does not affect the obligation to perform the rest. Where rights *in rem* are granted by the law (e.g. the right of an owner that no one shall trespass on his land), then the legal duty of performance is continuous; for persons are bound not only to forbear from trespassing once, but to continue to forbear. This is, perhaps, too obvious to need stressing.

---

[1] Thus the *Restatement of the Law of Contracts* gives twenty-one methods by which contractual rights may be extinguished: § 385.

[2] Cf. C.C., Art. 1234, which instances payment, novation, voluntary release, compensation, merger, loss of the *res*, avoidance or rescission, prescription.

On analysis, the cases of substituted performance really fall under other heads, for the 'substitution' must be due either to an agreement of the parties or to the operation of law—and both of these are discussed below. If I have contracted with Jones for the purchase of a German car, I may agree, if the performance of the contract is difficult, to accept in place of it an English car. This is, in reality, the destruction of the one obligation and the creation of another by the agreement of the parties. Set-off illustrates substitution by operation of law. If Jack owes Tom ten pounds and then, owing to other engagements between the same parties, Tom becomes indebted to Jack for five pounds, Tom can claim only five pounds.[1]

2. Consent

The great majority of rights may be waived by agreement between the parties.

Where rights arise from an agreement, the very terms which create the right may provide for its extinction in certain contingencies. Thus a condition subsequent may destroy the rights which have been created,[2] or a clause may give one of the parties, or both, the power to withdraw or to annul the agreement in certain circumstances.[3]

'Release' is the term used in many parts of the law to denote the surrender of a right. Thus if a simple contract is still executory on both sides, the parties may by agreement destroy the rights that they have just created. But the doctrine of consideration qualifies English law. My waiver of rights is consideration for your waiver, where both of us forgo something; but if a contract has been executed by A, A is not bound by his release of B, unless consideration exists or the release be made by deed or unless he is affected by some form of 'equitable estoppel'.[4] A promise to forgo part of a debt is not binding unless there be consideration for it. In systems which do not base the law of contract on consideration there is not this complication,[5] but

---

[1] In some systems of law, set-off operates only in an actual action between the parties: *Searles* v. *Sadgrove* (1855), 25 L.J.Q.B. 15. In German law there is an independent right of set-off: *BGB*. Art. 387. In French law, 'compensation' takes place as a matter of right by the sole operation of the law, even without the knowledge of the debtor: C.C., Art. 1290.

[2] Strictly a condition precedent does not destroy rights, but rather prevents them from arising.

[3] Conditions may also be implied by law. Thus a common carrier may be discharged from his obligation to deliver the goods safely, if they are lost through act of God or king's enemies.

[4] *Central London Property Trust Ltd.* v. *High Trees House Ltd.*, [1947] 1 K.B. 130; and *Combe* v. *Combe*, [1951] 2 K.B. 215; and § 96 *supra*.

[5] Cf. C.C., Arts. 1282 et seq.

the doctrine of *contrarius actus* has had great influence—an obligation made in a solemn form must be destroyed by the method by which it was created.

Novation is another method of discharge of rights by agreement, but it is more appropriate to rights *in personam*. Novation may take place in three ways.[1] Firstly, there may be a change of form, as when the duty to pay the price under a contract of sale is transformed into a promise to pay by *stipulatio*. Secondly, the subject-matter of the obligation may be altered, as when Jones agrees to accept Blackacre instead of Greenacre. Thirdly, the parties may be changed, either the right or the duty being transferred to one who previously was outside that particular contractual bond. James may release William from his duty, on condition that the duty is assumed by Philip: or Kenneth may assume the duty to pay Joseph instead of Jack, the original debtor. Technically, novation is really the cancellation of one complexus of rights and duties and the substitution of another for it.[2] Today assignment[3] has become so much simpler that there is not the same need for technical rules of novation as there was in primitive systems where the tie of *obligatio* was so intensely personal that it was considered unthinkable that a creditor could deal with a debt owed to him by assigning it to another.

3. *The exercise of a power by one party to destroy an obligation without the consent of the other*

In certain cases there may be a power in one party to avoid a contract without the other's consent. Thus to protect the inexperience of the infant, he may be favoured by the law with this power.[4] Again, one who has obtained rights by fraud, duress, or undue influence is liable to have those rights defeated by the exercise of a power of avoidance.

If there are reciprocal obligations which have been validly created, one who commits a breach of his duties may lose the right to call on

---

[1] C.C., Arts. 1271 et seq.; *Restatement of the Law of Contracts*, § 424.

[2] An exact analysis may become important in Private International Law—the debtor should be discharged according to the proper law of the contract and the creation of the debt would be governed by the proper law of the debt: *Re United Railways of Havana and Regla Warehouses Ltd.* (C.A.), [1959] 1 All E.R. 214.

[3] *Supra*, § 73.

[4] The common law rule gave power to avoid contracts which were neither for necessaries nor for the infant's benefit. But the rule has now been modified by statute: Sale of Goods Act, 1893, § 2.

the other for performance. This is sometimes termed discharge of contract by breach. Any breach of contract creates remedial rights; but in addition, my breach of a contract may destroy any claim (which I would otherwise have had) that the other party should perform his obligations. By discharge we must understand, not merely the right to bring an action under a contract because the other party has not fulfilled its terms (the contract being still in existence), but the right to consider oneself exonerated from any further performance under the contract—the right to treat the legal relations under the contract as having come wholly to an end.[1]

4. Impossibility of performance and frustration

If the fulfilment of a promise is impossible *ab initio* under all conceivable circumstances, most legal systems discharge the right to performance. More difficult problems arise when performance becomes impossible through a change of circumstances which occur subsequently to the creation of the right—supervening impossibility or *casus*. In Roman law *casus* would relieve only that party for whom performance was impossible, leaving the other to fulfil his obligations. This might easily lead to unjust results, but in the newer types of contract *bonae fidei* the claim would contain the words *ex fide bona*, and the *iudex* would condemn only for such sum as was reasonable after taking into account all the circumstances.[2] Modern Roman doctrine has emphasized the second tendency, and in French law today, where performance of the obligation is impossible because of *force majeure*, the obligation is discharged and the parties are put back as far as possible into their former position.[3] But the defence was narrowly construed and during the First World War jurists elaborated the doctrine of *imprévision* which was based partly on good faith and partly on the maxim *rebus sic stantibus*.[4] This, however, was applied mainly in administrative law.[5]

English law began with a very strict rule that although supervening

---

[1] Anson, *Contract*, ch. xv; *Restatement, Contracts*, § 397.

[2] W. W. Buckland, 46 *Harv. L. R.* (1933), 1281; R. Gottschalk, *Impossibility of Performance in Contract*; G. J. Webber, *Effect of War on Contracts*; R. G. McElroy, *Impossibility of Performance*.

[3] C.C., Arts. 1147–8; Amos and Walton, *Introduction to French Law*, 195–6.

[4] i.e. the theory that agreements should be binding only so long as conditions remain substantially the same. This doctrine was frequently urged in international law as an excuse for breaking a treaty.

[5] R. David, 28 *J. Comp. Leg.* (1946), 11 at 13. This volume also contains studies of frustration in Scots, S. African, and German law.

impossibility would be a defence for the breach of a duty laid down *by the law*, yet if the duty had been assumed *by contract*, then a party must pay damages if he cannot fulfil the promise.[1] The argument was that it was always possible for a party to a contract to protect himself by the insertion of a special clause. In spite of this doctrine, however, English law has gone very far in the creation of a doctrine of impossibility of performance. Death of the promisor destroys a duty to fulfil a contract for personal services: a serious illness may have the same effect,[2] or a relaxed throat may relieve a singer from the duty to take part in an opera.[3]

English law, however, frequently treats under one head problems that are not really the same: destruction of the subject-matter of the contract, supervening illegality, total failure of consideration, and the doctrine of commercial frustration. Different considerations apply in each of these cases, and the tendency to group them together under the heading of impossibility of performance has not led to clarity. This confusion was shown in the group of cases arising out of the postponement of the coronation procession. Is a contract discharged if it related to the hire of rooms from which the procession might be viewed, but did not specifically refer to the procession? It was not physically impossible to carry out the contract, for the rooms were available for use, but the Court of Appeal held that the contract was discharged on the ground that the circumstances, on the basis of which the parties had impliedly contracted, had been entirely changed.[4] Until 1942, English decisions left the parties as they were at the time the contract was discharged—if the whole rent or a deposit was by the terms of the contract payable on a date before the postponement was announced, then such sum must be paid. The Roman rule seems fairer, that the *iudex* should decide what was due *ex fide bona*. In 1942 the House of Lords[5] unanimously overruled the so-called rule in *Chandler* v. *Webster*.[6] It is true that both parties are released from further performance of the contract, but in quasi-contract the loser can recover where there has been a total failure of consideration. As Lord Simon pointed out, however, the English rule was not abstractly fair in all cases, for English law did not apportion a prepaid sum—if

---

[1] *Paradine* v. *Jane* (1647), Aleyn 26.
[2] *Robinson* v. *Davison* (1871), L.R. 6 Ex. 269.
[3] Even if the condition is due to the singer's failure to change wet clothes? Visc. Simon, *Constantine Line Ltd.* v. *Imperial Smelting Corp.*, [1942] A.C. 154 at 166–7.
[4] *Krell* v. *Henry*, [1903] 2 K.B. 740; A. D. McNair, 35 *L.Q.R.* (1919), 84.
[5] *Fibrosa Spólka Akcyjna* v. *Fairbairn Lawson Combe Barbour Ltd.*, [1943] A.C. 32.
[6] [1904] 1 K.B. 493.

there was a total failure of consideration, the whole sum had to be repaid even though the party had already been put to expense in preparing to carry out the contract. If there was not a total failure of consideration, then apparently nothing was repayable. This matter has now been covered by legislation[1] and the court is empowered to make a wider adjustment of the rights and liabilities of the parties. The statute does not define frustration, but rather regulates what is to happen, once it has occurred.

Commercial frustration frequently arises in time of war, for in many cases, although performance is physically possible, it would be so long delayed that to enforce the obligation would be harsh.[2] A doctrine of frustration was developed, but it is usually considered under the heading of impossibility of performance, and today it is becoming increasingly difficult to draw a clear line between the two doctrines. It is significant that the *Restatement* defines impossibility as not only strict impossibility, but also impracticability because of the extreme and unreasonable difficulty, expense, injury or loss involved.[3] The correct view seems to be that of Lord Sumner who describes the modern doctrine as 'a device by which the rules as to absolute contracts are reconciled with a special exception which justice demands'.[4] Lord Wright states that the court in the absence of express intention of the parties determines what is just.[5] To some judges this seems too great an interference with the autonomy of the will,[6] and hence a narrower doctrine is advanced on the basis of a term implied in the contract. One interpretation makes the basis of the implied term 'what the court thinks the parties ought to have agreed on the basis of what is fair and reasonable'[7]—on this objective test there seems little difference between the two theories.[8] The House of Lords seems now to have taken the view that the two theories reach the same result in the end; and that frustration will be found if, because of altered circumstances, performance would be something

---

[1] Glanville Williams, *The Law Reform (Frustrated Contracts) Act, 1943*.
[2] H. C. Gutteridge, 51 *L.Q.R.* (1935), 91 at 110.
[3] *Restatement of the Law of Contracts*, § 454.
[4] *Hirji Mulji* v. *Cheong Yue Steamship Co. Ltd.*, [1926] A.C. 497 at 510.
[5] *Legal Essays and Addresses*, 258.
[6] J. Stone, *Province and Function of Law*, 101.
[7] *Fibrosa Spólka Akcyjna* v. *Fairbairn Lawson Combe Barbour Ltd.*, [1943] A.C. 32 at 70.
[8] One difference is that, if the parties foresaw the contingency, and made no provision, the theory of the implied term would probably not allow of frustration: it might possibly be allowed on the objective theory. Cf. the discussion by Cheshire and Fifoot, *Law of Contract* (5th ed.), 467, of *W. J. Tatem Ltd.* v. *Gamboa*, [1939] 1 K.B. 132.

substantially different from what was contracted for. This may be put in a number of ways: the terms of the contract must be construed to see if they can be applied to the altered situation; is the fundamental nature of the adventure so altered by changed circumstances that fulfilment on the original terms is no longer possible? have later events so altered the circumstances that on a proper interpretation of the contract it could no longer be performed as bargained for when made?[1] The difficulty is to achieve a fair compromise and yet not to interfere too greatly with the security of contract. A party must not be allowed to escape from a contractual tie, merely because a change in the circumstances turns an anticipated profit into a loss. If a contract relates to the sale of German aniline dyes, the outbreak of war with Germany may render performance illegal and probably impossible: but if Jones contracts to sell dyes, the mere fact that the outbreak of war renders it excessively costly to fulfil the contract does not absolve him.[2] War casts a severe strain on whatever rules a legal system may adopt: currency control or a sudden leap in the exchanges may change entirely the relative position of the parties and there are frequently no specific provisions in the contract dealing with such contingencies. Sudden inflation may destroy the economic value of a creditor's rights. Hence the law must make a reasonable compromise between the desire to achieve justice and the necessity of upholding the sanctity of contract.

5. *Operation of law*

A right may be destroyed because a general rule of law is called into operation, or else because a change in the law destroys a particular right. To illustrate the former, a right may be extinguished because debtor and creditor become the same person (*Confusio*).[3] A man cannot be his own debtor. It was once held that Phyllis's right to sue Jack for negligence for personal injury would be destroyed by her subsequent marriage to Jack,[4] for the fiction is that for some purposes husband and wife are one person at law. Again, if a higher security is accepted instead of a lower, the lower security is

---

[1] See *British Movietone News Ltd.* v. *London and District Cinemas Ltd.*, [1952] A.C. 166; *Davis Contractors Ltd.* v. *Fareham U.D.C.*, [1956] A.C. 696; and *Tsakiroglou & Co.* v. *Noblee and Thorl GmbH.*, [1961] 2 All E.R. 179.
[2] *Blackburn Bobbin Co. Ltd.* v. *Allen & Sons Ltd.*, [1918] 2 K.B. 467.
[3] C.C., Art. 1300.
[4] *Gotliffe* v. *Edelston*, [1930] 2 K.B. 378: overruled *Curtis* v. *Wilcox*, [1948] 2 K.B. 474.

extinguished and merges in the higher (*Merger*). An instance of this is the extinction of a right of action for breach of a legal duty by the award of a judgment for damages. Set-off is another illustration of the operation of a rule of law. When a bankrupt is discharged there is a statutory release from debts and liabilities provable under the bankruptcy. If a deed or contract in writing be materially altered by addition or erasure, it may be discharged by operation of law.

Loss of rights by a change in the law hardly needs illustration. Where there are no constitutional safeguards, an omnicompetent parliament may sweep away whatever vested rights it pleases. In England there is a presumption of interpretation that statutes should, if possible, be so construed as not to have retrospective effect, but this is only a canon of interpretation which may be rebutted by the clear language of the statute.[1]

6. *Prescription*

Chinese law had no rules of prescription till 1930,[2] but most legal systems recognize that the passing of time may defeat the claims of the indolent. One who has enjoyed long possession does not necessarily possess the best title, but the effect of possible revivals at any time of 'stale claims' is so unsettling that it militates against an ordered community life. Hence the passing of time may create, transfer, or destroy rights. These rights may concern a claim *in personam* for compensation or the title to movable or immovable property. Hence two questions arise: why should the law prohibit actions for redress after a certain space of time? Why should continued possession (even where it is wrongful) be effective to defeat the rights of the true owner? The answer to the first question is that the law aids the vigilant and not the slothful. But both questions raise the same issues, and it is easier to proceed by discussing the second question. One argument in favour of prescription is that possession is prima facie evidence of ownership and that those who have held possession for a long time are normally the owners.[3] But owners do not need the benefit of the doctrine of prescription, though it is certainly sometimes easier to prove long possession than legal right, for a title, easily provable today, may be more difficult to prove in fifty years. Acquiescence by

---

[1] *Ward* v. *British Oak Insurance Co. Ltd.*, [1932] 1 K.B. 392.
[2] Tien-Hsi Cheng, 1 *Current Legal Problems* (1948), 170 at 178.
[3] Salmond, *Jurisprudence* (12th ed.), 436.

the claimant in the loss of his right needs a thorough explanation, if we are not to assume either that he was not interested in substantiating his claim, or that there were legal flaws in it which rendered a successful action impossible. It is noteworthy that international law recognizes the doctrine of prescription, basing it on two principles: firstly, that an unreasonable delay in presenting a claim may place the other party at a serious disadvantage, since he may be unable to produce evidence or witnesses which might have been available at an earlier period; secondly, that lapse of time may be evidence of a tacit abandonment of the claim.[1] Similarly English equity approves the maxim that it will aid the vigilant and not the indolent. 'A Court of Equity... has always refused its aid to stale demands, where the party has slept upon his right and acquiesced for a great length of time. Nothing can call forth this court into activity, but conscience, good faith, and reasonable diligence; where these are wanting, the court is passive, and does nothing.'[2]

In truth, the whole doctrine, like that of prohibiting actions after a certain length of time, is based on broad views of policy. It is unsettling to allow no time limit to legal claims, and indolence brings its own reward. The small percentage of cases in which there may be injustice is outweighed by the legal interest in establishing security. Where the period of limitation is too short (for example, the six months of the Public Authorities Protection Act, 1893)[3] injustice may be caused to a reasonably diligent plaintiff, but that is an argument against too brief a term, not against the institution of prescription itself. If statutes providing the rules of limitation of actions are not clear, then the object of reducing litigation may be defeated by arguments based on the meaning of the statute. This shows that acts of limitation achieve this purpose effectively only if they are efficiently drafted.[4]

The refusal to recognize stale claims may take various forms. Firstly, there may be limitation of actions. A statute may lay down that certain actions shall not be brought more than six years after the cause of action has arisen.[5] This destroys the *remedy*, but leaves

---

[1] B. E. King, 15 *Brit. Y.B.I.L.* (1934), 82; L. F. Vinding Kruse, *The Right of Property*, 366.

[2] Per Lord Camden, *Smith* v. *Clay* (1767), 3 Bro. C. C. 646.

[3] 56 & 57 Vict., c. 61, § 1. The period is now one year: Limitation Act, 1939, 2 & 3 Geo. VI, c. 21, § 21.

[4] e.g. in England there have been 100 reported decisions from 1957 to 1970 on the interpretation of these Acts—Note, 33 *Mod. L. R.* (1970), 318.

[5] Cf. 21 Jac. I, c. 16.

the right subsisting. If a creditor does not sue within the requisite period, his right still exists, although it is now imperfect since he can take no active steps to enforce it. But the existence of the debt is sufficient consideration to make enforceable a fresh promise to pay after the period has elapsed. If the claim is for the return of a chattel, under English law before 1939, only the remedy was extinguished. The original wrongdoer was protected because of the inability of the owner to sue him; but if the wrongdoer sold the chattel to an innocent purchaser after the period of prescription had elapsed, the innocent purchaser could be sued in conversion if he refused to restore the chattel to the true owner. This anomalous position was the logical result of the fact that the statute only barred an action for the original conversion and as title was not affected, a fresh conversion by a third party created another remedy.[1] This rule has now been abolished by the Act of 1939.[2]

Secondly, the law may not only prevent an action being brought after a certain length of time but also (where title to property is concerned) destroy the title of the owner whose goods have been adversely possessed by another for the requisite period, yet stop short of creating a legal title in the adverse possessor, and leave him in the position of having only the best possessory right.[3] This has sometimes been referred to as negative or extinctive prescription. Before the Limitation Act, 1939, came into force, this type of prescription applied only to real property, but it now applies to chattels as well.

Thirdly, there may be acquisitive prescription, in which, after the expiration of the necessary period, the law gives to the adverse possessor a full legal title—for example, *usucapio* in Roman law. English law, save where easements are concerned, has no doctrine of acquisitive prescription, nor can conclusive evidence of such an institution be discovered in Greek law.[4] Roman law kept quite

---

[1] *Miller* v. *Dell*, [1891] 1 Q.B. 468.

[2] Limitation Act, 1939, 2 & 3 Geo. VI, c. 21, § 3.

[3] Compare the English Real Property Limitation Acts of 1833 and 1874. The notion that possession for the requisite period conveys a 'parliamentary title' to the possessor is now regarded as incorrect: *Taylor* v. *Twinberrow*, [1930] 2 K.B. 16; *Kirk* v. *Sutherland*, [1949] V.L.R. 33.

[4] See P. Vinogradoff, *Historical Jurisprudence*, ii. 213. It is common, however, for systems of land title registration, like the *Torrens* systems, to provide for the acquisition of a title based upon mere adverse possession—see e.g. Transfer of Land Act, 1958 (Victoria, Act no. 6399). Division 5 of that Act provides for acquisition by possession; and Section 62 empowers the Registrar to make an order vesting an estate in fee simple in a claimant who bases his claim on adverse possession merely.

distinct the acquisition of title by the necessary period of enjoyment and the limitation of actions. *Usucapio* was based on the desire to remedy formal defects in transfer rather than to protect an adverse possessor. This is shown by the rules that the possessor must have good faith when possession began and that his holding must begin in some transaction which normally is a basis for the acquisition of ownership. Such requirements are not present in the English statutes which are based on a desire to preserve the *status quo* rather than to reward only the deserving.[1] Moreover in Rome a *res* that had been stolen or taken by force did not fall under the rules of *usucapio* until the 'vice' of the taking had been purged by the return of the *res* to the owner. The Romans also had other rules based on a desire to limit actions— thus *longi temporis praescriptio* was negative or extinctive and did not create *dominium* in the adverse possessor.

[1] M. J. Goodman, 33 *Mod. L. R.* (1970), 281; *Hayward* v. *Chaloner*, [1968] 1 Q.B. 107. 'The Statute of Limitations is not concerned with merits': per Lord Greene, *Hilton* v. *Sutton Steam Laundry*, [1946] 1 K.B. 65 at 73.

REFERENCES

BUCKLAND, W., 46 *Harv. L. R.* (1933), 1281.
McNAIR, A. D., 60 *L.Q.R.* (1944), 160.

XXI

THE CONCEPT OF PROPERTY

§113. Introduction

THE term 'property' has a bewildering variety of uses. Firstly, it sometimes means ownership or title and sometimes the *res* over which ownership may be exercised. Thus we may ask whether in a contract induced by fraud the property in the goods passed to the purchaser; or we may speak of Blackacre as property. Even in the sense in which property means ownership usage varies.[1]

A classical contrast is between property (in the sense of title) which creates rights *in rem* and obligation which creates rights *in personam*. But clearly the law of property does not include all rights *in rem*, at any rate if we define that term in the modern fashion as covering rights which bind persons generally. My right not to be defamed or imprisoned is not a property right, unless we make the term 'property' so wide as almost to deprive it of meaning.

On the other hand, the term 'property' is frequently used in a broad sense to include assets which the technique of the law would regard as mere rights *in personam*.[2] A share certificate is strictly only evidence of a right to a certain proportion of the funds of a company, yet we habitually speak of it as property. It would save confusion if the term 'patrimony'[3] were used to cover the whole of a person's assets instead of thus extending the term 'property'. Patrimony would include: (*a*) *dominium*; (*b*) proprietary interests less than ownership; (*c*) claims upon others, e.g. obligations.

---

[1] Austin, Lec. XLVII. (*a*) Sometimes ownership is confined to the greatest right of enjoyment known to the law, and servitudes are excluded; (*b*) sometimes life interests are described as property; (*c*) if the emphasis is placed on a contrast between property and possession, even servitudes are sometimes described as property in the sense that there is a legal title to them; (*d*) sometimes property means the whole of a man's assets, including both rights *in personam* and rights *in rem*—patrimony. Lord Porter has said: 'Property is not a term of art', *Nokes* v. *Doncaster Collieries*, [1940] A.C. 1014 at 1051. For a discussion of the meaning of 'acquisition of property' in § 51 (xxxi) of the Constitution of the Commonwealth of Australia, see *Minister of State for the Army* v. *Dalziel* (1944), 68 C.L.R. 261. *Infra*, § 115.

[2] *Infra*, § 118.

[3] Thus in French law patrimony is the totality of a man's assets and liabilities so far as they can be assessed in money; the term excludes political or family rights: Amos and Walton, *Introduction to French Law*, 16.

First we shall discuss the law of things, and then *dominium* or ownership.

§ 114. THINGS

Austin defined things as such permanent objects, not being persons, as are sensible or perceptible through the senses—permanent objects in the sense that they are perceptible repeatedly.[1] Dictionaries illustrate the very wide use of the word 'thing' in popular speech, but there are two elements that seem to be common to most usages of the word. Firstly, a thing must have a certain element of permanence. This was what Austin emphasized in order to distinguish a thing from a fact or an event. A puff of smoke would not normally be regarded as a thing as it is too transient, but the precise degree of permanence required is difficult to determine.[2] Secondly, it must have a certain element of physical unity. Where the unity is organic there is little difficulty—a sheep or a horse is undoubtedly a thing. Inorganic unity raises more difficult questions. A brick is a thing, yet, when a house is constructed of bricks, we regard the house itself as a thing. Indeed, if the house is on a farm we may go farther and regard the whole farm as a working unity. Thus, in common speech our use of the word 'thing' will vary according to our purpose at the moment. We may even call a collection of living units a thing, e.g. a flock of sheep. This approach has influenced the law, and the Romans distinguished between *res singulae* and *universitas rerum*.

The legal use is even broader than that of popular speech. 'A thing is, in law, some possible matter of rights and duties, conceived as a whole and apart from all others, just as, in the world of common experience, whatever can be separately perceived is a thing.'[3] In this sense every legal right has a *res* as its object. According to the classical analysis, a right-duty relationship concerns two persons, relates to an act or forbearance, with regard to some particular *res*. Thus the object of a right of ownership may be Blackacre, the object of my right not to be defamed is my reputation. In this sense, *res* concerns much more than is covered by the law of property, but as the analysis of a *res* is so bound up with this subject, it is more convenient to discuss it at this place. Unfortunately, however, legal usage is not consistent,

---

[1] *Jurisprudence*, i. 358; A. Kocourek, *Jural Relations*, ch. xviii.
[2] C. K. Allen, 28 *Calif. L. R.* (1940), 421 at 422.
[3] F. Pollock, *First Book of Jurisprudence*, 130.

and there are really many different elements of thought. A thing may mean:

1. A thing in the material sense which is corporeal and tangible and has an organic or physical unity, e.g. a horse or a block of marble.

2. A thing which is corporeal and tangible, but consists of a collection of specific things, e.g. a flock of sheep.

3. A thing which exists in the physical world but is not material in the popular sense, e.g. electricity.

4. A thing which is neither material, corporeal, nor tangible but is an element of wealth, e.g. a copyright or a patent. Buckland points out that although the Romans when classifying things had in mind material things, nevertheless in other parts of their writing a thing is treated as an element of wealth, an asset; this is an economic conception which is very different from the sense in which the word is used by Austin, who treats a thing as a permanent external object of sensation.[1]

5. A thing which is not material and which is not directly an economic asset or element or wealth, e.g. reputation. If every right concerns a *res* then we must admit this wider conception. The law of defamation binds others by a duty not unjustifiably to interfere with the thing in question, my reputation.

Some German writers suggest that a thing is 'a locally limited portion of volitionless nature'.[2] This may be true of the popular usage, but it is not of the legal. A slave may be a *res*, an idol may be a legal person. Law distinguishes not between those who possess volition and things which do not, but between legal persons to whom the law imputes a will (John Smith or an idol) and things which cannot hold rights but can merely be the objects thereof. Law in this instance has refined usage.

Again, it is inconvenient to say that a *res nullius* is not a thing until it has been acquired by someone.[3] It may be that, if the law specifically refuses to allow some *res* to be in any circumstances the object of a right,[4] it should fall outside the definition of a *res*. But whatever is a potential object of legal rights should be considered a *res*. A lion is a *res* even before it is caught.

[1] *Text-Book of Roman Law* (2nd ed.), 182.
[2] T. E. Holland, *Jurisprudence* (10th ed.), 97.
[3] C. K. Allen, 28 *Cal. L. R.* (1940) at 431.
[4] As in the *res communes* of Roman law—air, running water, and light.

Things may be divided as follows:

(a) Corporeal and Incorporeal

German law uses the word 'thing' only for *res* that are corporeal.[1] But it is not easy to determine the bounds of *corporeality*. If a corporeal *res* is one that can be touched and occupies space, what of electricity? It has been held by some German courts that since electricity is not a thing, appropriation of it is not theft. One definition of a thing is 'any object which loses its essential qualities by being subdivided'. But this is not very apt: Blackacre is undoubtedly a thing, yet it may be sub-divided without losing its quality as land.

English usage is wider. The law of real property[2] set the example of distinguishing between that which is corporeal and that which is incorporeal, but many interests of the latter type are included in the definition of land itself. Land, as defined in the Law of Property Act, includes 'a manor, an advowson, and a rent and other incorporeal hereditaments, and an easement, right, privilege or benefit in, over or derived from land'.[3] The distinction between land, houses, and things under the land (which are corporeal) and such things as rents (which are incorporeal) may be a convenient one, but it tends to confuse. From one point of view, land is a material *res* over which certain rights may exist. The Californian Civil Code defines land as the solid material of the earth, whatever be the ingredients of which it is composed. But legal systems have not relied on this materialistic philosophy.[4] Thus to remove garden soil is not to remove land. Kocourek defines land as three-dimensional space,[5] and English law with its doctrine that land extends *ad inferos et usque ad coelum*[6] gives to

---

[1] *BGB.* Art. 90; E. J. Schuster, *Principles of German Law*, 58. 'In the main classification with which Gaius and Justinian begin their discussion . . . the writers seem to have in mind physical things', but if we consider the meaning of *res* in that part of the *Institutes* dealing with the law of things, the word *res* seems to mean 'any right, any legally protected interest, the value of which can be expressed in terms of money for the purpose of *condemnatio* in an action': W. W. Buckland, *Main Institutions of Roman Law*, 91.

[2] Technically only chattels are things in English law, but it is convenient to discuss here also the problem of land.   [3] 15 Geo. V, c. 20, § 205 (1) ix.

[4] It seems that in Queensland all minerals are reserved to the Crown, and the definition of minerals is so wide that it includes most of the ingredients of which the soil is composed—theoretically, therefore, the landowner's right to the soil is restricted: T. P. Fry, *Freehold and Leasehold Tenancies of Queensland Land* (University of Queensland, 1946), 102.   [5] *Jural Relations* (2nd ed.), 335–6.

[6] Actually when the aeroplane made this doctrine a matter of practical importance the meaning of this maxim became a matter of dispute, but the knot was cut by legislation, so that the exact rule of the common law is still unsettled: R. A. Mace, 17 *Univ. of Cin. L. R.* (1948), 343; A. D. McNair, *Law of the Air*. See also *Kelsen* v. *Imperial Tobacco Co. (Great Britain and Ireland) Ltd.*, [1957] 2 All E.R. 343; *Woollerton and Wilson Ltd.* v. *Richard Costain Ltd.*, [1970] 1 All E.R. 483.

the humble plot-holder a sense of vast possession. Hence if I excavate Jones's block to a depth of 60 feet, and carry away the soil and clay, Jones's *land* still remains. As land is space, there is no reason why it should not be divided horizontally—thus A may own the minerals under the land, B the first floor of a building, C the second floor, and so on. Some of the modern arrangements for 'Own your own Flats' depend upon such a horizontal division of land being accepted. To define land in terms of space *simpliciter* seems, however, too wide. Even if the landowner has rights that extend *ad coelum*, land is necessarily based on some material part of the earth's surface. To own a cubic mile of air space near Mars is not to own land in the sense in which the term is normally used.

But, as we shall see in greater detail in discussing the law of property, there may be many rights over land. Smith may own Blackacre, Jones may have an easement over it, and Robinson a rent-charge. Smith, as owner, is in closest relation to the land and his rights are held to concern a corporeal hereditament. The rights of Jones and Robinson are held to be incorporeal hereditaments. In truth they are *iura in re aliena*, rights over a *res* which is owned by another. In each case the rights depend on the existence of the same *res*, the land—but the rights of the owner are the most extensive. A tithe, however, which is a mere right to a certain share of (produce), was regarded as an incorporeal *res* which could have an 'owner'. Once we speak of ownership of things which are not corporeal, where are we to stop? My reputation is a *res* in a broad sense, but it would be straining language to say that I own that incorporeal *res*. It is perhaps a pity that the word 'ownership' was not confined to corporeal things and another term used where incorporeal *res* are concerned.[1] It certainly is convenient to speak of ownership of a goodwill, but the goodwill is merely a mass of claims against another (or others) and a series of expectations that customers will continue to resort to the same firm. In a sense, of course, the real value of ownership of land is that it gives power to exclude others, but there is also in this case a relationship to a material *res* which is lacking in the instance of goodwill. But, as we shall see, English law has created many interests in land which may be held by different people and it is common usage to regard each of these interests as having an 'owner'. Unfortunately also, the ownership of corporeal things is sometimes spoken of as corporeal ownership, as if ownership itself were tangible; ownership

[1] A. H. Campbell, 7 *Camb. L. J.* (1940), 206 at 221.

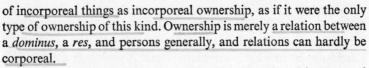

of incorporeal things as incorporeal ownership, as if it were the only type of ownership of this kind. Ownership is merely a relation between a *dominus*, a *res*, and persons generally, and relations can hardly be corporeal.

Similarly it is inaccurate to speak of corporeal and incorporeal rights. Since a right is merely a relationship between persons, with respect to a *res*, all rights are incorporeal. The right of ownership of Blackacre is just as incorporeal as my ownership of a patent—what distinguishes the two cases is that in the first ownership exists over a material *res*, whereas in the second the patent really consists of a bundle of claims to prevent others from using the process protected by the patent. When writers speak of a corporeal right, they concisely but inaccurately refer to a right over a corporeal thing: by an incorporeal right is meant a right over an incorporeal thing. The same confusion has arisen in private international law: sometimes the term immovables refers to immovable things in the material sense and sometimes to mere interests in immovable things. A mortgage is not an immovable in the first sense, but if it is a security over land, it may be in the second.

It is sometimes stated that the notion of an incorporeal thing is a refined conception of jurisprudence. It may be true that early law does not analyse with clarity, but interests in many incorporeal things are protected. In primitive law some of the few forms of individual property are myths, ceremonies, and chants—a primitive anticipation of copyright.[1] Medieval law is rich in incorporeal things.

The lawyer's business is not to make them things, but to point out that they are incorporeal. The layman who wishes to convey the advowson of a church will say that he conveys the church: it is for Bracton to explain to him that what he means to transfer is not that structure of wood and stone which belongs to God and the Saints, but a thing incorporeal.[2]

The feudal manor was really a bundle of rights over incorporeal things. The main difficulty in transfer is that while material things may be delivered, an incorporeal thing cannot—hence the need for the exercise of the right before the transfer is regarded as complete, the turning of beasts into the pasture or the presentation of a clerk to the church.[3]

[1] T. G. H. Strehlow, *Aranda Traditions*, 119–20.
[2] Pollock and Maitland, *History of English Law*, ii. 123.
[3] Ibid. 224.

(b) Chose in Action and Chose in Possession

The old rule of English law was that 'all personal things are either in possession or in action. The law knows no *tertium quid* between the two'.[1] A chose in action includes 'all personal rights of property which can only be claimed or enforced by action, and not by taking physical possession'.[2] But the meaning of the term has been modified in its long history and today there is no general agreement as to its exact limits. If John owes Paul ten pounds, Paul has a chose in action; the owner of a motor car has a chose in possession, for even although another may be unlawfully using it, the owner has the right of retaking the chattel, whereas a creditor is confined to suit in the courts. Patent rights, copyrights, probably rights of action for breach of contract, and a right of action for damages in tort are also choses in action.[3] The growing importance of negotiable instruments and company stock, the increase in value of authors' rights, bring it about that choses in action are playing a greater part in the economic life of today than in the past. A cheque or a bill of exchange is technically mere evidence of a right to sue the drawer: a company share is evidence of a right to receive dividends and to share in the property of the company, if it is dissolved while solvent. In truth, these choses do not seem to be things at all except in the broader sense. They are units of wealth—'a description, or delimitation, of the subject matter of a right'.[4] Some are documents of title (e.g. a bill of lading) and are frequently referred to as property, but this can hardly apply to a right of action for damages in tort. The attempt to treat all choses in action, however different they may be, as bound by the same rules, inevitably led to difficulties, and modern history shows a patchwork of statutory amendments dealing with particular problems. Just as the law has fallen into confusion in its attempt to distinguish between corporeal and incorporeal things, so it has created difficulties by the wide extension of the term 'chose in action'.

One mark of most modern forms of property is freedom of alienation—yet, a chose in action being an obligation, it was long held that this exclusively personal tie could not be assigned.[5] In the medieval

---

[1] Per Fry L.J., *Colonial Bank* v. *Whinney* (1885), 30 Ch. D. 261 at 285; P. Bordwell, 19 *N. Car. L. R.* (1941), 279.

[2] *Torkington* v. *Magee*, [1902] 2 K.B. 427 at 430; Elphinstone, 9 *L.Q.R.* (1893), 311.

[3] *Curtis* v. *Wilcox*, [1948] 2 K.B. 474 at 480.

[4] C. K. Allen, 28 *Calif. L. R.* (1940) at 426.

[5] *Novation* could, of course, destroy the old obligation and create a new one, but this is hardly assignment: *supra*, § 112.

period an additional argument against free transfer was that rights might be assigned to persons who could exercise illegitimate pressure on the person bound by the duty.[1] Today, paradoxically enough, that form of property which is most easily transferable, a negotiable instrument, falls under the heading of chose in action. The mark of a negotiable instrument is that a bona fide purchaser for value takes a good title, even though the title of the seller was faulty. Today many choses in action are really indistinguishable from things unquestionably accepted as personal property since they are transferable and have a market value; others fall more easily under the head of *obligatio* such as a right to sue for damages for an assault.

(c) Res mancipi et nec mancipi

Nearly all systems of law distinguish between two types of property, one of which is regarded as superior and is marked by special rules of transfer or succession.[2] The typical modern distinction is between movables and immovables: Roman law naturally had special rules relating to land, but the essential early distinction was that between *res mancipi* and *nec mancipi*. At the time this division became stereotyped, *res mancipi* included those forms of property which were economically most important to a primitive community—land, houses, slaves, beasts of draught and burden, and rustic servitudes,[3] while within *res nec mancipi* fell the less important types of property. The form of the ceremony suggests that land was not alienable when the distinction first arose, but later it was added to the list. Changes in economic life caused an overshadowing of the importance of these primitive types of property—moreover, the convenience of the simpler rules which were applied to *res nec mancipi* was recognized and the distinction was finally abolished by Justinian. In the same way, in English law real property was beset with a mass of technical rules from many of which personal property was free, and the modern tendency is to assimilate the law of realty to that of personal property, though important differences still remain.

(d) Movable and Immovable

The modern distinction, which is of great importance in private international law, is between movable and immovable property. The

[1] Holdsworth, op. cit. vii. 524. But a fear of maintenance was probably not the only reason, for in early times, while things were transferable, there was more difficulty in applying this to rights.
[2] H. J. S. Maine, *Ancient Law* (ed. Pollock), 283.   [3] Gaius, 2, 14a.

typical immovable is land and the things that are attached thereto. One suggested definition is that a thing is immovable if it cannot be moved without being divided into several units.[1] This hardly fits the case of land, for the removal of soil even to a great depth leaves the land still in existence—indeed the concept of land is that of space as much as the material of which that part of the earth is made. In its spatial aspect land is immovable—in its material aspect it may be removed, at least partially.[2] A house attached to land is an immovable in law, but obviously it may be moved in fact. The nature of an immovable cannot be understood unless we realize that, starting from a physical test, the law has gradually extended the notion. There is no *a priori* test, as the cases in private international law show—from a practical point of view we must accept the view of *lex situs*. Thus in many systems ships are immovable in law, though a vessel that is immovable in fact is of very little use. French law speaks of immovables by destination (for example, the horses and cattle that are placed on land for its economic exploitation) and immovables by declaration (for example, a person may impress on certain movables, such as shares in the Bank of France, the legal characteristics of immovables).[3] The old law of the Southern States in America treated the slave as an immovable, as he was attached to the land.

Land has certain characteristics which distinguish it from other forms of property. Firstly, though nothing may be eternal, land is more enduring than personal property, and hence future interests in land have a definite value. Moreover, the fact that land cannot be moved, combined with its relative permanence, makes it especially valuable as a security. Furniture may be surreptitiously hidden or accidentally destroyed, but the mortgagee does not need to worry lest the land be concealed, and the risks of destruction of the land (e.g. by incursion of the sea) are comparatively small. Again, land can be subdivided without necessarily losing its value. A father does not divide his motor car into two pieces for his sons, whereas half of his landed estate may be of great service to each. Land has one great disadvantage—flocks and herds may multiply by natural increase, whereas, save for expensive works of reclamation, the quantity of land remains the same. In the pastoral and agricultural eras, land is the main form of wealth and it is displaced only by the rising tide of industrialism.

---

[1] E. J. Schuster, *Principles of German Law*, 60.
[2] C. R. Noyes, *The Institution of Property*, 395; A. Kocourek, *Jural Relations* (2nd ed.), 334. [3] C.C., Arts. 517 et seq.

But, however far industry develops, land will still remain the essential foundation for most human undertakings—even the giant transports of the air still require land on which to rest and be reconditioned.

In contrast to modern systems, in Roman law the distinction between land and other property was comparatively insignificant. Thus a lease of land was not distinguished from the hire of a movable: the rights of succession were the same for both types of property.[1]

(e) Real and Personal Property

Bracton divided actions into real, personal, and mixed,[2] the first term being an adaptation of the Roman *actio in rem* and the second of the Roman *actio in personam*.[3] Broadly, a right *in rem* may mean either a power to recover a specific thing, or more often a right which avails against persons generally.[4] The Romans asked what was the nature of the right asserted—if the *intentio* claimed title to a specific *res*, the action was *in rem*; if the *intentio* was framed as an *obligatio* it was *in personam*. Hence when an owner sued to recover land, ox, sheep, or chariot the action was *in rem*—in other words, in this respect there was no difference between movables and immovables. English law looked not to the claim, but to the result of the action—if judgment was for the recovery of a specific *res* the action was real, if the judgment was for damages only it was personal. A real action in English law, then, is one in which a *res* may be specifically recovered. But, by an historical accident, land was the only *res* that could be specifically recovered, for in the case of movables the defendant might choose between returning the chattel and paying damages—hence land came to be described as real property, movables as personal property. The term 'real action' has a double meaning: it is an action which may result in a judgment for specific restitution or an action for the recovery of land. If this were the whole story, we could say that real property consists of immovables, personal property of movables. But unfortunately at the time that the terminology became fixed, the tenant, if ejected, could sue the landlord only for compensation—he could not get a judgment restoring the land, for he was not seised of the land. By the close of the Middle Ages the tenant was effectively

---

[1] Buckland and McNair, *Roman Law and Common Law*, 56. There were some differences, e.g. there was a longer period of *usucapio* for land: land could not be stolen; the possessory remedies were different.

[2] Lib. iii, cap. iii, par. i, fol. 101*b*.

[3] T. C. Williams, 4 *L.Q.R.* (1888), 394—this article is freely drawn on in this section.

[4] *Supra*, § 65.

protected, but it was then settled that a leasehold interest was only personal property.[1] Since, however, leasehold partook partly of the nature of land and partly of chattels, it received the name of chattel real. Personal property, therefore, in English law consists of movables and in addition leasehold interests.

This division into real and personal property has been of great importance in English law.[2] Before 1925, in England, the following were some of the differences between these two types of property. Firstly, the rules of descent on intestacy were different; secondly, personal property could only be absolutely owned, whereas a freehold could be split up into successive interests; thirdly, personal property was primarily liable for the payment of debts. The complexity of the law of real property led to statutory reforms in the nineteenth century, and an express object of the English consolidation of 1925 was to assimilate as far as possible the law of real and personal property, but important differences still exist.

(f) Miscellaneous Distinctions

Things may also be divided into fungible and non-fungible. The first consist of 'movable things which in ordinary dealings are usually determined by number, measurement or weight'.[3] Land is sold in specie, i.e. a particular plot is transferred and the purchaser does not merely buy one acre of English land; whereas in the case of butter, the trader normally orders not a specific piece but the quantity and quality which he desires—1 cwt. of Danish butter. In such a case the contract is performed by delivery of any butter that has the necessary characteristics. (Of course, there is no reason why a trader should not buy a specific parcel of butter, and in that case the contract will not be satisfied by the delivery of other butter, even if it be of the same quality).[4]

---

[1] Financial considerations played a part, for it was convenient to keep leasehold as a form of investment outside the strict rules of real property: Pollock and Maitland, *History of English Law*, ii. 113.

[2] The English lawyer is so used to this distinction that in Lord Kingsdown's Act, 1861, dealing with the wills of British subjects made abroad, the draftsman relied on the distinction between real and personal property, whereas it would have been more consonant with private international law to make the distinction that between immovables and movables: J. H. C. Morris, 62 *L.Q.R.* (1946), 170 at 175.

[3] *BGB.* Art. 91. A group of which 'any unit is from its nature or by mercantile usage treated as the equivalent of any other unit', Uniform Sales Act (America), § 76.

[4] Austin, ii. 780, emphasizes that the test is not the nature of the *res*, but the nature of the obligation in question.

A distinction often confused with that which has just been discussed is between things which are consumed by use and those which are not. The former may be defined as 'movable things intended to be used or enjoyed by means of being consumed or alienated'.[1] The purpose for which champagne is designed is drinking, and it ceases to exist as champagne immediately it is so used. Most movable property is subject in some degree to the ravages of time, but a gold candlestick or furniture may be used for generations without being destroyed, whereas *res quae usu consumuntur* do not survive a single 'use'. Money is not destroyed by use, but it is alienated—we cannot continually buy cigarettes with the same coin.

The main legal reason for classifying things is that dealings in them may be facilitated by the growth of such special rules as are necessary for each class.[2] But the methods of division vary so much in each system that it is impossible to do more than indicate some of the more important methods of classification.

§ 115. *Dominium* and Ownership

'Early law does not trouble itself with complicated theories as to the nature and meaning of ownership and possession',[3] but a very small degree of civilization will produce the phenomenon of a divorce between the two. Roman law made a very clear-cut division between *dominium* and *possessio*, much clearer than was the case in English law. The Romans began with a technical concept of *dominium* as the absolute right to a thing, *possessio* denoting rather mere physical control which had as such no legal consequences in early law; English law on the contrary 'reached the conception of ownership as an absolute right through developments in the law of possession'.[4] English medieval writers emphasize seisin and the right to possess, where Roman law spoke of *dominium*. 'The common law never had any adequate process in the case of land, or any process at all in the case of goods, for the vindication of ownership pure and simple.'[5] 'The best right to seisin is still the only form of ownership recognized by English law.'[6] One reason for this was that in Rome it was much

---

[1] *BGB.* Art. 92 (1).   [3] Austin, ii. 781.
[2] Holdsworth, *History of English Law*, ii. 78.
[4] Ibid. vii. 458–61.
[5] Pollock and Wright, *Possession*, 5. Cf. Pollock and Maitland, *History of English Law*, ii. 46.
[6] Holdsworth, op. cit. iii. 93. 'Indeed we may be left doubting whether there was any right in movable goods that deserved the name of ownership': Pollock and Maitland, op. cit. ii. 151.

easier to prove title than in early English law. *Usucapio* was a root of title and would cure formal defects (at least where there was good faith and *iusta causa*) within a remarkable short space of time, whereas before 32 Hen. VIII, c. 2, there was scarcely any limit to the tracing back of title to land in English law.[1] The Greeks took a relative view similar to English law—he was owner who could prove a better right to possession that anyone else.[2] Indeed, there is authority for saying that at one period the common law recognized not *dominium* and *possessio*, but seisin only.[3] Nevertheless, we must not conclude from this that today the position is necessarily the same. Holdsworth considers that the development of ejectment has introduced an absolute right of ownership—'a person who wishes to recover against the possessor must show, not merely a better right than the possessor, but an absolute right'.[4] This conclusion has, however, been questioned on the ground that few plaintiffs can ever show *dominium* in the Roman sense, because even a paper title covering sixty years would not necessarily exclude the possibility of an adverse claim.[5] With regard to chattels also, the concept of ownership has not been fully developed in English law.[6]

The Roman notion of *dominium* is thus absolute in the sense that it is not relative—a person either is *dominus* or he is not, for *dominium* can be acquired only in set ways. But both Roman *dominium* and English ownership are sometimes said to be absolute in another sense—that John may do as he likes with his own.[7] This statement was probably never true: at any rate it does not describe the situation today. The full rights of an owner are:

(a) the power of enjoyment (e.g. the determination of the use to which the *res* is to be put, the power to deal with produce as he pleases, the power to destroy);

(b) possession which includes the right to exclude others;

(c) power to alienate *inter vivos*, or to charge as security;

(d) power to leave the *res* by will.

---

[1] Buckland and McNair, *Roman Law and Common Law*, 64.
[2] P. Vinogradoff, *Historical Jurisprudence*, ii. 198.
[3] Holdsworth, op. cit. iii. 95.
[4] Ibid. vii. 79.
[5] A. D. Hargreaves, 56 *L.Q.R.* (1940), 376; for Holdsworth's reply see 56 *L.Q.R.* (1940), 479. But cf. the situation under '*Torrens*-type' land title registration systems.
[6] A. K. R. Kiralfy, 12 *Mod. L. R.* (1949), 424.
[7] Cf. the traditional definition that ownership is the right of enjoying or disposing of things in the most absolute manner. The French Code of 1804 emphasizes the absolute power of the owner much more than the German Code of 1900.

One of the most important of these powers is the right to exclude others. 'The property-right is essentially a guarantee of the exclusion of other persons from the use or handling of the thing.'[1] Use is not enough, for one may use property which one does not own, and use is not necessary, for many an owner does not use all the property he possesses. But every owner does not possess all the rights set out above—a particular owner's powers may be restricted by law or by an agreement he has made with another. Thus the law of nuisance limits the use to which my land may be put, and in most modern cities complex building regulations are in force. Power to alienate may be limited in the interests of the family as in France, where a father cannot dispose *inter vivos* or by will of more than a certain proportion of his estate.[2] The Nazi legislation of 1933, in order to create a strongly rooted peasantry, prohibited the alienation or division of farms of medium size; on death, the land descends *in toto* to one heir, and is put beyond the reach of creditors.[3] If the test of ownership were absolute power over property, there would be few owners in civilized states today.

Similarly, the owner may grant to another many of his rights and yet remain owner. X may lease his land for a pepper-corn rent for ninety years; make his land security for a debt; grant easements or allow another possession. In classical Roman law a quiritary owner might sell a slave to a purchaser for value, but, if the ceremony of *mancipatio* was not carried out, the *dominus* still remained owner until the period of *usucapio* had elapsed. '*Dominium* is the ultimate right, that which has no right behind it. It may be a mere *nudum ius* with no practical content, but it is still *dominium ex iure Quiritium*.'[4] The fact that an owner may cede so many rights and still remain owner raises difficulties of definition. From this angle Noyes regards ownership as a magnetic core which remains when all present rights of enjoyment are removed from it and which attracts to itself the various elements temporarily held by others as they lapse.[5] Thus if a lease expires, or an easement is lost, it is the owner of the land who benefits.

[1] J. H. Wigmore, *Select Cases on the Law of Torts* (1912), ii. 858, cited H. Cairns, *Law and the Social Sciences*, 60; F. S. Cohen, *Dialogue on Private Property, 9 Rutgers L. R.* (1954), 357.   [2] C.C., Art. 913.
[3] E. H. Kaden, 20 *Iowa L. R.* (1935), 350, discusses the Hereditary Peasant Farm Law. The heir can succeed only if he is agriculturally competent. One effect of this law was to create a landless proletariat of younger brothers who could be settled in neighbouring countries to extend German influence.
[4] Buckland, *Text-Book of Roman Law* (2nd ed.), 188.
[5] *Institution of Property*, 310. Cf. J. W. C. Turner, 19 *Can. B. R.* (1941), 342.

Austin distinguishes between ownership and a mere servitude by saying that the mark of a servitude is the rigorous limitation in set terms of the powers of a holder, whereas there is in every system some one mode of property in which the liberty of user is more extensive than in other cases—the powers of an owner are unlimited and indefinite save in so far as there is specific legal regulation or a specific right outstanding in a third party.[1]

To overcome these difficulties it is convenient to distinguish between:

(a) ultimate ownership, where but the residual core is left to the owner, the rights of present enjoyment being held temporarily by others;

(b) complete or beneficial ownership, where the owner enjoys all the rights and privileges which it is legally possible for an owner to have;[2]

(c) fractions split off from ownership, some or all of which may be held by persons other than the owner, so long as the 'magnetic core' remains in the owner.

To attempt to trace the history of ownership is full of peril, for we tend to look at early law through the spectacles of our modern culture and to fill the gaps in our facts with plausible conjectures. The early days of the clan seem very remote from our modern individualism. The *paterfamilias* had power over wife, descendants, and chattels, but rights over persons were not clearly distinguished from rights over property. The social unit governed itself, and it is idle to ask whether the control of the *paterfamilias* is best described as political power or private ownership, for in the realm of beginnings such questions are not asked. What was real was the actual power of the *paterfamilias*, tempered perhaps in its exercise by consultation with others.[3] Within the group, save for articles of personal use, there was little need to distinguish between *meum* and *tuum*—both persons and chattels were considered as belonging in the group rather than to particular individuals.[4] Indeed, until there is some form of organization above the

---

[1] Austin, Lects. XLVII, XLVIII. The Swiss Code regards ownership as the right to deal freely with a *res* within the limits of the law.

[2] Cf. *Restatement of the Law of Property*, p. 11.

[3] C. R. Noyes, *The Institution of Property*, 123; C. W. Westrup, *Introduction to Early Roman Law*, ii.

[4] Noyes, op. cit. 127–9. The learned author points out that if ownership means the separation of *meum* and *tuum*, then we see only the beginnings in the family group; if ownership requires a division between the property of different families, then we

family, it is difficult to see how the question of ownership can arise—within the group it is unnecessary, and until there is a co-ordinating power or the growth of a community, conflicts between groups are determined by force and not by law.

It is largely a matter of definition when we can conceive of property as actually beginning. The first step is to distinguish power over goods and slaves from power over free men. Two strains influence our modern English law—the doctrine of Rome and the practical influence of feudalism.

It has already been pointed out that the concept of *dominium* was much more developed than the notion of ownership in English law. It has been described as the 'ultimate right to the thing, or . . . what is left when all other rights vested in various people are taken out'.[1] While the powers of a *dominus* might be limited by law, there was no 'limited ownership' in the English sense—future interests could not be carved out of the land with the facility which the English doctrine of estates allows. A man might be bound by contract to reconvey property on the happening of a certain event, but (at least in classical law) there was no method by which a person could be made *dominus* only for a definite time. The usufructuary, the Roman equivalent of the English tenant for life, was not treated as owner, but as the mere holder of a servitude.[2]

The other strain which influences modern thought is that of feudalism, its most interesting theoretical contribution being the number of interests that could exist simultaneously in the same piece of land. Where a tenant held of his lord, who was *dominus* in the Roman sense? Where only two persons were concerned, it might be possible to speak of *dominium directum* and *dominium utile*, but what of a case where there were nine rungs in the feudal ladder?[3] Feudalism cannot be made to fit a Roman theory which demanded one absolute *dominus* and one alone. Logically it might have been possible to regard the king as *dominus* of all land which his tenants held, but to confine the term 'ownership' in this way seemed rather artificial to English law. In effect each person interested in the land had rights and duties which were laid down by the feudal bond.

require some co-ordinating agency above the family: there was little notion of alienation. The idea was of a politico-economic organism, not of a proprietary fund.

[1] Buckland and McNair, *Roman Law and Common Law*, 61.

[2] Op. cit. 70. In German law also, it is not possible to split ownership up into fragments or estates. Usufruct is treated as a mere servitude.

[3] Pollock and Maitland, *History of English Law*, i. 211.

Under the feudal system many interests of different *quality* were enjoyed simultaneously—under the modern doctrine estates may co-exist, provided the periods of enjoyment are different. Had the land itself been the subject of thought, English theory would probably not have become so complex; but once the lawyers began to play with that artificial entity, the estate, it was possible to carve out future interests with great facility. 'Proprietary rights in land are, we may say, pro-jected on the plane of time. The category of quantity, of duration, is applied to them.'[1] A Romanist would be very puzzled by a system which regards a tenant for life as an owner, or by the concept of remainders.

Once estates, instead of the land, became the immediate object of thought, it was easy to conceive of each estate as having an 'owner' —indeed, to speak of ownership of lesser interests such as legal charges. In a very real sense in English law limited ownership may exist. Indeed, estates in land almost shade off into servitudes. 'That English law should regard these tenants under leases for life as free-holders . . . is very remarkable: hirers are mingled with owners, because according to the great generalisation of English feudalism, every owner is after all but a hirer.'[2] The 'wonderful calculus of estates', which is still the distinctive feature of English law,[3] has great convenience, but terminology is determined by usage rather than by any general theory of ownership. We say that a tenant owns the leasehold, but not the land. On the other hand, when we speak of possession, the tenant possesses the land but not the freehold. It is impossible to fit the individualism of English law to the terminology of other systems. Here, as elsewhere, the division of law and equity makes the picture even more complex. What are we to think of ter-minology which speaks of the trustee as the legal owner and the bene-ficiary as the equitable owner? Once we think of each interest in land as having an owner, then it is perhaps natural to think of an owner of an interest at law, and the owner of an interest at equity, but it is very puzzling to those who build on the strict distinctions of Roman law.

Salmond treats ownership in its most comprehensive sense as the relation between a person and any right that is vested in him.[4] 'That which a man owns is in all cases a right': to speak of the ownership of

---

[1] Pollock and Maitland, *History of English Law*, ii. 10. See also C. R. Noyes, *Institution of Property*, 257–8. [2] P. Vinogradoff, *Villainage*, 330–1.
[3] Pollock and Maitland, op. cit. ii. 11.
[4] *Jurisprudence* (12th ed.), 250. In this edition the difficulties of Salmond's view are discussed.

a material object is merely to use a convenient figure of speech. To own a piece of land means in truth to own a particular kind of right in the land, namely, the fee simple of it. This dictum has been severely criticized by Cook.[1] There are many rights which a person may possess, and to use the word 'owner' to express the relationship between a person and a right is to introduce unnecessary confusion. In every system there is one method of enjoyment of property which is more extensive than others, and to this relationship the term 'ownership' is normally applied. A person *has* rights: ownership is the name given to one particular type of right or, more accurately, bundle of rights. Ownership of Blackacre gives to the owner many claims, privileges, powers, and immunities. What makes Salmond's argument seem plausible is that English law has not confined the term 'ownership' to enjoyment of material things. As we have pointed out, the law sometimes speaks of ownership of a copyright or a patent. In both cases there is no material object which is the subject-matter of ownership, for a copyright is merely a mass of claims and powers; but it was perhaps inevitable that the term 'owner' should be found a convenient one to denote the person who possessed the claims and powers in question. The Roman notion, however, is simpler since it confines *dominium* to absolute ownership of material things.[2]

For most purposes of jurisprudence, however, it is convenient to define ownership in terms of a relationship between persons with respect to a *res* which can be thought of as property, and where the relationship can be seen as a property relationship. Rights of ownership, as has been pointed out, like other rights are relations between legal persons. The distinguishing marks of the relations that are thought of as property, and the rights which are called rights of ownership in the law, turn on the one hand on the extent of the 'owner's' powers to exclude or permit others to enjoy the *res*, the subject of the right, and, on the other hand, on the nature of the *res* itself.[3]

§ 116. *IUS IN RE ALIENA*

An owner may transfer to another certain of the rights which inhere in him by virtue of his ownership. He may surrender possession by

---

[1] Introduction to W. N. Hohfeld, *Fundamental Legal Conceptions*, 12.

[2] K. Renner, *Institutions of Private Law*, 17, shows that this is the typical approach of continental codes, but English law with its broader use of the term is able to get closer to economic realities.

[3] Felix S. Cohen, *Dialogue on Private Property*, 9 *Rutgers L. R.* (1954), 357.

granting a lease of Blackacre to a tenant, pledge a gold watch as security for money, or grant to the owner of neighbouring land the right to use a path across his estate. *Iura in re aliena* may be described as encumbrances, as rights *in rem* over a *res* owned by another. The important test is that the right must 'run with' the thing encumbered —it must bind the *res* no matter into whose hands it may come. Thus an easement binds the servient tenement and a purchaser of it will be bound whether he was aware of the easement or not.

Encumbrances are not confined to real property. I may pledge personal property as security, for example, a string of pearls. Difficult questions arise, however, when we consider the creation of charges, not over real or personal property, but over rights *in personam*. Suppose A charges his book debts in B's favour; this limits his power of disposal over money paid to him. This charge may prevent other creditors seizing money paid to A until B is paid—in this sense the right avails against persons generally and seems to be a true encumbrance. But money possesses the peculiar character that one who gives value for it receives a good title even if the transferor is a thief —hence a charge cannot be as effective as an easement over land which will bind all purchasers. If A, in defiance of the charge, spends the money in order to buy meat, B cannot claim that the butcher took subject to the charge. In truth, an assignment of book-debts is not an encumbrance at all, but a transfer of certain rights *in personam* from one person to another,[1] a transfer the effectiveness of which will depend on the particular rules of the system in question.

There may be many types of encumbrances, but the three chosen for discussion are lease, servitude, and security.

(a) Lease

A lease may be defined as an agreement expressing an intention of the parties that the right to exclusive possession shall be granted by the owner of the land to the lessee, such possession to pass either at once or at an agreed future date.[2] If we wish to distinguish between a lessee and a mere lodger, we must ask whether exclusive possession, which creates an interest in land, is granted.[3] The tenant has the right

---

[1] Salmond, *Jurisprudence* (12th ed.), 241, gives a very wide definition of an encumbrance, but the difficulties are pointed out by A. H. Campbell, 7 *Camb. L. J.* (1940), 215–16.　　　　[2] G. C. Cheshire, *Modern Real Property* (8th ed.), 342.

[3] In *Shell-Mex* v. *Manchester Garages*, [1971] 1 All E.R. 841 at 843, Lord Denning rejects the older view that the decisive test is whether exclusive possession is given. The test is whether it is a personal privilege given to a person, or whether it grants an interest in land.

to exclude all persons from the land, including the owner save in so far as a power of entry has been reserved by the lease. In English law there are many differences between the rules relating to a lease of real property and a hire of movables; in Roman law *locatio-conductio* covered all forms of property.

In English law a lease creates a true encumbrance, for the tenant cannot be ejected from the land so long as the conditions of the lease are observed. If the owner sells the land to a third party, the purchaser takes subject to the lease, whether he was aware of its existence or not. Hence if either the owner or a third party unlawfully ejects the tenant, the latter may recover possession. In Roman law the lease did not create a true encumbrance, since if the tenant was ejected, he was confined to a claim *in personam* against the landlord for breach of contract. Incidentally, a tenant did not acquire possessory rights, and so was not as well protected as in English law.

(b) *Servitude*

The holder of a servitude has a right *in rem* which gives him the power either to put a *res* belonging to another to a certain class of definitely limited uses or else to prevent the owner of the *res* from putting it to a certain class of definitely determined uses. An owner is assumed to have all possible powers relating to a *res*, save in so far as these are limited by a definite prohibition of the law or by the right of another; the holder of a servitude is assumed to have no power over the *res* save such as are created by the facts that gave rise to the servitude.[1] Thus the holder of an easement to cross Blackacre may have only a power to pass on foot. A legal servitude is a true encumbrance because it will bind purchasers of the *res* even if they are ignorant of the existence of such a claim.

Grant of a power to cross land once or twice creates a mere licence: a servitude must relate to a possible series of acts or forbearances. No rigid definition is possible. There is no need for a servitude to be perpetual, but if it is too limited in time it ceases to be a true servitude—i.e. it is not called a servitude. As Austin puts it, the holder of a servitude has the right to put the subject generally to uses of a general class.[2]

Servitudes may inhere in a person only as owner of a particular

---

[1] Austin, ii. 794.
[2] Or else to prevent the owner doing acts of a general class. A servitude is a right to generically and not specifically determined uses: Austin, ii. 809.

piece of property—this is termed real servitude. Thus Jones, the owner of Blackacre, may have power to cross Greenacre, but if Blackacre is sold to Robinson, Jones loses the power and Robinson acquires it. Hence arises the metaphor of the dominant and servient tenement—as a figure of speech we may regard Blackacre as holding the easement and Greenacre as being subject to it. This only means that the easement inheres in the owner of Blackacre for the time being and binds the owner of Greenacre whoever he may be and whether he bought with knowledge of the easement or not. English law divides real servitudes into easements and profits. A profit is a right to take something off another's land,[1] provided the thing which is taken is capable of ownership. Thus A may have the right to take sand or turf or stones from the land of another. An easement is a privilege without a profit;[2] it may confer a limited right of user of another's land (e.g. to drive across it) or it may restrict the owner from using the land in certain ways (e.g. from building so as to obstruct the flow of light to a building on the adjoining land).[3] In English law real servitudes are limited to real property. It is difficult to see in the case of chattels how there could be a dominant and a servient chattel. Land is immovable, and a certain right over a neighbour's land may be reasonably necessary to the enjoyment of Blackacre. Chattels, however, are movable and juxtaposition of chattels is but temporary. Hence there seems no end to be served in inventing a law of 'real'[4] servitudes for chattels.

In contrast to real servitudes are personal servitudes, which inhere in a particular person as such and not merely in a person as the owner of certain land. (The use of the term personal has no reference to rights *in personam*; all servitudes create rights *in rem*). Post-classical writing in Roman law mentions *usufruct, usus,* and *habitatio* as examples. According to the definition suggested above *usufruct* should hardly be regarded as a servitude for it gives large and indefinite powers of enjoyment, whereas a servitude grants powers that are

---

[1] *Duke of Sutherland* v. *Heathcote*, [1892] 1 Ch. 475 at 484.

[2] Cheshire, *Modern Real Property* (8th ed.), 445.

[3] Roman law divided real servitudes into rustic and urban, but the exact principle of division is not clear. The urban servitudes mostly relate to buildings. The four early rustic servitudes were *iter, actus, via,* and *aquaeductus*. These were equivalent to English easements. Many of the other rustic servitudes were analogous to the profits of English law: W. W. Buckland, *Text-Book of Roman Law* (2nd ed.), 262.

[4] That is, real in the sense that the servitude inheres in the owner of a certain piece of property. Cf., however, *The Strathcona*, [1926] A.C. 108, where the purchaser of a ship with knowledge of a charter-party was held to be a constructive trustee. Apart from equity, covenants cannot 'run with a chattel'; but cf., *per contra*, *Port Line Limited* v. *Ben Line Steamers Limited*, [1958] 2 Q.B. 146.

strictly limited; moreover, usufruct exists only for a definitely limited period. The English lawyer treats the usufructuary as a limited owner —the nearest equivalent seems to be the life tenant. Bracton 'flirted' with the notion of calling a tenant for life a usufructuary, but he forbore.[1] In Roman law a personal servitude was limited to the life of the holder and was inalienable. Austin suggests that there was no theoretical reason why a personal usufruct should not be given to a certain person and his heirs,[2] for the adjective 'personal' is not meant to refer to the length of the interest but only to emphasize that the servitude does not inhere only in the owner of land as such.

Austin claimed that, since every servitude availed against persons generally, a servitude could impose on others only a negative duty; we can imagine a right against persons generally that they shall refrain from a certain course of action, but it is difficult to conceive of a right *in rem* which casts an active duty on persons generally.[3] As Roman law put it, *servitus in faciendo consistere non potest*. But a real servitude is said to be a right *in rem* because it will bind the owner of the servient tenement, whoever he may be. There is no difficulty in regarding the owner of the servient tenement as being under an active duty, say, to keep in repair a road over which a neighbour has the right of way. Indeed, the fact that such an example may be found in German law shows the danger of *a priori* reasoning that a certain type of servitude cannot possibly exist. Legal systems have a curious habit of giving the lie to bold generalizations.

(c) Security

An early method for the enforcement of debts was to seize the body of the debtor, and if we believe the accounts of early Roman law, unpaid creditors could do more than take it out of the hide of the debtor, for his very body could be cut in pieces.[4] The notion is rather that of a physical liability to suffer in the event of non-payment than of a legal duty to pay. If the creditor wished for security, then another person would stand as hostage, the liability being then transferred from the body of the debtor to that of the unfortunate hostage. This distinguished primitive rules from the modern law of surety, where

---

[1] Pollock and Maitland, *History of English Law*, ii. 8. There were detailed differences. Probably in early times the tenant for life was not liable for waste, whereas the usufructuary had to treat the *res* like a *bonus paterfamilias*; moreover, the tenant for life had seisin and in litigation he represented the land.

[2] *Jurisprudence*, ii. 820.

[3] Op. cit. 811.

[4] H. F. Jolowicz, *Historical Introduction to Roman Law*, 189.

the liability of the surety is secondary only, the debtor himself being primarily liable. Moreover, today there is a clear distinction between *surety*, in which one person guarantees the debt of another if that other defaults, and *security*, in which a particular *res* is charged with the debt. Suretyship is used today, but now that the power to imprison for debt has been so greatly circumscribed, in an economic sense the creditor has rights only against the property in the hands of the debtor or surety—for a discharge from bankruptcy may extinguish the debts even if only a proportion of them has been paid. It is the benefit of *real* security,[1] which alone is a true *ius in re aliena*, that a specific chattel or specific parcel of land is made subject to a charge for the debt.

There are various steps in the evolution of real security. One early method is that of *fiducia*—the title to the *res* is transferred to the creditor who binds himself by a *fiducia* to reconvey the *res* when the debt is paid. In this case, since the creditor owns the *res*, he has a *ius in re propria*. This form had, however, two disadvantages: the debtor lost the use of the *res* immediately the money was borrowed, and, as the creditor was the owner, he could pass a good title if he sold in breach of the *fiducia*.

A further development is to give the creditor possession alone, leaving the title of the *res* in the debtor. This protects the debtor from alienation by the creditor, but the latter has no power to realize the security on default. However, if a power of sale is given to the creditor on default by the debtor, this is a convenient form of security. *Pignus* in Roman law and the modern pledge or pawn illustrate this stage.

But neither of these forms of security was suitable for farm-land or for 'tools of trade', because, if the debtor lost control of these, his earning capacity was affected. In *hypotheca* the creditor was given possessory rights, but custody and physical control remained with the debtor until default was made in payment. A farmer by this method could borrow on the security of his land or cattle and remain in undisturbed occupation until he made default. Since pledge required surrender of the physical control to the creditor, only one pledge could be created, but with *hypotheca* it was possible to create successive charges. Both pledge and *hypotheca* are essentially *iura in re aliena*, for they give to the creditor rights *in rem*.

If we look at the mortgage historically, we see that it has passed

---

[1] The adjective *real* here means only that a right *in rem* is created over a *res*: it is not confined to *real* property in the English sense.

through two stages—firstly, that of the pledge, and secondly that of actual transfer of title to the creditor—and it will probably end by becoming a mere charge.[1] Even when at common law the mortgagee took a transfer of title, equity took the view that the debtor should be protected, and allowed recovery even after the date of repayment was passed. Once the Chancellor effectively protected the 'equity of redemption' it was true to say that the common mortgage by conveyance was 'one long *suppressio veri* and *suggestio falsi*'.[2]

In English law today some forms of real security vest possession in the creditor (e.g. pawn); others give the creditor legal title but leave the debtor in control until default. Lien at common law is the right of one in possession of goods to remain in possession until certain claims, which he has against the owner, are satisfied.[3] This 'possessory' lien is dependent on the retention of the goods by the creditor, and is only a right of retention. Once possession is lost the lien disappears, and there is no right of sale. In equity and maritime law, however, the creditor need not have possession of the *res*—his claim is rather that certain specific property should be primarily applied to the satisfaction of the debt. A maritime lien may arise from several causes, e.g. because of damage done by a collision, claims by seamen for wages, a bottomry bond,[4] salvage or moneys due to the master for wages or disbursements.[5] Since the lien grants a right *in rem*, it attaches to the ship, and thus the present owner of the ship may suffer in pocket, even although he himself was not personally responsible for the events which gave rise to the lien.[6] If I hire my car to Jones and he causes an accident, the car cannot be seized by the injured party, since his claim is merely *in personam* against Jones and not against me at all. But in maritime law, even although the collision was due to the negli-

---

[1] Hanbury and Waldock, *Mortgages*, 21–2; and under *Torrens*-type land title registration systems it has done so—see Transfer of Land Act, 1958 (Victoria—no. 6399) where § 74 (2) provides: 'any such mortgage or charge shall when registered have effect as a security and be an interest in land, but shall not operate as a transfer of the land thereby mortgaged or charged.'   [2] Maitland, *Equity* (2nd ed.), 182.

[3] A lien may arise (*a*) by operation of law, e.g. a lien of common carriers over goods for which the freight has not been paid; of an innkeeper over the goods of a guest till the lodging is paid; of a solicitor or artificer who has spent money or expended skill on the property of another; (*b*) by contract. *Caldwell* v. *Sumpters*, [1971] 3 All E. R. 892.

[4] A bottomry bond is an advance of money made to the master of a vessel on the security of the vessel and/or of its cargo and made in case of dire necessity. These bonds are of less importance now because wireless renders communication easier with the owners.

[5] The maritime lien has been described as one of the first principles of the law of the sea: *The Tolten*, [1946] P. 135.   [6] Griffith Price, 57 *L.Q.R.* (1941), 409.

gence of a charterer, the ship itself may, if necessary, be attached to satisfy the judgment. An innocent purchaser of a ship without notice of the lien may find that the vessel is bound by a bottomry bond. An equitable lien exists independently of possession, but it is not like the maritime lien, a perfect right *in rem*, as it does not bind a purchaser for value without notice—it is really a claim that according to the rules of equity certain property should be made subject to the particular charge in question, and as the claim is only an equitable one it may be defeated by one who obtains the legal estate without notice. Thus a vendor, even after he has parted with possession, has a lien in equity for the full amount of the unpaid purchase money.

§ 117. The Trust

One of the best demonstrations of the usefulness of the concept of the trust is an examination of the intricate devices used by other legal systems in an attempt to achieve what is so successfully done by the trust.[1] So accustomed were Englishmen to the trust that its curious nature and its practical contribution were not fully realized until Maitland wrote his classic papers.[2] Rather than attempt to fit the trust into the classifications of Roman law, it is better to deal with it separately.

It is difficult to see how the notion of the trust could have been satisfactorily developed without the separation of law and equity. To those who like their notions clear cut, a dual ownership, which is not co-ownership, is inconceivable. The ownership of the trustee recognized at law and the equitable duty imposed on the trustee of carrying out the terms of the trust have led to a useful division between responsibility and benefit of which English lawyers have not been slow to make use. If, of course, that were the whole story, the trust would be ineffective—an owner at law may pass a legal title, and the rights of the beneficiary might in that case be defeated. But equity evolved a formidable procedure of following the trust property, and the trust will bind the property no matter into whose hands it comes unless it be transferred to a bona-fide purchaser for value without notice.[3] Clearly, such equitable rights could hardly evolve save where there was a separation between two systems of law. The continental jurist is puzzled by any reference to a right that partakes of the nature of rights *in rem* and rights *in personam*. He asks: Who has the ownership? If it is given to the trustee, the beneficiary has a mere right *in*

---

[1] F. Weiser, *Trusts on the Continent of Europe.*   [2] *Collected Papers*, iii. 321.
[3] *Supra*, § 65.

personam; if to the beneficiary, then the trustee is a mere agent. There has been, in recent times, great interest on the Continent in the Anglo-Saxon trust,[1] but its true nature is often misunderstood.

The trust has served in many fields. Firstly, it has been used by associations as a means whereby the group property can be applied to the desired purposes—behind the hedge of trustees a community life may flourish, even although incorporation has not been granted.[2] Secondly, the problem of endowments and of gifts for charitable and religious purposes is made easy, for the property may be vested in trustees for such purposes (provided they be legal) as the settlor desires. Thirdly, the trust has been of great social importance in making possible a facile settlement of family property; the young have been protected from their inexperience; a married woman, through the help of equity, secured a certain measure of economic independence in spite of the common law rule which then vested her chattels in her husband. Indeed 'protective trusts'[3] have been developed by which the beneficiary is sheltered almost to an extreme degree, since it may be provided that, if he should attempt to assign his interest or should become bankrupt, his rights cease, but that thereafter the trustee shall have an absolute discretion to apply the income for his benefit. So far has the law allowed a parent to go in his desire to protect his child from rash speculation or extravagant living. In America some courts have even upheld clauses which provide that the income of the trust should not be subject to claims by creditors.[4] The creditor must be lucky enough to get the money after it is paid to the debtor, and before he has spent it. This carries protection to an extraordinary length and is hard to justify on any gounds of policy. How far is it 'desirable to permit one generation to give to the next generation the powers and privileges conferred by wealth and relieve it from the responsibility which ordinarily accompanies the ownership of property'?[5] If such devices were confined to beneficiaries under age, there would be little question; but they may be used to protect a beneficiary of any age.

---

[1] See, for example, P. G. Lepaulle, *Traité théorique et pratique des trusts*; W. Siebert, *Das rechtsgeschäftliche Treuhandverhältnis*; A. Nussbaum, 38 *Col. L. R.* (1938), 408.   [2] *Supra*, § 92.
[3] A. W. Scott, *Harvard Legal Essays* (ed. R. Pound), 419.
[4] Scott, op. cit. 423.
[5] Scott, op. cit. 432. For a more favourable view, see G. P. Costigan in *Legal Essays in Tribute to McMurray* (ed. M. Radin), 85. Costigan favours protective trusts so long as only a reasonable income is guaranteed and the creditors can seize anything above that limit.

Many systems of law possess some means of dealing with the reckless spendthrift,[1] but the institution of 'prodigality' has some advantages over that of the spendthrift trust: firstly, it is applied only to those cases where such control seems necessary; secondly, it may be applied against the will of the extravagant one, whereas in English law (while a settlor may, of course, draft a trust as he wishes when he gives property to another) there is no means of taking from an incompetent person the control of property which he owns. Although the trust has played its part in consolidating the family fortunes, the individualism of English law refuses to recognize that a man's family has any claim to prevent him from wasting his substance in riotous living.

There are two more fields where the trust has proved of great practical importance. The postponed trust for sale has rendered it easy to retain the business of a testator as a going concern until the moment arrives when it may be economically profitable to sell, without depriving the beneficiaries of the intermediate profits. Lastly, the trust has today become an instrument of 'high capitalism'.

What has made the trust so effective is the co-operation of the courts—in effect the court may be asked to supervise the execution of the trust deed. 'In no other circumstances can a private individual impose administrative duties upon the court to this extent, by his own volition.'[2]

§ 118. ANALYSIS OF PROPERTY IN THE MODERN WORLD

(a) Extension of the Term 'Property'

As we have already pointed out 'property' is an ambiguous term in English law, for its meaning varies according to the purpose in hand. This is an example of the 'instrumentalist' theory of definition—we cannot describe the real essence of the term property; we can define it only for a particular purpose and that definition is valid only within the given context. Firstly, there are technical reasons for an extension of the term in certain cases. To overcome the effect of the maxim that equity will protect only rights of property, there was a temptation to seek a tinge of property in what were really personal rights.[3] Some constitutions have a general clause prohibiting the taking of property without the payment of compensation, and very wide decisions have been made as to what is property within the

---

[1] L. Josserand, *Évolutions et Actualités*, 159.
[2] A. Nussbaum, 38 *Col. L. R.* (1938), 408 at 412.　　　　[3] *Supra*, § 65.

meaning of this rule. 'Property necessarily includes the right to con-tract.'[1] Examples such as these extend the term 'property' to cover whatever has a present or potential material value.[2]

Economically, the nature of property is being extended. The once overwhelming importance of landed property is now eclipsed by the growth of new forms of wealth. Much of the most valuable property today consists in the right to share in a particular fund, e.g. shares in a company. To the logic of the law a share certificate is theoretically mere evidence of a right to receive dividends and to share in the funds of the company if it be dissolved while still solvent. But economically the share certificate is itself property, since in most cases it has a market value and is fully transferable.[3] A railway ticket for one purpose is merely evidence of a contract: in the law of larceny it is property.

Some modern economists consider that we have in effect built a hierarchy of interests relating to funds, just as our ancestors built a feudal hierarchy upon the land.[4] In technical legal parlance, a claim can only be made against a legal person, but there are two practical factors to be noted. Firstly, now that imprisonment for debt has been largely abolished, a claim against John Smith is, in effect, a claim against such funds as he has under his control. If Smith cannot meet his debts he may go bankrupt, though his discharge may be postponed until he has paid, say, ten shillings in the pound. Personal liability for debts today means only a legal duty to pay which may be avoided by bankruptcy; it does not mean the physical liability of early law when the debtor suffered in person and the easy escape of bankruptcy was not available. Secondly, the frequent use of the device of incorpora-tion joined with limited liability allows a trader, not only to place his eggs in many baskets, but to confine his loss on any one venture to the eggs in that particular receptacle. John Smith may create three 'one-man' companies, make a fortune out of one, and leave his creditors to bear the loss on the other two. The device of 'holding' companies has rendered it possible for the corporation to limit its liability very successfully, and the parent company in control of subsidiaries has economic power and the prospect of taking such profit as there may

---

[1] *Dugger* v. *Insurance Co.* (1895), 95 Tenn. 245 at 252, cited C. R. Noyes, *Institution of Property*, 353.

[2] See *Minister of State for the Army* v. *Dalziel* (1944), 68 C.L.R. 261; and *Bank of New South Wales* v. *The Commonwealth* (1948), 76 C.L.R. 1.

[3] Cf. K. Renner's brilliant analysis in *The Institutions of Private Law and their Social Functions*.

[4] Cf. C. R. Noyes, *Institution of Property*, 504, 516.

be, but its possible loss on any particular venture is restricted to the capital invested therein. Thus from the economic point of view, incorporation means the limiting of liability to certain funds, and the modern system of 'holding' companies and 'interlocking' corporations means that a great number of these funds may be created. In many volumes of reported cases, nearly one-third of the litigants are corporations, and in each corporation many persons may have an interest. The invention of the share has made it easy to divide up the interest in these funds by any particular method desired. So much of our modern wealth is locked up in companies that our law of property seems very remote from that of Rome, where property consisted mainly of material things to which an absolutist concept of *dominium* could be applied. Now much wealth consists of paper which represents a claim of some sort upon corporation funds. Moreover, there has been a fundamental cleavage between ownership and control. In the days before the modern corporation, when an owner controlled his property, it was assumed that self-interest would ensure profitable use of it which would react to the advantage of the community. Now a corporation may be controlled by one interest holding a comparatively small block of shares. The classical study of Berle and Means[1] shows that where shareholders are widely dispersed, a holding of even five per cent of the voting stock may give control. By the device of 'pyramiding' or creating holding companies, the extent of financial power may be greatly increased; in one case an investment of less than twenty million dollars, controlled assets worth two billion dollars.[2] Thus the majority owners of the stock may lose effective power. What is in the financial interests of those in control may not assist the shareholders, especially as profits may be diverted to a subsidiary in which the controlling group has a larger interest. It is futile to attempt to approach this problem with the concepts of jurisprudence designed for a simpler economy.

In examining the break up of the old concept that was property and the old unity that was private enterprise, it is therefore evident that we are dealing not only with distinct but often with opposing groups—ownership on the one side, control on the other—a control which tends to move further and further away from ownership and ultimately to lie in the hands of the management itself, a management capable of perpetuating its own position. The concentration of economic power separate from

---

[1] *The Modern Corporation and Private Property.*
[2] Op. cit. 73; G. D. Hornstein, 92 *Univ. of Pa. L. R.* (1943), 1.

ownership has, in fact, created economic empires . . . relegating owners to the position of those who supply the means whereby the new princes may exercise their power.[1]

As in feudalism, ownership of land carried with it political power, so control of modern company groups gives power to command.

What some modern writers call 'intellectual' property has become more important in modern times. The extensive advertising and persuasive salesmanship of modern business has made increasingly valuable such forms of property as copyright, patents, and property in designs. To sell the 'moving picture rights' becomes the dream of a young novelist; international conferences are held with the object of securing as world-wide a protection as possible for the rights of an author. The normal right which an author or artist desires is the power to restrict reproduction of his work without consent in order that others may not unjustifiably profit from the toil of his brain. The rules of copyright achieve this end. Some systems of law have introduced *le droit de suite* which attempts to secure for the artist a fair return for his labours. Before he has achieved fame an artist is compelled to sell his work for very little: later, speculators may reap great profits. In France and Belgium the artist is entitled to a certain percentage of the sale price every time a work of this kind is sold by public auction.[2] In the sphere of literary copyright it has been suggested that lending libraries diminish an author's royalties because so many read the same copy, and that measures should be taken to recompense the writer. In addition to the financial interests of the author or artist, there is the desire of the creator that his work should not be mutilated or deformed. Jones may sell all the rights in his play, but feel that his reputation would suffer if the play is altered by inept producers and then presented under his name. As a French court has said: 'Independent of pecuniary interest there exists for the artist an interest more precious, that of reputation.'[3] Continental systems seem to have gone farther than English law[4] in modifying juristic concepts to protect the author. Logically it seems anomalous that an author

---

[1] Berle and Means, op. cit. 124. The learned authors conclude (p. 356) that the modern corporation should be operated not solely in the interests of the shareholders, or of the controlling group, but rather in the interests of the community itself.

[2] L. F. Vinding Kruse, *The Right of Property* (trans. P. T. Federspiel), 339, referring to the French law of 20 May 1920 and the Belgian law of 25 June 1921.

[3] Cited M. A. Roeder, 53 *Harv. L. R.* (1939), 554; Kruse, *The Right of Property*, 75 et seq.

[4] English law allows the author a remedy in defamation if an inferior story by another is put forward as a work of the plaintiff: *Ridge* v. *English Illustrated* (1913), 29 T.L.R. 592.

who has completely parted with his work should yet be able to prevent its deformation, but theory may invent an implied term in the contract that the work shall not be so treated as to injure the reputation of the author.

Copyright is not property in the material sense—it is a mere right to prevent reproduction without consent—but it is a most valuable economic asset. There must be originality, but there is no examination as in the case of patents by a public official before the patent is protected. A patent is available only where registration is granted: copyright exists without registration, and the question of originality is argued only if an action is brought for infringement.[1] Copyright may exist even where there is no literary value. Libraries for many years had committed breaches of copyright by providing photostats of articles to students and research workers—now a limited protection is given by the Act of 1956.[2] Once the period of copyright expires, anyone may reproduce the work without cost. Vinding Kruse suggests that the State should still exact a royalty and use it as a fund to assist creative work.[3]

The scientific discovery of the inventor may be protected by the law of patents. The interests to be reconciled are those of the inventor, the industrial expert who exploits it, and the public. The first and the last are usually less able to protect themselves. English law does not give protection to scientific discoveries as such—there must be a process which is patentable. Soviet and Czechoslovak law goes further than English law in protecting the discoverer of new scientific ideas.[4] Between the brilliance of the laboratory worker and the successful marketing of a commodity there is a wide gap which may require the expenditure of vast sums of money. A new drug must be subjected to wide clinical trials, and made the subject of a huge marketing campaign, before profit can be created by sales. Out of many discoveries there are few that return gain. Hence the entrepreneur, who must risk much, drives a hard bargain with the inventor. It is to the advantage of the community that there should be a government instrumentality, which can guide the inventor inexperienced in the ways of industry to make the best use of his discovery.[5]

---

[1] *Warwick Film Productions Ltd.* v. *Eisinger*, [1967] 3 All E.R. 367.
[2] 4 & 5 Eliz. II, c. 74.
[3] *The Right of Property*, 309. An interesting study of the functioning of copyright law with the conclusion (which few authors would accept) that copyright law is not really necessary is that of S. Breyer, 84 *Harv. L. R.* (1970), 281.
[4] S. J. Soltysinski, 32 *Mod. L. R.* (1969), 408.
[5] e.g. the National Resources and Development Corporation.

Is it in the interest of the community that a patentee should be able to withhold a patent from the community, e.g. if a monopoly buys up a patent which it does not intend to use, but which it wishes to prevent others from using?[1] Should the State have power to enforce compulsory licences in the interest of society?[2]

There are industrial secrets which cannot be, or are not, patented. How far should the law protect a manufacturer from industrial espionage, or the use of secrets obtained in confidence? The present law is rather confused—'property, contract, bailment, trust, fiduciary relationship, good faith, unjust enrichment, have all been claimed, at one time or another, as the basis of judicial intervention'.[3] In 1968 Sir Edward Boyle moved the second reading of the Industrial Information Bill, which was designed to protect this form of industrial 'property' which obviously may have great economic value, but the Bill was not passed, and the law still remains confused.

Another form of intangible property is the franchise—the licence obtained from the State to run a bus service, a television station, a taxi; these may have great economic value. Somewhat similar is the licence to practice certain professions, entry to which is limited by law to those with certain qualifications. This is a valuable right, but it is not a property right, for it cannot be sold or transferred to another. A doctor may sell his practice, but only to one who is professionally qualified. A barrister cannot sell his practice, for it is a personal pursuit.

(b) The Effect of Increasing Regulation by the State

The increasing interference by the State with the rights of owners and the rise of collectivist theories are modifying the notion of irresponsibility or absolute control and leading to the theory that property is a social responsibility. The modern inroads on the theory that an owner is one who can do as he likes with his own would have horrified Soames of Galsworthy's *Forsyte Saga*: to a Forsyte, even the Married Women's Property Act was an interference with the husband's right of property which contained a threat to the stability of society—apparently on the cynical view that wives with economic independence would not remain with their husbands, and thus endanger the family structure.

---

[1] W. Friedmann, *Law and Changing Society*, 78.
[2] Cf. Patents Act, 1949, §§ 16–19.
[3] Gareth Jones, 86 *L.Q.R.* (1970), 463.

The following are examples of State control which are now commonplace:

(i) Protection of the rights of certain tenants against the landlord, both as to the maximum rent payable and as to continuity of tenure. This is common with regard to cheaper residential and also agricultural tenancies.

(ii) Positive or negative rules concerning user. During a time of war, the need for the production of food may lead to strict rules concerning the method of dealing with agricultural land. Forestry is another example. From the seventeenth century Denmark had legislation controlling the rights of landowners to deal with forests—the community interest was regarded as superior to the individual rights of the owner. 'Protective' forests may be necessary to prevent erosion, or drifting sand, or to provide water catchments free of contamination by mud.

Town planning is not, as is sometimes suggested, an entirely modern concept. The central portions of Melbourne and Adelaide were 'town planned' from their inception, but the subsequent suburban growth on the fringes was for too long left to take care of itself. The object of town planning is to prevent development contrary to the public interest and to make long-term rules concerning roads, shopping centres, zoning of industrial and residential areas. Town planning requires great skill, but it is relatively easy to apply to a virgin area, compared with one that is already crowded with substandard housing. An interim development order may cover a huge area for which new buildings are planned, and there is often personal tragedy when a private dwelling is acquired to allow of development necessary for the community. All that society can do is to see that really adequate compensation is paid and that alternative housing is available in a community which is planned to conserve human values and not merely to provide bigger and better buildings.

Town planning, if it leads to expropriation, will necessitate compensation to the owner who has lost his property. But where a zoning restriction is imposed, an owner may suffer much loss without remedy. Property may be worth vastly more if it may be sold for offices, shops, or petrol stations, but if a limitation to residential purposes only is applied to an area, the landowner loses the chance of speculative profit.

(iii) Expropriation for community purposes—freeways, aerodromes, rehousing. In these cases compensation is normally payable. Danish law requires that the entire economic loss to the landowner should be paid—merely paying the market value of the land is not enough, for goodwill may be lost if the land on which there is a shop is compulsorily acquired. This is an area where the dispossessed owner may suffer great loss.

(iv) Normally, rights are given to public utilities to acquire easements, e.g. for drainage, telephone poles, or electric distribution systems. Where it is necessary to transmit high voltages on steel towers, this may lead to conflict between the economic interest of cheap electricity and the aesthetic desire to preserve the amenities of the landscape.

(v) The breaking up of large estates for 'closer settlement' is another example of state interference. This may be done either by a steeply graduated land tax that renders the large estate uneconomic, or else by direct expropriation and the division of the area into smaller farms.

(vi) Taxation may be used to redistribute property, e.g. succession and estate duties, land tax, income tax: taxation may be necessary to provide revenues for the State, but there are also other policies behind its imposition.

These examples of state regulation of the uses to which property may be put are of the utmost importance in conveyancing, and the task of the lawyer is thereby rendered more complex. It is of vital importance to a purchaser whether there is an interim development order, or whether a new freeway is planned which will take the front of his garden, or whether a house has been condemned as unfit for habitation.

§ 119. Theories of Property

There are two types of theories of property—one attempts to explain how property came to be, to describe the facts; the other passes an ethical judgment on those facts and attempts to justify (or condemn) the institution of private property. Sometimes, however, these two aims are combined: for example, a writer argues that property arose to reward private enterprise and that therefore it is ethically justifiable.[1]

---

[1] For a critical account of the traditional theories, see H. J. Laski, *A Grammar of Politics*, ch. v.

(*a*) One theory is that property arose by the taking control of a *res nullius—occupatio*. He who first reduces into possession a piece of property has the best of justifications for remaining in control.[1] But the acceptance of what has been flippantly termed 'the divine right of grab' is not so widespread today as once it was. Maine suggests that the doctrine that *occupatio* gives title is probably the result of later thought. 'It is only when the rights of property have gained a sanction from long practical inviolability, and when the vast majority of the objects of employment have been subjected to private ownership, that mere possession is allowed to invest the first possessor with *dominium* over commodities in which no prior proprietorship has been asserted.'[2] In a crowded world *occupatio* applies only to a relatively unimportant degree—less often does the vacant forest await the tiller. The theory of *occupatio* hardly provides a reasonable account of the origin of property, and it is even less satisfactory as a justification of property. Why should he who is lucky enough to seize a thousand acres become owner?

(*b*) Another theory regards property as the result of individual labour. Industry should be encouraged by granting to a worker the ownership of any *res* which is created by his toil. But this doctrine seems to imagine a simple state of society in which each man creates his own products. Things must be created out of something—if the material be a *res nullius*, there is something to be said for rewarding the work of the creator. What, however, if Peter makes a suit out of James's wool (*specificatio*)? Here the claim of the owner of the material and the right of the manufacturer come into conflict. The fact that there was a dispute between the Proculians and Sabinians shows that the answer to this problem is not easy, and Justinian's solution that the manufacturer gained title, if the *res* was a *nova species* and irreducible to its former state, is obviously a compromise.[3] In modern society it is impossible (at any rate in the industrial world) to say in more than a few cases what is the result of the labour of any one individual. Moreover, much wealth is not the result of labour at all, but of some fortunate accident, e.g. the increased value of land on which oil or coal is found. An owner may

---

[1] Huntington Cairns, *Law and the Social Sciences*, 61; Kant, *Philosophy of Law* (trans. W. Hastie), 82.

[2] H. J. S. Maine, *Ancient Law* (ed. Pollock), 269. Cf. J. Bentham, *Limits of Jurisprudence Defined*, 85: 'Till law existed, property could scarcely be said to exist. Property and law were born and die together . . . take away law and property is at an end.'

[3] W. W. Buckland, *Text-Book of Roman Law* (2nd ed.), 215.

neglect his land, but sell at a huge profit because a railway opens up that part of the country. The existence of this 'unearned increment' shows that wealth is not always the result of individual labour. Another factor to be considered is that what the community needs is not merely labour, but socially useful labour. The trafficker in drugs labours, but does not aid the community. Moreover, one who successfully acquires a fortune may withdraw his descendants from the labour market by removing from them the necessity of earning their daily champagne.

Nevertheless, the theory contains a grain of truth. Society needs labour and the occupations are still few where the intrinsic interest is so great that men will labour for the love of it. An incentive to toil must be provided, and the labourer should receive a just return. Conversely, society should demand from possessors of property service commensurate with the privileges they enjoy. 'No man . . . has a moral right to property except as a return for functions performed.'[1]

(c) According to the Hegelians some control of property is essential for the proper development of personality. The community has slowly evolved from status to contract, from group holding to individual property—liberty has grown in the process, and it is the control of property that makes men free. There is in this a valuable truth—he who is wholly dependent on property controlled by others in their own interest can hardly live the life of the free. But the argument does not justify, but rather criticizes, the present system which allows concentration of property in a minority of the community.[2] The Hegelian theory really leads to the conclusion that society should be so organized that every member can, by toil within his powers, acquire such property as is necessary for true self-realization.

(d) Some have considered that private property is a creation of the State and achieved only after a long struggle with the clan.[3] If we regard as the essential characteristic of private property the right to exclude others, to charge the res for debt, to alienate or leave by will, it is true that the State has provided the machinery by which these rights are enjoyed. The clan favours joint exploitation, dislikes alienation, and regards disposal by will as contrary to the interests of the family. Moreover, while the economic exploitation by the tiller of the

---

[1] H. J. Laski, *A Grammar of Politics* (5th ed.), 184.
[2] Cf. H. Rashdall: 'We cannot justify the whole capitalistic system *en bloc* by the bare formula that property is necessary to the development of individual character': *Property, its Duties and Rights*, 66. Cf. R. H. Tawney, *The Acquisitive Society*.
[3] E. Jenks, *Law and Politics in the Middle Ages*, 237–8.

soil may take place where there is no state, it is to the military exploits
of the State that the huge proprietary manor is due. But is not this
argument rather a case of *post hoc ergo propter hoc*? The State was
a resultant of social and economic forces and did not arise *ex nihilo*.
These same forces were tending to the creation of individual property.
The emergence of the State and the creation of private property were
the effects of the same causes and we can hardly say that one is the
creation of the other. Moreover, private property may exist even
where there is not a highly developed State, although protection of
the owner's right to exclude others can hardly be effective till there is
a developed legal order.

It is impossible to conceive of the modern forms of property in the
absence of a sophisticated set of legal rules with an effective sanction
behind them. Property today does not consist only of land and the
produce thereof—this might be defended by a strong right arm or a
horde of knights. Wealth that is built up by contract, that relies on
the company share or debenture, the security of the cheque or bill of
exchange, the television rights—all these assets are valuable only if
there is a stable business community with effective sanctions of law.
The modern company is a team and a hierarchy of interests has been
built on the 'fund' employed—it is obvious that an effective company
structure must depend on an effective Companies Act. The State,
therefore, may claim that it is a partner with the entrepreneur in the
creation of wealth, and therefore that the State can justifiably levy
its toll when necessary for what are deemed to be social ends.

(*e*) The increasing tendency in modern times is not to attempt to
justify the institution of private property by an *a priori* theory, but to
build doctrines on an analysis of the functioning and social effects
of the institution. This approach is sometimes called the functional
theory, and it lays down that property which is the result of effort
or involves the giving of service is ethically justifiable, but property
which is an undeserved claim on the wealth produced by others is
not.[1] If property is to be effective in encouraging production, then
society should see that it is distributed on proper principles. Duguit
would put it that property ceases to be a right and becomes a duty;
the owner is no longer free to exercise his arbitrary will but must
perform a social function.[2]

---

[1] R. H. Tawney, *The Acquisitive Society*; H. Cairns, *Law and the Social Sciences*,
75. 'The justification of property must depend not upon any *a priori* principle, but
upon its social effects': H. Rashdall, in *Property, its Duties and Rights*, 68.

[2] *Transformations du droit privé*. Duguit wished to subject everything to the rule of

Under any theory, some property must be available to the individual. Even under socialism there must be recognition of private property in articles for consumption and personal use. In the U.S.S.R. some writers speak of the resurgence of private property—it is now possible even to become a *rentier* in a small way by lending the State money.[1] The real question before the modern world is not whether property shall be destroyed but whether some of the excesses of private ownership of the means of production are to be cut down. No individual, however powerful he may be, can today create wealth without the help of the social framework and the co-operation of his fellows, and therefore society can well demand that, once created, wealth should be used for those purposes which will be of greatest benefit to the community. Duguit, however, goes too far in suggesting that there has been a complete revolution in the legal approach to property. The owner still has many 'sovereign' rights, though the area of complete freedom is being gradually restricted.

The modern theory thus seeks a justification of private property in the results that it achieves and criticizes the institution so far as it fails to achieve those results. Such an approach is closely linked with a functional study of what property means in the legal sense. Today we see the effective working of the institution of property, not in a mere analysis of concepts borrowed from Roman law, but in a realistic study of what legislatures and courts are actually doing.[2] Vinding Kruse has pointed out that the real task of the social sciences is to 'dedogmatize' the people—writing has been so full of ideological cant (whether capitalist, socialist, or communist in bent) that we do not accurately see whither the law is tending.[3] The old melodrama has too much influence. In some writings on the current scene, Big Business or the International Jew are cast to play the part of the villain; to others, Government Bureaucracy is destroying liberty of enterprise and the freedom of the individual; to a third group, Bolshevik Communism is a poison seeping through the world and destroying all that is lovely and of good repute. A realistic survey shows that we cannot explain the law of any country in terms of abstractions. Law is a compromise, and today there is in England what would have appeared radical socialism to the landowners of 1910. Beating the

---

law—not only the sovereignty of the State, but those relics of arbitrary power which an owner still possessed: Achille Mestre, *Archives de phil. du droit* (1932, 1–2), 163.

[1] S. P. Simpson and J. Stone, *Law and Society*, 1991.
[2] Cf. C. R. Noyes, *Institution of Property*, 419.
[3] *The Right of Property*, 5.

drum of propaganda may serve some purposes, but it neither advances
the study of jurisprudence nor gives a real appreciation of what is
happening in the world today. What is apparent is that absolute rights
are ceasing to exist, if they ever did exist, and are being replaced by
qualified rights the exercise of which is limited by the philosophy and
needs of the community in question.

§ 120. ACQUISITION *INTER VIVOS*

(*a*) *Original Acquisition*

A person is said to acquire derivatively when he accepts a conveyance of title from a previous owner: in original acquisition a *res* which
has no owner is reduced into possession and title acquired. The latter
was naturally more important in primitive times than today when the
world is crowded and most things are subject to ownership. In
English law, owing to the feudal doctrine that all land is held of the
king, land cannot become a *res nullius* and even in the case of personal property the list of such things is very limited.[1]

Occupatio was the term given in Roman law to the acquisition of
title in a *res nullius*. Apart from specific game laws, the birds of the
air are the property of him who first reduces them into possession. It
was generally considered that *occupatio* also applied to *res derelictae*—
when an owner abandoned his property, he lost title at once, and the
res was therefore open to acquisition by anyone. The Proculians,
however, held that an owner did not lose his property till some other
person reduced it into possession. On this theory, abandonment was
an example of *traditio incertae personae*—the owner by abandoning
the *res* manifested an intention to transfer title to the first taker. But
the Proculian view did not prevail,[2] although in English law there is
some authority for it.[3]

Accessio[4] may be an example either of original or derivative
acquisition according to the circumstances. If I darn my socks with
wool which is not mine, the wool 'cedes to', or is merged in, my socks

---

[1] Holdsworth, *History of English Law*, vii. 479.
[2] *Inst.* 2. 1. 47; *Dig.* 41. 7. 1. pr.; 41. 7. 2. 1.
[3] Holdsworth, op. cit. 495–6; see the *Arrow Shipping Co. Ltd.* v. *The Tyne Improvement Commissioners*, [1894] A.C. 508, per Lord Macnaghten, at 532; *A.-G.* v. *Trustees
of the British Museum*, [1903] 2 Ch. 598, at 608–9; *The Tubantia*, [1924] P. 78, at 87;
Johnstone & Wilmot Pty. Ltd. v. *Kaine*, [1928] 23 Tas. L. R. 43, at 56–8.
[4] 'Acquisition of property by its incorporation in what already belonged to the
acquirer': Buckland, *Text-Book of Roman Law* (2nd ed.), 208.

and I thereby become owner of it. If the wool was a *res nullius*, it is a case of original acquisition; if the wool belonged to another, I acquire title without his consent. If an island is created by natural forces in a river, a riparian owner[1] acquires a right to so much of the island as lies between the centre of the river and his own land. Since the island has no previous owner, this is a case of original acquisition.

(b) Acquisition of Title from Another without Consent

Normally we can acquire title to a *res* owned by another only with that other's consent. If a thief purports to transfer to a purchaser title in the *res* stolen, the maxim *nemo dat quod non habet* applies. But there are certain cases where an owner may lose title without his consent:

(a) By the happening of an event—a river in flood may tear away portion of A's land and cast it against the ground of B. The Romans applied the curious rule that B obtained title as soon as the portion had been there for a considerable time and trees carried with it had taken root in his ground.[2]

(b) By the operation of law—bankruptcy, execution against property, expropriation in the public interest.

(c) By the wrongful act of the acquirer—*specificatio*,[3] adverse possession bringing into play the rules of prescription.[4]

(d) By a wrongful act of one who has mere possession but not ownership of the goods.

Normally, an agent can pass title only if he has the authority of the owner so to do. The common law favours what Demogue has called static security, since it desires to protect the title of the real owner, even at the cost of rendering transactions slow and cumbersome by requiring the purchaser to investigate the title of him who purports to sell. The business world, on the other hand, favours dynamic security, emphasizing the necessity for speed of transactions and the protection of the purchaser in good faith even if this occasionally defeats the true owner's title. The concept of static security is seen in the land law, where rigorous investigation of the owner's title is necessary; that of dynamic security in the law relating to negotiable instruments, where a bona-fide purchaser for value (without notice of any flaw in the

---

[1] Whose lands are not *agri limitati.*
[3] *Supra*, § 119.
[2] *Dig.* 41. 1. 7. 2.
[4] *Supra*, § 112.

vendor's title) can rest assured that his title cannot be disturbed by any claim that the true owner gave no consent to the transfer. The use of money would be rendered difficult if the right of the holder of the coins had to be investigated before it was safe to deal with him— imagine a parchment title accompanying every pound note. The battle for the extension of the concept of negotiability to debenture bonds[1] illustrates in an interesting fashion the conflict of commerce with the law.[2] Again, the title of a true owner of any personal property might be defeated by sale in market overt;[3] the Factors Acts from 1824 onwards protect a purchaser who buys from a mercantile agent who is in possession of the goods with the consent of the owner, even although the agent had no power to sell.[4] With regard to land 'constructive notice' and the requirement of strict investigation may be a useful doctrine 'for title is everything and it can be leisurely investigated', but to apply these doctrines to commerce would be 'doing infinite mischief and paralysing the trade of the country'.[5]

Accessio[6] has become more important because of the ramifications of hire-purchase. If I take a flock of sheep on hire-purchase, who owns the natural increase? This clearly depends on the contract, but in the absence of a term relating to this, it has been held that the young belong to the lessee.[7] However, a contract between two parties does not affect the title of a third. If I obtain a truck on hire-purchase from A, and instal a new engine bought on hire-purchase from B, what are B's rights if A repossesses the truck? A Victorian court held that title to the engine would not pass unless the owner of the engine intended that. The onus lies on the owner of the vehicle to show that the engine cannot be identified and removed. Clearly the engine could be removed without damage to the rest of the vehicle, and therefore title was not lost by B.[8] On the other hand, it has been held in Canada that tyres fitted to a truck are governed by the doctrine of *accessio*.[9]

[1] *Crouch* v. *Crédit Foncier* (1873), L.R. 8 Q.B. 374; *Goodwin* v. *Robarts* (1875), L.R. 10 Ex. 337.
[2] R. S. T. Chorley, 48 *L.Q.R.* (1932), 51.
[3] Although under the Larceny Act, if a thief is convicted of larceny an order for restitution may be made by the court: Larceny Act, 1916, § 45 (1), (2).
[4] See 52 & 53 Vict., c. 45.
[5] Per Lindley L.J., *Manchester Trust* v. *Furness*, [1895] 2 Q.B. 539 at 545.
[6] *Supra*, § 119.
[7] *Tucker* v. *General Investment Trust Ltd.*, [1966] 2 All E.R. 508. See A. G. Guest, 27 *Mod. L. R.* (1964), 505.
[8] *Rendell* v. *Associated Finance Pty. Ltd.*, [1957] V.R. 604.
[9] Cited Guest, *supra*, at 509.

(c) Acquisition of Title by Consent of the Owner

The consent of the owner is expressed in a juristic act, but frequently, in addition to agreement, some systems require a delivery of the property (either with or without set formalities) before title will pass.[1] This has already been discussed in treating of the law of sale.[2]

The acquisition of title by the consent of the owner is a case of succession. In English law we cannot regard the acquisition of property by the adverse possessor as a true case of succession, for the possessor does not acquire a 'parliamentary conveyance' from the previous owner, but has merely the best possessory right based on the inability of anyone else to eject him by legal means.[3]

Succession may be either singular or universal.

In a singular succession . . . the same legal relationship passes from one subject to another: in a universal succession, the subject of the legal relationship remains the same. The essence of universal succession is that it is not strictly speaking a *succession* but a *continuation*. . . . It is in this sense that universal succession is said to be a succession to a personality and singular succession a mere succession to a right.[4]

The sale of a motor car is an example of singular succession: on the other hand, if A succeeds to the totality of rights held by, and duties binding on B, that is an instance of universal succession. There are few, if any, perfect examples of universal succession in actual legal systems. The trustee in bankruptcy acquires many of the rights of the debtor and is bound to some extent by his duties, but the bankrupt retains his personal rights (e.g. marital powers) together with some of his property (e.g. clothes, bedding, and tools of trade), and the trustee is not bound by a duty to pay all the debts but only to divide such assets as there may be proportionately among the creditors according to the priority of their debts. Personal rights are not normally transferred, though in some Australian aboriginal tribes when a man dies his younger brother takes over all the rights which the deceased possessed over his wife.[5] Another case that is sometimes termed universal

---

[1] 'In Bracton's eyes the necessity for a livery of seisin is no peculiarity of the land law': Pollock and Maitland, *History of English Law*, ii. 179.   [2] *Supra*, § 98.

[3] Cf. *Taylor* v. *Twinberrow*, [1930] 2 K.B. 16; *Fairweather* v. *St. Marylebone Pty. Co. Ltd.*, [1962] 2 All E.R. 288; but this is not so, of course, under *Torrens*-type land title registration systems.

[4] R. Sohm, *Institutes of Roman Law* (trans. Ledlie), 505.

[5] A. R. Radcliffe-Brown, 20 *Iowa L. R.* (1935), 286 at 287.

succession is the passing of the estate to the heir in Roman law; but this will be discussed in the next section.

§ 121. SUCCESSION ON DEATH

There are many theories concerning the evolution of succession on death and the development of the will. Our knowledge is as yet too scanty to tread with sure steps, and it is unwarrantable to assume that each race has passed through the same unilinear evolution. 'So long as it is doubtful whether the prehistoric time should be filled, for example, with agnatic *gentes* or with hordes which reckon by "mother right" the interpretation of many a historic text must be uncertain.'[1] Is family ownership the cause or the result of intestate succession?[2] No answer can be dogmatically given for primitive times.

Intestate Succession. Presumably intestate succession was prior to the origin of the last will and testament. Maine suggests as an analogy that the family was a corporation, or that the individual head of the family was a corporation sole whose rights and duties descended to the successor.[3] 'If the family was the owner of the property administered by a paterfamilias, its rights remained unaffected by the death of its temporary head.'[4] But care must be exercised in using the refined notions of advanced jurisprudence as analogies for primitive law.

There are many factors that may be considered when the law decides its rules of inheritance.[5] The law must consider the class of person most likely to be dependent on a testator, and also the type of relative whom an average property owner would be likely to favour. The rules of any one period will be determined largely by the structure of the family at the time. A patriarchal family will emphasize succession through males, those who practise mother right prefer succession through females. Modern systems favour *cognatio* or blood relationship at the expense of relationship through marriage, with one obvious exception—succession between husband and wife. Descendants are usually preferred to other blood relatives in accordance with the natural desires of man. But the estate may go to the eldest son (primogeniture), or be equally divided between sons, or be equally divided between sons and daughters, or be given to the

---

[1] Pollock and Maitland, *History of English Law*, ii. 237; A. S. Diamond, *Primitive Law*, 237.   [2] Pollock and Maitland, op. cit. 247.
[3] Maine, *Ancient Law*, ch. vi.   [4] Holmes, *The Common Law*, 343.
[5] T. E. Atkinson, 20 *Iowa L. R.* (1935), 185; Bentham, *Principles of Morals and Legislation.*

youngest son (ultimogeniture). Probably primogeniture arose, not so much from the desire of the father to keep the estate an undivided whole, as from the demand of the king or lord that the land should be under a strong hand—but in the feudal era there were not strict rules of inheritance, for each heir must make the best bargain he could with his lord.[1] However, primogeniture is practicable only in an ordered community: in a lawless one, it may be dangerous to allow the young son to take title—hence a tendency for the eldest male kinsman to assume control. This is termed *tanistry*. The rationale of ultimogeniture is said to be that the youngest son is most likely to be dependent, since an older child has probably already been settled in life by an advance from the father.[2]

One important factor is that either primogeniture or ultimogeniture keeps the estate of the deceased as a unit, whereas division among all the children soon leads to difficulties in an agricultural community, as the units of land become too small for subsistence. But where primogeniture exists, the elder may be forced to charge the land to provide for his brothers and sisters; where there is equal division, one child may buy out the others, again charging the land—this time for the purchase price.[3] Whatever be the system in force, the difficulty is to provide for all the children out of an estate normally designed as a single working unit.

How far should the law go in tracing kinship?[4] At Rome the Twelve Tables laid down that the nearest agnate took and in default the members of the same *gens*. It is often urged today that the law should set a narrow limit, especially as the growth of individualism has weakened the feeling of family solidarity. Uncertainty increases litigation if the law attempts to trace kinship too far, and some argue that the State should succeed in default of ascendants or descendants. But so long as there is power to make a will, most people will prefer to benefit a remote relative, a friend, or a charity in which they are interested, rather than let the money go to the coffers of the State.

Testate succession. It is impossible to be dogmatic concerning the origin of the will.[5] At Rome probably the first attempt to give the

---

[1] Pollock and Maitland, op. cit. 260–4.

[2] Ultimogeniture existed in many parts of Germany: Pollock and Maitland, op. cit. 280–1. For a criticism of the orthodox theories as to the causes of primogeniture and ultimogeniture, see H. Cairns, 20 *Iowa L. R.* (1935), 266.

[3] The position of the half-blood has led to many different solutions varying from equal rights with the whole blood to total exclusion.

[4] E. M. Meijers, 20 *Iowa L. R.* (1935), 341.

[5] Probably priestly exhortations played a large part—the desire of the Church

succession to one not within the family was by actual adoption. A further step was the actual 'sale' of the inheritance to the prospective heir—in Roman law by *mancipatio*. Possibly at the early stage the testator was then bereft of all his possessions and, like King Lear, was compelled to live on the charity of his beneficiary. Such a will was, of course, irrevocable. But the *mancipatio* soon became a mere formality, carried out only in order to give validity to the expression of the testator's wishes, and it was then accepted that the will became operative only on death. So long as the terms of the will were spoken, secrecy was impossible, but with the invention of writing it became the custom to seal the document and thus keep if from prying eyes. By slow degrees we reach the modern will which is secret, posthumous in operation, revocable, and ambulatory. The first two attributes have been explained. Today, since a will is only a signed and attested document, Brown may make a new will every day if he so desires—the irrevocable nature of the early *mancipatio* has disappeared. Ambulatory means that the will binds all property in the hands of the testator at his death, even if it was acquired only after the will was made. This seems, today, an obvious and reasonable characteristic of a will, but our ancestors found it difficult to see how a man could bind the disposition of property which he did not yet own.

There are several rules in Roman law which seem to show the influence of the early clan ownership of property. Firstly, there are relics of universal succession. Until the *beneficium inventarii* was granted by Justinian, the heir was liable in full for the debts, but thereafter his liabilities were confined to the assets received. Again, the primary purpose of the will was to nominate an heir or heirs in whom the succession would vest as a whole. If the heir did not accept, the whole will fell to the ground. The Roman maxim put it that inheritance was a succession to the entire legal position of the deceased.[1] There were, of course, certain rights that were not inheritable—usufruct was extinguished, a right to bring an action for *iniuria* lapsed unless *litis contestatio* had taken place.

Secondly, in a sense the *suus heres* was succeeding to property to which he had, as it were, a potential right. Hence the growth of rules to protect his interest. A *suus heres* must be expressly disinherited in the will. If a son was born after the will was made, the will was void.

to receive death-bed bequests would force the law to decide whether the claims of expectant heirs could be defeated: Pollock and Maitland, op. cit. 312 et seq.; Holdsworth, *History of English Law*, ii. 91; Cairns, 20 *Iowa L. R.* (1935), 266.

[1] 'Hereditas est successio in universum ius quod defunctus habuit.'

If a son felt he had been unjustly disinherited, he might bring the *querela inofficiosi testamenti* on the plea that the testator must have been insane to make such a will. If there were too many legacies the son might refuse to accept under the will, in which case the will would fall to the ground and the son would then receive his share according to the rules of intestate succession.[1]

By contrast the English rules seem very individualistic. Freedom of testation was carried so far that, for a death-bed whim, a testator might leave all his property to strangers and condemn his wife and children to penury. In 1900 New Zealand passed 'An Act to insure Provision for Testator's Families', and legislation in many parts of the Commonwealth now gives varying rights to a testator's family.[2] In England the law was changed in 1938 and the court was given power to award payment of a reasonable provision out of the net estate for a surviving spouse, an infant son, an unmarried daughter, or a child under a physical or mental disability.[3] The discretion which the Act confers on the court was severely limited, but doubtless it was thought wise to proceed slowly with the experiment.

In modern English law, if there is a will, the executor named therein calls in the assets and pays the debts. If the estate is insolvent, there are rules as to priorities—debts of the same rank are paid *pro rata*. Any surplus remaining after the estate is 'wound up' is distributed according to the directions of the will. By the use of the trust the testator may vest his property in trustees and direct them to pay the income to his beneficiaries, thus relieving them of responsibility. If there is no will, an administrator controls the estate and pays any remaining assets according to the rules of distribution on intestacy. The convenience of the personal representative is seen when we glance at systems the foundation of which is the existence of the heir as universal successor. Thus in French law the heir himself is liable for all the debts unless he specifically accepts only with the *beneficium inventarii*. This is justified by some French writers on the ground that it

---

[1] That is, when the *ius abstinendi* or right of refusal was granted.

[2] See B. Laskin, 17 *Can. B. R.* (1939), 181; Gray, ibid. 233; W. P. M. Kennedy, 20 *Iowa L. R.* (1934–5), 317; Mannie Brown, 18 *Can. B. R.* (1940), 261; and see e.g. Administration and Probate Act, 1958 (Victoria—no. 6191), Part V—Testator's Family Maintenance.

[3] The Inheritance (Family Provision) Act, 1938; G. W. Keeton and L. C. B. Gower, 20 *Iowa L. R.* (1935), 326; the Intestate's Estates Act, 1952 (15 & 16 Geo. VI and 1 Eliz. II, c. 64) extended those provisions to intestate estates and also made a number of amendments to the Inheritance (Family Provisions) Act, 1938. The test is not whether the testator acted reasonably, but whether reasonable provision was made: *In re Goodwin (deceased)*, [1969] 1 Ch. 283.

is morally right for the heir to pay the debts of the testator even if the estate be insolvent, but cynics reply that the moral duty is effective only in cases where ignorance of the law caused a failure to take advantage of the *beneficium inventarii*.[1] Moreover, there are in French law few rules dealing with proportional payment of debts where the estate is insolvent—bankruptcy applies only to merchants. If there are several coheirs, a creditor of the deceased must sue each coheir for that proportion of the debt which corresponds to the heir's share of the inheritance; similarly debtors of the deceased must pay each heir only his due proportion of the debt. The courts have boldly filled many of these gaps in the code,[2] but the law still seems very complicated when compared with the English system. The German Code also builds on the concept of universal succession, but there are not so many technical difficulties as in French law. It certainly is an 'imperative necessity in an economic system based largely upon credit that the debts survive the debtor'[3] and most systems recognize this; but is there any need to enlarge the fund available by making the heir liable in full unless he takes special steps to protect himself?

A legacy is an example of singular succession, and is a deduction from the estate left to the heir in favour of another. 'A legacy is a gift, chargeable only on a *heres*, usually of *res singulae*, having an assignable money value'—thus speaks Buckland for Roman law.[4] In English law the term 'legacy' is inapplicable to gifts of real estate, and the gift is not chargeable on the *heres* but is a direction in the will to the personal representative.

The institution of the will has been strongly attacked, even before the days of socialism.[5] Inheritance is said to be one of the chief causes perpetuating the unequal distribution of wealth. Whatever view be taken, there is no doubt that the modern State with its steeply graduated succession duties makes a noble (or ignoble, according to the scope of our expectations) attempt to redistribute property. In U.S.S.R. the first decree flatly declared: testate and intestate succession are abolished. This, however, cut across a deeply rooted

---

[1] M. Rheinstein, 20 *Iowa L. R.* (1935), 431 at 439.
[2] J. P. Niboyet, ibid. 416.
[3] Rheinstein, ibid. 468.
[4] *Text-Book of Roman Law* (2nd ed.), 334.
[5] Mirabeau wrote: 'What is a testament? It is the expression of the will of a man who has no longer any will, respecting property which is no longer his property; it is the action of a man no longer accountable for his actions to mankind; it is an absurdity, and an absurdity ought not to have the force of law' (cited in *Rational Basis of Legal Institutions*, 453). Yet Mirabeau himself made a will.

sentiment, and in 1945 the rights of parents, brothers, and sisters were recognized—thus inheritance survives even in a communist regime.[1]

[1] V. Gsovski, 45 *Mich. L. R.* (1947), 291, 296; Simpson and Stone, *Law and Society*, 2000.

REFERENCES

ALLEN, C. K., 28 *Calif. L. R.* (1940), 421.
AMOS, M. S., and WALTON, F. P., *Introduction to French Law*, chs. iv, v.
AUSTIN, J., *Jurisprudence*, Lectures 47, 48.
CAMPBELL, A. H., 7 *Camb. L. J.* (1940), 206.
CHORLEY, R. S. T., 48 *L.Q.R.* (1932), 51.
COHEN, F. S., *Dialogue on Private Property* (1954), 9 Rutgers L. R. 357.
LASKI, H. J., *A Grammar of Politics*, ch. v.
MAINE, H., *Ancient Law*, ch. vi.
MAITLAND, F. W., *Collected Papers*, iii. 321.
NIBOYET, J. P., 20 *Iowa L. R.* (1935), 416.
NOYES, C. R., *Institution of Property*.
POUND, R., *Philosophy of Law*, ch. v.
Property, its Duties and Rights.
RHEINSTEIN, M., 20 *Iowa L. R.* (1935), 431.
ROEDER, M. A., 53 *Harv. L. R.* (1940), 554.
SCOTT, A. W., *Harvard Legal Essays* (ed. R. Pound), 419.
VINDING KRUSE, L. F., *The Right of Property*.
VINOGRADOFF, P., *Historical Jurisprudence*, ii. 197–228.
WEISER, F., *Trusts on the Continent of Europe*.
WESTRUP, C. W., *Introduction to Early Roman Law*, ii. *Joint Family and Family Property*.
WILLIAMS, T. CYPRIAN, 4 *L.Q.R.* (1888), 394.

XXII

THE CONCEPT OF POSSESSION

§ 122. INTRODUCTION

As with most words in the English language, the word 'possession'
has a variety of uses and a variety of meanings. Reference to any
reasonably comprehensive English dictionary provides sufficient
illustration. As a noun from the transitive verb *to possess*, 'possession' is given as: the action or fact of possessing something or of
being possessed. Depending on the context, the lexicographer may
be found to give meanings such as the following: the holding of
something as one's own; actual occupancy as distinguished from
ownership; a territory subject to a sovereign ruler or state; the fact or
action of a demon possessing a person or the fact of being possessed
by a demon; the action of an idea or feeling possessing a person; the
action of keeping oneself under control—as in self-possession.[1] The
lexicographer, in attempting to assign the meaning of the word as
used in English law, may well find himself saying something like the
following: 'The visible possibility of exercising over a thing such
control as attaches to lawful ownership; the detention or enjoyment
of a thing by a person himself or by another in his name; the relation
of a person to a thing over which he may at his pleasure exercise
such control as the character of the thing admits, to the exclusion
of other persons. . . .'[1]

It should be clear at the outset, then, that different meanings may
be ascribed to the word 'possession', depending upon context and
use, and that the search for one 'proper' meaning for the word is
likely to be a fruitless one.[2] It may be objected, however, that it is the
concept of possession in the law that is of interest here, and not the
varied uses to which the word 'possession' may be put in the English
language. It may be, and has been, urged that there is a unitary
concept of possession so far as the law is concerned, and that the
analysis and explanation of that concept is the proper function of

---

[1] *The Shorter Oxford English Dictionary* (3rd ed.), vol. ii, 1550.
[2] 'The term *possession* is always giving rise to trouble. The meaning of possession
depends on the context in which it is being used': per Lord Parker, *Towers & Co. Ltd.*
v. *Gray*, [1961] 2 W.L.R. 553 at 557–8.

jurisprudence. It is not difficult to demonstrate, however, that the search for a unitary concept of possession in the law is one doomed to frustration, if it is assumed that every time the word 'possession' is used in legal reasoning it refers to or names that unitary concept. Further it is not difficult to demonstrate that the example of the lexicographer's definition of possession in the law given above is inadequate, misleading, and that it produces confusion in legal reasoning. Before examining the use either of the word or of the concept or concepts of possession in the law, it is proper to demonstrate that the word and concept are important in many aspects of the law as described or discovered in textbooks, statutes, or judicial pronouncements.

Possession, even without ownership, may have the utmost practical importance. Possession may create ownership, either by *occupatio*[1] (the taking control of a *res nullius*) or by the expiration of a period of acquisitive prescription.[2] Moreover, possession is prima facie evidence of ownership, and he who would disturb a possessor must show either title or a better possessory right. A chimney sweep who finds a ring may not be the owner of the ring, but his possessory right allows him to recover to the value of the stone set in the ring from a jeweller who refuses to return it after it is handed to him for examination.[3] In technical language, the *ius tertii* cannot be pleaded against a possessor. If Jones possesses a car and I, having no title, take it from him, it is no defence for me to prove that Jones is not the true owner. He may be a thief, but whatever the power of the owner to recover the car, Jones's possessory right is superior to mine.

In Roman law one who brought an action for *furtum* had to show that his interest had been honestly secured,[4] but in English law there is no theoretical[5] reason why a thief should not sue a second thief who takes from him the *res* in question, for even a wrongful possession is good against all but the true owner or one claiming through him or one claiming a prior possessory right. Some systems carry their theories so far that in a possessory action title is irrelevant. Thus, if I, as dispossessed owner, retake a chattel, the previous possessor may recover it from me by a possessory action—my only remedy is a real action based on my title. But here the law must effect a

---

[1] *Supra*, § 120.
[2] *Supra*, § 112. To use the language of English law, seisin is a root of title.
[3] *Armory* v. *Delamirie* (1721), 1 Strange 505.　　　　[4] *Dig.* 47. 2. 12. 1.
[5] Obviously in practice the first thief would not desire to call attention to his possession of the *res*.

delicate compromise, which rather confuses the theory of possession. It would be thought absurd in the English world if an owner had no right to retake the purse seized from him or to eject a trespasser who entered his house during his absence. Sometimes the solution is sought in the doctrine that possession seized by violence is not true possession, but this produces internal conflict with what is usually taken to be the central notion of possession, however convenient the result may be in allowing the owner to act effectively.[1] The problem when self-help should be allowable is always a difficult one. English law allows title to chattels to be set up as a defence in a possessory action[2]—if I retake my own chattel, I can defeat the previous holder's action of trespass by proof of my title.

In the light of such difficulties the question 'Why should the law protect possession as such, even though it may have been seized unlawfully?' became a favourite one for jurists and philosophers. Would it not be sufficient to protect only ownership or at least a possession that was lawfully justifiable? Three main reasons for the protection of possession were advanced. Firstly, it aids the criminal law by preserving the peace.[3] Interference with possession almost inevitably invites violence, not only in primitive times but even in the more civilized world of today. Order is best secured by protecting a possessor and leaving the true owner if there is one to seek his remedy in a court of law. Secondly, possession is protected as part of the law of tort. 'These rights of action are given in respect of the immediate and present violation of the possession of the bankrupt independently of his rights of property—they are an extension of that protection which the law throws around the person.'[4] And thirdly, possession is protected as part of the law of property. The law does not always know that the possession in question is unlawful. In times when proof of title was difficult and transfers of property required intricate formalities, it would have been unjust to cast on every man whose possession was disturbed the burden of proving a flawless title. Ihering's doctrine that in most cases possessors are the rightful owners may not be historically accurate, but it is convenient for the law to regard possession as well founded, at least until a superior title

---

[1] *Infra*, § 123.
[2] O. W. Holmes, *The Common Law*, 210. Holmes wrote that this has *always* been the position in English law, but Maitland, *Collected Papers*, i. 426, shows that it was not true in Bracton's time.
[3] Pollock and Maitland, *History of English Law*, ii. 30–46; Holmes, *The Common Law*, ch. vi.   [4] *Rogers* v. *Spence* (1844), 13 M. & W. 571 at 581.

is shown to exist. English law provides illustrations of each of these reasons for the protection of possession. Thus disseisin was regarded as a crime. While an owner who had been wrongfully dispossessed of *land* might retake possession peaceably, the Statutes of Forcible Entry made it an indictable misdemeanour to use force.[1] The tort of trespass turns upon interference with another's possession; but an *owner* is not liable in tort (even if he may be criminally responsible under the Statute referred to) if he uses only reasonable force in retaking his land.[2] So far as recaption of *chattels* is concerned, so long as an owner uses only reasonable force, he is liable neither civilly nor criminally.

The peculiar historical evolution of the English law of property has given increased point to the protection of possession. Ownership in English law may almost be described as the ultimate or best right to possession.[3] Hence 'the law protects seisin because the person seised is owner till someone else proves a better right to seisin; and therefore to ask why the law protects seisin amounts to asking why the law protects ownership'.[4] Possession is a 'root of title', and all possession is regarded as just till it is shown to be otherwise. Whatever may be the case in other systems, no student of English law can neglect the importance of possession, for the learning of seisin and possession covers a great part of the law of property.[5]

Many other speculative questions may be, and have been, pursued with respect to the notion of possession. Is possession limited to the control of material things? Can A possess a fishery? If B pollutes the stream, can A bring trespass, the gist of which is an interference with possession? Roman law at first denied that there could be possession of a mere *ius* such as a servitude, but later writers used the term *quasi-possessio*. English law treated certain incorporeal rights as analogous to possessory rights over material things, provided there was a power of excluding others from the enjoyment of the right.[6] Many theorists would confine the use of the word possession to contexts where material things were involved and, instead of speaking of a possessory right to an *incorporeal res*, would refer to the *de facto* use and enjoyment of the content of a right, without having a legal claim

---

[1] 5 Rich. II, st. 1, c. 7.
[2] *Hemmings* v. *Stoke Poges Golf Club*, [1920] 1 K.B. 720.
[3] *Supra*, § 115.   [4] Holdsworth, *History of English Law*, iii. 95.
[5] The story is well told by Pollock and Maitland, *History of English Law*, ii. 46 et seq.
[6] Pollock and Wright, *Possession*, 35; *Nicholls* v. *Ely Beet Sugar Factory Ltd.*, [1936] Ch. 343 at 347 et seq.

thereto.[1] But the cost of consistency with theory is a clumsy circum-
locution, and the convenience of speaking of possession, e.g. of a
servitude, is so great that the term 'possession' tends to be used more
widely.

It is necessary now to demonstrate that, in spite of the importance
of the general notion of possession as indicated by the brief discussion above, the search for an exhaustive and exclusive definition of
possession along the lines illustrated at the beginning of this chapter
is doomed to failure. Few parts of English law have been so influenced by Roman law doctrines, and in particular, by nineteenth-
century German views on Roman law, as has the law of possession.[2]
The story of the last hundred years or so can be told in terms of a
struggle between convenience and theory—theory seeking to discover
a unitary concept in the interests of consistency and harmony, and
the judges seeking to dispose of particular cases so as to achieve
justice in each case, on the one hand, and to establish rules for the
just disposition of other cases on the other. One thing is clear; and
that is that 'English law has never worked out a completely logical
and exhaustive definition of "possession" '.[3]

§ 123. THE STRUGGLE OF CONVENIENCE AND THEORY

Why should such a notion as possession be surrounded with complexity?[4] One reason is that there is an inevitable and continuing
conflict between the logic of the law and the demands of convenience
in particular cases. Law in its early stages is fluid, and later a theory
is invented as a means of rationalizing decisions that have already
been reached. Many of the fundamental problems of the law of
possession are not clearly examined until the 'classical period' in a
nation's legal history, when analytical genius, discontented with the
law as a collection of rules, attempts to discover a logical structure
around which the rules may be grouped. If such a theory is discovered in the law of possession and wins acceptance, then rules that
cannot be reconciled with it are dubbed 'logical anomalies' or

---

[1] A. H. Campbell, 7 *Camb. L. J.* (1940), 222–3.

[2] O. W. Holmes, *The Common Law*, 206–13.

[3] *U.S.A.* v. *Dollfus Mieg et Cie S.A.*, [1952] A.C. 582 at 605—and see D. R. Harris,
'The Concept of Possession in English Law', *Oxford Essays in Jurisprudence* (1961), 69.
Harris presents the thesis that 'the English decisions preclude us from laying down any
conditions, such as physical control or a certain kind of intention, as absolutely
essential for a judicial ruling that the man possesses something'.

[4] Much of the material in this section was published in 1 *Res Judicatae*, (1935), 187,
and the editor of that journal is thanked for his permission to republish.

'historical exceptions'. The law is not static, however, and the pressures of practice tend to create further exceptions, which sometimes eat away the theory itself. There may even be two or more theories of the law, each battling for supremacy.

In one sense possession began as a fact—the fact of physical control. Before there was law there was possession. That fact could produce consequences. Felix Cohen asked the question, to a student posing as a reasonable wolf in a society consisting of wolves and sheep, 'Now, suppose you had to decide whether to kill a sheep yourself or to take mutton out of the jaws of other wolves who have made a kill. Let's assume, in spite of Kipling, that the wolves are not concerned about law or ethics. What considerations might lead you to respect the first occupancy of your fellow wolves and to go out after your own mutton?'[1]

Whatever it may be possible to say of the pre-law situation,[2] it is clear that, once law arises to protect possession by rules, then its primary concern is with the relations between persons (legal units[3]) in the legal system with respect to things; and not primarily with the relations between persons and things. If this is so then not merely the nature of the thing concerned, and what is done or may be done to it, are important, but also the nature of the person or persons concerned, their relationships *inter se*, and the consequences of the rules provided or of the remedies for their breach. This will be illustrated more fully in a later section.

Without doubt most legal systems have built upon the notion of physical control in developing rules which have the term 'possession' as a necessary part of their expression. The concentration upon the notion of physical control attracted special attention to the relations of persons to things. In the refinement of rules in the development of English law a number of terms came to be accepted, and some clarification of those terms is desirable.

Thus it is said we may have the following relations of a person to a thing:[4]

(*a*) Custody—where the holder either lacks full control or else has

---

[1] *Dialogue on Private Property* (1954), 9 Rutgers L.R. at 386.

[2] And there, even among wolves, it seems likely that no such notion as possession would be necessary merely to describe the relations between a wolf and a thing but would become necessary only when the relations between wolves or the wolf in possession and other predators were to be considered.

[3] See Ch. XVI *supra*.

[4] All writers do not use these terms in the exact sense set down.

no *animus* to exclude others, for example, a customer examining a ring in the presence of the jeweller.[1]

(*b*) Detention—full physical control in fact which for some reason is not regarded as possession in law.

(*c*) Possession—legal possession. In most cases the legal notion of possession is built on the popular notion of physical control, but each legal system has 'anomalous' cases either where a person in full physical control in fact is denied possession in law, or where one who does not have physical control in fact at all is accorded the rights of possession.

(*d*) Ownership.[2]

This table gives a more definite meaning to the terms 'custody' and 'detention' than is usual. Sometimes the two terms are used as synonyms. *Constructive possession* is a phrase that is often used in the books, but there are so many different approaches that the term is best left unused.[3]

As the praetor at Rome began to protect possession, it became necessary to refine the notion. Buckland thinks that in the classical era possession was regarded primarily as a matter of fact, however hard it might be to reconcile this with the artificial notions already springing up. As Paul said: 'The same possession cannot be in two persons any more than you can be considered to stand in the place in which I am standing, or to sit in the place in which I am sitting.'[4] A *captivus* on his return to Roman soil automatically reacquired the rights which he had lost by being taken prisoner, but, since possession was regarded as a matter of fact, it vested in him only when actual control was obtained.[5]

The theory of the nineteenth-century Romanists was mainly concerned with the attempt to discover a logical method of distinguishing between detention and possession. At Rome the possessor had two

---

[1] A person who is given by the owner permission to eat his lunch in a car and listen to the radio is not to be deemed to be in possession of the car, since he was given the key only to open the door and not for the purpose of driving the car: *Hollingsworth* v. *Bean*, [1970] V.R. 819.   [2] *Supra*, § 115.

[3] Salmond, *Jurisprudence* (12th ed.), 276, treats constructive possession as covering those cases where the law grants possession to one who is not in actual physical control. Clerk and Lindsell, *Torts* (11th ed.), 458 n., write that a person has constructive possession: (*a*) when he has lost possession and no one else has acquired it; (*b*) when his servant is in charge of a *res*. Pollock and Wright, *Possession*, 25–7, confine it to cases where there is a mere right to recover possession.

[4] *Dig.* 41. 2. 3. 5. (The translation is that of F. de Zulueta in his edition of *Dig.* 41. 1. and 41. 2. to which the author acknowledges his debt.)

[5] *Dig.* 41. 2. 23 pr. and 1.

practical advantages—he had a right to the protection of the praetor's interdict, and, if he could show good faith and *iusta causa* he could acquire ownership on the expiration of the necessary period of time.[1]

Savigny maintained that the distinction between detention and possession follows from a proper analysis of the latter concept and built his doctrine on Paul's text, '*apiscimur possessionem corpore et animo, neque per se animo aut per se corpore*'.[2] The classical theory, therefore, is that possession is made up of two elements: firstly the *corpus* or element of physical control; secondly the *animus* or intent with which such control is exercised. Savigny thought that since the detentor and possessor have the same physical relation to the *res*, the differences between them must be found in the mental element. The intent, which distinguishes a possessor, is the *animus domini*—the desire to hold for oneself and not on behalf of another. This theory explains why the tenant, the borrower, and the agent did not have possession in Roman law, for they did not intend to hold in their own right. The compilers of the *Digest* seem to have emphasized the importance of the element of *animus*—indeed some of the texts seem to go to extraordinary lengths.[3] On the other hand, Savigny's theory was faced with the difficulty that in certain cases Roman law gave a non-owner possessory rights:[4] these examples Savigny explained away as anomalies which he termed instances of derivative possession.

Ihering adopts a more objective theory. 'A man possesses who is, in relation to the thing, in the position in which an owner of such things ordinarily is, *animus* being merely an intelligent consciousness of the fact.'[5] Ihering's theory can explain exactly those cases which Savigny found difficult, but, on the other hand, it cannot account for those cases where the law refuses possessory rights to those who are in effective physical control. The anomaly on his view is that not every detentor is a possessor and he seeks to explain these 'exceptions'.[6]

---

[1] The Romanists talk of: (*a*) *detentio* or *possessio naturalis*; (*b*) *possessio* or *possessio civilis* which was hardly distinguishable from *possessio ad interdicta*; (*c*) *possessio ad usucapionem*. But the terminology is by no means fixed. A complication is introduced by the fact that the praetor would protect only possession that had been acquired in certain lawful ways—*nec vi, nec clam, nec precario*.   [2] *Dig.* 41. 2. 3. 1.

[3] Whether these references to *animus* are interpolated or not is another question. Paul, in particular, emphasizes the element of *animus*.

[4] e.g. the pledgee, precarist, the stake-holder, and one who held under *emphyteuta*.

[5] Buckland, *Text-Book of Roman Law* (2nd ed.), 198, summarizing the theory of Ihering. Savigny's theory triumphed in the first draft of the German Civil Code, but in the final draft the term 'possession' was applied even to those who held for another, and the distinction between mediate and immediate possession was introduced.

[6] e.g. he argued that many tenants in the early days were probably of servile status. See E. Ehrlich, *Fundamental Principles of the Sociology of Law*, 381.

Does Paul's analysis of *animus* and *corpus* satisfactorily explain the law? Holdsworth thought that, in addition, Roman law required a cause or special reason why possession should be protected, the exact limits of possession varying with the needs of the moment; 'but unfortunately for the interpretation of (Roman) texts, they have fallen into the hands of German legal philosophers, who have constructed from them logical theories which never wholly fit the actual rules, because those rules were, like the rules of English law, made to fit the illogical facts of life.'[1] Some of these complicating factors are now discussed.

(*a*) Firstly, in Roman law the notion that proprietary capacity was essential to possession became firmly established and this cut across the notion of possession as mere physical control. The rule that those in the *potestas* of another could not possess led to a certain divorce between actual control and legal possession, thus creating confusion in the texts.[2] A master possessed what was held by his slave, the theoretical solution being that the master had the *animus* and the slave provided the *corpus*. Since the slave was himself possessed by the master, it was not a very violent extension to say that the master possessed a *res* in the hands of a slave who was himself possessed.[3] But as acquisition through a slave became more and more common, it became inconvenient to require the master to have a specific *animus* directed to every *res*,[4] and it was laid down that the master possessed whatever was acquired by the slave in connection with the *peculium*. As acquisition through those not within the bonds of the family was gradually allowed, convenience dictated an even broader rule and so some texts boldly state that the agent provided both *animus* and *corpus*.[5] This was a case where the classical rule was almost eaten away by exceptions.

(*b*) Secondly, we note the influence of the mode of acquisition of possession on the concept of possession itself. If it is assumed that the essence of possession is control, the question whether possession has been lawfully acquired or not may be relevant when the law considers whether it should protect that control, but, if we are determining

---

[1] *History of English Law*, vii. 467.
[2] Paul, h.t. 1. 4, writes that a wife possesses what was given to her by her husband, although the gift was forbidden by law since a *matter of fact* cannot be invalidated by law. Ulpian, h.t. 29, illustrates the two views.
[3] Paul, h.t. 3. 12.
[4] The early rule required either previous authorization or subsequent ratification by the master.
[5] Cf. h.t. 34. 1.

whether the taker has in reality acquired possession, the lawfulness of its inception should be irrelevant. The thief acquires possession, although his taking is a crime. In practice, however, there is an inevitable tendency for 'the right to possession to acquire importance at the expense of possession itself'[1]—'possession borrows a great deal from right . . . possession is not merely a matter of physical fact but also of right'.[2] At Rome one of the most important practical results of possession was the protection afforded by the interdict of the praetor. The praetor laid down that he would not protect the possession of one who had acquired it *vi, clam aut precario*. According to logical analysis one who takes by force or steals secretly acquires possession; but, since the praetor would not protect such a holding, there was a tendency, instead of saying that the praetor would protect only certain forms of possession, to limit the definition of possession itself to control which had not commenced in certain unlawful ways. This was an illogical, though convenient, policy. Ulpian considered that one who has lost possession by violence should be considered as still in possession.[3] If my house is seized in my absence, I retain possession until I know of the intrusion and have had a reasonable time in which to eject the trespasser.[4] Clearly this doctrine cannot be carried too far or possession would mean only control that has been lawfully acquired. The strict doctrine is that of Gaius that any loss of *corpus* involved loss of possession. To reconcile the texts, we can only suppose that Gaius' doctrine was applied to movables and that, where immovables were concerned, the rules were broadly interpreted for the benefit of the owner. In the post-classical era, if a third party seized land held by a tenant the owner did not lose possession until he was aware of the intrusion and had failed within a reasonable time to assert his rights.[5]

Just as the law weights the dice against one who has seized secretly

---

[1] Pollock and Wright, *Possession*, 83.
[2] Papinian, *Dig.* 41. 2. 49 pr. and 1.　　　　　　　　　　　[3] h.t. 17 pr.
[4] Ulpian, h.t. 6. 1. Cf. *Browne* v. *Dawson* (1840), 12 A. & E. 624, where a schoolmaster after dismissal broke into, and held control of, his old rooms for eleven days, but it was held that nevertheless he had not acquired possession. Cf. Maitland, *Collected Papers*, i. 456: 'Practically for the last three hundred years and more, theoretically as well as practically for the last fifty years and more, we have had no action in which an ejected possessor could recover possession from the owner who ejected him: certainly this is a fact which deserves the consideration of all who are troubled with theories of possession' (written in 1888).
[5] The classical view was that the owner supplied the *animus* and the tenant the *corpus* and therefore that loss of *corpus* entailed loss of possession: Africanus, *Dig.* 41. 2. 40. 1; Paul, h.t. 3. 8; Pomponius, h.t. 25. 1; Buckland, *Main Institutions of Roman Law*, 111.

or by force, so it favours one who takes lawfully; even if we regard control as a pure matter of fact, one whose holding is lawful is less likely to be disturbed than one who has no title. Where one has a right to enter, entry into any part of the house gives possession of the whole, whereas the possession of a trespasser extends no further than it does in fact.[1] '*De facto* as well as *de iure* there is much to be presumed in favour of him who comes by title, nothing for him who comes by wrong.'[2]

(c) Thirdly, what may be called the legal concept of inertia plays its part. If possession is once proved to exist, it is assumed to continue until it is ended either by abandonment on the part of the owner, or by seizure by another. Savigny considered that possession continued only so long as physical power to deal with the *res* could be reproduced at any moment.[3] If all power to enjoy, now or in the future, is lost, possession ceases—e.g. if a ring is dropped into the sea. But a London citizen retains possession of his house even while he is absent in Paris, for he may return at will. Holmes suggests, however, that Savigny's statement is rather too absolutely phrased and gives the following example. The finder of a purse leaves it at his country house, while he languishes behind the bars of a prison. English law at least would treat him as in possession, even though he could not reproduce his physical power of enjoyment at the moment. If a burglar began to break in, the finder would be in possession until the thief had actually seized the purse.[4]

Roman law sometimes referred to these cases as being possession held *animo solo*. The possession of summer pastures was held to be retained *animo solo* during the winter, and the jurists went even further than Holmes in the example just cited, for they considered that seizure by a stranger did not end the possession of the previous holder until he was excluded on his return or acquiesced in the trespass.[5] Paul in one text writes that, since both *animus* and *corpus* are necessary for possession, both must disappear before possession is lost.[6] This, however, cannot be accepted as a general rule. If possession is lost merely by consent of the holder, then the notion of possession would not be that which we understand it to be. Apart from the exceptions introduced for convenience, the true rule is that

---

[1] Pollock and Wright, *Possession*, 79. Cf. Paul, h.t. 3. 1, and Celsus, h.t. 18. 4.
[2] Pollock and Wright, op. cit. 62.
[3] Savigny on *Possession* (trans. Perry), 253–4, citing Paul, h.t. 3. 13.
[4] *The Common Law*, 237–8. *Wuta-Ofei* v. *Danquah* (J.C.), [1961] 3 All E.R. 596.
[5] Pomponius, h.t. 25. 2.   [6] h.t. 8.

loss of *corpus* involves loss of possession, whether the owner is aware of it or not. But is mere change of *animus* enough? Do I cease to possess the forged banknote in my pocket, merely because I think that I have thrown it away, when in reality I have thrown away a true note? Where the physical control is reduced to vanishing point, or exists only by a fiction of the law, a mere change of *animus* may be sufficient (e.g. a determination not to return to the summer pastures). But where there is real physical control, English law would normally require loss of that control before possession was regarded as ending.[1] The law is seeking a convenient solution of practical problems and does not make too sharp a separation of *corpus* and *animus*.

Just as the notion of *corpus* is modified for convenience, so is that of *animus*. The classical analysis would require a specific *animus* directed to the *res* in question and some Roman texts approve this doctrine—the possessor of land does not possess the treasure buried in the land, unless he is aware of its existence.[2]

§ 124. ILLUSTRATIVE CASES AND RULES

To see how the common law stands, in the light of the theories influenced by the Roman law, it is necessary to review briefly some illustrative cases. These fall conveniently into separate groups.

Larceny cases

Larceny, of course, requires—(a) a taking—'without a claim of right made in good faith', (b) and the carrying away of something capable of being stolen, (c) without the consent of the owner, (d) and with the intent, at the time of such taking, permanently to deprive the owner thereof (the owner here includes any 'part-owner, or person having possession or control of, or a special property in, anything capable of being stolen').[3] The legislative form provided by the Larceny Act, 1916, was not intended to change the common law of larceny, but merely to consolidate it. Traditionally larceny had turned upon a notion of taking possession unlawfully and at the time of such taking to intend permanently to deprive the person entitled to possession of the thing concerned.[4]

---

[1] There is some authority for the view that possession cannot be lost even by wilful abandonment. See Pollock and Wright, *Possession*, 124, and *Johnstone & Wilmot Pty. Ltd.* v. *Kaine*, [1928] 23 Tas. L.R. 43.   [2] Paul, h.t. 3. 3.

[3] The Larceny Act, 1916, § 1; 6 & 7 Geo. V, c. 50.

[4] The Theft Act, 1968, has modified the law, but the old cases throw light on the theory of possession.

Reg. v. *Riley*[1]

In this well-known case the accused drove off amongst his own lambs, but without knowing it, a lamb belonging to the prosecutor. After he had discovered the error he sold the lamb with his own. He was convicted of larceny. The court rationalized the decision by relying on a notion of 'continuing trespass' based on the ground that the accused had undoubtedly made himself liable in trespass when he first drove off the lamb even though he did not know that he had the lamb at the time.

R. v. *Ashwell*[2]

In this case the accused had asked the prosecutor to lend him a shilling. In a poor light the prosecutor pulled from his pocket what he thought was a shilling and handed it to the accused. Later the accused discovered that he had been given a sovereign by mistake, but he none the less spent the sovereign and thereby converted it. He was convicted of larceny of the sovereign. In the last resort the conviction was affirmed by an equally divided Court for Crown Cases Reserved consisting of fourteen judges. The conviction involved a decision that the accused did not take possession of the sovereign until he knew it was a sovereign, although the judges who so held gave different reasons for saying that he had not taken possession until that time—at which time he took it *animo furandi.*

R. v. *Moore*[3]

The prisoner had picked up and converted to his own use a bank note which had been dropped on the floor of his shop. He converted the bank note in spite of the fact that he knew the owner of it could be found. It was held that he was rightly convicted of larceny—that is, that he had not obtained possession of the note while it was lying on the floor of his shop before he had discovered it, and further that the owner's possession was in some way extended, at least fictionally, after he had lost the note in the accused's shop.

Merry v. *Green*[4]

An action for assault and false imprisonment—the defence was that the assault and imprisonment were justified because the plaintiff had committed larceny. The relevant facts were that the plaintiff had purchased a bureau at an auction and subsequently discovered a purse in a secret drawer. The purse contained money and other valuables. The plaintiff appropriated that property to his own use. At first instance the plaintiff obtained judgment in his favour. On appeal the matter was sent back for a new trial because it was not clear from the evidence just what the terms

---

[1] (1853), Dears. 149.   [2] (1885), 16 Q.B.D. 190.
[3] (1861), Le. & Ca. 1.   [4] (1841), 7 M. & W. 623.

of sale of the bureau had been. In his judgment Baron Parke laid it down that if the auctioneer had sold the bureau with express notice that the purchaser was not gaining title to the contents of it, if there happened to be any, then the plaintiff's appropriation of the purse and other valuables could constitute larceny—that is to say that the mere delivery of the bureau did not necessarily carry with it delivery of possession of its contents, at least if it was made clear that the contents were not being sold with the bureau.

Cartwright v. Green[1]

A bureau was delivered to a carpenter for repairs. The carpenter discovered money in a secret drawer which he appropriated to his own use. It was held that he committed larceny by feloniously taking the money into his possession. In this case of course the carpenter was merely a bailee of the bureau but none the less by the ordinary rules would be held to have possession of it. It follows from the decision that he did not obtain possession of the money when he obtained possession of the bureau, but only at the time he discovered it and wrongfully formed the intention to convert it to his own use.

R. v. Rowe[2]

The accused had taken pieces of iron which he found on the bed of a canal when the canal was drained of water. The iron had fallen overboard from barges. The accused was convicted of larceny of the iron from the company which owned the canal—that it to say that the company had had possession of the iron merely because it was resting upon the company's land.

R. v. Hudson[3]

By mistake a department of the government posted the accused a letter in which was a cheque intended for someone else. The accused appropriated the cheque to his own use and it was held that he was guilty of larceny. Although the accused had received possession of the letter innocently, the view taken was that he could not have been said to have acquired possession of the cheque until he was aware of its existence and at the time he became aware of its existence he took it *animus furandi*.

Possession of drugs

Warner v. Metropolitan Police Commissioner[4]

The appellant collected two boxes which had been left for him at a café, and when he was stopped by the police, one of the boxes was found to

[1] (1802), 8 Ves. 405.   [2] (1859), 1 Bell. 93.
[3] [1943] K.B. 458.   [4] [1969] 2 A.C. 256.

contain drugs. His defence was that he thought both boxes contained scent. Clearly the accused had physical control of both boxes. The argument turned therefore on the *animus* necessary to constitute possession—must the accused be aware that drugs were in the box?

(*a*) At Quarter Sessions it was considered that mere control of the box was enough.

(*b*) Lord Morris in the House of Lords admitted that some *animus* was necessary. If a stranger hides something in your stable without your knowledge, you are not in possession of it:[1] but the appellant was in possession of the contents of the box, although he did not know precisely what they were. Lord Guest agreed, basing an argument on policy. It would be too difficult to secure conviction if the Crown had to prove specific knowledge of the contents. 'I am unable to see how, if I know that I have a parcel in my possession, I am not also in possession of its contents.'

(*c*) Lords Reid, Pearce, and Wilberforce required a more specific *animus*. 'Could it be right that if the appellant had taken possession of the parcel of scent and thereafter the drugs had been slipped in without his knowledge, he would be innocent . . . but that if the drugs had been slipped in without his knowledge before he took possession then he would be guilty?' This was the approach of Lord Reid. Lord Pearce stated: '. . . the difference between scent and tablets is a sufficient difference in kind to entitle the accused to an acquittal if on the whole of the evidence it appears that he may have genuinely believed that the parcel contained scent, and that he may not have had any suspicion that there was anything illicit in the parcel and that he had no opportunity of verifying its contents.'

Hibbert v. *McKiernan*[2]

The appellant had been convicted for the larceny of golf balls, the property of the secretary and members of a golf club. He had taken the golf balls, which had been abandoned by their original owners, while he was trespassing on the golf links owned by the members of the golf club. It was held that the appellant had been rightly convicted—that is to say that the golf balls he had taken had been, at the time of his taking, in the possession of the secretary and members of the club although no one knew where they were or how many balls might be at any time lying abandoned on the various parts of the links.

Ruse v. *Read*[3]

The respondent had been acquitted of larceny in the following circumstances. He had, while drunk, taken a bicycle from a public place, and it

---

[1] This seems to be one of the two points on which there was unanimity: the other was that, although there was misdirection of the jury, the appeal was dismissed as no reasonable jury could have accepted the appellant's story.

[2] [1948] 2 K.B. 142.   [3] [1949] 1 K.B. 377.

was accepted at first instance that at the time of taking he had no larcenous intent. When sober he found he had the bicycle and panicked. He consigned it by rail to a non-existent person at a railway station some distance away. The magistrates had held that he had no intention of permanently depriving the owner of his property and was incapable of forming such an intention at the time of taking the bicycle. On appeal it was held that the original taking of the bicycle had been a trespass and, although not then felonious, the subsequent misappropriation of the machine on the following day amounted to larceny and the respondent should have been convicted. *R. v. Riley* (*supra*) was followed.

R. v. Harding[1]

The Court of Criminal Appeal upheld a conviction for larceny of a mackintosh from the servant of the person who would, for other purposes, have certainly been held to be not only the owner but the possessor of the mackintosh. It was held that the servant had a 'special property' in the mackintosh so that she could properly be named as the prosecutor in a case of larceny.

Rose v. Matt[2]

The respondent, when purchasing some goods, deposited a clock which he owned, with the vendor, as security for the price of the goods he was purchasing. It was agreed between them that the vendor would be entitled to sell the clock if the respondent did not pay for the goods within one month. The respondent later returned to the vendor's shop and took the clock without paying the price of the goods. On appeal it was held that the respondent should have been convicted of larceny.

The finding cases

In all these cases the issues are civil and not criminal ones, and are between two of more persons claiming to be entitled to the benefits of possessory enjoyment of a chattel—the assumption being that, if there is a true owner, he cannot be found.

Bridges v. Hawkesworth[3]

The plaintiff found a parcel of notes on the floor of the defendant's shop. It was held that the plaintiff had acquired a good title to them, as against the defendant, as he was the first to acquire possession of the notes. The defendant had not previously acquired possession because he had not known of the notes' existence until after they were found by the plaintiff.

---

[1] (1929), 21 Cr. App. R. 166.   [2] [1951] 1 K.B. 810.
[3] (1851), 21 L.J.Q.B. 75.

Elwes v. *Brigg Gas Co.*[1]

The plaintiff, a tenant for life in possession, had leased an area of land to the defendant company for the purpose of erecting gas works. In the lease all mines and minerals were reserved to the lessor. The lessor retained certain supervisory rights over the gasholders and other structures to be built by the defendant company. In the course of the defendant company's excavation of the land a prehistoric boat was found some six feet below the surface. It was held that the plaintiff was entitled to the boat as against the tenant company. The judgment is an unsatisfactory one in that it does not make clear which of several possible grounds for the decision is the one to be relied on. It does, however, assert clearly enough that the plaintiff was in possession of the boat for one reason or another before it was found by the defendant company, and that it made 'no difference' in these circumstances that the plaintiff was not aware of the existence of the boat.[2]

South Staffordshire Water Company v. Sharman[3]

Sharman was employed by the plaintiffs to clean out a pool on land owned and occupied by the plaintiffs. He found certain gold rings in the mud at the bottom of the pool. It was held that the plaintiff company was in first possession of the rings, and that Sharman therefore had acquired no possessory title to them as against the plaintiff.

Willey v. Synan[4]

The boatswain of a ship found some coins on board during the voyage. When the ship arrived at port the coins were delivered to the collector of customs. In an action against the collector by the boatswain who found the coins, it was held that the boatswain had not made out his claim. On appeal two members of the court were prepared to hold[5] that the boatswain had never had possession of the coins because he had found them in the course of his employment and his finding of them put them in the possession of his employers.[6]

Hannah v. Peel[7]

The plaintiff, a soldier, found a brooch in a house where he was billeted. The house had been requisitioned at the beginning of the 1939–45 war and, it may be supposed, both at the time of and for some time before the finding of the brooch the house was in the possession of the Crown. The Crown made no claim to the brooch. The defendant was the owner of the house but he had never gone into physical occupation of it before it was

---

[1] (1886), 33 Ch. D. 562.   [2] At 568–9.   [3] (1896), 2 Q.B. 44.
[4] (1936), 57 C.L.R. 200.   [5] Rich and Dixon JJ.
[6] And see *McDowell* v. *Ulster Bank* (1899), 33 Ir. L.T. 225.
[7] [1945] 1 K.B. 509.

requisitioned for the army. It was held that the plaintiff was entitled to
the brooch as against the defendant, the owner of the house—that is, the
owner of the house had never been in possession of the brooch before it
was found. In the course of the judgment stress was laid on the two points:

(*a*) that the brooch was on the surface and was not embedded in the
land, and

(*b*) that the owner of the house had never at any stage gone into physical
occupation of it before the brooch was found.

Grafstein v. Holme & Freeman[1]

An employee of a storekeeper found a locked box in the basement
rubbish of the store premises. He brought the box to his employer who
told him to put it aside on a shelf. Some two years later the employee
opened the box and found that it contained some $38,000 in bank notes.
It was held that the employer was entitled to the money, as against the
employee who had found it, on the basis that the employer had, when the
finding of the box had been communicated to him, taken lawful possession
not only of the box but also of its contents. His possession of the money
therefore was prior to any claim to possession that the finder may have
made arising out of his discovery of the contents after opening the box.
It is significant that the court came to this conclusion expressly without
relying on any arguments which turned upon the master-and-servant
relationship involved.

Armory v. Delamirie[2]

The plaintiff, a chimney-sweep's boy, found a jewel and took it to a goldsmith to find out what it was. The goldsmith refused to return it to him.
It was held that as against the goldsmith the plaintiff was entitled to the
jewel and he could maintain an action of trover against the defendant
goldsmith.

Cases where possession follows title

It has already been noted that a person in possession is deemed to
be the owner of the thing possessed save as against a person who can
show a better title or who claims under a better title. Cases like
R. v. Rowe, Hibbert v. McKiernan, Elwes v. Brigg Gas Co., and *South
Staffordshire Water Co. v. Sharman*[3] show that a person may be held
to be in possession of a chattel merely because it is on land owned
and occupied (possessed) by him.[4] It is clear of course that those

---

[1] (1958), 12 D.L.R. (2nd) 727.   [2] (1721), 1 Strange 505.
[3] All noted *supra*.   [4] Cf. *Hannah v. Peel (supra)*.

cases rest upon a presumption, for it is obvious that the mere owner-ship and occupancy or possession of land does not necessarily carry with it the possession of chattels upon that land. If I drive my motor car upon the land of a friend possession of it does not pass to him while it is on his land. All those cases attribute possession to the owner of the land merely on the presumed non-existence of anyone with a better claim who, depending upon the circumstances, may have had and retained possession of it. Just as title may be attributed on the basis of possession, so may possession be attributed on the basis of title, and the following cases illustrate the kinds of relation-ships which may be involved.

In re Cohen[1]

Cohen and his wife had lived in a flat which was owned by the wife. After they both had died, a large sum of money was discovered hidden in various parts of the flat. There was no evidence as to the origin of the money, or as to when, or by whom, or for what purpose the money had been secreted. It was held that the lawful possession of the money must be attributed to the wife as the owner and one of the occupiers of the premises on which it was found, and that as between the estate of the husband and the estate of the wife it must be treated, therefore, as having been the property not of the husband but of the wife.

Ramsay v. Margrett[2]

In this case a wife agreed to buy from her husband some furniture and other chattels which were in the house occupied by both of them. She paid the purchase price agreed upon and her husband signed a receipt acknow-ledging the sale. The chattels concerned were not in any way moved from the positions in the house which they had previously occupied. In an action between the wife and an execution creditor of her husband's, it was held that the wife had possession of the goods (at least so far as the Bills of Sale Act, 1878, was concerned), that the situation of the goods was consistent with their being in the possession of either the husband or the wife and the law attributed possession to the wife who had legal title to them.

French v. Gething[3]

Furniture was given, by deed, by a husband to his wife, but remained in the matrimonial home undisturbed. A third person recovered judgment

---

[1] [1953] Ch. 88. Cf. *Moffatt* v. *Kazana*, [1968] 3 All E.R. 271; *Corporation of London* v. *Appleyard*, [1963] 2 All E.R. 834.
[2] [1894] 2 Q.B. 18.   [3] [1922] 1 K.B. 236.

against the husband and seized the furniture on a writ of execution against the husband alone. Under the Bills of Sale Act, 1878, a deed of gift, if the husband remained in possession of the furniture, was nothing more than an unregistered bill of sale and hence invalid. If the goods, on the other hand, were in possession of the wife then the judgment creditor would not be able to attach them. It was held that as the wife was the legal owner of the furniture, in the circumstances, she was the possessor of it also.

Landlord and tenant

It is trite law that it is essential to the creation of a tenancy of a corporeal hereditament that the tenant should have the right to the exclusive possession of the premises concerned.[1] A tenancy relationship between landlord and tenant may be brought to an end in a number of ways other than by the mere expiration of the term. If the tenant surrenders possession to the landlord and that surrender is accepted, then the tenancy is at an end.[2] It should be noted it is not merely the right to possession but the delivery of possession itself that is comprehended by the rule and that only if the surrender of possession is accepted by the landlord does it work a surrender of the lease itself.[3] The tests of just what would be held to constitute an actual change of possession from tenant to landlord were the subject of litigation on a number of occasions and, *inter alia*, it was held that if the tenant returns the keys of the premises concerned and if the landlord accepts them with the intention of accepting and taking possession, then possession was effectively transferred.[4] But it was held that the landlord's consent to the delivery of the keys was essential to enable such a method of transferring possession to be treated as effective in law.[5] The central notion behind these cases was that the landlord had to be shown to be accepting and taking physical control over the premises once more to the exclusion of the tenant.

Under the early Rent Restrictions Acts in England[6] rents were controlled and the rights of landlords to evict tenants were restricted. If the landlord came into or obtained possession of premises which were controlled under that legislation, then the controls no longer applied. It was provided that the expression 'possession' should be

---

[1] H. A. Hill and J. H. Redman's *Law of Landlord and Tenant* (13th ed.), 11.
[2] Ibid. 473.
[3] *Cannan* v. *Hartley* (1850), 9 C.B. 634, n. (*a*).
[4] *Dodd* v. *Acklom* (1843), 6 Man. & G. 672; *Natchbolt* v. *Porter* (1689), 2 Vern. 112.
[5] *Cannan* v. *Hartley* (*supra*) at 648; *Furnivall* v. *Grove* (1860), 8 C.B. (N.S.), 496.
[6] See the Rent and Mortgage Interest Restrictions Act, 1923, 13 & 14 Geo. V, c. 32.

construed as meaning 'actual possession'. There are several reported cases concerned with the application of those provisions.[1]

Thomas v. *Metropolitan Housing Corporation Ltd.*[2]

It was held that the landlord had regained 'actual possession' when the tenant had dropped the key of the leased premises into the letter box at the office of the landlord's agent—even though the office was closed for the week.[3]

The case of *Wrightson* v. *McArthur and Hutchisons (1919) Ltd.*[4] provides an interesting comparison.

Certain goods, being set aside by the defendant as security for debt, were locked in a room in premises owned by and in the possession of the defendants and the key to that room was given to the plaintiff. It was held that on delivery of the key possession of the goods passed to the plaintiff and was subsequently retained by him although the goods remained upon the premises possessed by the defendants.[5]

Bailment

Bailment is a transaction that is *sui generis*. It often arises out of a contract, and in such a case the contractual terms may be all important—but analytically it falls under the heading of property. In the law of real property we distinguish between a contract which creates rights *in personam* and a conveyance which creates rights *in rem*. In the law of personal property the distinction is rather blurred, as the contract itself may transfer title. Bailment is really a transfer of an interest in property—the extent of that interest will depend on the nature of the bailment. In the gratuitous bailment revocable at will, the bailee's rights are subject to the pleasure of the bailor: in pledge, the pledgee has the right to retain the *res* till the debt is paid.[6]

---

[1] See e.g. *Jewish Maternity Society's Trustees* v. *Garfinkle* (1926), 42 T.L.R. 589; *Thomas* v. *Metropolitan Housing Corporation Ltd.*, [1936] 1 All E.R. 210; *Holt* v. *Dawson*, [1940] 1 K.B. 46; *Goodier* v. *Cooke*, [1940] 2 All E.R. 533. But note that the sections concerned were repealed by the Increase of Rent and Mortgage Interest (Restrictions) Act, 1938, § 3, and the Rent and Mortgage Interest Restrictions Act, 1939, § 2, Schedule 2.

[2] *Supra.*

[3] See the full discussion of these cases in Dias and Hughes, *Jurisprudence*, 316–21.

[4] [1921] 2 K.B. 807.

[5] Cf. *Ancona* v. *Rogers* (1876), 1 Ex. D. 285.

[6] Winfield, *Province of the Law of Tort*, 97.

That the bailee has a proprietary interest may be seen from the following considerations:

(a) Historically the bailee exercised nearly all the rights of ownership and as late as Blackstone it was thought that the bailor had only a chose in action.[1]

(b) The bailee has the remedies of trespass and trover against third parties, at least where the bailment is for a fixed term.[2]

(c) The bailee cannot at common law commit larceny of the *res* bailed,[3] and in some circumstances the owner may be guilty of larceny by taking the *res* from the bailee with intent to defraud.[4]

(d) The bailee has an insurable interest.

(e) Some bailees, such as the pledgee, have a common law (and in some cases statutory) right to sell on default.

(f) The common carrier, the innkeeper, and the artificer have a common law lien—which is a proprietary right.

Subject to the rights of the bailee the bailor retains his interest and the bailor may recover the *res*, even though the contract of bailment was illegal, provided that the bailor 'does not seek, and is not forced, either to found his claim on the illegal contract, or to plead its illegality in order to support his claim'.[5]

In the last resort bailment rests on possession and upon the distinction between possession and title. Any person is to be considered as a bailee who otherwise than as a servant either receives possession of a thing from another or consents to receive or hold possession of a thing for another upon an undertaking with the other person either to keep and return or deliver to him the specific thing or to (convey and) apply the specific thing according to directions antecedent or future of the other person.[6] It is important to remember that the gratuitous bailee at will, being in possession, may avail himself of possessory remedies such as trespass but that the bailor may also

---

[1] 2 *Comm.*, 453. J. B. Ames supported this view: 3 *Harv. L. R.* (1890), 313 at 345. This view is now rejected: *Bristol and West of England Bank* v. *Midland Rly. Co.*, [1891] 2 Q.B. 653.

[2] *Lotan* v. *Cross* (1810), 2 Camp. 464—*aliter* for gratuitous bailment at will.

[3] There is the exception of breaking bulk laid down in the *Carrier's Case* (1473), 64 Selden Society, 30. The other exceptions, based on fraud, really depend on the principle that fraud may negative the owner's consent to the passing of the property—this is based on the doctrine that no bailment is created.

[4] *R.* v. *Wilkinson* (1821), R. & R. 470; *Rose* v. *Matt*, [1951] 1 K.B. 810.

[5] *Bowmakers Ltd.* v. *Barnet Instruments Ltd.*, [1945] K.B. 65 at 71. This decision raises difficulties which are discussed by C. J. Hamson, 10 *Camb. L. J.* (1949), 249.

[6] Pollock and Wright, *Possession*, 163. And see G. W. Paton, *Bailment in the Common Law* (1952).

avail himself of those remedies although he is not in possession but has merely a right to possession.

Miscellaneous cases

Ancona v. Rogers[1]

Goods owned by A were put by her agent in rooms in the house of B—with B's permission. The rooms were locked by A's agent and he took away the key. It was held that A was in possession of the rooms.

The Tubantia[2]

A salvage company had located and marked a wreck with buoys, and had spent large sums diving and cutting open the holds of the sunken ship. Work was suspended during the winter, to be resumed in the summer. The company was held to be in possession of the wreck.

Young v. Hichens[3]

Plaintiff had drawn his sean and net around a large number of fish but had left an opening of about forty feet which he was about to close with a 'stop' net. He had two boats in the opening with men splashing the water to frighten the fish away from the opening. It was held that at that stage of the operation the plaintiff had not reduced the fish into his possession.

Moors v. Burke[4]

Where legislation[5] provided that if any person is in actual possession of goods suspected of being stolen that person may be . . . etc., the facts were that Burke, who was employed on the wharves where he had the right to use a clothes locker, was found to have goods suspected of being stolen in his locker. He was held not to be in 'actual possession' of the goods because he shared the locker with another and so could not be said to have exclusive control of the goods concerned while they were in the locker.

Sloan v. McGowan[6]

Some trunks were deposited by the defendant in a warehouse for storage. The trunks contained goods which were suspected of being stolen. The trunks were locked and the defendant had retained the keys. The storeroom where they were contained goods deposited by other persons as well. It was held that the defendant was not in actual possession of the trunks within the meaning of the section of the Police Offences Act referred to in the previous case.

[1] (1876), 1 Ex. D. 285.   [2] [1924] P. 78.
[3] (1844), 6 Q.B. 606, 115 E.R. 228.   [4] (1919), 26 C.L.R. 265.
[5] Police Offences Act, 1915 (Victoria), § 40.   [6] [1926] V.L.R. 227.

Johnson v. *Kennedy*[1]

Some wheat suspected of being stolen was found on premises jointly occupied by a husband and wife. The wife claimed that some of the wheat was hers and the husband claimed the remainder. It was not clear which wheat was claimed by either. It was held that neither husband nor wife was shown to be in 'actual possession' of the wheat, or any part of it, within the meaning of the Police Offences Act section referred to above.

M'Attee v. *Hogg*[2]

Section 21 of the Salmon Fisheries (Scotland) Act, 1868, made any person who buys, sells, or exposes for sale, or has in his 'possession' salmon taken within a particular time, liable to a penalty. 'The allegation ... is that these men were in possession of certain fish at a time when it was illegal to have them in possession. Of that they were convicted. . . . Take this case: Suppose five men went down together to the river to take fish and caught two, and were met when on the way up with the fish, would not all five men be in possession of the fish although some of them may never have touched them? They certainly would.' Per the Lord Justice-Clerk (Lord MacDonald), at p. 69.[3]

Collector of Customs (*N.S.W.*) v. *Southern Shipping Co. Ltd.*[4]

A consignment of tobacco was delivered to the defendant company for shipment out of the State of New South Wales. The defendant put the tobacco in a store, on the wharf from which shipment would be made, owned by the Maritime Services Board. The store was locked and the keys were lodged in the customs office which was itself locked overnight—so that the keys to the store were not available to the defendant except in an emergency. During the night (of Easter Saturday/Sunday) the store was broken open and the tobacco was stolen. Sec. 60 (1) of the Excise Act 1901–52 (C'wealth) casts certain liabilities upon persons who have . . . 'the possession, custody or control of excisable goods' . . . It was held (*inter alia*) that defendant did not lose possession of the tobacco when it was locked in the store and the keys locked in the customs office.

From those illustrative cases and rules, a surprising number of propositions about possession can be extracted—for example:

(i) Possession of a chattel is not acquired when mere physical control is taken; such acquisition waits upon knowledge by the taker of the nature of the thing acquired: see e.g. *R.* v. *Ashwell*; *R.* v. *Hudson*.

---

[1] [1922] V.L.R. 481.   [2] (1903), 5 F. (Ct. of Sess.) 67.
[3] Quoted by Burrows, *Words and Phrases Judicially Defined* (1944), iv. 309.
[4] (1962), 36 Aust. L.J.R. 15 (High Court of Australia).

(ii) The owner and possessor of land may be in possession of a chattel on his land in spite of the fact that he does not know the nature of the thing or even that it exists: see e.g. *Elwes* v. *Brigg Gas Co.*; *R.* v. *Rowe*; *South Staffordshire Water Co.* v. *Sharman.*

(iii) The owner and possessor of a shop is not in possession of chattels on the floor of his shop until he knows of their presence there: see e.g. *R.* v. *Moore*; *Bridges* v. *Hawkesworth.*

(iv) The owner of a house, who may well have been in possession of the house for the purpose of taking action against a trespasser, may not be in possession of a chattel found on the premises if he has never physically occupied the house: *Hannah* v. *Peel.*

(v) The owner and possessor of land may not be in possession of chattels on his land even though he owns those chattels—another person, not on the land, may be in possession of them: *Ancona* v. *Rogers*; *Wrightson* v. *McArthur & Hutchisons.*

(vi) The finder of a lost chattel obtains possession of it, and hence title to it as against those who have no claim to it prior to his: *Armory* v. *Delamirie.*

(vii) A finder of a chattel who finds in the course of his employment does not obtain possession of it—his master does: *Willey* v. *Synan.*

(viii) As between two or more persons who are in apparent physical control and enjoyment of the use of chattels, the owner of the chattels is in possession of them: *Ramsay* v. *Margrett*; *French* v. *Gething.*

(ix) As between two or more persons apparently in physical control and enjoyment of the use of land (which is owned by one of them) and of chattels upon that land, where ownership of the chattels is in doubt, the owner of the land is in possession of the chattels and hence is presumptively the owner of them: *Re Cohen.*

(x) To acquire possession of a thing it is necessary to exercise such physical control over the thing as the thing is capable of, and to evince an intention to exclude others: *The Tubantia*; *Young* v. *Hichens.*[1]

(xi) But possession may be acquired of a thing, by transfer from another in possession, without any change in the physical control of the thing concerned: *Ramsay* v. *Margrett*; *French* v. *Gething.*[2]

This list could be extended almost indefinitely.

---

[1] And cf. *Pierson* v. *Post* (1805), 3 Caines 175 (Supreme Ct. of New York); *Littledale* v. *Scaith* (1788), 1 Taunt. 243 n.; 127 E.R. 826; *Hogarth* v. *Jackson* (1827), M. & M. 58, 173 E.R. 1080; *Hamps* v. *Darby*, [1948] 2 K.B. 311.

[2] Cf. *In re Stoneham*, [1919] 1 Ch. 149; *In re Ridgway* (1885), 15 Q.B.D. 447; *Cochrane* v. *Moore* (1890), 25 Q.B.D. 57.

§ 125. ANALYSIS OF POSSESSION

It should be obvious that the concept of possession in the law is not a simple concept which can be satisfactorily described in terms of facts grouped into essential and differentiating criteria for the purposes of definition—at least not when the law is seen as a process for regulating relations between persons and for resolving disputes between them. Holmes saw one important aspect of the complicating factors concerned when he said: 'The word "possession" denotes such a group of facts. Hence, when we say of a man that he has possession, we affirm directly that all the facts of a certain group are true of him, and we convey indirectly or by implication that the law will give him the advantage of the situation. Contract, or property, or any other substantive notion of the law, may be analysed in the same way, and should be treated in the same order. The only difference is, that, while possession denotes the facts and connotes the consequences, property always, and contract with more uncertainty and oscillation, denote the consequence and connote the facts.'[1] But he produced, none the less, an over-simplification which, having shed some light, obscured further investigation. Thus one might describe 'possession' as a word which serves as a useful symbol to refer to the link between diverse conditions of fact and equally diverse consequences in the law—as Ross does with the concept of ownership.[2] A diagrammatic illustration can be given as follows:

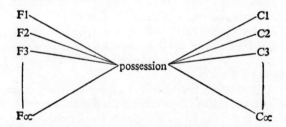

(Where F = conditioning fact and C = legal consequences)

Then possession merely stands for the systematic connection that F1 as well as F2 – – – Fоc entail some or all of the legal consequences C1 – – – Coc. As a technique of presentation this is expressed then

[1] *The Common Law*, 214–15.
[2] A. Ross, *On Law and Justice*, 171.

by stating in one series of rules the facts that 'create possession', and in another series the legal consequences that 'possession' entails.[1]

Some jurists, frustrated in the search for a conceptualized[2] group of facts which would take account of $F1 - - - F\infty$, which Holmes had assumed to exist, turned to look for some unifying similarity in the legal consequences to be discovered in $C - - - C\infty$. If it were possible to generalize the totality of legal consequences and find perhaps the 'essence' of the notion of possession in that generalization, then such a search might succeed in satisfying the ordering mind of the jurist. But even this is not possible, for the systematic connection between $F1 - - - F\infty$ is not with the totality of $C1 - - - C\infty$, but with some number of C's less than that totality. That is, there is not merely a diversity of F's defying the search for an essence, there is a diversity of C's also and the question is open at both ends. Thus the remedies that are said to be open to possessors are sometimes open to persons who are not in possession—e.g. the gratuitous bailor at will, the servant who has mere custody of her master's mackintosh.

Further, the systematic connection is circular in nature, because although the legal consequences are said to flow from the establishment of the conditioning facts, the characterization of the conditioning facts as constituting possession or not may well vary with the legal consequences. That is sufficiently established by comparing the trends of the larceny cases summarized above, the finding cases, the cases which go to the establishment of title, and the landlord and tenant cases, one with another. Again a man may be held to be in possession for one purpose where, for another, he would not be held to be in possession although the facts proved were unchanged. Consider, for example, the situation of the defendant in *Moors* v. *Burke* (*supra*) if he had been, on the facts shown, suing, for trespass to chattels, someone who had damaged the goods in his locker, or the position of the defendant in *Wrightson* v. *McArthur & Hutchisons* (*supra*) if that company had been proceeding against a person for trespass to the goods which had been contained in the locked room.

Some insight is gained by such a presentation as Ross outlines, but it does not go far enough. As Kocourek[3] demonstrates, the F's are conceptual in nature, and, lying behind them again, are extra-legal facts—the raw facts seen from outside the legal system as it were, which give rise to relations which must be regulated by the legal system.

---

[1] To adapt Ross's statement from ownership to possession.
[2] To use Ross's word.　　　　　　　　　　[3] *Jural Relations*, ch. xx.

It is often said that: 'Possession is a fact to which the law attaches certain consequences.'[1] In the light of the preceding discussion it can be seen that such an assertion presented in the form of definition leads to confusion, for it invites definition of an Aristotelian kind by identifying the 'fact' by reference to essence and differentia, and the search for those is a fruitless one. At the same time, in priority of history and of logic, the fact comes before the law. A typical set of facts which called for rules of law to regulate relations arising out of those facts, provided the core notion around which the various uses of the word 'possession' in rules of law tend to group themselves. Thus, when a *res* which has never been in the physical control of any person is first 'taken' into physical control by some person for himself[2] in circumstances where resistance can be expected if others attempt to interfere with that physical control, we see something which in the ordinary use of English would be called 'possession' of the thing— and possession has been created. When, however, in a legal system rules are provided to protect such a possessor in his possession, very quickly something more is added than the mere attachment of legal consequences to the 'fact' of possession. Legal relations, rights, duties, powers, immunities, etc., are established between the possessor and all other persons.

When legal relations are established, in general they continue and are supported by the system which established them unless and until some change occurs in the facts or the law which is thought sufficient to disturb them. It is not surprising, therefore, to find that the facts which will be held to create possession for the first time[3] need not be shown to continue for possession to be held to continue—for once established it is the *right to possession* which becomes important so far as legal relations are concerned. If I leave my car unlocked outside my host's house while I dine, I am not in physical control of it nor can I be expected to resist interference with it, yet I do not lose possession of it in the eyes of the law (my legal relations are not changed with respect to my possession of it) even if I have left it upon my host's land. So the change of facts which will be held to bring about loss of possession is not the mere discontinuance of the facts which created possession in the first place. Loss of possession involves a change in pre-existing legal relations with respect to a thing and

---

[1] As in the second edition of this work at 453.

[2] As with the wolves and the mutton mentioned at p. 558 (*supra*).

[3] See e.g. *Littledale* v. *Scaith* (1788), 1 Taunt. 243 n., 127 E.R. 826; *Hogarth* v. *Jackson* (1827), M. & M. 58, 173 E.R. 1080; *Pierson* v. *Post* (1805), 3 Caines 175.

raises different questions from the creation of possession of a thing with respect to which there have been no pre-existing legal relations.[1]

Similarly the transfer of possession from one person to another may be effected by changing the legal relations of persons with respect to the thing, by means permitted by the legal system, without in any way changing the physical conditions affecting the thing or the persons concerned.[2]

Just as with the concept of ownership[3] then, the way out of the confusion engendered by the struggle between convenience and theory already outlined is to recognize that possession in the law always involves legal relations between persons. Where those relations are in dispute there will be various values, sometimes competing, to be considered when establishing the precise relations to be recognized or enforced by the legal system, and when fixing the tests by which the relations concerned are to be recognized. No doubt, almost always, the basic values suggested by Felix Cohen[4] will be involved: simplicity, certainty, promotion of the community's economy, economy of effort in administration, acceptability as consonant with a general sense of fairness. But the precise rules, which include possession in their expression, developed in different parts of the legal system are affected by further complicating factors, for different purposes are pursued in the development of different rules and those purposes affect the development of the rules themselves.

A mere glance at the cases and rules summarized in the preceding section reveals that the tests for recognizing possession vary in response (*inter alia*) to the pressures of different purposes being pursued in different parts of the law. Thus in the larceny cases there is the desire to see that people who take things to which they have no justifiable claim (who have the minds of thieves)[5] shall not escape retribution.[6] In cases like *Moors* v. *Burke*,[7] there is the desire to limit

---

[1] If, as seems obvious, possession once gained can be lost or abandoned absolutely (i.e. not to another person), then there can be a series of 'creations' of possession with respect to the one thing, but each 'creation' involves the establishment of fresh possessory relations where there were none immediately before the act of 'creation'— see *The Tubantia*, [1924] P. 78, but cf. *Johnstone & Wilmot Pty. Ltd.* v. *Kaine*, [1928] 23 Tas. L.R. 43.

[2] See *Ramsay* v. *Margrett* (*supra*), *French* v. *Gething* (*supra*).

[3] *Supra*, § 115.

[4] *Dialogue on Private Property* (1954), 9 Rutgers L.R. 357.

[5] *Hibbert* v. *McKiernan* (*supra*) per Goddard C.J.

[6] In contrast with a 'system-made pressure' of not so long ago when there was a tendency to find some technical ground to prevent very harsh punishment being inflicted for a minor transgression: see Kenny's *Outlines of Criminal Law* (17th ed.), § 221, pp. 238–9.   [7] *Supra*, 575 n. 4.

the harsh application of a statutory rule which cuts across traditional notions affecting the administration of justice in the criminal law. In the landlord and tenant cases there are varying pressures from times when there is a special need to protect the interests of tenants to other times when it is felt that landlords have been too restrictively treated by the law.[1]

In the finding cases the task facing the courts is really to allocate rights to physical control and enjoyment of things where no such control existed before in the parties concerned. The real nature of the task is obscured by the search for a pre-existing 'possessory title', and the assumption that the thing must belong to one or another of the parties prohibits a solution which may in some cases be the most desirable: an allocation of the future rights among those parties in shares.[2]

To the objective observer there is a further complicating factor. In most cases the court does not have all the facts before it, but only those facts which are known to the litigating parties and are thought by them to be relevant to their claims in the light of the legal authorities. Thus a variety of persons in different proceedings could be held to be in possession of a thing, without the actual extra-legal facts being changed at all, depending upon the nature of the litigation, and upon the information disclosed to the court about the relevant physical facts and about the legal relations affecting the persons concerned.

This can be demonstrated by supposing any number of possible sets of facts under any one of which different persons could be held to be possessors. For example, suppose A is in lawful possession of a large purse which he has in his pocket. The purse and contents are owned by B but B is not at the relevant time entitled to possession of them. B is married to C and is living with him in a flat owned by C. A, on visiting B and C one evening, because the purse is bulky and puts his clothes out of shape, hides the purse under his hat in C's cloakroom. On this information is there any doubt that in an issue as to possession, between a finder of the purse and A, A would be held to have been all the time in possession of it? As between C and a stranger who finds the purse, if information about A and B is not

---

[1] And further complicated by awareness of the special interests of persons in a position of near helplessness—e.g. the wives of tenants. See *Middleton* v. *Baldock*, [1950] 1 K.B. 657; *Errington* v. *Errington*, [1952] 1 K.B. 290; *Bendall* v. *McWhirter*, [1952] 2 Q.B. 466; R. E. Megarry, '*The Deserted Wife's Right to Occupy the Matrimonial Home*', 68 *L.Q.R.* (1952), 337, 379.   [2] See Kocourek, loc. cit.

disclosed, C will be held to be in possession of it. If all suddenly die and the purse is found, then, if the only information disclosed is that C owned the flat, C will be held to have had possession of the purse. If in those circumstances the only information disclosed is that B owned the purse, then B will be held to have been in possession of the purse—and so on.

In the light of the preceding discussion, the discovery that the word 'possession' wears varying shades of meaning in different legal contexts should not surprise nor greatly disturb the student of law. The compulsive search for one unitary 'concept' of possession[1] or for one proper meaning of the word 'possession' is a profitless one.[2] The elucidation of the precise meanings conveyed by the word 'possession' may well be best pursued by the method urged by Professor Hart.[3] Thus given a rule that 'Delivery' means 'voluntary transfer of possession from one person to another',[4] to elucidate the term 'possession' or the expression 'transfer of possession' one should identify the conditions under which such a statement as 'A *transferred possession* to B and so effected delivery' is a true or valid statement in the light of the rules and authorities applicable within a given legal system.[5]

There are very many rules which use the word 'possession', however, and an account of the law of possession which limited itself to a series of precise statements as to the conditions under which all the possible uses of the word would be valid or invalid, would be so detailed and unwieldy as to be useless to all but practitioners faced with particular cases and searching for precise authority in a wilderness of single instances.[6] 'It is the task of legal thinking to conceptualise the legal rules in such a way that they are reduced to systematic order and by this means to give an account of the law in force as plain and convenient as possible.'[7] Where the law of possession is concerned, this task still awaits its master.

---

[1] Except perhaps as a move for sweeping law reform in the interest of tidiness and simplicity alone.

[2] 'Preoccupation with the search for some common feature is apt in either case to divert us from the important inquiries which are (1) what for any given legal system are the conditions under which possessory rights are acquired and lost; (2) what general features of the given system and what practical reasons lead to diverse cases being treated alike in this respect.' H. L. A. Hart, *Definition and Theory in Jurisprudence* (1954), 70 *L.Q.R.* 37, at p. 44.

[3] Loc. cit.; and see D. R. Harris, 'The Concept of Possession in English Law', *Oxford Essays in Jurisprudence*, ch. iv.

[4] Sale of Goods Act, 1893, s. 62—repeated in many Acts throughout the common law world, e.g. s. 3 (1) of the Goods Act, 1958 (Victoria—no. 6265).

[5] And see § 4 and § 18 *supra*.   [6] And then only if superbly indexed.

[7] A. Ross, *On Law and Justice*, 171; and see Hart, *supra*.

Even if, at any one point of time, the only completely accurate way to elucidate all the different uses of the word 'possession' in the law were to provide the unwieldy account indicated above, to do so and to deny the value of any more general statement would be to throw the baby out with the bath water. The living law involves processes of change and development. At few points are those processes irrational or arbitrary. They turn upon general ideas, however vague, which provide direction for thought in the absence of more precise and authoritative directions provided by the legal system.

With perhaps only one general exception, the idea, however vague and imprecise, which colours and gives a family relationship to all the uses of the word 'possession' in the law, is the recognition of a relation between persons where one has taken or has control of a thing and is to be protected in his enjoyment of it unless more is shown. The general exception, of course, is that the legislator[1] may stipulate a meaning or use for the word which takes it out of the family relationship. This is frequently done and for a variety of purposes: e.g. it may be desired to give to certain persons not in any then accepted sense 'in possession' legal benefits which are ordinarily afforded possessors only. Usually, however, the warning signal of a fiction will be given and the legislator will say that the persons concerned are to be *deemed to be* in possession.

§ 126. MEDIATE AND IMMEDIATE POSSESSION

Plures eandem rem in solidum possidere non possunt.[2] Must this well-worn adage be modified by a recognition of mediate and immediate possession? Salmond writes: 'One person may possess a thing for or on account of someone else. In such a case the latter is in possession by the agency of him who so holds the thing on his behalf. The possession thus held by one man through another may be termed *mediate*, while that which is acquired or retained directly or personally may be distinguished as *immediate* or *direct*.'[3] Salmond instances three types of mediate possession: firstly, that acquired through an agent or servant; secondly, that held through a borrower, hirer, or tenant where the *res* can be demanded at will; thirdly, where the chattel is lent for a fixed time or delivered as security for the repayment of a debt.

---

[1] Whether judge or legislature—more often, these days, the latter.
[2] *Dig.* 41. 2. 3. 5.   [3] *Jurisprudence* (12th ed.), 282.

The distinction between mediate and immediate possession is in many ways a useful one and is explicitly recognized by German law.[1] In English law, however, in all the cases mentioned, possession is granted to one person and one person alone: the common law needs no theory of mediate and immediate possession. In the master and servant relationship the servant does not possess the master's goods received from him, though the servant does possess goods given to him by a stranger, until by some act he has appropriated them to his master. In the case of bailor and bailee it is the latter who has possession.[2] In the case of landlord and tenant the tenant has possession of the land. Maitland has pointed out the confusion that arose in early English law because of the difficulty of applying the strict terminology of Rome to the intricacies of the feudal system.[3] Who was *dominus*, and who had *possessio*? To adapt Roman theory to feudal conditions, some distinguished between the *dominium directum* of the lord and the *dominium utile* of the vassal, the *possessio civilis* of the lord and *possessio naturalis* of the vassal. In modern English law the doctrine of the exclusiveness of possession is saved by a rather narrow distinction—the landlord is seised or possessed of the freehold and the tenant possesses the land.

It has already been noted[4] that it is an essential characteristic of a lease that the tenant should have exclusive possession. It is difficult to reconcile all the cases dealing with the distinction between tenants and licensees and between tenants and mere lodgers. In many of the infinity of possible sets of facts which can give rise to litigation, it is often difficult to decide whether or not the owner granted exclusive control to another—especially where neither party directed his mind to the notion of exclusive control at the time of the agreement.[5] The tenant's possession of the land is no empty figment: he desires and has the power to exclude the landlord during the currency of the lease, save in so far as a power of entry has been reserved. The landlord's interest in the freehold is evidenced by the existence of a written lease or the receipt of rent or both. A tenant has a sufficient possessory right to bring trespass against the landlord.[6] If furniture

---

[1] *BGB.* Art. 868. Cf. C.C., Art. 2228: 'Possession is the retention or enjoyment of a thing or of a right which we have or which we make use of, either ourselves or through another person who holds it or makes use of it in our name.'   [2] *Supra*, § 124.

[3] *Collected Papers*, i. 352.   [4] *Supra*, § 124.

[5] See e.g. the cases noted in H. A. Hill and J. H. Redman's *Law of Landlord and Tenant* (13th ed.) at 12–15 and 18. The courts treat the question as to whether exclusive possession was granted or not as one of fact.

[6] *Gordon* v. *Harper* (1796), 7 T.R. 9.

leased with the house is converted, the landlord cannot bring trover, for he has not a right to immediate possession; if they are stolen, he cannot describe the goods as his in an indictment for larceny.[1]

Confusion of terminology may lead to genuine misunderstanding. Plaintiff agreed to sell the defendant an orchard, described as being in occupation of A, and promised that the purchaser should have 'possession' on the day appointed for completion. The defendant refused to complete unless the tenant was ejected, but the court found against him on the ground that there was a broad distinction between possession and occupation.[2]

Difficulties have already been noted, however, in the adoption of a theory that the common law always regards possession as exclusive. The law sometimes allows possessory remedies to those admittedly not in possession.[3] Thus where there is a simple bailment determinable at will, either the bailor or the bailee may maintain trespass against a stranger. The theory that the bailee does not acquire possession in such a case does not help, for on that basis the bailee would be unable to sue in trespass. Similarly a servant has been allowed to sue for trespass to the goods of his master.[4]

Again, as has been seen,[5] the larceny cases give rise to similar difficulties. It is well established that an indictment may lay the 'property' of the goods in the real owner, a bailee or a servant—and this use of the term 'property' is practically equivalent to possession.[6] Hale places the rule on a reasonable basis—the felon may be indicted for stealing the goods of either the bailor or the bailee, and 'it is good either way' for the property is still in the owner and the bailee has possession.[7] But the language of the books has not always been as uniform as this. When a parcel was stolen from a stage coach, Hotham B. allowed the property to be laid in a servant driving the coach, but he did so on the practical grounds that it would be

[1] *R.* v. *Belstead* (1820), R. & R. 411; *R.* v. *Brunswick* (1824), 1 Mood. 26.

[2] *Lake* v. *Dean* (1860), 28 Beav. 607. And see the awkward case of *Fairweather* v. *St. Marylebone Property Co. Ltd.*, [1962] 2 All E.R. 288 (H.L.).

[3] We can hardly say that *anyone* with a right to immediate possession can bring trespass, for that conflicts with too many established rules. 'It is difficult to see how there can be a forcible and immediate injury *vi et armis* to a mere legal right': Pollock and Wright, *Possession*, 145. If, in general, a wrong to a mere right of possession were sufficient for trespass and theft, why is conversion by a bailee not trespass and theft? (op. cit. 146).

[4] *Moore* v. *Robinson* (1831), 2 B. & Ad. 817. Winfield, *Text-Book of the Law of Tort* (4th ed.), 309, suggests that this case would probably not be followed today, as it depended on the view that the master of the ship was a bailee.

[5] *Supra*, § 124.   [6] Pollock and Wright, op. cit. 139.

[7] *Pleas of the Crown*, i. 513; ii. 181; approved by Parke B. in *Manders* v. *Williams* (1849), 4 Ex. 339 at 344–5.

inconvenient to require the names of all the owners of a stage coach to appear in the indictment.[1] It is authoritatively stated that this case depended on special considerations,[2] but in 1929 the Court of Criminal Appeal carried the doctrine even further.[3] The prisoner forced a maid to deliver to him her master's coat and it was held correct to lay the property in the servant. This decision has been severely criticized. If the maid has possession of her master's coat which had not been delivered to her but was hanging in the hall, then logically a servant should have possession of goods delivered to him by the master—yet it is well known that the rule is otherwise. Does this case sweep away the 'six hundred year old distinction' between a servant's custody and possession?[4] It can be explained only by saying that, when it is a question of determining whether the prosecutor has the property, the court allows even custody to be treated as possession; whereas when it is a case of theft by the servant, the law is stricter. It is certainly disconcerting, after having emphasized that the servant has only custody of the master's goods delivered to him by the master, to explain in the next breath that when it comes to indicting a thief, the law allows the servant to be regarded as in possession.

› These difficulties merely reveal that some of the rules of law as authoritatively stated may be mutually inconsistent in some of their detailed applications and so need to be embroidered with exceptions, and that 'possession' may be used in different contexts for different purposes and with different meanings. They do not force us to adopt the classification of 'mediate' and 'immediate' possession.

› *Prescription.* Is it necessary to use the concept of mediate and immediate possession to explain the operation of the rules of prescription as between landlord and tenant, bailor and bailee? Salmond suggests that

title by prescription is based on long and continuous possession. But he who desires to acquire ownership in this way need not retain the *immediate* possession of the thing. He may let his land to a tenant for a term of years, and . . . prescription will continue to run in his favour. . . . For all the purposes of the law of prescription mediate possession in all its forms is as good as immediate. . . . As between landlord and tenant, prescription, if it runs at all, will run in favour of the tenant; but at the same time it may run in favour of the landlord as against the true owner of the property.[5]

---

[1] *R. v. Deakin* (1800), 2 Leach 862.
[3] *R. v. Harding* (*supra*, § 124).
[5] *Jurisprudence* (12th ed.), 284, 286.

[2] Pollock and Wright, op. cit. 139.
[4] Note in 46 *L.Q.R.* (1930), 135.

Another way of explaining the same rules is to emphasize that the tenant possesses the land and the landlord the freehold. The tenant, although he has the *animus* to exclude the landlord from the land during the term of the lease, has no intent to possess the freehold. The only way in which the landlord can show intent concerning, and physical control of, the freehold is to secure written evidence of his right (e.g. a lease) and to exact rent. If a stranger exacts rent, then he is showing an intent adverse to the interest of the freeholder and, in the absence of steps by the landlord, time may begin to run against the latter. If there is no lease in writing, and the tenant refuses to pay rent, he is showing not only an intention to enjoy possession of the land but also a desire to exclude the landlord from the freehold itself. If the latter neglects either to obtain written acknowledgement of his title, or to exact rent, then time may begin to run in favour of the tenant. Similarly, if I have seized land, time may continue to run in my favour if I place a tenant on the land, for the tenant's intent is confined to exclusive control of the land during the currency of the lease and is not directed to the freehold. The rules of English law are not as simple as is here suggested,[1] but they can be explained as easily without, as with, the doctrine of mediate and immediate possession.

Turning next to bailment, the rules are specific. The bailee has full possession but recognizes the title of the true owner. Conversion can take place only if the bailee does some positive act inconsistent with the title of the true owner. Technically prescription does not apply to this case, but only limitation of actions. The bailor may sue for conversion within six years of the act complained of, or, if he chooses, he may, even after the action in conversion is barred, make a formal demand for the return of the *res*, and on refusal by the bailee, sue in detinue.[2] The Limitation Act, 1939, has, however, changed this rule, and now where there are successive conversions time runs from the first, provided the chattel has not returned into the possession of the owner.[3]

In order to avoid misunderstanding, it is emphasized that it is not suggested that the distinction between mediate and immediate possession could not be useful in an attempt to impose some general order upon the variety of rules relating to possession. The only point the

---

[1] G. C. Cheshire, *Modern Real Property* (5th ed.), 821.

[2] *Wilkinson* v. *Verity* (1871), L.R. 6 C.P. 206; *Goulding* v. *Vict. Rly. Commissioners* (1932), 48 C.L.R. 157.

[3] Limitation Act, 1939, 2 & 3 Geo. VI, c. 21, § 3.

writer is making in this Section is that the rules of English law can be explained without such a doctrine.[1]

[1] Many cases can be cited in favour of Salmond's approach, e.g. the dicta of Crompton J. in *Marvin* v. *Wallis* (1856), 6 El. & Bl. 726. But this was in reality a case of constructive delivery of possession. The same applies to *Elmore* v. *Stone* (1809), 1 Taunt. 458. The point is discussed in *Dollfus Mieg Co.* v. *Bank of England* (1950), 66 T.L.R. 675.

REFERENCES

Dias, R. W. M., and Hughes, G. B. J., *Jurisprudence* (1957), ch. xi.

Goodhart, A. L., *Essays in Jurisprudence and the Common Law*, 75.

Harris, D. R., 'The Concept of Possession in English Law', *Oxford Essays in Jurisprudence* (1961).

Kocourek, A., *Jural Relations* (2nd ed.), ch. xx.

Maitland, F. W., *Collected Papers*, i. 329.

Pollock, F., and Maitland, F. W., *History of English Law*, ii. 30–46.

—— and Wright, S., *Possession in the Common Law*.

Riesman, D., 52 *Harv. L. R.* (1939), 1105.

Savigny, F. K. von, *Possession* (trans. E. Perry).

XXIII

THE LAW OF PROCEDURE

§ 127. INTRODUCTION

ONE of the orthodox classifications is that which distinguishes between substantive and procedural law, but it is difficult to draw a clear line between them. One suggested test is that substantive law determines rights, procedural law remedies; this, however, is inaccurate.[1] Firstly, the whole law of remedies does not belong to procedure, and secondly, there are rights in the realm of procedure just as in that of substantive law. Thus, to take the first point, substantive law itself recognizes both antecedent and remedial rights, i.e. those which exist independently of wrongdoing and those that arise from the wrongful act or omission of another.[2] A power to recover damages is a remedial right, but it does not fall under the heading of procedure. If we adopt the view of those realists who deny that antecedent rights exist at all (since in effect the law consists only of remedies), then any definition of procedure which described it as covering all remedies would entail almost the total disappearance of substantive law. Secondly, the law of procedure creates rights—or more accurately claims, liberties, powers, and immunities—just as does the substantive law. There is a claim to demand an answer which a witness is under a duty to give, the privilege of a witness to refuse to answer a question which might incriminate. The distinction between substance and procedure must be sought elsewhere than in the division between right and remedy.

English usage sometimes speaks of practice and procedure, sometimes of practice in a wide sense as including 'all the proceedings by which a cause is brought to judgment and execution',[3] sometimes it distinguishes practice, pleading, and evidence. Procedure has been defined as the body of rules that govern the process of litigation:[4] practice as the rules 'that make or guide the *cursus curiae*, and regu-

---

[1] Salmond, *Jurisprudence* (11th ed.), 503. This passage is changed in 12th ed. 461.
[2] *Supra*, § 65.
[3] Per Willes J. cited Lord Chelmsford, *A.-G.* v. *Sillem* (1864), 10 H.L.C. at 768–9.
[4] Salmond, op. cit. 461.

late the proceedings in a cause within the walls or limits of the court itself'.[1] On this usage procedure is a wider term than practice: the former covers everything from the issue of the writ to execution, the latter only the proceedings in an actual trial. A Victorian court held that the phrase 'practice and procedure' covered the manner in which a decree for the dissolution of marriage is made and the period to elapse before it is made absolute.[2] To define *procedure* as court *process* is really a description of it in terms of itself, but it is difficult to discover any purely logical test that will make a clear-cut division. Thus the rules of evidence regulate the process of the court, but a power to make rules governing procedure has been held not to cover the rules of evidence.[3] Judges continually advert to the distinction between 'substance' and 'procedure', between 'right' and 'remedy', but they never venture upon a general principle which affords a test for deciding into which of these categories a given rule falls.[4] Indeed, some authors deem it the safer course to demonstrate the meaning of procedure by a wearisome enumeration of the particular rules which have been held to fall under that head. It is impossible to make valid generalizations, because in different systems of law the line is drawn now here, now there. Moreover, if we look at the course of history, we see that in the middle period substantive law is inextricably intertwined with procedural formalities. The method by which a right can be enforced naturally determines to some extent the nature of the right. At some periods procedure seems to become almost an end in itself and 'substantive law has at first the look of being gradually secreted in the interstices of procedure'.[5] Even in modern England although the 'forms of action are dead . . . their ghosts still haunt the precincts of the law. In their life they were powers of evil, and even in death they have not wholly ceased from troubling'.[6] Today we regard limitation of actions as belonging to procedure, but the barring of an action for conversion results in an important restriction of the true owner's power. Whether I possess a right of appeal or not is sometimes regarded as a question of substantive law, but the failure to carry out the necessary procedural formalities may destroy my right. If a right can be proved in only one way, it is easy (and almost

---

[1] Per Lord Westbury, *A.-G.* v. *Sillem* (1864), 10 H.L.C. at 723.

[2] *White* v. *White*, [1947] V.L.R. 434.

[3] *Wm. Cook Pty. Ltd.* v. *Read*, [1940] V.L.R. 214.

[4] Cheshire, *Private International Law* (6th ed.), ch. xviii. Cf. A. V. Dicey, *Conflict of Laws* (7th ed.), R. 204; per Lush L.J., *Poyser* v. *Minors* (1881), 7 Q.B.D. 329 at 333; note in 47 *Harv. L. R.* (1933), 315.

[5] Maine, *Early Law and Custom*, 389.   [6] Salmond, 21 *L.Q.R.* (1905), 43.

true) to say that the right does not exist unless that proof is avail-able.[1] If an action can be brought on a certain type of contract only if it is in writing, then we are tempted to say that any contract not thus evidenced is void in substantive law. But this is not quite accurate, as is demonstrated by decisions in Conflict of Laws. In other cases, rules of substantive law masquerade as rules of evidence. Thus there is a conclusive presumption of law that no child under eight can possess the *mens rea* necessary for a criminal conviction—this is undoubtedly a rule of substantive law relating to the criminal liability of minors.[1]

Yet we cannot take the easy course of denying that there is any real difference between substance and procedure, unless we are willing to jettison many important rules. Thus in Conflict of Laws, matters of procedure are governed by the *lex fori* and matters of substance by the proper law of contract. An accurate delimitation of what falls under the head of procedure is necessary if injustice is to be avoided. If too wide a definition is given to procedure, a remedy may be refused on a contract which is valid by its proper law. In England the Statute of Frauds requires certain contracts to be in writing be-fore an action can be brought. To prevent the statute being used as a protection for sharp dealing this section has been held to relate to procedure only. But what may be a reasonable rule for English con-tracts produces anomalous results when it is applied to a contract valid by its proper law, for it is impossible to sue in England unless the procedural requirements of the *lex fori* are observed.[2] Cheshire[3] approves the dictum of Cook[4] that the line between substance and procedure cannot be drawn in the same place for all purposes.

Again, Order 54 R. 23 of the Rules of the Supreme Court laid down that appeals in practice and procedure should lie, not to the Divisional Court but directly to the Court of Appeal—hence it was necessary to evolve definite rules by which the limits of practice and procedure could be determined. But, although in these two cases practical results flow from the definition of procedure adopted, it cannot be said that satisfactory tests have been evolved.

The drawing of precise distinctions is always a difficult matter for the law. Few would deny that there is a distinction between night and day, between minority and maturity, and yet in each case it is so

---

[1] Salmond, *Jurisprudence* (12th ed.), 463.
[2] *Leroux* v. *Brown* (1852), 12 C.B. 801.   [3] *Conflict of Laws* (3rd ed.), 829.
[4] *Logical and Legal Bases of the Conflict of Laws*, 189.

hard to determine the precise moment of transition that arbitrary rules have been created to determine the exact boundary line. In the definition of burglary night is defined as the period between 9 p.m. and 6 a.m., and minority ends at eighteen years. Unfortunately no statute has drawn definite lines to mark the boundaries of substance and procedure. The modern revolt against authority is leading many to reject the most useful classifications merely because they are difficult to formulate.[1] The legal distinction between substance and procedure is not an *a priori* one, but is pricked out by each system along the lines that appear expedient. Yet, although based on pragmatic tests, the division between substantive and procedural law is an essential one, as can be shown by a practical example. In a question concerning conflict of laws there is sometimes only one point of substance, but many problems in procedure. The convenience of leaving these questions to be determined according to *lex fori* shows the absurdity of rejecting the distinction between substance and procedure.

The practical problems which face a plaintiff are the choice of a court, a decision as to the most appropriate form of action, the issue of a summons to get his opponent before the court, and the most skilful use of the rules governing pleading and proof in the hope that he may secure judgment and, if necessary, execution. Once judgment has been given the question of the possibility of appeal will arise. Yet not all these problems can be regarded as falling under the head of procedure. Whether an action lies in equity or at common law, in England or in France, is determined by substantive law. The rules that mark the boundaries of contract and tort have in England been influenced by procedural requirements, but they can hardly be placed under the law of procedure. Forms of action are difficult to classify: the detailed rules belong to process, the broad distinction between trespass and case to substantive law. In the last analysis it is a question of convenience precisely where the line is drawn.

The functional test to which all procedural rules should be subjected is their practical efficiency in providing machinery for the prompt and reasonably cheap settlement of disputes on lines that do justice to both parties.[2] Jurisprudence has often failed to realize the practical importance of procedural problems. 'The substantive

---

[1] E. Ailes, 39 *Mich. L. R.* (1941), 392.

[2] For a comparative study of the rules of procedure in America and Germany, see E. H. Schopflocher, *Wisconsin L. R.* (1940), 234.

law which defines our rights and duties is, of course, important to all of us, but unless the adjective law of procedure is a working machine, constantly translating these obligations in terms of Court orders and actual execution, the substantive law might just as well not exist.'[1]

§ 128. SUMMONS

In modern times the efficient powers of the State render comparatively simple the problem of forcing another to submit to the jurisdiction of the court; but in primitive law there was no judicial machinery which could be used to enforce the appearance of a reluctant defendant. Thus, at the time of the Twelve Tables, a claimant orally requested his opponent to follow him to the court and, in a case of refusal, a claimant could use physical force, unless a *vindex* could be found who would guarantee the appearance of the defendant.[2] So long as even a vestige remains of the theory that litigation depends on consent, the court is faced with difficulty even after a defendant has appeared, if he refuses to co-operate. What has solved this problem is the threat of judgment by default against a defendant who, after due notice, fails to appear or to take a necessary procedural step. Today, in a civil case, a defendant is not threatened with arrest or other dire penalty if he does not enter an appearance, but only warned that judgment may be given against him.

§ 129. PLEADING AND PRACTICE

The first step, then, is to serve the defendant with a writ, notifying him of the claim that is to be made against him. A modern action may be divided into two parts: the procedural steps necessary before the trial opens and the actual trial itself. The details of every system vary greatly. In Rome a trial was divided into the preliminary procedure before the praetor and the final stage where the facts were found and judgment given by a private *iudex*. On the Continent today, sometimes the evidence is gathered and committed to writing in preliminary proceedings and the judge who ultimately tries the action may see none, or only a few, of the witnesses face to face. In England, in general, all evidence is given in open court.

---

[1] C. P. Harvey, 7 *Mod. L. R.* (1944), 42 at 49–50; and see J. Frank, *Courts on Trial,* where the late judge analyses the defects of the present system and advocates a series of reforms.

[2] H. F. Jolowicz, *Historical Introduction to Roman Law,* ch. xii.

The purpose of pleading is twofold: firstly, to eradicate (as far as possible) irrelevancy and to isolate the issues which are in dispute; secondly, to give reasonable notice to the other party of the claim against him so that he may prepare his reply. The rules of pleading should aim at ease of trial, reasonable cost, and justice to both parties. If the rules become too strict, the pitfalls of pleading may prevent the merits of the issue from being discussed: if the rules are too elastic, the result may be confused trials, unfair surprise, costly adjournments, and many appeals. To effect a delicate balance between precision and flexibility, between technicality and regard for the practical issues, is no easy task. An interesting contrast is provided by the rules of procedure in equity and the common law. Equity aimed at perfection and thus 'precluded itself from attaining the more possible, if more mundane, ideal of substantial justice'.[1] Eager to decide on the real merits of the case, the Chancellor allowed an intolerably slow procedure, advantage of which was taken by those who had no defence and merely wished to postpone the evil day of reckoning. Costs multiplied and sometimes exhausted the whole estate. On the other hand, the common law procedure was technical and archaic and frequently justice was defeated by skilful use of the rules of special pleading; but the rules were directed to a speedy decision of issues and costs were less burdensome than in equity

Those who have listened to a verbal quarrel between two neighbours know how far the discussion may range from the point which was the first matter of dispute. Even where the issue is fairly simple, such as the question whether a motor car driver was guilty of negligence, a trial would be long if every fact had to be proved. Hence the convenience of allowing the plaintiff to formulate his claim, the defendant to reply and ultimately for the parties to 'agree to differ' on one or more points. Firstly, in reply to a claim, a defendant at common law may traverse the allegations of the plaintiff, i.e. deny the truth of his assertions. This raises an issue of fact. Secondly, the defendant may confess and avoid, i.e. admit that the plaintiff's facts are true but assert that they are only half the story. A defendant sued for negligent driving may admit the negligence but plead that the plaintiff really brought about his own injury by contributory negligence; or, if sued for breach of contract, a defendant may admit the making of a contract and its breach, but plead facts which

---

[1] Holdsworth, *History of English Law*, ix. 373. For a critical survey of the modern problem, see S. P. Simpson, 53 *Harv. L. R.* (1939), 169.

rendered it impossible to perform the contract. Thirdly, instead of raising an issue of fact, the defendant may object in point of law—plead that, even if the plaintiff's story is true, no legal liability has been created.[1]

The defect of the old common law rules of pleading was that they were too narrow, and a party was forced to make an awkward choice since 'he could not both demur and plead, nor could he traverse any allegation to which he also pleaded by way of confession and avoidance'.[2] The rules had the merit of simplifying the contest by narrowly isolating the material issues, but in practice they frequently led to a decision on a technicality, the real merits of the case being unconsidered. The Judicature Commissioners in their report of 1868–9 advocated a system 'which combined the comparative brevity of the simpler forms of common law pleading with the principle of stating, intelligibly and not technically, the substance of the facts relied upon as constituting the plaintiff's or the defendant's case, as distinguished from his evidence'.[3] This is the basis of the modern English rules of pleading.

In England today what may be called 'pre-trial procedure' is becoming increasingly important. The slow majesty of a trial with its rigid rules is neither necessary nor desirable in all cases, and actually, out of every hundred actions commenced by writ in the Supreme Court, only one comes to trial.[4]

§ 130. PROOF

The problem of proof is always a difficult one. For a primitive court it is wellnigh insoluble owing to lack of ability to analyse the evidence, the prevalence of perjury, and the natural fear of any court which lacks an assured position lest some powerful member of the community should be offended by its decision. Hence comes escape from the judgment of man to that of God—the ordeal which has played such a great part in European legal history.[5] The ordeal by oath may be useful, if it is used where there is no evidence, or where the facts are exclusively within the knowledge of one party, but there is always the danger that a weak court may resort to it, even where

---

[1] The demurrer, as it was termed.
[2] W. B. Odgers, *Principles of Pleading and Practice* (17th ed.), 128.
[3] Cited Holdsworth, *History of English Law*, ix. 407.
[4] Master W. Valentine Ball, 51 *L.Q.R.* (1935), 22–3.
[5] A. S. Diamond, *Primitive Law* (2nd ed.), ch. xxx.

there is evidence, in order to avoid either the difficulty of deciding or the danger which may result from a decision against a popular figure.[1] Compurgation (or wager of law) was theoretically available in England in the actions of debt and detinue till 1833—the party, on whom lay the burden of proof, took the oath together with twelve witnesses who swore that he was to be believed. This naturally gave an opening for 'licensed perjury', which was frequently used to defeat just claims.

There were forms of ordeal other than the oath—the red-hot iron, water, swallowing the consecrated bread—and their exact operation still puzzles us today. The effectiveness of some forms depended on the existence of a feeling of guilt; for example, fear dries the mouth and renders it more difficult to swallow a dry morsel of bread. But a psychological explanation cannot be applied to all; thus in the ordeal by water, two different theories appear in history: according to the first the accused was guilty if he floated (the water-god rejected the guilty) and innocent if he sank; the second acquitted the prisoner only if he floated. One wonders whether the unfortunate prisoner did not suffer in either case on the first theory. Such evidence as there is shows that many escaped the ordeal, though today we would think that the ordeal by hot iron would be difficult to pass if rigorously administered.[2] A recent case in the Privy Council shows that the 'witch doctor' is not averse from aiding the test of heaven by deft manipulation of a harmless substance and arsenic,[3] and probably those who administered the ordeal were not always impartial or unaffected by the result. The ordeal was not confined to criminal cases.

In modern times proof is made by means of the production of evidence—which term 'as used in judicial proceedings, means the facts, testimony and documents which may be legally received in order to prove or disprove the fact under inquiry'.[4] Evidence may be either oral (words spoken by a witness in court), documentary (the production of admissible documents), or material (the production of a physical *res* other than a document). A witness's description of a

[1] Diamond, op. cit. 383.

[2] 'Such evidence as we have seems to show that the ordeal of hot iron was so arranged as to give the accused a reasonable chance of escape': Pollock and Maitland, *History of English Law*, ii. 596. C. K. Allen, *Legal Duties*, 262, asks: 'How was it arranged? By corruption of the officiating clergy? Thaumaturgy always has its commercial aspects. Perhaps this was in the mind of William Rufus when, after fifty men sent to the ordeal of iron had all escaped, he waxed satirical about the judgments of heaven.'

[3] *Fakisandhla Nkambule* v. *R.*, [1940] A.C. 760.

[4] S. L. Phipson, *Evidence* (9th ed.), 2; cf. J. H. Wigmore, *On Evidence* (3rd ed. 1940), vol. i, § 1; R. Cross, *Evidence*, ch. i.

murder which he witnessed is oral evidence; a blackmailing letter which the victim sent to the prisoner is documentary evidence; the knife with which the murder was committed is material evidence.

The task of a claimant is to prove such facts in issue as are necessary to his claim and of which he bears the burden of proof. Direct evidence proves the existence of a given thing or fact either by the production of the thing or by the oral evidence of a witness (or the admissible declaration of a person not before the court), who has seen the thing or observed the fact.[1] But, if only direct evidence could be accepted, courts would be seriously handicapped. In the criminal law, the more serious the crime, the less likely is direct evidence to be available because of the precautions which the criminal will take. In the civil law it is unlikely that such an act as adultery can be proved by direct evidence. Thus a rule that no cardinal was to be convicted of adultery save on the evidence of seven eyewitnesses meant, in effect, immunity for the cardinal.[2] Hence circumstantial evidence is admitted—other facts are proved from which the existence of the fact in issue may either be logically inferred, or at least rendered more probable. To prove that a prisoner consumed five double whiskies during the afternoon is not direct evidence that he was drunk at four o'clock when he drove negligently, but it aids in rendering the fact of drunkenness more probable. There has been much dispute concerning the relative weight of direct or circumstantial evidence, but the truth is that either form may be of very little or very great cogency. The direct evidence of witnesses may be most conflicting, sometimes because of perjury, sometimes through honest mistake. Thus in the *Tichborne Case*, where a butcher claimed to be a long-lost baronet, 212 witnesses appeared for the Crown and 256 for the defence. Four large groups gave the following evidence: (1) the claimant is not Roger Tichborne; (2) he is Arthur Orton; (3) he is not Arthur Orton; (4) he is Roger Tichborne.[3] On the other hand, circumstances may mislead or false clues may have been laid by the wrongdoer to cast suspicion on another.[4]

Admissibility. In general, the law uses the general test of logical relevance in determining what is admissible, but it excludes certain forms of evidence which would be used by the layman in reaching a

---

[1] J. H. Wigmore, op. cit., §§ 24 and 25.
[2] C. S. Kenny, *Criminal Law* (17th ed.), 481 n. 5.
[3] Ibid. 431, discussing *Reg.* v. *Castro* (1874), L.R. 9 Q.B. 350.
[4] Kenny, op. cit. 432: 'as when Joseph's silver cup was placed in Benjamin's sack, or when Lady Macbeth "smeared the sleeping grooms with blood".'

conclusion. 'Relevant' means what logically is probative (i.e. will aid in proving the desired conclusion), 'admissible' what is legally receivable in a court of law.[1] Logically, any evidence should be allowed which directly proves or disproves the fact in issue, or else proves facts rendering the existence of facts in issue more probable or improbable. When we say that one fact is evidence of another, we mean merely that it furnishes a premiss or part of a premiss from which the existence of the other fact is a necessary or probable inference, and 'judicial evidence is for the most part nothing more than natural evidence restrained or modified by rules of positive law'.[2] The English rules are stricter than those of other systems in ruling out certain types of evidence, this being due partly to the fact that the jury was so extensively used as the fact-finding body and judges feared that the jury might place undue weight on certain types of evidence which are notoriously untrustworthy. Thus hearsay is excluded,[3] since the person who made the original remark cannot be cross-examined and it is well known that a story 'grows in the telling'. The average man in determining whether to suspect another of a crime examines carefully his past record and character, but English rules exclude, in general,[4] proof that the prisoner had previously been convicted of crime in order that the jury may not 'give a dog a bad name and hang him'. Again, the average man considers the opinions of others as well as their testimony concerning facts which they observed, but English law generally debars a witness from expressing mere opinion unless he possesses expert knowledge on the point at issue.

Method and burden of proof. In every mature system there are technical rules concerning the method by which certain facts should be proved. Of some facts no proof need be given since they are assumed to be within the judicial knowledge of the court—in English law, however, this class is limited to facts so notorious that to require proof would be merely a waste of time. Thus there is no need to prove

---

[1] S. L. Phipson, *Evidence* (9th ed.), 57; cf. J. H. Wigmore, op. cit., §§ 9, 10, 12, and 28.

[2] W. M. Best, *Evidence*, § 34, cited Phipson, op. cit. 50. But in some cases the law may admit evidence that logically seems irrelevant.

[3] There are exceptions, e.g. certain types of dying declarations; and see Z. Cowen and P. B. Carter, *Essays on the Law of Evidence* (1956), ch. i. See also the Civil Evidence Act, 1968, and the Criminal Evidence Act, 1965, where the problem of business and computer records is dealt with.

[4] But similar facts may be proved to rebut a defence of ignorance, accident, mistake, etc.: *Makin* v. *A.-G. for N.S.W.*, [1894] A.C. 57; and see Cowen and Carter, op. cit., ch. iv.

the imputation of the term 'frozen snake' in a libel action.[1] But of other facts evidence must be given—in general, the burden of proof lying on him who in substance asserts as part of his plea the affirmative of any issue. 'Omnia praesumuntur pro negante.'[2] 'Ei qui affirmat non ei qui negat incumbit probatio.' This is an ancient rule founded on the common-sense approach that the proof of a negative is extraordinarily difficult and should not be forced on a person without very strong reasons.[3] In a civil case a reasonable preponderance of probability is sufficient for a verdict,[4] but in a criminal case the Crown must prove the guilt of the prisoner beyond reasonable doubt.[5] The Court of Appeal in *Ginesi* v. *Ginesi*[6] laid down that the same strict proof is necessary in the case of a matrimonial offence as in a criminal case. The Australian High Court rejected this view. Dixon J. stated that *Briginshaw* v. *Briginshaw*[7] was 'a well-considered decision based on as complete an examination and survey of the subject as we could make. So much cannot be said of *Ginesi* v. *Ginesi*.'[8] The present position of English law is uncertain, as can be seen from the judgments of the Court of Appeal in *Bastable* v. *Bastable*.[9]

In English law the influence of the jury may be seen in the fact that the 'day in court' is a typical feature of English procedure. If the jury is to be used as the fact-finding body, then all the evidence must be rehearsed before it, and it is obviously better for the jury to see the witnesses than merely to use records of their testimony. In some continental countries the examination of witnesses may proceed by easy stages, and the judge who conducts the final trial may not see many of the witnesses, being satisfied with a transcript of their evidence. If a witness lives in a town other than that where the trial is taking place, expense is saved by arranging for his examination in the local court. But although such methods of examining witnesses may shorten the actual trial, the serious disadvantage is that the trial judge has not necessarily seen all the witnesses in the box and has not had the opportunity of drawing from their demeanour inferences as to the

[1] *Hoare* v. *Silverlock* (1848), 12 Q.B. 624 at 633.
[2] Cf. Paul, *Dig*. 22. 3. 2.
[3] Cf. Visc. Maugham, *Constantine Line* v. *Imperial Smelting Corp.*, [1942] A.C. 154.
[4] Per Willes J., *Cooper* v. *Slade* (1856), 6 H.L.C. 746 at 772; *Helton* v. *Allen*, [1940] A.L.R. 298.
[5] In *Sodeman* v. *R.*, [1936] 2 All E.R. 1138, the J.C. accepted the view of the High Court that, while the Crown must prove the guilt of the prisoner beyond a reasonable doubt, a prisoner who pleads insanity does not have to satisfy this heavy burden but need only prove his case on a preponderance of probability.
[6] [1948] P. 179. [7] A previous decision of the High Court: (1938), 60 C.L.R. 336.
[8] *Wright* v. *Wright* (1948), 77 C.L.R. 191 at 211. [9] [1968] 1 W.L.R. 1684.

truth of their statements. The day in court illustrates the dramatic value of a trial. Vyshinsky emphasizes that an important aim of the public administration of justice is to inculcate discipline.[1]

A court may leave each of the parties to prove his own case, acting merely as an impartial umpire to see that the 'rules of the game' are observed, and taking no active part in the discovery of the truth. This is sometimes called the 'contest' or 'sporting' theory of justice. Or the court may regard its duty as being the discovery of the truth; thus the Soviet Court is regarded as 'an active governmental agency which investigates, tests and decides in accordance with the policies of its government; the parties, defence as well as prosecution, are there merely to assist the court in establishing the truth. But it is the *court* and *not the parties* that carries on the judicial inquiry.'[2] Earlier Russian writers frankly regarded the provincial court as an instrument of class vengeance upon the enemies of the State—which is far removed from the contest theory which lays down that the task of the judge is to secure the observance of every rule of procedure and evidence (whether it be in favour of one side or the other), and to stress that the guilt of the prisoner must be proved beyond all reasonable doubt. Vyshinsky claims, however, that under the Stalin constitution, adversary procedure has been adopted as a constitutional principle.[3] Thus the contest theory emphasizes that the defence must have equal rights with the prosecution, and that a barrister should be allowed to defend even those accused of crimes against the State. This seems axiomatic in England, but the position is not so in all countries.[4] Where the inquisitorial method is adopted, the court regards itself as responsible for discovering the truth. This theory led in the past to torture as a means of extracting a confession,[5] but in most countries torture has now disappeared. Too close a co-operation between the prosecution and the court detracts from that impartiality which should mark the judge.[6]

---

[1] *Law of the Soviet State*, 517.

[2] J. Zelitch, *Soviet Administration of Criminal Law*, 210.

[3] *Law of the Soviet State*, 519.

[4] For a discussion of Russian theories, see Zelitch, op. cit. 251 et seq.; J. N. Hazard, *Law and Social Change in the U.S.S.R.* (1953); *Soviet Codifiers Release the First Drafts* (1959), 8 *Am. J. Comp. Law*, 72; H. J. Berman, *Soviet Law and Government* (1958), 21 *Mod. L. R.* 19; *The Comparison of Soviet and American Law* (1959), 34 *Ind. L. R.* 559.

[5] It has been suggested that, once the jury was in use, there was less temptation to use torture, for what jury would believe a confession obtained by such means?

[6] M. Ploscowe, 29 *Minn. L. R.* (1945), 376, emphasizes this point with regard to French criminal trials.

While in criminal cases English law favours the contest theory,[1] in civil cases powerful inquisitorial processes are available to the litigant. These were first developed by Chancery and were probably borrowed from canon law.[2] A defendant is forced to reply on oath to such interrogatories as a Master allows and must make an affidavit of, and produce, such documents as are relevant. These weapons are now available in common law actions. On the Continent we see the same apparent paradox as in England, but with exactly the opposite results—for while the court directly seeks the truth in criminal cases, in civil cases it leaves the parties to their own devices. In England the position is not really so paradoxical, however, for the 'inquisitorial processes' are moved by the litigant. The court does not really initiate or directly pursue the search for truth; its role remains one of deciding the issues joined by the parties.

The task of proof is rendered easier (whatever the theory on which the court acts) by the use of legal presumptions. A legal presumption is an inference which the law directs should be drawn from a specific fact.[3] Thus if it is shown that a child is under eight years of age, English law directs the conclusion to be drawn that he is incapable of *mens rea* and therefore cannot be convicted of a crime. This particular presumption is conclusive, that is, it is forbidden to introduce rebutting evidence to show that the child was possessed of malice. Other legal presumptions provide merely prima facie evidence, i.e. the presumption is regarded as sufficient proof of the fact unless and until it is rebutted by other evidence.[4] From legal presumptions there should be distinguished mere presumptions of fact, 'inferences which the mind naturally and logically draws from given facts, irrespective of their legal effect'.[5] There has been much dispute whether the application of *res ipsa loquitur* raises a legal presumption of negligence or only an inference of fact which the tribunal may reject even in the absence of explanation by the defendant.[6]

[1] The prisoner has the right to be silent, to make a statement not on oath, or to give sworn evidence and thereby be subject to cross-examination: see the discussion by A. R. N. Cross and R. H. Field in 11 *J. Soc. Public Teachers of Law* (1970), 66, 76.
[2] M. S. Amos, *The Future of the Common Law*, 33; R. M. Jackson, *The Machinery of Justice in England*, 59.   [3] J. F. Stephen, *Evidence*, Art. 1.
[4] Conclusive presumptions are sometimes termed *praesumptiones iuris et de iure* and rebuttable ones *praesumptiones iuris sed non de iure*.
[5] S. L. Phipson, *Evidence* (9th ed.), 4; cf. Wigmore, op. cit., § 249.
[6] *Barkway* v. *S. Wales Transport*, [1950] A.C. 185. The wittiest comment is cited by W. L. Prosser, 37 *Calif. L. R.* (1949), 183 at 232: '*loquitur, vere; sed quid in inferno vult dicere?*'; *Dorset Yacht Co.* v. *Home Office* (C.A.), [1969] 2 All E.R. 564; *Ludgate* v. *Lovett* (C.A.), [1969] 2 All E.R. 1275; *Colvilles Ltd.* v. *Devine*, [1969] 2 All E.R. 53. The Australian High Court rejects the view that the onus of proof, or indeed of

The presumption of innocence is an illustration of a rebuttable presumption. Although we flatter ourselves that it is a traditional ornament of English law, the doctrine is rather more modern than is usually supposed.[1] Allen states that it is only when society is strong enough to put away fear that it can afford to give suspected persons treatment that is really generous.[2] Savage treatment of prisoners may be due to the desire to preserve a weak social structure rather than to the love of cruelty for its own sake.

Competency. Not all witnesses are competent. Even if the evidence which John wishes to give is legally admissible, he may be prevented by a rule of law from appearing as a witness in that particular suit. At one time English law went so far in its distrust of biased evidence as to debar nearly all those who were most likely to have direct knowledge of the necessary facts—e.g. neither the party to a civil case nor his wife could give evidence on oath. But the law came to recognize that, while interest may create bias and so affect the *cogency* of evidence, wholesale exclusion is likely to do more harm than good and, accordingly, the rules were recast in the nineteenth century.[3] Competency should be distinguished from compellability. In general, all competent witnesses are compellable—i.e. they can be punished for refusal to answer a relevant question which has been allowed by the court. But there are exceptions.[4] Thus a witness may be willing but not competent (for example, one with an intellect so defective that he cannot understand the nature of the oath); or competent but not compellable; or competent but protected from answering a particular question on the plea of privilege.

Cogency. Once the evidence is received there is the difficult problem of analysing it and determining its weight. There are legal rules which act as a check, but the task of sifting truth from falsehood, of inferring the known from the unknown, is determined mainly by the common sense, experience, and subtlety of the tribunal. 'To the hungry furnace of the reasoning faculty the law of evidence is but a stoker.'[5] The fallibility of human testimony is a well-recognized fact today. Apart altogether from perjury and the unconscious twist

explanation, is cast on the defendant: *Government Insurance Office of N.S.W.* v. *Fredrichberg* (1968), 118 C.L.R. 403.

[1] C. K. Allen, *Legal Duties*, 253; and see *Esso Petroleum Ltd.* v. *Southport Corporation*, [1956] A.C. 218 (and in the Court of Appeal where the onus was placed on the defendant, [1954] 2 Q.B. 182). [2] Op. cit. 272.
[3] See Phipson, op. cit., ch. xl; cf. Wigmore, op. cit., §§ 575–87, 600–20.
[4] The wife is not compellable in some cases, but the detailed rules cannot here be stated. [5] J. B. Thayer, *Preliminary Treatise on Evidence* (1898), 271.

to our recollection which bias gives, great inaccuracies exist even in
the evidence of disinterested third parties. When a witness makes
a simple statement—'the prisoner is the man who drove the car after
the robbery'—he is really asserting: (a) that he observed the car; (b)
that the impression became fixed in his mind; (c) that the impression
has not been confused or obliterated; (d) that the resemblance between the original impression and the prisoner is sufficient to base
a judgment not of resemblance but of identity.[1] Scientific research
into the nature of the eye has shown how comparatively easy it is for
vision to be mistaken,[2] lack of observation and faulty memory add to
the difficulties. Experiments by criminologists have shown the high
percentage of error in the reports of a class of students witnessing an
unexpected incident.[3] Borchard, in discussing sixty-five established
cases of error in criminal convictions, points out that many of these
arose from faulty identification and that in eight of the cases there
was not the slightest resemblance between the real criminal and the
person who was falsely convicted.[4] In one case, on the evidence of
six girls, sitting on the steps of a factory, a man was convicted of
indecently exposing himself from the window of a train travelling at
thirty miles an hour. On appeal, tests were carried out in the locality
and it was shown to be impossible to make any identification whatever from the place where the girls were sitting.[5] In the hands of an
experienced practitioner, cross-examination is a valuable weapon to
sift out the truth, but it cannot always be relied on to defeat either
a skilful perjurer, or one who has formed a wrong conclusion as to
what he saw and with honest stubbornness sticks to his story. In
certain cases in the criminal law where evidence is likely to be un-
reliable, there must be corroboration and in others the court must
warn the jury of the danger of convicting in the absence of it.[6]

In previous ages, torture was regarded as an aid to the discovery of
the truth, in spite of the well-known and natural propensity of men

[1] Per Evatt J., *Craig* v. *The King* (1933), 49 C.L.R. 429 at 446; Barry J., 11 *A.L.J.*
(1938), 314.   [2] J. Hodgson, 7 *Medico-Legal and Crim. R.* (1939), 108.
[3] R. H. Gault, *Criminology*, 380.   [4] *Convicting the Innocent.*
[5] Barry J., op. cit. See also L. R. C. Haward, 'A Psychologist's Contribution to Legal
Procedure', 27 *Mod. L. R.* (1964), 656.

[6] Thus corroboration is necessary in trials for perjury: the jury must be warned where
the witness is an accomplice and in certain sex offences. Traditionally corroboration
was necessary in treason but the Treason Act, 1945 (8 & 9 Geo. VI, c. 44) amended
the Treason Act and made trials for treason similar to trials for murder. It therefore
became necessary no longer to have more than one witness to an act of treason to
produce a conviction. That Act was passed shortly before the infamous Joyce (Lord
Haw Haw) was brought back to England, after being captured on the Continent at
the end of the 1939–45 war, to stand his trial for treason.

to say anything to end the almost intolerable agony. Today, scientific devices are being advocated. The 'lie-detector' has sprung into prominence, if not into universal acceptance,[1] and psychologists claim a high percentage of accuracy for the use of word-association tests designed to discover the emotional reactions of the prisoner.[2] Scopolamin is a drug which induces a state almost of unconsciousness, but leaves the subject able to answer questions, although unable to fabricate or invent.[3] But none of these devices is yet sufficiently proved to be able to be used with any confidence in a court of law.[4]

The most striking advance in the problem of proof today is the significant evidence which can be drawn by science from material things. The increase in knowledge of the physiologist and the pathologist, the physicist and the chemist has led to astounding results being achieved from meagre clues. The use of the so-called invisible rays has, for example, made easier the detection of forgeries,[5] and the truths of scientific achievement are more wondrous than the fabled exploits of fiction. The use of expert evidence is essential in many cases; e.g. in what Ormrod J. described as the first occasion in which a court in England had been asked to determine the sex of an individual, nine doctors of high standing gave evidence, and it was agreed by counsel on both sides that articles in learned journals could be used without formal proof.[6]

How far is the jury a competent body to determine the cogency of evidence? This question is often debated, and opinions range from lyrical praise of this palladium of our liberties to sneering references to its propensity to favour a pretty woman or to mulct a railway company in damages. In cases of serious crime most English writers

---

[1] The theory of the lie-detector is that, when a guilty suspect is asked a question concerning the crime, his emotional reaction will be different from that which occurs when he is asked an irrelevant question. The emotions affect breathing, blood-pressure, and heart-beat, and the contrivance attempts to measure the difference between the reaction to the irrelevant question and that which concerns the crime. See P. V. Trovillo, 29 *J. Crim. Law and Crim.* (1939), 848.

[2] Thus A. R. Luria tested criminal suspects and believed it was possible, with a fair measure of success, to detect consciousness of guilt by psychological tests: H. Cairns, *Law and the Social Sciences*, 204.   [3] Cairns, op. cit. 216.

[4] It would seem that in cases of disputed paternity, the court should pay attention to scientific proof that the defendant could not possibly be the father, on account of his blood group, yet in the *Chaplin Case* the verdict was given in defiance of the evidence: S. B. Schatkin, 32 *Virg. L. R.* (1946), 890; but times are changing rapidly and verdicts of that kind are less likely now or in the future—see L. R. Bowen, *Blood Tests and Disputed Parentage*, 18 *Mod. L. R.* (1958), 111.

[5] C. A. Mitchell, 3 *Medico-Legal and Crim. R.* (1935), 3; Laurie, 4 ibid. (1936), 208. For an account of the *Ruxton Case*, where it was necessary to identify the dismembered remains of two bodies, see R. Crichton, 4 ibid. 144.

[6] *Corbett* v. *Corbett (otherwise Ashley)*, [1970] 2 All E.R. 33.

favour the retention of the jury, though a minority would modify the requirement of unanimity by allowing a majority decision. In civil cases opinion is more divided. Perhaps the main argument in favour of the jury is that it ensures the participation of citizens in the administration of justice—this tempers the law by the views of the common man and educates the common man in the views of the law.[1] Another argument, often advanced by members of the Bar, is that nothing controls the personal idiosyncracies of judges in their conduct of trials so effectively as the presence of a jury which must judge the issues of fact. Leaving theoretical arguments aside, we find that the use of the jury is declining both in criminal and civil cases. In certain indictable cases a summary court may try the case summarily if the prisoner consents, and in 1935 only one-eighth of the indictable cases were tried by jury. In civil cases in the King's Bench Division the proportion of jury cases was only slightly higher and since that time has dwindled away to a minute percentage as almost all actions for personal injuries are tried without juries, while in the County Court it sank to 0·006 per cent.[2] Traditionally the verdict of the jury must be unanimous, but both in civil and criminal cases, majority verdicts have been introduced by statute in many jurisdictions.[3]

On the whole, the English laws of evidence require a very high standard of proof and few desire that in criminal cases there should be a substantial change in the rules. In civil cases, however, the rigid rules of evidence greatly increase the cost of an action and sometimes cause delay.[4]

§ 131. Appeal

Once a plaintiff has secured judgment he may proceed to execution if the judgment is not satisfied, unless execution is stayed because of an appeal. No court is perfect, and the possibility of review is a valuable safeguard of justice. *Adolf Beck's Case* showed the necessity for a right of appeal in criminal cases, and the Court of Criminal Appeal

[1] A. I. Vyshinsky, *Law of the Soviet State*, 506–7; for France, see M. Ploscowe, 29 *Minn. L. R.* (1945), 376.

[2] R. M. Jackson, 1 *Mod. L. R.* (1937), 132, 177. For general discussion of the value of trial by jury, see Jackson, 6 *Camb. L. J.* (1938), 367; H. Mannheim, 53 *L.Q.R.* (1937), 99, 388; M. D. Howe, 52 *Harv. L. R.* (1939), 582; Evatt J., supplement to 10 *A.L.J.* (1936–7), 49; Sir Patrick Devlin, *Trial by Jury* (1956); G. Williams, *The Proof of Guilt* (2nd ed. 1958).

[3] See D. M. Downie, 44 *A.L.J.* (1970), 482; Criminal Justice Act, 1967, s. 13.

[4] For a critique of the general machinery of English law, see C. Mullins, *In Quest of Justice*; R. M. Jackson, *The Machinery of Justice in England.*

was established in 1907. To create a right to one appeal is reasonable; to allow three courts in an ascending hierarchy to decide a matter seems an excess of caution; but to have a hierarchy of four or more courts seems to be based only on a desire to aid the legal profession.[1] A commentator in the *Law Quarterly Review* asks whether English legal procedure is as satisfactory as it is frequently claimed to be, in the light of the fact that the decision of a preliminary point, whether Scottish or English law applied, cost thousands of pounds, as the matter was argued in three courts from October 1966 to March 1970.[2] In continental courts there is usually only one appeal, sometimes two, but rarely more.[3]

When there is an appeal it should be possible to find the legal basis on which the lower court acted. The actual decision will be a matter of record (e.g. that the defendant pay the complainant £120), but on the return of an *order nisi* in one case, the affidavit of each party differed greatly as to the evidence given in the original proceedings. When application was made to the magistrate, he confessed that he did not remember and had kept no notes.[4] The higher court was therefore reduced to following the rule of practice that the affidavit which best supported the decision of the court should be accepted.

Appeal may take various forms. It may be an entirely new trial of questions of fact,[5] or it may be limited to questions of law.[6] The appeal may be as of right or only by leave of the court which gave the judgment or of the higher court. In English law only the parties can appeal—no state official (who is not a party) has the power to refer what he regards as an erroneous legal decision to a higher court. The court which hears the appeal may have the power, if it disagrees with the decision of the lower court, to enter final judgment, or it may be

---

[1] Under the Rating and Valuation (Apportionment) Act the local rating authorities draw up preliminary special lists; the local Assessment Committee hears objections; there is then an appeal through Quarter Sessions, the Divisional Court, and the Court of Appeal to the House of Lords: Mullins, *In Quest of Justice*, 382. In *Bell* v. *Lever Bros.*, [1932] A.C. 161, the appellant succeeded although only three judges out of nine were in his favour. The English Administration of Justice Act, 1969, permits in certain cases an appeal direct to the House of Lords.

[2] 86 *L.Q.R.* (1970) at 291, referring to *James Miller and Partners Ltd.* v. *Whitworth Street Estates (Manchester) Ltd.*, [1970] 2 W.L.R. 728.

[3] R. C. K. Ensor, *Courts and Judges*, 13. Russia allows one appeal: A. I. Vyshinsky, *Law of the Soviet State*, 520.

[4] *Buzatu* v. *Vournazos*, [1970] V.R. 476.

[5] As when Quarter Sessions try an appeal from a court of summary jurisdiction: 4 & 5 Geo. V, c. 58, § 37 (1).

[6] Thus an appeal lies from the Court of Criminal Appeal to the House of Lords only if the certificate of the Attorney-General be obtained that an important principle of law is involved: 7 Edw. VII, c. 23, § 1 (6).

confined to sending the case back to the original court for decision
on the lines laid down. The Court of Cassation in France is not an
ordinary appellate court according to English notions. Its real function is not to hear an appeal between the parties but rather to decide
an abstract question of law. This is shown by several factors: firstly,
questions may be referred to it either by the parties or by the *pro-
cureur général*, whose task it is to watch for weak decisions or to
refer points on which there is little authority to the superior court.
Secondly, if a case is referred, otherwise than by the parties, any
decision reached has no effect on their rights, the task of the court
being limited to the statement of a principle of law. Thirdly, if a case
is referred by the parties, even then the court does not deliver final
judgment, but, if it disapproves of the legal principle on which the
original court based its decision, it refers the case, not to the original
court, but to another of the same rank. Moreover, this lower court
may refuse to apply the principle adopted by the Court of Cassation
in which case the matter is reconsidered by the plenary chamber of
the latter court. If we add the fact that reference to the Court of
Cassation does not act as a stay of execution, then certainly we would
agree that this rather clumsy procedure is not designed to encourage
appeals from private persons.[1] The real function of the court is to
advise on abstract questions of law rather than to effect a final
adjustment between two particular parties. But the advantage of the
system is that a formulation of legal principle on a doubtful point
may be obtained otherwise than at the expense of two unfortunate
litigants, whereas in England a conflict of decisions in lower courts
may long leave the law doubtful, because no hardy warrior has
hazarded his fortune by appealing to the higher courts. An experiment well worth watching has been going on for some time in the
State of New South Wales where, pursuant to the Legal Assistance
Act, 1943–57,[2] Government funds are made available to defray the
costs of appeals in appropriate cases where doubtful points of law
are involved.

[1] R. C. K. Ensor, *Courts and Judges*, 44 et seq.
[2] Act no. 17 of 1943 as amended by Act no. 63 of 1957.

REFERENCES

AILES, E. H., 39 *Mich. L. R.* (1941), 392.
BALL, W. V., 51 *L.Q.R.* (1935), 13.
COHN, E. J., 8 *Mod. L. R.* (1945), 97.
DEVLIN, SIR PATRICK, *Trial by Jury* (1916).
DIAMOND, A. S., *Primitive Law*, ch. xxx.
HARVEY, C. P., 7 *Mod. L. R.* (1944), 42.
HODGSON, S., 7 *Medico-Legal and Criminological R.* (1939), 108.
JACKSON, R. M., *The Machinery of Justice in England.*
KENNEDY, W. B., 8 *Mod. L. R.* (1945), 18.
MULLINS, C., *In Quest of Justice.*
SIMPSON, S. P., 53 *Harv. L. R.* (1939), 169.
WIGMORE, J. H., *Evidence* (3rd ed. 1940).
WILLIAMS, G., *The Proof of Guilt* (2nd ed. 1958).

INDEX OF CASES

A

B

C

D

F

G

H

I

J

K

L

N

O

P

R

S

X

Y

Z

INDEX